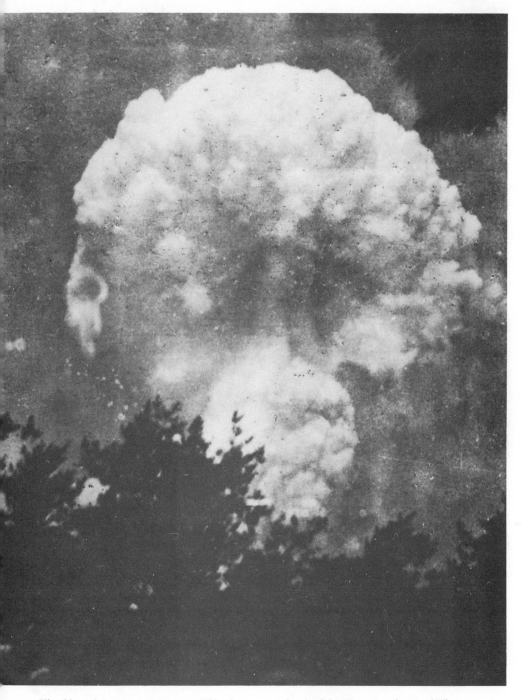

Hiroshima, 6 August 1945, 8:15 A.M. This picture was taken by Seizō Yamada—then a middle-school student—when he was fishing with a friend at Mikumari ravine located 7 kilometers east-northeast of Hiroshima (Fuchū town, Aki county). Frightened by a flash and explosion, he looked up to find the surrounding trees shaking and a huge cloud blowing up.

Hiroshima, Miyuki Bridge, 6 August 1945, 11 A.M. The injured people escaping to this bridge located 2.2 kilometers south-southeast from the hypocenter. Those who were able to move proceeded to Ujina. The wounded were later taken by boat to Ujina, Ninoshima Island, and Saka town and admitted to the relief stations. (Photograph by Yoshito Matsushige.)

Nagasaki, 7 August 1945, two days before the bombing. The Urakami river *(center)* flows into Nagasaki bay; factories and residences line the basin. (Photograph by United States Army #.)*

*The # sign denotes documents or photographs returned to Japan by the United States (see Postscript). (Ed.)

Nagasaki, 11 August, 1945, two days after the bombing. (Photograph by United States Army #.)

Nagasaki, Iwakawa township as seen from Hamaguchi township, 10 August 1945, 11 A.M. The heavy overcast of smoke from fires cut off the sunlight. The narrow path, along which the wounded are being carried on stretchers, leads to Nagasaki Railway Station. (Photograph by Yōsuke Yamahata.)

Hiroshima, Atomic Bomb Dome. The ruins of Sei Hospital *(right, front)* are located directly beneath the epicenter. The branches of the trees have been blown away instantaneously by the blast, but the trunks and part of the walls are still standing. The board tied to the post in the lower right corner bears the message that its writer still lives. (Photograph by Shigeo Hayashi.)

Hiroshima, Shimomura Clock Store, Hirataya township (800 meters from the hypocenter), early October 1945. The blast from the right completely destroyed the first floor; only the distorted outer shell of the second floor and the clock tower remain. (Photograph by Shigeo Hayashi.)

Nagasaki, in the vicinity of Hamaguchi township, 10 August 1945. The corpse *(center)* is that of a person who failed to escape from the indoor air-raid shelter and was burned to death. The girl standing on the right and staring vacantly is thought to be a member of the girls volunteer corps who came looking for her friends. (Photograph by Yōsuke Yamahata.)

Nagasaki, in the vicinity of Yamazato township, early in September 1945. Two girls returning home with bags of rice rations. There were only a few distribution points, so that people had to travel far for their rations. (Photograph by Eiichi Matsumoto.)

(left) and *(right)*. Nagasaki, Refugees at Ibinokuchi (1.5 km south of the hypocenter), 10 August 1945, morning. The injured people coming here immediately after the exposure spent one night in this district. They are all from the vicinity of Iwakawa township. The girl about to drink water from the canteen was unable to move because her hip was bruised. (Photographs by Yōsuke Yamahata.)

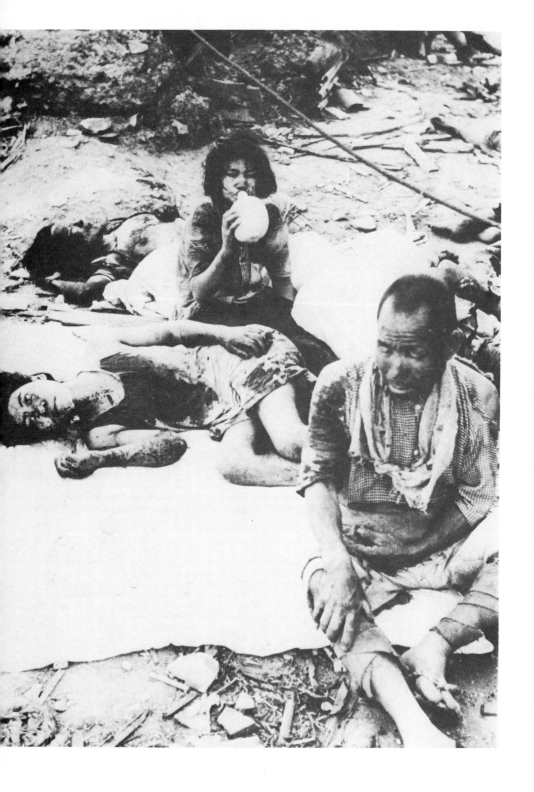

Nagasaki, in the vicinity of Iwakawa township (700 meters south-southeast from the hypocenter), 10 August 1945. The burned corpse is presumably that of a mobilized student who was exposed to the atomic bomb while walking along the prefectural highway. (Photograph by Yōsuke Yamahata.)

Nagasaki, in front of Urakami Railway Station, 10 August 1945. The first-aid party from Mitsu-bishi Heavy Industries' Nagasaki Shipyard started their activities in early morning, but it reportedly took from one to two hours to bring in a seriously injured patient. The concrete wall on the right is a part of the Mitsubishi Urakami branch hospital, and the steel-frame structure in the background is the number 3 factory of the Mitsubishi Steel Works. (Photograph by Yōsuke Yamahata.)

Marked thermal burns covering the occipital area, back, and buttocks, and the dorsal portion of the thigh of a soldier exposed within 1 kilometer of the hypocenter in Hiroshima, 7 August 1945, Ninoshima Quarantines; his waist was protected by a waistband. (Photograph by Masayoshi Onuka.)

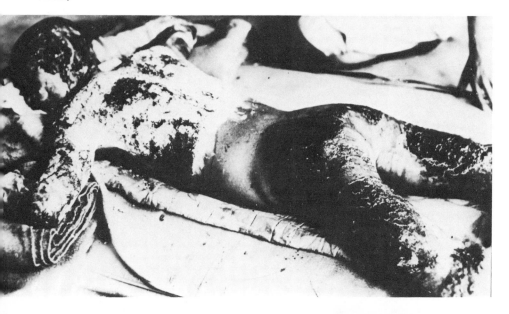

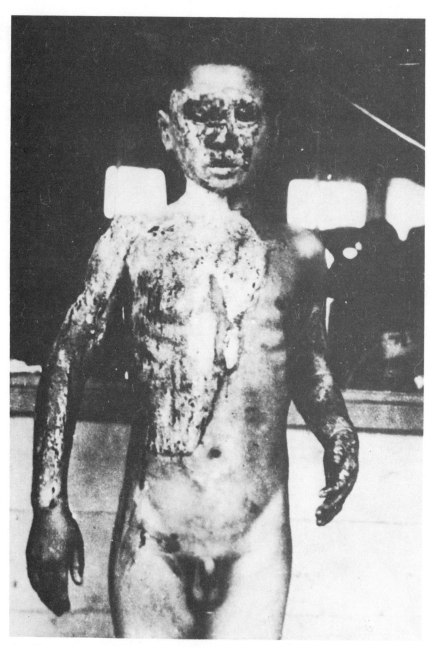

Thermal burns on the face, the upper half of the body, and the upper extremities of a sixteen-year-old male, 11 August 1945, Ōmura Naval Hospital, Nagasaki. It is clear that the thermal rays originated from the upper right. Desquamation of the epidermis of the upper half of the body is shallow but covers a wide area. (Photograph by Masao Shiotsuki.)

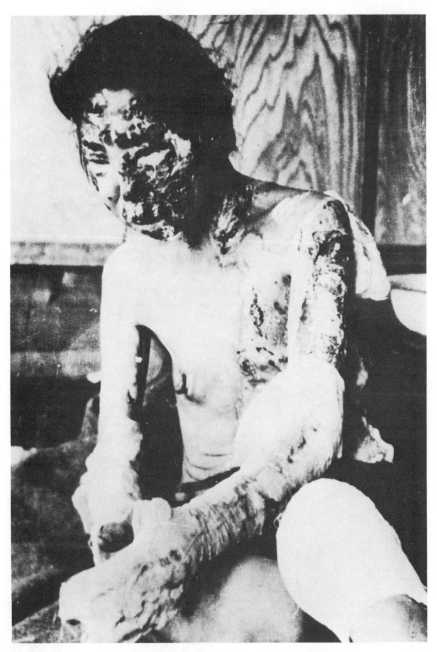

Thermal burns on the face and upper half of the body of a forty-five-year-old woman, exposed 1.6 kilometers from the hypocenter in Nagasaki. The burns are especially marked on the left side; gauze has been placed on her forearms for treatment. She died on 15 October 1945, Ōmura Naval Hospital. (Photograph by Masao Shiotsuki.)

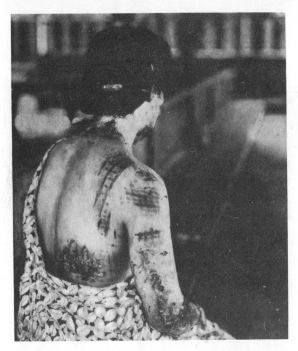

Burned areas on the back and on the dorsal portion of the upper arm show that thermal rays penetrated only the black or the dark-colored parts of the clothing worn at the time of exposure. Hiroshima, 3 September 1945, Hiroshima First Army Hospital Ujina branch. (Photograph by Masao Tsuzuki and Gon'ichi Kimura.)

Thermal burns on the dorsal side of the lower extremities, with signs of keloid formation. Hiroshima (900 meters from the hypocenter), mid-October 1945, Hiroshima First Army Hospital Ujina branch. #

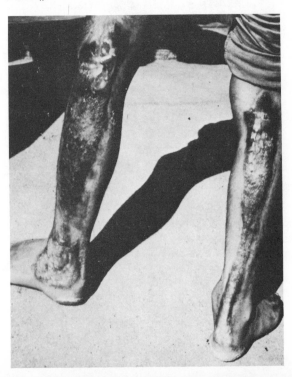

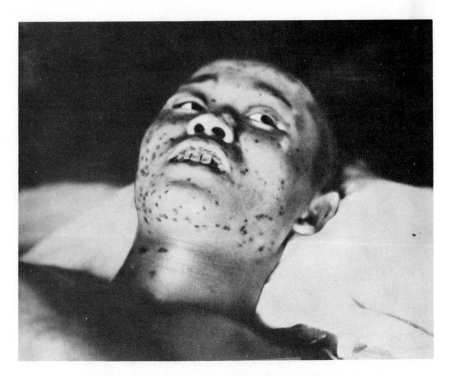

Subcutaneous hemorrhage appearing on patient's face. Epilation (18 August), gingival hemorrhage, purpura (29 August), fever (31 August), oropharyngitis and hemorrhagic tendency (1 September). Patient died 3 September 1945, Hiroshima First Army Hospital Ujina branch. (Photograph by Masao Tsuzuki and Gon'ichi Kimura.)

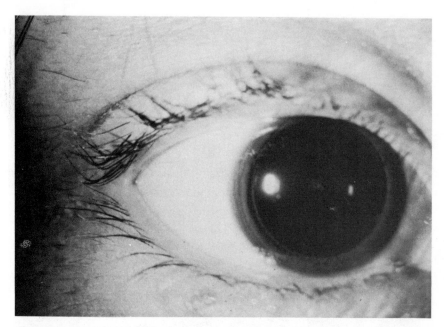

Atomic bomb cataract, April 1966. Right eye of case 1. Exposed in Hiroshima at the age of one year and eleven months (900 meters from the hypocenter). *(a)* Under oblique illumination, a small dark area is visible on the inner surface of the posterior polar capsule. *(b)* Narrow slit figure; a cavity is found in the small dark area. (Courtesy of Tsugio Dodo.)

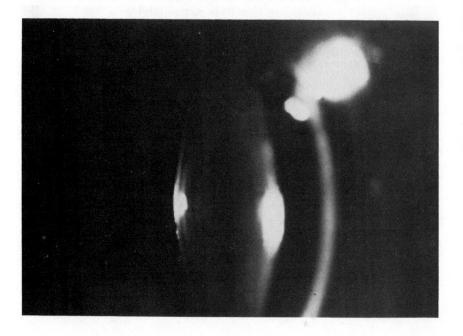

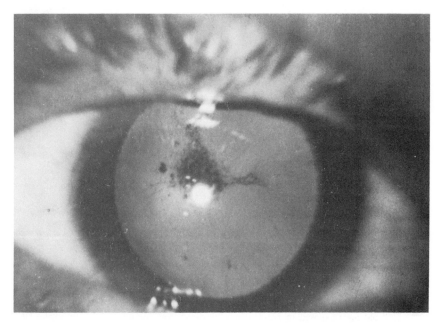

Atomic bomb cataract, April 1966. Right eye of case 2. Exposed in Hiroshima at age forty, 820 meters from the hypocenter. Marked cataract of both eyes. *(a)* Opacity of vitreous body as observed by transillumination. *(b)* Narrow slit figure. Note opacity on the anterior surface of the posterior polar capsule. (Courtesy of Tsugio Dodo.)

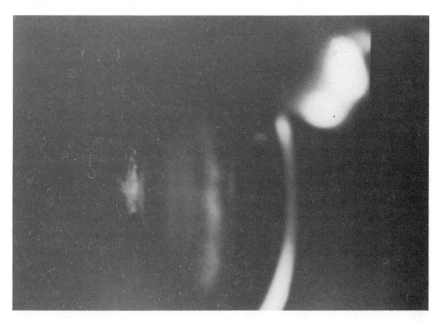

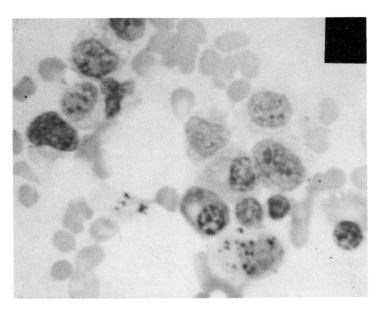

Bone marrow smear of femur, stained with Geimsa's stain, shows only a few reticulum cells, young myeloid cells, and plasma cells. From a twenty-two-year-old male exposed in Hiroshima 1 kilometer from the hypocenter; he died on 1 September 1945. (Tokyo Imperial University series.)

Histological specimen of femoral bone marrow: normal hematopoietic tissue has been lost and replaced by reticulum cells and plasma cells; note erythrophago-cytosis by macrophages. From a thirty-nine-year-old male exposed in Hiroshima 1 kilometer from the hypocenter; he died on 12 August 1945. (Yamashina's series, case 5.)

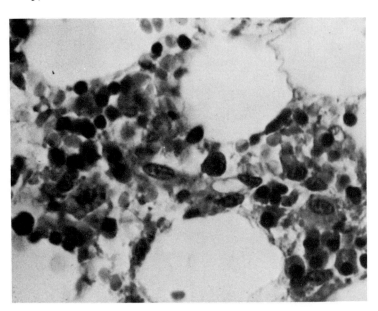

HIROSHIMA
AND
NAGASAKI

THE COMMITTEE

FOR THE COMPILATION

OF MATERIALS ON DAMAGE

CAUSED BY

THE ATOMIC BOMBS

IN HIROSHIMA AND NAGASAKI

TRANSLATED BY

EISEI ISHIKAWA

AND

DAVID L. SWAIN

HIROSHIMA AND NAGASAKI

THE PHYSICAL, MEDICAL, AND SOCIAL EFFECTS OF THE ATOMIC BOMBINGS

BASIC BOOKS, INC., PUBLISHERS
NEW YORK

Library of Congress Cataloging in Publication Data

Hiroshima-shi Nagasaki-shi Genbaku Saigaishi
  Henshū Iinkai.
  Hiroshima and Nagasaki.

  Translation of: Hiroshima Nagasaki no genbaku
saigai.
  Bibliography: p. 641
  Includes index.
    1. Hiroshima-shi (Japan)—Bombardment, 1945.
  2. Nagasaki-shi (Japan)—Bombardment, 1945.
  3. Atomic bomb—Physiological effect. 4. Atomic
  bomb—Blast effect. I. Title. [DNLM: 1. Atomic
  warfare. 2. Radiation effects. 3. Radiation
  injuries. WN 610 C734h]
  D767.25.H6H67 1981   940.54'26   80-68179

  ISBN: 0-465-02985-X   AACR2

Hiroshima Nagasaki no Genbaku Saigai
edited by The Committee for the Compilation of Materials
on Damage Caused by the Atomic Bombs
in Hiroshima and Nagasaki

Originally published in Japanese by Iwanami Shoten, Publishers, Tokyo, 1979

Chapter 10 of the Japanese edition is the
introduction in this edition; chapters 14 and 15
of the Japanese edition have been combined and
are now chapter 13; chapter 16 of the Japanese
edition is chapter 14 here.
Printed in the United States of America
DESIGNED BY VINCENT TORRE
10 9 8 7 6 5 4 3 2

CONTENTS

PART II

INJURY TO THE HUMAN BODY

Contents

PART III

THE IMPACT ON SOCIETY AND DAILY LIFE

PART IV

TOWARD THE ABOLITION OF NUCLEAR ARMS

Contents

LIST OF FIGURES

FOREWORD

Peace is not to be had merely by desiring it. Too many obstacles stand in the way. But if all the nations and the peoples of the world will determine the conditions for building peace and will work steadily and with all their might to fulfill those conditions, peace is by no means beyond our reach. Today, when the development of nuclear weapons with massive destructive and killing power proceeds unchecked, the building of peace must be made the top priority of all mankind. Einstein has clearly warned us:

The release of atomic energy has so changed everything that our former ways of thinking have been rendered obsolete. We therefore face catastrophe unheard of in former times. If mankind is to survive, then we need a completely new way of thinking.*

At 8:15 A.M. on 6 August 1945 in Hiroshima, and then at 11:02 A.M. on 9 August 1945 in Nagasaki, atomic bombs were dropped for the first time in human history. Measured by the capacities of today's nuclear weapons, these first bombs were small indeed. Even so, in an instant, living things were robbed of life, bodies were burned and broken, and material objects were reduced to dust and ashes, as whole cities were laid waste. Even now, the dreadful scars remain in the bodies, and in the hearts, of the world's first A-bomb victims. The horrors visited upon Hiroshima and Nagasaki would be no less grave in any other nuclear war—and they teach us that mankind must never again risk waging war with nuclear weapons. The people of our cities did not have to wait for Einstein's warning: they learned this lesson tragically, through experience.

Yet the citizens of Hiroshima and Nagasaki have risen above grief and hate to a belief in mankind's essential unity, and with one voice they proclaim, "No more Hiroshimas. No more Nagasakis." And in order that man will never repeat these disasters, they have unceasingly called for the elimination of nuclear weapons from the face of the earth.

Every year since 1947, the city of Hiroshima on 6 August and the city of Nagasaki on 9 August have held ceremonies, scheduled at the specific bombing times, to mourn and honor those sacrificed in the bombings and to memorialize

---

* Quoted by Georg Picht in Georg Picht and Wolfgang Huber, *Was heist Friedensforschung?* [What Is Peace Research?] (Stuttgart: Ernst Klett Verlag; Munich: Kösel-Verlag, 1971), p. 32.

the cause of peace. The mayors of the two cities have repeatedly issued peace declarations, directed both to Japan and to the whole world, renewing our common pledge to peace.

For a while after the bombings, neither Hiroshima nor Nagasaki began to rebuild: the damages were simply too massive and too stunning. In 1949, however, the rebuilding of the two cities was considered in the National Diet. In May of that year, a law was passed to rebuild Hiroshima as a symbol of the ideal of a genuine and lasting peace; a similar law was enacted to rebuild Nagasaki as a symbol of the ideal of lasting peace as expressed in the promotion of international culture. In the spirit of these laws, both cities constructed, in their central bombed areas, peace parks as memorials both to the A-bomb dead and to the cause of peace. To keep the memory of A-bomb realities alive for succeeding generations, Hiroshima erected the Peace Memorial Museum and the Peace Memorial Hall in its Peace Park; and in its Peace Park, Nagasaki constructed the International Cultural Hall. Annually, more than two million people from Japan and other lands visit these memorials. For these visitors, the horrors of atomic catastrophe become vividly real—and peace becomes a matter of urgent necessity.

The currents of contemporary global politics, however, are working against the aspirations of those who seek peace. Nuclear arms have become a mark of national power and pride, and no one seems to know how to stop the nuclear arms race. The current stockpiles of nuclear arms are said to be enough to wipe out the whole human race. If present trends are not reversed, they clearly spell doom for mankind. Peace will not be granted by someone else; we must secure it with our own hands.

In 1976 the mayors of Hiroshima and Nagasaki visited the United Nations to represent the aspirations of the citizens of our cities and to disclose both the realities of A-bomb damages as well as our common quest for peace to the President of the General Assembly, to the Secretary-General, and to the permanent representatives to the United Nations from twelve nations. Again, in 1978 the two mayors were able to attend the United Nations Special Session on Disarmament and appeal for the abolition of nuclear weapons. At that time the two cities also sponsored an exhibition of A-bomb photographs at the United Nations headquarters. Those who viewed the photographs were able easily to visualize themselves suffering the same horrors in the future—if nuclear weapons are not abolished. We have been doing all in our power to convey the A-bomb realities to people everywhere, simply because we fear for the future of all mankind, including ourselves.

On the other hand, the A-bomb catastrophe has become more remote with each passing year. The A-bomb victims themselves are aging, and younger people who know nothing of war now constitute over half of our own populations. Thus, it is clear that we must make a renewed effort to keep alive the A-bomb experience. There are still many areas of that total experience that have not been fully clarified. Even so, Hiroshima and Nagasaki have joined in the publication of this comprehensive compilation of the findings that are so far scientifically confirmed; and we have done so out of the conviction that, in the present state of international policy in regard to nuclear arms, there is not a moment to lose.

Finally, we wish to express our sincere appreciation to the thirty-four specialists who, despite their many other responsibilities, prepared the various sections; and especially to the three editors—Soichi Iijima, formerly president of Hiroshima University and presently professor of pathology at Nagoya University; Seiji Imahori, president of Hiroshima Women's University; and Kanesaburo Gushima, president of Nagasaki University—for their painstaking devotion to the task of compiling this volume; to Iwanami Shoten, Publishers, for their recognition of the importance of this venture and their unflagging commitment to its successful completion; and to all others who in many ways cooperated in making this publication possible.

TAKESHI ARAKI, *Mayor*
City of Hiroshima

HITOSHI MOTOSHIMA, *Mayor*
City of Nagasaki

June 1979

PREFACE TO THE ENGLISH EDITION

In 1945 the first three atomic bombs in human history were produced by the United States; one of these was exploded experimentally at its Alamogordo testing grounds in the desert of New Mexico. The remaining two were used against Japan that same year: one bomb, using uranium 235, was dropped on Hiroshima on 6 August; the other, using plutonium 239, was dropped on Nagasaki on 9 August. Compared with the technologically far superior and incredibly more destructive nuclear weapons manufactured and stockpiled today by a few countries, the earliest atomic bombs were rudimentary indeed. Nonetheless, the first—and, we pray, the last—atomic bombs ever used in warfare did, in fact, inflict massive damages on whole cities, their peoples, and all living things in the bombed areas. In the extremely brief time span of 0.2–3 seconds, hundreds of thousands of people were obliterated along with their homes and places of work; many thousands more of the survivors suffered serious physical and psychological injuries which are not all healed even today, over thirty-five years later; and the genetic damages may well last for several generations, if not indefinitely.

There are at least some people who will think that, in terms of the number killed and of the scale of destruction, wars in the past have repeatedly involved far greater slaughter and desolation; that what happened over a generation ago on a relatively small island in the Far East is the kind of tragedy that inevitably occurs in wars, and it was certainly unfortunate; but that Hiroshima and Nagasaki have rebuilt handsomely and more than recovered their populations and prosperity, so there is no use in dredging up old grudges. It is by no means our intent to prolong bitterness or to settle old scores. The threat of nuclear holocaust, however, spreads increasingly over the world like a dark stormcloud; and the projected destruction of the newer nuclear arms would exceed that suffered by Hiroshima and Nagasaki by several hundred thousand, if not several million, times. Faced with such a real and horrendous threat, it certainly is not useless to make known to the widest possible world audience the nature and extent of damage caused by those first rudimentary atomic bombs. Indeed, if the future of the human race is to be safeguarded, the destructive dimensions of those "small" bombs and the depths of misery they caused must be clearly recognized. For our part, as human beings and as scientists, we believe that it is our inescapable duty to report accurately and objectively the full spectrum of the Hiroshima and Nagasaki experiences while the memories and records of that fateful August and subsequent years are still accessible. This duty is all the more compelling when the aftereffects of the first atomic bombs have yet to come to an end.

Such considerations as these prompted and guided the work of compiling this book. Throughout, we have had the unfaltering support of the citizens of Hiroshima and Nagasaki, whose fervent wish and prayer are "No more Hiroshimas, no more Nagasakis." Commissioned by the two cities, the editorial committee (Soichi Iijima, Seiji Imahori, Kanesaburo Gushima) had the expert cooperation of thirty-four specialists in producing the original Japanese edition, *Hiroshima–Nagasaki no Genbaku Saigai,* which was published in July 1979 by Iwanami Shoten, Publishers, in Tokyo. The plan and procedures of that process are explained in detail in the postscript, and thus need not be repeated here.

The English translation was done by Dr. Eisei Ishikawa, professor of pathology at Jikei University School of Medicine, and David L. Swain, editor of the *Japan Christian Quarterly.* Born in Stockton, California, Dr. Ishikawa spent his youth in the United States; before completing his high school education there, he went to his homeland, Japan. An outstanding scientist, Dr. Ishikawa is highly proficient in English and has long played an influential role in the Japanese Pathological Society. Mr. Swain came to Japan from the United States in 1953. Active for over two decades in church and university programs in Japan, he is unusually knowledgeable in the history of Japanese science and technology and has engaged in the translating, editing, or writing of nearly a dozen important books. Dr. Ishikawa was responsible for the natural science sections of this book; Mr. Swain, for the social science sections. For their labors in making the original Japanese material available in English translation to a wider audience, we wish to express the heartfelt appreciation of the editorial committee and of the citizens of Hiroshima and Nagasaki. We must also mention our appreciation of Dr. Takeshi Ohkita and Assistant Professor Minoru Yuzki, of Hiroshima University's Research Institute of Nuclear Medicine and Biology, as well as of Dr. Akio A. Awa and Mr. Kenji Joji, of Radiation Effects Research Foundation, for their constant cooperation in this effort.

While this translation follows the Japanese original faithfully, a few changes in the arrangement of materials have been made to facilitate the English-language reader's understanding. In the Japanese edition, chapter 10 ("The Atomic Bomb and Society: Challenge of Our Time") was the introduction to part III on the social effects of the atomic bombings; in the English-language edition, this chapter was moved up front to be the introduction ("The Atomic Bomb: Challenge of Our Time") to the entire book, and for this purpose was expanded and rewritten slightly. Owing to this change, chapters 11, 12, and 13 in the Japanese original are chapters 10, 11, and 12, respectively, in this edition. In part IV, chapter 14 of the Japanese edition was condensed and combined with chapter 15 of the original to form chapter 13 of this edition. Accordingly, chapter 16 in the Japanese edition is here chapter 14. Also, this preface was written for this edition.

The English-language edition has been made available through an arrangement between Basic Books, Inc., Publishers, in New York and Iwanami Shoten, Publishers, in Tokyo. On behalf of Basic Books, Erwin Glikes initiated the project, Martin Kessler handled its details, and Phoebe Hoss was responsible for editorial work. We have been particularly impressed with the devoted, painstaking care that Mrs. Hoss gave to the complex editorial details. Messrs. Shigeki Kobayashi, Hiromi Katayama, and their colleagues at Iwanami Shoten, after seeing the original Japanese edition to successful completion, continued to give their unstinted cooperation to the tasks of producing this English edition. The editorial committee is extremely grateful for the sustained cooperation of all these persons.

We sincerely pray that this book will contribute to the lasting peace and happiness of all peoples on this earth. If in this book there is a power that can touch deeply the hearts and minds of readers, it is surely a power that stems from the grievous recollection that the lives of countless people were tragically ended by the blazing inferno and the deeply penetrating, fatally ruinous radiation of the first—and, again we pray, may they be the last—atomic bombs ever used in human warfare.

*The Committee for the Compilation
of Materials on Damage Caused by
the Atomic Bombs in Hiroshima
and Nagasaki*

12 February 1981

HIROSHIMA
AND
NAGASAKI

Introduction

The Atomic Bomb: Challenge of Our Time

What Is Atomic Destruction?

The names Hiroshima and Nagasaki are known around the world—yet most people remain ignorant of the reality and the meaning of atomic destruction. Those who dropped the first atomic bomb worked thereafter to demonstrate its destructive powers and to justify its use as a way of ending the war quickly so as to limit the number of combat casualties. Nuclear bombs have thus become generally accepted. They have been developed and stockpiled by the United States of America and the Soviet Union on the premise that they effectively deter other countries from using them. When other major powers* acquired nuclear capability, they extended the nuclear threat to fearful proportions. The two great superpowers have sought to check the further spread of nuclear capability through a nuclear nonproliferation pact, but this effort is not convincing since it does not restrict them from adding to their own nuclear weapons. The peoples of the world who have learned the lessons of Hiroshima and Nagasaki, however, see nuclear arms no longer as useful deterrents but as dangerous weapons that could annihilate the human race. Thus, they recognize that the time has come to reverse the tide of world events.

* The United Kingdom, France, the People's Republic of China, and India, in chronological order.

The citizens of Hiroshima and Nagasaki have since the last world war consistently called for the elimination of all nuclear weapons; and each year on the anniversaries of the dropping of the first atomic bombs, their cities issue peace declarations. These people know from experience that such weapons threaten human existence and should never be used for any reason. The vast majority of the citizens of each city were A-bomb victims and as such have harbored great indignation about the use of the bombs as being unforgivably inhumane. Immediately after the war their anger was directed solely toward those who had dropped the bombs. As time passed, their wrath turned, through reflection, on their own government for having brought Japan into the war and for committing wholesale murder in the name of the state. This attitude, in turn, was later modulated into a call to ban all nuclear weapons, as the people of Hiroshima and Nagasaki came to understand that everything possible must be done to build world peace. With this understanding, they have thus persistently appealed to the nuclear powers to abandon their large-scale programs for expanding nuclear capability.

The suffering experienced by the A-bomb victims was beyond imagination, a blow unprecedented in human history. In the decade after 1945, when they most needed help, the Japanese government gave none. The victims felt that others did not understand the horrors of atomic destruction, and thus saw themselves as terribly alone and abandoned. A turning point in this mood came in 1954 when the United States conducted a hydrogen bomb test on Bikini Atoll in the Marshall Islands in the Pacific Ocean. A total of 290 people were affected—239 inhabitants of three atolls in the area, of whom 46 died during the period 1954–66; 28 American meteorological observers on Longelap Island; and 23 crewmen of the Japanese fishing vessel *Fukuryū Maru No. 5* ("Lucky Dragon No. 5"), one of whom died from radiation injury soon after the ship returned to its home port in Japan. The A-bomb victims of Hiroshima and Nagasaki quickly identified with these new victims. Indeed, they came to feel a new responsibility to promote solidarity among all peoples for the sake of world peace. Many Koreans and other foreigners had been victims of the atomic bombs in Hiroshima and Nagasaki; and citizens of the two cities now assumed the responsibility of extending help to these victims. Bikini became the occasion for the founding of a nationwide people's movement to ban the bomb, and the call for "No more Hiroshimas" and "No more Nagasakis" escalated. Even so, these appeals as well as efforts to clarify the extent and severity of A-bomb damages did not lead to a broad public understanding of the horrors of atomic destruction.

Immediately after the atomic bombings, Japanese medical scholars and natural scientists, while extending all possible care to the A-bomb injured, exerted strenuous efforts to determine the details of the atomic disasters.

During the early postwar months their labors yielded a considerable volume of solid research and surveys, the most important of which were later compiled by the Science Council of Japan (SRIABC 1951; CRIABC 1953).* Allied Occupation policies, however, imposed strict controls on all Japanese research into A-bomb affairs: under directives issued in late November 1945 by the General Headquarters (GHQ), Japanese scientists could neither undertake studies of A-bomb damages without permission nor could they publish their findings. Given these restrictions, their work was seriously curtailed until the conclusion of the San Francisco Peace Treaty in 1951.† Despite these limitations, many scientists managed to sustain their efforts; and their findings, particularly those revealing the marked increase in radiation aftereffects in 1946, contributed greatly to the medical treatment of exposed victims. With the signing of the San Francisco Peace Treaty, the Japanese regained the freedom to conduct scientific research openly and to publish their results. Since 1954, research on A-bomb damages has progressed rapidly in almost every field, in alliance with movements to secure relief for A-bomb survivors and to ban all nuclear weapons.

Only limited social studies were conducted during the first fifteen years after 1945; but since 1960, Japanese scholars have engaged in extensive research and surveys in order to ascertain how seriously atomic destruction damaged the social fabric. Confirming the actual conditions of the A-bomb victims became a matter of common commitment; deepening and transmitting the A-bomb experience, a common goal. As the real situation of the victims became more generally known, people began to realize that nuclear weapons endanger all mankind—and must be eliminated as soon as possible. An objective account of the realities of the Hiroshima and Nagasaki bombings, then, was clearly a necessary step on the way to banning all nuclear arms.

To assess the overall physical, medical, and social impact of the atomic bombings is not merely to recall the events of 1945; it is also to develop a new outlook on nuclear weapons in order to turn current world thinking away from their proliferation and toward their abolition. That task, however, is fraught with difficulties, especially in the area of social research. Indeed, the fact that there is so little basic research on the social dimensions of the atomic bombings clearly exposes the crisis of the atomic age.

---

* Nihon Gakujutsu Kenkyū Kaigi (Scientific Research Council of Japan) was the prewar/ wartime agency that advised the Japanese government on academic and scientific affairs. In July 1948 a law was passed combining it and another body (Nihon Gakushiin [Japan Academy]) to form Nihon Gakujutsu Kaigi (Science Council of Japan). Elections were held to select thirty members each for its seven sections (three in humanities, four in science)—a total of 210 members; and the Science Council of Japan began operations from June 1949. (The Japan Academy became independent again in 1956.)

† Details are given in part IV, chapter 13.

Atomic Destruction of Daily Life and Society

It is natural, when the destruction and casualties of war are extensive, for the impact on society to be great as well. In the case of an atomic bombing, however, a community does not merely receive an impact; the community itself is destroyed. Within 2 kilometers of the atomic bomb's hypocenter all life and property were shattered, burned, and buried under ashes. The visible forms of the city where people once carried on their daily lives vanished without trace. The destruction was sudden and thorough; there was virtually no chance to escape. Everything was utterly wiped out. Just as the demise of the irrigation system of Mesopotamia turned once fertile fields into a desert, so the cities of Hiroshima and Nagasaki were reduced to wastelands in an instant. Damage outside the 2-kilometer radius was also extensive. Houses were burned and flattened for several kilometers from the hypocenter, and radioactive fallout covered even wider areas. Citizens who had lost no family members in the holocaust were as rare as stars at sunrise.

Moreover, Hiroshima was hit by a violent typhoon on 17 September 1945. Floodwaters swept away over half the city's bridges; boats were often the only means for crossing the seven branches of the Ōtagawa river which courses through the city's delta center. Railroads and motor roads were ripped to pieces, making the transport of goods and materials extremely difficult. Had the atomic bomb not already demolished the city's services, the typhoon's damage might have been somewhat ameliorated. But there were no policemen, firemen, or community organizations to deal with broken dikes; there were no maintenance crews to clear off railways buried by earth and sand; there was no city hall to order emergency repairs to damaged highways. And it was not just a matter of reeling under the typhoon itself; the atomic bomb had blasted and burned hospitals, schools, city offices, police stations, and every other kind of human organization. In Nagasaki, it was the same; the bombed area was no longer fit for human habitation.

The atomic bombs, then, not only devastated the daily lives of citizens; they also permanently changed the structures of society. Hiroshima had once flourished as a castle town in the Tokugawa era (1603–1868), while Nagasaki was once Japan's primary port for foreign trade. Their populations had long and proud traditions of community organization maintained by the people themselves. Family, relatives, neighbors, and friends relied on a broad range of interdependent organizations for everything from birth, marriage, and funerals to firefighting, productive work, and daily living. These traditional communities were completely demolished in an instant. Those who survived were at a loss to know how to function. Had Japan at the time been a mature modern society, national and local governments might have set up the necessary agencies for social relief on which the people could have relied. But once emergency hospitals and first-aid stations were closed down, the people were left with virtually no means of relief from public sources. The responsibilities of wartime administration did not include looking after ordinary citizens in need.

The seriousness of atomic destruction cannot be understood unless, in addition to injuries suffered by individual persons, one also takes into account the damage done to the whole social fabric. Where household heads or spouses were injured or killed by the bomb, and even if other family members had escaped injury or death, the entire household suffered. It could no longer function properly as a corporate body. Many stores, factories, and offices were forced to close down due to lost personnel. Over half of the schools and other community organizations met a similar fate. When the key members of a community are wiped out or wounded, the community itself disintegrates, and traditional society collapses.

The Difficulties of Conducting Social Surveys of Atomic Destruction

Despite the setback caused by Occupation restrictions, important gains in physical and medical research of A-bomb damages were made. Developments in these areas are explained in part IV, chapter 13, and the principal findings are reviewed in parts I and II.

On the other hand, while the importance of surveys of how atomic destruction affected the daily life of society has often been stressed, the overall picture is still far from clear. There are several reasons for this situation.

The first is that the government of Japan at the time was extremely bureaucratic; the very idea that it should protect the rights and the livelihood of its citizens did not exist in its administrative organs. Had the government possessed some system for compensating the family survivors of those killed in the bombings, it would have carried out surveys to check on background, income, and cause of death of the victims; but there was no provision for condolence payments to survivors, and thus no need for surveys. Accordingly, no thorough ones were conducted. It was the same with the surviving A-bomb victims. They had to manage somehow with what was left of the traditional communities to which they belonged; the government took no

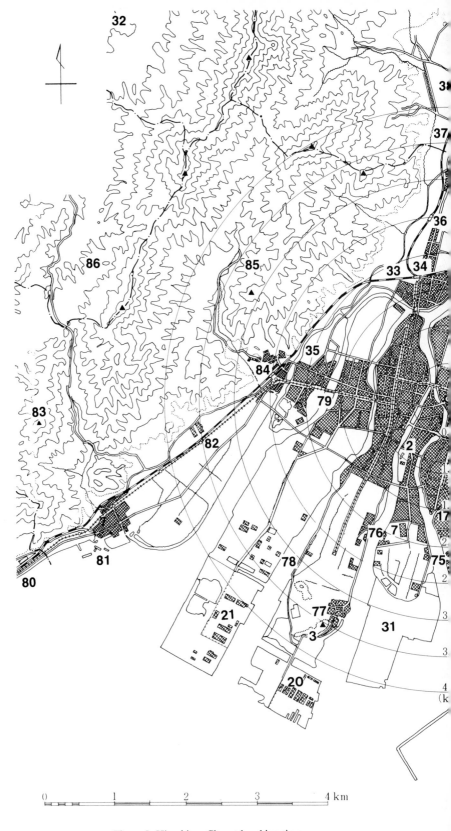

0   1   2   3   4 km

Figure I. Hiroshima City at bombing time.

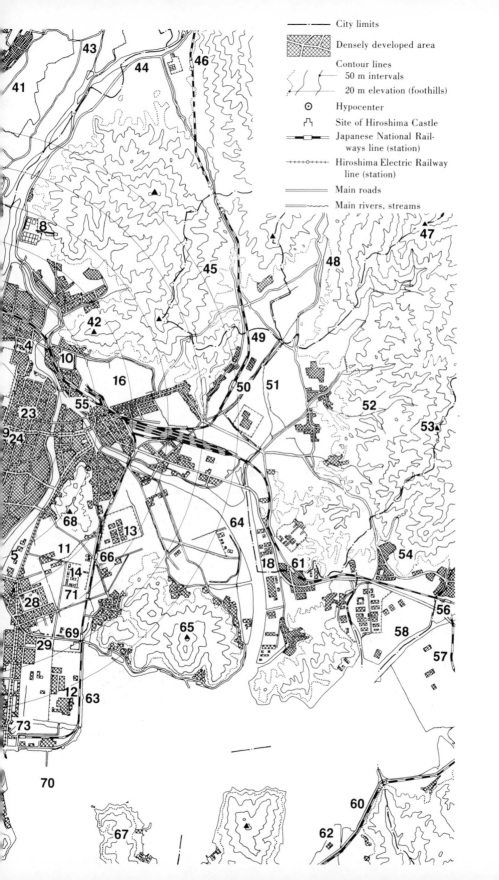

—·—	City limits
▨	Densely developed area
	Contour lines
	50 m intervals
	20 m elevation (foothills)
⊙	Hypocenter
⊓	Site of Hiroshima Castle
━◼━	Japanese National Railways line (station)
+++o+++	Hiroshima Electric Railway line (station)
═══	Main roads
══	Main rivers, streams

1. Hiroshima City Office
2. Hiroshima Pretectural Office
3. Hiroshima District Meteorological Observatory
4. Hiroshima Communications Bureau
5. Hiroshima District Monopoly Bureau
6. Hiroshima District Court/Court of Appeal
7. Hiroshima Prison
8. Hiroshima Municipal Filtration Plant
9. Chūgoku Regional Military Headquarters
10. Second Army Headquarters
11. Army Marine Communications Regiment
12. Army Marine Training Division
13. Hiroshima Army Ordnance Supply Depot
14. Hiroshima Army Clothing Depot
15. Hiroshima Army Provisions Depot
16. Eastern Drill Ground
17. Hiroshima Red Cross Hospital
18. Tōyō Kōgyō Co., Ltd.
19. Fukuya Department Store
20. Mitsubishi Heavy Industries Hiroshima Shipyard
21. Mitsubishi Heavy Industries Hiroshima Machine Tool Works
22. Chūgoku Power Distribution Company
23. Hiroshima Central Broadcasting Station (NHK-Hiroshima)
24. Chūgoku Shinbun News Publishing Company
25. Hiroshima Electric Railway Company
26. Hiroshima University of Literature and Science
27. Hiroshima Higher Normal School
28. Hiroshima Higher School
29. Hiroshima Prefectural Women's College
30. Hiroshima Technical College
31. Army Air Field
32. Numata Town
33. Sanyō Main Line
34. Yokogawa Station
35. Yamate River
36. Mitaki Station
37. Kabe Railway Line
38. Gion Town
39. Aki-Nagatsuki Station
40. Shimo-Gion Station
41. Yasu River
42. Mt. Futaba
43. Furu River
44. Ōta River
45. Nakayama Village
46. Hesaka Station
47. Mt. Takao
48. Nukushina Village
49. Geibi Railway Line
50. Yaga Station
51. Nukushina River
52. Fuchū Town
53. Mt. Chausu
54. Funakoshi Town
55. Hiroshima Station
56. Kaitaichi Station
57. Kaitaichi Town
58. Seno River
59. Yano Town
60. Kure Railway Line
61. Mukainada Station
62. Saka Town
63. Ujina Railway Line
64. Enkō River
65. Mt. Ōgon
66. Kami-Ōkō Station
67. Kanawajima Island
68. Hijiyama Hill
69. Tanna Station
70. Ujina Port
71. Shimo-Ōkō Station
72. Ujina Island
73. Ujina Station
74. Kyōbashi River
75. Motoyasu River
76. Honkawa River
77. Eba Hill
78. Tenma River
79. Fukushima River
80. Inokuchi Village
81. Kusatsu Harbor
82. Miyajima Streetcar Line
83. Mt. Onigajō
84. Koi Station
85. Mt. Chausu
86. Ishiuchi Village

responsibility for these people. As Hiroshima and Nagasaki had been battle-fields, it would have been only natural for the government to care for A-bomb victims as it did for military personnel; but it lacked such concern, and made no surveys as a preliminary to rendering aid.

A second reason for lack of information is that the atomic bomb was a totally new experience in human history. What to survey, and how to survey it, could be judged only in part from previous war damages; a complete investigation was impossible. In order to determine the number of A-bomb victims, it was necessary to determine the amount of radiation one would have to have received to qualify as a victim. The fact that radioactivity was carried by rainfall far outside the immediate bombed areas complicated this problem. Secondary victims among those entering the cities after the bombings—involving factors of date, time, place, and kind of work or activity—made the matter even more complex. A further complication arose from the fear that doctors and nurses involved in the long-term care of A-bomb victims—not only those in the two bombed cities but even those who fled to Tokyo—would also become contaminated by radiation. Secondary victims were not only those touched by radiation; many children and elderly people evacuated from the two cities prior to the bombings became orphaned when their families in the cities were wiped out. At the same time traditional society was breaking down. According to how one defines orphaned children and the elderly, their numbers and the relief measures needed vary widely. As deaths apparently related to the atomic bombings continued long after 1945, it is necessary to select a clear cut-off date (year and month) in order to determine how many deaths were directly caused by, or related to, the atomic bombings. Deaths occurred steadily into 1946 and after; by 1950 the count had risen by several tens of thousands. Even after that year, many died from leukemia and other malignancies—diseases that were thought to be related to the atomic bombings. These various factors distinguish atomic warfare from ordinary wars. It is important to establish clearly the numbers of those killed by the bombings themselves as well as of those who died with acute symptoms after the bombings; but, as it is impossible to diagnose each case individually, the number of deaths with acute symptoms is calculated as of the selected date.

A third reason for the incomplete picture of A-bomb damage is that the sufferings of the A-bomb victims were complicated by psychological problems—a special characteristic of such damage. Because the magnitude of atomic destruction exceeds all human imagination, the A-bomb victims suffered extreme psychological shock; and the shock intensified their suffering. To make matters worse, keloid scars developed later on burned areas of their bodies, and the incidence of leukemia rose. Psychologically, the victims

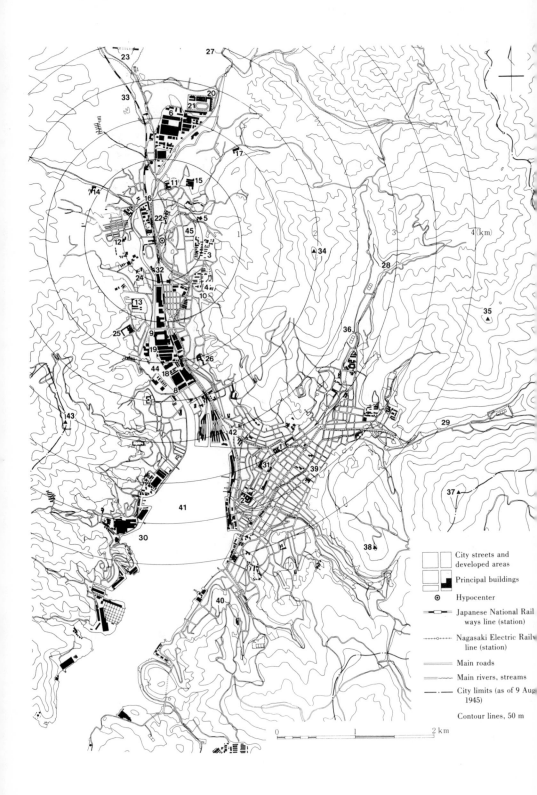

City streets and
developed areas

Principal buildings

Hypocenter

Japanese National Rail
ways line (station)

Nagasaki Electric Railw
line (station)

Main roads

Main rivers, streams

City limits (as of 9 Aug
1945)

Contour lines, 50 m

0   1   2 km

Figure II. Nagasaki City at bombing time.

1. Nagasaki City Office
2. Nagasaki Prefectural Office
3. Nagasaki Medical University
4. Nagasaki Medical University Hospital
5. Urakami Cathedral
6. Mitsubishi Heavy Industries Nagasaki Ordnance Factory, Ōhashi Plant
7. Mitsubishi Heavy Industries Nagasaki Shipyard, Ōhashi Parts Plant
8. Inasa Bridge
9. Yanagawa Bridge
10. Sannō Shrine
11. Yamazato Primary School
12. Shiroyama Primary School
13. Keiho Middle School
14. Nagasaki Commercial School
15. Nagasaki Technical School
16. Ōhashi Bridge
17. Urakami First Hospital
18. Mitsubishi Heavy Industries Nagasaki Shipyard, Saiwaimachi Plant
19. Mitsubishi Steel Manufacturing Co. First Nagasaki Plant
20. Nishi-Urakami Primary School
21. Nagasaki Normal School
22. Urakami Prison
23. Mitsubishi Heavy Industries Nagasaki Ordnance Factory, Sumiyoshi Tunneling Works
24. Chinzei Middle School
25. Fuchi Primary School
26. Zenza Primary School
27. Urakami Reservoir
28. Nishiyama Reservoir
29. Hongōchi Reservoir
30. Mitsubishi Heavy Industries Nagasaki Shipyard
31. Shinkōzen Primary School
32. Mitsubishi Electric Corporation, Nagasaki Foundry
33. Nagasaki Main Line
34. Mt. Konpira
35. Mt. Hōka
36. Nishiyama District
37. Mt. Hiko
38. Mt. Atago
39. Nakashima River
40. Ōura District
41. Nagasaki Port
42. Nagasaki Station
43. Mt. Inasa
44. Urakami River
45. Urakami District

were burdened with almost inconsolable hopelessness and anguish—which have been termed "keloid of the heart" and "leukemia of the spirit." The complexity of psychological shock makes it most difficult to measure and evaluate in qualitative, quantitative, and chronological terms.

The A-bomb experience was brutalizing. In a sociopsychological survey of the households of 332 A-bomb victims and those of 268 nonvictims conducted in Kure City in October 1952, Seiichi Nakano (1954, pp. 29–39) found that, among surviving victims who had been within 1 kilometer of the hypocenter at bombing time, the tendency was for children to abandon parents and for husbands to abandon their wives (mothers' attitudes toward children was different) and seek only their own escape. Such behavior destroys one's trust in human relations and gives rise in time to "keloid of the spirit," and was in clear contrast to the behavior of nonvictims. The depth of such inner suffering can hardly be measured quantitatively on a universal scale.

The A-bomb victims' strong sense of mission to abolish all nuclear weapons everywhere stems from the extremity of their suffering, and their plight and their purpose have deeply moved many thousands of people. Even so, the A-bomb victims' energetic efforts to share their experiences have not been as fruitful as they hoped. When others have been deaf to their arguments, the victims have been tempted to conclude that "unless you are an A-bomb victim, you can't understand." It is, after all, an almost hopeless task to communicate ideas and feelings about the A-bomb experience to the nations of the world that are in a headlong race to expand and upgrade their nuclear arsenals. Thus, the victims have converted these ideas and feelings into a rationale to ban all nuclear weapons.

The fourth reason for incomplete data on A-bomb damage derives from the restrictions imposed by the Allied Occupation of Japan. On 6 September 1945, the General Headquarters of the Occupation forces issued a statement that made it clear that people likely to die from A-bomb afflictions should be left to die. The official attitude in early September was that people suffering from radiation injuries were not worth saving. Then, on 19 September, a press code was adopted that imposed prior censorship on all radio broadcasts and on newspapers, magazines, and other print media (Central Liaison Office 1947, p. 260). As a result, all reports, commentaries, and treatises dealing with A-bomb damages, including even those about medical treatment of A-bomb-related symptoms, were prohibited. Except for a brief time before the press code was imposed, all accounts of A-bomb damages disappeared from newspapers, magazines, and academic journals.

On the other hand, articles that publicized the power of the atomic bomb were warmly welcomed by GHQ. A group of American reporters who visited Hiroshima on 3 September 1945 expressed satisfaction with the complete destruction of the city. At a press conference held at the prefectural office, *New York Times* reporter W. L. Laurence noted the total devastation of the city and its population and extolled the obvious superiority of the bomb's potential. Some Japanese reporters present at this press conference raised questions from the standpoint of the bomb's victims—Would Hiroshima be uninhabitable for seventy-five years? Would the atomic bomb contribute to world peace?—but Laurence refused to respond to such questions. His concern was solely with the might of the bomb; its victims interested him only as proof of that might. Hiroshima's desolation and the cause of peace were of no interest to him. This singular focus on the atomic bomb's power was not limited to *Times* reporter Laurence; it was the policy of the Occupation and of the United States government at that time.

In any case, GHQ restrictions on reporting A-bomb damages effectively postponed serious research by social scientists. In 1949, for example, Hiroshima University planned to open a peace research center, but this plan was lost to oblivion.

In Hiroshima and Nagasaki there were many Japanese military personnel and government-conscripted workers, and a number of foreigners as well. The A-bomb victims had come from many different places all over Japan, and many of them had now returned to their native towns and provinces or had moved elsewhere. Thus, a survey of the A-bomb's aftermath could not be done without help from the national government. The state should, of course, have conducted a thorough survey of those victimized in the war it had itself started; although it did form an academic study group soon after the atomic bombings, it excluded the social sciences and humanities from this group and did not even attempt to determine the number of A-bomb victims. The peoples of Hiroshima and Nagasaki, as well as their municipal and prefectural governments, made repeated requests for surveys; but the national government consistently turned down these requests. Finally, in 1965—twenty years after the atomic bombings—the Ministry of Health and Welfare, backed by a National Diet decision, conducted a survey of the conditions of people holding A-bomb health books (certificate-record books issued under the 1957 A-bomb Victims Medical Care Law). This was the first survey of this kind made by the national government. A summary report of this initial survey, issued in 1967, was so far removed from reality that it was roundly condemned by specialists and A-bomb victims' associations alike. Even researchers involved in the survey criticized it. The full report, therefore, was not published at this time (Yuzaki 1977*b*, pp. 279–313). Since then no fully adequate national survey of A-bomb victims has been made, despite repeated demands from the Science Council of Japan. The Ministry of Health and Welfare in 1975 did conduct the Survey of A-bomb Victims

Conditions, and the results were published in 1977; but this, too, was inadequate.

Despite so many adverse circumstances, the A-bomb victims' needs and the concern of scientists blended to spur surveys of the victims' social situation, bit by bit, following conclusion of the San Francisco Peace Treaty that ended the Allied Occupation. As noted earlier, from 1954 serious research by natural scientists gradually got under way, and social surveys were begun in connection with the nationwide movement to aid A-bomb victims; then, in the 1960s extensive studies were conducted by social scientists. Also in that decade, the decline in the number of victims, due to aging and dying, became marked, while the memories of surviving victims began to fade. Thus, records of the A-bomb damages in Hiroshima and Nagasaki, as well as thousands of personal testimonies, were collected and published; and efforts to reconstruct the actual configurations of the two cities' bombed areas were promoted. Furthermore, the disputes that erupted and divided the antinuclear movement by the early 1960s, served to stimulate reassessment of the whole movement and thereby drew attention to the A-bomb experience. Studies of all these sources progressed, and many research reports were published to commemorate the thirtieth anniversary (1975) of the atomic bombings. Nonetheless, more remained obscure concerning the social dimensions of A-bomb damage than was clarified.

The devastation of community structures by atomic bombing was sweeping and multifaceted. The deaths and the dissolution of whole families, along with the physical and spiritual suffering that continues even today, amount to a consummate tragedy beyond what anyone could have imagined before the bombs were dropped. The task of assessing so massive a breakdown accurately and comprehensively has for many years been almost impossible. The compiling and sorting of relevant data remains inadequate. All who would, through systematic research, draw lessons from the A-bomb experience still labor under painful limitations. In part III, too, we have not been able to escape all those limitations; yet we have done our best to compile the best results of all accumulated social research and to outline the main problems encountered along the way.

* * *

This book consists of the following parts:

Part I (chapters 1–6) focuses on the atomic bomb's enormous power and special features to give a detailed but compact description of various kinds of physical destruction.

Part II (chapters 7–9) explains in detail the various damages to the human body caused by atomic bombs—external wounds, burns, and radiation injuries. These chapters cover both the immediate effects of the bombings and the long-term aftereffects that continue to the present day.

Part III (chapters 10–12) treats the overall collapse of society that resulted from atomic destruction, ranging over many aspects of daily life and community relationships, with careful attention to the difficulties described in the preceding paragraphs.

Part IV (chapters 13–14) summarizes efforts to survey and analyze A-bomb damages as well as efforts to provide adequate relief and medical care to the A-bomb victims, and then traces the growth of the antinuclear movement and the evolution of peace education—all from the crucial perspective of the aim to rid the earth of all nuclear weapons.

The ruins of the Urakami Cathedral in Nagasaki (approximately 500 meters from the hypocenter, April 1958). (Photograph by Sadao Tsuba.)

PART I

PHYSICAL ASPECTS OF DESTRUCTION

Chapter 1

Atomic Bombing—
Hiroshima
and Nagasaki

6 August 1945: Hiroshima

In the early morning of 6 August 1945, a United States Army weather observation plane took off from the Tinian* air base toward the Japanese interior. As the plane neared Hiroshima City at an altitude of 10,000 meters, it sent a message to the B-29 *Enola Gay,* which was following it and carrying the atomic bomb: "Fair weather, ready for air raid." At 7:09 A.M. the air-raid alert was sounded by the Hiroshima Chūgoku Regional Military Headquarters, but it was called off at 7:31 since the weather observation plane had turned back and flown away. The people in the city were on their way to work. At 7:00 A.M. workers had started tearing down buildings as part of the city's self-defense measures; and many volunteers and students, who had come from both inside and outside the city, were at work in the open. When the air-raid alert was called off, there was a brief moment of relief among these people. It did not last long—at 8:15 A.M. the whole city was instantaneously covered by a bluish-white glare.† The *Enola Gay,* together with two

---

* Tinian is one of the Mariana Islands and is approximately 2,740 kilometers from Hiroshima (see map in figure 6.3). It took B-29s about six and one-half hours to fly nonstop over this distance.

† Hiroshima Prefectural Office 1976, p. 484; Hiroshima City Office 1971, p. 59.

weather observation planes, invaded the skies of Hiroshima from the northeast and released the atomic bomb at 8:15:17 A.M. (Tinian time, 9:15:17 A.M.) at an altitude of 9,600 meters: the atomic bomb exploded 43 seconds later (Knebel and Bailey 1960). Records on the time of the explosion vary from 8:15 to 8:18 A.M.,* but the official time according to Hiroshima City is 8:15 A.M.

With the explosion of the atomic bomb, the epicenter instantaneously reached a maximum temperature of several million degrees centigrade and an atmospheric pressure of several 100,000 bars; with the formation of a fireball, powerful heat rays and radiation were emitted in all directions within a short interval. Radiation extended not only directly from the burst point but also from the surface of the ground—from fission fragments and the residue of neutron-induced radioactive materials. The shock waves propagated by the explosion and the tremendous blast that followed almost instantaneously demolished buildings and killed many people. The survivors suffered the agonies of thermal burns and radiation exposure, whose effects were in many cases delayed.

News of the atomic bombing was briefly announced at 6 P.M. by Radio Newscast of the Japan Broadcasting Corporation: "August the 6th. Hiroshima was attacked by B-29s this morning at 8:20. The planes have turned back after dropping incendiary bombs. Damage is now being investigated." The news of the bombing was dispatched from Osaka and reported by newspapers throughout Japan on the following day (Hiroshima Prefectural Office 1976, p. 99).

On 6 August (7 August in Japan), U.S. President Harry S. Truman had stated clearly that the bomb used on Hiroshima was an atomic bomb. The Japanese Imperial Headquarters' announcement was made at 3:30 P.M. on 7 August: "Yesterday Hiroshima was considerably damaged by the attack of B-29s. Our enemies have apparently used a new type of bomb, but details are now being investigated" (Hiroshima Prefectural Office 1976, p. 94).

The altitude of the atomic bomb burst point and the location of the hypocenter (the point on the ground directly below the burst point) can be assumed from the shadows cast by objects that had been scorched by thermal rays.

The altitude of the burst point was estimated to be 577 ± 20 meters (Kimura and Tajima 1953, p. 83) and 570 ± 20 meters (Kanai 1953, p. 92) from the investigation made in 1945, but it was changed to 606 meters (Arakawa and Nagaoka 1959) in 1959, and to 580 meters (Woodbury and Mizuki 1961) in 1961. In 1969 a composite evaluation of these data was made, with the conclusion that the altitude of the burst point was 580 ± 15 meters (Hubbell, Jones, and Cheka 1969). At the present time this figure is considered to be the most reliable.

* Glasstone 1962, p. 672; Hirose and Sugito 1953, p. 212; Hiroshima District Meteorological Observatory 1953, p. 119; Uda, Sugahara, and Kita 1953, p. 98.

Figure 1.1. Hiroshima, about 1 hour after the bombing on 6 August 1945. (Photographed from a U.S. bomber above the Seto Inland Sea, about 80 kilometers from the hypocenter.) From documents returned to Japan by the United States.

There have been many estimates about the location of the hypocenter. These are included within the limits of coordinates 744. 30 ± 0.05 (abscissa), and 1261. 70 ± 0.05 (ordinate) on Map L902 of the U.S. Army Map Service (figure 1.2). The estimate made in 1945 (Kimura and Tajima 1953) was almost identical to the composite evaluation in 1969 (Hubbell, Jones, and Cheka 1969), the hypocenter being situated at coordinates 744.298 (longitude 132°27′29″ E) × 1261.707 (latitude 34°23′29″ N)—a difference in radius of about 15 meters. This point is located on the ground of the Shima Hospital, 160 meters southeast from the center of the Atomic Bomb Dome.

9 August 1945: Nagasaki

A hot morning in Nagasaki. Several air-raid alarms and alerts from early morning. Since alerts and alarms had been repeatedly announced every day,

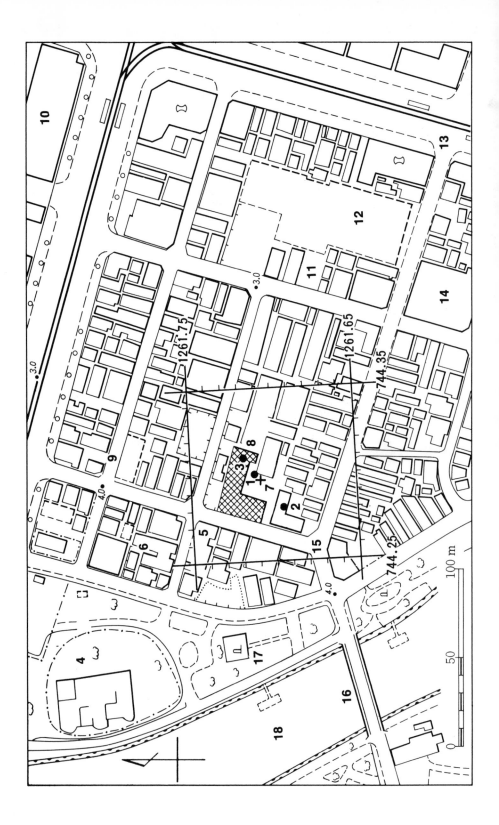

Figure 1.2. Hypocenter in Hiroshima: 1—as estimated by Kimura and Tajima (1953, p. 83) (744.30, 1261.71); 2—as estimated by Arakawa and Nagaoka (1959) (744.281, 1261.696); 3—as estimated by Woodbury and Mizuki (1961) (744.31, 1261.72); +—as estimated by Hubbell, Jones, and Cheka (1969) (744.298, 1261.707).

1. As estimated by Kimura and Tajima 1953 (744.30, 1261.71).
2. As estimated by Arakawa and Nagaoka 1959 (744.281, 1261.696)
3. As estimated by Woodbury and Mizuki 1961 (744.31, 1261.72)
   + As estimated by Hubbell, Jones, and Cheka 1969 (744.298, 1261.707)
4. Atomic Bomb Dome
5. Saikōji Temple
6. Sairenji Temple
7. Ōtemachi Township
8. Shima Hospital
9. Saikumachi Township
10. Bus Terminal
11. Kamiyachō Township
12. Hirogoku Building
13. Hondōri Shopping Street
14. Uneed Supermarket
15. Yokomachi Township
16. Motoyasu Bridge
17. Memorial Tower to the Mobilized Students
18. Motoyasu River

Figure 1.3. Nagasaki, 9 August 1945. A few minutes after the bombing. (Photographed from a U.S. bomber.) From documents returned to Japan by the United States.

people accepted them like the daily mail and returned to work when the alarms were called off. In the city, people were lining up to receive their rations, classes were going on in the schools, and patients were being treated in the hospitals.

Two planes—the B-29 bearing the atomic bomb and a weather observation plane—had left the Tinian air base in formation flight early in the morning and, at 9:50 A.M., were over Kokura,* their first target. The skies of Kokura, however, were covered by heavy clouds; and after circling the area for about 10 minutes, the planes headed for Nagasaki, their second target (Chinnock 1970). The Sixteenth Army Headquarters announced the air invasion (Nagasaki Shiyakusho 1977, pp. 137–59). The second atomic bomb exploded in the skies over Nagasaki City at 11:02 A.M.

According to the memorandum (Marx 1971) written by one of the crew on the weather observation plane, the atomic bomb had been dropped in the following way. Since the skies over Nagasaki were covered by clouds, the bomb was to be released by radar. Then a gap appeared between the clouds, through which could be seen below the Mitsubishi Heavy Industries Nagasaki Arsenal. The atomic bomb was instantly released, and the B-29 made a quick turn to escape. The time was 0:02 P.M. in Tinian (11:02 A.M. in Japan).

As to the actual time of the bombing, there are many records, as in Hiroshima. The automatic instruments at the Nagasaki Meteorological Station indicated sharp fluctuations of pressure at 10:54 A.M. It was found later, however, that the clock attached to the recorder was inaccurate; and the time was corrected to 11:05 A.M. The time was recorded as 11:02 A.M. by the vibration meter at the Onsendake Meteorological Station in Unzen, located at about 38 kilometers from Nagasaki City, and as 11:07 A.M. at the Saga Meteorological Station, about 70 kilometers from Nagasaki.† The head of the Nagasaki Meteorological Station reported the time of the explosion to be 10:59 A.M. (Nakamura 1953, p. 177). There also is a record of 10:58 A.M. (Glasstone 1962), but Nagasaki City has adopted 11:02 A.M. as the time.

There have been many estimates of the height of the burst point. The estimated height was 490 ± 25 meters in a study (Kimura and Tajima 1953, p. 83) carried out in the same year. Estimated values made in 1966 and 1969 were 500 ± 9 meters (Hubbell et al. 1970) and 504 ± 10 meters (Hubbell,

---

* Kokura is situated in the northeast of Fukuoka Prefecture in the island of Kyushu. An arsenal was built here in 1933. Since then, the city had come to assume a strategic aspect as an army base. In 1963 the adjacent five cities were merged to form a new city, Kitakyushu, a major trade and industrial center with a population of well over one million.

† NGO International Symposium on the Damage and Aftereffects of the Atomic Bombing, Nagasaki Preparatory Committee and Expert Committee for the Preparation of the Nagasaki Report 1977b.

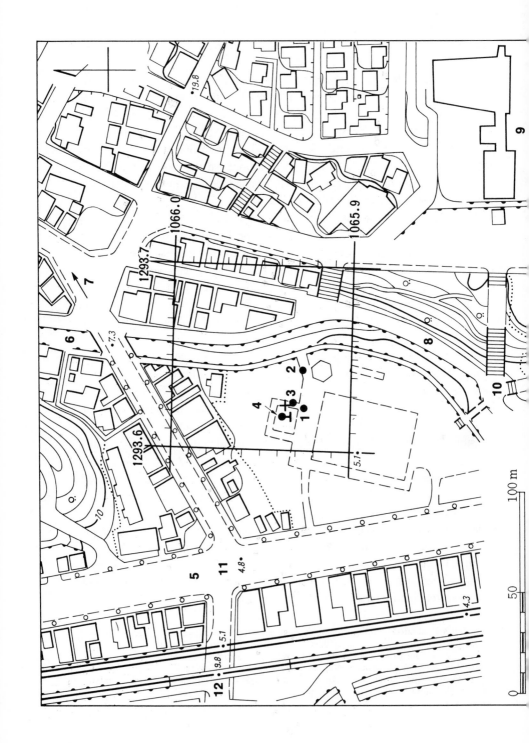

Jones, and Cheka 1969), respectively. Analysis of all data in 1976 revealed the estimated height to be 503 ± 10 meters (Kerr and Solomon 1976); this figure is at present the most reliable.

The assumed location of the hypocenter is shown on Map L902 of the U.S. Army Map Service (figure 1.4; hypocenter indicated by a + mark). The location was obtained from a reanalysis of the available data in 1976 (Kerr and Solomon 1976) and can be considered fairly accurate. The hypocenter in Nagasaki is located at coordinates 1293.624 ± 0.007 (longitude 129°51′56″4 E) × 1065.936 ± 0.008 (latitude 32°46′12″6 N)—a difference in radius of about 7 meters. This site is approximately 90 meters east-southeast of a main intersection in the township of Matsuyama, and about where the Hypocenter Monument at Heiwa Kōen (Peace Park) is now.

Figure 1.4. Hypocenter in Nagasaki: 1—as estimated by Kimura and Tajima 1953 (p. 83) (1293.623, 1065.926); 2—as estimated by Hubbell et al. 1970 (1293.644, 1065.927); 3—as estimated by Hubbell, Jones, and Cheka 1969 (1293.626, 1065.932); 4—as estimated by Kerr and Solomon 1976 (1293.624, 1065.936).

1. As estimated by Kimura and Tajima 1953 (1293.623, 1065.926)
2. As estimated by Hubbell et al. 1970 (1293.644, 1065.927)
3. As estimated by Hubbell, Jones, and Cheka 1969 (1293.626, 1065.932)
   + As estimated by Kerr and Solomon 1976 (1293.624, 1065.936)
4. Hypocenter Monument
5. Route 206
6. Matsuyama Bridge
7. To Urakami Cathedral
8. Shimonokawa River
9. Nagasaki International Cultural Hall
10. Midori Bridge
11. Matsuyama-machi Intersection
12. Nagasaki Main Line

Chapter 2

The Atomic Bomb and Thermal Radiations

The Atomic Bomb

Uranium 235 (^{235}U) and plutonium 239 (^{239}P) were used in the atomic bombing of Hiroshima and Nagasaki, respectively. Neutrons are collided onto the nucleus of each of these isotopes, causing an explosive chain reaction of nuclear fission and releasing a large amount of energy. The energy released in both Hiroshima and Nagasaki was long thought to be the equivalent of 20 kilotons of conventional high explosive trinitrotoluene (TNT) (Hirschfelder et al. 1950). It has been recently estimated, however, to have been 12.5 ± 1 kilotons in Hiroshima and 22 ± 2 kilotons in Nagasaki (Auxier et al. 1966; Penny, Samuels, and Scorgie 1970). The energy released by 20 kilotons of TNT is about equivalent to the energy released at the time of complete nuclear fission of 1 kilogram of uranium 235 (Hirschfelder et al. 1950).

The power of the atomic bomb as usually expressed in equivalents of TNT is merely a comparison of total amounts of energy and ignores the essential qualitative difference between an atomic bomb and a conventional bomb. The content of the energy yield by nuclear fission of uranium 235 is of special importance. The emitted fission fragments have marked radioactivity, and about 17 percent of the total energy released by nuclear fission is the result of radiation. It is, therefore, inadequate to evaluate the power of the atomic bomb in terms of the energy released by TNT.

Figure 2.1. A full-size model of the atomic bomb that was dropped on Hiroshima. (Photograph contributed by Wide World Photos, Inc.)

Figure 2.2. A full-size model of the atomic bomb that was dropped on Nagasaki. (Photograph contributed by Wide World Photos, Inc.)

The type of atomic bomb ("Little Boy"*) dropped on Hiroshima is shown in figure 2.1. The size of the bomb was 3 meters in length by 0.7 meter in diameter, and the weight, 4 tons. Figure 2.2 is the atomic bomb ("Fat Man"†) dropped on Nagasaki; it measured 3.5 meters in length by 1.5 meters in diameter and weighed 4.5 tons.

* "Little Boy" was the name, used by scientists in the United States, for the uranium bomb, in reference to Franklin D. Roosevelt.
† "Fat Man" was the name for the plutonium bomb, in reference to Winston Churchill.

Formation of Fireball and Release of Thermal Radiations

Though the explosion of the atomic bombs in Hiroshima and Nagasaki has not been scientifically observed, experiments using standard atomic bombs with similar energy (equivalent to 20 kilotons of TNT) have been carried out in the United States. From these experiments it has been possible to study the atomic bombs used in Japan (Glasstone 1962, pp. 316–68; Hirschfelder et al. 1950).

One characteristic of the atomic bomb is the extremely high temperature it produces as compared with conventional explosives. The maximum temperature at the bursting point reaches several million degrees centigrade, while that of the conventional explosive is about 5,000° C. At the high temperatures of an atomic bomb all materials composing it become an ionized gas, and electromagnetic waves of short wave length of about 0.01–10 nanometers (1 nanometer = 10^{-9} meters) is released. These waves are instantly absorbed by air within a few meters; and as the temperature rises, a fireball forms.

Thermal radiations responding to temperature are then released from the fireball. The energy of thermal radiations, as in the air burst of the atomic bomb, is about 35 percent of the whole energy. An enormous amount of energy of about 7×10^{12} calories is, therefore, released as thermal radiations from the standard atomic bomb. Men and animals in Hiroshima and Nagasaki were seriously injured by thermal burns, and buildings and trees were scorched and burned.

The burst point probably reached a temperature of several million degrees centigrade within one millionth of a second after the explosion; and 0.1 millisecond later, an isothermal sphere, with a radius of about 15 meters and a temperature of about 300,000° C., was formed. The temperature inside such a sphere is almost uniform, and the shock front coincides with the surface of the fireball.

Thereafter, with the movement of the shock front, or wave, a tremendous pressure rapidly builds up, and the fireball now consists of two concentric regions—an inner hot region and an outer region of somewhat lower temperature.

For some time the fireball continues to expand, but the shock spreads more rapidly. With the spread of the shock front, the temperature of the air surrounding the fireball rises and becomes luminous. Then the temperature of the air decreases gradually; and as it does, it loses this luminescence so that it is possible to see the inner region of the hot fireball. This moment is referred to as the *breakaway*. In the standard atomic bomb, the breakaway is reached 15 milliseconds after the explosion.

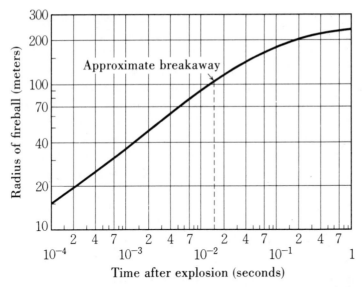

Figure 2.3. Variation of radius of luminous fireball with time in a 20-kiloton explosion (Glasstone 1962, p. 74).

Figure 2.4. Variation of apparent fireball surface temperature with time in a 20-kiloton explosion (Glasstone 1962, p. 75).

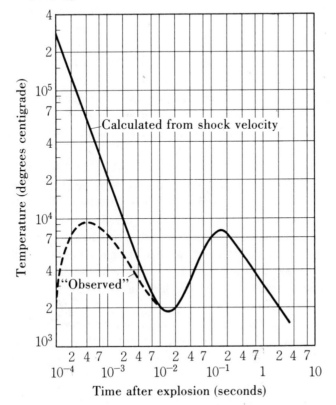

Even after the breakaway, the fireball at the center gradually increases in size and reaches its maximum size 1 second after the explosion. The variation in size of the fireball with time is shown in figure 2.3. The observed variation of fireball surface temperature 0.1 millisecond to 15 milliseconds after the explosion is represented by the broken curve in figure 2.4.

When the temperature of the outer region of the fireball approaches a temperature of about 1,800° C. (about 15 milliseconds after the explosion), the surface temperature again starts to rise. In about 0.2 seconds after the explosion, it reaches a temperature of about 7,700° C. and then gradually falls. About 10 seconds later, the brightness of the fireball disappears completely.

Among the thermal radiations emitted by the fireball, ultraviolet rays of short-wave length are considerably absorbed in air and ozone and attenuate during transmission. The thermal rays that extended a great distance from the fireball surface were near-ultraviolet ray, visible ray, and infrared ray.

Ultraviolet rays and near-ultraviolet rays were almost completely emitted within 15 milliseconds (time to temperature minimum in figure 2.4) after the explosion, and the total energy of ultraviolet rays and near-ultraviolet rays reaching the ground was extremely small. It can, therefore, be assumed that the heat rays causing thermal burns in human subjects were infrared rays emitted in vast amounts 0.2 to 3 seconds after the explosion.

Distance-dependent Attenuation of Thermal Radiations

The degree of damage to material caused by thermal radiations emitted from the fireball depends on the amount of heat energy received by its surface and on their wavelength. The latter is dependent on the temperature of the fireball.

Thermal radiation energy per unit area attenuates with the distance from the burst point. There are two attenuations: one is inversely proportional to the square of the distance; and the other is brought about by absorption and scattering in radiation's passage through the air.

Absorption and scattering occur from nitrogen and oxygen molecules in the air, or from dust particles and vapor in the air. In general, attenuation is greater with dust particles and water vapor. When the range of vision is poor due to dust particles and fog, the distance covered by thermal radiation is extremely decreased.

In order to estimate the degree of attenuation, the term *visibility* is sometimes used to describe the range of vision. By visibility is meant the maximum distance at which it is possible to discern a large dark object (such as a tree) on the horizon with the daytime sky in the background. When the air is exceptionally clear, the visibility is about 40 kilometers; when clear, about 20 kilometers; and when there is a light haze, about 5 kilometers.

The weather was fine at the time of the bombing both in Hiroshima and Nagasaki. The visibility was recorded by the Hiroshima District Meteorological Observatory, which is located on Eba hill about 3.6 kilometers south-southwest from the hypocenter. According to the observatory report, the visibility north of Eba hill at 8 A.M. was over 20 kilometers; at 9 A.M., 2 kilometers; and between 11 and 12 A.M., 1 kilometer, as it was enveloped in fire and smoke (Uda, Sugahara, and Kita 1953).

The situation was presumably similar in Nagasaki, although this was not recorded. The visibility at the time of the bombing in both cities can be considered to have been over 20 kilometers. Table 2.1 gives the calculations

TABLE 2.1
Estimated Thermal Energy on the Ground

Distance from Hypocenter (m)	Slant Distance from Epicenter* (m)	Thermal Energy (cal/cm²)†	
		Visual Range (20 km)	Visual Range (30 km)
0 Hiroshima	580	96	100
Nagasaki	500	222	229
500 Hiroshima	766	53	56
Nagasaki	707	107	112
1,000 Hiroshima	1,156	22	23
Nagasaki	1,118	39	42
1,500 Hiroshima	1,608	10	11
Nagasaki	1,581	18	20
2,000 Hiroshima	2,082	5.5	6.3
Nagasaki	2,062	9.6	11
2,500 Hiroshima	2,566	3.3	3.9
Nagasaki	2,550	5.7	6.7
3,000 Hiroshima	3,056	2.1	2.6
Nagasaki	3,041	3.6	4.4
3,500 Hiroshima	3,548	1.4	1.8
Nagasaki	3,536	2.4	3.1
4,000 Hiroshima	4,042	1.0	1.3
Nagasaki	4,031	1.7	2.2

* Factors for geographical features and altitude are ignored.
† Total energy of Hiroshima bomb is estimated as 13 kilotons of TNT, and Nagasaki bomb as 22 kilotons. Estimation was carried out on the assumption that the thermal energy was 35 percent of total energy: 4.5×10^{12} cal in Hiroshima and 7.7×10^{12} cal in Nagasaki.
Source: N. Shohno and S. Iijima, *Kakuhōshasen to Genbakushō* [Nuclear Radiation and Atomic Bomb Disease] (Tokyo: Nihon Hōsō Shuppan Kyōkai, 1975), p. 97.

Figure 2.5. A roof tile. Bubbles appearing on its surface due to thermal radiation. Nagasaki, collected at a spot 270 meters from the hypocenter. Photographed in July 1967.

of thermal radiation energy by distance from the hypocenters when visibility is 20 and 30 kilometers.

Reflection and absorption occur on the surface of the material hit by thermal radiation, while a few rays fall through. The degree of absorption depends upon the nature and color of the material or object. For example, much more heat is absorbed by a black cloth than by a white cloth. The absorbed heat raises the temperature of the material or object.

A point of special importance about the thermal radiation of the standard atomic bomb is that a large amount of thermal radiation is emitted within a short period of time (about 0.2 to 3 seconds following explosion). The amount of heat escaping by conduction within such a short time is minimal, and the enormous energy absorbed is localized on the surface of the material or object and thus results in an extremely high surface temperature. In the atomic bombings of Hiroshima and Nagasaki, the ground surface at the hypocenter is believed to have reached a temperature of 3,000° to 4,000° C. The heat rays caused thermal burns on the exposed skin of people within the limits of about 3.5 kilometers of the hypocenter in Hiroshima and of about 4 kilometers in Nagasaki. Though thermal burns were sometimes seen on skin covered by clothing, the skin of those wearing white clothing, with its high rate of reflection, was relatively protected; while that of those wearing black, with its high rate of absorption, had many marked thermal burns (see frontispiece, photograph 17).

Other objects, such as electric light poles and trees, within a radius of 2.9 kilometers (Hiroshima) and of 3.4 kilometers (Nagasaki) of the hypocenter were charred on the surface facing the burst point, and roof tiles showed blistered surfaces (figure 2.5). This phenomenon was seen within 1 kilometer of the hypocenter as a result of a temperature of over 1,800° C.

Chapter 3

Blast Caused by the Atomic Bomb Explosion

Formation of Shock Wave (Blast Wave) *

Shock wave is caused by an atomic explosion in air. At a certain distance from the burst point, the air following the shock front becomes more concentrated and reaches a higher temperature than the air before passing of the shock front. At the beginning it travels along the same direction as the shock front at a slower speed. The maximum velocity (wind velocity) of the air movement depends on the peak pressure, falls at a point far from the burst point. Though the velocity of the shock wave is greater than the velocity of sound near the burst point, it becomes slower with increasing distance from the burst point, and is about equal to the sound velocity at a distant point (figure 3.1). The wind caused by the passage of the shock wave ceases to blow soon after and then blows slightly toward the hypocenter.

The Mach effect occurs in the atomic explosion in air. In other words, at a point where the distance from the hypocenter is greater than the height of the burst point, the primary wave front occurring from the explosion in air and the wave front reflected from the ground surface fuse and form a new shock front (Mach stem). Its pressure is generally greater than the primary wave front and adds much greater lateral load to objects on the ground.

* Brode 1955; Hirschfelder et al. 1950; Los Alamos Scientific Laboratory 1944; Newmark and Hansen 1961.

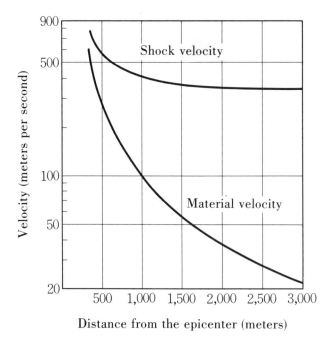

Figure 3.1. Decrease, according to distance from the hypocenter, in shock velocity and in material velocity (Hirschfelder et al. 1950).

Damages Caused by Blast

Approximately 50 percent of an atomic bomb's latent energy is considered to become energy of the blast. In Japan, the atomic bomb's blast caused structural damage over a wide area, not only destroying structures but also killing men and animals. Near the hypocenter, people were blown against the walls by a powerful blast or were crushed to death under collapsed houses. Many people were injured by glass splinters and other flying débris even at distances far from the hypocenter. Fire broke as houses collapsed, and spread on a large scale because of inadequate and damaged fire-fighting facilities.

FRACTURE OF BUILDINGS BY BLAST PRESSURE

The total energy released by the atomic bomb was much greater than the conventional bombs of 500 kilograms or 1 ton in use at that time. The blast effects also covered a much wider area of ground. K. Mutō and K. Umemura (1953, p. 184) compared the blast pressure of the atomic bomb with that of conventional bombs. With the atomic bomb in Hiroshima, the common wooden houses collapsed completely within a radius of 2 kilometers, while with 1 ton of a conventional bomb similar destruction would occur within a radius of only 40 meters. On the other hand, with the atomic bomb in Nagasaki, timber and lumber were crushed to pieces within 1 kilometer of the hypocenter. Similar destruction using 500 kilograms of a conventional bomb would occur within a radius of 10 meters.

The duration of blast pressure is several milliseconds with a conventional bomb (Mutō 1941), while that of the atomic bomb is about 1 second. Blast pressure produced by the atomic bomb is thought to act upon the structures during this time in the following way.

When the shock front reaches the structure, the pressure on the wall of the structure becomes two to five times that of the shock front and has a powerful impulsive force. Until the shock front has passed through the structure, a force pushes the structure in the opposite direction from the hypocenter owing to the difference in pressures on front and back faces of the structure. If, with the passing of the shock front, the window and other parts are not destroyed by blast pressure, and if inside and outside pressures are not balanced, the entire structure collapses from outside pressure. Furthermore, a continuous force from the strong wind blowing in the advancing direction of the shock wave acts upon the structure (Hirschfelder et al. 1950). Basically, a structure is destroyed either by impulse—the accumulation of energy within it—or by outside pressure, depending on the relation between the duration of the latter and proper vibrations within the structure itself. When the vibrations of structure are periodically longer than those of the blast pressure, destruction is caused by impulse. When the cycle of blast pressure exceeds the vibration cycle of the structure itself, destruction is determined by the maximum pressure acting upon the structure. This latter is the more common cause of structural breakdown after an atomic bomb explosion (Mutō 1952).

Table 3.1 shows the general relationship between the damages and the estimated values of maximum pressure and wind velocity produced by the blast of a standard atomic bomb exploded at an altitude of 600 meters. Since the actual damages occurring in the two cities differed to some extent, the conditions encountered will be described in detail.

STRUCTURAL DAMAGES

Wood-frame Houses. Though many of the wood-frame houses were burned down by the fire occurring simultaneously with the explosion, damages caused to houses only by blast in both cities, were as follows.

According to the investigation made by Y. Kondō and S. Saka (1953, p. 195) in Hiroshima, at 2 kilometers from the hypocenter 10 percent of the houses showed complete collapse, and 40 percent partial damage and damage

TABLE 3.1

Damages from Blast Pressure Caused by a Standard A-Bomb

Maximum Blast Pressure (kg/cm²)	Maximum Velocity (m/sec)	Distance from Hypocenter (km)	Extent of Damage
3.5	440	0	Iron bridge floor sideslipped.
2.4	330	0.3	Total collapse of strong steel structures; roofs and walls blown away.
1.9	280	0.5	Except for ferroconcrete, earthquake-proof structures, the buildings *demolished almost completely.*
1.5	200	0.8	
1.0	160	1.0	Ferroconcrete chimneys 20 cm thick collapsed.
0.76	130	1.2	Brick walls 30 cm thick cracked.
0.53	94	1.5	Multistory brick buildings destroyed completely.
0.48	86	1.6	*Serious damage* suffered within this distance: all buildings seriously damaged and beyond repair.
0.38	72	1.8	
0.30	60	2.0	Multistory brick buildings destroyed heavily.
0.22	45	2.3	Wooden buildings collapsed.
0.17	38	2.5	
0.16	36	2.6	*Half-damage* suffered within this distance: all buildings unusable without repair; wooden structures beyond repair.
0.13	30	3.0	Possible outbreak of fire when houses collapsed.
0.12	28	3.2	*Partial damage* suffered within this distance: wooden buildings usable if repaired.
0.11	26	3.5	Slight damage on doors; moderate breakage in plastering; window glass completely broken.
0.10	25	3.6	*Slight damage:* cracks in plastering, broken window glass, etc.
		approximately 15	

Sources: J. O. Hirschfelder, D. B. Parker, A. Kramish, R. C. Smith, and S. Glasstone (eds.), *The Effects of Atomic Weapons*, revised edition. (Washington, D.C.: U.S. Government Printing Office, 1950).
N. Shohno and S. Iijima, *Kakuhōshasen to Genbakushō* [Nuclear Radiation and Atomic Bomb Disease] (Tokyo: Nihon Hōsō Shuppan Kyōkai, 1975), p. 92.

of frame; while at 4 kilometers there was neither collapse, partial damage, nor damage of frame, with only damage to fittings. Kondō and Saka (1953, p. 195) considered the range of collapse (fall-down) to be about 2.5 kilometers.

M. Uda, Y. Sugahara, and I. Kita (1953, p. 98) indicated the range of collapse of houses to be 2.5 to 3 kilometers, severe damage 3 to 4 kilometers, moderate damage 4 to 5 kilometers, and light damage 5 to 10 kilometers. In some cases windows were broken at a far distance of 27 kilometers. The damage criteria are given in table 3.2.

TABLE 3.2
Classification of Residential Destruction

Classification	Pillars	Roofs	Walls	Fixtures	Windowpane	Condition
Collapse	broken	broken	collapsed	—	broken	uninhabitable
Severe damage	broken	broken	broken	—	broken	heavily damaged; uninhabitable
Moderate damage	unhinged, inclined	broken	broken	—	broken	half-destroyed; uninhabitable
Light damage	—	damaged	damaged	—	broken	slightly damaged; inhabitable

Source: M. Uda, Y. Sugahara, and I. Kita, "Meteorological conditions related to the atomic explosion in Hiroshima," in CRIABC* (1953), Vol. I, p. 98.
* For such abbreviations, see Bibliography, page 641.

The damage occurring in Nagasaki was described by Mutō and Umemura (1953, p. 184). Houses within 1 kilometer of the hypocenter completely lost their original shape, and wooden material had crumbled to pieces. Though the joints were mainly damaged and collapsed within 1 to 2 kilometers, the smaller portions were almost intact, as in the trusses. The framework of the houses suffered little within 2 to 4 kilometers; but nearly all the walls, ceilings, and floors were damaged, and there were cracks at the center of narrow pillars. The damage found at more distant areas is shown in table 3.3.

TABLE 3.3
Damage by the Blast to Buildings on the Outskirts of Nagasaki

Location	Distance from Hypocenter (km)	Seriously Damaged (%)	Partially Damaged (%)	Windowpanes Broken (%)	Not Damaged (%)
Fukuda	6	0.4	67.9	12.3	19.4
Higashi-Nagasaki	8	0.7	18.0	25.4	55.7
Kōyagi	10	1.2	20.2	10.0	68.6
Ōkusa	12	3.2	16.2	19.5	61.1
Iōjima Island	12	0	36.5	41.7	21.8

Source: Nagasaki Shiyakusho, A-bomb Survivors Measures Department, *The A-bombed Area Map* (1974).

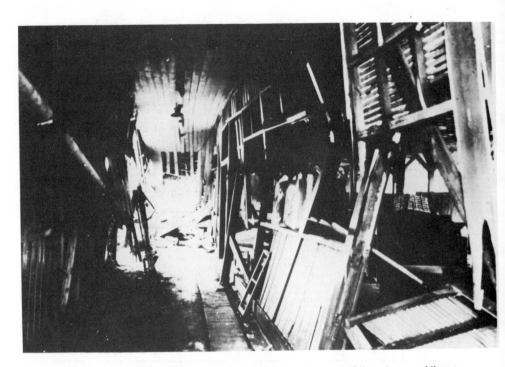

Figure 3.2. Interior of the Hiroshima District Monopoly Bureau building, about 2.3 kilometers from the hypocenter, October 1945 (The United States Strategic Bombing Survey, Physical Damage Division 1947a, p. 113). Photograph preserved at the National Archives and Record Service, Washington, D.C.

Figure 3.3. Destroyed wooden house of three stories located about 2.4 kilometers from the hypocenter, Nagasaki, September 1945. (Photograph by Eiichi Matsumoto.)

Damage to wooden houses and residences was caused by displacement of the main portions of the structure, which led to fracture of pillars and destruction of roof truss joints. These damages were also commonly caused by damage to and separation of structural joints.

Figure 3.2 shows a damaged wooden structure—the Hiroshima District Monopoly Bureau located about 2.3 kilometers from the hypocenter. Note the fracture of the narrow pillars resulting from displacement of the entire building. Figure 3.3 shows a three-story wooden residence located 2.4 kilometers from the hypocenter in Nagasaki. The roof is markedly damaged, and the entire structure is distorted.

Reinforced-concrete Building. Since the explosion occurred in air, the force acting on structures near the hypocenter was mainly vertical, while the horizontal force increased with distance. Consequently, in buildings near the hypocenter the roof slabs showed a concave deformity, and the weak ones were broken. In buildings far from the hypocenter, roof slabs and outer walls were destroyed, and pillars were sheared.

In Hiroshima many reinforced-concrete structures were standing near the hypocenter. Investigations by Kondō and Saka (1953, p. 195) show that the radius of destruction was approximately 500 meters and attic slabs, girders, and beams were destroyed by a vertical force. Only the attic was damaged in buildings designed to be earthquake-resistant. Though several buildings within this radius collapsed, they were built partly of bricks or were not of earthquake-resistant design.

Such an example is shown in figure 3.4. The structure of the head office

Figure 3.4. Hiroshima Gas Company building, 250 meters from the hypocenter, October 1945. (Photograph by Shigeo Hayashi.)

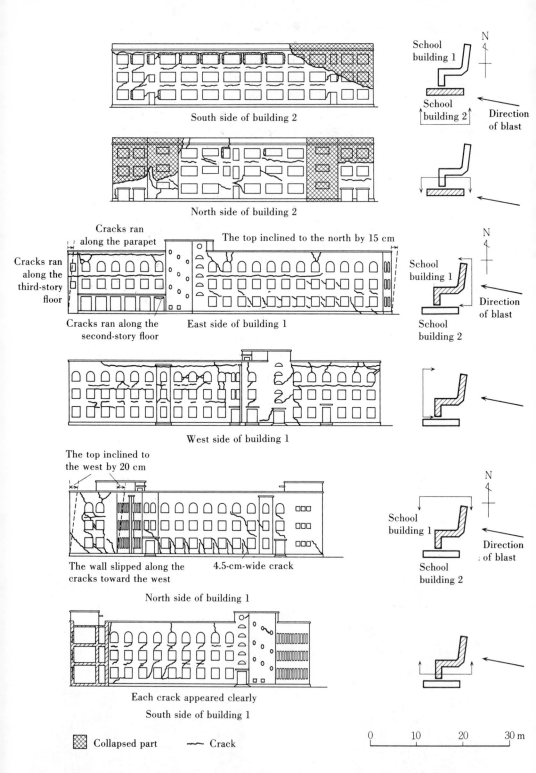

South side of building 2

North side of building 2

Cracks ran
along the parapet

The top inclined to the north by 15 cm

Cracks ran
along the
third-story
floor

Cracks ran along the
second-story floor

East side of building 1

West side of building 1

The top inclined to
the west by 20 cm

The wall slipped along the   4.5-cm-wide crack
cracks toward the west

North side of building 1

Each crack appeared clearly

South side of building 1

School
building 1

School
building 2   Direction
                    of blast

School
building 1

Direction
of blast

School
building 2

School
building 1

Direction
: of blast

School
building 2

N

N

N

⬚ Collapsed part   〜 Crack

0   10   20   30 m

Figure 3.5. Damage to the Shiroyama Primary School building, Nagasaki, about 500 meters
from the hypocenter. (The United States Strategic Bombing Survey, Physical Damage Division
1947c, pp. 49–50.)

of the Hiroshima Gas Company located 250 meters from the hypocenter had a reinforced-concrete frame and a curtain wall made of bricks.

In Nagasaki, the radius of destruction was considered to be 750 meters (Kondō and Saka 1953, p. 195), and the number of structures with reinforced concrete frames within this radius was less than that in Hiroshima. The buildings within this radius were those of the Chinzei Middle School (about 500 meters from the hypocenter; its attic collapsed), Shiroyama Primary School (about 500 meters; partial collapse), and Nagasaki Medical University Hospital (about 750 meters; crack in part of parapet and slabs). The walls facing the hypocenter were destroyed at a distance of 1 kilometer from the hypocenter. All windows were blown away, and the window frames facing the hypocenter were also destroyed within 2 kilometers (Mutō and Umemura 1953, p. 184).

The damaged condition of Shiroyama Primary School is shown in figure 3.5. Figure 3.6 is a photograph of the completely collapsed portion. Since this building was located about 500 meters from the hypocenter, the blast pressure came obliquely from above. Cracks were found in the slabs of both buildings. Figure 3.7 shows that the roof slabs of the school building on the north were first compressed and bent by the downward blast pressure and then pushed upward by the blast pressure after the windows were blown away. The whole building was tilted in a direction away from the hypocenter, and shear cracks were found on the outer wall.

Figure 3.8 shows the damaged condition of the Chinzei Middle School, a

Figure 3.6. Shiroyama Primary School, Nagasaki. The east edge of the school building 2, as viewed from the south side of the school's grounds, located about 500 meters from the hypocenter. (Photograph taken in September 1945 by Eiichi Matsumoto.)

Figure 3.7. Broken ceiling slabs of the third floor of Shiroyama Primary School building I. (Photograph taken in October 1945 by Shigeru Miki.)

four-story reinforced-concrete building with its roof supported by steel and wooden trusses. Note that the roof trusses are destroyed, and the second or third stories slant in the opposite direction from the hypocenter. The pillars on all floors were either destroyed or extensively cracked. Note the cracks on a pillar of the first floor (figure 3.9). The first-floor slabs dropped down into the basement floor from imbalance of pressure between both floors.

Steel-frame Construction. Steel-frame constructions were more damaged than reinforced concrete ones. Since a steel frame has little resistance to a horizontal force, many structures in distant areas showed deformation in a

Figure 3.8. Chinzei Middle School, Nagasaki, located about 500 meters from the hypocenter. (Photograph taken in October 1945 by Shigeo Hayashi.)

Figure 3.9. Pillar cracks on the first floor of Chinzei Middle School. (Photograph taken in September 1945 by Torahiko Ogawa.)

direction away from the hypocenter. In the vicinity of the hypocenter, the roof trusses under the roof were fractured by a horizontal force and collapsed under the force driving down onto the roof. In steel-frame constructions, the damage to the framework was greater among those that used corrugated sheet iron compared with those that used corrugated asbestos cement. In structures containing corrugated asbestos cement, the asbestos was instantly crushed to pieces by the blast pressure, so that the force acting upon the framework did not increase. On the other hand, when corrugated sheet iron was used, the sheet iron was not readily destroyed, and the great force acting on roof and walls caused marked destruction of framework.

There were more industrial buildings in Nagasaki than in Hiroshima, and many heavy steel-frame structures with overhead traveling cranes and buildings of light steel-frame construction. The damage to steel-frame constructions in Nagasaki was reported by Mutō (1941, 1952) and by Mutō and Umemara (1953, p. 184). In the vicinity of 1 kilometer from the hypocenter, the framework was tilted obliquely, and many roof trusses were destroyed. The structural materials were greatly deformed even at a distance of 1.5 kilometers from the hypocenter, and the entire building was tilted in the same direction as the blast. Marked damage was seen up to a distance of 1.8 kilometers.

Figure 3.10 is a photograph of the Mitsubishi Steel Works building situated about 700 meters from the hypocenter in Nagasaki. The structure of the collapsed building is shown in figure 3.11. After receiving a powerful horizontal force, this building slanted in the same direction as the blast, and the roof trusses below the roof collapsed and were destroyed by the vertical force. Corrugated sheet iron was used for side walls and roof.

The building seen in figure 3.12 was located about 550 meters from the hypocenter in Hiroshima. The side wall and the roof, which were of corrugated sheet iron, were deformed by a powerful blast in a direction away from the hypocenter.

Brick and Stone Structures. Brick and stone are weak in the face of a strong horizontal force. Both roof and floors collapsed after the collapse of the wall facing the blast. The radius of destruction in Hiroshima was about 1.5 kilometers (Kondō and Saka 1953, p. 195); and there was also fairly large damage between 1.5 and 2 kilometers (Mutō and Umemara 1953, p. 184).

Other Structures. As to bridges, the sidewalk of the Aioi bridge in the vicinity of the hypocenter in Hiroshima was damaged. The high railings of some of the bridges had collapsed in many districts. In Nagasaki an iron bridge approximately 250 meters from the hypocenter moved about 70 centimeters downstream, while the Shiroyama bridge located approximately 500 meters from the hypocenter moved toward the right bank. The decks fell off two of the bridges (Aoki, Yamada, and Murakami 1953, p. 190).

Figure 3.10. Mitsubishi Steel Works Second Foundry, located about 700 meters from the hypocenter. (Photograph taken in October 1945 by Shigeo Hayashi.)

Figure 3.11. Collapse of a steel frame structure, Mitsubishi Steel Works, Nagasaki. (The United States Strategic Bombing Survey, Physical Damage Division 1947b, p. 151.)

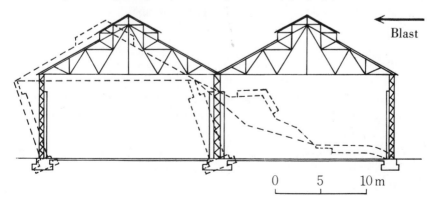

Figure 3.12. Ruined steel structure, about 550 meters from the hypocenter, Hiroshima, October 1945. (Photograph by Shigeo Hayashi.)

The trunks of nearly one half of the trees were broken within 2 kilometers of the hypocenter in Hiroshima, while in Nagasaki nearly all the trees came down or were broken within 0.3 to 1 kilometer of the hypocenter. Iron and wooden electric light poles came down up to 2 kilometers from the hypocenter in Hiroshima (Mutō and Umemura 1953, p. 184).

Reservoirs for water-supply and filtration plants, located far from the hypocenter, were hardly damaged, though there was occasional breakage of pipes caused by collapse of residences and other structures. The water pipes of the burned-down houses were all damaged, and the waterworks could not be used due to leakage of water (Hirschfelder et al. 1950).

ESTIMATION OF BLAST SPECIFICITY IN HIROSHIMA AND NAGASAKI

In Hiroshima, Kondō and Saka (1953, p. 195) calculated the blast pressure from the radius of destruction of reinforced concrete constructions and of collapse of wooden residences; and from destroyed portions of reinforced concrete constructions, they obtained an estimated pressure of 0.3 to 0.6 kilogram per square centimeter at a distance of 240 meters from the hypocenter. T. Hirono and K. Aihara (1953, p. 164) investigated the fallen handrails of bridges and damaged stone columns of shrines and estimated the blast pressure to be 0.6 kilogram per square centimeter at a point 1 kilometer from the hypocenter, and 1 kilogram per square centimeter at the hypocenter. From the damages occurring in Hiroshima, K. Aoki, J. Yamada, and E. Murakami assumed the height of the explosion to be 600 meters and estimated the blast pressure at twelve different locations (figure 3.13a).

In Nagasaki, Hirono and Aihara (1953, p. 164), referring to the destruction of the gatepost of the Nagasaki Medical University, estimated the blast pressure to be about 1 kilogram per square centimeter at a point 500 meters from the hypocenter and about 1.4 kilograms per square centimeter at the hypocenter. According to M. Majima, T. Tsutsui, and Y. Suga (1953, p. 183), the blast pressure, as estimated from the way the tombstones tumbled, was about 0.13 kilogram per square centimeter at 1 kilometer from the hypocenter. Aoki, Yamada, and Murakami also estimated the blast pressure at seven different locations in Nagasaki (figure 3.13b).

As in figures 3.13a and 3.13b, at a point 500 meters from the hypocenter, the blast pressure was 0.14 kilogram per square centimeter in Hiroshima; while in Nagasaki it was 0.5 or 0.28 kilogram per square centimeter. In Hiroshima at 850 meters from the hypocenter, the blast pressure was 0.23 kilogram per square centimeter, and at 1 kilometer in Nagasaki the pressure was 0.33 kilogram per square centimeter. Aoki, Yamada, and Murakami mentioned that the blast pressure in Nagasaki was much greater than that in Hiroshima. Considering the disastrous damage, Hirono and Aihara (1953, p. 164) also noted a greater blast pressure in Nagasaki than in Hiroshima; but when calculations were made on definite examples, no great difference could be detected. In both cities, the blast pressure was about 1 kilogram per square centimeter at the hypocenter.

The velocity of blast pressure, according to the calculation made by Hirono and Aihara, was 700 to 780 meters per second in the vicinity of the hypocenter in Hiroshima; and the average up to 50 kilometers was 330 meters per second, nearing the sound velocity. Since the average velocity at 4.5 kilometers from the hypocenter was 650 meters per second in Nagasaki, the velocity at the hypocenter was thought to be about three times that of sound velocity. The velocity of blast was estimated to be about 75 meters per second at a point 400 to 500 meters from the hypocenter in Nagasaki (calculated from cracks on chimneys).

COMPARISON OF STRUCTURAL DAMAGE IN HIROSHIMA AND NAGASAKI

The differences in structural damage occurring in the two cities were attributable to the following factors: (1) differences in destructive power according to type and scale of bomb and detonation height; (2) differences in range of blast effects owing to the terrain in the vicinity of the hypocenter and to

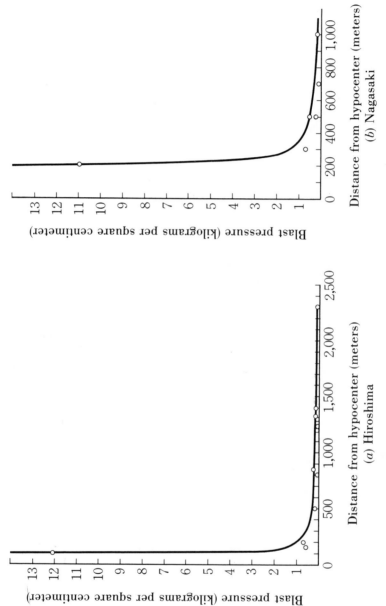

Figure 3.13. Estimated blast pressure in Hiroshima and Nagasaki (Aoki, Yamada, and Murakami 1953, p. 190).

the layout of the city; and (3) differences in distribution of structures and structural design. The scale of the bomb was about 12.5 kilotons in Hiroshima and about 22 kilotons in Nagasaki (Auxier et al. 1966; Penny et al. 1970) (see page 30). The detonation height was about 580 meters and 500 meters in Hiroshima and Nagasaki, respectively (Hubbell, Jones, and Cheka 1969; Kerr and Solomon 1976) (see chapter 1). The terrain in the vicinity of the hypocenter in Hiroshima was a flat plain containing a congested administrative and commercial district. On the other hand, Nagasaki lay in a series of narrow valleys stretching north and south, with mountains to the east and west. The hypocenter was located away from the center of the city in a district of schools, industrial plants, and homes. Consequently, the buildings in Hiroshima were mostly of reinforced concrete and were concentrated in the vicinity of the hypocenter. There were also light steel-frame constructions in the surrounding area. In Nagasaki, factories lined the Urakami river basin, and most of them were of heavy and light steel-frame construction. There were hospitals and many schools built of reinforced concrete in the vicinity of the hypocenter.

The U.S. Strategic Bombing Survey (1946, p. 30; 1947a, p. 96) investigated the designs of structures in both cities and estimated the mean distance where structural damage occurred (table 3.4). Data were lacking for those not indicated.

The studies indicated that reinforced concrete in Nagasaki was damaged over a radius three times greater than in Hiroshima. The range of damage for other structures in general was greater in Nagasaki, but about the same for light steel-frame constructions in both cities.

The great difference in damage to reinforced-concrete constructions in the two cities was attributable to the difference in scale and detonation height of the bomb. Reinforced-concrete constructions are less resistant to horizontal force than to vertical force. The closer to the ground a bomb is when it is detonated, the greater is the horizontal force, and the greater is the radius of damage. Mutō and Umemura (1953, p. 184) noted that the vertical pressure was pronounced near the hypocenter in Hiroshima, while the horizontal pressure was great in Nagasaki. Also, the effects of local terrain cannot be disregarded. In Nagasaki, there were many undulations where great damage occurred in reinforced-concrete constructions. The Nagasaki Medical University Hospital was located halfway up a hill 750 meters from the hypocenter, and the damage to it was comparatively great for its distance from the hypocenter. The damage of construction was estimated to be similar to that found in sites located 500 meters from the hypocenter in Hiroshima (Kondō and Saka 1953, p. 195).

The damage to one-story brick-wall structures and wooden structures was

TABLE 3.4

Average Distance at Which Buildings of Various Kinds Were Damaged in Hiroshima and Nagasaki

Classification of Structures	Average Distance (m)	
Multistory quakeproof buildings	Hiroshima	150
	Nagasaki	—
Multistory steel-frame reinforced-concrete buildings (both resistant and nonresistant to earthquakes)	Hiroshima	210
	Nagasaki	600
One-story heavyweight steel-frame buildings	Hiroshima	—
	Nagasaki	1,200
One-story lightweight steel-frame buildings	Hiroshima	1,650
	Nagasaki	1,620
Multistory brick-wall buildings	Hiroshima	1,710
	Nagasaki	—
One-story brick-wall buildings	Hiroshima	2,190
	Nagasaki	2,550
Wooden buildings (except residences)	Hiroshima	2,610
	Nagasaki	2,820
Wooden residences	Hiroshima	2,190
	Nagasaki	2,460

Source: The United States Strategic Bombing Survey, *The Effects of Atomic Bombs on Hiroshima and Nagasaki* (Washington, D.C.: U.S. Government Printing Office, 1946), p. 30. The United States Strategic Bombing Survey, Physical Damage Division. *Effects of the Atomic Bomb on Hiroshima, Japan.* (Washington, D.C.: U.S. Government Printing Office, 1947), Vol. I, Section X, p. 96.

slightly greater in Nagasaki. One reason for this difference was that the scale of the bomb dropped on Nagasaki was greater, but nothing is known about the other determining factors.

The damage to one-story, light steel-frame structures was about the same in both cities (table 3.4). The many structures that were crowded together inside the factories in Nagasaki were thought to have had a shielding effect.

Chapter 4

Composite Damage Caused by Heat Rays, Blasts, and Fires

Complex of Damages

The damage in Hiroshima and Nagasaki was caused by a combination of heat rays, blasts, and fires, and was more extensive than the total sum of these effects. Fire occurred from primary ignition by thermal ray and from secondary ignition following structural destruction.

The total area reduced to ashes by blasts and fires was about 13 square kilometers in Hiroshima and about 6.7 square kilometers in Nagasaki. In spite of the fact that the total energy of the atomic bomb used on Nagasaki was greater than that on Hiroshima, the burned-down area in Hiroshima was greater as a result of differences in topography and distribution of buildings.

With the outbreak of conflagration, the air in this area became heated, causing a rapid rush of air upward, with cold air flowing in from all directions. This phenomenon is called a *fire storm* and it may extend a fire. The topographical differences in the two cities affected the fire storms in each.

In Hiroshima, conflagration broke out 30 minutes after the explosion, and a fire storm started to blow, reaching a velocity of 18 meters per second two to three hours later. From 11 A.M. to 3 P.M. a violent whirlwind blew locally from the center toward the northern part of the city (Hirschfelder et al. 1950; Uda, Sugahara, and Kita 1953, p. 98). The wind finally calmed down and became mild by about 5 P.M. Everything within a radius of 2 kilometers of the hypocenter was completely burned to ashes by the fire storm. Though the fire storm in Nagasaki was not so evident as that in Hiroshima, about two hours after the explosion when the fire became violent, a southwest wind blew between the hills at a velocity of 15 meters per second. This wind extended the fire toward the north of the valley, where there were fewer residences. About seven hours later, the direction of the wind changed to the east, with also a drop in velocity (Hirschfelder et al. 1950).

In a conflagration the minute particles of carbon produced by fire and others are blown up into the cold air, where water vapor is formed, and rain may be precipitated. Between 9 A.M. and 4 P.M. in Hiroshima, "black rain" containing radioactivity poured down over a large area from north of the hypocenter to the west (Uda, Sugahara, and Kita 1953, p. 98). Also, in Nagasaki, the "black rain" came down on the Nishiyama district, located east of the hypocenter, about 20 minutes after the explosion (see page 101).

The fire-fighting facilities were almost totally destroyed in Hiroshima and Nagasaki. In Hiroshima, 70 percent of the facilities were destroyed, and 80 percent of the firemen suffered from the disaster (Hirschfelder et al. 1950). Even where both facilities and firemen escaped disaster, blocked roads interfered with fire-fighting activity. In Nagasaki, firemen from other districts could not get within 2 kilometers of the hypocenter. One of the reasons for the expansion of fire was that water pipes were broken, causing loss of water pressure and water supply. The water pipes on the ground were cut off when

Figure 4.1. Hiroshima in utter ruins, October 1945. (Photograph by Shigeo Hayashi.)

structures collapsed or were melted by fire, while most underground pipes were damaged by irregular movements of the earth.

Table 4.1 shows the conditions of structural damages occurring in Hiroshima and Nagasaki. The structural damage in Hiroshima was approximately three times greater than that in Nagasaki.

TABLE 4.1

Damage to Buildings in Hiroshima and Nagasaki

	Number of Buildings before the Bombings	Completely Destroyed/ Burned (%)	Completely Destroyed (%)	Half-Destroyed/ Half-Burned/ Slightly Damaged (%)	Total
Hiroshima	approximately 76,000	62.9	5.0	24.0	91.9
Nagasaki	approximately 51,000	22.7	2.6	10.8	36.1

Source: Hiroshima Shiyakusho, *Hiroshima Shisei Yōran* [Hiroshima City Almanac], 1946 ed. (Hiroshima, 1947), p. 55. Nagasaki Shiyakusho, *Nagasaki Shisei Yōran* [Nagasaki City Almanac], 1949 ed. (Nagasaki, 1949), p. 96.

Damages in Hiroshima

Hiroshima City is built on a delta at the mouth of the Ōta river, which flows into the Seto Inland Sea from the northern mountains. The east and

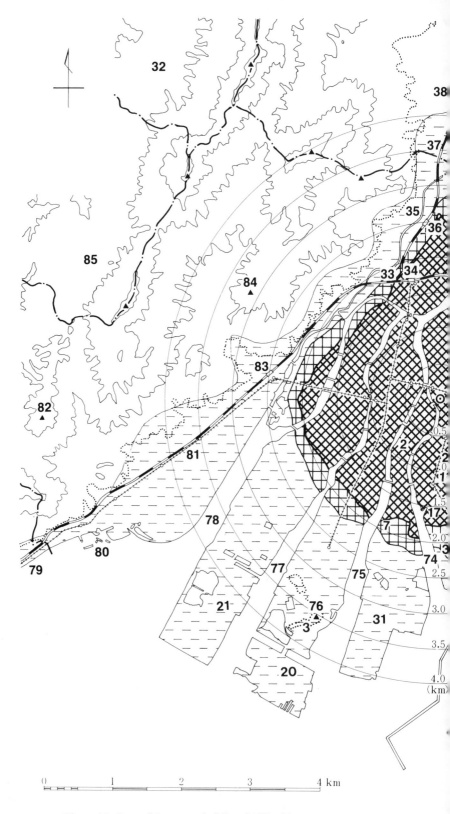

Figure 4.2. State of damage to buildings in Hiroshima.

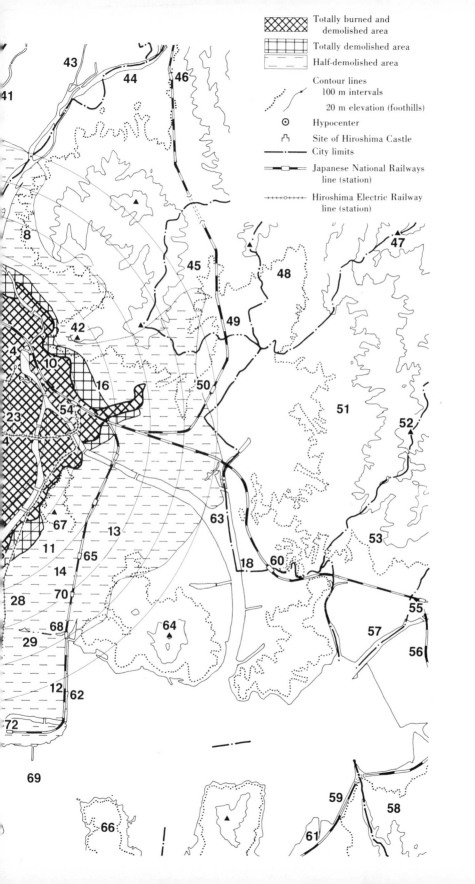

Totally burned and demolished area

Totally demolished area

Half-demolished area

Contour lines
100 m intervals
20 m elevation (foothills)

⊙ Hypocenter

♫ Site of Hiroshima Castle

City limits

Japanese National Railways line (station)

Hiroshima Electric Railway line (station)

west are walled off by hills, and the southern delta area faces the Seto Inland Sea. Since the explosion occurred at the heart of this fan-shaped, flat city, the damage extended throughout the city unrelated to direction. The degree of damage decreased with distance from the hypocenter, but 92 percent of the total structures (76,327) were damaged to some extent (table 4.1). It is no exaggeration to say that the whole city was ruined instantaneously (figure 4.1).

Figure 4.2 shows the destruction of Hiroshima City by degree of damage. *Completely destroyed/burned* means a state of damage in which houses and buildings were reduced to utter ruins in the disastrous conflagration that soon followed the explosion. As for reinforced concrete constructions, however, they are included in this category if they were totally destroyed with only the external shell remaining. The outer walls were markedly damaged, and the interior was gutted by fire. The Hiroshima Municipal Office located 1 kilometer from the hypocenter is one such example. These conditions were found in all districts within a radius of 2 kilometers from the hypocenter.

Completely destroyed means that wooden structures were beyond repair and that reinforced-concrete constructions were damaged beyond use. In table 3.1 this collapse is indicated as half-damage. It was encountered at a maximum distance of about 2.8 kilometers of the hypocenter.

Half-destroyed means that the damaged wooden structure could be repaired for use and is compatible to the partial damage indicated in table 3.1. The term *slightly damaged* is used when the degree of destruction is slightly lighter than that of half-destruction—as when a wooden structure could be used after repair. Half-destruction occurred within a radius of 4 kilometers from the hypocenter; thus, the degree of damage of almost the entire city of Hiroshima was greater than partial destruction.

Slightly damaged structures occurred over a distance of about 5 kilometers, and broken windows were seen even at a distance of 27 kilometers southwest (Uda, Sugahara, and Kita 1953, p. 98).

Though many fires broke out in districts farther than 2 kilometers, the majority resulted from secondary causes. Spontaneous ignition of straw roofs, timbers, and trees was observed at a distance of about 3 kilometers (Uda, Sugahara, and Kita 1953, p. 98). Primary ignition by heat rays under certain conditions occurred at distances up to about 3 kilometers. Since various structures and objects were burned down up to a distance of about 3 kilometers (Kikuchi 1953), secondary ignition must have also occurred in these areas.

Figure 4.3. The area around Urakami river, Nagasaki, reduced to cinders and ashes, September 1945. (Photograph by Torahiko Ogawa.)

Damages in Nagasaki

Nagasaki City is built around the Nakashima river basin, the Urakami river basin, and Nagasaki bay into which both rivers flow. The city's two basin districts (Nakashima river district and Urakami river district) are separated by a hill about 200 meters above sea level (maximum height in the area 360 meters). The commercial center, the prefectural and municipal offices, and other government offices were concentrated in the Nakashima river district. Along the Urakami river district lies a relatively broad expanse between hills running north and south. There were intermittent rows of factories from the west bank of the Nagasaki bay, and there were also many residences and schools in this district.

The atomic bomb exploded at a height of about 500 meters above the center of the Urakami river district. Consequently, the damages caused by heat rays and blast were almost entirely restricted to this area (figure 4.3), while the Nakashima river district was fairly well shielded by the hills. However, 36 percent of the total structures in both districts were damaged (table 4.1).

Figure 4.5 shows the destroyed condition of Nagasaki City by degree of damage: it is apparent that the damage extended toward the south rather than to the north. This was due to the concentrated distribution of buildings in the south.

The completely demolished area extended up to 2.5 kilometers from the hypocenter toward the south, which exceeds the 2-kilometer radius in Hiroshima. While the area within a radius of 2 kilometers was uniformly destroyed in Hiroshima, the conditions varied by location in Nagasaki. This difference

Figure 4.4. Nagasaki Prefectural Office, September 1945. Foreground shows the ruins of Nagasaki Local Court. (Photograph by Torahiko Ogawa.)

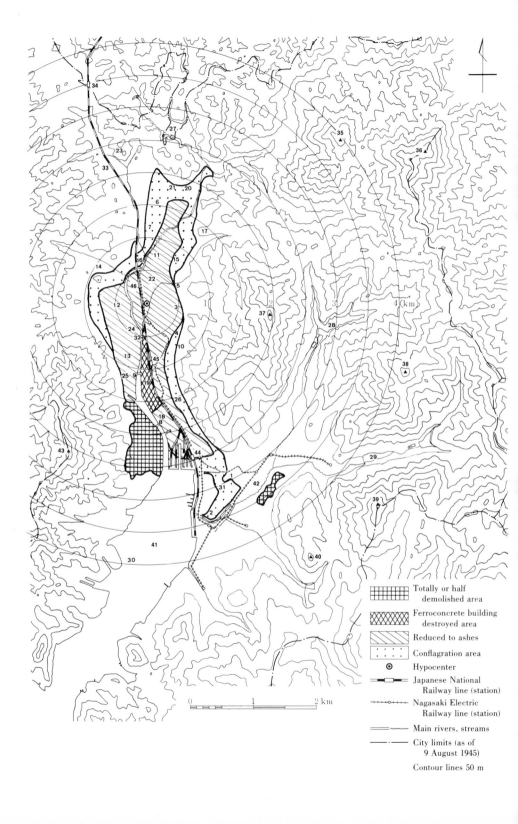

	Totally or half demolished area
	Ferroconcrete building destroyed area
	Reduced to ashes
	Conflagration area
⊙	Hypocenter
	Japanese National Railway line (station)
	Nagasaki Electric Railway line (station)
	Main rivers, streams
	City limits (as of 9 August 1945)

Contour lines 50 m

Figure 4.5. Damage to buildings in Nagasaki.

1. Nagasaki City Office
2. Nagasaki Prefectural Office
3. Nagasaki Medical University
4. Nagasaki Medical University Hospital
5. Urakami Cathedral
6. Mitsubishi Heavy Industries Nagasaki Ordnance Factory, Ōhashi Plant
7. Mitsubishi Heavy Industries Nagasaki Shipyard, Ōhashi Parts Plant
8. Inasa Bridge
9. Yanagawa Bridge
10. Sannō Shrine
11. Yamazato Primary School
12. Shiroyama Primary School
13. Keiho Middle School
14. Nagasaki Commercial School
15. Nagasaki Technical School
16. Ōhashi Bridge
17. Urakami First Hospital
18. Mitsubishi Heavy Industries Nagasaki Shipyard, Saiwaimachi Plant
19. Mitsubishi Steel Manufacturing Co. First Nagasaki Plant
20. Nishi-Urakami Primary School
21. Nagasaki Normal School
22. Urakami Prison
23. Mitsubishi Heavy Industries Nagasaki Ordnance Factory, Sumiyoshi Tunneling Works
24. Chinzei Middle School
25. Fuchi Primary School
26. Zenza Primary School
27. Urakami Reservoir
28. Nishiyama Reservoir
29. Hongōchi Reservoir
30. Mitsubishi Heavy Industries Nagasaki Shipyard
31. Shinkōzen Primary School
32. Mitsubishi Electric Corporation Nagasaki Foundry
33. Nagasaki Main Line
34. Michinoo Station
35. Mt. Tenjiku
36. Mt. Hoba
37. Mt. Konpira
38. Mt. Hōka
39. Mt. Hiko
40. Mt. Atago
41. Nagasaki Port
42. Nakashima River
43. Mt. Inasa
44. Nagasaki Station
45. Urakami Station
46. Urakami River

was mainly due to the differences in distribution of structures and terrain in Nagasaki.

The maximum distance at which partial destruction was observed was about 4 kilometers toward the south. Broken windows were reported to have been seen even at a distance of about 19 kilometers (Nakamura 1953, p. 177). In Nagasaki fires broke out approximately 90 minutes after the explosion at several locations quite far from the hypocenter. These fires triggered widespread conflagration. The Nagasaki railroad station, located 2.5 kilometers south of the hypocenter, started to burn at about 0.30 P.M. At about the same time, a fire broke out from the Nagasaki Prefectural Office, 3.3 kilometers from the hypocenter (figure 4.4). This fire was fanned by a west wind and spread to private homes nearby. A wide area had been burned down by 8:30 P.M., when the fire was extinguished. Though the exact time remains unknown, fires broke out from many objects at different locations: a hemp palm in front of the City Auditorium (3.1 kilometers south-southeast); an electric light pole at the corner of the Nagasaki City Office (2.9 kilometers south-southeast); and the upper end of an electric light pole near Michinoo (3.4 kilometers north of the hypocenter). From the conditions of these fires, it can be assumed that the fires were caused by heat rays first acting on combustible material, which smoldered for a while and then burst into flames (Nagasaki Shiyakusho 1977, pp. 190–95, 262–66).

Chapter 5

Radiation from the Atomic Bomb

The radiation released by the air burst of the atomic bomb can be divided into two categories: initial radiation, which is emitted within 1 minute after the explosion; and residual radiation, which is emitted later than 1 minute after the explosion. An enormous amount of radiation was released by the atomic bomb—a crucial difference from the conventional bomb. People exposed to the radiation were seriously injured and suffered thereafter for a long period. The power and the characteristics of both initial and residual radiations will be explained in this chapter. Since the injuries to the human body are to be described in part II, little reference to them will be made here; but this chapter contains an outline of injuries to animals and plants (pages 80–86).

Initial Radiation

The initial radiation of the atomic bomb consists of alpha particles, beta particles, gamma rays, and neutrons. Alpha rays are released from uranium and plutonium, which have escaped fission, and beta rays from fission products. Since the ranges in air of alpha and beta particles are short, these rays emitted immediately after the explosion failed to reach ground. Consequently, gamma rays and neutrons as initial radiation had considerable effects on the human body, animals, and plants. The energy of these rays was comparable with about 3 percent of the total energy emitted by the explosion (Glasstone 1962, p. 370).

GAMMA RAYS

Gamma rays are produced during nuclear fission of uranium and plutonium, and when neutrons released by fission are absorbed by surrounding atomic nuclei, and from a variety of products of nuclear fission. Since the majority of gamma rays produced by fission of uranium and plutonium are absorbed by bomb materials, the main gamma rays reaching the ground are those of the products of nuclear fission.

NEUTRONS

Neutrons are electrically neutral elementary particles, and atomic nuclei are generally composed of protons and neutrons. Since the interaction of the neutron and material fluctuates greatly according to the velocity of the neutron, neutrons are often classified as fast and slow. For example, the velocity of 1 mega-electronvolt fast neutron is 1.4×10^7 meters per second; but a thermal neutron of about 0.025 electronvolt, playing a main role in nuclear reactors, is a slow neutron with a velocity of 2.2×10^3 meters per second.* Most of the neutrons in an A-bomb are fast neutrons released simultaneously with nuclear fission. Though some of these neutrons are delayed by elastic collisions with the nuclei present in the bomb materials and cause a chain reaction of nuclear fissions, most neutrons are emitted into the air. The neutrons scattered in air are slowed down by collisions with the nuclei of nitrogen and oxygen, and some are absorbed by the nuclei of nitrogen.

When the neutrons reach the ground, and when they collide with, and are absorbed by the nuclei in it, most of the material that have absorbed these neutrons become radioactive. This process is called *induced radioactivity*. When the components of the ground and of man-made structures are activated, they continue to emit radiation for some time; this is called *residual radioactivity*.

INITIAL RADIATION DOSE

On 10–11 August, several days after the bombing in Hiroshima, radioactivity was detected in soil at different locations several hundred meters from the hypocenter, and also at a distance of 2,400 meters to the west (Arakatsu et al. 1953, p. 5; Yamaoka et al. 1953, p. 1). The locations near the hypocenter exhibited induced radioactivity, and the one 2,400 meters away was radioactive from nuclear fission products (fallout). On the fourth day after the bombing in Nagasaki (13 August), induced radioactivity was confirmed in the soil samples taken near the hypocenter (Nishina Memorial Foundation 1973, pp. 114, 181).

---

* An *electronvolt* is a unit of kinetic energy: 1.6×10^{-19} joules.

In clarifying the injuries to the living body caused by atomic bomb radiation, it is necessary to estimate as accurately as possible the radiation dose an individual has received instantaneously. One must then determine the in-air dose at the radiation site and the location of the subject at the time of exposure (especially shield effects). Thus, it is important to decide the accurate location of the burst point. Once the distance between burst point and exposed location is known, it is possible to calculate the in-air dose of gamma rays and neutrons at that point. In order to obtain accurate figures, this dose should be compared with the actually measured values or estimated values obtained by other methods. Great efforts have been made to estimate the dose by measuring induced radioactivity at various locations in Hiroshima and Nagasaki and through experiments applying gamma rays and neutrons emitted from a nuclear reactor.

In-Air Dose. Information on radiation exposure in Hiroshima and Nagasaki began to be collected soon after the explosion. Several days after the bombing in Hiroshima, it was noticed that unused films, X-ray films, and sensitive papers had been blackened by gamma rays; and estimations of gamma-ray doses were attempted but proved unsuccessful. Among the samples collected between 13 and 14 August in Hiroshima, abnormally strong beta particles were detected in the bones of a horse. Radioactivity was also found in sulphur from a porcelain insulator attached to an electric light pole. These were all induced radioactivity from neutrons (Arakatsu et al. 1953, p. 5). Since induced radioactivity (phosphorus 32; half-life 14.3 days) was detected in human bones on 16 August, the bones of the victims were collected until early September (Yamazaki, Sugimoto, and Kimura 1953, p. 16). Based on these measured values of radioactivity, the total number of fast neutrons at the hypocenter in Hiroshima was estimated to be 1.2×10^{12} (neutrons per square centimeter) (Sugimoto 1953, p. 19), and slow neutrons to be 9×10^{12} (neutrons per square centimeter). In Nagasaki the total number of neutrons was estimated to be 8×10^{12} (neutrons per square centimeter) from the measurements of radioactivity in bone on 23 October near the hypocenter (Shinohara et al. 1953c, p. 41). It was, however, difficult to obtain the estimated in-air dose for various distances from the hypocenter. Based on the experimental data in the United States after 1955, dosimetry studies for estimating the actual exposure dose of subjects have been carried out at the Oak Ridge National Laboratory (ORNL) since 1956; and in 1957 the T57D (tentative 1957 dose) by distance was proposed for the first time by E. N. York (Ritchie and Hurst 1959; and York 1957).

On the other hand, continuous efforts to estimate the in-air dose have also been made in Japan. It was found from the basic studies made in the period 1958–60 that the exposure dose of neutrons could be estimated by a radiochemical method. Iron material used for construction contains minute amounts of nonradioactive cobalt; and when neutrons are absorbed, radioactive cobalt 60 is produced. The number of neutrons at the time of the bombing can be estimated from the radioactivity of cobalt 60 (Saito 1961, p. 142). In 1962 iron materials were collected from buildings situated at varying distances from the hypocenter, and estimations were made about the exposure of neutrons by distance (Hashizume et al. 1967).

At about the same time, estimations of initial gamma-ray doses by thermoluminescence measurement were made on bricks and tiles collected at various distances from the hypocenter. *Thermoluminescence* is a weak light emitted by an oxide heated to a temperature of about 300° C. Since the luminosity is proportional to the latent energy retained in the matter or substance by exposure to radiation, it is possible to estimate the initial gamma-ray exposure of each location. This attempt proved unsuccessful since the tiles used for study were greatly affected by the fire, which continued for long hours after the explosion (Hashizume et al. 1967; Higashimura, Ichikawa, and Sidei 1963). This method, however, yielded good results later, when structural materials saved from the fire were used for study (Hashizume et al. 1967; Ichikawa, Higashimura, and Sidei 1966). The National Institute of Radiological Sciences (NIRS) succeeded in obtaining in-air dose corresponding to distance from the previously estimated values in Hiroshima and Nagasaki (Hashizume et al. 1967).

In 1966 the Oak Ridge National Laboratory, after having continued its study on radiation-dose estimation, reported the tentative 1965 dose (T65D).

Figure 5.1 shows the T57D and the T65D and the dose estimated by the NIRS.* The figures for T65D values by distance from the hypocenter are indicated in table 5.1. As shown in the figure, the T65D curve is lower than the T57D curve in Hiroshima; and the NIRS curve is within the estimated error limits of T65D. Both T65D and T57D curves are about the same in Nagasaki, and the estimated gamma-ray dose of NIRS is similar to the T65D curve. Although the neutron doses obtained by the NIRS at two different places in Nagasaki are about 17 percent and 42 percent higher than the T65D neutron dose, the ratio of neutron dose to the entire radiation dose is small. In regard to the radiation hazard in both cities, the T65D is the most widely used in-air dose at present (Auxier et al. 1966; Milton and Shohoji 1968).

Shielding. The in-air dose of gamma rays and neutrons previously mentioned is the dose given to subjects without any shielding. Although this dose may serve as a scale for estimating exposure dose, the shielding effects of houses, shelters, and buildings must also be considered. The shielding effects of various obstacles to initial gamma rays are shown in table 5.2.

* Auxier 1975; Auxier et al. 1966; Hashizume and Maruyama 1975b.

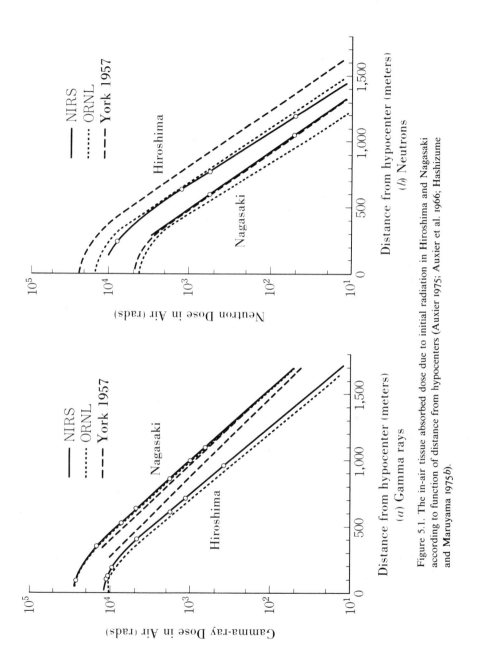

Figure 5.1. The in-air tissue absorbed dose due to initial radiation in Hiroshima and Nagasaki according to function of distance from hypocenters (Auxier 1975; Auxier et al. 1966; Hashizume and Maruyama 1975*b*).

TABLE 5.1

*The Dose in Tissue from Air (rads) in Tentative 1965 Dose (T65D)
in Both Cities as a Function of Distance from Each Hypocenter**

Distance from Hypocenter (m)	Hiroshima		Nagasaki	
	Gamma Rays (rads)	Neutrons (rads)	Gamma Rays (rads)	Neutrons (rads)
0	10,300	14,100	25,100	3,900
100	9,660	13,100	23,500	3,570
200	8,040	10,600	19,500	2,790
300	6,050	7,700	14,700	1,910
400	4,220	5,090	10,400	1,190
500	2,790	3,150	7,090	703
600	1,780	1,870	4,720	398
700	1,110	1,080	3,110	221
800	685	613	2,040	121
900	419	344	1,340	66.1
1,000	255	191	888	35.9
1,100	155	106	588	19.5
1,200	94.6	58.9	391	10.6
1,300	57.7	32.6	262	5.8
1,400	35.2	18.1	176	3.2
1,500	21.6	10.1	119	1.7
1,600	13.2	5.6	80.7	1.0
1,800	5.0	1.7	37.6	0.3
2,000	1.9	0.5	17.8	0.1
2,500	0.2	0.0	2.9	0.0
3,000	0.0	0.0	0.5	0.0

* The figures below three ciphers in significant figures have been omitted.
Source: R. C. Milton and T. Shohoji, "Tentative 1965 radiation dose (T65D) estimation for atomic bomb survivors, Hiroshima and Nagasaki," ABCC TR (1968) 1–68.

TABLE 5.2

Shielding Effect against Initial Gamma Rays

Material	Thickness Reducing Radiation Dose by 90% (m)
Iron	0.09–0.13
Concrete	0.30–0.45
Soil	0.45–0.65
Water	0.65–0.92
Wood	1.25–1.75

Source: S. Glasstone, ed., *The Effects of Nuclear Weapons*, rev. ed. (Washington, D.C.: U.S. Atomic Energy Commission, 1962), p. 384.

TABLE 5.3

Average Penetration Coefficient for Those Who Suffered inside Wooden Houses or in Light Frame Buildings

Radiation	Hiroshima	Nagasaki
Gamma rays	0.904	0.813
Neutrons	0.716	0.351

Source: R. C. Milton and T. Shohoji, "Tentative 1965 radiation dose (T65D) estimation for atomic bomb survivors, Hiroshima and Nagasaki," ABCC TR (1968) 1–68.

The extent of shielding at the time of the explosion varied greatly. It is difficult to reproduce the actual conditions of individual exposure and to estimate the exposure dose as affected by various shields. Studies on this problem have been carried out from 1952 at the Atomic Bomb Casualty Commission (ABCC) and at the Oak Ridge National Laboratory. At present the actual exposure dose (T65D) is estimated by taking into account the Japanese style of structure, a person's position inside a building and his or her distance from any windows, and the shape of a structure and its location (Auxier 1975, p. 1; Milton and Shohoji 1968). When the accurate shielding conditions were not clear, the mean penetration coefficient was used (table 5.3).

The Dose Received by the Main Organs of the Body (Organ Dose). Even when the in-air dose of gamma rays and neutrons received by human subjects, that is the dose acting on the skin surface, in studying radiation injury, one still needs to know the dose absorbed by various organs.

The study made at the National Institute of Radiological Sciences showed that when one is exposed from one direction outdoors, the gamma rays and neutrons received by the center of the body would diminish to about one half and one tenth of those acting on the surface (table 5.4).

TABLE 5.4

Ratio to In-Air Dose of the Dose Absorbed by Various Parts of the Human Body

Radiation	Ovary	Testis	Thyroid	Bone Marrow	Fetus	Lungs
Gamma rays	0.5	0.6	0.7	0.6	0.3 − 0.5	0.6
Neutrons	0.1	0.4	0.4	0.2	0.1	0.2

Source: T. Hashizume and T. Maruyama, "Dose estimation of human fetus exposed in utero to radiations from atomic bombs in Hiroshima and Nagasaki," *Journal of Radiation Research* (Tokyo) 14 (1973): 346. T. Hashizume and T. Maruyama, "Physical dose estimates for A-bomb survivors—Studies at Chiba, Japan," *Journal of Radiation Research* (Tokyo) 16 (1975 Supplement): 12. T. Hashizume, T. Maruyama, and K. Nishizawa, "Estimation of exposed radiation dose of atomic bomb survivors," in *Genbaku Shōgaishō Chōsa-Kenkyū-han Hōkoku* [Report of the Study Group for Atomic Bomb Disease] (Nihon Kōshū Eisei Kyōkai, 1977), p. 15. T. Hashizume, T. Maruyama, K. Nishizawa, and K. Fukuhisa, "Mean bone marrow dose of atomic bomb survivors in Hiroshima and Nagasaki," *Journal of Radiation Research* (Tokyo) 18 (1977): 67. T. Hashizume, T. Maruyama, K. Nishizawa, and A. Nishimura, "Estimation of absorbed dose in thyroids and gonads of survivors in Hiroshima and Nagasaki," *Acta Radiologica* 13 (1974): 411.

Residual Radiation

The sources of residual radiation are fission products (mainly beta particles and gamma rays), uranium and plutonium escaping fission (mainly alpha particles and gamma rays), and radioactive isotopes induced by the interaction of neutrons with bomb fragments and with substances in the air or on earth (beta particles and gamma rays). In exposure to residual radiation are included external exposure mainly to gamma rays from outside of the body and internal exposure to beta particles and gamma rays from radioactive substances taken into the body.

INDUCED RADIOACTIVITY

Most of the substances by absorbing neutrons emitted by the atomic bomb through fission reaction of uranium and plutonium change into radioisotopes. These substances continue to emit beta particles, and frequently gamma rays as well, for a long time. The neutron-induced radioactive materials are an important source of residual radiation in the bombed area.

The radioactive weapon residues turned into vapors as a result of high temperatures and became a constituent of the fallout together with fission products. It was this fallout ("ashes of death"), together with radioactive materials in soil, rubble, and structural materials, that proved harmful to the human body. Although the atomic bomb emitted both fast neutrons with high energy and slow neutrons with low energy, the slow neutrons (low-speed neutrons of about 0.2 electron-volts, 6.3 kilometers per second) were the main source of induced radioactivity.

The intensity of induced radioactivity in substances irradiated by neutrons can be calculated from the energy of neutrons and the total number of neutrons in the substance. The total number of slow neutrons at the hypocenter was estimated to be about $4-6 \times 10^{12}$ in Hiroshima and about 2×10^{12} in Nagasaki.[*] These figures—together with the estimated values[†] of radioactivity produced by irradiating thermal neutrons known from nuclear reactor onto soil, tiles, bricks, and asphalt—were used to estimate the induced-radioactivity intensity at the hypocenter.[‡] Table 5.5 gives an outline of the intensity of various radioisotopes. Aluminum 28 (^{28}Al; half-life 2.3 minutes), manganese 56 (^{56}Mn; half-life 2.6 hours), and sodium 24 (^{24}Na; half-life 15 hours) have a short half-life and disappeared almost completely 100 hours or more after the explosion. Scandium 46 (^{46}Sc; half-life 83.9 days), cobalt 60 (^{60}Co; half-life 5.26 years), and cesium 134 (^{134}Cs; half-life 2.05 years) have a long half-life— hence the importance of these elements, however minute in quantity. The radioisotopes mentioned here were the products of neutron irradiation in the soil and emitted beta particles and gamma rays. Table 5.5 shows the values at the hypocenter, and their intensity away from the hypocenter can be calculated according to distances.

In order to determine their effects on the human body, it is necessary to estimate the exposure dose of gamma rays emitted by these radioisotopes. The significant effects on ground are attributable to gamma rays emitted from radioisotopes at depths of several centimeters.

* Arakawa 1962; Hashizume et al. 1969; Shohno 1967, pp. 75, 118.
† Arakawa 1962; Hashizume et al. 1969.
‡ Hashizume et al. 1969; Shohno and Iijima 1975.

TABLE 5.5

Estimated Intensity of Radioactivity from Major Radioisotopes Induced at the Hypocenter Immediately after the Bombing (in units of microcuries per gram*)

	Aluminum 28	Manganese 56	Sodium 24	Scandium 46	Cobalt 60	Cesium 134
Soil: Hiroshima	226.27	1.23	0.77	5.88×10^{-5}	5.62×10^{-6}	2×10^{-7}
Nagasaki	115.13	0.88	0.27	5.42×10^{-5}	3.51×10^{-6}	
Roofing tile: Hiroshima		16.3	0.81	17×10^{-5}	1.3×10^{-5}	5×10^{-7}
Brick: Hiroshima		12.3	1.13	11×10^{-5}	1.1×10^{-5}	2×10^{-7}
Concrete: Hiroshima		3.32	0.38	9×10^{-5}	0.8×10^{-5}	4×10^{-7}
Asphalt: Hiroshima		3.99	2.06	2×10^{-5}	2.2×10^{-5}	1×10^{-7}

* A *microcurie* is one millionth of a curie and denotes the specific radioactivity induced in each isotope; a *curie* is the official unit of radioactivity (3.70×10^{10} distintegrations per second).

Source: T. Hashizume, T. Maruyama, Y. Kumamoto, Y. Kato, and S. Kawamura, "Estimation of gamma-ray dose from neutron-induced radioactivity in Hiroshima and Nagasaki," *Health Physiology* 17 (1969): 761.

N. Shohno and S. Iijima, *Kakuhōshasen to Genbakushō* [Nuclear Radiation and Atomic Bomb Disease] (Tokyo: Nihon Hōsō Shuppan Kyōkai, 1975), pp. 118–24.

TABLE 5.6

Dose Rate of Gamma Rays of Induced Radioactivity Estimated (in rads per hour) Recorded 1 Meter over the Hypocenter in Hiroshima Immediately after the Bombing

	Manganese 56	Sodium 24	Scandium 46	Cobalt 60
Soil	4.6	2.8	81.6×10^{-6}	10.6×10^{-6}
Roofing tile	2.7	0.3	33.6×10^{-6}	3.4×10^{-6}

Source: T. Hashizume and T. Maruyama, "Dose estimation from residual and fallout radioactivity: A simulated neutron activation experiment," *Journal of Radiation Research* (Tokyo) 16 (1975, Supplement): 32.

The estimated values of gamma-ray dose rate 1 meter aboveground immediately after the explosion at the hypocenter in Hiroshima are shown in table 5.6 (Hashizume and Maruyama 1975). Based on experiments carried out on the surface and underground at various depths with gamma-ray sources of varying energies, these values are estimated on the assumption that the covered soil or tiles were 1.4 centimeters thick in Hiroshima. Of others not seen in this table, the dose rate of cesium 134 is negligible; and although the dose of aluminum 28 could become great, its half-life is only 2.3 minutes, so that it almost completely loses its radioactivity in about one hour. The possibility that *early entrants** were affected by these two radioisotopes is but small. When considering their effects on the directly exposed subjects at the hypocenter, aluminum 28 cannot be disregarded (527 rads per hour in Hiroshima and 268 rads per hour in Nagasaki) (Shohno and Iijima 1975).†

Induced radioactivity in soil decreases with the half-life specific to each isotope. Figure 5.2 shows the chronological changes of gamma-ray dose rate at the hypocenter in Hiroshima. The solid lines indicate the chronological decrease in dose rate of manganese 56, sodium 24, scandium 46, and cobalt

Figure 5.2. Changes by time of gamma-ray dose at 1 meter above the ground at the hypocenter in Hiroshima (estimated from induced radioactivity in soil).

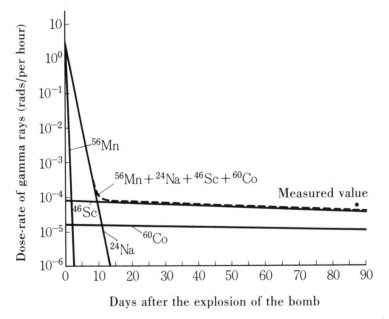

* *Early entrants* were people who entered any area within a radius of about 2 kilometers of the hypocenter from the date of the bombing until 20 August 1945 in the case of Hiroshima and until 23 August 1945 in the case of Nagasaki.

† A *rad* is a unit of energy absorbed from ionizing radiation: (1 rad = 0.01 gray = 0.01 J/kg). (Ed.)

60; while the broken line indicates that of all four grouped together. This estimated curve coincided fairly well with the value (Pace and Smith 1959) of 78 microrads per hour (70 microrads per hour when 8 microrads per hour of natural radiation are subtracted) actually measured on day 87 after the explosion. When the dose-rate curve is integrated for a definite period, the total amount of gamma rays received during this period can be obtained. The dose for 100 hours after the explosion is especially high, and this is followed by a rapid decrease. Even at 100 hours or more after the explosion, if a minute dose were taken to be of significance as compared with natural radiation, one would not be able to disregard the effects of cobalt 60 and scandium 46. The total gamma-ray dose from induced radioactivity up to 100 hours after the explosion 1 meter above the ground at the hypocenter in Hiroshima averaged about 100 rads (Takeshita 1975). Since the total number of neutrons rapidly decreased away from the hypocenter, the total gamma-ray dose from induced radioactivity decreased: for example, about 20 rads at a distance of 500 meters (Takeshita 1975), and about 1 rad at 1,000 meters (Shohno 1967).

The total number of neutrons at the hypocenter in Nagasaki was estimated to be about one third that in Hiroshima. On the other hand, the manganese content in the soil of Nagasaki was about twice that of Hiroshima. Consequently, the total gamma-ray dose up to 100 hours after the explosion 1 meter above the ground at the hypocenter in Nagasaki was estimated to be about 40 rads, and those at 500 meters and 1,000 meters from the hypocenter, 7 rads and 0.4 rad, respectively (Shohno 1967; Takeshita 1975).

Judging from the preceding results, for a person who entered the area around the hypocenter 1 hour after the explosion and remained there for about 5 hours, the exposure dose to induced radioactivity would be approximately 20 rads; while one who entered there the following day and stayed for about 8 hours, would be exposed to less than 10 rads. The exposure dose in Nagasaki was approximately 40 percent that in Hiroshima. However, this dose includes only radiation induced in soil; the actual exposure dose must include residual radiations from building materials.

FALLOUT

The fallout contains nuclear-fission products of uranium and plutonium, isotopes that have escaped fission, and weapon residues activated by neutrons. These minute particles are blown high into the air, into the atmosphere, and then gradually descend or come down concentrated on a specific area.

In Hiroshima, a mild wind was blowing toward the west at the time of the explosion, and the "black rain" fell from the north to the west of the hypocenter (figure 6.1). Thus, radioactivity was detected throughout a wide area in the part where rain fell (Pace and Smith 1959; Yamazaki 1953,

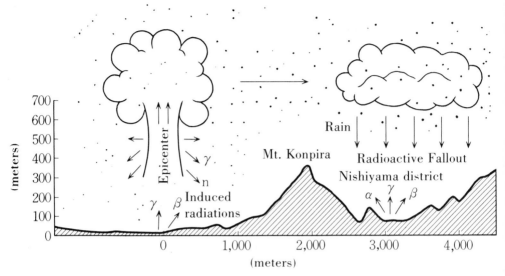

Figure 5.3. Topographical section of Nagasaki and residual radiation (NGO International Symposium 1977*b*, p. 24).

p. 25). In Nagasaki, a 3 meter-per-second wind was blowing toward the east-northeast at the time of the explosion, and the rain together with the fallout came down concentrated near the Nishiyama water reservoir about 3 kilometers east of the hypocenter. High radioactivity was detected at the Nishiyama district (Pace and Smith 1959; Shinohara et al. 1953*b*, p. 45) (figure 5.3).

About 200 different kinds of isotope were produced by the explosion of the atomic bombs. Although most of these isotopes were radioactive, those with a short half-life had attenuated by the time of the measurement; and only those with a long half-life were detected. Radiochemical analysis of soil at the Nishiyama district revealed strontium 89 (^{89}Sr; half-life 52.7 days), barium 140 (^{140}Ba; half-life 12.8 days), praseodymium 144 (^{144}Pr; half-life 17.3 minutes), zirconium 95 (^{95}Zr; half-life 65.5 days), strontium 90 (^{90}Sr; half-life 29 years), cesium 137 (^{137}Cs; half-life 30 years), celium 144 (^{144}Ce; half-life 284 days), and also plutonium 239 (^{239}Pu; half-life 2.4×10^4 years) which had escaped fission. Excepting for plutonium 239, all these isotopes emit beta particles or gamma rays, but the intensity of radioactivity as a whole attenuates rapidly.

According to the actual gamma-ray dose rate at 1 meter aboveground as measured by the Japan–United States Joint Commission between 3 and 7 October 1945, a maximum 0.045 milliroentgen per hour was recorded in the area 3 to 4 kilometers to the west of the hypocenter in Hiroshima and a maximum 1 milliroentgen per hour at the Nishiyama district in Nagasaki (figure 5.4). Since the estimated value of the total exposure dose from the fallout 1 hour after the explosion up to the present contains uncertain elements, such as washing away by rain (Takeshita 1960), the values vary from one

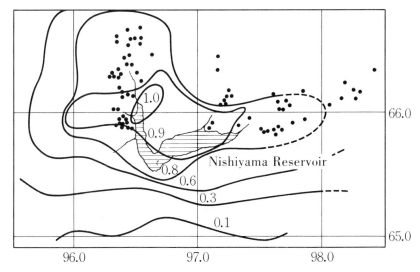

Figure 5.4. Isodose curves of gamma rays from radioactive fallout in Nishiyama, Nagasaki (milliroentgens per hour) 3–7 October 1945, about two months after the atomic bomb (Pace and Smith 1959).

report to another.* In Hiroshima the maximum value was from 4 to 40 rads; and in the Nishiyama district, Nagasaki, 48 to 149 rads.† Special note should be taken of the high values measured in Nagasaki.

RESIDUAL RADIOACTIVITY IN THE BODY

As previously mentioned, exposure to residual radioactivity is both external and internal. Radioactive substances enter the body by inhalation, through food and drinking water, and through the skin.

There are several reports on the estimates of internal exposure of the residents of the Nishiyama district in Nagasaki (Shohno 1967; Takeshita 1960). Since 1969 radioactive substances in the body have been measured with the human counter (Okajima et al. 1978).‡ This study was repeated up to 1971, and it was confirmed that the amount of cesium 137 in the residents of the Nishiyama district was nearly twice that in other districts. The amount of cesium 137 contained in soil and agricultural products in this district was also significantly greater than that in other districts. These facts indicate that the residents of this district have been receiving a greater internal exposure than those living in other districts.

* Arakawa 1962; Okajima 1975; Shohno 1967; Shohno and Iijima 1975, pp. 118–24; Takeshita 1960; Takeshita 1975.

† This is an estimate based on data at 15 centimeters above ground and will presumably be reduced by one half at 1 meter (Pace and Smith 1959).

‡ *Human counter* (or *whole body counter*) is an instrument designed to measure the radioactivity in the human body. In principle, a detector placed near the body can measure this radioactivity in an iron room.

Radiation Effects on Animals and Plants

The Biological Science Division (zoology, botany, and entomology) of the Special Committee for Atomic Bomb Casualty Investigation and Research of the Scientific Research Council of Japan had already completed its preparation for surveys to be carried out in early September of 1945. However, the railroad was cut off by the Makurazaki typhoon on 17 September, and the weather conditions did not improve after the typhoon passed Hiroshima. The rainfall continued for many days, and the greater part of the city was flooded, greatly hampering the on-site survey.

ZOOLOGICAL SURVEY*

The primary on-site survey was carried out from 22 September to 22 October 1945 in Hiroshima, and from 3 to 15 October in Nagasaki. This survey focused on three areas: information collected about the damages occurring immediately after the explosion; on-site survey of fauna; and experimental observations of the effects of radiation on animals. Observations were continued after the primary survey, and in October 1947 the second on-site survey of the conditions of fauna was carried out in Hiroshima.

Fauna. Fauna were examined right after the explosion in Hiroshima, but the only method of obtaining information was from first-hand accounts of conditions at that time.

Right after the explosion, mosquitoes disappeared from the vicinity of Hakushima-cho (about 1 kilometer northeast of the hypocenter) but did not disappear from the grounds of the Hiroshima University of Literature and Science (present-day Hiroshima University, located 1.5 kilometers south of the hypocenter). Mosquitoes were thought to have decreased in the vicinity of the Miyuki bridge (1.8 kilometers south-southeast of the hypocenter), but other observers denied this. No changes were noted on the west side of Hijiyama hill (1.8 kilometers southeast of the hypocenter) or in Funairi district (2 kilometers southwest of the hypocenter). Mosquitoes, however, remarkably increased in number a few days later in all districts. Although opinions vary about whether the number of flies decreased or remained the same, the great increase in their number several days after the explosion was similar to that of mosquitoes.

As to fish, almost all the carps and *Carassius auratus* (crucian carp) kept in a shallow pond on the west side of Hijiyama (1.8 kilometers from the hypocenter) were killed, and many were also killed near Koi (2 to 2.5 kilome-

* Ichikawa 1953, p. 247; Katashima 1977; Maekawa 1953, p. 21; Okada 1953*a*, p. 217; Okada 1953*b*, p. 42; Uda, Sugahara, and Kita 1953, p. 98.

ters west of the hypocenter); though those kept in deep ponds escaped death in both districts. Death was considered to have resulted from the enormous blast pressure, since the air bladders of the dead fish were greatly damaged. Neither dead frogs nor lizards were seen.

There were many dead birds with hemorrhage, epilation, and lost feathers. The number of crows and sparrows decreased temporarily even near Koi. Fragmentary records on dogs, cats, rats, laboratory rabbits, laboratory mice, goats, and hogs were found, but the conditions of their exposure were unknown. It was said that rats remained the same before and after the explosion.

There were 301 army horses in the city at the time of the explosion; and since the stables were near the hypocenter, of 184 injured war horses 120 were killed, 12 wounded, and 52 missing. On the other hand, of the 600 to 800 horses coming into the city from other districts, from 60 percent to 70 percent suffered from injuries. According to a report made on 30 wounded horses that were taken in and treated for a month, the characteristic findings consisted of thermal injuries, leukopenia, fever, suppurative conjunctivitis, loss of appetite, and loss of weight (Ichikawa 1953, p. 247). Autopsies were performed on 2 horses that died ten days and twelve days after exposure, and on another 2 horses that were exposed on the road at about 1.5 kilometers from the hypocenter and recovered temporarily but were killed at the end of September. All four showed thermal injuries and other lesions of radiation injury.

In the primary on-site survey, plans were made to collect animals and plants in soil by digging up 1 square meter, to a depth of 30 centimeters, at intervals of 500 meters within 4 kilometers in radius of the hypocenter, and also to observe the animals living in ponds and fire-prevention water tanks. The initial purpose was not fully attained owing to the flooding of these areas and the overflow of the ponds and water tanks.

As to animals and other insects in soil, earthworms, bombardier beetles, earwigs, and beach fleas were collected near the torii* of the former Gokoku shrine (500 meters east of the hypocenter), on the grounds of this shrine, and at places 300 and 500 meters, and 2 kilometers distant from the hypocenter. Chrysalises were also found.

Also in Nagasaki, earthworms, bombardier beetles, tiger beetles, and moths were collected at the top of the hill on which stood the Urakami Roman Catholic Cathedral (the Cathedral of the Archdiocese of Nagasaki; 600 meters east-northeast of the hypocenter), on the grounds of Nagasaki Medical University (the present Nagasaki University School of Medicine; 600 meters east-southeast of the hypocenter), and in the vicinity of Urakami. None of these specimens showed structural or ecological abnormalities.

* A *torii* is the gateway to a Shinto temple. (Ed.)

Since a great number of earthworms *(Terricola)* were alive near the hypocenter and lacked structural and ecological abnormalities, it is likely that they were hardly affected by the atomic bomb.

As to small aquatic animals, there were many water fleas, whirligig beetles, predaceous diving beetles, *Saldula saltatoria,* and larvae of various mosquitoes in the vicinity of Aioi bridge (300 meters northwest of the hypocenter), on the grounds of the former Gokoku shrine, and in ponds and water tanks, at distances of 1, 1.5, 2, 2.5, and 4 kilometers from the hypocenter in Hiroshima. A great number of *Turbellaria* and *Sinotaia quadratus historica* were collected near Urakami in Nagasaki.

Experimental Observations. The following experiments were carried out to see the effects of radiation on animals.

The external appearance of the earthworms was normal; but in order to obtain information on radiation effects, the tenth joint from the caudal end was amputated, and regeneration of the frontal portion was observed. The regenerative process was normal; and one month later five new joints were formed, including the caudal end. Sections of the regenerating tissue revealed normal interior structures. The *Turbellaria* collected from a brook near the Urakami Roman Catholic Cathedral and kept for four years did not show any external abnormalities. The chrysalis, which was assumed to have been exposed, was bred and grew into an imago.

Mating experiments were carried out on laboratory rabbits and mice that survived in the laboratory of the Hiroshima University of Literature and Science. Mating between a survived female rabbit and a non-exposed male rabbit from a different source yielded 4 offspring on 23 November, three months after the exposure. When another surviving male rabbit was mated with 4 female rabbits from different sources, 2 of the female rabbits gave birth on 28 February of the following year to 4 and 5 offspring, respectively. On 18 February 1946, the mice bore 5 offspring. All these animals were found to be in good health.

Studies on the genetic effects of atomic-bomb radiation were carried out with 41 varieties of vinegar flies *(Drosophilae)* collected on the grounds of the Hiroshima University of Literature and Science and several other locations. Mutations were observed; but, in consideration of the distance between the area where the flies were collected and the hypocenter, one cannot hastily conclude that these mutations were caused by the direct effects of the atomic bomb.

For the purpose of knowing the effects of residual radioactivity near the hypocenter, *Drosophilae* of 2 species and 10 varieties were brought from Kyoto University between 7 and 15 September and were exposed to the residual radioactivity, for 2 to 5 days, 100 meters east of the hypocenter. No mutations, however, could be seen in any of the varieties.

The second on-site survey on fauna was carried out two years later in October 1947 at Hiroshima. As in the primary survey, observations were made on collected small animals in both soil and water. This survey covered a wide area from the hypocenter to the Ujina district (4 kilometers south of the hypocenter). The results indicated that fauna at the hypocenter had recovered to a degree that did not differ from that in other districts.

BOTANIC SURVEY*

The survey on the effects of the atomic bomb on plants in Hiroshima began in mid-September of 1945. The aforementioned survey by the Biological Science Division was carried out in mid-October in Nagasaki and late in October in Hiroshima. The second survey was made late in April 1946 in both cities, and was continued up to 1950 in Hiroshima.

The survey was carried out in five different areas divided according to distance from the hypocenter; and several locations not affected by the fire were selected in each area. This survey studied damaged plants, malformed plants, and the later renewal of vegetation in Hiroshima.

The following is a brief outline of related subjects from the Collection of the Reports on the Investigation of the Atomic Bomb Casualties of the Science Council of Japan (1953).

Damaged Plants. The degree of damage to plants gradually diminished with distance from the hypocenter. Within 1 kilometer of the hypocenter, herbs withered and trees came down or were broken and burned, but the burned thick trunks and roots frequently remained standing. Thus, it was possible to know how trees were distributed before the explosion and also how damaged they were. On the basis of the damage to trees and herbs, one can judge that plants were damaged, especially from thermal radiation, over a distance of several kilometers from the hypocenter. The burned condition of bamboo tree trunks indicated the range distance to be 5 to 6 kilometers in Nagasaki and 7 to 8 kilometers in Hiroshima. From the burned condition of the leaves of rice plants, the range distance in Hiroshima was thought to be about 5.7 kilometers to the north, about 4.5 kilometers to the east, and about 4 kilometers to the west.

The degree of damage was quite different by direction. At places far from the hypocenter, only the side of the tree trunk facing the hypocenter was burned, while the opposite side was frequently normal in appearance. In some trees there were no branches on the side facing the hypocenter, while the other side had many branches.

Damage to plants was found only in the portions exposed aboveground,

* Fujita, Andō, and Tanaka 1977, p. 12; Nakayama 1953, p. 239; Ogura 1953, p. 225; Shimotomai et al. 1953, p. 227; Suita 1953, p. 235.

and portions underground were not directly damaged. Consequently, the root and the underground stalk put forth new buds even in those whose aboveground portion was completely burned. New buds were found coming out from the stumps of trees, which were standing burned without any branches. These sights were seen two months after exposure to the atomic bomb at the time of the primary survey. New buds did not sprout from the damaged side of trees within 700 meters of the hypocenter. Regeneration differed greatly by species of plants: some regenerated rapidly, while others withered. Broad-leaved trees in general regenerated actively, especially *Cinnamomum camphora* (camphor tree), *Melia azedarach* var. *japonica* (chinaberry), willow, *Robinia pseudoacacia* (black locust), Chinese parasol, fig tree, hemp palm, sago palm, ginkgo, eucalyptus, *Euonymus japonica* (spindle tree), *Fatsia japonica, Celtis sinensis* var. *japonica* (nettle tree), *Nerium indicum* (oleander, rosebay), azalea, and bamboo. Among the herbs that regenerated rapidly, there were sweet potato, taro, *Cyperus rotundus* (coco-grass), *Lycoris radiata,* canna, *Oxalis martiana, Polygonum cuspidatum* (Japanese knotweed), *P. multiflorum, Eleusine indica, Lygodium japonicum, Ophiopogon japonicus* (dwarf lilyturf), and *Liriope graminifolia* (big blue lilyturf). The poorly resistant herbs were needle-leaved trees such as Japan cedar and pine. Cedar and pine forests far from the hypocenter were frequently reddish in color, and trees apparently normal during the first year sometimes withered the following year. This tendency was especially marked with *Pinus densiflora* (Japanese red pine).

Small herbs were found already growing near the hypocenter when the survey was made two months after the explosion. This growth probably resulted from the sprouting of seeds that had dropped on the shallow layered soil before exposure. Some examples are pumpkin, *Pharbitis nil* (morning-glory), *Cassia obtusifolia, Erigeron bonariensis, Portulaca oleracea,* radish, *Brassica campestris* var. *Komatsuna, B. juncea,* buckwheat, and *Ricinus communis* (castor-oil plant). In the spring of the following year many kinds of herbs not seen in the autumn of the year before were found. These were also thought to have sprouted from unharmed seeds before the exposure. Plants in reservoirs, ponds, and swamps were hardly damaged.

Malformed Plants. Although abnormal types and malformations were seen in the herbs sprouting in the spring of the following year at several places within 1 kilometer of the hypocenter, they were hardly encountered at other locations and had almost completely disappeared three to four years later. In the Nishiyama district in Nagasaki, where the residual radioactivity from fallout was strong, these phenomena, though not prominent, had already been noted during the primary survey. Abnormalities included growth retardation, fasciation, malformation, and variegation, with the latter being most

Figure 5.5. Malformed flowers of *Veronica persica Poir* after A-bomb radiation. The farthest left one is a normal flower (Shimotomai et al. 1953, p. 227).

prominent. As to variegation of leaves, the white portion took a linear, spotty, and cloudy form and turned completely white (albino) in extreme cases. The shade of white varied. The variegated leaves were seen in *Clerodendron trichotomum*, taro, amaryllis, *Cerastium holosteides, Stellaria media* (chickweed), *Houttuynia cordata, Erigeron bonariensis, Veronica persica*, and *V. arvensis;* and albino was seen in *Cyperus rotundus* (nut grass). Fasciation occurred in the stem of *Veronica persica* and in inflorescence of *Capsella bursa-pastoris* (shepherd's-purse). Malformed flowers were found in *Veronica persica* (figure 5.5), *Oxalis martiana*, and *Lycoris radiata*. There were many stem-growth abnormalities of *L. radiata* near the hypocenter in Nagasaki, but the degree of abnormality differed by distance and location. *L. radiata* was probably in a preparatory stage of putting out floral stems from the tuber underground at the time of the exposure, and the floral stems were affected by A-bomb radioactivity. Some of the offspring from abnormal *Tradescantia reflexa* showed no blooms by the usual culture. Bloom was made possible with the appliance of artificial photoperiodic effect (24 hours' exposure); in other words, this was an abnormal photoperiodic plant. The pollen of the artificially bloomed flower was examined and revealed chromosomal abnormality and a high incidence of pollen malformation.

Renewal of Vegetation. The renewal of vegetation was studied in Hiroshima for five years after the atomic bombing. This renewal in the city was much quickened by the heavy rain following the Makurazaki typhoon, approximately one month after the explosion. *Euxolus viridis, Euxolus ascendens, Digitaria adscendens*, and *D. violascens* grew profusely; and in June of the following year, *Erigeron canadensis, Veronica persica, Persicaria longiseta, Portulaca oleracea*, and twenty-five other species were found in the ground of Shima Hospital located at the hypocenter. *Pteridium aquilinum, Phytolacca americana*, and *Oxalis martiana* grew thickly at places where other species were not found. Liverwort and *Funaria hygrometrica*, which are usually uncommon in the city, appeared at some places, and *Digitaria adscendens* and

Euxolus viridis predominated for three years (1947). From the third year, new plants such as *Lolium temulentum* (darnel), *Lepidium perfoliatum,* and *Sisymbrium altissimum* began to appear. *Aster subulatus,* whose growth previously was limited to the land near the sea, was also found here and there inside the city. This growth was attributable to the wide dissemination of seeds in the city, which was well ventilated by the loss of houses and buildings. *Erigeron canadensis* and *E. bonariensis* predominated in place of *Euxolus ascendens* and *Digitaria adscendens,* thus completely changing the scene. Many buds sprouted from the trunks and near the roots of the damaged trees. Although urban restoration was begun in the vicinity of stations at Hiroshima, Yokogawa (3 kilometers northwest of Hiroshima Station) and Koi (6 kilometers west of Hiroshima Station) and in the surroundings of the city such as Ujina port, the herbs continued to grow at the center of the city. Wheat, Indian corn, foxtail millet, beans, and vegetables were grown on a small scale around the irregularly distributed shacks. In 1947 the people obtained a rich harvest of wheat, tomato, eggplant, and soybean, which surpassed that in the nearby villages. Although tomatoes were formerly difficult to raise inside the city owing to damage by blight and insects, there was an ample harvest of them throughout the city. At about the same time, the people started to grow *Pinus Thunbergii, Cryptomeria japonica, Mahonia japonica,* gold-leaf plant, and hemp palm. In 1948, houses and buildings rapidly increased in number; and urban construction was well underway by the following year. Consequently, vegetation was destroyed; and by the end of 1950, it was difficult for one to retain the early post-atomic bomb images of the city.

Chapter 6

Meteorological Conditions on the Day of the Bombing

*Meteorological Conditions in Hiroshima**

The weather on 6 August was fine in the Hiroshima area. At 8 A.M. the temperature was 26.7 degrees centigrade; atmospheric pressure (sea level), 1,018 millibars; humidity, 80 percent; and visibility, fair. Land and sea breezes developing along the Seto inland coast are especially prominent in Hiroshima during August and cover a distance of several kilometers inland. These breezes were about to change at the time of the explosion, and the sea breeze was starting to blow. Although a northerly wind was blowing in the northern part of Hiroshima and a southerly wind to the south of the central area, the condition as a whole was calm. The atomic bomb exploded about 1 kilometer south of the front where the north and south winds came into contact. Meteorological conditions as indicated in table 6.1 were recorded at the Hiroshima District Meteorological Observatory, located 3.6 kilometers southsouthwest of the hypocenter.

Immediately after the explosion, a huge "mushroom cloud" was seen hanging over the skies of Hiroshima. Approximately half an hour later, a conflagration broke out and then a fire storm began to blow. Between 11 A.M. and 3 P.M., when the fire reached its peak, a strong whirlwind (tornado) developed

* Uda, Sugahara and Kita 1953, p. 98.

TABLE 6.1

Weather Conditions on 6 and 7 August 1945 in Hiroshima

Date	Time	Atmospheric Pressure (at sea level) (mb)†	Temperature (°C)	Humidity (%)	Wind Direction	Wind Velocity (m/sec)	Precipitation	Weather‡	Cloudiness	Cloud Forms§	Sunshine (true solar time)	Notes
6 August	0	16.4	25.6	87	NNE	1.5		○	0	—	—	*6 August* — $\delta°$ ○¹ a — Faint red sky. Slight morning dew.
	1	16.0*	25.0	88	NNE	2.0		○	0	—	—	
	2	16.1	24.7	90	NNE	2.0		○	0	—	—	—∞^0—$\infty^0 \equiv 4^h50^m$— Invisible haze which had continued from the 5th hovered over the whole city. Fog was observed at 04:50.
	3	16.1*	24.2	92	NNE	1.5		○	2	C	—	
	4	16.7*	23.9	93	NNE	2.5		○	2	C, Sk	—	
	5	16.9*	23.7	93	NNE	2.3		⊕	4	Kc, Sk, Sc	—	
	6	17.5	23.6	94	NNE	2.3		⊕	8	Sc, Ck, Sk, K, C	—	
	7	18.0*	24.7	89	NNE	1.3		⊕	8	Cs, Kc, Sk	0.10	—∞^1 (N) 8^h15^m— At 08:15, the haze thickened in the northern part of the city.
blast wind arose	8	18.1*	26.7	80	N	0.8		⊕	10	C, Cs, K	0.99	
	8.15	18.1*	26.8*	80*	W	1.2		—	—	—	1.00	
	8.18	18.1*	26.9*	80*	W	1.2		—	—	—		
	8.20	unknown	27.0*	80*	unknown	1.2		—	—	—		—∞^2 10^h50^m—∞^1 12^h50^m— At 10:50, the haze became more dense, but thinned slightly at 12:50.
	8.30	unknown	27.0*	81*	unknown	1.0		—	—	—		
	9	18.0	27.3	79	SW	1.7	no rainfall	◎	9	Kn, C	0.80	
	9.30	18.4*	28.4*	70*	SSW	2.3	observed	⊖	—	—		—∞^0 16^h45^m— The haze became invisible but remained.
	10	18.5	29.3	67	SW	2.5	at Eba	—	7	Kn	1.00	
	10.30	18.1*	29.6*	67*	WSW	2.3	district	⊖	—	—		
	11	17.7*	30.0	65	W	2.8		⊖	5	Kn, C	1.00	The haze became invisible but remained.
	11.30	17.1*	30.4*	64*	WSW	3.2		—	—	—		
	12	16.7	30.7	64	SSW	3.3		⊖	6	Kn	1.00	m^0 5^h50^m—6^h15^m 05:50–06:15 Observed mammatus with a cloud amount less than one tenth of the sky.
	13	16.1*	30.7	64	SW	3.7		◎	8	Kn, C	1.00	
	14	15.9	31.0	66	SW	3.2		⊖	6	Kn, C	1.00	
	15	15.3*	30.3	70	SW	3.8		⊖	7	Kn, C, Kc	0.90	T_2^0 $10^h02^m10^h03^m10^h07^m$ . . . 10^h40^m Thunder began rolling intermittently from 10:02 to 10:03 in the sky over Hiro-
	16	15.2*	30.7	65	SW	4.0		⊖	5	Kn, C	1.00	
	17	15.1*	29.7	72	SW	5.5		⊖	4	Kn, K	1.00	
	18	15.5	28.3	78	SW	5.2		⊖	4	Kn, K, Kc	0.40	

Time	Pressure*†	Temp.	Humidity	Wind dir.	Wind speed	Weather‡	Cloud amount	Cloud type§	
19	16.1*	28.2	77	SSW	3.0	◎	9	K, Cs, Kn	—
20	16.4*	27.5	83	SSE	5.2	◎	9	Sk, K, Cs	—
21	17.3	26.9	79	S	3.7	◎	10	Sk	—
22	17.2	26.7	78	S	2.3	◎	9	Sk	—
23	17.3*	26.6	78	SW	1.5	◎	10	Sk	
24	16.9*	26.5	75	WSW	2.5	◎	10	Sk	
7 August 1	17.1*	26.3	76	WSW	3.0	◎	10	Sk	
2	17.2	26.5	70	WSW	2.2	◎	10	Sk	
3	17.1*	26.0	72	WSW	2.3	◎	10	Sk	
4	17.3*	25.7	76	WSW	1.2	◎	10	Sk	
5	17.5*	25.6	78	WSW	1.3	◎	10	Sk	
6	18.0	25.6	82	—	0.0	⊖	10	K, Kc	
10	18.5	30.3	61	SE	3.0	○	3	K	
14	16.3	29.4	56	SSW	4.2	○	2	K	
18	15.5	28.8	62	SSW	3.8	○	1	K	

Notes (right-hand column):

shima City. At 10:07 it began roaring again and continued till 10:40.

𝝘° NNW 10ʰ52ᵐ Tᵒ11ʰ09ᵐ

10:52 Thunder and lightning occurred in the north-north-western direction.

11:09 Thunder rolled.

7 August

—∞⁰—|∞|⁰ 11ʰ30ᵐ—

Haze continued from the 6th.

11:30 Haze cleared off at and around the meteorological observatory, but it still hung along the rivers.

—∞⁰ 20ʰ30ᵐ—

20:30 Haze appeared again at and around the meteorological observatory.

◊° 5ʰ50ᵐ—6ʰ40ᵐ

05:50–06:40 Pure air. Visibility was up to 50 km.

◊° 10ʰ45ᵐ—19ʰ40ᵐ

10:45–19:40 Pure air. Visibility was up to 50 km.

δ° ⌒ᵗ p

Faint sunset glow. Slight evening dew.

Visibility in the direction of the areas on fire was worst from 11:00 to 12:00 when it was about 1 km.; in other directions it was 20 km.

* Automatically recorded.
† 1,000 millibars must be added to the numbers given when reading the atmospheric pressure.
‡ Weather symbols: ○ Fair and clear ◐ Fine ⊕ Cloudy ◎ Slightly cloudy ⊕ Thundery 𝝘°Thunder and lightning
§ Cloud symbols: C: Cirrus Cs: Cirrostratus Ck: Cirrocumulus Kc: Altocumulus Sc: Altostratus Sk: Stratocumulus K: Cumulus Kn: Cumulonimbus
Source: M. Uda, Y. Sugahara, and I. Kita, "Meteorological conditions related to the atomic bomb explosion in Hiroshima," in CRIABC (1953), vol. I, p. 98.

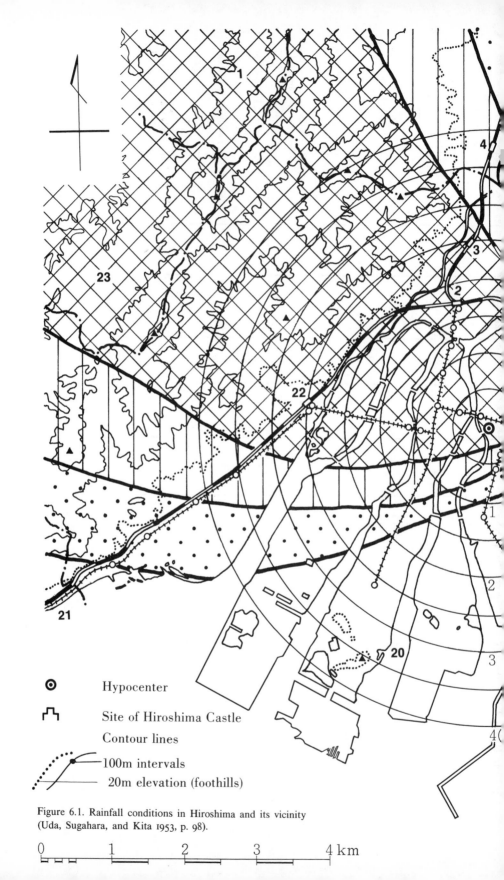

Figure 6.1. Rainfall conditions in Hiroshima and its vicinity
(Uda, Sugahara, and Kita 1953, p. 98).

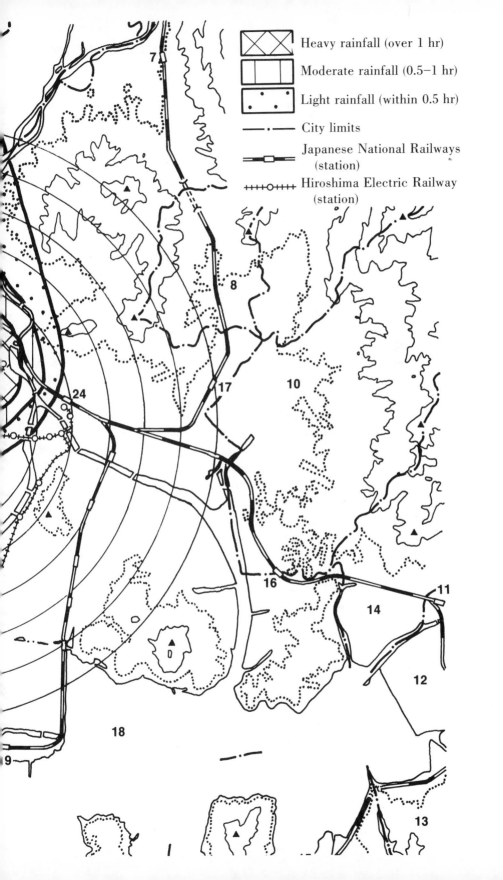

Heavy rainfall (over 1 hr)

Moderate rainfall (0.5–1 hr)

Light rainfall (within 0.5 hr)

City limits

Japanese National Railways (station)

Hiroshima Electric Railway (station)

locally in the central part toward the northern half of the city. The whirlwind developed near the front. Rumbling of thunder was heard between 10 and 11 A.M. The sea breeze became strong with the fire and calmed down at night, but did not change into a land breeze.

Black clouds and smoke moved toward the northwest; and since there was a fall of "black rain," it was assumed that a southeast wind of 1 to 3 meters per second was blowing. Meteorological data of high altitudes were not recorded. From about 20 to 30 minutes after the explosion, black clouds (nimbostratus) moved gradually toward the north-northwest and resulted in a shower (9 A.M.–4 P.M.), as indicated in figure 6.1. The conditions of the shower and the direction of flow of the blown-up scattered material are shown in figure 6.2. Heavy rain continued for one hour or more over an elliptical area, 19 × 11 kilometers, toward the northwest, including the destroyed area within 2 kilometers of the hypocenter. A light rain fell in an area measuring 29 × 15 kilometers.

One must not overlook the fact that the muddy rain contained the fallout. This rain was sticky, and the people at that time thought that oil had been dropped. A black spotty pattern remained wherever a raindrop struck. It was said that the river was as black as if Chinese ink had been dropped. The temperature fell rapidly in the midst of the big rainfall, and many people were shivering in midsummer. A large quantity of fish were found dead in the river where "black rain" poured. Diarrhea was noted among the cattle that ate grass contaminated by the muddy rain. Many residents in the Koi and Takasu districts (2.5 to 4 kilometers west of the hypocenter) complained of diarrhea. The rainfall in the area of heaviest downpour was estimated to be 50 to 100 millimeters in 1 to 3 hours. The area where dusty ash fell extended several kilometers outside the rainy area. Light, heavy, small, and large paper materials were found scattered throughout a distance of 30 kilometers to the north. This phenomenon has also been recorded in Shimane Prefecture at a distance of more than 50 kilometers. The scattered materials fell before the "black rain" and were also confirmed during the rain.

1. Numata Town	9. Nukushina Village	17. Yaga Station
2. Yokogawa Station	10. Fuchū Town	18. Ujina Port
3. Mitaki Station	11. Kaitaichi Station	19. Ujina Station
4. Aki-Nagatsuka Station	12. Kaitaichi Town	20. Ōta River
5. Shimo-Gion Station	13. Yano Town	21. Inokuchi Village
6. Gion Town	14. Funakoshi Town	22. Koi Station
7. Hesaka Station	15. Saka Town	23. Ishiuchi Village
8. Nakayama Village	16. Mukainada Station	24. Hiroshima Station

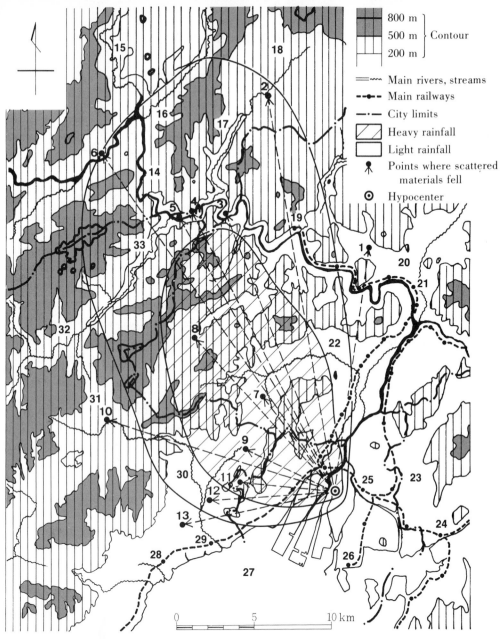

Figure 6.2. Area of rainfall and directions of scattered materials in Hiroshima and its surrounding counties (Uda, Sugahara, and Kita 1953, p. 98). 1. Kameyama 2. Tosaka 3. Ana 4. Usa 5. Sakaichi 6. Tonoga 7. Tomo, Ōtsuka 8. Toyama 9. Ishiuchi 10. Sagotani 11. Yamada 12. Takai 13. Itsukaichi

1. Kameyama	9. Ishiuchi	17. Youro River	25. Ujina Station
2. Tosaka	10. Sagotani	18. Yamagata County	26. Hatsukaichi Station
3. Ana	11. Yamada	19. Aki-Imuro Station	27. Itsukaichi Station
4. Usa	12. Takai	20. Asa County	28. Yahata River
5. Sakaichi	13. Itsukaichi Town	21. Kabe Station	29. Saeki County
6. Tonoga	14. Ōta River	22. Yasu River	30. Yuki
7. Tomo, Ōtsuka	15. Takiyama River	23. Kaitaichi Station	31. Minochi River
8. Toyama	16. Kake Town	24. Hiroshima Station	

The "black rain" continued for about 30 minutes to an hour and was followed by intermittent rains. A forest fire in the Koi district west of the city was extinguished by this rain.

According to data kept at the Hiroshima District Meteorological Observatory, the rainfall after 6 August was as follows:

0.4 mm	18 August
16.5 mm	25 August
1.8 mm	26 August
30.6 mm	27 August
44.7 mm	30 August
37.9 mm	31 August
over 10 mm	1–4 September
over 10 mm	9 and 11 September
31.9 mm	14 September

In other words, there was a dry condition for about two weeks after the explosion. This area was hit by the Makurazaki typhoon between 16 and 18 September, with a rainfall of 219 millimeters. Most of the bridges in Hiroshima were lost, and roads and railroads were cut off by the storm on the night of the seventeenth. Rescue activity was greatly hindered, since the trains were unable to move until November. At the western part of Hiroshima Prefecture, the Ōno Army Hospital collapsed and was washed away. Ten scientists participating in the third survey team of Kyoto Imperial University were killed during this accident (see page 505).

Meteorological Conditions in Nagasaki

9 August was a hot summer day in Nagasaki. A thick morning mist started to clear gradually from about 7 A.M. At 11 A.M. the temperature was 28.8 degrees centigrade; atmospheric pressure (sea level), 1,014 millibars; and humidity, 71 percent. The meteorological conditions on 9 August as recorded by the Nagasaki Marine Observatory (formerly called the Nagasaki Meteorological Station, located on top of the "Donnoyama"* 4.5 kilometers south-southeast of the hypocenter at 131.5 meters above sea level) are seen in table 6.2 (Nagasaki Shiyakusho 1977, p. 137). The weather map (figure 6.3) at 6 A.M. on the same day showed a distribution of atmospheric pressure characteristic for summer—an overall high atmospheric pressure from the Pacific Ocean.

* A mountain in the southern district of Nagasaki. (Ed.)

TABLE 6.2
Weather Conditions in Nagasaki on 9 August 1945*

									Hours							
	8	9	10	11	12	13	14	15	16	17	18	19	20	21	22
Wind direction	ESE	ESE	—	SW	SW	SW	SW	SW	WSW	SW	SW	SW	WW	WSW	SW
Wind velocity (m/s)	1.2	1.8	0.3	3.0	3.7	4.2	4.3	5.0	6.0	3.3	6.2	7.2	2.0	5.0	1.5
Temperature (° C)	25.7	27.3	28.0	28.8	29.4	29.9	29.9	29.9	29.3	28.5	27.2	26.4	25.7	25.2	24.9
Humidity (%)	91	76	76	71	68	58	65	63	66	68	78	80	84	88	91
Weather†	○	◎	⊕	○	○	⊕	◎	○	○	○	⊕	○	○	○	◎
Atmospheric pressure at sea level (mb)‡	15.0	15.3	15.3	14.0	13.9	13.6	13.3	13.0	12.7	12.7	12.8	12.7	13.0	13.2	13.5
Sunshine (h)	1.00	1.00	0.70	0.69	1.00	1.00	1.00	1.00	1.00	0.88	1.00	0.30	—	—	—
Precipitation	—	—	—	—	—	—	—	—	—	—	—	—	—	—	—

N.B. Fog on the ground: 04:40–04:50. Moderately foggy in the morning. A cumulonimbus cloud arose in the morning. Fire broke out. A doughnut-shaped cloud appeared. Slightly foggy in the afternoon.

* Data from Nagasaki Meteorological Station.
† ○ Fair and clear ⊕ Fine ◎ Cloudy ⊕ Slightly cloudy
‡ 1,000 millibars must be added to the figures when reading the atmospheric pressure.
Source: Nagasaki Shiyakusho, *Nagasaki Genbaku Sensaishi* [RNAWD] (Nagasaki: Nagasaki Kokusai Bunka Kaikan, 1977), vol. I, p. 137.

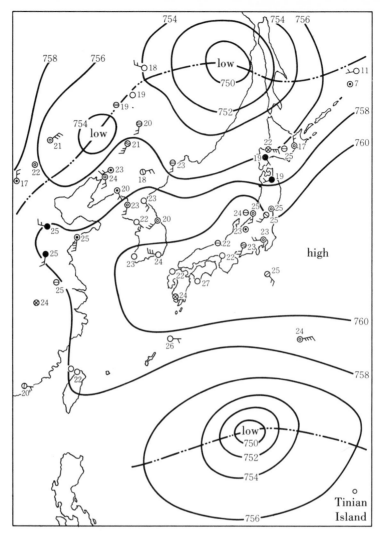

Symbol	Description	Symbol	Description	Symbol	Description	Symbol	Description
O	Fair and clear	◐	Slightly cloudy	◉	Cloudy	⊙	Fog
①	Fine	⊗	Middle cloud overcast	●	Rain		

Symbol	Wind speed (m/sec)	Wind scale	Symbol	Wind speed (m/sec)	Wind scale
O	0.0-0.5	0			
O⌐	0.6-1.7	1	O⫰⫰⫰⌐	12.5-15.2	7
O⟍	1.8-3.3	2	O⫰⫰⫰⫰	15.3-18.2	8
O⟍	3.4-5.2	3	O⫰⫰⫰⫰	18.3-21.5	9
O⟍	5.3-7.4	4	O⫰⫰⫰⫰	21.6-25.1	10
O⟍	7.5-9.8	5	O⫰⫰⫰⫰⫰	25.2-29.0	11
O⟍	9.9-12.4	6	O⫰⫰⫰⫰⫰	29.1<	12

Figure 6.3. Weather map, 6:00 A.M., 9 August 1945. Figures show temperature and atmospheric pressure in mm Hg. (Chūō Kishōdai 1945).

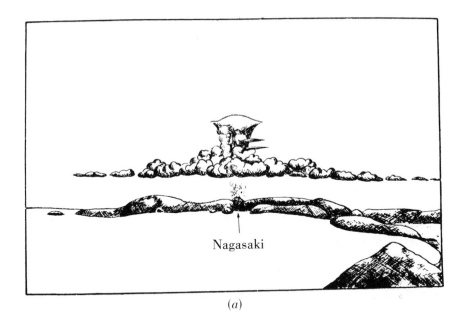

(a)

(b)

Figure 6.4. "Mushroom cloud" as viewed from Mt. Unzen (Y. Ishida 1953, p. 139).

The heliograph of the observatory recorded a figure of 0.70 at 10 A.M. and 1.00 at noon, indicating that the clouds were in a process of decreasing at the time of the explosion (table 6.2). The weather at 11 A.M. was recorded to be fair (cloud 0.1–0.2).

As already mentioned in chapter 1, the skies over Nagasaki were covered by clouds, but a gap was found between the clouds just before the bombing. The photograph of the atomic bomb cloud taken from the plane a few minutes after the bombing shows thick clouds besides the mushroom cloud (figure 1.3). There is disagreement on the cloud conditions of the day. Some victims said that the weather was fine at the moment of explosion; others thought it might have been cloudy. In any case, it is judged there were no clouds below 500 meters of the burst point.

Automatic records of temperature and humidity indicated no changes at the time of the explosion.

The cloud formed by the Nagasaki A-bomb explosion (mushroom cloud) was sketched at about 11:40 A.M. and 0:10 P.M. as observed from the Onsendake Meteorological Station at Mount Unzen, 45 kilometers east of the hypocenter (Ishida 1953, p. 139). Figure 6.4*a* was sketched at about 11:40 A.M., showing the cumulonimbus and black smoke rising right below the cloud. The cloud bottom was estimated to be 1,200 to 1,300 meters, and the cloud top, 4,000 to 5,000 meters. At about 0:10 P.M., the cloud started to go out of shape toward the east-northeast (figure 6.4*b*), and a light rainfall was noted between 1:50 and 2 P.M. at Mount Unzen.

The mushroom cloud was assumed to have moved as indicated in figure 6.5.* *A* is the area where there was rain in Nagasaki; *B* is the position of the cloud at 11:40 A.M. (figure 6.4*a*); *C*, at 0:10 P.M. (figure 6.4*b*); and *D*, at 2 P.M. passing by the vicinity of Mount Unzen. The area covered by *D'* is that of the lower air cloud seen from the Onsendake Meteorological Station.

Light objects, such as black dust and ashes and paper fragments, were blown high up into the sky near the hypocenter. They were then carried away by a southwest wind and were recorded to have fallen toward the northeast of Nagasaki on the villages of Yagami, Toishi, Koga, Kikitsu, Tayui, and Enoura and even as far away as Isahaya City as shown in figure 6.6 (Nagasaki Shiyakusho 1977, p. 205).

Right after the bombing, 3 radiosondes,† each tied on a parachute, were dropped from the weather observation plane at an altitude of 4,000 to 5,000 meters. They were gradually carried away toward the east and dropped on

---

* NGO International Symposium on the Damage and Aftereffects of the Atomic Bombing 1977*b*, p. 38.

† These radiosondes were dropped with a special view to observing in detail atmospheric pressure, temperature, radiation dose, and other effects of the explosion.

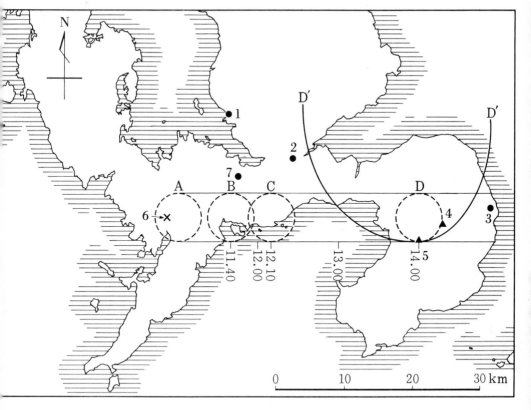

Figure 6.5. Drift of the huge atomic cloud (NGO International Symposium 1977*b*, p. 38).

1. Ōmura City
2. Isahaya City
3. Shimabara City
4. Mt. Unzen
5. Mt. Kinugasa
6. Hypocenter
7. Tarami Village

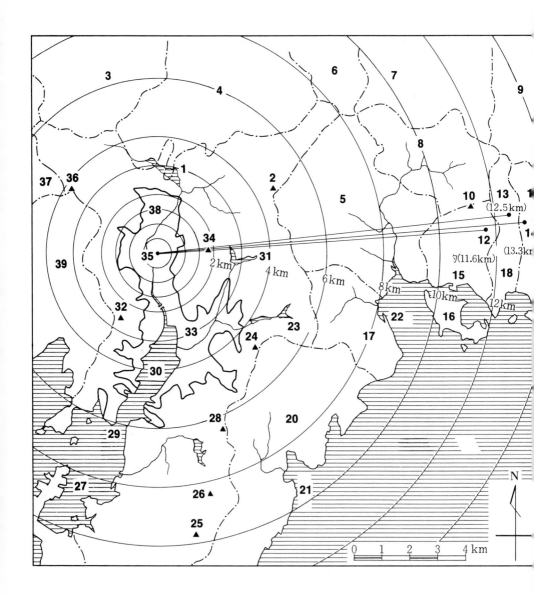

three spots as shown in figure 6.6 (Nagasaki Shiyakusho 1977, p. 217). The distance from the hypocenter was about 11.6 to 13.3 kilometers toward the east. One parachute was presumed to have dropped on spot 1 around 11:30 A.M. to noon, and the remaining two on spots 2 and 3 between noon and 1 P.M. From these data, the wind velocity is estimated to have been about 3 meters per second east or east-northeast, which almost coincides with the record in table 6.2.

There was quite a rainfall at Mount Konpira less than 2 kilometers east of the hypocenter and at Nishiyama district 3 kilometers east of the hypocenter.

The rain started to fall approximately 40 minutes after the explosion in the vicinity of Mount Konpira. Off and on there were intermittent showers until night. The rain was frequently admixed with ashes (black rain). A great amount of black rain fell from 20 minutes after the explosion on Nishiyama district located right behind the east side of Mount Konpira. Concentrated amounts of radioactive materials were assumed to have fallen here.

Figure 6.6. Points where radiosonde fell (Nagasaki Shiyakusho 1977, p. 217): first point, Kamikōchi, Toishi village; second point, Hotogi, Tayui village; third point, Dake, Enoura village.

1. Urakami Reservoir
2. Mt. Hoba
3. Togitsu Village
4. Nagayo Village
5. Yagami Village
6. Ōkusa Village
7. Kikitsu Village
8. Koga Village
9. Isahaya City
10. Mt. Funaishi
11. Enoura Village
12. Kamikōchi (first point)
13. Hotogi (second point)
14. Dake (third point)
15. Toishi Village
16. Makishima Island
17. Himi Village
18. Tayui Village
19. Tachibana Bay
20. Mogi Town
21. Shiomizaki
22. Aba
23. Hongōchi Reservoir
24. Mt. Hiko
25. Mt. Kumagamine
26. Mt. Tomachidake
27. Kōyagi Island
28. Mt. Tōhakkei
29. Kōzakibana
30. Nagasaki Port
31. Nishiyama Reservoir
32. Mt. Inasa
33. Nakashima River
34. Mt. Konpira
35. Hypocenter
36. Mt. Iwaya
37. Shikimi Village
38. Urakami River
39. Fukuda Village

Thermal burns on nineteen-year-old man exposed to the atomic bomb about 1 kilometer from the hypocenter in Nagasaki August 1945. (Photograph by Masao Shiotsuki.)

PART II

INJURY TO
THE HUMAN
BODY

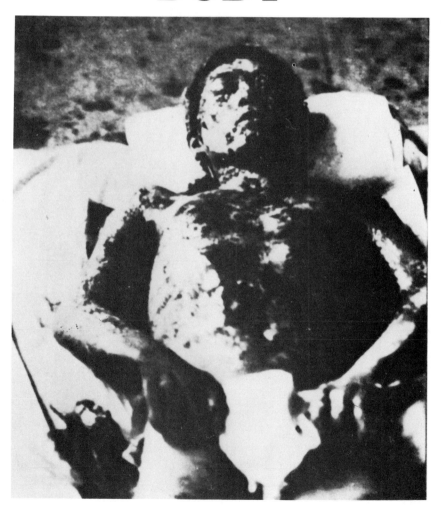

Chapter 7

Injury to the Human Body Following Exposure to the Atomic Bomb

As already noted in part I, the explosion of the atomic bomb released thermal rays, blasts, and radioactive rays, which acted directly, simultaneously, and in complex fashion on the human body to cause thermal injury, blast injury, and radiation injury. Indirectly they damaged the human body by destroying the natural environment. Injury by exposure to an atomic bomb first occurred in August 1945 at Hiroshima and Nagasaki, and its effects are still in evidence. This miserable injury resulted from a catastrophe never before experienced by mankind. Following the proposal of the Special Committee of the Science Council of Japan on the Investigation of the Atomic Bomb Casualties (1951), this condition will be called *atomic bomb injury* or *atomic bomb illness* (Science Council of Japan 1951).

The atomic bomb casualties occurred almost immediately after the explosion; and the thermal rays, radioactive rays, and blasts became attenuated with distance from the burst point. The injurious action was weakened with shielding, which absorbed or reflected the energy of the blast. The severity of early-stage atomic bomb injury was roughly in inverse proportion to the distance between the site of exposure and the hypocenter. Figure 7.1 (Oughter-

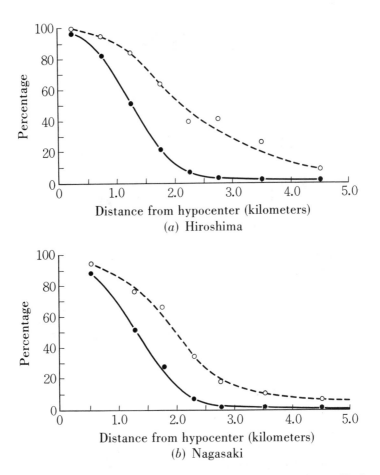

Figure 7.1. Relation of casualty (○---○) and mortality (●---●) rates to distance (Oughterson and Warren 1956, p. 30).

son and Warren 1956, p. 30) gives the relation of casualty and mortality rates to exposure distance (Joint Commission). As can be seen in this figure, both injury and mortality rates fell with increasing distance from the hypocenter. Even when the distance from the hypocenter was equal, the degree of injury differed according to shielding conditions. Table 7.1 shows the difference in degree of injury by site of exposure to the atomic bomb.

As indicated in figure 7.1 and table 7.1, a high mortality rate, especially instant death and death on the same day, was brought about by exposure to the atomic bomb. A 50 percent death rate is presumed in those exposed within 1.2 kilometers of the hypocenter, and a higher rate of 80 percent to 100 percent is presumed in those exposed at shorter distances. Even among those escaping instant death or death on the day of exposure, the mortality rate later became extremely high in those exposed at close distances and in those sustaining severe injuries. M. Masuyama (1953, p. 510), going through the inquiry records of the Kabe Police Station of Hiroshima Prefecture examined the day-by-day situation of the exposed survivors who escaped to the Kabe district. According to his report, the daily increase in total number of deaths can be expressed by a definite exponential function curve, and the number of deaths reduced by half every six days (figure 7.2). In this group, 50 percent of those seriously injured died by the sixth day; another 25 percent died by the seventh to twelfth day; and more than 90 percent, by the fortieth day.

Although the conditions of death differed somewhat according to distance from the hypocenter, to shielding conditions, and to the nature and the severity of injury, an outline of the situation was as indicated in tables 7.2 to 7.7. (Summary Report of Investigation of Atomic Bomb Casualties [Science Council of Japan 1951]). This survey covers the deaths occurring one to two months after the exposure.

Materials on the early-stage mortality rate of the general public cannot be said to be sufficient. According to the survey made by the medical survey team of Tokyo Imperial University (November 1945) on the conditions of

TABLE 7.1

Types and Severity of A-bomb Injury in Relation to Exposure Conditions, Hiroshima

Distance from hypocenter (km)		0 — 1	1 — 2	2 — 3	3 — 4	4 — 5	5 — 6
Outdoors (unshielded)	blast injury	high	low				
	burn	high	moderate	low			
	radiation injury	high	moderate	low			
Outdoors (shielded)	blast injury	low					
	burn	low					
	radiation injury	moderate	low				
Inside (wooden house)	blast injury	high		moderate		low	
	burn	low					
	radiation injury	moderate	low				
Inside (concrete building)	blast injury	low					
	burn	low					
	radiation injury	moderate	low				

N.B. Mortality rate: high, 50–100%; moderate, 10–50%; low, 0–10%.

Source: Science Council of Japan, *Genshibakudan Saigai Chōsa Hōkokusho* [SRIABC] (Tokyo: Nihon Gakujutsu Shinkōkai, 1951), p. 41.

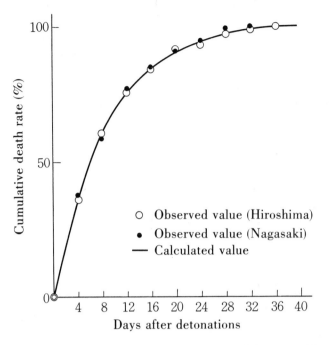

Figure 7.2. Cumulative death rate of atomic bomb victims. (Motosaburō Masuyama, Tokyo Imperial University) (Masuyama 1953, p. 510).

death of those living in twenty-eight small districts within 2 kilometers of the hypocenter, there were 507 deaths, among whom 358 died on the day of exposure, out of a total of 898 examined. The total number of deaths and the number of deaths on the day of exposure were divided into four groups according to distance from the hypocenter, and then the total mortality rate and the mortality on the day of exposure by distance from the hypocenter were calculated, as shown in table 7.8 (Kajitani and Hatano 1953, p. 522; Science Council of Japan 1951, pp. 29–30).

From the preceding data obtained at a time of much confusion and difficulty, one can grasp an outline of the general situation of those killed and wounded by exposure to the atomic bomb in Hiroshima and Nagasaki. Neither the whole picture of the killed and wounded at the initial stage of casualty nor accurate figures on the total number of those suffering or dying from atomic bomb illness have been obtained to date. The following factors made it extremely difficult to grasp the actual conditions at that time: (1) the extensive destruction of local society; (2) disorganization of war mobilization following Japan's miserable defeat in the Second World War; and (3) limitations on investigating atomic bomb casualties imposed during the United States occupation of Japan. Notwithstanding these disadvantages, attempts were made repeatedly, soon after the explosion and up to the present, to determine

TABLE 7.2

Casualties among the Groups Exposed Outdoors to the Atomic Bomb, Hiroshima

Group	Situation	Location; Distance and Direction from Hypocenter (km)	Number Exposed	Died				Survived			Mortality Rate (%)
				6 August	Within One Week	Within Two Weeks	Later than Two Weeks	Radiation Illness	Injured	Not Injured	
Hijiyama Girls' High School students	on the school ground	Military District Headquarters; 0.8 NE	52	10	42	0	0	0	0	0	100.0
Labor service corps from Ogata Village, Ōtake	dismantling houses	Koami-cho; 0.9 W	87	80	3	0	4	0	0	0	100.0
Labor service corps from Kuba Village, Ōtake	loading a barge with roofing tiles	near the Tenma Bridge; 1.1 W	101	43	38	10	0	10	0	0	90.0
Labor service corps from Ōtake, Morimoto Group	resting on road; most resting in the shade of two-story houses	near the Tenma Bridge; 1.1 W	30	4	1	0	21	4	0	0	84.0
Labor service corps from Ōtake, Nagato Group	resting on road; most resting in the shade of two-story houses	near the Tenma Bridge; 1.1 W	165	2	4	0	72	87	0	0	47.2
Labor service corps from Ōtake, Hino Group	walking on road	Fukushima-cho; 2.3 W	580	2	7	0	0	0	568	3	1.6

Source: Science Council of Japan, *Genshibakudan Saigai Chōsa Hōkokusho* [SRIABC] (Tokyo: Nihon Gakujutsu Shikōkai, 1951), p. 24.

TABLE 7.3

Casualties among the Groups Exposed to the Atomic Bomb inside Wooden Houses, Hiroshima

Name of Building	Structure	Distance and Direction from Hypocenter (km)	Number Exposed	Died			Survived				Mortality Rate (%)
				Instantly	Not Instantly but Soon	Total	Radiation Illness	Injured	Not Injured	Total	
First Hiroshima Army Hospital	Single-story	0.5 N	750?	600?	150?	749	0	0	1	1	99.9
Lodging for an itinerant theatrical troupe	Two-story	0.7 E	17	13	4	17	0	0	0	0	100.0
Second Hiroshima Army Hospital	Single-story	1.0 N	402	90?	213?	303	—	—	—	99	75.3

Source: Science Council of Japan, *Genshibakudan Saigai Chōsa Hōkokusho* [SRIABC] (Tokyo: Nihon Gakujutsu Shinkōkai, 1951), p. 25.

TABLE 7.4

Casualties among the Groups Exposed to the Atomic Bomb inside Concrete Buildings, Hiroshima

Name of Building	Structure	Direction and Distance from Hypocenter (km)	Number Exposed	Died			Survived				Mortality Rate (%)
				Instantly	Soon after the Explosion	Total	Radiation Illness	Injured	Not Injured	Total	
The Bank of Japan, Hiroshima Branch	three-story	0.4 SE	75	33	10	43	23 } 6		3	32	57.3
Hiroshima Central Telephone Office	seven-story	0.5 SE	150	?*	?*	50	93?		7	100?	33.3
Chūgoku Power Distribution Company	five-story	0.8 S	183	48	16	64	51 } 3		65	119	34.9
Hiroshima Telephone Office, Fukuromachi	seven-story	0.9 SE	95	36	53	89	5 }		1	6	93.7
Broadcasting Station	two-story	1.0 E	31	2	0	2	6	2	21	29	6.5
Communication Bureau	four-story	1.4 N	245	11	4	15	1	5	224	230	6.1
Japan Red Cross Hospital, Hiroshima	three-story	2.0 S	480	2	0	2	0	many	—	478	0.4

TABLE 7.5

Casualties among the Groups Exposed to the Atomic Bomb inside Various Types of Buildings, Nagasaki

Name of Building	Structure	Direction and Distance from Hypocenter (km)	Number Exposed	Died			Survived			Mortality Rate (%)
				Instantly	Not Instantly but Soon	Total	Injured	Not Injured	Total	
Air-raid shelter near the prison	underground tunnel	0.1 NE	50	42	1	43	2	5	7	86.0
Shiroyama Primary School	three-story concrete building	0.4 W	151	52	79	131	9	11	20	86.7
Chinzei Middle School	five-story concrete building	0.5 SW	91	46	30	76	14	1	15	83.5
Annex to Chinzei Middle School	single-story wooden house	0.5 SW	27	22	5	27	0	0	0	100.0
Mitsubishi Steel Manufacturing Company plant	slate-roofed, iron-frame, partially concrete building	0.6–1.0 S	1,720	by 15 September		883	—	—		51.3
				by 15 October		915	—	—		53.2
Nagasaki Medical College Hospital	three-story concrete building	0.8 SE	243		—	69			174	28.4
Fuchi Primary School	two-story concrete building	1.2 SSE	66	4	18	22	30	14	44	33.3
Mitsubishi Ordnance Factory, Mori-machi Works	slate-roofed, iron-frame, concrete building	1.0–1.5 S	2,201	by 1 September		170?	—	—		7.7
				by 1 October		600?	—	—		27.2?
Mitsubishi Ordnance Factory, Ōhashi Works	slate-roofed, iron-frame, concrete building	1.2–1.7 N	6,028	by 15 September		479	—	—		7.9
				by 15 October		1,200?	—	—		19.9?

Source: Science Council of Japan, Genshibakudan Saigai Chōsa Hōkokusho [SRIABC] (Tokyo: Nihon Gakujutsu Shinkōkai, 1951), p. 27.

TABLE 7.6

Mortality Rate of Primary School Children, Nagasaki, 31 October 1945

Distance from Hypocenter (km)	Number of Schools	Number of Pupils	Number Killed	Mortality Rate (%)
0–1	3	1,807	770	42.6
1–2	2	2,679	652	24.3
2–3	4	3,351	153	4.6
3–4	6	5,835	46	0.8
4 or more	12	8,054	32	0.4
Total	27	21,726	1,653	7.6

Source: Science Council of Japan, *Genshibakudan Saigai Chōsa Hōkokusho* [SRIABC] (Tokyo: Nihon Gakujutsu Shinkōkai, 1951), p. 29.

TABLE 7.7

Mortality Rate of Primary School Teachers, Nagasaki, 31 October 1945

Distance from Hypocenter (km)	Number of Schools	Number of Teachers	Number Killed	Mortality Rate (%)
0–1	3	96	56	58.3
1–2	2	63	11	17.5
2–3	4	92	1	1.1
3–4	6	158	5	3.2
4 or more	12	252	1	0.4
Total	27	661	74	11.2

Source: Science Council of Japan, *Genshibakudan Saigai Chōsa Hōkokusho* [SRIABC] (Tokyo: Nihon Gakujutsu Shinkōkai, 1951), p. 29.

TABLE 7.8

Comparative Mortality Rates of Those Exposed within 2 Kilometers of the Hypocenter, Hiroshima, 6 August 1945 and through November 1945

Distance from Hypocenter (km)	6 August Mortality Rate (%)	Total Mortality Rate (%)
0–0.5	90.4	98.4
0.6–1.0	59.4	90.0
1.1–1.5	19.6	45.5
1.6–2.0	11.1	22.6
Total	39.8	56.5

Sources: T. Kajitani and S. Hatano, "Medical survey of acute effects of the atomic bomb in Hiroshima," in CRIABC (1953), vol. I, p. 522. Science Council of Japan, 1951. *Genshibakudan Saigai Chōsa Hōkokusho* [SRIABC] (Tokyo: Nihon Gakujutsu Shinkōkai, 1951), pp. 29–30.

the number of those killed and wounded. According to the report of the Special Committee of the Science Council of Japan on the Investigation of the Atomic Bomb Casualties (1951), the total number of deaths during the early stage (up to the end of 1945) following exposure to the atomic bomb in Hiroshima was estimated to be approximately 100,000 (announced by the Hiroshima Prefecture, 25 August and 30 November 1945). A stochastic study by the Joint Commission led by M. Masuyama and M. E. Habel was made of approximately 6,000 dwellings each in Hiroshima (December 1945) and Nagasaki (January 1946). Since their figures (Hiroshima, 68,670–58,580 deaths and 72,880–68,810 injuries; Nagasaki, 37,507–29,398 deaths and 26,709–23,469 injuries) did not include military personnel and the unknown, they were lower than the actual figures. The Hiroshima City Survey Section investigated the number of casualties until 10 August 1946 and completed its inquiry the following year. The data were then lost and were not discovered for twenty years (see table 7.9). Table 7.10 represents similar data (December 1945) in Nagasaki, which were confirmed by the Nagasaki City Commission for Preservation of A-bomb Material and reported by Nagasaki City. In the report (Hiroshimashi-Nagasakishi, p. 31) sent to the Secretary-General of the United Nations by both cities in the autumn of 1976, the total deaths following exposure to the bomb by the end of 1945 totaled 140,000 (± 10,000) in Hiroshima and 70,000 (± 10,000) in Nagasaki.

According to the results obtained from observations made on atomic bomb

TABLE 7.9

Total Number of Casualties due to the Atomic Bomb, Hiroshima, 10 August 1946*

Distance from Hypocenter (km)	Killed	Severely Injured	Slightly Injured	Missing	Not Injured	Total
Under 0.5	19,329	478	338	593	924	21,662
0.5–1.0	42,271	3,046	1,919	1,366	4,434	53,036
1.0–1.5	37,689	7,732	9,522	1,188	9,140	65,271
1.5–2.0	13,422	7,627	11,516	227	11,698	44,490
2.0–2.5	4,513	7,830	14,149	98	26,096	52,686
2.5–3.0	1,139	2,923	6,795	32	19,907	30,796
3.0–3.5	117	474	1,934	2	10,250	12,777
3.5–4.0	100	295	1,768	3	13,513	15,679
4.0–4.5	8	64	373		4,260	4,705
4.5–5.0	31	36	156	1	6,593	6,817
Over 5.0	42	19	136	167	11,798	12,162
Total	118,661	30,524	48,606	3,677	118,613	320,081

* Military personnel not included.
Source: Hiroshima Shiyakusho, *Hiroshima Genbaku Sensaishi* [RHAWD], (Hiroshima, 1971), vol. I.

TABLE 7.10
Number of Casualties due to the Atomic Bomb in Nagasaki*
as of 31 December 1945

Killed	73,884
Injured	74,909
Affected	120,820

* It is unknown whether floating population, such as military personnel and other volunteer corps, is included.
Source: Nagasaki City A-bomb Records Preservation Committee.

injury from a medical standpoint, the general course of this condition in those exposed can be divided into the following four stages, as abstracted from the Summary Report of Investigation of Atomic Bomb Casualties:

1. *Stage 1—Early or Initial Stage*

The greatest number of casualties occurred immediately after the explosion to the end of the second week; and at this stage various injurious actions of the atomic bomb explosion simultaneously led to the onset of symptoms. Approximately nine tenths of the fatal cases died during this stage, and the majority (about 90 percent) of these injured who received medical care for several days after the explosion, complained of thermal injury.

2. *Stage 2—Intermittent Stage*

Many moderate injuries caused by radioactivity were encountered from the beginning of the third week to the end of the eighth week; and the remaining fatal cases, or one tenth, died. From the general course taken by the victims, stages 1 and 2 may be considered as the acute stage of atomic bomb injury.

3. *Stage 3—Late Stage*

From the beginning of the third month to the end of the fourth, all symptoms from injury showed some improvement, although a few cases terminated in death from complications. By the end of the fourth month (early December 1945), those suffering from the disaster in both cities had recovered to a certain degree, and the course of the atomic bomb injury itself had come to a near end.

4. *Stage 4—Delayed Effects*

After five months or more, there were various delayed effects: some—such as distortion, contracture, keloid, and so on—following recovery from thermal injury or mechanical injury; some—such as anemia—as a result of blood disorder caused by radiation injury; and some originating in disturbances of the reproductive function—such as sterility—may occur at this stage. There are, however, not a few items that must be continuously examined during the following few months.

These categories of atomic bomb injury summarize the many medical observations made at that period and reflect the actual conditions of the exposed. In reality, however, these stages were not the end of the injury to the human body following the explosion; and various delayed effects began to appear after certain periods of latency. Even today, more than thirty years since the explosion, these effects have not come to an end. The first case (Ikui 1967, p. 160) of atomic bomb cataract in Hiroshima was discovered in the autumn of 1948, and this was followed by many reports (Hirose and Fujino 1950) on this condition in both cities. Leukemia in those exposed to the atomic bomb first appeared in 1945 in Nagasaki (Misao, Haraguchi and Hattori 1953, p. 1041) and in 1946 in Hiroshima (Yamawaki 1953, p. 387). Its incidence rose gradually thereafter, reached its peak between 1950 and 1953, and has maintained its high percentage ever since. Slightly after the peak of leukemia, a general trend in the increase of various cancers (thyroid, breast, lung, and salivary gland cancer) was found among the exposed. Microcephaly and developmental disturbances were encountered among infants exposed in utero, and these conditions were studied for genetic effects. If injuries to the body immediately after the explosion and those up to six months after it, and also their direct aftereffects are to be called atomic bomb injuries *of the acute stage,* late effects may be called atomic bomb injuries *of the late stage.* Fortunately investigations to date have revealed no harmful genetic effects in either the first filial generation (F_1) or the second filial generation (F_2), but further investigations and studies on atomic bomb illness must be continued for several generations to come (Tsuzuki 1954*a*).

Atomic bomb illness not only is a pathological condition that the human race has confronted for the first time but also possesses a specific characteristic unlike the usual war damage and injury (Iijima 1977, p. 18). In the first place, the energy causing vital damage is vast. Not until August in the year of 1945 had mankind ever experienced large-scale thermal radiation and blast; and, together with radioactivity, these caused the deaths of 140,000 in Hiroshima and 70,000 in Nagasaki. In the second place, atomic bomb illness is the first and only example of heavy lethal and momentary doses of whole body irradiation. It destroyed the actively regenerating cells in the body and greatly devastated the vital defensive mechanism. These heavy doses were the main reason for the poor repair, the prevalence of infection, and the extremely high mortality in atomic bomb injury. The atomic bomb not only brought tragic and horrible injuries to the exposed but also hindered the basis for the reparative and regenerative processes of the living body. Thirdly, whole body irradiation injured the nuclei of the cells and their component DNA (deoxyribonucleic acid) and may lead to the induction of malignancies (cancer and leukemia) and to alteration of genes. One should never forget that such momentary injurious action of an atomic bomb can have aftereffects for years and generations to come. We should look squarely at the facts and bear the heart-heavy responsibility for seeing that such a disaster will never again befall the human race.

Chapter 8

Body Injury in the Initial Stage— Acute Stage of Atomic Bomb Injury

As explained in the previous chapter, atomic bomb casualties result from the simultaneous effects of heat rays, blasts, and ionizing radiation. The acute stage of atomic bomb injury can be considered a complex result of these actions, and injuries to the human body may be classified as follows according to their mechanism of each (Science Council of Japan 1951, p. 8).

1. Atomic bomb thermal burns
   a. Primary thermal burns: flash burns
   b. Secondary thermal burns: scorched burns
                                 contact burns
                                 flame burns
2. Atomic bomb trauma
   a. Primary injury: blast injury
   b. Secondary injury: buried injury
                          compression injury
                          fragment injury
3. Atomic bomb radiation illness
   a. Primary radiation illness
   b. Secondary radiation illness

Atomic Bomb Thermal Injury

THERMAL RAY ENERGY EMITTED BY THE ATOMIC BOMB

At the time of an explosion, the internal temperature of the fireball at the point of explosion reaches a temperature of over 100,000°C., but the surface temperature of the fireball comes down to 7,700°C., within 0.2 second. Radiation of heat rays fades in 3 seconds. The atomic bomb as an injurious heat source is characterized by the action of intensive heat rays within an extremely short period of time. According to the experimental study of H. E. Pearse and H. D. Kingsley (Morton, Kingsley, and Pearse 1952; Pearse and Kingsley 1954), the most intensive injury (burn) following the atomic bomb explosion occurs 0.1 to 0.2 second after the explosion and reaches its maximum by 0.5 second. Among the heat rays, which reach a great distance, are near-ultraviolet rays, visible rays, and infrared rays; but from the relation between time and dose, it may well be considered that the main rays causing thermal injury are the infrared rays. This thermal-ray energy subsides while transmitted through the atmosphere and becomes extremely small with distance from the hypocenter. Although the degree of subsidence varies according to meteorological conditions, the thermal-ray energy received at various locations in Hiroshima and Nagasaki is assumed to have been as shown in table 2.1. As a result of the enormous heat rays emitted within a short period, the temperature at the site of explosion in the two cities reached 3,000°C. to 4,000°C.; and primary atomic bomb thermal injury of the skin caused by heat rays was found in those exposed within 3.5 kilometers of the hypocenter in Hiroshima, and in those within 4 kilometers in Nagasaki.

PRIMARY THERMAL INJURY (BURN) AND SECONDARY THERMAL INJURY (BURN)

Primary atomic bomb thermal injury (flash burn) is a thermal burn caused by the direct action of heat rays upon the human body. On the contrary, secondary atomic bomb thermal injury is a thermal burn brought about indirectly from a fire caused by atomic bomb thermal rays. The latter includes scorched burns, contact burns, and flame burns, among which flame burns are thought to have occurred most frequently.

Secondary thermal burns are frequently encountered in civil life, while primary burns are injuries of a special nature and not ordinarily experienced in everyday life. Studies on primary atomic bomb thermal injury or flash burn actually were initiated after the Hiroshima-Nagasaki casualties. The relationship between calory per unit area and the nature of thermal burns was clarified through the experiments made by J. H. Morton, J. B. Perkins, H. E. Pearse, and H. D. Kingsley (table 8.1). In a comparison of tables 8.1 and 2.1, both data almost agree with the facts that severe thermal burns of

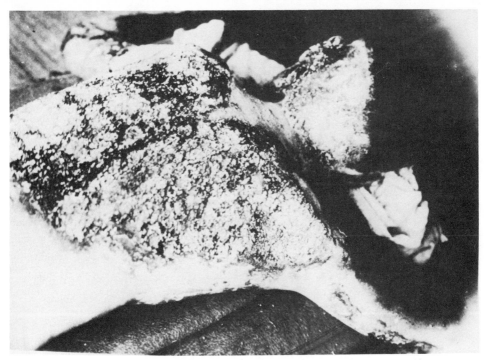

Figure 8.1. Thermal burns, mid-August, 1945; victim exposed 500 meters from the hypocenter in Hiroshima. (Photograph by Masao Tsuzuki and Gon'ichi Kimura.)

over grade 5 occurred within 1 and 1.5 kilometers of the hypocenters in Hiroshima and Nagasaki, and those of grades 1 to 4, 3.5 and 4 kilometers from the hypocenters.

The uniform alteration of epidermal tissue as well demarcated from normal deeper tissue is a characteristic feature of flash burns. When injury to the epidermis is greater than grade 2, a coagulation necrosis (death of tissue with coagulation) occurs; and when it is greater than grade 5, there is usually

TABLE 8.1

Classification of A-bomb Flash Burns and Intensity of Radiant Heat Energy

Severity	Appearance of Burned Skin	Nomenclature	Estimated Intensity of Radiant Heat Energy (cal/cm²/0.3 sec)
1	Erythema	Red Burn	2.3
2	Patchy coagulation	Spotted white burn	4.5
3	Uniform coagulation	White burn	7.5
4	Steam bleb, or blister	Blebbed white burn	10.0
5	Carbonization	Charred burn	19.0

N.B.: The sun's radiant heat energy on a 1 cm² vertically oriented area of the spherical segment of outer space for a duration of 0.3 sec is approximately 0.01 cal/cm². The energy used to heat the earth's atmosphere and surface is 0.007 cal/cm²—that is, about 66% of the 0.01 cal/cm² (H. Mizutani and T. Watanabe, *Chikyū* [Constitution of the Earth], Tokyo: Iwanami Shoten, 1978, p. 170). With this knowledge, one can have some realization of the tremendous intensities of heat shown in the table.

Source: J. H. Morton, H. D. Kingsley, and H. E. Pearse, "Studies on flash burns; threshold burns," *Surgery, Gynecology and Obstetrics* 94 (1952):317.

carbonization with sparse edema and exudation. The injured lesion is covered by an eschar;* and when the wound is shallow, desquamation† occurs within a few days or weeks, leaving a reddish, light black-brown, shiny surface. Regeneration starts from the basal layer and forms a clear demarcation with the necrotic tissue. When the necrosis reaches a deeper level, epithelial regeneration is evoked from the surrounding epidermis and leaves a scar. Extremely intense thermal energy leads not only to carbonization but also to evaporation of viscerae (Tsuzuki 1954*a*).

THE ACTUAL CONDITIONS OF THERMAL BURNS IN HIROSHIMA AND NAGASAKI

The thermal burns at the time of explosion in Hiroshima and Nagasaki appeared in a mixed form of primary and secondary thermal injuries. Some people with primary thermal injury and trauma were trapped in the flames during the fire, while in others garments (especially areas of black) were burned by the thermal rays. The exposed victims escaping early death mostly suffered from flash burns. The rate of both types of thermal injury in the survivors twenty days after exposure is indicated in table 8.2 (Hanaoka 1964, p. 541).

TABLE 8.2

Cause of Burns in Twenty-day Survivors

	Number of Burns Observed	Flash (%)	Flame (%)	Flash and Flame (%)
Hiroshima	1,921	83.2	1.9	14.9
Nagasaki	1,004	90.9	3.4	5.7

Source: A. W. Oughterson and S. Warren, *Medical Effects of the Atomic Bomb in Japan.* (New York: McGraw-Hill, 1956), p. 102.

The exact number of instant deaths, day 1 deaths, or early deaths is unknown. When groups were examined in such places as schools or factories where the general conditions could be grasped, it was found that 90 percent to 100 percent of those receiving severe thermal injuries from exposure within 1 kilometer of the hypocenter without shielding died within a week. The mortality rates at an early stage among those exposed at distances of 1.5 to 2 kilometers from the hypocenter were about 14 percent for the shielded and approximately 83 percent for the unshielded. In light of the severity of radiation injury at this distance, the mortality rate from thermal injury under an unshielded condition is assumed to have been about 70 percent (Oughterson and Warren 1956, p. 103). The relation between incidence of flash burns and

* An *eschar* is a dry scab that forms on skin after a burn. (Ed.)
† *Desquamation* is the shedding, or peeling, of skin. (Ed.)

trauma, and distance from hypocenter as calculated from twenty-day survivors, is shown in table 8.2 (Joint Commission). Tables 8.3A and 8.3B give the results of the investigation made by the Tokyo Imperial University team (Iijima 1967*b*).

CLINICAL COURSE OF ATOMIC BOMB THERMAL INJURY

One characteristic noted during atomic bomb thermal injury is that it did not simply develop as a thermal burn, but the majority of casualties were simultaneously injured by the blast as well as by ionizing radiation. Of the victims receiving severe thermal burns in the central district, their clothes were completely burned, and they themselves were blown away by the blast. The exposed skin was burned, inflamed, and desquamated; and in many people skin became loosened and dropped down in flaps. Most of the victims received direct thermal injuries to the viscera and died instantly or soon after the explosion. Demarcation and falling-off of burned necrotic tissue took time in victims receiving moderate thermal injury at the hypocenter and up to about 2 kilometers away. Furthermore, since all had received varying degrees of ionizing radiation, there were many complications with suppuration of the injured surface due to delayed healing owing to altered tissue reaction and also to lowered resistance to infection. The fact that normal recovery processes were delayed by suppuration led to debility and poor prognosis (Science Council of Japan 1951, p. 13). Malnutrition—at a time when the food situation was poor, and drugs were in short supply—also influenced the recovery process. There were marked scar formations and pigmentation, or even depigmentation. Many of these victims developed contracture of scars and keloid (see pages 186–96).

Atomic Bomb Trauma (Injury from Blasts)

ATOMIC BOMB BLAST AND TRAUMA

According to the report (Tanaka 1953, p. 25) made by the Special Committee for Atomic Bomb Casualties on damage to buildings, the pressure directly below the burst point was assumed to be 4.5 to 6.7 tons per square meter in Hiroshima and 6.7 to 10 tons per square meter in Nagasaki, and it was maintained for approximately 0.4 second. In Hiroshima, all wooden buildings within a distance of 2 kilometers from the hypocenter collapsed and were burned down. Most concrete buildings escaped complete destruction but were greatly damaged, being gutted by fire and their windows broken. Wooden buildings within 2 to 4 kilometers collapsed or were greatly damaged, according to distance; while broken windows were found up to a distance of 16

TABLE 8.3A

Number of Persons with Burns from Different Causes (Tokyo Imperial University First Survey, October–November 1945)

Distance from Hypocenter (km)	Primary Burns*				Primary and Secondary Burns†			
	Outdoors	In Shade	Indoors	Total	Outdoors	In Shade	Indoors	T
0–0.5		1 (50.0)	3 (100.0)	4 (80.0)		1 (50.0)		(2
0.6–1.0	5 (22.7)‡	26 (76.4)	20 (60.6)	51 (57.3)	17 (77.2)	7 (20.5)	10 (30.3)	3 (3
1.1–1.5	35 (20.3)	32 (64.0)	70 (66.6)	137 (41.8)	137 (79.6)	18 (36.0)	31 (29.5)	18 (5
1.6–2.0	172 (33.2)	45 (70.3)	89 (65.9)	306 (42.6)	345 (66.6)	16 (25.0)	40 (29.6)	4C (5
2.1–2.5	159 (36.2)	38 (55.0)	38 (76.0)	235 (42.1)	277 (63.0)	28 (40.5)	10 (20.0)	31 (5
2.6–3.0	64 (65.3)	12 (63.1)	16 (69.5)	92 (65.7)	32 (32.6)	5 (26.3)	6 (26.0)	4 (3
3.1–3.5	31 (93.9)	2 (10.0)	5 (83.3)	38 (92.6)	2 (6.0)			(
3.6–4.0	4 (100.0)			4 (100.0)				
Total	470 (36.5)	156 (65.0)	241 (67.8)	867 (46.0)	810 (62.9)	75 (31.2)	97 (27.3)	98 (5

* Primary burns are burns by thermal rays from the A-bomb.
† Secondary burns are burns by fire other than thermal rays.
‡ Figures in parentheses are percentages of incidence.
Source: T. Kajitani and S. Hatano, "Medical survey on acute effects of atomic bomb in Hiroshima," in CRIABC (1953), vol. I, p. 522.

TABLE 8.3B

Region of Burns (Tokyo Imperial University's First Survey, October–November 194

	Head		Face		Neck		Upper Body	
	Outdoors	Indoors	Outdoors	Indoors	Outdoors	Indoors	Outdoors	Indoo
Number of persons	179 (11.7)*	44 (12.3)	1,030 (67.4)	127 (35.7)	643 (42.1)	78 (21.9)	724 (47.4)	91 (25.6
Total	223 (11.8)		1,157 (61.5)		721 (38.3)		815 (43.3)	

* Figures in parentheses are percentages of incidence.
Source: T. Kajitani and S. Hatano, "Medical survey on acute effects of atomic bomb in Hiroshima," in CRIABC (195 vol. I, p. 522.

| | Secondary Burns† | | | | | | | Total Burns | | | |
| | From Clothes on Fire | | | By Flame | | | | | | | |
oors	In Shade	Indoors	Total	Outdoors	In Shade	Indoors	Total	Outdoors	In Shade	Indoors	Total
									2	3	5
	1 (2.9)	2 (6.0)	3 (3.3)			1 (3.0)	1 (1.1)	22	34	33	89
						4 (3.8)	4 (1.2)	172	50	105	327
1)	2 (3.1)	1 (0.7)	4 (0.5)		1 (1.5)	5 (3.7)	6 (0.8)	518	64	135	717
6)	1 (1.4)	1 (2.0)	5 (0.8)		2 (2.8)	1 (2.0)	3 (0.5)	439	69	50	558
0)	2 (10.5)		4 (2.8)			1 (4.3)	1 (0.7)	98	19	23	140
		1 (16.6)	1 (2.4)					33	2	6	41
								4			4
4)	6 (2.5)	5 (1.4)	17 (0.9)		3 (1.2)	12 (3.3)	15 (0.7)	1,286	240	355	1,881

| Lower Body | | Upper Limbs | | Lower Limbs | | Total | |
doors	Indoors	Outdoors	Indoors	Outdoors	Indoors	Outdoors	Indoors
3 (4.4)	11 (3.0)	1,271 (83.2)	230 (64.7)	707 (46.3)	105 (29.5)	1,526	355
79 (4.1)		1,501 (79.7)		812 (43.1)		1,881	

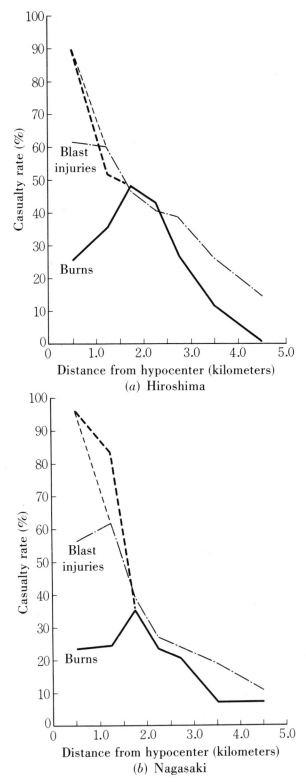

Figure 8.2. Incidence of blast injuries and burns by distance (---: probable incidence in the innermost zones, if one assumes that all those who died were injured by blast and radiant heat) (Oughterson and Warren 1956, pp. 43–44).

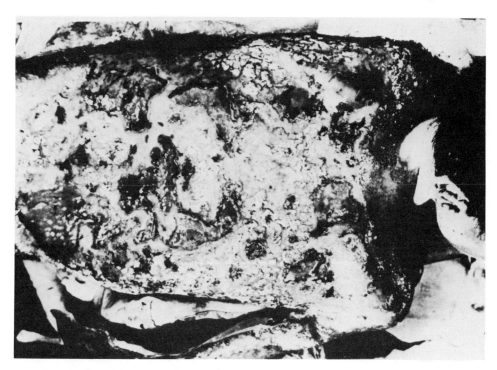

Figure 8.3. Severe burns, Nagasaki. (Photographed by Kyushu Imperial University Survey team.)

kilometers. Although in geography Nagasaki differs somewhat from Hiro-shima, its casualties were essentially the same notwithstanding the fact that the explosion was greater in Nagasaki (see chapter 3).

Injuries to the human body by the blast can be divided into primary injuries caused directly by the blast and secondary injuries caused by destruction of dwellings and buildings. From the power of the blast, it can readily be understood that primary or blast injury occurred mainly in the vicinity of the hypocenter, but in actuality the condition of the direct effects of the blast on human bodies has not been fully clarified. Some people were blown far away by the blast that caused damage to their viscera. The usual type of blast injury, such as injury and hemorrhage of viscera (brain, lung, liver) without apparent trauma of the covering skin, could not be found. Among the corpses of those dying instantly or on the same day of the explosion, there were some without severe thermal burns or contusions, but there were actually some with their viscera hanging out; on the other hand, there were in the central district many victims with severe, ugly thermal burns. This peculiar distribution of injuries suggests that the atomic bomb blast acted somewhat differently from more conventional explosions. The actual facts, however, cannot be fully extracted from the materials left for study (Summary

Report of Investigation of Atomic Bomb Casualties [Science Council of Japan 1951, p. 3]).

Although it is said that petechiae* of the pleura, especially right underneath the ribs, and sometimes injuries of the large intestine, liver, spleen, kidney, and bladder are found in blast injury, only a few findings have been confirmed by autopsies performed during the early stages in Hiroshima and Nagasaki. Since rupture of the tympanic membrane is also a sign of blast injury, examination of the tympanic membrane of the survivors was carried out by the Joint Commission. The incidence of injury was much lower than expected; 1 percent (Hiroshima) and 8 percent (Nagasaki) within 1 kilometer of the hypocenters, and 0.1 percent at 1.5 kilometers or more of the hypocenter in both cities. The incidence of blast injury in victims indoors was higher than that in those outdoors. As calculated from the data of the Joint Commission, the rates of injury within 5 kilometers of the hypocenter in both cities were 69 percent in concrete buildings, 52 percent in Japanese-style wooden houses, and 34 percent and 17 percent, respectively, outdoors with and without shieldings (Oughterson and Warren 1956, p. 38). These data indicate that most traumas were compatible with secondary injury rather than with blast or primary injury. On the other hand, these are figures for exposed survivors and do not account for the effect of blast injury on the victims dying instantly or on the same day. According to the medical aid record soon after the explosion, there was a high incidence—10 percent to 40 percent—of injury to or perforation of the tympanic membrane; and not a few people had actually witnessed others being blown away or had been blown away themselves. The high mortality at the center of the explosion was caused by intense thermal injury along with primary or secondary injuries.

SECONDARY INJURY AND CLINICAL COURSE

The majority of the exposed who had escaped instant or early death suffered from secondary injuries (bruises, lacerations, cut wounds, and fractures). According to the record (as of 13 August 1945) kept at the Ninoshima Provisional Field Hospital (Army Medical School 1953, p. 285) in Hiroshima, the injuries found in those hospitalized consisted of thermal burns (50.2 percent), traumas (33.3 percent), and both thermal injury and trauma (16.5 percent). Traumas (as of 15 August 1945) included contusions (53.8 percent), cut wounds mainly due to glass fragments (34.7 percent), and fractures (11.5 percent). If we include those with mild injury who were not hospitalized, open wounds caused by broken pieces had the highest incidence. A survey (Kajitani and Hatano 1953, p. 522) made by the Tokyo Imperial University team on 5,000 people (October to November 1945) revealed 2,379 wounded

---

* *Petechiae* are small spots on a surface of the body; each is caused by a tiny hemorrhage. (Ed.)

persons (46.4 percent), including 1,598 with open wounds (31.2 percent); 383 with contusions (7.4 percent); 259 with contusions and open wounds (5 percent); 68 with fractures (1.3 percent); and 5 with dislocations (0.1 percent). Injuries to blood vessels and peripheral nerves were caused by large flying fragments. Wounds from glass splinters were frequent and led to multiple small lacerations or to cut wounds with embedded splinters. Although these multiple wounds themselves were not fatal, they caused great pain and agony. With the fall of individual resistance following radiation injury, the wounds became infected and frequently led to gangrenous changes.

Atomic Bomb Radiation Illness

RADIATION AND EXPOSURE DOSE OF THE ATOMIC BOMB

Although there was some difference between the uranium bomb (Hiroshima) and the plutonium bomb (Nagasaki), gamma rays and neutrons were the main agents in the radiation emitted by fission, fission products, and induced-radioactive materials to exert their effects on land. The actual exposure dose of radiation becomes the main concern in consideration of its effects on the human body. Since these values could not be measured in Hiroshima and Nagasaki soon after the explosion, one can only estimate the doses by the various available methods. For such an estimate, it is necessary to know the in-air dose of gamma rays and neutrons at various points on the ground, to reconfirm the position of each exposed victim at the time of the explosion, and also to ascertain the shielding conditions and their effects. In order to obtain the in-air dose, one must determine the dose of gamma ray-neutron emitted by the atomic bomb; one must also obtain an accurate location of the explosion, the distance from the point of explosion, and the attenuation of gamma ray-neutron in response to the atmospheric conditions. The estimation of radiation dose has been continued since 1952. A theoretical calculation was made from the structure and the nature of the atomic bomb in Hiroshima and Nagasaki, and an analysis was attempted from the measurement of radiation effects found in exposed objects in both cities. Since 1955, data obtained from nuclear tests by the United States have been added; and these led to the proposal of the T65D dose by the Oak Ridge National Laboratory (see figure 5.1 and table 5.1). From about 1970, investigations on the estimation of radiation dose (organ dose) in various organs of exposed victims have been undertaken. Estimations of radiation dose are still underway; and although they are not complete, it is now possible to obtain more information on the radiation dose (including its nature) received during exposure at Hiroshima and Nagasaki.

General discussions and detailed descriptions of the injurious effects of radiation on the vital tissues of animals, especially the human body, can be found elsewhere. The casualties in Hiroshima and Nagasaki, where the victims received a single large dose of total-body irradiation, was the first and greatest such experience that mankind has ever encountered. It can thus be said that the data of observations made in both cities constitute the starting point in this new field (White 1975).

Table 8.4 shows the relation between effect and radiation dose of a single total-body irradiation. Injury to blood cells, especially to lymphocytes, appears after a single total-body irradiation of 10 roentgen; and with more than 100 roentgen, red blood cells, white blood cells, and platelets are injured. This condition is followed by destruction of gastrointestinal mucosa; and when a greater dose is given, there is an onset of fatal changes in the central nervous system. Radiation effects appear more gradually in humans than in experimental animals, and the LD_{50} (radiation dose causing death in one half of those receiving irradiation within a 60-day period) can be recognized in the area of 200 to 600 rads. Such acute radiation effects are composed of vascular and cellular injuries; and since the former is basically caused by endothelial injury, both can be considered cellular injury.

When the radiation penetrates the cell, radiation particles running at a

TABLE 8.4

Whole-Body Doses of Radiation and Their Acute Effects

Dose (Roentgen)*	Biological Effects
Less than 1	No detectable effect.
10	Barely detectable qualitative changes in lymphocytes.
100	Mild acute radiation (illness) in some. Slight diminution in white cell counts. Possible nausea and vomiting. Possible transient suppression of hemopoietic activity.
1,000	Depression of blood cell and platelet formation. Damage to gastrointestinal mucosa. Severe-acute radiation (illness). Death within 30 days.
10,000	Immediate disorientation or coma. Death within hours.
100,000	Death of some micro-organisms.
1,000,000	Death of some bacteria.
10,000,000	Death of all living organisms. Some denaturation of proteins.

* A *roentgen* is equivalent to 0.9 rad.

Source: S. Warren, *The Pathology of Ionizing Radiation* (Springfield, Ill.: Charles C Thomas, 1961).

high speed cause ionization and excitation along the locus of radiation in the cell leading to damage of molecules or of molecular groups. The penetrating particles lose their energy as they progress, and the loss of energy can be expressed as *linear energy transfer* (LET). LET differs according to mass, electric charge, and speed of the particles. Particles of low speed, large mass, and electric charge have, in general, a higher LET than those with high speed, small mass, and no electric charge. When a heavy particle penetrates a cell, a concentrated ion is produced; while in gamma rays, the ionization concentration is small, the energy absorbed by tissue is small, and the distance is that much longer. The LET differs according to the nature of radiation; and even if the absorption dose is the same, there is a difference in concentration of electrolytic dissociation. This difference can be expressed as *relative biological effectiveness* (RBE). Generally, biological effectiveness varies greatly; and although expressing it quantitatively has some disadvantages, it is usually compared with the irradiation effect of X-rays of 150 to 300 kilo-electronvolts when passing through a 1-millimeter copper filter. *Rem* is the dose unit including relative biological effectiveness and is obtained by multiplying the absorption dose (rad) by the RBE.

There is still much to be learned about the essential qualities of molecular alteration and destruction occurring in cells penetrated by radiation. One action of radiation is the formation of free radicals; and when radiation acts on water, which is abundant in cells and tissue, free hydrogen radicals and a hydroxyl group are formed. These free radicals have a strong oxidation and reductional action, produce peroxide by reacting with water, and combine with DNA, RNA, and other important molecules to make them inactive, or invade the membrane structures of cells to suppress their function. DNA is itself highly sensitive to radiation; and when a solution containing DNA is irradiated, the DNA molecule is altered and loses its function as a template for synthesizing a new DNA chain. Destruction of the DNA chain by radiation can be seen in the cells; and, as it differs from DNA injury caused by ultraviolet rays, its repair is difficult. Cell death, loss of mitotic function, or latent cellular injuries accompanied by abnormalities of molecules and membranes occur as a result of irradiation.

The sensitivity of human cells varies from one cell to the other. Cell nuclei are much more sensitive than the cytoplasm, and actively proliferating cells are more sensitive to radiation than are nonproliferating cells. The most radiosensitive cells in the human body are lymphocytes, young blood cells (hemoblasts or proliferating blood cells in bone marrow), mucosal epithelial cells of the intestines, spermatogonia of the testicles, and follicle cells of the ovaries. These are followed in sensitivity by mucosal epithelial cells of the urinary bladder, of the esophagus, of the stomach, and of the oropharynx, by epidermis of skin, hair bulb, and sebaceous gland, and by epithelial cells of the eye lens (White 1975).

ATOMIC BOMB RADIATION ILLNESS IMMEDIATELY AFTER EXPLOSION

Following the explosion in Hiroshima and Nagasaki, the authorities soon knew that it had been caused by an atomic bomb, and turned their attention to radiation injuries of the human body. Observers' records of the clinical symptoms of radiation injury immediately after the explosion are found in Medical Investigation Report on A-Bomb Casualty of Hiroshima (30 November 1945 [Army Medical School, Provisional Tokyo First Army Hospital 1953, p. 285]). This report classified radiation injury into stage 1 (6–17 August), stage 2 (18 August to early September), and stage 3 (early September to late September). The following is an abstract of the symptoms in stage 1 and stage 2.

Stage 1.   On the day of the explosion, all medical facilities were overcrowded with the wounded, so that it was impossible to make any detailed observations. Although it was difficult to gain accurate information on the early symptoms of radiation injury, it can be said that nausea, vomiting, polydipsia,* anorexia (loss of appetite), general malaise, fever (sometimes high fever), and diarrhea were the characteristic early features of this condition. Nausea and vomiting were most striking on the day of the explosion and were found in 31 percent of the survivors and in 16.6 percent of those terminating in death. Vomiting continuing overnight or longer was relatively rare. It started 30 minutes to 3 hours after exposure to the atomic bomb and occurred two or three times and in some cases more than ten times. On the other hand, nausea continued for two to three days in the majority of cases and even for two weeks in some cases. Loss of appetite was noted mostly on the first day and was found in 34.8 percent of the survivors and in 6.2 percent of those dying. General malaise showed the highest incidence on the first day and affected 23 percent of the survivors and 5.7 percent of the dead. The incidence of these symptoms was lower in those who were dying, but they were already too far gone to be able to supply such information.

Among the military personnel of the Chūgoku III Corps and 121 Corps with relatively mild injury observed after 10 August in the branch hospitals of the Hiroshima First Army and the Hiroshima Second Army hospitals, 67 exposed within 1 kilometer of the hypocenter and 20 patients from the Kushigahama branch of Hiroshima First Army Hospital complained of frequent watery stools on the day of the explosion or at least by four days later. Diarrhea was sometimes complicated by mucus and hemorrhage and was accompanied by a high fever of 38°C. to 41°C. The stools were like

* *Polydipsia* is excessive or abnormal thirst. (Ed.)

those seen in bacterial dysentery, but bacterial examination yielded negative results. Polydipsia and general malaise set in; and the patients died in seven to ten days, and many suffered from cerebral symptoms, such as convulsions (clonic convulsions of extremities) and delirium.

Among the 181 fatal cases recorded up to 17 August, 159 had fever; 85, diarrhea (hemorrhagic stools, 16); 22, hemorrhagic diathesis;* 2, petechiae of skin; and 1 case each had nasal bleeding and gingival hemorrhage. The white cell count in the few cases examined showed low figures, between 300 and 400.

Stage 2. Epilation† appeared by the middle of the second week in the early cases and by the fifth week in the late cases. This condition occurred most frequently on the fourteenth and fifteenth days and was mainly located on the scalp; while in marked cases areas of the cheek, jaw, axilla, and genitals were the sites of susceptibility. Coarse hair and eyebrows were relatively resistant. Hair bulbs were not attached to the hairs that fell off. The incidence of epilation was 41.4 percent among the survivors and 54.8 percent among the fatal cases.

Fever was frequently seen five to seven days after the onset of epilation; and simultaneously or one to two days later there were not a few cases with hemorrhagic diathesis, purpura of the skin, gingival bleeding, nasal bleeding, melena, hematuria, and sometimes hemoptysis.‡ Gingivitis was encountered in 10.1 percent of the survivors and in 20.8 percent of the dead; while tonsillitis was found in 24.3 percent of the survivors and in 21.3 percent of the fatal cases. At first there was redness of the gums, and this turned to purple-red within a few days, and was accompanied by swelling, pain, and hemorrhage. Gangrenous ulcers covered by a pseudomembrane were seen in severe cases. Tonsillitis in severe cases demonstrated purulent and later pseudomembranous and gangrenous changes.

INCIDENCE AND CLINICAL COURSE OF ATOMIC BOMB RADIATION ILLNESS

Prodromal symptoms such as nausea, vomiting, and general malaise appeared temporarily soon after the explosion, and were followed by early diarrhea and fever in victims near the hypocenter. After a short latent period, hemorrhagic diathesis, hemorrhage, oropharyngitis,§ epilation, and fever appeared in victims receiving a low dose of radiation (Kikuchi and Kimoto

* *Hemorrhagic diathesis* is a syndrome showing a tendency to spontaneous bleeding, resulting from weakness of blood vessels, or a clotting defect, or both.

† *Epilation* is the removal of hair by the roots (see pages 133–36, 174). (Ed.)

‡ *Purpura* is a condition where parts of the body are covered by merged petechiae; in *melena* there is a passage of dark colored, tarry stools stained with altered blood or with blood pigments; in *hematuria,* blood is discharged in the urine; *hemoptysis* is spitting of blood, or blood-stained sputum. (Ed.)

§ *Oropharyngitis* is an inflammation of the mucous membrane of the mouth and the portion of the pharynx between the soft palate and the epiglottis. (Ed.)

1947, p. 1580). The following is an outline of the Joint Commission's report on the incidence and course of the symptoms on the twentieth day after the explosion in Hiroshima and Nagasaki (Oughterson and Warren 1956).

Nausea, vomiting, and *anorexia* appeared as early as thirty minutes to three hours after the exposure, but the majority were noted within twenty-four hours. These symptoms became apparent on the day of the explosion in 71 percent of the exposed in Hiroshima and in 69 percent in Nagasaki. They continued for 2.3 days in Hiroshima and for 2.7 days in Nagasaki. The incidence of vomiting in those within 1 kilometer of the hypocenter was 35 percent and 27 percent in Hiroshima and Nagasaki; and of anorexia, 48 percent and 37 percent, respectively. At a distance of more than 5 kilometers, both symptoms tended to decline; 1 percent to 2 percent for vomiting and 5 percent to 7 percent for anorexia (figure 8.4). In general, women were more resistant to these symptoms than were men.

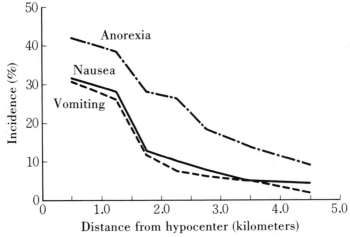

Figure 8.4. Incidence of nausea, vomiting, and anorexia by distance (Hiroshima and Nagasaki combined) (Oughterson and Warren 1956, p. 130).

The incidence of *diarrhea* in the survivors at day 20 was 37 percent (Hiroshima) and 33 percent (Nagasaki); and if it is restricted to those exposed within a distance of 1 kilometer, it was 50 percent and 43 percent, respectively. In Hiroshima, however, an incidence of 30 percent still occurred in victims exposed at a distance of more than 5 kilometers. The relation between diarrhea and shielding effects was not clear in both cities. *Bloody diarrhea* was noted in 11 percent of those within 1 kilometer of the hypocenter and in 1 percent beyond 5 kilometers whose shielding effects were much more evident. Among the 2,500 twenty-day survivors with diarrhea in Hiroshima and the 2,100 in Nagasaki, the rate of bloody diarrhea was 16 percent in Hiroshima and 13 percent in Nagasaki (figure 8.5).

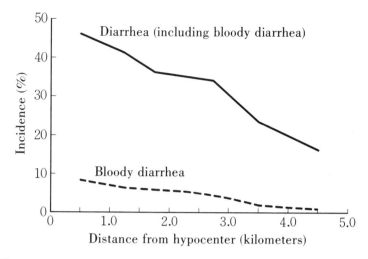

Figure 8.5. Incidence of diarrhea and bloody diarrhea by distance (Hiroshima and Nagasaki combined) (Oughterson and Warren 1956, p. 157).

Although the earliest signs of *ecchymosis** and/or *petechiae* appeared on the third day, the peak of the disorder was reached between 20 and 30 days, and the average was 25 days. The incidence within 1 kilometer of the hypocenter in Hiroshima was 49 percent and, beyond 5 kilometers it was 0.5 percent, with a marked decrease beyond 1.5 kilometers. The incidence in Nagasaki was lower. Hemorrhage occurred frequently on heads, faces, chests, and upper arms. Its course varied, and the lesions were frequently complicated by necrosis and infection (figures 8.6, 8.7, and 8.8).

In many cases, *epilation* appeared earlier than purpura and abruptly started from about the second week; it was correlated to distance from the hypocenter and to shielding conditions. In Hiroshima, epilation occurred on day 17.2 (average) in those exposed within a distance of 1 kilometer and on day 28.1 (average) in those between 1.5 and 2 kilometers. The incidence within 1 kilometer in Hiroshima was 69 percent and in Nagasaki, 32 percent; and in districts 3 or more kilometers from the hypocenter, it was approximately 2 percent in both cities. When the victims were exposed outdoors or inside of wooden buildings at a distance of 1 kilometer or less, epilation appeared in 76 percent and 45 percent in Hiroshima and Nagasaki, respectively. On the other hand, among those exposed in concrete buildings, the incidence was somewhat lower: 53 percent and 21 percent in Hiroshima and Nagasaki, respectively. Epilation continued for 1 to 2 weeks on the average (figure 8.9), and regeneration took place after 8 to 10 weeks, with the majority of survivors recovering by 12 to 14 weeks. Epilation occurred most frequently on the head, first

* *Ecchymosis* is a purplish patch caused by extravasation of the blood into the skin; ecchymosis differs from petechiae only in size.

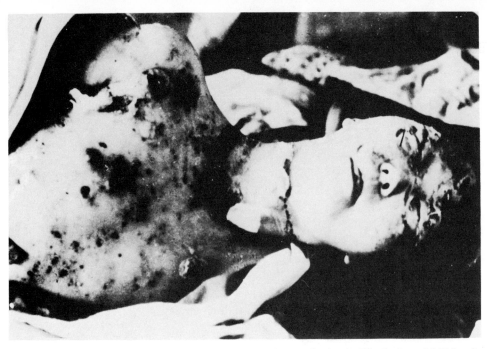

Figure 8.6. Purpura, Nagasaki, August 1945. (Photograph taken by Kyushu Imperial University Survey team.)

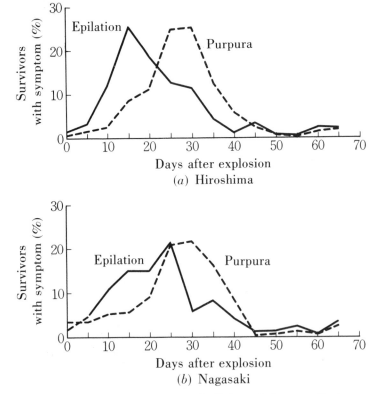

Figure 8.7. Days from explosion to onset of epilation and of purpura (Oughterson and Warren 1956, p. 134).

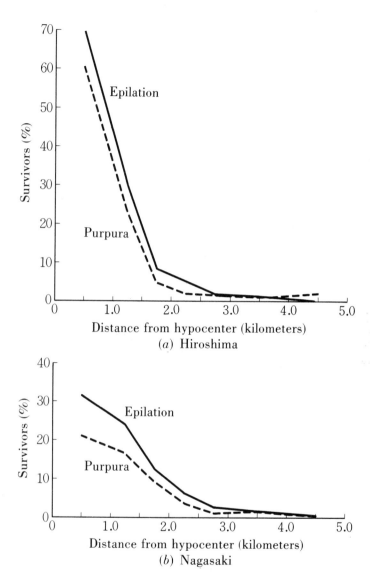

Figure 8.8. Incidence of epilation and purpura by distance (Oughterson and Warren 1956, pp. 134–35).

appearing on the forehead and then extending to the occipital and the parietal areas. Coarse hair, the eyebrow, axillary hair, and the pubes were fairly resistant. The remaining hair, which did not fall off, frequently showed specific deformations (Shirai 1956).

Epilation and *purpura* were frequently accompanied by oropharyngeal lesions. In Hiroshima, these lesions were seen in 56 percent of the survivors

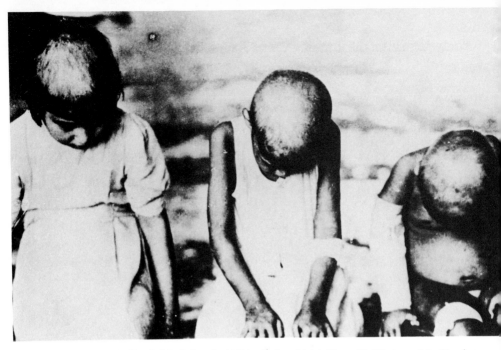

Figure 8.9. Depilated girls *(left and middle)* and a boy *(right)*, Nagasaki. (Photograph by Kyushu Imperial University Survey team.)

who suffered epilation and had been exposed within 5 kilometers of the hypo-center, but in only 11 percent of the survivors without epilation or purpura. The figures in Nagasaki were 53 percent and 12 percent, respectively. It can thus be said that epilation, purpura, and oropharyngeal lesions are the three main symptoms of acute atomic bomb radiation illness. Oropharyngeal symptoms appeared from a few days after the explosion up to five weeks, and peaked at the fourth week. The incidence was 61 percent within 1 kilometer and 7 percent beyond 5 kilometers in Hiroshima. The figures in Nagasaki were about the same (figure 8.10). At the beginning there were reddening and pain of pharynx and palate, and these symptoms rapidly progressed to hemorrhage, necrosis, and formation of ulcers. Victims with marked ulceration often died. The clinical course was dominated by nutritional conditions and recovery of bone marrow function. It took two to three weeks for improvement even in those showing a tendency to recover. Necrotic gingivitis was noted in 6 percent (Nagasaki) and in 10 percent (Hiroshima) of the oropharyngeal lesions (figure 8.10).

Hemorrhage (bleeding) occurred as a result of decreased platelets, necrosis of mucosa and other tissues, ulceration, and infection. Nasal bleeding (epitaxis) and uterine hemorrhage were often hard to stop, causing great loss of blood. Hemorrhages from mouth, rectum, urethra, and respiratory passages as well as from traumas were not rare. In relation to radiation injury, ocular hemorrhage—especially retinitis, with hemorrhage and white spots—was of special note. The eyeground changes were caused by anemia and hemorrhagic

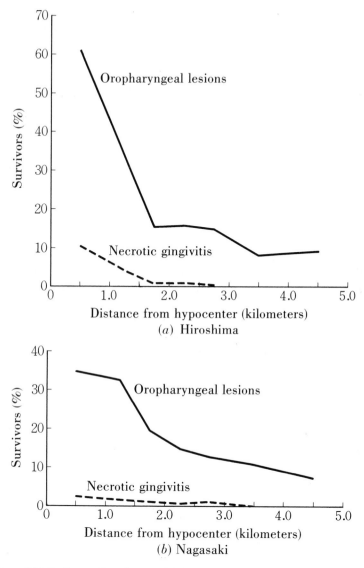

Figure 8.10. Incidence of oropharyngeal lesions and necrotic gingivitis by distance (Oughterson and Warren 1956, p. 144).

diathesis but also occurred as a consequence of septicemia accompanying atomic bomb radiation illness.

Fever was also a result of various factors having an intimate relation to infection. Fever was found in 35 percent (Hiroshima) and in 10 percent (Naga-saki) of the 20-day survivors within 1 kilometer of each hypocenter; while the figures were 5 percent (Hiroshima) and 0.5 percent (Nagasaki) at 5 kilometers or beyond. From the severity of exposure, those receiving a large dose of radiation showed signs of nausea and vomiting within a few hours, and then fever. In severe cases, there was staged elevation of body temperature from five to seven days which continued until death. In slightly milder cases, both nausea and vomiting soon ceased and temporarily entered into a latent phase without fever. Fever, however, reappeared, together with epilation and purpura. Diarrhea occurred before epilation and was sometimes accompanied by fever. The type of fever varied from one case to another. In general, fever became prominent when a new symptom set in and continued until death. Fever dropped rapidly to normal with the restoration of white blood cell count.

This has been a summary of the report made by the Joint Commission. The results of the investigation carried out by the Tokyo Imperial University team on 4,406 survivors following exposure to the atomic bomb in Hiroshima between 15 October and 16 November 1945 are shown in tables 8.5 and 8.6 (Kajitani and Hatano 1953, p. 522). Among the 4,406 survivors, those with one or more symptoms of epilation, skin petechiae, and gangrenous or hemorrhagic stomatitis (this was defined as radiation illness in this investigation)

TABLE 8.5

Relation between Radiation Illness and Sex

Distance from Hypocenter (km)	Radiation Illness		Hair Epilation		Sugillation (ecchymosis)		Total Number of Persons Examined	
	Male	Female	Male	Female	Male	Female	Male	Female
0–0.5	16 (84.2)*	6 (75.0)	15 (78.9)	6 (75.0)	7 (36.8)	2 (25.0)	19	8
0.6–1.0	111 (82.2)	119 (72.1)	100 (74.0)	111 (67.2)	54 (40.0)	47 (28.4)	135	165
1.1–1.5	150 (35.5)	174 (33.1)	123 (29.1)	134 (25.5)	60 (14.2)	72 (13.7)	422	525
1.6–2.0	90 (13.0)	117 (14.9)	55 (7.9)	79 (10.0)	30 (4.3)	39 (4.9)	690	784
2.1–2.5	46 (7.9)	62 (10.7)	33 (5.7)	42 (7.2)	10 (1.7)	16 (2.7)	577	579
2.6–3.0	8 (3.6)	10 (3.5)	2 (0.9)	7 (2.4)	5 (2.2)	3 (1.0)	220	282
Total	421 (20.4)	488 (20.8)	328 (15.8)	379 (16.1)	166 (8.0)	179 (7.6)	2,063	2,343

* Figures in parentheses are percentages of incidence.
Source: T. Kajitani and S. Hatano, "Medical survey on acute effects of atomic bomb in Hiroshima," in CRIABC (1953), vol. I, p. 522.

TABLE 8.6

Frequency of Symptoms of Radiation Illness by Distance from Hypocenter

Distance from Hypocenter (km)	Epilation	Purpura	Stomatitis	Diarrhea	Fever	Nausea, Vomiting	Anorexia	Malaise	Number of Persons Examined
0–0.5	21 (77.7)*	9 (33.3)	17 (62.9)	10 (37.0)	18 (66.6)	16 (59.2)	13 (48.1)	12 (44.4)	27
0.6–1.0	211 (70.3)	101 (33.6)	150 (50.0)	126 (42.0)	167 (55.6)	161 (53.6)	140 (46.6)	147 (49.0)	300
1.1–1.5	257 (27.1)	132 (13.9)	187 (19.7)	176 (18.5)	209 (22.0)	177 (18.6)	173 (18.2)	192 (20.2)	947
1.6–2.0	134 (9.0)	69 (4.6)	93 (6.3)	99 (6.7)	109 (7.3)	63 (4.2)	112 (7.5)	127 (8.6)	1,474
2.1–2.5	75 (6.4)	26 (2.2)	59 (5.1)	56 (4.8)	64 (5.5)	31 (2.6)	59 (5.1)	81 (7.0)	1,156
2.6–3.0	9 (1.7)	8 (1.5)	10 (1.9)	13 (2.5)	9 (1.7)	4 (0.7)	8 (1.5)	7 (1.3)	502
Total	707 (16.0)	345 (7.8)	516 (11.7)	480 (10.8)	576 (13.0)	452 (10.2)	505 (11.4)	566 (12.8)	4,406

* Figures in parentheses are percentages of incidence.
Source: T. Kajitani and S. Hatano, "Medical survey on acute effects of atomic bomb in Hiroshima," in CRIABC (1953), vol. I, p. 522.

numbered 909; and the relationships between the prevalence of these symptoms, distance from the hypocenter, and sex are shown in table 8.5. Table 8.6 gives a comparison of incidence of varying symptoms and distance from the hypocenter.

ACUTE BLOOD INJURY

Blood injury, especially to the bone marrow, is one of the most important elements of radiation illness. It has been mentioned that injury of the blood cells forms the background of such symptoms as hemorrhagic diathesis, purpura, other hemorrhages, stomatitis, and fever. The severity of acute injuries differed from case to case; and an outline of these changes will be described by dividing them into the following four categories: very severe, severe, moderately severe, and mild (Oughterson and Warren 1956; Wakisaka 1953, p. 346).

Very Severe Group.   The very severe group includes those receiving probably 450 to 600 rads, or more, near the hypocenter and dying within fourteen days. Table 8.7 contains the data of hematological examination of patients

TABLE 8.7

Blood Findings in Very Severe Cases in Hiroshima during the First Week after the Explosion *

Case	Day after Explosion		Red Cell Count (in millions)	Hemoglobin (%)	White Cell Count	Platelets	Other Injuries
	Examined	Died					
1	6th	9th	4.10	42	400	61,540	Burns and wour
2	6th	9th	4.69	50	150		Burns and wou
3	6th	?	3.75	40	250		Burns and wour
4	6th	11th	4.20	45	400		Burns
5	6th	8th	2.65	32	400	87,400	Burns
6	6th	8th	3.28	43	150		Burns
7	6th	8th	2.82	40	300		Wounds
8	7th	8th	4.13	40	400		Burns
9	7th	9th	3.26	40	300		Wounds
Normal range			4.00–5.00	80–100	6,000–8,000	150,000–200,000	

* These patients were exposed in the Banker's Club, a three-story concrete building, 240 m from the hypocenter (Iwakuni Naval Hospital).
Sources: K. Nakao, G. Kobayashi, S. Katō, Y. Yano, and M. Komiya, "Hematological studies of A-bomb radiation injuries," in CRIABC (1953) vol. I, p. 649. A. W. Oughterson and S. Warren, *Medical Effects of the Atomic Bomb in Japan* (New York: McGraw-Hill, 1956), p. 193.

exposed in the Chūgoku Naval Supervision Office (Banker's Club, three-story concrete building). This examination was carried out on 12–13 August at the Iwakuni Naval Hospital (Nakao 1953, p. 361; Nakao et al. 1953, p. 649). Among those exposed at such a close distance, a marked decrease in white cell count and moderate anemia were already detected by the sixth or seventh day; and as can be seen in figure 8.11, many victims showed further decrease in the number of white blood cells by the time of death. Of special note were a drop in lymphocytic ratio, a nuclear shift to the left of neutrophils,

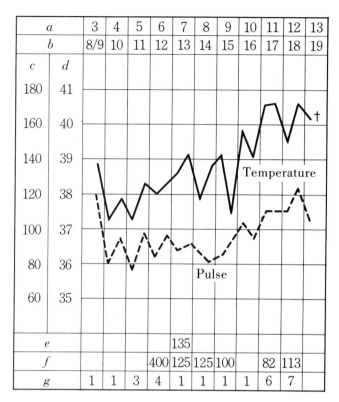

a	3	4	5	6	7	8	9	10	11	12	13
b	8/9	10	11	12	13	14	15	16	17	18	19

c	d
180	41
160	40
140	39
120	38
100	37
80	36
60	35

Temperature

Pulse

† (Termination)

e					135						
f				400	125	125	100		82	113	
g	1	1	3	4	1	1	1	1	6	7	

a	Day after explosion	e	Red cell count (10^4)
b	Date	f	White cell count
c	Pulse	g	No. diarrhea
d	Temperature (°C.)	†	Termination

Figure 8.11. Temperature chart for a fatal case with typical radiation injury (Oughterson and Warren 1956, p. 177). This patient, a twenty-seven-year-old man, was exposed in the Banker's Club, 240 meters from the hypocenter; he had no burns. (Iwakuni Naval Hospital.)

the entry of metamyelocytes and nucleated erythrocytes into the peripheral blood, and giant neutrophils from abnormal mitosis. These findings of white blood cells are often encountered in animals given a high dose of radiation. Although there was a slight drop in the number of red blood cells, one must also keep in mind the effects of hemorrhage from trauma, or of dehydration following thermal burns and diarrhea. Platelet count was examined in only two cases: both showed a moderate decrease. Bone marrow puncture was carried out in two cases; and, according to K. Nakao's description (1953, p. 361; Nakao et al. 1953, p. 649), the marrow was almost devoid of hemoblasts (hematopoietic precursor cells), showing an extreme condition of myelophthisis.* Although epilation and hemorrhagic diathesis were not apparent in these cases, hemorrhagic findings were found at autopsy.

* *Hemoblasts,* or hemocytoblasts, are cells from which it is assumed that all other blood cells derive; *hematopoietic* refers to blood cell production; *myelophthisis* is a reduction in production of blood cells by the bone marrow. (Ed.)

The twenty-seven-year-old male shown in figure 8.11 was exposed on the first floor of the Chūgoku Naval Supervision Office and received contusions of the head, face, and neck, bruises on the hands, but no thermal injury. He was then admitted to the Iwakuni Naval Hospital on 9 August 1945. The chief complaints were anorexia, diarrhea, coughing, and stomatitis, and blood-tinged sputum was noted one day prior to death. He died thirteen days after exposure to the atomic bomb. This case is considered to be typical of a high-dose, total-body irradiation.

The white cell count right after the explosion in the most severe cases in Nagasaki was recorded at the Ōmura Naval Hospital (Hanaoka 1964, p. 541) (table 8.8). The distance from the explosion in these cases is unknown,

TABLE 8.8

White Cell Counts in Very Severe Cases in Nagasaki*

| Case | Day after Explosion | | White Cell Count |
	Examined	Died	
1	1st	2nd	2,200
2	2nd	?	200–530
3	1st	2nd	1,670
4	2nd	?	830
5	2nd	2nd	1,300–1,600
6	2nd	2nd	600–1,000
7	2nd	2nd	400–500
8	2nd	2nd	530–1,040
9	2nd	2nd	830
10	2nd	2nd	300
11	2nd	2nd	715
12	8th	8th	430–500
13	9th	9th	1,700
14	9th	9th	500

* From Ōmura Naval Hospital.
Source: A. W. Oughterson and S. Warren, *Medical Effects of the Atomic Bomb in Japan* (New York: McGraw-Hill, 1956), p. 205.

but all terminated in death. Since all but two cases had thermal burns covering a large part of the body, it can be assumed that they were exposed outdoors within a distance of 1 kilometer of the hypocenter. A marked decrease in the number of white blood cells was already observed one to two days after the exposure.

Severe Group. One half of the patients in this group died within forty days after exposure, while the remaining patients showed improvement. There were symptoms of epilation, fever, hemorrhage, and oropharyngitis, often accompanied by infection. The typical course taken by two patients and

TABLE 8.9A

Serial Blood Findings in a Fatal Severe Case—Fourteen-year-old Boy*

Date of Examination	Red Cell Count (in millions)	Hemoglobin (%)	White Cell Count	Platelets	Remarks
11 August	4.06	70	4,200	203,000	high fever pharyngitis (15 August) epilation (17 August)
20 August	3.37	60	1,100	168,000	
21 August	3.91	65	1,000		
23 August	2.05	51	350		nasal bleeding
25 August	1.69	48	170		
26 August					purpura, hematuria
27 August	2.68	70	120		died

* From Saijō Sanatorium, Hiroshima.
Source: K. Nakao, G. Kobayashi, S. Katō, Y. Yano, and M. Komiya, "Hematological studies of A-bomb radiation injuries," in CRIABC (1953), vol. I, p. 649.

TABLE 8.9B

Serial Blood Findings in a Nonfatal Case with Severe Radiation Injury—
Twenty-five-year-old Man*

Date of Examination	Red Cell Count (in millions)	Hemoglobin (%)	White Cell Count	Platelets	Bone Marrow Nucleated Cell Counts
4 September	2.60	68	900	200,000	4,000
8 September			1,400		
19 September			2,800		
27 September	2.79	51	4,600		
23 October	3.30	74	10,400		75,000

* From Ujina Hospital, Hiroshima.
Source: A. W. Oughterson and S. Warren, *Medical Effects of the Atomic Bomb in Japan* (New York: McGraw-Hill, 1956), p. 183.

the hematology of the fatal and the improved cases are shown in tables 8.9A and 8.9B, respectively (Nakao et al. 1953). Although the distance from the hypocenter was unknown for the boy in table 8.9A, nausea, vomiting, and anorexia appeared right after the explosion, and then were followed by high fever on the sixth day, by pharyngeal pain on day 9, and by epilation on the eleventh day. Hemorrhagic tendency including nasal bleeding became prominent from the seventeenth day, and he finally died on the twenty-first day (27 August 1945). In this case, anemia and leukopenia progressed with the lapse of time. Among the white blood cells, the lymphocytes were the first to decrease; and there was a subsequent decrease in neutrophils. The man in table 8.9B was exposed on the second floor of a wooden house at a distance of about 960 meters from the hypocenter. He had cut wounds from glass on his right upper arm and bruise wounds on his right shoulder. After having recovered from general malaise, which had been noted on the day of the explosion, he was at work clearing away the wreckage outdoors from the fourth to the eighth day. Epilation appeared on his head on day 14 and was followed by fever on the twenty-first day and skin purpura on the following day. He was hospitalized on 30 August 1945, at which time the gingiva was already swollen. On the twenty-sixth day he complained of pharyngeal pain and gingival bleeding, and a high fever of 40°C. was noticed on the following day (2 September) and continued until 14 September. The fever rapidly fell to normal, and he was discharged on 3 October. As seen in table 8.9B, the white cell count was 900 with no neutrophils on 4 September (twenty-ninth day). Bone marrow puncture on the same day revealed a cell count of only 4,000, with mature neutrophils being extremely few. The production of cells of the red blood series was also suppressed. On 27 September both series showed improvement on bone marrow examination, and they returned to almost normal on 23 October.

As mentioned previously, nausea, vomiting, general malaise or diarrhea occurred on the day of explosion in the majority of the cases in this group, while there was some improvement of symptoms in some cases. From about the tenth to the fourteenth day, however, there were epilation, marked malaise, persistent fever, decrease in number of white cells followed by anemia, decreased number of platelets, gingivitis, oropharyngitis, and skin purpura. In patients surviving over twenty days, the lowest count of platelets was found about the fourth week, but the drop of red cell count continued until the seventh week. The symptoms started to improve with the recovery of white cell and platelet counts.

The distribution of red cell count in the severe cases in the third and fourth weeks is shown in table 8.10A. When dividing this group into two,

TABLE 8.10A

Distribution of Lowest Red Cell Counts in Severe Cases during the Third to the Fifth Week in Hiroshima; Comparison of the Degree of Anemia between Fatal Cases and Survivors

Red Cell Count (in ten thousands)	Fatal Cases	Recoveries
100–200	3	5
201–300	14	12
301–400	7	7
Over 401	1	3
Total	25	27

Source: A. W. Oughterson and S. Warren, *Medical Effects of the Atomic Bomb in Japan* (New York: McGraw-Hill, 1956), p. 196.

the 25 cases that died later and the 27 cases that recovered, one can hardly note any difference in the degree of decrease of red blood cells; thus, it is difficult to take the red cell count as an index for prognosis. Examination of reticulocytes,* however, revealed no case with a value higher than 0.4 percent in the fatal cases (9 cases), while one half (7 out of 13) of those recovering showed figures over 0.4 percent. This fact suggests a difference in hematopoietic function of bone marrow. The white cell count was less than 1,000 in 21 out of the 25 fatal cases, and those with a count of less than 500 (56 percent of fatal cases) had a poor prognosis (table 8.10B). The

TABLE 8.10B

Distribution of Lowest White Cell Counts in Severe Cases during the Third to the Fifth Week in Hiroshima; Comparison of the Degree of Leukopenia between Fatal Cases and Survivors

White Cell Count	Fatal Cases	Recoveries
0–500	14	1
501–1,000	7	8
1,001–2,000	4	10
Over 2,001	0	4
Total	25	23

Source: A. W. Oughterson and S. Warren, *Medical Effects of the Atomic Bomb in Japan* (New York: McGraw-Hill, 1956), p. 206.

platelet count was less than 100,000 in 12 fatal cases three to six weeks after exposure to the atomic bomb in Hiroshima, and 10 out of the 12 cases showed a count lower than 25,000. At about the same period, the platelet count was less than 100,000 in 16 out of 24 severe cases that recovered later, while it was less than 25,000 in only 5 cases. The data of the clotting time during four to five weeks after the explosion have been recorded by the Kumamoto Medical School team (table 8.11) (Oughterson and Warren 1956). In table 8.11, the white cell count was selected as standard for determining the degree of radiation injury, and the corresponding average bleeding and clotting time are indicated. From these data it is evident that vascular injury and altered blood coagulation became more conspicuous with the decrease in the number of white blood cells.

Moderately Severe and Mild Groups. The moderately severe cases include those who were considerably injured but survived for more than forty days. Their mortality was about 10 percent. In the mild cases are included patients

* A *reticulocyte* is a young red blood cell with a network of precipitated basophilic substance (by special staining) and occurring during the process of active blood regeneration.

TABLE 8.11

Hemorrhagic Tests in Twenty-two Severe Cases during the Fourth to the Fifth Week in Nagasaki*

Number of Cases	Bleeding Time (mean) (Duke Method)	Clotting Time (mean) (Sahli–Fonio Method)	White Cell Count (mean)	Rate of Epilation
14†	21 minutes	14 minutes	570	9/14
5	9.8 minutes	12.6 minutes	1,600	4/5
3	6.8 minutes	11.7 minutes	2,633	0/3
Normal Japanese	3–6	6–10		

* From Nagasaki Medical University and Kumamoto Medical College.
† Of these, 6 patients were positive in Rumpel-Leede test.
Source: A. W. Oughterson and S. Warren, *Medical Effects of the Atomic Bomb in Japan* (New York: McGraw-Hill, 1956), p. 220.

who received mild injury and survived for more than four months. The symptoms in the moderately severe cases appeared more gradually than those in the severe cases, and recovery occurred early. Fatal cases (10 percent) terminating after forty days or later died not from the direct effects of radioactivity but rather from various factors inhibiting recovery, such as poor nutritional conditions, shortage of medical supplies, and complications (for example, infection). The symptoms in the mild cases were much milder than those in moderately severe cases. The general trend of hematological changes in both groups was that the milder the injury, the greater the individual difference and fluctuation of blood changes.

In general, both red cell count and hemoglobin showed the lowest values (average red cell count 3,000,000) from the sixth to the ninth week (mid-September to early October) and did not return to normal even at twelve weeks (late October). As to white cell count in both cities, the lowest value was seen during the fourth week (table 8.12). When the clinical course was smooth, the patient started to recover about four weeks later, and the white cell count returned to almost normal by the early part of October. Skin petechiae and gingival bleeding of a mild degree occurred in both groups. In a comparison of the average platelet counts of the 101 cases with symptoms of radiation illness and the 55 cases with only trauma (Ōmura Naval Hospital, October to November), it was noted that the average value in the former group was slightly lower than that in the latter group. The data (Misao et al. 1953, p. 1021) on twelve patients followed by the Kyushu Imperial University team (Misao Medical Clinic) from the fourth to the eighth week after the explosion showed normal bleeding and clotting time; while capillary fragility was mildly abnormal up to the sixth week but returned to normal in the seventh week with a parallel change in average platelet count.

TABLE 8.12

*Average Weekly White Cell Counts
in Moderately Severe and Mild
Cases*

Week after Explosion	Average White Cell Count	
	Hiroshima	Nagasaki
1st	4,200*	
2nd	2,400*	
3rd	2,400	5,300*
4th	1,800	2,500
5th	2,400	2,700
6th	3,400	4,700
7th	5,000	4,800*
8th	5,300	8,500*
9th	6,700*	8,500
10th	8,600*	7,100*
11th	7,400	7,600
12th	6,800	5,800*

* Fewer than 10 cases.
Source: A. W. Oughterson and S. Warren, *Medical Effects of the Atomic Bomb in Japan* (New York: McGraw-Hill, 1956), p. 207.

Correlation between Hematological Changes and Symptoms in Atomic Bomb Radiation Illness.   In figure 8.12 are found the mortality (those dying soon after the explosion are not included) and the incidence and transition of epilation, oropharyngitis, and skin petechiae as compared with hematological changes (average white cell count, red cell count, and nucleated cell count in marrow) according to the degree of severity of radioactivity illness classified as: I, very severe; II, severe; III, moderately severe; and IV, mild. When excluding the victims dying soon after the explosion (assumed to be 60 percent to 70 percent of the dead within four months), there were two peaks of high mortality: the first peak appeared on the eighth to ninth day, and the second peak, from the fourth to fifth week. From the standpoint of radiation injury, the first peak reflected the death of those receiving the severest injuries. The bone marrow was remarkably damaged resulting in panmyelophthisis* and also extreme reduction in the number of white cells in the peripheral blood (figure 8.12b, white blood cell [I]). The second peak coincided with the stage when skin petechiae and oropharyngitis appeared. The decrease in white cells was at its peak at this stage (figure 8.12b, white cell [III–IV]), and the cellular damage of marrow was marked (figure 8.12c). As shown

* *Panmyelophthisis* is general suppression of the bone marrow. (Ed.)

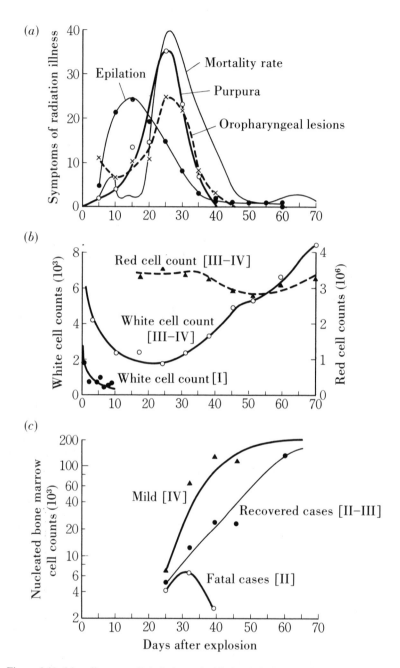

Figure 8.12. Mortality rate, clinical signs of radiation injuries, and hematopoietic cell counts of survivors during the first 10 weeks after the Hiroshima atomic bomb (Ohkita 1975).

in this figure, the number of nucleated cells in the marrow increased, and the symptoms started to show improvement with the recovery of hematopoietic function. Epilation was an important symptom of radiation illness and also a sign of bone marrow injury.

SECONDARY RADIATION ILLNESS

Secondary radiation illness is caused by the action of radiation from various neutron-induced radioisotopes in air and on earth or in fallout composed of nuclear fission products, uranium and plutonium escaping fission, and atomic bomb residues with neutron-induced radioactivity (Tsuzuki 1954a). In other words, this condition, as discussed in chapter 5, is caused by residual radiation; and the victims in Hiroshima and Nagasaki were not only exposed to the actions of gamma rays and neutrons emitted by the atomic bomb but were also injured to some extent by secondary radiation. Another portion of the population was not affected by primary atomic bomb radiation but was assumed to have received only secondary radiation. At the time of the explosion, these people were at a distance beyond the effects of the primary radiation; and they either came or stayed near the hypocenter after the explosion when the remaining radioactivity had not decreased, or they were living in the suburbs of Hiroshima and Nagasaki, where the fallout was heavily distributed. As related in chapter 5, it was difficult to estimate the radiation dose received by these people. The people entering into the city one hour after the explosion and staying for about five hours near the hypocenter in Hiroshima would have received about 20 rads, while those entering the next day and staying for eight hours would have received less than 10 rads. The residual radiation dose in Nagasaki is regarded as approximately 40 percent of that in Hiroshima. The total external radiation dose from fallout and induced radioactivity one hour after the explosion to infinite time is estimated at 4 to 40 rads in Hiroshima, while that from mainly fallout in the Nishiyama district of Nagasaki is 48 to 149 rads (see chapter 5). Although this dose is extremely low compared with that of primary radiation, it is not negligible when considering external as well as internal irradiation effects.

Survey records of the Army Medical School, Provisional Tokyo First Army Hospital (1953, p. 285), the Kyoto Imperial University team (Hiroshima), and the Kyushu Imperial University team (Nagasaki) show that great attention was paid to the people entering into both cities at an early stage after the explosion. The Army Medical School, Provisional Tokyo First Army Hospital team examined the clinical symptoms, blood sedimentation rate, and white cell count in the peripheral blood of those entering the city on the day of the explosion or one to two days later and staying for several days or frequently going in and out of the district near the hypocenter. This study was carried out between 3 September and 2 October on 230 soldiers, 20 occupants of the Ujina district, and 36 occupants of Ishiuchi village, Saeki County. Among these people are included a noncommissioned officer and a bank clerk who were not directly exposed to the atomic bomb. The noncommissioned officer worked for several days after the explosion at a distance of 0.9 to 1.6 kilometers from the hypocenter and complained of diarrhea and anorexia from 11 August; he had skin petechiae on 6 September. His white cell count was 3,200, and his red cell count 440 $\times$ 10^4 on 24 September. The bank clerk came to the city on 10 August and was working 500 meters from the hypocenter. He felt malaise on 25 August, and his white cell counts on 5, 17, and 26 September were 2,500, 3,700, and 4,700, respectively. Ishiuchi village is located within the district where the "black rain" fell, and the people entering the city at an early stage were probably affected by the fallout, since there were many who complained of diarrhea and malaise.

According to the investigation carried out by the Kyoto Imperial University team on twenty early entrants in Hiroshima City, a white cell count of 2,000 to 3,000 was found in three and a count of 3,000 to 4,000 in one (Mashimo et al. 1953, vol II, p. 769). Wakisaka (1953, p. 346) estimated the incidence of those with a white cell count of less than 5,000 to be about 32.3 percent.

The Kyushu Imperial University team record (T. Sawada et al. 1953, p. 1054) of Nagasaki showed that the white cell count was normal, being 4,400 to 8,200 (average 6,350) in eight adults who had been far from the hypocenter at the time of the explosion and resided in the hypocenter from right after the explosion or from the following day (30 August). In the thirteen who entered the city three days after the explosion and stayed at the Nagasaki Medical University as members of the Kyushu Imperial University first-aid team, the white cell count ranged between 5,200 and 8,200, with the average being 6,440 (7 to 8 September). However, the six adults who had been in the city or in the suburbs at the day of the explosion and then stayed in the hypocenter for several hours after the explosion, had a white cell count of 3,000 to 7,320 (average 4,600, 30 August), with three being less than 3,200.

Contamination from the fallout was especially marked in the Koi and Takasu districts (Hiroshima) and the Nishiyama district (Nagasaki). Early in October 1945, the Army Medical School, Provisional Tokyo First Army Hospital team (1953, p. 285) made a survey of the residents of the Furue district in Furutamachi township. Excluding the early entrants, seven residents of this district complained of marked malaise, headache, and abnormal menstruation right after the rainfall. The white cell count ranged from 5,800 to 11,600, with three out of the seven showing counts of over 10,000.

Detailed periodical observations of the residents in the Nishiyama district were made by the Kyushu Imperial University team.* Later the Kyoto Imperial University team headed by Kikuchi (1953a, p. 871) also participated in this survey. Hematological studies were continued until October 1960. According to the report prepared by the Kyushu Imperial University team, the majority of residents living in the Nishiyama district showed leukocytosis 50 to 80 days after contamination, with the extreme cases revealing a high count of 30,000 to 50,000. In the first investigation held on 1 October 1945, the increase in number of white blood cells was greatest in children under age fifteen and was followed by that in older youths and adults. Although no increase was found at that time in those over age fifty, it began to appear among the aged from January 1946, while leukocytosis tended to decline in children. The Kyoto Imperial University survey (February 1947) revealed an increase in the number of leukocytes in about 51 percent of the residents in the Nishiyama district. The peripheral blood smear showed an increase in number of eosinophils, a shift to the left of neutrophils, and sometimes few metamyelocytes. A mild hyperchromic anemia was seen in approximately 30 percent of the cases, and erythrocytosis (over 5.5 million) in 10 percent. There were no changes of reticulocytes and platelets. By 1953 the white cell count in this district returned to almost normal, and no changes were detected by the survey of 1960.

The mechanisms concerned in the aforementioned leukocytosis have not been clarified, but the possibility of the effects of radiation nuclide contained in the fallout cannot be denied (Irie and Matsuura 1967). By using the whole-body counter and radiochemical analysis of urine, S. Okajima and K. Takeshita (Okajima et al. 1975) have been measuring the residual radioactivity of radiation nuclide in the body of the residents in the Nishiyama district since 1969. Their data reveal a significantly higher concentration of cesium 137 in residents of this district than in the non-exposed population. At that time, however, the radiation dose was very low compared to the maximum permissible exposure recommended by the International Commission on Radiological Protection (ICRP), and no medical effects were seen among the residents.

DISTURBANCES OF REPRODUCTIVE FUNCTION

Since spermatogonia of the testis and follicular cells of the ovary are radio-sensitive, disturbance of reproductive function was an inevitable consequence of exposure to the atomic bomb.

Males. Loss of sexual desire was not uncommon during the two to three

---

* Irie et al. 1956, p. 1539; Irie and Matsuura 1967; Nakajima et al. 1953, p. 949; Shinohara et al. 1953a, p. 979.

months after the explosion. Investigations of the sperm (spermatozoa) of the exposed in Hiroshima were carried out several times by the Tokyo Imperial University team.* The first survey was made on 124 cases between the latter part of October and mid-November of 1945. As shown in tables 8.13 and 8.14, the number of spermatozoa decreased in proportion to nearness to the hypocenter. Since fewer than 5,000 spermatozoa per 1 cubic centimeter of sperm are tantamount to sterility, and since counts of 5,000 to 10,000 constitute relative sterility, approximately one third of the cases were in a state of sterility. Although the decrease in the number of spermatozoa ran parallel to the incidence of other symptoms of radiation illness, it was not related to the degree of thermal injury and, basically, showed an intimate correlation with distance. The degree of decrease in the number of spermatozoa was marked in those under age twenty and in those over forty.

Spermatozoa are renovated in about a month, which is longer than for leukocytes. Twelve men between the ages of twenty and forty were examined in May 1946. Six were devoid of spermatozoa; three had fewer than 1,000;

TABLE 8.13

Relation between Distance from Hypocenter and Counts of Spermatozoa, Hiroshima

Counts of Spermatozoa (per cm³)	Distance from Hypocenter (km)						Total Men Examined
	0–1.0	1.0–1.5	1.5–2.0	2.0–2.5	2.5–3.0	3.0–3.5	
0–5,000	19	13	8	3	0	0	43
5,000–10,000	0	4	3	1	2	0	10
10,000 or over	3	15	23	21	5	4	71
Total men examined	22	32	34	25	7	4	124

Source: M. Ōkoshi, S. Asakura, and T. Kaseki, "Seminal findings in Hiroshima A-bomb survivors," in CRIABC (1953), vol. I, p. 720.

TABLE 8.14

Relation between Age and Counts of Spermatozoa, Hiroshima

Counts of Spermatozoa (per cm³)	Age				Total Men Examined
	Under 20	21–30	31–40	40 and over	
0–5,000	13	13	13	4	43
5,000–10,000	2	2	4	2	10
10,000 and over	11	31	23	6	71
Total men examined	26	46	40	12	124

Source: M. Ōkoshi, S. Asakura, and T. Kaseki, "Seminal findings in Hiroshima A-bomb survivors," in CRIABC (1953), vol. I, p. 720.

* Ishikawa 1953, p. 724; Ishikawa and Asakura 1953, p. 727; Ōkoshi, Asakura, and Kaseki 1953, p. 720.

one, between 1,000 and 5,000; one, between 5,000 and 10,000; and one over 10,000. There was a drop in sperm count in the victims exposed within 1.5 kilometers of the hypocenter. In June 1947, thirty-two men were examined (fourteen to forty-four years old; twenty unmarried, twelve married, with eleven having children; the wives of four of the eleven became pregnant after the explosion). Sperm counts of fewer than 5,000 were found in ten, of 5,000 to 10,000 in three, and over 10,000 in nineteen. A drop in sperm count was frequently encountered in men exposed within a distance of 1 kilometer of the hypocenter. Later surveys revealed that although there were a few cases with sterility, the majority returned to almost normal in five years.

Women. Menstrual disorder was the most prominent symptom appearing right after the explosion. A survey was carried out until November 1945 by the Tokyo Imperial University team (Mitani et al. 1953*a*, p. 735; 1953*b*, p. 738) on 504 women exposed to the atomic bomb in Hiroshima (table 8.15).

TABLE 8.15

Menstrual Disorders among Women Exposed to Atomic Bomb, Hiroshima

Distance from Hypocenter (km)	Regular Menstruation	Irregular Menstruation					Total Women Examined
	I	II	III	IV	V	Number of Women Examined*	
0–0.5	0	1	2	0	1	4 (100.0)	4
0.5–1.0	6	20	4	2	2	28 (82.3)	34
1.0–1.5	28	73	24	4	9	110 (79.7)	138
1.5–2.0	42	81	31	6	16	134 (76.1)	176
2.0–2.5	39	35	13	3	12	63 (61.7)	102
2.5–3.0	19	8	1	2	5	16 (45.7)	35
3.0–3.5	5	2	1	1	0	4 (44.4)	9
3.5–4.0	1	1	0	0	0	1 (50.0)	2
4.0–4.5	1	0	1	0	0	1 (50.0)	2
4.5–5.0	2	0	0	0	0	0 —	2
Total women examined	143 (28.4%)	221	77	18	45	361 (71.6%)	504

* Figures in parentheses are percentages of total number of women examined.
Source: Y. Mitani, M. Itô, S. Nozu, T. Ikuishi, M. Iwai, M. Iwadate, and E. Watanabe, "Effects of A-bomb Exposure on female sexual function in Hiroshima," second report, in CRIABC (1953), vol. I, p. 738.

According to their data, 71.6 percent who had menstruated regularly before the explosion, showed menstrual disorder after exposure (II: amenorrhea from right after exposure; III: amenorrhea after one menstruation; IV: amenorrhea after two or more menstruations; V: early menstruation, prolonged menstruation, or irregular bleeding). The incidence of abnormal menstruation correlated with distance from the hypocenter. Examination of the relationship between menstrual disturbance and various injuries revealed that the former occurred frequently in patients with radiation illness and occurred less with thermal injury, trauma, and with no symptoms, in that order. Approximately 78 percent of those women with abnormal menstruation returned to normal by March 1946. Y. Mitani et al. concluded that "although there was a temporary castrated condition, there were no residual signs of marked ovarian disorder." The data of a similar survey made about Nagasaki by K. Kaida et al. of the Kyushu Imperial University team between 1 and 20 November 1945 is shown in table 8.16.

TABLE 8.16

Changes in Menstruation and Amenorrhea in Relation to Distance, Nagasaki

Distance from Hypocenter (km)	Number of Women	Change in Menstruation		Amenorrhea for More than 1 Month	
		Number	Percentage	Number	Percentage
0–0.9	11	11	100.0	9	81.8
0.9–1.8	80	70	87.5	60	75.0
1.8–2.9	50	33	66.0	31	62.0
2.9–3.9	83	41	49.4	27	32.5
3.9 and more	102	26	25.5	18	17.6
Total	326	181	55.5	145	44.5

Source: A. W. Oughterson and S. Warren, *Medical Effects of the Atomic Bomb in Japan* (New York: McGraw-Hill, 1956), p. 162.

TABLE 8.17

Clinical Symptoms Observed among Exposed Pregnant Women according to Distance from the Hypocenter, Hiroshima

Distance from Hypocenter (km)	Number of Cases	Acute Radiation Illness	Diarrhea	Malaise, Fever	Burn	Trauma	No Symptoms
0–0.5	0						
0.5–1.0	1	1			1		
1.0–1.5	22	7	4	1	9	10	10
1.5–2.0	56	6	21	10	10	26	19
2.0–2.5	97	4	26	27	14	39	40
2.5–3.0	74	1	19	21	3	14	33
3.0–3.5	20		6	6	2	2	8
3.5–4.0	27		7	5		3	15
4.0–4.5	18		3	4	1		11
4.5–5.0	15		3	5		1	7
5.0–6.0	10		1	2		1	7
6.0–7.0	7		1	3			3
Total	347	19	91	84	40	96	153

Source: Y. Mitani, M. Itō, S. Nozu, T. Ikuishi, M. Iwai, M. Iwadate, and E. Watanabe, "Effects of A-bomb exposure on the female sexual function in Hiroshima," second report, in CRIABC (1953), vol. I, p. 738.

Disorders of Pregnancy, Puerperium, and Delivery. Evacuation of pregnant women in Hiroshima was so complete that relatively few were exposed to the atomic bomb. A total of 347 pregnant women were examined by the members of the Tokyo Imperial University team (Mitani et al. 1953*a*, p. 735; 1953*b*, p. 738); see tables 8.17, 8.18, and 8.19. Excluding the cases with

TABLE 8.18

Effects of the Explosion on Pregnancy in Relation to Exposure Distance, Hiroshima

ance from center (km)	Number of Cases	Miscarriage and Premature Parturition	Stillbirth	Normal Termination	Abnormalities soon after the Bombing*
0–1.0	—				
1.0–1.5	16	1		15	premature parturition: 1 case at 9 months
					threatened abortion: 2 cases at 3 and 5 months
1.5–2.0	49	3	1	45	premature parturition: 2 cases at 8 and 9 months
					threatened abortion: 2 cases at 6 and 9 months
2.0–2.5	85	4 (2)†	1	80	
2.5–3.0	68	3	3	62	
3.0–3.5	20	2	1	17	
3.5–4.0	23	3		20	
4.0–4.5	18			18	
4.5–5.0	14		1	13	
5.0–6.0	9			9	
6.0–7.0	7			7	
Total	309	16 (2)	7	286	premature parturition: 3 cases
					threatened abortion: 4 cases

hese abnormalities were observed for several days after the detonation.
umbers in parentheses indicate artificial abortions.
rce: Y. Mitani, M. Itō, S. Nozu, T. Ikuishi, M. Iwai, M. Iwadate, and E. Watanabe, "Effects of A-bomb exposure on the female sexual function in Hiroshima," second
in CRIABC (1953), vol. I, p. 738.

TABLE 8.19

Effects of the Explosion on Pregnancy by Gestational Term at the Time of Bombing, Hiroshima

Gestational Term (month)	Number of Cases	Miscarriage and Premature Parturition	Stillbirth	Normal Termination	Abnormalities soon after the Bombing*
I	39	3		36	
II	48	3 (1)†	2	43	
III	74	4	1	69	threatened abortion: 1 case
IV	48	2 (1)	1	45	
V	49	1	1	47	threatened abortion: 1 case
VI	29		1	28	threatened abortion: 1 case
VII	13		1	12	
VIII	9	1		8	premature parturition: 1 case
IX	7	2		5	premature parturition: 2 cases
					threatened abortion: 1 case
X	5			5	
Total	321	16 (2)	7	298	premature parturition: 3 cases
					threatened abortion: 4 cases

* These abnormalities were observed for several days after the detonation.
† Numbers in parentheses indicate artificial abortions.
Source: Y. Mitani, M. Itō, S. Nozu, T. Ikuishi, M. Iwai, M. Iwadate, and E. Watanabe, "Effects of A-bomb exposure on the female sexual function in Hiroshima," second report, in CRIABC (1953), vol. I, p. 738.

artificial abortion, the incidence of miscarriage, premature delivery, and still-birth was 6.8 percent of 309 cases (table 8.18). This figure is not high compared to the nationwide average, which was 10 percent at that time. The 177 cases investigated by the members of the Kyushu Imperial University team in Nagasaki showed abnormal deliveries in 25.4 percent of the cases (table 8.20).

TABLE 8.20

Miscarriage and Premature Parturition in Relation to Exposure Distance, Nagasaki*

Distance from Hypocenter (km)	Number of Pregnant Women	Miscarriages		Premature Parturition		Total Abnormal Terminations	
		Number	Percentage	Number	Percentage	Number	Percenta
0–0.9	5	5	100.0	0	—	5	100.0
0.9–1.8	14	8	57.1	6	42.9	14	100.0
1.8–2.9	20	14	70.0	1	5.0	15	75.0
2.9–3.9	35	3	8.6	0	—	3	8.6
3.9 and over	103	3	2.9	5	4.9	8	7.8
Total	177	33	18.6	12	6.8	45	25.4
Attributed to causes other than the explosion		3		2		5	

* These pregnant women were attended for 3 months after the explosion.
Source: A. W. Oughterson and S. Warren, *Medical Effects of the Atomic Bomb in Japan,* (New York: McGraw-Hill, 1956), p. 163.

The Pathology of Atomic Bomb Injury (Acute Phase)

Pathological investigations of atomic bomb injury were carried out by many universities and institutions soon after the atomic bombing in Hiroshima and Nagasaki. The pathological changes lying at the base of various symptoms occurring after exposure to the atomic bomb have been accurately observed, and autopsies were of great help in clarifying their essential qualities.

A total of 213 autopsied cases (Hiroshima, 145 cases; Nagasaki, 68 cases) were reported to the Special Committee for Atomic Bomb Casualty Investigation and Research of the Scientific Research Council of Japan up to April 1947. The name of the reporter, the name of the institute, the place of autopsy, the number of cases, and the days after exposure to the atomic bomb are shown in tables 8.21A and 8.21B (Kinoshita and Miyake 1951, p. 79). The days after the explosion were divided into four stages, following Miyake's

TABLE 8.21A
Autopsy Cases in Hiroshima

Doctor Reporting (Institution)	Place	Number of Cases	Days after the Explosion			
			1–14	15–35	36–60	61–120
uo Kusano (Tokyo Imperial University's stitute of Infectious Diseases)	Saijō Sanatorium	21	3	16	2	
uo Kusano (Tokyo Imperial University's stitute of Infectious Diseases)	Miyajima Island	1		1		
irō Kuno (Iwakuni Naval Hospital)	Iwakuni	2	2			
uo Kayashima (Beppu Naval Hospital)	Beppu	1		1		
Nagato (Kure Naval Hospital)	Kure	1				1
o Shinoi (Tokyo Medical College)	Tokyo	1				1
ashi Miyake (Tokyo Imperial University)	Hiroshima	26		26		
ashi Miyake (Tokyo Imperial University)	Tokyo	2		2		
hi Ōhashi (Army Medical School)	Hiroshima	20	12		6	2
shi Tanabe (Okayama University Medical hool)	Okayama Army Hospital	8		6	1	1
o Hamasaki (Okayama University Medical School)	Okayama	2		2		
ta Tamagawa (Hiroshima Medical College)	Hiroshima	19		7	8	4
eyasu Amano (Kyoto Imperial University)	Hiroshima	25	3	10	12	
aku Ono (Kyushu Imperial University)	Fukuoka	2		1	1	
io Miyazaki (Tokyo Medical and Dental llege)	Tokyo	1		1		
hiko Ishibashi (Chiba Medical School)	Chiba	1			1	
a Abe (Tohoku Imperial University)	Sendai	1			1	
un Kinoshita (Osaka Imperial University)	Osaka	3			3	
aya Araki (Kyoto Prefectural Medical hool)	Hiroshima, Kyoto	8		1	1	6
Total		145	20	73	37	15

ource: R. Kinoshita and M. Miyake, "Pathological investigation of atomic bomb injuries," in SRIABC (1951), p. 79.

TABLE 8.21B
Autopsy Cases in Nagasaki

Doctor Reporting (Institution)	Place	Number of Cases	Days after the Explosion			
			1–14	15–35	36–60	61–120
Masashi Miyake (Tokyo Imperial University)	Nagasaki, Ōmura	6			5	1
Ureshino Naval Hospital	Ureshino	2		2		
Atsuo Fujita (Hario Marine Corps)	Hario	5	5			
Takeo Iemori (Yamaguchi Medical College)	Nagasaki	13			13	
Kōsaku Ono (Kyushu Imperial University)	Nagasaki	14		10	2	2
Kōsaku Ono (Army Rescue Team)	Nagasaki	10		10		
Kitasu Suzue (Kumamoto Medical College)	Nagasaki	18		18		
Total		68	5	40	20	3

Source: R. Kinoshita and M. Miyake, "Pathological investigation of atomic bomb injuries," in SRIABC (1951), p. 79.

classification (1953a 1953b, p. 375; 1967): stage I covers up to 14 days afterward; stage IIa, 15 to 35 days; stage IIb, 36 to 60 days; and stage III, 61 to
120 days. Table 8.22 shows age and sex distribution of the autopsied cases.

TABLE 8.22
Sex and Age Distribution of Autopsy Cases

| | Sex | Age in Years | | | | | | Total | Unknown |
		0–10 (months)	1–15	16–30	31–45	46–60	61 and over		
Hiroshima	Male	0	12	53	25	9	2	101	2
	Female	2	3	17	9	6	4	41	1
	Total	2	15	70	34	15	6	142	3
Nagasaki	Male		2	14	9	3	2	30	
	Female		9	9	10	2	3	33	5
	Total		11	23	19	5	5	63	5

Source: R. Kinoshita and M. Miyake, "Pathological investigation of atomic bomb injuries," in SRIABC (1951), p. 79.

FATAL CASES SOON AFTER THE EXPLOSION (STAGE I)

There were 25 autopsied cases of those who died within two weeks from
immediately after the explosion. (Hiroshima, 20 cases; Nagasaki, 5 cases).
Among these cases, complete records on name, age, sex, distance from hypocenter, situation at time of bombing, date and time of death, clinical symptoms,
and microscopic slides have been preserved in 12 autopsied by K. Yamashina
between 10 and 15 August at the Ninoshima Quarantine (Iijima 1967b; Yamashina 1967). The data of these cases are shown in tables 8.23, 8.24, and 8.25.

Pathological Findings of Thermal Injuries. As shown in table 8.24, 11
out of Yamashina's 12 cases showed thermal injuries; only 6 cases out of
the 25 autopsied cases were free from thermal injuries (Hiroshima, 3 cases;
Nagasaki, 3 cases); and as previously noted, it is evident that thermal injury
was one of the main causes of early death in those exposed near the hypocenter.
According to Yamashina's record, thermal injury often appeared on the bare
skin of the face, the occipital, nuchal and cervical areas, the upper portion
of the chest and back, and of the hands and legs. The main factors contributing
to the high incidence of thermal injuries were: the burst point was at a
high altitude; the heat rays at short distances acted as though poured from
above; and garments were of light texture due to hot weather, so that much
bare skin was exposed. The degree of thermal injury was described as second
degree (formation of vesicles) or third degree (necrosis, formation of ulcers),
but in general it can be said that the surface of thermal injury was wide
and shallow with clear-cut borders. The external appearance of the thermal

TABLE 8.23
Autopsy Cases Performed by Yamashina, Hiroshima

Case	Age	Sex	Location at Time of Bombing	Distance from Hypocenter (m)	Exposed Condition	Time of Death	Date
1	13	Male	around Kokutaiji	1,300	outdoors	24:00	9 August 1945
2	24	Male	Zaimoku-cho	800	indoors, second floor of a house which collapsed	19:50	10 August 1945
3	15	Male	behind City Hall building	1,000	outdoors, wearing a white sports shirt	10:10	11 August 1945
4	32	Male	behind City Hall building	1,000	outdoors, standing with his back toward the hypocenter, naked to waist	12:00	11 August 1945
5	39	Male	the 10th Corps	1,000	indoors, beside the window of collapsed barracks	14:20	12 August 1945
6	13	Female	10, Takaramachi-Higashi	1,500	outdoors, wearing white clothes	14:30	12 August 1945
7	34	Male	the 10th Corps	1,000	washing at a lavatory, wearing a khaki uniform	02:25	13 August 1945
8	28	Male	in front of north barracks	1,200	outdoors (the barracks collapsed)	03:30	14 August 1945
9	25	Male	on grounds of north barracks	1,500	outdoors	05:50	14 August 1945
10	24	Female	Senda-machi	2,000	outdoors, wearing a one-piece summer dress	11:00	14 August 1945
11	25	Male	Nakajima-shinmachi	1,200	outdoors	23:00	14 August 1945
12	33	Male	north of hypocenter	700	outdoors	07:30	15 August 1945

Source: K. Yamashina, "Pathology of early effects from exposure to the atomic bomb," *Journal of the Hiroshima Medical Association* (special series) 20 (1967): 115.

TABLE 8.24

Clinical Symptoms of Autopsies Performed by Yamashina, Hiroshima

Case	Age	Sex	Burns	Trauma	Other Symptoms	Leukocyte Counts
1	13	Male	Third degree: face, nape, occipital region, back of limbs	None	(no description)	
2	24	Male	None	Contusion of right scapular region, forearm, left elbow, occipital region, and legs	impaired hearing, fading consciousness (final stage), nausea, tiredness, anorexia	9,500 (10 August)
3	15	Male	Third degree: face, head, neck, nape, anterior chest, scapular region, arms, right leg	None	nausea, vomiting, fever (38–39° C), diarrhea, fading consciousness (from earlier stage)	
4	32	Male	Second to third degree: face, neck, right anterior chest, back to occipital region	None	nausea, vomiting, thirst, anorexia, diarrhea (frequently), fever (38–40°C)	
5	39	Male	Second to third degree: face, right scapular region	Fracture of right leg, contusion of shoulder and right chest	nausea, headache, fever	
6	13	Female	Second degree: face, nape, neck, scapular regions, arm, back of the hands	None	nausea, vomiting, diarrhea, excited state since three days after bombing followed by fading consciousness	
7	34	Male	Second degree: occipital region, scapular region	Contusion of occipital region and right leg, rupture of spleen	nausea, vomiting, diarrhea, fever (39° C), cerebral symptoms before death	
8	29	Male	Second degree: right side of face, right chest, back, abdomen	None	nausea, vomiting, high fever since three days after bombing, fading consciousness (final stage)	
9	25	Male	Second degree: mouth, right scapular region	Fracture of left thigh	nausea, diarrhea (frequently), thirst, high fever, proteinuria	7,500 (13 August)
10	24	Female	Second degree: face, neck, both forearms, legs	None	diarrhea (frequently), fever (39.2° C), albuminuria, excited state before fading consciousness and death	9,500 (14 August)
11	25	Male	Third degree: left side of face, scapular region and abdominal wall, left hand, upper and lower limbs	None	fever (38.5–41° C), albuminuria, cerebral symptoms before death	5,500 (14 August)
12	33	Male	Third degree: face, left side of occipital and scapular region, right limbs, right side of chest	None	vomiting, diarrhea (frequently), remittent high fever	

injury differed greatly according to the degree of penetration and varied especially when complicated by bacterial infection.

Histologically, the epidermis was destroyed with necrosis and desquamation, and the subcutaneous tissue was frequently exposed. The wound surface was damaged and somewhat edematous but, as a whole, had a dry appearance. The entire layer of the epidermis was not necrotic and frequently revealed a still living basal layer. In these areas, there was sometimes an increase in melanocytes* with marked pigmentation, while other areas showed loss of melanocytes and depigmentation. According to S. Minami (1953, p. 1134), atomic bomb thermal injuries of the skin have been described differently by different authors: "the skin tended to turn black," "first became black and then formed vesicles," "the black color was due to dust." Although "the actual facts remain unclear," the superficial necrosis of the slightly dry skin and the focal increase in melanocytes apparently intensified the black color.

Pain following thermal injury in those exposed to the atomic bomb was milder than that of common heat injury, while edematous swelling around the wound two to three days later was especially conspicuous (Kikuchi and Kimoto 1947, p. 1580). In other words, the reaction consisting of congestion, edema, and cell infiltration was more remarkable in the surrounding tissue than in the focus of thermal injury. In these areas, thrombosis of vessels was sometimes found together with emigration of histiocytes and monocytes. When complicated with bacterial infection, the necrosis extended into the deeper tissue and was accompanied by marked congestion and hemorrhage. Only few polymorphonuclear cells were usually found as a result of radiation injury of the bone marrow. In the acute form of burn, necrosis of the skin extended into the deeper dermis, leaving only shadows of hair follicles and sweat glands. Colonies of bacteria were found on the necrotic surface, but they remained in only the superficial layer because of its dryness (Sugiyama et al. 1953, p. 895).

Changes Found in Hematopoietic Organs. The most significant change in stage I was seen in the lymphatic tissues (thymus, spleen, lymph node, tonsil, lymphatic apparatus of digestive tract) and bone marrow, which are related to the production and function of blood cells. The marked drop in number of lymphocytes soon after exposure has already been mentioned. Corresponding with this, there was a remarkable change in the *spleen*. Pure changes consisting of almost complete loss of lymphocytes from the spleen occurred in the cases without thermal injury (Yamashina's case 2, a twenty-four-year-old male, and case 1 of Kyoto Imperial University, a forty-two-

---

* A *melanocyte* is a skin cell that synthesizes a black pigment and causes color variations in the skin. (Ed.)

TABLE 8.25

Microscopic Findings in the Autopsies Performed by Yamashina

Case	Age	Sex	Spleen	Bone Marrow	Thymus Lymphoid Tissue Lymph Node	Liver	Kidney	Gastro-intestinal Tract	Lung	Others
1	13	Male	normal size soft consistency follicles clearly seen	red marrow	thymus 15 g	cloudy swollen	cloudy swollen	diffusely hyperemic distal colon edematous	emphysematous static congestion	many petechiae on mucosa (++) right pleural effusion (+)
2	24	Male	follicles atrophic		lymph nodes atrophic	central congestion slightly yellowish	slightly cloudy	petechiae on stomach	focus of tuberculosis emphysematous	petechiae on serosa (+)
3	15	Male	70 g follicles atrophic		thymus 14 g tonsils hypertrophic lymph nodes atrophic	930 g cloudy swollen	L: 110 g R: 120 g cloudy swollen pelvic hemorrhage	distal colon edematous lymphoid follicles prominent	petechiae on pleura emphysematous	petechiae on serosa (++) meningeal edema and hyperemia
4	32	Male	80 g follicles not clear		lacunar tonsillitis lymph nodes atrophic	1,210 g cloudy swollen	L: 160 g R: 120 g cloudy swollen pelvic hemorrhage	ileum hyperemic colon edematous	petechiae on pleura emphysematous	petechiae on mucosa and serosa (++) cloudy meninx
5	39	Male	65 g firm consistency follicles not clear	yellow marrow	lymph nodes slightly atrophic	1,350 g anemic swollen lobule unclear	L: 140 g cloudy petechiae of pelvis	stomach: mucosal bleeding duodenum petechiae ileum anemic colon normal	slightly emphysematous	hemorrhage in myocardium (++) mucosal petechiae subarachnoideal hemorrhage
6	13	Female	60 g anemic follicles not	grayish-yellow marrow partly myeloid	lymph nodes slightly atrophic	1,100 g anemic swollen	110 g each cloudy petechiae of	lymphoid tissue of ileum hyperemic	petechial bleeding (++)	petechiae on pericardium

			rupted follicles not clear		generally atrophic	yellowish-brown cloudy	K: 140 g markedly cloudy parenchyma pelvic hemorrhage	...ach and duodenum colon edematous	...bronchus congestion in lower lobes	...hemorrhage pia mater hyperemic petechiae on serosa
8	29	Male	95 g follicles not clear	yellow marrow	involuted thymus fatty tissue lymph node atrophic	1,695 g cloudy swollen	L: 180 g R: 160 g cloudy swollen petechiae of pelvis	petechiae in stomach fresh ulcer at cardiac region intestines not remarkable	tuberculosis in lung apex	hemorrhagic diathesis (++)
9	25	Male	135 g splenomegaly	yellow marrow	lymph nodes not swollen	1,800 g cloudy swollen	L: 170 g R: 160 g cloudy parenchyma	ulcer in colon lymphoid tissues of intestine swollen	no abnormality	hemorrhagic diathesis (++)
10	24	Female	60 g follicles not clear	yellow marrow	lymph nodes not swollen	965 g congestion of nutmeg liver	L: 110 g R: 95 g slightly cloudy petechiae of pelvis	lower part of ileum hyperemic petechiae colon markedly edematous	petechiae on pleura bronchial hyperemia tuberculosis	hemorrhagic diathesis (++) edema on legs (+) petechiae in white matter
11	25	Male	220 g	yellow marrow soft	lymph nodes not swollen	cloudy swollen	L: 150 g R: 140 g cloudy petechiae of pelvis	hemorrhagic fleck in stomach petechiae and erosion in small intestine	congestion and edema	hemorrhagic diathesis (++) gingivitis stomatitis
12	33	Male	95 g follicles not clear		lymph nodes not swollen	1,700 g fatty degeneration	L: 175 g R: 160 g cloudy petechiae of pelvis	petechiae in ileum colon edematous and pseudomembrane formation	congestion	hemorrhagic diathesis (++)

Source: K. Yamashina, "Pathology of early effects from exposure to the atomic bomb," *Journal of the Hiroshima Medical Association* (special series) 20 (1967): 115.

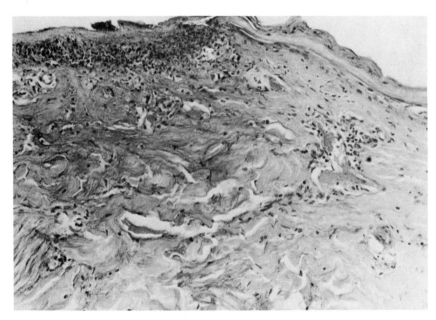

Figure 8.13. Burned skin, showing necrosis and foliation of epidermis, from a man of thirty-two exposed to the atomic bomb 1,000 meters from the hypocenter; he died on 11 August 1945. (Case 4 from Yamashina's series, Hiroshima.)

year-old male). Case 1 of Kyoto Imperial University, exposed 400 meters from the hypocenter, showed an extremely destroyed spleen. The follicles were completely devoid of lymphocytes, and there was only a reticular structure. The red pulp had lost its cellular elements and also revealed a reticular structure. It was difficult to detect the distribution of sinuses, since the entire spleen was homogenously occupied by reticulum cells and endothelial cells. The central arteries in the follicular area and the sinus endothelial cells were the only hallmarks suggestive of a spleen (Amano 1964, p. 630). Yamashina's case (figure 8.14), exposed at a distance of 800 meters from the hypocenter, also showed similar destructive changes. Only a few lymphocytes appeared to have degenerated and undergone lytic changes surrounding the central artery and plasma exudation in the subendothelia of the central artery. The spleens in the other cases at this stage basically showed similar loss of lymphocytes; but there were also congestion of the red pulp as an effect of thermal injury and frequently signs of erythrophagocytosis and hemosiderin in reticulum cells (macrophages of red pulp).* These changes indicate membrane injury to red blood cells induced by radiation and the intact function of

---

* *Erythrophagocytosis* is a condition in which erythrocytes (red blood cells containing hemoglobin and carrying oxygen) are engulfed by phagocytes; *hemosiderin* is a pigment found in phagocytic cells resulting from the phagocytic digestion of the effete erythrocytes; *macrophages* are large phagocytic cells.

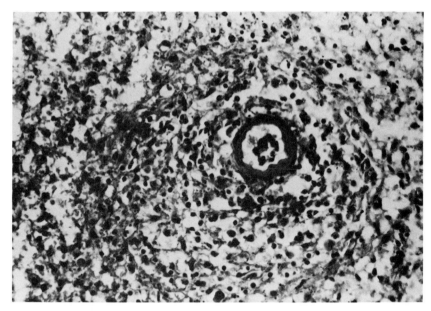

Figure 8.14. Depletion of lymphocytes from the Malpighian body in the spleen of a twenty-four-year-old man exposed to the atomic bomb at 800 meters from the hypocenter; he died on 10 August 1945. (Case 2 from Yamashina's series, Hiroshima.)

macrophages in the spleen. There was marked infiltration of plasma cells in two cases of Yamashina's series—case 9, a twenty-five-year-old male, 1,500 meters from hypocenter; case 11, a twenty-five-year-old male, 1,200 meters from hypocenter (Yamashina 1967)—which led to an increase in weight of the spleen—to 135 grams in the former, and to 220 grams in the latter. In 1949, A. A. Liebow, S. Warren, and E. DeCoursey described the appearance of large, atypical cells in the spleen in Yamashina's case 3 (a fifteen-year-old male, 1,000 meters from the hypocenter).

Lymph Nodes, Tonsils, and Lymphatic Apparatus. The number of lymphocytes also decreased conspicuously. The lymph follicles in lymph nodes became indistinct, and small vessels in the cortex were remarkably dilated. The lymph nodes were of small size due to the decrease in lymphocytes, while tissue mast cells* were seen between the collapsed reticulum cells. Necrosis and bacterial infection were found in some of the tonsils. The function of the *thymus* was not fully understood at that time; and although attention had not been paid to this organ, a decrease in lymphocytes was described in the thymus—weighing 14 grams and 15 grams, respectively—in cases 1 and 3 of Yamashina's series (S. Ōhashi and M. Miyake [*see* Army Medical School 1953, p. 285]).

* A *mast cell* is a connective tissue cell capable of elaborating cytoplasmic granules that contain histamine and heparin.

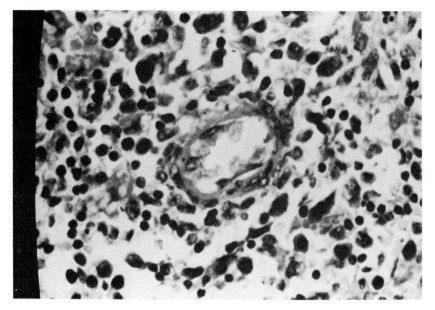

Figure 8.15A. Atypical cells in the white pulp of spleen from a fifteen-year-old boy exposed to the atomic bomb 1,000 meters from the hypocenter; he died on 11 August 1945. (Case 3 from Yamashina's series, Hiroshima.)

Figure 8.15B. Proliferation of plasma cells in the spleen from a twenty-five-year-old man exposed to the atomic bomb 1,200 meters from the hypocenter; he died on 14 August 1945. (Case 11 from Yamashina's series, Hiroshima.)

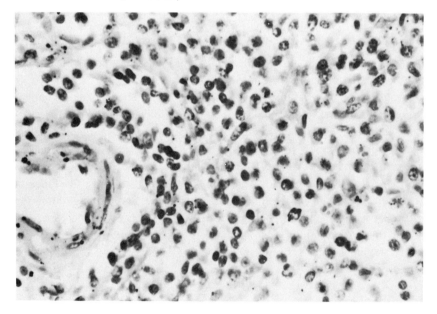

The *bone marrow* was examined in only seven cases in stage I. Six cases were those from Yamashina's series, and the bone marrow was taken from the femur, where fatty marrow with poor hematopoiesis is usually found. Bone marrow rich in hematopoietic tissue such as that of flat bones (sternum, vertebrae) was examined in the two cases autopsied at the Hiroshima Sanatorium (case 1, a nineteen-year-old male, died on 16 August; case 3, a thirty-two-year-old female, died on 18 August (figure 8.16B); distance from hypo-

Figure 8.16A. Degenerated bone marrow showing a fatty marrow with few plasma and reticulum cells, from a thirteen-year-old girl exposed to the atomic bomb 1,500 meters from the hypocenter; she died on 12 August 1945. (Case 6 from Yamashina's series, Hiroshima.)

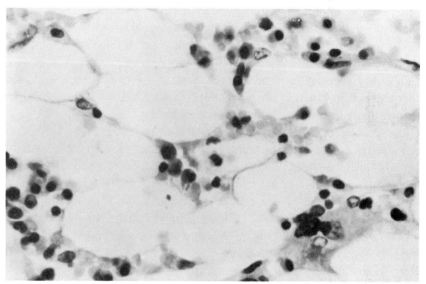

Figure 8.16B. Proliferation of reticulum cells in the bone marrow of a thirty-two-year-old woman exposed to the atomic bomb at an unidentified place; she died on 18 August 1945. (Case 3 of Hiroshima Sanatorium; contributed by N. Kusano.)

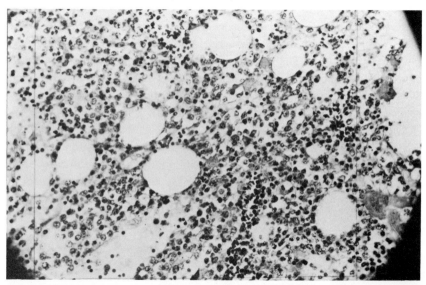

center unknown in both cases). According to N. Kusano's report (1953*b*, p. 1346), in case 1 there was a general decrease in cells, with scattered nodular islets of grouped cells. There were also congestion, moderate dilatation of veins, and mild hemorrhage. About one half of the cells were composed of small and large plasma cells, with a small number of myeloid cells and sparse polymorphonuclear leukocytes. Eosinophils were more prominent than usual, but the number of erythroblasts ranged within a normal limit. There were no normal megakaryocytes, with only few degenerated ones being found. Reticulum cells showed marked vacuolization, while some demonstrated moderate erythrophagia and mild hemosiderosis. It has been described in case 3 that there was diffuse proliferation of cells. They consisted mainly of myeloblasts, plasma cells, and proliferating nonphagocytizing reticulum cells with rather basophilic cytoplasm. There were only a few myelocytes, leukocytes, and erythroblasts. Although a considerable number of megakaryocytes were found, they were far from normal, showing conspicuous degeneration and characteristic destruction of nuclei. Reticulum cells showed vacuolization. Nuclear destruction was not an uncommon finding.

The histological specimen of the bone marrow obtained at the earliest period after exposure to the atomic bomb was that of Yamashina's case 5 (a thirty-nine-year-old male, 1,000 meters from hypocenter, died on 12 August). In the fatty marrow, hematopoietic foci consisted of very few erythroblasts with pyknotic nuclei, plasma cells, and reticulum cells with erythrophagia. It has already been mentioned that a description of the bone marrow of a severe case obtained by aspiration at a similar stage was made by K. Nakao (1953, p. 361; Nakao et al. 1953, p. 649). In the two cases at Iwakuni Naval Hospital, the nucleated cells in the marrow were so few that it was difficult to detect any cells on stained blood films. Young proliferative blood cells completely disappeared from the marrow. The number of polymorphonuclear leukocytes decreased to $\frac{1}{50}$ to $\frac{1}{100}$ of that of normal, and the number of erythroblasts to $\frac{1}{50}$ to $\frac{5}{100}$ of that of normal, with "normochromic" erythroblasts predominating and an absence of young cells. On the other hand, there was an increase in reticulum cells and plasma cells. Megakaryocytes numbered only $\frac{2}{100}$. The data obtained by aspiration and the histological figures of the bone marrow of Yamashina's cases and those of the Hiroshima Sanatorium show that varying degrees of destruction occurred in the marrow at an early stage after exposure.

Changes of the Digestive Tract. The gland cells of the small intestines, especially those of the ileum, are extremely sensitive to radiation. This phenomenon is related to the rapid turnover and the active mitoses of these cells. In the small intestines of stage I autopsy cases (Yamashina's cases 2– 7; figure 8.17), atypical cells and abnormal mitotic figures were found in

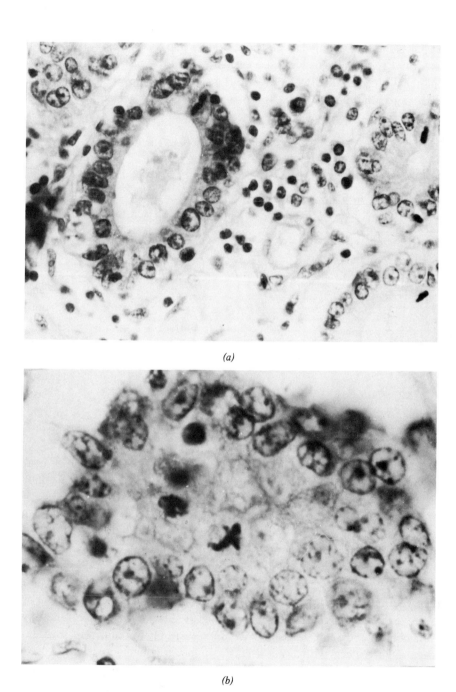

(a)

(b)

Figure 8.17. Small intestine: Cell division *(a)* and abnormal cell division *(b)* in the gland of Lieberkühn, from a boy aged fifteen who was exposed to the atomic bomb 1,000 meters from the hypocenter; he died on 11 August 1945. (Case 3 from Yamashina's series, Hiroshima.)

the crypts of intestinal glands (Liebow, Warren and DeCoursey 1949). Similar abnormal epithelial cells were also encountered in the gastric mucosa. These epithelial changes of the digestive tract indicate that not only do the cells receiving radiation injury die and desquamate but the goblet cells are also injured, resulting in abnormal regeneration. There were other changes such

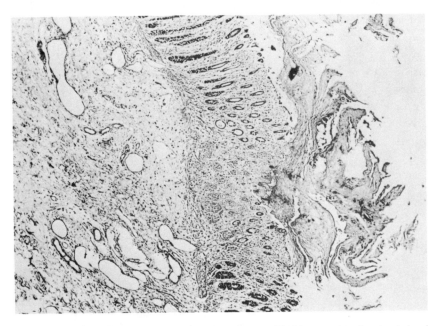

Figure 8.18. Ulcer of large intestine from a fourteen-year-old girl exposed to the atomic bomb 1,800 meters from the hypocenter in Hiroshima; she died on 23 August 1945. (From documents returned to Japan by the United States.)

as edema and petechial hemorrhage of the digestive tract, with the former being marked in the colon and the latter in the gastric mucosa.

In the cases from day 7 and on, ulcerative changes were found in the stomach, the small intestine, or the colon. In 1945, S. Ōhashi and M. Miyake (Army Medical School 1953, p. 285), reviewing Yamashina's series, described that the most outstanding findings were the pseudomembranous change or ulcer formation in the intestine appearing in three cases with a relatively long clinical course in the early stage. In case 9 (day 8), numerous soybean-sized shallow ulcers with a yellow-gray pseudomembranous coating or erosive changes were found along the cecum and the upper colon. In case 11 (day 9), shallow ulcers the size of a red bean or a broad bean occurred in the duodenum and the proximal portion of the jejenum, while in case 12 (day 9) there were changes of pseudomembranous colitis. The site of ulcer formation sometimes coincided with that of lymphatic apparatus. The surface of the ulcers was covered by necrotic tissue, with only a few cells (polymorpho-nuclear leukocytes extremely few) being seen in these areas. Liebow, Warren and DeCoursey (1949) noted abnormal epithelial cells in the small intestine (giant nucleated or binuclear cells) and focal ulceration in a case at Nagasaki (day 11). A large number of bacilli was detected at the site of the ulcer, where there were no leukocytes. Radiation injury of epithelial cells and lack of leukocytes can be considered to have triggered the formation of ulcers.

A marked change of the esophagus was seen in case 1 (a nineteen-year-old male, died on 16 August), autopsied at Hiroshima Sanatorium. In this case there were also gangrenous tonsillitis and findings of pseudomembranous inflammation extending from the upper esophagus to the pharynx. The covering epithelia of the esophagus had completely fallen into necrosis and was covered by large colonies of bacilli. There was only congestion without any cellular reaction.

Changes of Gonads and Endocrine Glands. Changes of the *testicles* appeared as early as four to five days after exposure (Yamashina's cases 1 and 2). The changes consisted of degeneration and desquamation of seminiferous epithelium (spermatogonia), with a slight decrease in spermatids and sperms (figure 8.19). On the other hand, there seemed to be an increase in Sertoli cells. The *ovaries*, although only a few cases could be examined, have been

Figure 8.19. Ablation [detachment] of the seminiferous epithelia in the testis of a thirty-two-year-old man exposed to the atomic bomb 1,000 meters from the hypocenter; he died on 11 August 1945. (Case 4 of Yamashina's series, Hiroshima.)

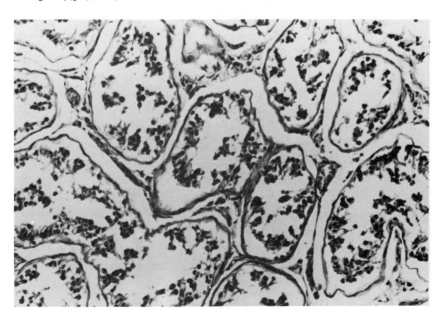

described as showing pyknotic nuclei of primary follicles and nuclear destruction in some cases. In the *adrenals,* there were atrophy of the cortex, decreased amount of lipoid in the outer zone of cortex, interstitial edema, increased pigmentation in the reticular zone, and in some cases infiltration of plasma cells. In the *pituitary glands,* basophilic cells showed vacuolar changes, pyknotic nuclei, and poorly staining cytoplasm (figure 8.20). The capillaries in

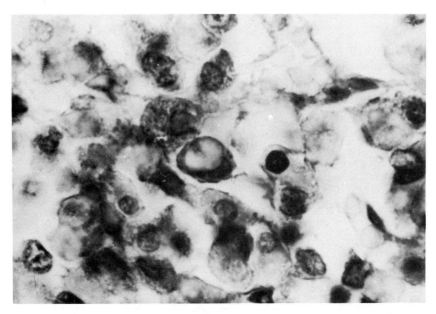

Figure 8.20. Pituitary gland showing vacuolation of basophilic cells, from a thirty-nine-year-old man exposed to the atomic bomb 1,000 meters from the hypocenter in Hiroshima; he died on 12 August 1945. (Case 5 of Yamashina's series, Hiroshima.)

the interstitial tissue were, in general, remarkably dilated. Vacuolar change of basophilic cells usually occurs in burns; but since these changes were also seen in cases without burns, radiation effect cannot be excluded (Miyake 1953*b,* p. 375). The *thyroid* revealed decreased contents of colloid, basophility of colloid, and often atrophic follicles. Ōhashi and Miyake have pointed out vacuolar changes and desquamation of epithelial cells, while Amano noted furrows of the wall of follicles.

Other Pathological Changes and Early Radiation Death. Various pathological changes were found in other organs and tissues. Those who received thermal injuries demonstrated loss of water and concentration of blood accompanied by changes suggestive of circulatory shock. Other changes such as anemia, hemorrhagic diathesis, leukopenia,* infection, and diarrhea were con-

---

* *Leukopenia* is reduction in quantity of leukocytes in the blood. (Ed.)

sidered to have contributed to shock and imbalance of electrolytes. It was extremely difficult to clarify the cause of death in those terminating in the early stage without any thermal injuries or obvious fatal traumas. Such a case of early radiation death can be represented by case 2 of Yamashina's series (a twenty-four-year-old male, 800 meters from the hypocenter, died on 10 August). The main findings at autopsy are shown in table 8.26. Besides

TABLE 8.26

Pathological Findings of Case 2 Autopsied by Yamashina

1. Multiple contusions on face, right shoulder, right forearm, left elbow, and both legs.
2. Contused wounds of the head; a crushed wound of soft tissue about 1 cm in diameter, with a lentil-sized defect of skull on the occipital region, and a small intramuscular bleeding lesion on the left temporal region.
3. Right pleural cavity containing a small volume of bloody fluid.
4. Pericardial petechial and myocardial hemorrhage.
5. Pleural petechiae and hemorrhage in pulmonary parenchyma.
6. Bilateral lungs with disseminated fibrous and fibrocaseous tubercules and mild emphysematous lesion.
7. Liver and kidneys showing mild parenchymal degeneration.
8. Spleen with depletion of lymphocytes and obscure lymphatic nodules.
9. Systemic lymph nodes showing marked atrophy.
10. Bone marrow markedly deteriorated.
11. Adrenals slightly atrophic.
12. Stomach with numerous mucosal petechiae.
13. Small intestine with abnormal epithelium and containing ascarids.

Source: Hiroshima University, Research Institute for Nuclear Medicine and Biology, *Report on the Scientific Materials and Data of Atomic Bomb Disasters. On the returned materials from the Armed Forces Institute of Pathology,* report no. 1 (Hiroshima: Hiroshimadaigaku Genbaku Hōshanō-igaku Kenkyūsho, 1973), p. 95.

injury to bone marrow and lymphatic tissue and hemorrhagic diathesis, no pathological changes were suggestive as the direct cause of death in this particular case. There is some doubt about traumatic injury of the brain (no description of the brain); but if such injury can be excluded, death may have been caused by direct radiation injury or radiation shock. Although the existence of a nonresponsive bacterial infection cannot be denied, there is no evidence to support it as the cause of death. A few similar cases were also encountered in those of stage II*b*.

CRITICAL STAGE TO RECOVERY STAGE—PATHOLOGY OF STAGE II

The main cause of death in stage I was thermal injury; and with the lapse of time, radiation injury became manifest with the appearance of serious symptoms. Bone marrow injury, epilation, fever, oral and pharyngeal changes, and bloody diarrhea occurred more markedly in stage II*a*. On the other hand, signs of recuperation began to appear during the later phase of this stage and continued to stage II*b*. Basically, the pathological changes in this stage were characterized by severe hemorrhagic diathesis and altered defensive mechanism of the body caused by atomic bomb radiation and accompanying infection.

Epilation and Changes in the Skin. Epilation appeared approximately fourteen days after exposure to the atomic bomb, as though it were an advanced notice of serious dysfunction of the bone marrow. Pathologically, epilation is caused by an inhibition in the ability of the hair matrix to differentiate and proliferate into the sheath-shaped cellular tissue forming the hair bulb (outer and inner root sheath). Atrophy of the inner root sheath, which produces hair, was especially remarkable. The hair matrix was also atrophic. Not only the hair root but also the entire epidermis, the epithelial cells of sweat glands, and the sebaceous gland all demonstrated marked atrophy (figure 8.21). From these findings, it can be assumed that epilation is a partial phenomenon of radiation injury to the entire skin (Matsusaka 1972).

In an examination of skin that had escaped thermal injury in stage I, a relatively remarkable change could already be detected. According to the 1945 study of Ōhashi and Miyake (*see* Army Medical School 1953, p. 285), conspicuous changes were found histologically in the skin, where no gross findings of thermal injury, or only mild changes, were evident. These changes consisted of disappearance of nuclei from cells of the granular layer, vacuolar changes of the prickle cells, pyknotic nuclei of basal cells, atrophy of sweat gland and sebaceous gland, hyalinization of connective tissue of hair bulb, atrophy of inner hair root sheath, degeneration of cells of outer hair root

Figure 8.21. Atrophy of hair follicle in the skin of a forty-five-year-old man exposed to the atomic bomb 1,000 meters from the hypocenter; he died on 2 September 1945, in Hiroshima. (From documents returned to Japan by the United States.)

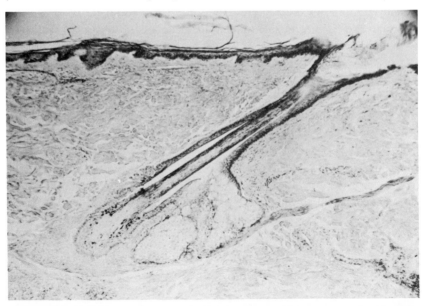

sheath, and congestive capillaries in dermis. Epilation in stage II was probably brought about by the progress of these changes. Besides epilation, these dermal changes led to ulcer formation, which was not directly related to thermal injury. As the ulcers showed no signs of leukocytic reaction, there may have been deteriorated function of bone marrow and infection along with radiation injury.

Changes in Hematopoietic Organs, Especially in Bone Marrow. The destruction of hematopoietic organs became much more conspicuous in stage II*a*. At the end of this stage, variegated regenerative and reparative changes were admixed with infection. The regenerative and reparative process appeared somewhat earlier in the lymphocytic series as compared with those of the myeloid series. Although only sparse lymphocytes were seen in the *spleen* in stage II*a*, lymphocytes of the follicles recovered somewhat, and the atrophic follicles maintained their original structure up to a certain point. These signs indicate that the lymphatic tissue recovers and can send out lymphocytes into the circulation at an earlier phase than the bone marrow (Amano 1964, p. 630). Hyalinous deposits were found in the walls and surrounding tissue of central arteries of splenic follicles.

According to Miyake's description (1953*b*, p. 375) of the *bone marrow* from stages II to III, myeloid cells almost completely disappeared from the marrow in stage II*a*, it was aplastic, and there was slight proliferation of reticulum cells and plasma cells (figure 8.22). There was also loss of erythroblasts and megakaryocytes accompanied by capillary congestion and marked hemorrhage. About one week before entering stage II*b*, the first cells to

Figure 8.22. Bone marrow showing hyperplasia of plasma cells and reticulum cells, from a man exposed to the atomic bomb 1,000 meters from the hypocenter in Hiroshima; he died on 1 September 1945, at the age of twenty-seven. (From documents returned to Japan by the United States.)

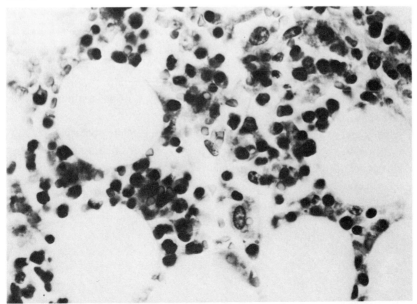

appear were myelocytes and monocytes, then followed by erythroblasts and megakaryocytes. Although the maturation process was insufficient, the bone marrow in stage II*b* revealed myeloblasts, myelocytes, stab cells, and polymorphonuclear leukocytes. In stage III, there was excessive proliferation of these cells, while some megakaryocytes showed figures of degeneration. The changes of hematopoiesis, reproductive organs, and skin according to the stage of progress are shown in table 8.27 (Miyake).

TABLE 8.27

Process of Injury, Regeneration, and Reconvalescence Caused by A-Bomb Radiation in Various Cel

Stage Cell	I	II*a*	II*b*	III
Myelopoietic	pre-aplastic	aplastic-regenerative	reconvalescence	hyperplastic
Erythropoietic	pre-aplastic	aplastic-regenerative		reconvalescen
Megakaryopoietic	pre-aplastic	aplastic-regenerative	reconvalescence	
Lymphocytopoietic	aplastic		reconvalescence	
Spermatogenetic	pre-aplastic	disturbance of maturation	disturbance of maturation	reconvalescen
Oogenetic	pre-aplastic	disturbance of maturation	disturbance of maturation	reconvalescen
Skin, hair-root	pre-aplastic	epilation	reconvalescence	

Pre-aplastic stage: Primitive proliferating cells have been destroyed, whereas mature cells remain undestroyed.
Aplastic stage: Both primitive and mature cells have disappeared; no new cells yet formed.
Stage of regeneration or stage of disturbance of maturation: Primitive cells initiated to proliferate; maturation of cells not yet completed.
Stage of reconvalescence or stage of hyperplasia: Mature cells also appear, and even increase.
Source: M. Miyake, "Pathology of atomic bomb injuries: Acute and subacute stage," in PSH (1953), p. 375.

On the other hand, Liebow, Warren, and DeCoursey (1949) classified into four types the histopathological changes of the bone marrow fifteen days or more after exposure: type A—marrows showing marked hypoplasia;* type B—marrows showing marked focal reticulum hyperplasia;† type C—marrows showing focal myeloid regeneration; type D—marrows showing myeloid hyperplasia. Comparing these four types with Miyake's stages, A and B are found in stage II*a;* B and C between the end of stages II*a* and II*b,* and D in stage III. S. Amano (1956, p. 1725) classified the bone marrow changes into the following three types: *a*—aplastic bone marrow; *b*—aplastic bone marrow with focal regeneration; and *c*—bone marrow with suppressed maturation. The changes occurring in the bone marrow will be summarized with special reference to Amano's description.

Since there was almost complete disappearance of hemoblasts (hematopoietic precursor cells), aplastic bone marrow contained neither granulocytic, erythrocytic, nor platelet series (megakaryocytes), and there was also a prominent depletion of lymphocytes. The only cellular element seen were phagocytic

* *Hypoplasia* is defective development. (Ed.)
† *Hyperplasia* is abnormal multiplication of normal cells. (Ed.)

reticulum cells and plasma cells, with the latter predominating around blood vessels. In ordinary cases, proliferation of fatty tissue is frequently found in bone marrow—a sign of depletion or loss of hematopoietic cells. However, in the aplastic marrow of those exposed to the atomic bomb in Hiroshima and Nagasaki, the interstitium was watery and gelatinous, and there were hemorrhage and fibrin deposits. These specific findings of aplastic marrow were characteristic features of bone marrow injury caused by the atomic bomb. Bacterial colonies were seen in the marrow of cases with bacteremia. They caused tissue necrosis but lacked leukocytic reaction in the surrounding tissue. Bone marrow with marked hemorrhage grossly resembled a red marrow.

By the end of stage II*b*, patchy figures or islets of cellular regeneration appear in the aplastic marrow (figure 8.23). Although Liebow et al. described hyperplasia of reticulum cells, it is not clear what is meant by reticulum cells. Amano attached importance of regeneration of monocytes preceding regeneration of the neutrophilic series. Regeneration of hematopoietic cells occurred in small groups of cells of the same series. The site of regeneration of various cells did not indicate any selectivity to a specific structure as observed in normal ontogenesis, and seemed to occur at random in clusters.

In the bone marrow with suppressed maturation, the regenerating cells did not reach their ultimate stage of maturation, and were not sent into the peripheral blood, but accumulated in the marrow. Suppression of maturation occurred in all blood cell series, including neutrophils, erythrocytes, and platelets. Since regeneration of neutrophils occurred first and was followed later by erythroblasts and megakaryocytes, suppressed maturation of the neutrophilic series was the most prominent feature in the marrow. This appears to be hyperplasia and focally closely simulates a leukemic change. Repair of the basic structure of the bone marrow is not complete and shows imperfect formation of sinusoids and admixture of fatty tissue and postnecrotic cicatrical fibrotic lesions. These were the characteristic features of bone marrow injury of this type.

Hemorrhage and Infection of Organs. Hemorrhage and infection occurred in various organs as a result of severe injury to the bone marrow and its accompanying functional insufficiency. These symptoms were most frequently encountered in stage II and were important causes of death. Hemorrhage covering a wide area was found in the serosa (pericardium, pleura, peritoneum) and mucosa (digestive tract, respiratory passage, genitourinary tract). Myocardium, lungs, kidneys, and intracranium were also the sites of hemorrhage, which, depending on its site and amount, sometimes proved fatal.

Among the various infections, oropharyngitis was most frequently seen. Necrotizing tonsillitis occurred in the majority of cases, followed by infection

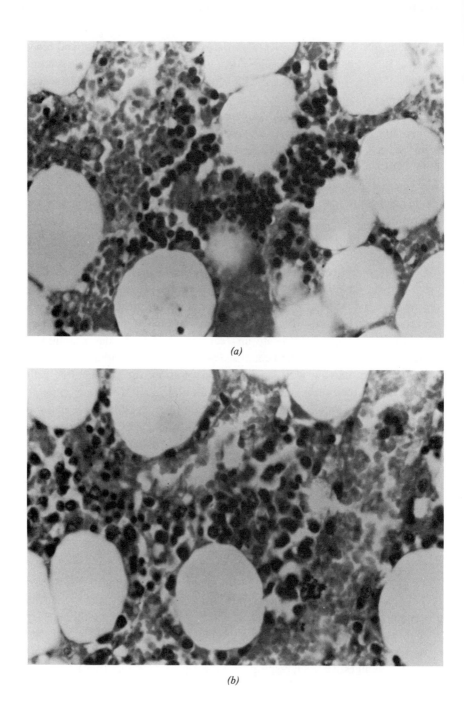

(a)

(b)

Figure 8.23. Bone marrow: regeneration of erythroblasts *(a)* and of granulocytes *(b);* both are from a man aged twenty-eight who was exposed to the atomic bomb 8oo meters from the hypocenter in Hiroshima. (Contributed by Tetsurō Shimamine, Tokyo Imperial University.)

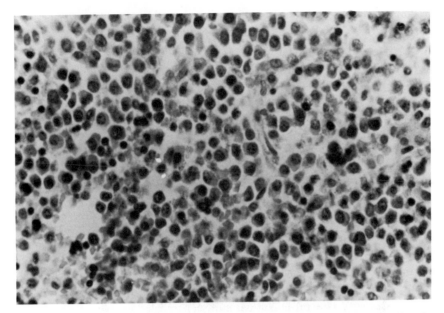

Figure 8.24. Bone marrow: hyperplastic regeneration of granulocytes eight weeks after the bombing; from a sixteen-year-old boy exposed to the atomic bomb 1,600 meters from the hypocenter in Nagasaki. (Contributed by Tetsurō Shimamine, Tokyo Imperial University.)

of large intestine, esophagus, bronchus, lungs, uterus, and urinary tract. These sites became the portal of entry and caused generalized infection (septicemia, bacteremia) in not a few cases. The characteristic features of the infected sites were marked gangrenous or necrotic changes, hemorrhage, active exudation of fibrin, and lack of neutrophilic reaction—that is, it was a condition of aleukocytic inflammation.

Fifty cases (Hiroshima Sanatorium [Kusano 1953b, p. 1346], Tokyo Imperial University [1953, p. 1394], Okayama University Medical School [Tanabe 1953, p. 1483], Hiroshima Medical College [Tamagawa 1953a, p. 1497]) were selected from the autopsy cases in stage IIa, and the incidence of various pathological changes was examined. Hemorrhagic diathesis or hemorrhage occurred in almost all cases. Among the various infections, gangrenous, hemorrhagic infection of oral cavity and pharynx—such as necrotizing tonsillitis—was encountered in 33 cases, the incidence of which is compatible with that of epilation (36 cases). This infection was followed by skin ulcer (10 cases), necrotizing, ulcerative changes in large intestine (9 cases), similar changes of small intestine (6 cases), necrotizing esophagitis (5 cases), and gastric ulcer (2 cases). The common findings of the lungs were pulmonary edema (16 cases), hemorrhagic foci (4 cases), and pneumonia (7 cases). The high incidence of pulmonary edema is noteworthy, in contrast to the frequency of emphysema in stage I. Although the participation of infection cannot be denied in those described as pulmonary edema or pulmonary hemorrhage, the main cause of pulmonary edema can be assumed to be cardiac insufficiency and vascular injury of the lungs following radiation. Pulmonary infection (aleukocytic pneumonia) became more apparent in stage II*b,* and the severe changes of the oropharynx in stage II*a* were considered as the portal of entry of the generalized infection (bacteremia) in many cases. Thermal injury was the cause of death in 6 cases, and trauma in 5 cases, the signs of which are quite different from those in stage I.

Thirty cases (Hiroshima Sanatorium [Kusano 1953*b,* p. 1346], Tokyo Imperial University, [1953, p. 1394], Okayama University Medical School [Tanabe 1953, p. 1483], Hiroshima Medical College [Tamagawa 1953*a,* p. 1497], and Kyoto Imperial University [Sugiyama et al. 1953, p. 895]) in stage II*b* were examined as in stage II*a.* Epilation tended to decrease with 12 cases, but there were still 22 cases with lesions of the oropharynx. The number of pulmonary infections increased with 17 cases, and the incidence of fibrinous or ulcerative colitis rose with 11 cases. In other words, there was an increase in the cases with visceral inflammatory lesions, including even nephritis.

The noteworthy visceral change in stage II was jaundice: it developed in 11 out of 50 cases in stage II*a* and in 4 out of 30 cases in stage II*b.* Although the cause of jaundice was obscure, findings of ordinary hepatitis were not seen. Since there were many cases with findings of hemosiderosis of the liver and other organs, it can be considered that acceleration of hemolysis, hemorrhagic diathesis from platelet injury, and deteriorated liver cell function may contribute to this condition. Deteriorated liver cell function might result from marked congestion, from generalized infection, and furthermore, from malnutrition. Malnutrition was the result of food shortage during the war and played an important role in the clinical history of those exposed to the atomic bomb.

Gonads and Endocrine Glands. Atrophy of the *testes* was prominent in stage II with the wall of the seminiferous tubules being almost completely occupied by Sertoli cells, and spermatogonia and other cells were hardly discernible (figure 8.25). In some cases, irregular-shaped giant cells and multinucleated cells surrounded by Sertoli cells were found in the center of atrophic seminiferous tubules. The testes in stage II*b* demonstrated atrophic and destroyed seminiferous tubules with thick basal membrane. Atrophy of the *ovaries* became more prominent as compared with that in stage I, and there was also depletion of follicles. Acidophils predominated in the *pituitary glands* with the least number of chromophobes. Paranuclear vacuoles were frequently seen in the basophils. It has already been mentioned that M. Miyake considered the vacuolar change in the basophils to be a result of radiation injury. Liebow, Warren, and DeCoursey (1949), however, interpreted this change

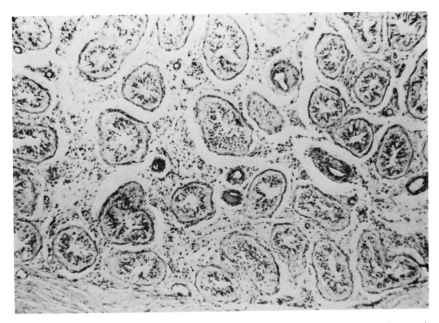

Figure 8.25. Testis showing atrophy, from a twenty-five-year-old man exposed to the atomic bomb 1,000 meters from the hypocenter in Hiroshima; he died on 22 September 1945. (From documents returned to Japan by the United States.)

in basophils to be secondary to atrophy of gonads ("castration cells"). Atrophy of the *adrenal cortex* was extremely marked, together with diminution of lipoid content. No definite changes were found in the *thyroid,* but atrophy of follicles and alteration of colloid were frequent findings.

LATE PHASE OF ACUTE STAGE—PATHOLOGY OF STAGE III

According to the autopsy findings in stage III, these cases may be roughly divided into three groups: (1) those with visceral infection, (2) those showing aggravation of chronic disease such as pulmonary tuberculosis, and (3) those showing general improvement of injury sustained from exposure to the atomic bomb but complicated accidentally by other diseases. One case developed leukemia. In the first group, most cases revealed pulmonary gangrene or necrotizing pneumonia, and fibrinous necrotizing colitis; but with the gradual regeneration and recovery of bone marrow, leukocytic reaction began to appear in these lesions. The following is a description of the bone marrow of a case eighty-eight days after exposure in Nagasaki: "The bone marrow of the femur showed dilatation of engorged capillaries, and although erythropoiesis could not be seen in-between fatty tissue, there was regeneration of myelopoiesis (leukocytopoiesis).* These regenerative foci were mainly com-

* *Myelopoiesis* is the formation of blood cells in the bone marrow; *leukocytopoiesis* is the production of leukocytes. (Ed.)

posed of myeloblasts, scanty myelocytes, and an admixture of cells with fragmented nuclei. There were only a few small megakaryocytes having pyknotic nuclei and suppressed maturation (K. Ono et al. 1953*b*, p. 1011)." Recovery of leukocytic reaction was insufficient. S. Matsuoka (1959, p. 919) noted characteristic foci of proliferating cells in the marrow of those exposed to the atomic bomb and used the term "blast focus" for such a lesion.

In the Collection of the Reports on the Investigation of the Atomic Bomb Casualties, the term *cachectic condition* has been used in describing the pathological condition of those in months 3 to 4. Observations were made mainly by Urabe and Keuke, who stated that the characteristic features were composed of progressive emaciation, dry skin and mucosa, frequent subicteric* conditions, edema in places, occasional ascites,† frequent persistent diarrhea, marked anemia, and disturbances of liver and renal functions (Urabe and Keuke 1953*a*, p. 684; 1953*b*, p. 697). These cases did not necessarily have incurable wounds or purulent complications; but when they did have trauma, the condition of the wound became poor and showed no tendency to cure. The victims with these symptoms showed no response to therapy and died. Among the 141 patients with severe injuries from the atomic bomb admitted to the Nagasaki City Shinkōzen Hospital, 15 demonstrated typical cachectic conditions, while 7 more cases also showed a similar tendency. The marked anemia, malnutrition, and persistent infection under a deteriorated function of bone marrow are considered to be the essential qualities of the cachectic condition.

The case in which leukemia developed was that of a nineteen-year-old male, who was exposed to the atomic bomb in Nagasaki approximately 1,000 meters from the hypocenter while working in an arsenal plant. There was no trauma, with only a small thermal injury of the right foot. He had noted anorexia for two to three days following exposure, but soon recovered and was living an ordinary life. On 28 August, he noted epilation; this condition was followed by onset of fever on 3 September and by skin petechiae and pharyngeal pain on 6 September. Examination of blood revealed a red cell count of 3.15 million, a white cell count of 850, and 22,600 nucleated cells in bone marrow. He was admitted to hospital on 8 September; and after three weeks of therapy he had improved, with his red cell count reaching 3.92 million, and his white cell count, 5,500, on 30 September. He was discharged on the same day and returned to normal life. In early November he complained of malaise at labor service; and on 6 November he noted headache, febrile sense, gingival swelling and hemorrhage, pharyngeal swelling and hemorrhage. Other signs and symptoms, such as high fever and skin

---

* *Subicteric* denotes a tendency to jaundice. (Ed.)
† *Ascites* is an accumulation of serous fluid in the peritoneal cavity.

petechiae (7 November) and bloody stool (9 November), appeared, and examination of blood showed a red cell count of 3.04 million and a white cell count of 0.39 million. Since the latter was monocytic, a diagnosis of monocytic leukemia was made. He took a rapid downhill course and died on 16 November, ninety-nine days after the explosion. The femur of this case showed a red marrow with general features of a regenerative marrow. There were scattered foci of patchy, grayish-white lesions composed of monocytoid leukemic cells. These lesions lacked fatty tissue and were demarcated by engorged capillaries. The growth was almost completely made up of leukemic cells with only a few erythroblasts and small megakaryocytes having degenerative nuclei. Normal myeloid cells (leukocytic series) could hardly be detected.*

PATHOLOGY OF THE CENTRAL NERVOUS SYSTEM

Changes occurring in the central nervous system, especially in the brain, after exposure to the atomic bomb have been carefully examined and described by many authors, including specialists in the field of neuropathology: K. Okada, Y. Shimazono, and S. Hakamada (1953, p. 757); H. Shiraki (1953, p. 759; Shiraki and J. Andō [1956]; Shiraki et al. 1958a); C. Tamagawa et al. (1952b); and Y. Uchimura and Shiraki (1952a; 1952b). Under the Joint Commission program, a systemic study of the brains of 49 cases was made with the cooperation of American and Japanese scientists: H. Shiraki, Y. Uchimura, S. Matsuoka, S. Takeya, C. Tamagawa, K. Koyano, S. Amano, M. Araki, W. W. Ayres, and W. Haymaker (Shiraki et al. 1958a). The forty-nine cases consisted of thirty-three from Hiroshima and sixteen from Nagasaki. Forty-seven cases were those sixteen to sixty-nine days after the explosion, and two cases were those with chronic aplastic anemia developing four years and nine months and six years and three months after exposure. Seven cases were within 1 kilometer of the hypocenter; thirty-one cases were between 1 and 2 kilometers; one case, 2.7 kilometers; for the remaining ten cases, distances are unknown.

The main cerebral changes consisted of traumatic injury to brain and meninges; of subarachnoidal, intraventricular, and perivascular hemorrhage from hemorrhagic diathesis; of anoxic changes due to marked anemia (formation of glial nodules, degenerative changes of nerve cells); and of marked nuclear swelling of astrocytes in the globus pallidus and the substantia nigra. Although swelling of the nuclei of astrocytes in the brain stem is known to be related to liver dysfunction, there was no clear-cut correlation between nuclear change and jaundice. Changes of cerebral vasculature, especially small vessels, in radiation injury attracted much attention; and, in fact, accelerated

* Misao, Haraguchi, and Hattori 1953, p. 1041; Ono et al. 1953a, p. 1000, and 1953b, p. 1011.

permeability of small vessels was extremely prominent and a common finding in the brain of those exposed to the atomic bomb. Such vascular changes, however, may occur in a hemorrhagic condition and anemia, so that it was difficult to decide from just the autopsy findings how much radiation participated directly in inducing such a lesion.

ATOMIC BOMB INJURY, ESPECIALLY INJURY IN THE ACUTE STAGE AND INDUCED RADIOACTIVITY

The role played by induced radioactivity in atomic bomb injury should also be mentioned. In the initial pathological surveys made on atomic bomb injury at Hiroshima and Nagasaki, it was S. Amano who attached great importance to the pathogenetic role played by the activity of neutrons and neutron-induced radioactivity of various elements of the body. He mentioned the opposing opinions held by the American scientists and the Kyoto Imperial University members about whether the pathogenetic action of the atomic bomb was triggered by gamma rays alone or by secondary radioactivity following neutrons (Amano 1964, p. 630). Contrary to the passive evaluation of induced radioactivity made by the American team at that time, Amano emphasized that neutrons alone acted on the body as the most important factor of injury. Amano's assertion was based on the results of measuring induced radioactivity from various tissues of the body during autopsy (M. Shimamoto and G. Unno) and also on the specificity of pathological changes (Sugiyama et al. 1953, p. 895).

On the other hand, in 1967, M. Miyake, H. Sugano, T. Yokoyama, K. Yamaguchi and M. Hara stated that, although various values of induced radioactivity per gram of bone tissue of those exposed to the atomic bomb had been reported at that time, there were no definitive values. These researchers then attempted to estimate the induced radioactivity in the bodies of experimental mice. In this experiment, a neutron dose compatible with that 1 to 1.5 kilometers from the hypocenter in Hiroshima (approximately 140 rads of fast neutron, of which 27 percent were thermal neutrons) was irradiated. The radioactive elements detected were manganese 55, sodium 24, chlorine 38, and phosphorus 32 (and, theoretically, calcium 49) among which phosphorus 32 and sodium 24 were to become a subject of discussion from the standpoint of energy and half-life. Beta rays amounted to 23 rads of sodium 24 and to 34.4 rads of phosphorus 32; and these were extremely small, compared to the initial radiation. Gamma rays were much smaller; and it was concluded that the role played by induced radioactivity in the acute stage of atomic bomb injury was almost negligible.

As for injuries of blood and hematopoietic tissues following irradiation by neutron beam, there are the experimental studies carried out by Hanaoka

(1959; 1964, p. 541), one of Amano's collaborators. Although a relatively marked secondary radioactivity was recognized for up to forty hours in the bone of mice irradiated with neutron-gamma rays, Hanaoka states that their effects are minimal at least in acute radiation injury, but that continuous irradiation of beta or gamma rays in the body, especially in bone marrow, may play an important role in inducing leukemia. He further mentioned the possibility of genetic effects.

Chapter 9

Aftereffects and Genetic Effects

Keloid

The victims who received marked primary thermal burns or flash burns in the central areas of Hiroshima and Nagasaki, near the hypocenters, were simultaneously injured by a tremendous blast and radiation; and most of them were killed instantly or died on the same day, or at least near the end of stage I. Those who suffered thermal injury in areas 1,000 to 2,000 meters from the hypocenter, had heated or charred garments and varying degrees of secondary thermal injury (contact burns, flame burns) in addition to moderate flash burns. These secondary injuries were similar in nature to the injuries in cases of flame burn and resembled grade 3 or grade 4 thermal burns, in which great damage occurs in the deeper dermis and in subcutaneous tissue. Since these lesions were frequently complicated by flash burns, they took a long time to heal. It cannot be denied that the poor living conditions during and after the war also contributed to this long healing time and led to the suppuration of burns, to delayed repair of wounds, and to the formation of thick scars in subcutaneous tissue (figure 9.1). Then scar tissue contracted, resulting in deformity or functional disturbance. These aftereffects were most marked on face, neck, and fingers.

At first the majority of flash burns (primary thermal injury), frequently occurring in districts within 2,000 to 3,000 meters of the hypocenter, healed within a relatively short time with the formation of simple, thin scars. It is

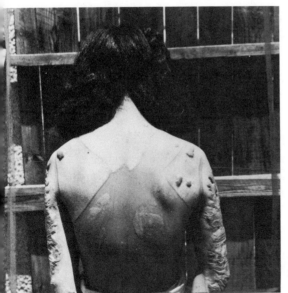

(a)

Figure 9.1. Keloid formation on burned skin.
Photographs taken (a) on July 1947 in Hiroshima
and (b) on February 1947 in Nagasaki.
(Selected from Masao Tsuzuki's collection.)

(b)

noteworthy, however, that the scars caused by flash burns had markedly altered to become keloids after more than three to four months (Tsuzuki 1954*c*).

The development of scars and keloids has been reported by S. Hatano and T. Watanuki (1953, p. 621) for Hiroshima and by R. Shirabe and H. Tezuka (1959) for Nagasaki.

In December 1946, Hatano and Watanuki, in their investigation of atomic bomb casualties in Hiroshima, noted a high incidence of keloids among students (primary and middle school). The conditions at the time of the explosion are shown in table 9.1. Among the survivors, the cases actually examined totaled 426, including 388 thermal burns, 63 radiation illnesses, 39 traumas, 5 without trauma, and 247 with keloid developing from the surface of thermal burns (table 9.2). The incidence of keloid in students exposed outdoors at a distance of 1.6 kilometers was 89.1 percent (41 out of 46 burned); at 2.1 kilometers, 94.5 percent (52/55) and 87.1 percent (95/109); and at 2.3 kilometers, 32.6 percent (51/156). The one person burned indoors at 1.2 kilometers had keloids. Of the 19 burned in shade outdoors at 1.3 kilometers, 7 had keloids (36.8 percent); and of the 2 in shade at 2.1 kilometers, none had keloids. The total keloids and thermal burns in the 239 cases developing these conditions after thermal burns received outdoors were 697 and 2,128, respectively. They were distributed as follows:

	Number of Keloids	Number of Thermal Burns	Percentage
Face	131	334	39.2
Neck	89	292	30.4
Upper arm/ shoulder	140	276	50.7
Forearm	115	235	48.9
Hand	83	281	29.5
Back	19	94	20.2
Chest	27	63	42.8
Thigh	39	94	41.4
Lower leg	23	83	27.7
Foot	13	67	19.4
Hip	9	26	34.6
Abdomen	4	22	18.1

Table 9.3 shows the number of days from thermal burn to the development of keloid. The highest incidence was found between 61 and 90 days (October–November 1945) from the date of injury, and keloids tended to develop when the thermal burns were about cured.

TABLE 9.1
Casualties among Pupils and Students in Hiroshima

Name of School	Number of Cases	Distance from Hypocenter (km)	Exposed Condition	Survived	Killed	Mortality Rate (%)
Second Hiroshima Prefectural High School (first year)	308	0.6	outdoors	0	308	100.0
Hiroshima Municipal Girls' High School (first year)	277	0.6	outdoors and in shade	0	277	100.0
Hiroshima Municipal Girls' High School (second year)	264	0.6	outdoors and in shade	0	264	100.0
Hiroshima Municipal Ship-building School (first year)	200	0.8	outdoors	0	200	100.0
First Hiroshima Prefectural Girls' High School (fourth year)	40	0.8	indoors	0	40	100.0
First Hiroshima Prefectural High School (third year)	40	0.9	outdoors	0	40	100.0
First Hiroshima Prefectural Girls' High School (first year)	250*	0.9	outdoors	0	250*	100.0
First Hiroshima Prefectural High School (first year)	150*	1.2	outdoors	0	150*	100.0
First Hiroshima Prefectural High School (first year)	150*	1.2	indoors	17	133*	88.6
Second Hiroshima Prefectural Girls' High School (second year)	37	1.3	outdoors	1	36	97.2
Hiroshima Prefectural Commercial High School (second year)	44	1.3	outdoors	0	44	100.0
Third Primary School (boys)	72	1.3	outdoors	1	71	98.6
Third Primary School (girls)	139	1.3	outdoors and in shade	68	71	51.0
First Hiroshima Prefectural High School (third year)	75	1.6	outdoors	74	1	1.3
Second Hiroshima Prefectural Girls' High School (first year)	71	2.1	outdoors	70	1	1.4
Second Hiroshima Prefectural Girls' High School (second year)	40*	2.1	in shade	40*	0	0
Hiroshima Prefectural Commercial High School (first year)	250*	2.1	outdoors and in shade	over 233	below 17	6.8†
Hiroshima Prefectural Commercial High School (second year)	200*	2.1	outdoors and in shade	over 185	below 15	7.5†
Second Hiroshima Prefectural High School (second year)	200*	2.3	outdoors	200*	0	0
Hiroshima Municipal Ship-building School (first year)	140	3.5	indoors	139	1	0.7

* Approximate.
† Including those dead at home and other places.
Source: S. Hatano and T. Watanuki, "A-bomb disaster investigation report—fourth investigation: Chiefly concerned with occurrence of keloids due to thermal burns of atomic bomb," in CRIABC (1953), vol. I, p. 621.

TABLE 9.2

Occurrence of Keloids as the Sequelae of Burns and Traumatic Injuries among Pupils and Students

Name of School	Distance from Hypocenter (km)	Number of Persons Exposed	Exposed Condition		Number of Persons with Burns	Number of Persons with Keloids Caused by Burns*	Number of Persons with Trauma	Number of Persons with Keloids Caused by Trauma	Number of Persons with Radiation Injury	Number of Persons without Injury
First Hiroshima Prefectural High School	1.6	46	outdoors		46	41 (89.1%)	1	0	9	0
Second Hiroshima Prefectural Girls' High School	2.1	56	outdoors	55	55	52 (94.5%)	0	0	5	0
			in shade	1						1
Hiroshima Prefectural Commercial High School	2.1	125	outdoors	109	109	95 (87.1%)	12	0	4	0
			in shade or indoors	16	2	0	10	0	0	4
Second Hiroshima Prefectural High School	2.3	159	outdoors		156	51 (32.6%)	3	0	5	0
First Hiroshima Prefectural High School	1.2	16	indoors		1	1 (100%)	9	1	16	0
Third Primary School	1.3	24	in shade		19	7 (36.8%)	4	1	24	0

* Figures in parentheses are percentages of persons with burns.

Source: S. Hatano and T. Watanuki, "A-bomb disaster investigation report—fourth investigation: Chiefly concerned with occurrence of keloids due to thermal burns of atomic bomb," in CRIABC (1953), vol. I, p. 621.

In August 1946 at Nagasaki, Shirabe and Tezuka asked patients to come to the hospital through a notice in the newspaper; and they found keloid in 106 cases (67.1 percent) among 158 with thermal burn scars and in 24 cases (21 percent) out of 114 cases with traumatic scars. Keloids developed more frequently in females than in males (females, 74.3 percent; males, 62.0 percent) and most commonly in teenagers, especially in males. The majority of cases were at a distance of 1.6 to 2 kilometers from the hypocenter (males, 55.5 percent; females, 56.6 percent).

KELOIDS AND HYPERTROPHIC SCARS

The results of the reports by Hatano and Watanuki (1953, p. 621) and Shirabe and Tezuka (1959) are apparently similar. The incidence of keloids, however, was about 63 percent (247 out of 388) among all students with thermal burns in Hiroshima; while this condition was found in 67.1 percent of those with thermal burn scars in Nagasaki. The incidence of keloids out of the total number of thermal burns (755 cases) in the latter was low—about 14 percent. One of the reasons for this great difference may be attributed to the way in which *keloid* is defined.

Keloid describes an overgrowth of scar tissue on the wound surface during the reparative process following thermal burn. In this condition the tissue forms, on the skin surface, an irregularly shaped protrusion which resembles the shell and legs of a crab. On the other hand, the term *hypertrophic scar* is used for a simple heaping up of thickened scar tissue, and its differentiation from keloid has frequently caused confusion. M. Tsuzuki (1954c), after actually seeing and hearing the discussions of thermal burn scars—especially keloidal changes—concluded that the ambiguous definition for this condition was probably one of the reasons for the great confusion. From June to July 1947, at the time when H. E. Pearse of Rochester University came to Japan to investigate thermal scars, joint studies were made in Hiroshima and Nagasaki; and after many discussions the researchers arrived at the conclusion that, as a general concept, atomic bomb thermal burns should at least be classified into hypertrophic and keloidal types. On this basis, Tsuzuki proposed that thermal scars be classified into the following four types—(1) skin pigmentation or depigmentation, (2) simple scar, (3) hypertrophic scar, and (4) keloid. He had made this suggestion in an article, written with M. A. Block in 1948 (p. 417), on burn scars sustained by atomic bomb survivors.

Later, in 1952, W. Wells and N. Tsukifuji described three types of scars: (1) hypertrophic (2) keloid, and (3) excessive. Tsuzuki (1956, p. 1459), after reviewing these studies, finally came to the conclusion that scars formed as an aftereffect of atomic bomb thermal burns should be divided roughly into hypertrophic and keloid. In other words, a hypertrophic scar was to be consid-

TABLE 9.3

Days of Development of Keloids after the Bombing

Days after Bombing	Number of Persons with Keloids	Percentage of Distribution
1–30	11	4.6
31–60	81	33.8
61–90	86	35.9
91–120	27	11.2
121–150	17	7.1
151–180	3	1.2
181–210	3	1.2
211–240	2	0.8

Source: S. Hatano and T. Watanuki, "A-bomb disaster investigation report—fourth investigation: Chiefly concerned with occurrence of keloids due to thermal burns of atomic bomb," in CRIABC (1953), vol. I, p. 621.

ered as an aftereffect of a secondary thermal burn; and since the injury extended into the deeper subcutaneous tissue, the scar was formed not only in the skin but also in the deeper tissue—resulting in thickening and protrusion from the skin surface, followed by contraction, consolidation, and contracture. Keloid, on the other hand, was an aftereffect of primary thermal burns sustained by survivors at a distance of about 2 kilometers from the hypocenter. These burns apparently healed in a relatively short time and left a thin scar which eventually became elevated from the skin surface. It had a shiny, red-copper surface and a rubbery consistency, could be moved away from the deeper tissue, and was accompanied by stinging pain and itching. The thickening was located in the skin and defined from the surrounding tissue. Keloids developing in atomic bomb survivors were different from those found in other conditions; they covered a larger area and were much thicker.

According to the preceding classification of keloids found in atomic bomb thermal burns, the keloids mentioned in the report by Hatano and Watanuki (1953, p. 621) could include hypertrophic scars. When the incidence of keloids is reviewed, with special attention to protrusion from the skin surface, the figures in Hiroshima would be 54.4 percent (Block and Tsuzuki 1948, p. 417) and 59 percent (Harada 1967). Y. Itō at the Hiroshima Red Cross Hospital examined 606 cases of thermal injuries between September 1945 and February 1946 and found 210 cases (34.7 percent) of keloid among them. From these data, it can be said without question that the incidence of hypertrophic scars and keloids was extremely high as an aftereffect of atomic bomb injury, especially of thermal injury (Tezuka 1967).

CLINICAL COURSE OF KELOIDS

Keloids resulting from atomic bomb injury followed a definite course both in its development and in its recurrence in response to operative procedures and other new stimuli. These keloids gradually became stable and tended to disappear. The development of keloids and hypertrophic scars reached a peak 61 to 90 days after injury and declined remarkably after 150 days or more. As previously shown by the survey made by Hatano and Watanuki (table 9.3), the lesion became pale, rather flat and thin, and paresthesia* also tended to show some improvement with the lapse of time. According to the survey made by C. Tamagawa and G. Katsube (1953, p. 1190) on 200 cases, the clinical course taken by the patients was as shown in table 9.4; and in relation to the clinical course, histopathological findings also

TABLE 9.4

Changes of Clinical Findings of Keloids in the Representative Case

Time of Observation	Ridge of Skin	Color	Tonus of Skin
December 1945	Started to swell	Red	Tensive
May 1946	Reached maximum elevation	Red	Marked tension
July 1946	Flattened partly	Reddish purple	Majority of keloids still tensive; some wrinkled
October 1946	Small keloids flattened out	Purple	Tension slightly diminished
January 1947	Big keloids shrank and wrinkled	Purplish blue	Wrinkled

Source: C. Tamagawa and G. Katsube, "Study on keloids due to the A-bomb exposure," in CRIABC (1953), vol. II, p. 1190.

demonstrated a definite change. H. Tezuka (1967), in his investigation of cases at Nagasaki mentioned that when the 164 cases with keloid not receiving operation and taking a natural course were re-examined thirty months later, all keloids were smaller in size and more prominent in males than in females. The rate of cure was somewhat higher in the younger generation; the size of the lesions was much smaller in those exposed more than 2.6 kilometers from the hypocenter; and the rate of cure was lower in survivors who had been exposed between 1.6 and 2.5 kilometers. A long-term observation between 1946 and 1956 revealed a relatively rapid decrease in size of atomic bomb keloids after its peak in 1946–47, and frequently transformation to ordinary scars. The percentage of the remaining keloids fell year by year; and by February 1956, keloids were found in 55 out of 1,175 with thermal burn scars (4.7 percent) and in 15 out of 1,703 with traumatic scars (0.9 percent). Wells and Tsukifuji (1952) also noted atrophy of protruding scars from the second year and flattening of the lesions—with gradual disappearance—in about two thirds of the cases after four years.

* *Paresthesia* is an abnormal sensation, such as burning or prickling or as though insects were crawling on one's skin. (Ed.)

Keloids frequently recurred after surgical therapy such as resection and skin transplantation. According to Shirabe and Tezuka (1959), in the operations carried out during the early stage, recurrence of keloids was found in a high percentage (62 percent) on the wound surface of the resected portion where skin was grafted, and in the area where skin grafts were taken. This proportion fell to about 20 percent in the cases that were operated on more than eighteen months following exposure to the atomic bomb. G. Katsube (1953, p. 1317) observed elevation of suture during plastic surgery of thermal and traumatic injuries and considered this to be a characteristic feature of keloid. Elevation is a kind of over-repair or keloidlike reaction, which is observed most frequently between six and fourteen months after exposure and runs nearly parallel to the development of keloids. T. Harada (1967), examining scars in the non-active phase after 1955, recognized four types of scar: keloid, hypertrophic, strand-shaped, and contracted. Compared with scars of the early stage, the keloid type showed a prominent protrusion in the early stage, but those with mild elevation were found to transform into strand shapes or to contract. Even at this stage, however, a cicatrical protruding reaction was seen during resection or operation in all cases with prominent keloids from the early stage. This reaction ran parallel with the degree of elevation of the scar in the early stage.

ETIOLOGY AND PATHOGENESIS OF ATOMIC BOMB KELOIDS

The etiology of atomic bomb keloids is unknown. In the first place, the cause of ordinary keloids is also unclear: of the many theories on their etiology, none is decisive. Discussion of atomic bomb keloids has focused on whether thermal rays or radiation itself acted as a key cause, or on whether the participation of these elements could be discounted. The American scientists were mainly of the latter opinion for the following reasons: (1) In the Japanese the incidence of keloids among the exposed was not so high compared with that of keloids occurring in other circumstances; and thus keloids cannot be regarded as a specific aftereffect of atomic bomb injury. (2) Even if their incidence were somewhat higher, this could be considered as a consequence of thermal burns covering a large area of the body, of general lack of nutrition, and of prolonged healing due to lack of proper medical treatment during the early stage (Liebow, Warren, and DeCoursey 1949; Wells and Tsukifuji 1952). On the other hand, most of the Japanese scientists who were actually investigating and treating atomic bomb survivors with keloid confirmed its intimate relation with exposure to the atomic bomb. These scientists recognized a great prevalence of keloids among the exposed survivors who had sustained primary thermal burns within 1.5 to 3 kilometers of the hypocenter. Furthermore, the keloids actually became prominent from six to fourteen months later and subsided thereafter with the lapse of time.

According to M. Tsuzuki (1954c), many survivors with keloids were found among those who received thermal burns at a distance of about 2 kilometers from the hypocenter. In other words, Tsuzuki's report accounts for the high incidence of keloids in survivors who had received both thermal burns and radiation injuries. Simple flash burns that promptly cured and formed scar tissue frequently transformed into keloids, which were prominent and covered a large area of the body with marked elevation. Since a keloid itself is a pathological proliferation of dermal tissue, it must be admitted that the dermal layer of the skin, even though somewhat injured, was in a state where regeneration and repair could be fully expected. Tsuzuki further added that importance should be attached to the thermal action of the atomic bomb, although radioactivity cannot be disregarded. R. Shirabe (1967) stressed the difference in hypertrophic state between thermal scars in atomic bomb injury and those not related to radiation. He further stated that it was impossible to consider the hypertrophic condition of thermal scars as entirely unrelated to radiation. The possibility of endocrine disorder due to irradiation (hyperactivity of thyroid gland; hypofunction of parathyroid and adrenals) in accelerating keloid formation was suggested. The correlation between radiation and keloidal conditions was emphasized by G. Katsube (1953, p. 1317). Measuring the radioactivity of keloid tissue, Katsube confirmed the parallel relationship between radiation dose and degree of scar hyperplasia, and concluded that the cause of keloid may well be radioactivity of a heavier dose than is normally in living body and scar tissue. T. Yonezawa, S. Chin, and A. Takejima (1949) also stressed the effect of radiation.

It was C. Tamagawa* who carried out detailed histopathological studies on atomic bomb keloids from an etiological standpoint. During a four-year period from January 1946, Tamagawa examined the resected tissues of keloid in 420 cases and classified them into three types: (1) simple fibroma, (2) fibroma with marked hyalinization, and (3) polymorphic sarcomatous. Keloid is a lesion showing proliferation of fibrocytes, which are the main components of subcutaneous tissue, and increased connective tissue matrix and fibers. Differing from ordinary granulation tissue, keloid is characterized by wide and large fibrous bundles. Tamagawa postulated that proliferation of fibrocytes in such a state exceeds the limits of repair or reaction and gradually acquires a neoplastic character. This conclusion is especially likely when one observes the third type composed of large, irregularly shaped fibrocytes. In the development of keloids from the early stage to the height of the proliferating stage, the first change noted was the proliferation of capillaries, which guides the proliferation of fibrocytes. These fibrocytes originate from the adventitial cells, and proliferate excessively beyond the limits of repair, leading to a tumorous transformation. Tamagawa also noted frequent perinuclear hy-

* 1950a, 1950b, 1953b, 1958; Tamagawa et al. 1950, 1952a; Tamagawa and Oda, 1959.

dropic degeneration in the epidermis; he considered this change to reflect the effects of radiation. Although he had feared that skin cancer or sarcoma might develop later, fortunately neither did so.

S. Iijima (1967) re-examined the histological slides left by both Tamagawa and Harada. Iijima considered that the vascular system plays the leading role in the development and the subsequent changes of keloids, and that the most essential change in keloid transformation is the arterial character of new capillaries in the granulation tissue. These new arteries originate in the upper dermis immediately beneath the epidermis. From there an arteriole extends almost perpendicularly into the deeper layer, and the fibrous tissue surrounding the arteriole forms into bundles. The keloid owes its pinkish color to one form of arterial congestion. With the lapse of time, there is progressive collagenization of fibrous bundles and gradual atrophy of arterial blood vessels, and at the end there remain only hypertrophic, hyalinized fibrous bundles. For keloidal changes to develop, it is necessary that the surface of the thermal burn be in the first place repaired and then covered by the epidermis, which the point of origin being in the upper dermis. A sort of activation of the epidermis and of the upper layer of the dermis is thought to induce keloidal changes, but the actual state of the control mechanism, or its failure, remains to be clarified in the future.

Blood Disorder

As already mentioned in chapter 8, hematopoietic organs (bone marrow, lymph node, lymphatic tissue of spleen) were among the systems greatly damaged by atomic bomb radiation. Since young blood cells were destroyed—resulting in decrease in number of, or in death of, cells—the patients showed various symptoms originating in decrease in number of blood cells soon after the explosion: infection and deteriorated vital defense mechanisms, with fewer white cells; hemorrhagic tendency, with decreased platelets; and anemia, with fewer red blood cells. Besides these quantitative changes in blood cells, diseases such as leukemia and other tumors caused by qualitative changes of blood cells began to appear later.

RESULTS OF GROUP HEMATOLOGICAL EXAMINATIONS

Not including the special cases, the disorders that were a matter of life or death in the early stage after the explosion, passed their peak after two months and then gradually showed improvement. Under the very poor nutritional conditions following the war, however, physical recuperation of the exposed victims was extremely inhibited. The purposes of the hematological examinations carried out on those exposed included detection of blood changes, early detection of blood diseases, and stabilization of general health. These studies were started soon after the explosion and are still being continued.

The hematological findings observed in the survivors one and two years after the explosion are found in the reports made by members of the Kyoto Imperial University team (T. Kikuchi et al. 1953*b*, p. 834; 1953*c*, p. 859; 1953*d*, p. 850). Kikuchi et al. carried out a physical checkup on 523 exposed survivors (356 were exposed within 2 kilometers of the hypocenter) in Hiroshima between August and September 1946. These were compared with 173 healthy residents of Hiroshima and its suburbs who had not been exposed to the atomic bomb. In the exposed group, frequent complaints of general malaise and dizziness were noted; and although few, some complaints indicated mild prolongation of bleeding time. Other examinations revealed reduction of red cell count, elevation of color index, and reduction of white cell and platelet counts. Statistically, a significant difference was found between the preceding data and those of the controls. Bone marrow puncture was carried out on 17; and although a few cases showed bone marrow insufficiency, the majority were within a normal limit. No conspicuous changes were seen in the functional tests (phagocytosis, migration) of leukocytes. Physical checkups were also made on 172 survivors between 30 November and 6 December 1946 in Nagasaki and were compared with 45 non-exposed residents in Nagasaki. Although some of the exposed had anemia, leukopenia, and low platelet count, there was no significant difference between the two groups.

In October 1947, two years after the explosion, physical checkups were again made on 243 exposed victims. There were still some who complained of general malaise, dizziness, and palpitation, with occasional hemorrhagic diathesis. Hematological examination revealed anemia, low white cell count, and low platelet count, and prolongation of bleeding time in some cases. In general, the values of hematological examination were closer to those of the controls as compared with the data obtained one year after the explosion (figure 9.2). A similar investigation made by F. M. Snell, J. V. Neel, and K. Ishibashi (1949) on the exposed, twenty to thirty-three months after the explosion in Hiroshima, also confirmed low red cell count, low hemoglobin and hematocrit, and mild reduction in number of lymphocytes, as compared with residents in Kure City.*

* Kure City is located about 30 kilometers east-southeast of Hiroshima City, and its western part faces the Bay of Hiroshima. With the establishment of a naval station in 1899, the city enjoyed a rapid growth as a naval port city. At the height of the Second World War, its population numbered some 400,000. After the war, however, it fell by one half, as a result of the Japanese Navy's disbandment and a massive air raid which was a catastrophe for the city.

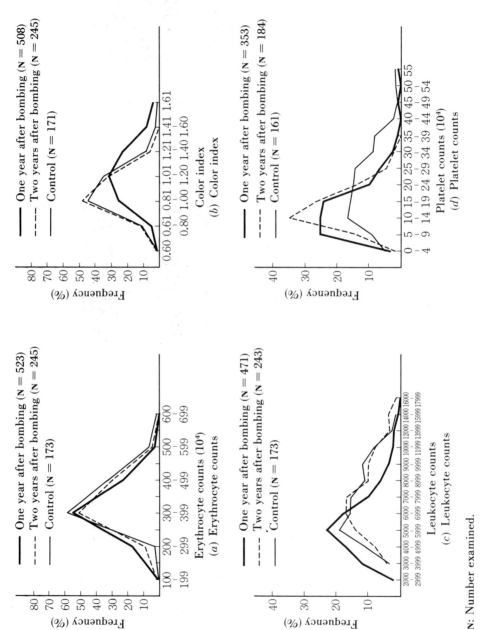

N: Number examined.

Figure 9.2. Hematological data in the first and second years after the bombing in Hiroshima (Kikuchi et al. 1953c, p. 859; and Wakisaka 1964, p. 600).

The hemoglobin content, the white cell count, and differential counts of white cells in the exposed at Nagasaki were examined five times between August 1946 and February 1956 (Kageura et al. 1955; Tomonaga 1957). The survey carried out in 1956 included examination of bone marrow in 65 cases (32 were exposed within 1.5 kilometers of the hypocenter). Peripheral blood smears revealed a significantly high incidence of anemia and an increase in eosinophils up till 1953, but no significant difference could be seen in 1956. In the bone marrow, however, maturation of granulocytes and megakaryocytes was somewhat suppressed in the victims nearer the hypocenter. At about the same time (ten to eleven years after the explosion), hematological examinations were made on the exposed survivors living in Hiroshima, Tokyo, and the Tōkai and Kinki areas.* When observed overall, the distribution of red cell count, hemoglobin, and white cell count showed no difference from those of the control. On close examination, however, it was noted that the incidence of one type of anemia generally seen in radiation injury was still slightly higher among the exposed survivors.† Later surveys have reported the gradual decline of such a characteristic type of anemia (Wakisaka 1961, p. 600).

From the preceding data, it can be summarized that, although the injury to hematopoietic organs by atomic bomb radiation was a matter of life or death at the early stage of exposure, the majority of victims had recovered by the end of one year. The few cases that took time to recuperate can be ascribed to differences in radiation dose, to degree of thermal burns and trauma, to presence of complications, to individual vitality or lack of it, and to postwar living conditions.

The periodical checkups of the exposed that are still being done, have shown that the incidence of low white cell count and anemia, and of anemia during pregnancy and its recovery, have no direct correlation to the exposure†† It cannot, however, be denied that in some cases an irreversible injury remained in the hematopoietic cells or hematopoietic tissue or organs following atomic bomb injury and later apparently developed blood disorders.

* Kōno 1957; Kurokawa 1957; Miyata 1957; Setsuda 1957; Wald 1957.

The *Tōkai area* is part of the Chūbu district of Honshu, the main island of the Japanese archipelago. This area particularly includes the two prefectures of Shizuoka and Aichi on the Pacific coast (there are forty-seven prefectures in Japan). The term "Tōkai area" denotes a topographical, climatic, economic, and cultural division of Central Japan. This area is remarkable for an influx of population attributable to its being Japan's leading industrial zone. The *Kinki district* is located a little to the west of the central part of Honshu and includes two urban prefectures (Osaka and Kyoto) and five prefectures. It has become a megalopolis of many cities, large and small, linked by a complete traffic network. This district is especially distinguished for its rich cultural heritage, as represented by Nara and Kyoto, Japan's ancient capitals.

† Hibino 1956, p. 249; Torii 1957; Watanabe 1958, p. 477; Watanabe 1959a, p. 128; Watanabe 1965, p. 485.

†† Ohkita and Takahashi 1970; Ohkita and Takahashi 1972; Taketomi et al. 1976a; 1976b; 1978b.

SPECIFIC AFTEREFFECTS IN BLOOD

Leukemia, multiple myeloma, malignant lymphoma, polycythemia vera, myelofibrosis, and aplastic anemia are all specific blood disorders that are considered to be related to exposure to the atomic bomb. The first three will be discussed later (pages 255–75).

Polycythemia vera is a slowly progressing condition in which there are abnormal increase in production of blood cells, increased red cell count, increased white cell count, increased platelet count in peripheral blood, and an increased circulating blood volume. The cause of this condition is unknown; it is thought to be a neoplastic disease of the bone marrow. Generally, the term *polycythemia* is used in its broad sense to include symptomatic polycythemia, which does not have a neoplastic character, and is treated differently from polycythemia vera. The first five cases of polycythemia vera occurring in the exposed were reported by R. M. Heyssel, A. B. Brill, L. A. Woodbury, E. T. Nishimura, T. Ghose, T. Hoshino, and M. Yamasaki (1969). The five cases were all exposed at a distance of more than 2.3 kilometers from the hypocenter and cannot be thought to have had any direct relation with atomic bomb radiation. S. Hibino, K. Yamasaki, and S. Kurita* reviewed, mainly through literature, 134 cases of polycythemia vera reported in Japan during a fifty-year period from 1909 to 1959, and found 17 cases who were exposed to the atomic bomb among the 83 cases reported after the Second World War. Among the 17 cases, 8 were exposed less than 2 kilometers from the hypocenter, and the remaining 9, at a distance of more than 2 kilometers. The incidence per million would be 156 (2 cases) within 1 kilometer of the hypocenter, 47 (5 cases) between 1 and 1.5 kilometers, 5.6 (1 case) between 1.5 and 2 kilometers, and 11 (9 cases) from 2 to 10 kilometers, showing an extremely high incidence in those exposed near the hypocenter. During the ten years after 1950, the incidence of polycythemia vera was 16.5 among the exposed and only 0.07 among the non-exposed.

T. Hoshino (1962) found 100 cases (70 males, 30 females) of polycythemia in its broad sense among about 10,000 exposed survivors during a three-year period from 1958. From the distribution of cases according to distance, this condition was thought not to be related to radiation dose, and none was diagnosed as polycythemia vera. Most of these cases were complicated with diabetes, obesity, hypertension, proteinuria, and gastroduodenal ulcers and were considered a sort of stress polycythemia caused by mental stress. T. Hoshino, S. Kawasaki, H. Okada, T. Yamamoto, and K. Kimura (1968) mention that only the seven cases with swollen spleens in Hibino's review came under the category of polycythemia vera, and since they were all exposed far from the hypocenter, there was no relation to exposure. The same research-

* Hibino and Yamasaki 1961; Hibino, Yamasaki, and Kurita 1962, pp. 647–89.

ers discovered twelve cases of polycythemia vera among the citizens of Hiroshima between 1950 and 1960. Only two cases had been exposed within 2 kilometers of the hypocenter, five cases over 2 kilometers, and five were not exposed at all. Although the incidence was slightly high in those exposed, the cases were too few to warrant any conclusions.

This condition was not found among the exposed survivors in Nagasaki. From the records of periodical physical checkups of about 40,000 exposed survivors in Hiroshima (1973), Y. Taketomi, T. Abe, N. Kamada, A. Kuramoto, H. Takahashi, T. Ohkita, C. Ito, and H. Kimura (1978a) obtained 438 cases agreeing with the criterion of polycythemia in its broad sense. Follow-up studies on these cases up to 1977 revealed only one case that could be diagnosed as polycythemia vera, and this survivor had been exposed at a distance of 2.3 kilometers from the hypocenter.

Idiopathic myelofibrosis is a chronic progressive condition in which there is abnormal proliferation of blood elements and also of fibroblasts forming the supporting tissue of bone marrow, and ultimately results in fibrosis of bone marrow tissue. This disease belongs among myeloproliferative diseases such as polycythemia vera, chronic myeloid leukemia, and leukemia. Pathologically, it can be divided into two stages: (1) when proliferation of various cells is dominant in the marrow; and (2) when fibrosis of the marrow dominates. The disease takes a slow course, and its morphology varies from case to case. Since fibrosis of the marrow sometimes occurs secondarily in leukemia, it is not infrequently difficult to differentiate this condition from other related disorders.

The first pathoanatomical study on the specific features of fibrosis occurring in bone marrow of atomic bomb survivors was reported by T. Yamamoto (1957). He studied four cases exposed within 1 kilometer of the hypocenter and dying from five to seven years after the explosion. The clinical diagnoses were aplastic anemia in three cases and chronic myeloid leukemia in one case. Later, R. E. Anderson, T. Hoshino, and T. Yamamoto (1964) and Anderson (1971) reported twelve patients with marked myelofibrosis, among whom ten were survivors of the atomic bomb. From the observations made through autopsies, it can be said that the incidence of myelofibrosis was higher in those exposed nearer the hypocenter. According to S. Watanabe (1959b; 1964), the degree of myelofibrosis found in autopsy cases of leukemia at Hiroshima showed no definite difference between exposed and non-exposed.

As already mentioned, not only was the number of cases of polycythemia vera and essential myelofibrosis insufficient, but there also remain many complicated problems concerning their diagnosis: thus, it is difficult to make any direct correlation between exposure to atomic bomb radiation and these specific disorders. From the intimate relationship between chronic myeloid leukemia, which belongs to the same disease group of myeloproliferative disorders, and exposure to radiation, the existence of a similar cause-and-effect relation in regard to these other two diseases cannot be denied. This problem should be pursued in the days to come.

The pathological status of *aplastic anemia* is that hematopoietic insufficiency is chronic and involves a marked drop in production of white cell, red cell, and platelet series. Autopsies performed during the early stage after the explosion revealed varying degrees of damage in bone marrow, and conditions that were similar to those of the marrow in aplastic anemia.

Bone marrow injuries that occurred during the acute stage usually recovered and regained their hematopoietic function in the survivors. On the other hand, not a few cases, especially those exposed to high doses, may be classified as atypical *leukemia* or a *myeloproliferative disorder* from the present diagnostic standard. These cases had been dealt with as aplastic anemia right after the explosion; and the problem whether aplastic anemia does occur as a late effect of exposure to atomic bomb radiation has been a matter of concern for a long time. The incidence of this condition, from October 1950 to December 1973, in the exposed and the non-exposed, was compared by M. Ichimaru, Y. Tomonaga, M. Matsunaga, N. Sadamori, and T. Ishimaru (1978*b*). The relation between radiation dose and the incidence of this condition was also examined, but neither a significant difference in incidence between exposed and non-exposed, nor a rise in incidence with increased radiation doses, was found.

Recently, N. Kamada and H. Uchino (1976) reported that a high incidence of chromosome abnormality of bone marrow cells is still found in the survivors who were exposed within 1 kilometer of the hypocenter in Hiroshima (14 out of 26 cases) (see pages 318–19). These abnormal chromosomes were all of the stable type, and some clones transmitted the same chromosome abnormality to the daughter cells after cell division. When these cases were observed periodically, the incidence of chromosome abnormality in bone marrow was found to be constantly over 10 percent. All persons with the chromosome abnormality, however, showed normal hematological values and were in good health.

In recent years lymphocytes, which are one type of leukocyte, have been found to be composed of several kinds of cell partaking in the different immunological functions; and development of new methods for examining their functions is now under way. Chromosome abnormality is still found in the lymphocytes of survivors of the atomic bomb who received a high dose of radiation within a short distance of the hypocenter (see pages 315–18). What kind of functional change does such a variation bring about in lymphocytes, and what are the effects on the immunological capacity of the living body?

If this capacity is altered or inhibited, what should be done? These are all subjects for immediate and intensive study.

Ocular Lesions

Ocular lesions following exposure to the atomic bomb consisted of (1) direct injury immediately after the explosion, (2) partial lesions of atomic bomb radiation illness, and (3) delayed effects. The injuries encountered immediately after the explosion were thermal burns, especially of the eyelids, mechanical injuries of the eye by blast, ocular trauma from glass splinters and other foreign bodies, and lesions of cornea, conjunctiva, and retina from flash.* Ocular lesions accompanying atomic bomb radiation illness also resulted from anemia, hemorrhagic tendency or hemorrhage, and infection. Besides so-called atomic bomb radiation cataract, deformation of eyelids from scar following cure of thermal burns, and subsequent changes of the cornea and conjunctiva are all aftereffects. Since exposure to an atomic bomb is said to accelerate aging, the problems whether ocular accommodation is affected by exposure, and whether the incidence of senile cataract is higher among those exposed, are subjects for discussion among other aftereffects of the atomic bomb.

Atomic bomb cataract was the first aftereffect to be noted, and the most frequent one, among the Hiroshima and Nagasaki casualties. The lens of the eyes are especially sensitive to radiation compared with other tissues of the eye, and has been an important subject in the study of aftereffects. In mid-September, approximately forty days after the explosion in Hiroshima, T. Fukuoka and T. Nita of Tokyo Imperial University, Department of Ophthalmology (1953) reported a case of cataract in a seventy-year-old male which was assumed to be due to atomic bomb radiation. There was much room for doubt, since the latent phase was much too short for radiation cataract to occur. Confirmable cases of atomic bomb cataract were discovered and first recorded by H. Ikui (1967) in the autumn of 1948 (Hiroshima) and by K. Hirose and S. Fujino (1950) in June 1949 (Nagasaki). These were followed by the reports made by D. G. Cogan, S. F. Martin, and S. J. Kimura (1949), T. Dodo (1962; 1967) and Dodo and S. Toda (1963, pp. 400–408), T. Tokunaga (1953; 1959; 1962; 1963; 1968), Y. Masuda (1955; 1962; 1966) and Masuda and Y. Shōji (1972, p. 346), S. Sugimoto (1971; 1973), and other Japanese ophthalmologists** and by investigations and surveys by the Atomic Bomb Casualty Commission.†

* Fukuoka and Nita 1953, p. 753; Ikui 1967; Tamura et al. 1953a, p. 1116; 1953b, p. 1117.
** Asayama and Tsukahara 1955; Maetani 1955.
† Hall, Miller, and Nefzger 1964; Miller, Fujino, and Nefzger 1967, 1968.

CLINICAL FEATURES OF ATOMIC BOMB CATARACTS

In *cataract* the ocular lens becomes opaque. Although a number of causes of this disease have been mentioned to date, most authors agree that the clinical symptoms are similar to those seen in radiation cataract not caused by an atomic bomb. According to the report made by D. G. Cogan, D. D. Donaldson, and A. B. Reese (1952) on the clinical manifestations of twenty cases of radiation cataract, including ten cases of atomic bomb cataract, the clinical findings did not differ by type of radiation. The characteristics mentioned were doughnut-shaped configuration, as observed with the ophthalmoscope, and sharply demarcated anterior boundary of the opacity and bivalve configuration of the opacity beneath the posterior capsule, as observed with the slit-lamp biomicroscope. Opacity in the posterior pole of the lens, however, is not only found in atomic bomb cataract; a similar change is also seen in pigmentous degeneration of retina and in senile cataract occurring from the posterior pole: thus, it is necessary to differentiate these conditions from atomic bomb cataract by closely examining their past histories and other parts of the eye. It is sometimes difficult to decide whether only mild change of the lens was caused by atomic bomb radiation, since similar changes were also found in non-exposed persons. R. M. Sinskey (1955), in his survey on 3,700 exposed and 164 non-exposed survivors in Hiroshima (May 1951 to December 1953), mentioned that the presence of granules in only the posterior subcapsular axial region was not sufficient, and that a definite tiny subcapsular plaque located axially as seen with a slit-lamp should be detected to justify the diagnosis of atomic bomb cataract. He found polychromatic granular plaques on the posterior capsule in 139 (84 percent) out of 165 exposed victims, among whom 90 percent to 100 percent showed epilation of the scalp within one to three months after the explosion. On the other hand, similar changes were encountered in only 16 (10 percent) out of 164 non-exposed persons. According to the survey made by Tokunaga (1959) on 1,600 exposed and 125 non-exposed between July 1953 and December 1956 at Nagasaki, the main changes of the lens following atomic bomb radiation were: (1) punctate opacities in disjunction zones, (2) vacuoles in the cortex, (3) subcapsular punctate opacities at the posterior pole, and (4) subcapsular tufflike opacities of the posterior pole. Among the four figures, (1) and (4) were characteristic of radiation injury of the lens; while (2) developed in various types of cataract other than radiation cataract; and (3) occurred as a physiological change in 7.4 percent of the non-exposed controls. Tokunaga further classified atomic bomb cataract by degree of severity: mild type I and mild type II from the degree of subcapsular punctate opacity at the posterior pole; and moderate type I, moderate type II, and a severe type depending on the degree of tufflike opacity at the posterior pole.

The diagnostic standards for atomic bomb cataract when Dodo (1962) investigated 128 exposed survivors between October 1957 and September 1961 at Hiroshima, were: (1) localized opacity on the inner surface of the posterior capsule, sometimes showing polychromatic sheen depending on the direction of observation; and (2) punctate or massive opacity situated anterior to the posterior capsule. In this study, 248 eyes of 128 survivors were examined to reveal 58 eyes (23.4 percent) with atomic bomb cataract. The degree of severity of cataract was classified into minute, slight, moderate, and severe degrees, which are shown in table 9.5. By *minute* is meant that there is a localized

TABLE 9.5

Classification of Radiation Cataracts of Hiroshima Survivors by Severity

Findings	Minute	Slight	Moderate	Severe
Localized opacity on inner surface of posterior polar capsule	+	+	+	+
Opacities located in subcapsular cortical layer of posterior polar region	−	+ (punctate)	+ (small clumps)	+ (large)
Shadows on transillumination	−	+	+	++
Photographic reproduction by transillumination	impossible	impossible	possible	possible
Subjective visual disorders	−	−	−	+
Incidence in 58 eyes with radiation cataract	33 (56.9%)	15 (25.9%)	4 (6.9%)	6 (10.3%)

Symbols: + = positive; − = negative; ++ = more positive than +.
Source: T. Dodo, "State of A-bomb cataracts at the Department of Ophthalmology, Hiroshima University during the recent four years," *Journal of the Hiroshima Medical Association* 15 (1962): 878.

opacity with polychromatic sheen on the inner surface of the posterior capsule, which can only be detected by slit-lamp biomicroscopy; while *slight* indicates minute punctate opacity anterior to the posterior capsule and sometimes an extremely dim shadow by ophthalmoscopy. In *moderate* degree an ovoid opaque shadow on transillumination with a diameter of less than 1 millimeter is seen on the central axis of the lens, while a localized massive opacity is found anterior of the plaque on the posterior capsule, as seen with the slit-lamp biomicroscopy. *Severe* means that there is a rather large, ovoid, opaque shadow on transillumination at the posterior pole. The opaque shadow has a diameter of several millimeters, and processes are frequently seen extending toward the axis. As compared with these marked findings in the posterior pole, opacity can hardly be found on the anterior capsule and the anterior subcapsular region.

A shadow on transillumination can be confirmed in those demonstrating more than moderate opacity, and photographic reproduction by transillumination is possible. Visual disturbance occurs only in patients with severe opacity. Figure 9.3 is a schematic representation of varying severity in atomic bomb

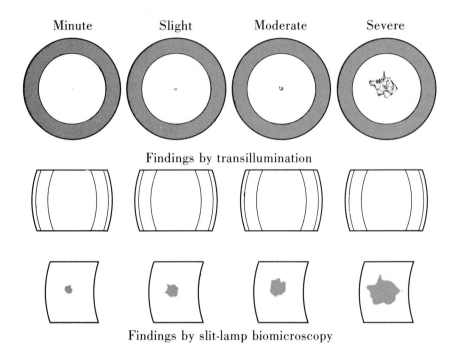

Figure 9.3. Schematic representation of the degree of severity of atomic bomb cataracts (Dodo 1962).

cataract. Among the frontispiece photographs are two typical cases of atomic bomb cataract (Dodo 1967). The first case (photograph 20) is a patient with moderate atomic bomb cataract of both eyes. She had been exposed to the atomic bomb outdoors at 900 meters from the hypocenter in Hiroshima when she was one year and eleven months old. The visual acuity was 1.2 for both eyes when this photograph was taken in April 1966 at age twenty-two. The second case (photograph 21) is that of a patient who, at the age of forty, had been exposed to the atomic bomb outdoors while standing under the eaves at a distance of 820 meters from the hypocenter in Hiroshima. Atomic bomb cataract of both eyes appeared after nearly complete epilation. This photograph of the right lens was taken in April 1966 at the age of sixty, and the visual acuity was 0.4 corrected. The visual acuity of the left eye was 1.0 corrected in 1959 at the time when the lens was extirpated.

HISTOPATHOLOGY OF ATOMIC BOMB CATARACTS

S. J. Kimura and H. Ikui (1951) reported the histopathological changes in the lens of a twenty-two-year-old male who had noted visual disturbance two years after the explosion at Hiroshima and who had his lens extracted from the left eye two years and two months later. According to this report, the middle one third of the posterior lens capsule was wrinkled, thickened, loose, and separated from the underlying cortex by empty spaces, some of which contained amorphous debris. The covering epithelium showed degenerative changes. The epithelial cells at the equator and the lens fibers were irregular in shape and arrangement.

Histopathological studies were also done by Dodo (1962), Y. Fujinaga (1969), and Tokunaga (1959). Their observations confirmed the prominent changes occurring in the posterior subcapsular cortex, which coincide with the clinical findings. Histopathological features in compliance with the type of radiation were not noted.

PREVALENCE OF ATOMIC BOMB CATARACTS

The incidence and the degree of severity of atomic bomb cataracts ran parallel with radiation doses, as in other atomic bomb radiation illnesses. There was also a correlation with age at time of exposure, and with distance from the hypocenter, with shielding conditions, presence and degree of epilation, and other symptoms of acute radiation illness.

In P. G. Fillmore's survey (1952) made at the Hiroshima Atomic Bomb Casualty Commission five years after bombing, 85 of the 98 cases with atomic bomb cataracts were discovered among 869 survivors who had been exposed within 1 kilometer of the hypocenter. The incidence was calculated to be 9.8 percent. Between June 1953 and October 1954, there were 116 patients (26.6 percent) with atomic bomb cataracts out of 435 exposed survivors who had been seen at the Ophthalmology Clinic of Hiroshima Red Cross Hospital (Kandori and Masuda 1956). Eighty-seven (54.7 percent) of the 159 exposed were within 2 kilometers of the hypocenter, and 30 (10.8 percent) of the 277 survivors were exposed at a distance of more than 2 kilometers. The visual acuity of the cases with cataracts in this survey was well preserved, with 53.5 percent having normal vision. The survey made by the Department of Ophthalmology of Hiroshima University during a four-year period from 1957 to 1961 resulted in the detection of atomic bomb cataracts in 32 (25 percent) of 128 patients and 58 (23.4 percent) of 248 eyes examined. The incidence within 1 kilometer of the hypocenter was 70 percent and 30 percent between 1 and 2 kilometers and fell rapidly at a distance of more than 1.6 kilometers.

In order to exclude the intervention of senile changes of the lens and consequent error, a survey of those exposed during infancy was made by the members of Hiroshima University (Department of Ophthalmology) from February 1958 to June 1959, with the intention of accurately grasping the true facts of the effects of atomic bomb radiation on the lens (Toda et al. 1964). As can be seen from the results in table 9.6, the incidence of atomic

TABLE 9.6

*Frequency of A-bomb Cataracts among Survivors
Exposed during Infancy in Hiroshima*

Distance from Hypocenter (km)	Number of Eyes Examined	Number of Eyes with A-bomb Cataracts*	
		Definite	Suspected
0–1.0	18	10 (55.6)	2 (11.1)
1.0–1.2	20	10 (50.0)	0
1.2–1.4	18	4 (22.2)	2 (11.1)
1.4–1.6	50	6 (12.0)	1 (2.0)
1.6–1.8	30	0	0
1.8–2.0	38	1 (2.6)	2 (5.3)
2.0–3.0	56	0	1 (1.8)
Total number	230	31 (13.5)	8 (3.5)

* Figures in parentheses are percentages of eyes examined.
Source: S. Toda, Y. Hosokawa, K. Chōshi, A. Nakano, and M. Takahashi, "Ocular changes in A-bomb survivors exposed during infancy," *Nihon Ganka Kiyō* [Folia Ophthalmologica Japonica] 15 (1964): 96.

bomb cataracts was 13.5 percent, including 58.1 percent of very mild cases, 29 percent of mild, and 12.9 percent of moderate; and no marked or severe cases were found. The prevalence fell markedly for exposures at distances of more than 1.6 kilometers.

In Nagasaki, detailed observations were made by Tokunaga (1959) between 1953 and 1956 on 1,600 exposed survivors and 125 non-exposed controls. The incidence within 1.8 kilometers of the hypocenter was 57.4 percent, and 45.8 percent within 2.4 kilometers. The limit of the distance from the hypocenter at which atomic bomb cataract could occur was thought to be 1.8 kilometers, statistically. Hirose and Okamoto (1961) made a survey on the correlation between estimated exposure dose and the incidence of lenticular opacity of the posterior pole in 178 survivors in whom the estimated exposure dose was known (table 9.7). This study was carried out on 775 persons visiting the Nagasaki Atomic Bomb Casualty Commission between November 1959 and August 1960. The survivors in group I were exposed within 2 kilometers of the hypocenter and had suffered the course of acute radiation illness, while those in group II, although exposed within 2 kilometers, had not had a similar course of acute radiation illness.

TABLE 9.7

Frequency of Lens Opacity of Posterior Polar Region in Relation to Estimated Radiation Doses and Exposure Status

Estimated Radiation Dose (rads)	Group I (%)*	Group II (%)†	Number of Opacities per Number of Examined
0–49	17.4	5.3	5/42 (11.9%)
50–99	22.2	31.3	9/34 (26.5%)
100–199	56.5	41.9	26/54 (48.1%)
200–499	58.1	42.9	21/38 (55.3%)
500 and over	90.0	—	9/10 (90.0%)
Total	48/105 (45.7%)	22/73 (30.1%)	70/178 (39.3%)

* With acute radiation symptoms.
† Without acute radiation symptoms.
Source: I. Hirose and A. Okamoto, "Interrelationship between lenticular turbidity of the posterior pole and estimated exposure doses of the atomic bomb survivors in Nagasaki" (preliminary report), *Nagasaki Medical Journal* 36 (1961): 781.

S. Kawamoto, T. Fujino, and H. Fujisawa (1964), in the study made between August 1963 and March 1964 on 266 persons who had been exposed in utero at Nagasaki, mentioned that the incidence of posterior subcapsular opacity was 11.1 percent where the mother had been exposed within 2 kilometers of the hypocenter, and 7.8 percent where the mother had been exposed between 3 and 4.999 kilometers of the hypocenter. Although the prevalence was 3.7 percent in the controls (their mothers were not in Nagasaki at the time of the explosion), no significant statistical difference between the in utero exposed and the non-exposed was found.

CLINICAL COURSE OF ATOMIC BOMB CATARACTS

In general, atomic bomb cataracts occurred several months or years after exposure. Severe cases appeared within ten months, while the latent period of mild or moderate cases was assumed to be longer than ten months (Tokunaga 1962). W. T. Ham (1953) re-examined this condition in seventy survivors, six years after exposure and found slight improvement of opacity in 2 percent, very slight change in 17 percent, and no change in 36 percent. On the other hand, the opacity had progressed very slightly in 15 percent, slightly in 26 percent, and markedly in 4 percent. In Y. Masuda's survey (1962), observations were made on the conditions of twenty-one survivors among seventy-five Hiroshima patients with atomic bomb cataracts occurring from one and one-half years to nine years later. He found no change in four cases, transformation in eight, improvement in four, and progression in five. The ten-year observation (1959–69) of atomic bomb cataracts in Hiroshima by Y. Fujinaga (1970) revealed no progression of the lesions.

At the present, lenticular opacity occurring after radiation is thought to progress slowly for a long time and then to stop. When atomic bomb cataracts are followed for a long term, however, a small number eventually demonstrate stronger opacity, while some others show improvement. As in senile cataracts, extirpation of the lens is carried out on patients complaining of visual disturbance and difficulty in everyday life. The postoperative course has usually been good.

OTHER AFTEREFFECTS ON THE EYES

In 1958 at Hiroshima, examinations for ocular accommodation were carried out to discover whether exposure to an atomic bomb accelerates aging of the eyes. A. Koyama and S. Seki (1959) examined 139 exposed survivors between twenty and thirty-five years of age and 350 non-exposed of the same age group, and found no difference between the groups. According to a similar investigation made by I. Hirose et al. (1967) on a total of 1,974 exposed survivors (954 examined between September 1959 and February 1960 at Hiroshima; 1,020 examined between November 1959 and 1960 at Nagasaki), no definite difference in accommodating function could be obtained. From these results, however, Hirose et al. could not assert that exposure to the atomic bomb had no effect whatsoever on the aging phenomenon of accommodating function.

It is also essential to know whether the incidence of senile cataract, an aging phenomenon of the lens, is higher among those exposed. As no accurate detailed data on this subject have been obtained to date, it remains to be studied in the future.

Aftereffects among Exposed Women

It has already been mentioned in chapter 8 that exposure to the atomic bomb caused disorders of the ovaries and led to abnormal menstrual cycles and other symptoms immediately after the explosion.* This section is concerned mainly with the delayed effects of exposure in women's reproductive system.

AMENORRHEA IN EXPOSED WOMEN

Excluding women who were going through menopause or were pregnant or lactating, H. Sawada (1960, p. 1158) made a survey on 880 exposed survivors (within 2 kilometers of the hypocenter) who had visited the Atomic Bomb

---

* Hatanaka 1953, p. 1326; Mitani 1955; Mitani et al. 1953, pp. 735, 738.

Casualty Commission between 1949 and 1957. Approximately one half—with women over forty years old predominating—had experienced amenorrhea right after the explosion. When the samples were divided into two groups according to whether they had symptoms of acute radiation illness or not, the incidence of amenorrhea was 69 percent in those who had symptoms and a lower 33.7 percent in those without symptoms. The incidence of amenorrhea was especially high, being 96.3 percent in the exposed women over age forty-five. Amenorrhea was generally temporary and continued in the majority of women for less than six months. The average duration of amenorrhea among women with acute radiation symptoms was 5.87 months, and that among women without symptoms was 4.67 months. The majority of women who were over age forty-five went into menopause.

The mean age of menopause in exposed women was 47.35 years (45.9 years in those with symptoms of acute radiation illness; 48.5 years in women without symptoms), while the mean age in non-exposed women was 49.3 years. This tendency was especially definite in women entering menopause right after the explosion, with the mean age of those with symptoms of acute radiation illness being 44.85 years and 45.24 years for all women who were exposed.

A similar survey was made by K. Yamaoka et al. (1955) on 389 exposed women who had visited the Hiroshima Citizens Hospital during a two-year period from 1953. The results coincided with Sawada's data, with the incidence of amenorrhea being 70 percent within 1 kilometer of the hypocenter, 60 percent within 1.5 kilometers, 28 percent within 2.5 kilometers, and 11 percent at 5 kilometers. The duration of amenorrhea was up to three months in 36.4 percent, up to six months in 28.9 percent, up to one year in 24.8 percent, and on rare occasions as long as five years. Other symptoms frequently noted were irregular menstruation, dysmenorrhea, irregular genital bleeding, opsomenorrhea, frigidity, and "Hiroshima disease," a sort of vegetative dystonia.*

MENARCHE AFTER EXPOSURE TO THE ATOMIC BOMB

According to the observations made by T. Shōji and H. Kariya (1947) in September 1946 at Hiroshima, the average age of menarche in survivors receiving trauma or thermal burns was 15.55 years and in those without trauma or thermal burns, 15.24 years. On the other hand, the figures for students were 14.16 years in non-exposed students in Hiroshima and 14.70 years in Iwakuni (Yamaguchi Prefecture). These data show that exposure to the atomic bomb delayed menarche.

Y. Mitani and members of the Department of Obstetrics and Gynecology

---

* *Opsomenorrhea* is delayed menstruation; *dystonia* is abnormal tonicity of a tissue or a body.

at Nagasaki University (Mitani 1953; 1954; 1956, p. 1673) made four surveys on 21,792 exposed young girls from 1947 to 1953. No definite effects of the atomic bomb on menarche were found in the young and healthy girls. The first survey carried out in December 1947 consisted of 2,067 students in Nagasaki, among whom was noted no difference in period of menarche by distance from the hypocenter. A similar result was obtained from the second survey in December 1949 on 2,567 students in Nagasaki and in Isahaya City as controls. The third survey in June 1951 consisted of 7,860 girls; and more controls were added to the fourth survey carried out in June 1953, totaling 9,298. Each survey revealed no correlation between distance from hypocenter and period of menarche.

Applying E. L. Kaplan's (1948) method, Sawada (1960) calculated and compared the ages at the time of menarche in 1,007 girls who had been exposed within 2 kilometers of the hypocenter in Hiroshima and in 993 non-exposed girls. The age of the exposed was 14.71 years and that of the controls 14.57 years; thus, there was hardly any difference between the two groups. Through periodic checkups held at the Atomic Bomb Casualty Commission, K. Monden (1955) examined the skeletal development of 610 exposed girls who were born between 1936 and 1945 and 590 controls of the same age group. By applying the fact that menstruation does not occur before the appearance of sesamoid bones (eleven years and nine months to twelve years and three months), and before intercristal length of the iliac reaches 23 centimeters, he estimated the age of menarche and then compared it with the controls. The mean age of menarche was 14.09 years in the exposed girls and 14.1 years in the non-exposed; hence, there was no difference between the two groups.

FERTILITY AFTER EXPOSURE TO THE ATOMIC BOMB

Although fertility of exposed women was feared to have been affected by the explosion, J. V. Neel and W. J. Schull (Neel et al. 1953*a*; Neel and Schull 1956) in their analysis of births between 1948 and 1953, found no difference in termination of pregnancy of exposed and non-exposed women. D. G. Seigel (1966), by checking the census register ("Koseki") for the years 1945 to 1961, examined the birth histories of the exposed women and controls (only persons born between 1900 and 1945 and with marital history were selected from the Atomic Bomb Casualty Commission-National Institute of Health, Japan, Life Span Study Samples). He found no alteration in fertility either by marital age or by distance from the explosion. In the surveys made by N. Seto (1954, p. 864 and 1955, p. 123) on 410 exposed women in the cities of Ōtake and Hiroshima, the conception rate was rather higher even in those exposed at a near distance as compared with the controls (211 women).

By examining birth certificates between January 1951 and August 1955 in Hiroshima, S. Nishida (1957) found a low birth rate in both exposed and controls, with the number of newborns from primaparas being remarkably low, especially in women aged ten to twenty at the time of exposure near the hypocenter. These results, however, were consequences of artificial abortion and not of low fertility.

A. Tabuchi and K. Kinutani (1965) and Tabuchi (1955) of Hiroshima University compared the number of pregnancies in exposed women (174 were married before exposure, and 98 after exposure) and of those in the controls, in a study carried out between January 1958 and 1961. The number of pregnancies after exposure in previously married women did not differ from that of the controls, indicating a lower conception rate than before the explosion. This lower rate was either because they had enough children or because of their ages. The number of pregnancies in the exposed women who married after the explosion was somewhat fewer than in the controls but showed no significant difference statistically. A similar survey was made by W. J. Blot and H. Sawada (1971) by interviewing married women (2,400 survivors in 1962 who were under age forty in August 1945) in the Atomic Bomb Casualty Commission Adult Health Program at Hiroshima and Nagasaki. This survey was carried out between 1962 and 1964, and analyses have led to the following results: (1) There was a consistent significant difference between the samples in Hiroshima and Nagasaki, with a much higher conception potential in women at Nagasaki. (2) The incidence of sterile women and zero pregnancy showed no significant difference by radiation dose. (3) In women with histories of pregnancy and delivery, the mean pregnancy rate, birth rate, and time interval from the first pregnancy to first birth did not differ significantly in either the high-dose group (over 100 rads) or the low-dose group (0–9 rads). Blot and Sawada have stressed that there is no evidence of fertility being suppressed for a long period of time in women exposed to high radiation doses.

STERILITY AND INFERTILITY AFTER EXPOSURE TO THE ATOMIC BOMB

A married woman who had been exposed to the atomic bomb under the age of forty-eight years, and who had not become pregnant without birth control for over three years after marriage or over five years after the last delivery, was defined as being sterile. H. Hamaoka (1959) investigated the incidence of sterility among exposed women in Hiroshima (1955–57) and found that although the incidence of sterility was high among the exposed, this was due to other factors than exposure to the atomic bomb. Sterility before exposure was mainly caused by tuberculous disorders, while sterility after exposure was attributable to appendicitis and to disorders of the genital organs. Three of the seven cases of primary sterility were a consequence of ovarian disorders and were not related to exposure. Infertility was detected in eight exposed women, indicating no increase in incidence by exposure as compared with the controls.

CLINICAL COURSE OF PREGNANCY AND ABORTION; PREMATURE BIRTH AND STILLBIRTH

The incidence of toxemia in pregnancy, of anemia, and of lowered pulse pressure was rather high among the exposed as compared with the controls in patients hospitalized at Hiroshima University Hospital. The incidence of abnormal delivery and delayed delivery did not differ.

N. Seto's survey (1954–1955) on the exposed women in Hiroshima shows no increase in abortions or in immature deliveries irrespective of whether a woman was married before or after exposure to the atomic bomb. In an investigation based on birth and death certificates between January 1951 and August 1955, Nishida (1957) found it difficult to clarify the effect of exposure on abortion, since many artificial abortions were carried out at that time. There was, however, a slight increase in abortions at the first pregnancy (four to nine months) after the explosion in women who were exposed near the hypocenter, but the figures did not significantly differ from those of the controls. Although the incidence of stillbirths during the last month of pregnancy was not affected by exposure, the causes of abortions were most often death in utero, malformation, and intracranial hemorrhage. There were also many cases of eclampsia and pre-eclampsia during pregnancy among the exposed women. In the survey made by S. Ishizu (1960) in 1958, a higher incidence of stillbirths was noted in women who were married before the explosion and when both husband and wife were exposed to the atomic bomb, and in women who were married after the explosion but were exposed under age nineteen or over age thirty. The relation to distance from hypocenter was not evident. An examination of birth and death certificates between January 1950 and June 1959 in Hiroshima found that stillbirths increased in number up to 1955 and decreased thereafter.

The number of natural stillbirths was 69.4 in 1,000 pregnancies, while that of artificial abortion was 57.18 in the exposed women. These figures are higher than those found in the controls, being 66.24 and 54.33, respectively. Surveys by home interviews showed that abortions and stillbirths were found more frequently in women who had experienced at least one birth, and who had been exposed to the atomic bomb under age nineteen or over age thirty. Many women complained of unstable emotions.

The stillbirth rates during a five-year period (1948–52) in Hiroshima and Nagasaki are shown in table 9.8 (Neel et al. 1953*b*).

TABLE 9.8

Frequency of Stillbirths in Hiroshima and Nagasaki

Mothers' Exposure	Fathers' Exposure					
	Hiroshima			Nagasaki		
	1	2 + 3	4 + 5	1	2 + 3	4 + 5
1	381/16,166 (2.4%)	38/1,578 (2.4%)	14/700 (2.0%)	263/13,446 (2.0%)	44/1,981 (2.2%)	4/374 (1.1%)
2 + 3	148/5,502 (2.7%)	54/2,328 (2.3%)	18/493 (3.7%)	171/8,527 (2.0%)	89/3,951 (2.3%)	12/502 (2.4%)
4 + 5	85/2,691 (3.2%)	11/552 (2.0%)	26/663 (3.9%)	31/1,211 (2.6%)	4/270 (1.5%)	4/196 (2.0%)

1. Non-exposed.
2. Exposed 2,545 m and more from the hypocenter.
3. Exposed between 1,845 m and 2,544 m from the hypocenter. No symptoms observed.
4. Exposed within 1,844 m of the hypocenter. No symptoms observed.
5. Radioactive symptoms observed within a few months of the bombings.
Source: J. V. Neel, N.E. Morton, W. J. Schull, D. J. McDonald, M. Kodani, K. Takeshima, R. C. Anderson, J. Wood, R. Brewer, S. Wright, J. Yamazaki, M. Suzuki, and S. Kitamura, "The effect of exposure of parents to the atomic bombs on first-generation offspring in Hiroshima and Nagasaki," *Japanese Journal of Genetics* 28 (1953): 211.

SEX RATIO OF NEWBORNS

The question whether a change in sex ratio might occur when either one or both parents are exposed to radiation is concerned with the genetic effects of exposure rather than with its aftereffect on the vital functions of the exposed mothers themselves. The sex ratios of those born to the exposed as well as stillbirth rates were subjects of great interest from the standpoint of radiation-induced, sex-linked lethal mutations (Schull and Neel 1958). Although it was at first thought that the theoretical estimation by Neel and Schull could be confirmed by actual survey materials, evidence supporting changes in sex ratio of children born to the exposed could not be obtained through repeated surveys. After reviewing the sex ratios in 47,624 children born between 1956 and 1962 in Hiroshima and Nagasaki, Schull, Neel, and A. Hashizume (1966) concluded that "there were no findings to support their previous data suggesting the possible effects of radiation exposure on sex ratio." Tabuchi and members of Hiroshima University's Department of Obstetrics and Gynecology (1965, p, 205) also carried out similar investigations but reached no definite conclusions. It was found, however, that there were more male stillbirths than female in the exposed women.

BIRTH WEIGHT OF NEWBORNS

Table 9.9 was taken from the survey made by Neel et al. (1953*b*) between 1948 and 1952. Although no significant effect of exposure on birth weight could be found, the birth weight of an infant whose father had been exposed

TABLE 9.9

*Weight of Live Births in Hiroshima and Nagasaki**

Mothers' Exposure	Fathers' Exposure					
	Hiroshima			Nagasaki		
	1	2 + 3	4 + 5	1	2 + 3	4 + 5
1	15,240 (3,066 g)	1,499 (3,057 g)	667 (3,032 g)	13,062 (3,079 g)	1,921 (3,079 g)	366 (3,077 g)
2 + 3	5,244 (3,066 g)	2,222 (3,098 g)	461 (3,081 g)	8,290 (3,071 g)	3,819 (3,111 g)	488 (3,099 g)
4 + 5	2,537 (3,042 g)	527 (3,075 g)	617 (3,118 g)	1,171 (3,085 g)	265 (3,092 g)	189 (3,188 g)

1. Not in Hiroshima or Nagasaki at the time of the bombings.
2. In one of the two cities, 2,545 m or more from the hypocenter. No symptoms observed.
3. In one of the two cities 1,845–2,544 m from the hypocenter. No symptoms observed.
4. In one of the two cities within 1,844 m of the hypocenter. No symptoms observed.
5. In one of the two cities. Symptoms developing within a few months of the bombings (epilation, petechiae, gingivitis, or any combination of these.
* The total number of infants in each class; in parentheses, their average weight in grams.
Source: J. V. Neel, N. E. Morton, W. J. Schull, D. J. McDonald, M. Kodani, K. Takeshima, R. C. Anderson, J. Wood, R. Brewer, S. Wright, J. Yamazaki, M. Suzuki, and S. Kitamura, "The effect of exposure of parents to the atomic bombs on first-generation offspring in Hiroshima and Nagasaki," *Japanese Journal of Genetics* 28 (1953): 211.

was significantly greater than that of an infant whose father had not been exposed. On comparing exposed and non-exposed groups, a mutual relationship was noted between the effects of exposure on the father and the mother. The two phenomena were considered to have resulted from the age difference of the mothers in the exposed groups.

The surveys on exposed women in Ōtake City made by the Department of Obstetrics and Gynecology of Hiroshima University in 1956 and 1960 revealed many low birth weights. A similar investigation in 1958 on exposed women living in Kaita Town (Hiroshima Prefecture) found a great number of immature newborns among the first children after the exposure of their mothers. In the analysis of birth certificates in Hiroshima by Nishida (1957), the mean birth weights of newborns whose mother or parents had been exposed were lighter than those of the controls but showed no significant difference statistically.

EARLY DEATH AND DEVELOPMENTAL DISORDERS IN NEWBORNS

Early deaths were not infrequent in newborns whose mother or parents had been exposed. The majority died within a year at a rate like that of the controls (Nishida 1957).

T. Funahashi (1955*b*) examined the relation between the developmental status of the 61 first children after their mothers' exposure to the atomic bomb within 3 kilometers of the hypocenter in Hiroshima and found breadth of shoulders, relative breadth of shoulders, and upper arm circumference to be less developed in the child whose mother had been exposed within 2 kilometers of the hypocenter than among the controls. A definite relation was noted between the time interval after exposure in pregnancy and the constitution of the child.

Although many observations have been made on chromosome abnormalities and malformations in children whose mothers had been exposed to the atomic bomb, their relation to exposure remains obscure. I. Hayashi et al. (1955) made a pathological survey on 887 fetuses and newborns from September 1949 to December 1953, and it was confirmed that no characteristic malformations resulted from the exposure. The incidence of malformation, however, was 18.5 percent in the exposed cases and 11 percent in the controls, with a significant difference between the two groups. In the exposed cases there was a gradual decline in number of malformations, especially in the complicated ones with the lapse of time after exposure. A correlation was also found between distance from hypocenter and incidence of malformation. The frequency of malformation of various organs was seen in the following order: bone, heart and large vessels, central nervous system, digestive tract, genitourinary system, and respiratory tract.

Exposure in Utero

Fetuses in utero were also affected by the atomic bombings on Hiroshima and Nagasaki. When severely injured, the mother died, or either death of fetus or abortion occurred; but not a few babies were born after a normal length of pregnancy. These are referred to as children exposed in utero, and they have since matured into adults and are still living. In general, young and proliferating cells and tissues are sensitive to radiation effects, and organs at an important stage of development are also very sensitive to relatively low doses of radiation. Irradiation during the fetal stage is, therefore, more serious than in the fully developed adult and results in developmental abnormalities of the body through cellular and tissue damage. Under certain conditions, such disorder may remain for a long time. Microcephaly remains one of the ill-fated aftereffects of exposure in utero to the atomic bomb in Hiroshima and Nagasaki. One who meets these unfortunate microcephalics has no alternative but to consider the atomic bomb attack on Hiroshima and Nagasaki to have been a crime. There are no accurate data on the exact number of those exposed in utero at the time of the bombing in August 1945. The survey made by the Atomic Bomb Casualty Commission when the national census was taken in 1960 revealed 2,310 survivors who had been exposed in utero in Hiroshima and 1,562 in Nagasaki.

COURSE AND TERMINATION OF PREGNANCY AFTER EXPOSURE IN UTERO

An outline of the exposed conditions of the pregnant women in Hiroshima and Nagasaki and the effect of exposure on the course and termination of pregnancy have already been mentioned in chapter 8. A more detailed survey of these conditions was made by J. N. Yamazaki, S. W. Wright, and P. M. Wright (1954). They found 98 who had been pregnant on 9 August 1945 among 1,774 women of childbearing age who had survived within 2 kilometers of the hypocenter in Nagasaki. One hundred and thirteen women who had been exposed at a distance of 4 to 5 kilometers of the hypocenter were used as controls. Table 9.10 shows the incidence of fetal deaths (abortion, stillbirth);

TABLE 9.10

Fetal Mortality among Irradiated and Control Groups

Meters	Group	Number of Conceptions	Number of Abortions	Number of Stillbirths	Fetal Mortality (%)
0–2,000	Major radiation signs	30	3	4	23.3
0–2,000	No major radiation signs	68	1	2	4.4
4,000–5,000	Controls	113	2	1	2.7

Source: J. N. Yamazaki, S. W. Wright, and P. M. Wright, "Outcome of pregnancy in women exposed to the atomic bomb in Nagasaki," *American Journal of Diseases of Children* 87 (1954): 448.

table 9.11, the mortality rate of newborns and infants; and table 9.12, the child morbidity rate up to five years after birth. From these data one can note the high rate of disorders occurring during pregnancy and in fetuses when the mother was exposed within 2 kilometers of the hypocenter and showed signs of acute radiation illness. As to the 30 mothers who had been

TABLE 9.11

Neonatal and Infant Mortality among Irradiated and Control Groups

Meters	Group	Mothers*	Neonatal Deaths	Infant Deaths	Mortality (%)
0–2,000	Major radiation signs	23	3	3	26.1
0–2,000	No major radiation signs	65	3	0	4.6
4,000–5,000	Controls	110	1	3	3.6

* Mothers of living infants; stillbirths and abortions excluded.
Source: J. N. Yamazaki, S. W. Wright, and P. M. Wright, "Outcome of pregnancy in women exposed to the atomic bomb in Nagasaki," *American Journal of Diseases of Children* 87 (1954): 448.

TABLE 9.12

Child Morbidity among Irradiated and Control Groups

Meters	Group	Mothers*	Mental Retardation in Children	Alive and Normal Child after 1 Year of Life	Rate of Mental Retardation (%)
0–2,000	Major radiation signs	16	4	12†	25
0–2,000	No major radiation signs	60	1	59‡	1.6
4,000–5,000	Controls	106	0	106§	0

* Includes mothers whose children were alive at time of examination.
† Nystagmus, corneal opacity, and pupillary membrane in one child.
‡ Urinary incontinence in one child.
§ Unilateral cataract in one child.
Source: J. N. Yamazaki, S. W. Wright, and P. M. Wright, "Outcome of pregnancy in women exposed to the atomic bomb in Nagasaki," *American Journal of Diseases of Children* 87 (1954): 448.

exposed within 2 kilometers of the hypocenter and demonstrated such symptoms of acute radiation illness as epilation, hemorrhagic diathesis, hemorrhage, and oropharyngitis, there were 7 fetal deaths (23.3 percent), 6 neonatal and infantile deaths (26.1 percent), and mental retardation in 4 out of the remaining 16 cases, with an overall morbidity and mortality of 60 percent.

MORTALITY RATE OF CHILDREN EXPOSED IN UTERO

The children exposed in utero who survived have grown and reached ages thirty-two to thirty-three in 1978. H. Kato (1971) made a survey of the mortality rate of the children after birth, which included approximately 1,300 children exposed in utero in Hiroshima and Nagasaki and covered a period of twenty-four years after birth, to 1969. There were 196 deaths among 1,292 with the greatest number of deaths (104) less than one year after birth, followed by those (70) between one and nine years after birth. The mortality rate as a whole ran parallel with radiation doses; but under the age of one year, a significant increase in mortality was confirmed in respect to radiation doses. Although there was no relation between death and radiation dose for the following nine years, a significant increase in mortality was noted with increase of radiation dose after age ten. C. Miki (1960) investigated the trend of deaths in children who were born between 6 August 1945 and 14 May 1946 to mothers exposed in Hiroshima. The highest mortality rate was found within one year after birth, and mortality gradually decreased by the age of three years, when the cause of death was similar to the controls. The mortality rate for children of preschool age, however, was higher than that for the controls, especially for boys. This difference disappeared gradually after age seven. One infant died of myeloid leukemia; and deaths from malignancies, including leukemia, were noted in children of preschool age.

GROWTH DISORDERS

Following the survey made by Yamazaki, S. W. Wright, and P. M. Wright (1954), G. Plummer (1952) examined 205 children who had been exposed in utero during early gestation in Hiroshima. He found 7 children with mental retardation among 11 who had been exposed in utero within 1.2 kilometers of the hypocenter. The mean head circumference of the 7 children was less than 45 centimeters, while that of 171 normal children who had also been exposed in utero was 48.6 ± 1.3 centimeters. Children exposed in utero tended to be smaller than the average. R. W. Miller (1956) obtained similar results.

In 1955, T. Funahashi (1955*a*) of Hiroshima University's Department of Obstetrics and Gynecology carried out an anthropometric study on nine-to-ten-year-old children who had been exposed in utero and were living in Ōtake City and Hiroshima City. Another group of forty-eight children was used as a control. Boys exposed in utero during early gestation revealed a narrow pelvis and were brachycephalic, while those exposed in utero during late gestation had relatively narrow shoulders. The pelvis and shoulders of boys exposed in utero within 2 kilometers of the hypocenter were generally narrower than those of the controls. Measurements of the head and other indices of growth in eight cases were inferior to those of the controls; while, aside from indices of the skull, six cases showed better growth than the controls.

Since growth is thought to stop at about age eighteen, G. Hirai (1964) re-examined in 1963 the growth of children who had been exposed in utero. The selected cases consisted of 536 children (227 males and 309 females) who had been exposed in utero within 3 kilometers of the hypocenter in Hiroshima, and 473 (147 males and 326 females) non-exposed children of the same age group as controls. In many children who had been exposed in utero, stature, weight, head circumference, girth of chest, upper arm circumference, thigh circumference, and breadth of shoulders were smaller compared with standard measurements. This tendency was especially prominent in children who had received large doses of radiation in utero before the fifteenth week of pregnancy. When periodical changes in growth were observed over six to seventeen years, it was noted that the children exposed in utero whose growth was still inhibited, tended to develop in a way similar to the controls. Twelve cases were markedly microcephalic and were emotionally and intellectually retarded. Autosomal trisomy 21 was seen in one of these cases.*

The Atomic Bomb Casualty Commission established a long-term fixed population of 1,608 children who had been exposed in utero in Hiroshima

---

*Autosomal trisomy 21 is known as "Down's syndrome," or "Mongolism." An *autosome* is any chromosome that does not determine sex; in *trisomy,* there are three—rather than the normal two—of a given chromosome; 21 denotes the chromosome's number.

and Nagasaki, and has continually examined and observed these children at about the time of their birthdays from ages nine to nineteen. According to the analyses made by Wood et al. (1967*b*) (table 9.13), retarded growth was most prominent in those exposed near—especially within 1.5 kilometers—the hypocenter, and they were retarded in stature, weight, and head circumference. Periodical observations (Connor, Kawamoto, and Omori 1971) from ten to seventeen years of age revealed a small body and head in those who had received large doses of radiation in utero at age ten; and a similar tendency was found at age seventeen. The growth in general, and the maximum growth rate during the seven-year period, however, did not differ from either in those receiving low doses of radiation. These results coincide with those reported by Hirai (1964).

TABLE 9.13

*Mean Measurements of Survivors (at the age of 17) Who Were Exposed in Utero by Distance from the Hypocenter**

Measurement	City	Sex	1,500 m	1,500–1,999 m	Not in City
Head circumference (cm)	Hiroshima	Male	53.9	55.1	55.1
		Female	53.1	54.0	54.2
	Nagasaki	Male	53.8	54.9	55.4
		Female	53.7	54.8	54.5
Standing height (cm)	Hiroshima	Male	163.4	165.4	165.5
		Female	151.3	153.9	153.8
	Nagasaki	Male	161.0	162.3	166.7
		Female	151.5	155.1	152.9
Body weight (kg)	Hiroshima	Male	51.3	54.2	54.2
		Female	46.1	48.4	49.0
	Nagasaki	Male	50.5	52.8	54.9
		Female	45.6	50.8	48.3
Chest circumference (cm)	Hiroshima	Male	77.2	78.3	78.0
		Female	71.9	73.4	73.1
	Nagasaki	Male	78.7	81.0	82.0
		Female	77.6	79.9	79.7

* All values in the table are mean values.
Source: J. W. Wood, R. J. Keehn, S. Kawamoto, and K. G. Johnson, "Growth and development of children exposed in utero to the atomic bombs in Hiroshima and Nagasaki," *American Journal of Public Health* 47 (1967): 1374.

In relation to growth in general, there are some reports on the skeletal system of children exposed in utero to the bomb. One of them is the survey of W. W. Sutow and E. West (1955) on the development of skeletal abnormalities in two groups of children exposed in utero within 2 kilometers, and at distances of 4 to 5 kilometers, of the hypocenter. The results showed no difference between the two groups. Another survey was made by W. J. Russell et al. (1973) on bone maturation. This study was carried out on 556 children in Hiroshima and Nagasaki who had been exposed to the atomic bomb in utero and controls; and it was found that epiphyseal closure of the hands developed six to seven months later in boys and eight to nine months later in girls, as compared with previous reports on normal children.

THE ADULT STAGE OF THOSE EXPOSED IN UTERO

After collecting the results of the survey made by the Atomic Bomb Casualty Commission, Kato in 1973 reported the late effects of exposure in utero. The effects encountered up to that time in those receiving high doses of radiation in utero were: (1) increased incidence of retarded growth and development (stature, head circumference) and of microcephaly (Blot and Miller 1972; Miller and Blot 1972); (2) increased mortality, especially of infants; (3) temporary fall of antibody production (Kanamitsu et al. 1966); and (4) increased frequency of chromosome abnormality in peripheral lymphocytes (Bloom, Neriishi, and Archer 1968). There was, however, neither increased incidence of leukemia or cancer (Jablon and Kato 1970*a*; Takamura and Ueda 1960) nor alteration in fertility (Blot, Moriyama, and Miller 1972; Blot et al. 1975) nor sex ratio (Jablon and Kato 1970*b*) of those born to exposed women.

MICROCEPHALY

Microcephaly denotes a head circumference less than two standard deviations below the age- and sex-specific mean head size and is frequently accompanied by mental retardation (figure 9.4). As already mentioned, microcephaly occurred relatively often among those exposed in utero in Hiroshima and Nagasaki and is one of the most important aftereffects of the atomic bomb.

Frequency of Microcephaly. At the Atomic Bomb Casualty Commission, Miller (1956) found 33 cases of microcephaly (two or more standard deviations below normal) among 169 children exposed in utero in Hiroshima. These 33 cases included 15 with mental retardation, 18 with normal mental development, and 13 with a head circumference three or more standard deviations below normal. Wood et al. (1967*a*) found 33 cases of microcephaly among 183 children exposed in utero in Hiroshima. Fourteen of the 33 showed it to a marked degree. As to the children exposed in utero in Nagasaki, G. N. Burrow, H. B. Hamilton, and Z. Hrubec (1964; 1965) pointed out the low mean head circumference in the heavily exposed group (within 1.5 kilometers, more than 50 rads). Kawamoto (1966) reported 7 instances of microcephaly among 102 exposed in utero within 2 kilometers of the hypocenter

Figure 9.4. Microcephaly in a child exposed in utero (*left*, Group I–Case 10 in table 9.15); non-exposed friend on the right.

in Nagasaki, and another 5 among 173 at a distance of 2 to 3 kilometers of the hypocenter.

In the survey of children exposed in utero in Hiroshima in 1963, Tabuchi and Hirai (1965) and Tabuchi et al. (1967) found 45 cases (8.3 percent) of microcephaly among 545 children exposed in utero within 3 kilometers of the hypocenter; the 45 included 12(2.2 percent) with marked microcephaly. As compared to the 13 cases (2.7 percent) of microcephaly among 473 non-exposed children, the incidence of this condition among those exposed in utero is extremely high (table 9.14). With the cooperation of the Kinoko-kai,* survey and medical care for those with microcephaly were continued up to 1965 by the Department of Obstetrics and Gynecology of Hiroshima University (44 cases are still alive).

Medical Findings of Microcephaly. Tabuchi et al. (1967)—with the cooperation of R. Fumizawa (Kinoko-kai), T. Akinobu (Chūgoku Broadcasting Corporation), M. Harada (Miyazaki University), and Y. Yorita and M. Yokozaki (Hiroshima A-Bomb Survivors Health Control Clinic)—carried out a

---

* Kinoko-kai, or Mushroom Club, is a group of parents of microcephalic children. It was organized in 1965 and has been supported since then by the Hiroshima Study Association, a group of writers and journalists in Hiroshima.

TABLE 9.14
Incidence of Microcephaly Due to Exposure in Utero

	Total Number Exposed	Microcephaly		Male			Female		
		a	b	Number Exposed	Microcephaly a	b	Number Exposed	Microcephaly a	b
Persons exposed in utero (0–3 km)	545	45 (8.3%)	12 (2.2%)	232	18 (7.8%)	5 (2.2%)	313	27 (8.6%)	7 (2.2%)
Fetal age ATB*									
0–3 mos.	152	26 (17.1%)	10 (6.6%)	62	11 (17.7%)	3 (4.8%)	90	15 (16.7%)	7 (7.8%)
4–7 mos.	211	15 (7.1%)	2 (0.9%)	93	6 (6.5%)	2 (2.2%)	118	9 (7.6%)	7 (7.8%)
Distance from hypocenter									
0–1 km	12	6 (50.0%)	6 (50.0%)	5	3 (60.0%)	3 (60.0%)	7	3 (42.9%)	3 (42.9%)
1–1.5 km	108	24 (22.2%)	6 (5.6%)	52	9 (17.3%)	2 (3.8%)	56	15 (26.8%)	4 (7.1%)
1.5–2 km	137	6 (4.4%)		58	2 (3.4%)		79	4 (5.1%)	
Non-exposed controls	473	13 (2.7%)		147	3 (2.0%)		326	9 (2.8%)	

a. Number of persons with microcephaly (below M–2σ†); figures in parentheses are percentages of the total number exposed.
b. Number of persons with severe microcephaly (below M–3σ); figures in parentheses are percentages of the total number exposed.
* ATB: at time of bombing.
† M: mean circumference of head; σ: standard deviation of the mean.
Source: A. Tabuchi and G. Hirai, "Studies on developmental disturbances in children exposed in utero to the atomic bomb," *Journal of the Hiroshima Obstetrical and Gynaecological Society* 4 (1965): 236.

detailed clinical survey on twelve cases with marked microcephaly, four cases with mental retardation following exposure at the infant stage, and nineteen cases exposed in utero but without microcephaly. All twelve cases with conspicuous microcephaly were within the twenty-fourth week of gestation at the time of the explosion, with eleven being within the fifteenth week. They were exposed within 1.5 kilometers of the hypocenter, and the majority of their mothers had suffered from acute radiation symptoms. There was no particular relation between the mother's age and number of deliveries she had had. The children with severe microcephaly were small in stature, and the majority had a head circumference three or more deviations below normal. They were usually retarded mentally (I.Q. 13.6–25.5), and social adaptability was low. Chromosome testing revealed trisomy 21 in one case. There were no cases with phenylketonuria,* and neither microcephaly nor other malformations were found among their siblings.

Further detailed examinations, including X-ray, were made on the aforementioned cases: nine cases with marked microcephaly (group I), four cases exposed and mentally retarded (group II), and four cases exposed in utero but without microcephaly (group III). The results are summarized in tables 9.15, 9.16, and 9.17.

Observations made by the Atomic Bomb Casualty Commission on microcephaly in children exposed in utero have also confirmed myopia, strabismus, microcornea, nystagmus, dislocation of hip joint, defect of pharynx, funnel chest, and mongolism. Also found were diseases such as nephritis, urinary tract infections, hepatitis, liver cirrhosis, acute poliomyelitis, tuberculosis, chronic gastritis, otitis media, and marked tendency to obesity. Autopsy reports of cases with microcephaly in Nagasaki described small cranium, poorly developed cerebral hemisphere, heterotopic gray substance in lateral ventricle, defect of mammillary body *(corpus mamillare),* microphthalmia, microcornea, yellow spot defect, congenital cataract, latent spina bifida, retarded growth of bone, and retarded physical growth (Yokota et al. 1963; Ōtsuru 1968).

Incidence of Microcephaly and Exposed Radiation Dose. From the preceding information it is clear that microcephaly had been induced by exposure in utero to the atomic bomb, and there is a significant correlation between exposure dose and frequency of microcephaly as well as between the latter and gestational age at exposure. In 1972, R. W. Miller and W. J. Blot (1972, p. 784) again investigated the relation between microcephaly and exposure dose of radiation. The subjects consisted of 388 persons in Hiroshima and 99 in Nagasaki, who had been exposed in utero, and of the controls. The

---

* *Phenylketonuria* is a congenital flawed metabolism of the acid phenylalanine, which is often associated with mental defects. (Ed.)

TABLE 9.15

Abnormal X-ray Findings in Persons Exposed in Utero

Group I. Severe Microcephaly (head size $\leq M-3\sigma$) with Mental Retardation

Case	Head				Spine			Chest	Extremities		Others	Remarks
	High Tentorial Attachment	Calcification	Sella Turcica	Others	Thoracic Vertebrae	Lumbar Vertebrae	Rib	Lung Field	Deformity of Small Finger	Transverses Line at Epiphysis of Radius		
1	(+)		small				thin				absence of foot phalanges	
2	(+)		small									
3	(+)											
4	(+)		small					pendulous heart, diaphragmatic tenting		(+)		
5	(+)		irregular						short			
6	(+)			front parietal osteoma					short	(+)		
7	(+)		deep									
8	(+)											
9	(+)											
10	(+)										*Luxatio Coxae Congenita*	
11												by 1965 x-ray findings

Group II. Microcephaly (head size $<M-2\sigma \sim >M-3\sigma$) with Mental Retardation

1	(+)			
2	small	convergence of vascular grooves		
3		shallow occipital fornix fossa		
4	small			short second phalanx of left fifth toe transverse line of fibula

Group III. Exposed in Utero but without Microcephaly

1	(+)	irregular prominent occipital eminence	(+)	
2		small (irregular)		
3				
4				

Cases with no abnormal findings not listed. All cases had 8 carpal bones.

Source: A. Tabuchi and G. Hirai, "Studies on developmental disturbances in children exposed in utero to the atomic bomb," *Journal of the Hiroshima Obstetrical and Gynaecological Society* 4 (1965): 236. A. Tabuchi, G. Hirai, S. Nakagawa, K. Shimada, and J. Fujitō, "Clinical findings on microcephalic children exposed in utero," ABCC TR (1967) 28–67.

TABLE 9.16

Degenerative Signs

---

(1) Head
   Hair: Curly. Alopecia. Scanty pigmentation.
   Brachycephaly: Oxycephaly. Scaphocephaly. Flat occiput.
   Asymmetry: Megacephaly. Microcephaly. Tumor.
(2) Face
   Eye: Strabismus (divergent, convergent). Narrow palpabral fissure. Cataract. Corneal opacity.
      Abnormality of iris. Epicanthus. Mongoloid. Nonmongoloid.
   Nose: Saddle nose. Prominence of root of nose. Large. Small. Curved concha.
   Mouth: Gothic palate. Odontoloxia. Harelip. Cleft palate. Uvula bifida. Micrognathia. Mega-
      loglossia.
   Pinna: Small. Large. Low position. Bent. Lop ear. Nodular.
   Skin: Hemangioma. Vascular engorgement.
(3) Fingers and palm print
   Digitus varus of 5th finger. Brachydactylia. Arachnodactylia. Short 2nd phalanx. Polydacty-
   lia. Syndactylia. Adactylia. Wide thumb. Simian crease (complete, incomplete). Axial trira-
   dius (t).
(4) Upper and Lower Extremities
   Cubitus valgus. Cubitus varus. Limitation of extension. Limitation of flexion.
(5) Trunk
   Heart murmurs. Pigeon breast. Funnel chest. Asymmetry. Umbilical hernia. Accessory
   mamma. Pterygoid neck.
(6) Skin
   Leukoplakia. Café. Pigmented nevi. Hypertrichosis. Hemangioma. Skin sinus.
(7) Genitourinary Organ
   Hernia. Cryptorchidism (left, right). Hypospodias. Vaginal fistula. Aproctia. Hermaphro-
   dism.
(8) Viscera
   Brain. Skull film. Pneumoencephalography. Angiography. Chest and abdomen. Physical
   examination. Roentgenography.

Source: M. Arima, "Morphological abnormalities noted among those exposed in utero with A-bomb disturbances—especially in comparison with general feeble-minded patients," *Nagasaki Medical Journal* 43 (1968): 873.

mothers of the former had been exposed within 2 kilometers of the hypocenter. The controls consisted of 1,010 children whose mothers were either remotely exposed (3 to 5 kilometers), or who were not in the city at the time of explosion. Forty-eight persons with microcephaly (mental retardation in 10) were found among those exposed in utero in Hiroshima, and 15 (mental retardation in 4) in Nagasaki. The highest incidence of microcephaly, especially when accompanied by mental retardation, was encountered in those who had been exposed within the eighteenth week (especially three to seventeen weeks) of gestation (table 9.18). In Hiroshima a significant increase in frequency of microcephaly was already seen in those whose mothers had received low doses (10 to 19 rads) of radiation. In general, the frequency of microcephaly increased with the increase of exposure dosage. The thirty-seven mothers who had received over 50 rads within the eighteenth week

Degenerative Signs and Diseases Observed in Persons Exposed in Utero

Case	Head	Mouth	Eyes	Ears and Nose	Skin	Spine and Extremities	Urogenital Organ	Viscera and Blood	Past History
					Group I. Severe Microcephaly (head size $\leq$M-3σ) with Mental Retardation				
1	Brachycephaly, Flat occiput	Chronic gingivitis	Epicanthus, myopia	Saddle nose, flat root of nose	Pigmentary abnormality of whole body (+++) Hypertrichosis (++)	Scoliosis, cubitus valgus	Right double pyelo-ureter	Anemia (pernicious?)	Epilepsy at age 8
2	Brachycephaly	3⌐labial displacement. ₂T₂ defects	Strabismus, myopia	Lop ear	Abnormality of pigmentation (leukoplakia, nevus pigmentation) (++)	Brachydactylia, axial triradius t', absence of 2–5 phalanges of right foot	(−)	Hyperactive tendon reflexes	Convulsions
3	Flat occiput	Facial abnormalities, protrusion of lips	?	?	(−)	Dislocation of hips	Urobilinuria	Leukocytosis	
4	Brachycephaly, alopecia, occipital deformity	Odontoloxia, mild micrognathia 5|5 malposition 2|2 tion	Myopia	Prominence of root of nose, curved concha, small pinna	Leukoplakia, pigmentation (++)	Irregular simian line, axial triradius t', decreased equilibrium function	(−)	Pendulous heart, diaphragmatic tenting	Bronchial pneumonia
5	Brachycephaly	Gothic palate, gingivitis, rotated teeth, excessive overbite	Hyaline remnant, fibrosis of medullated nerve, myopia	Bent pinna, dysfunction (extravestibule)	Pigmentary abnormality of whole body (leukoplakia, pigmentation) (+++)	Inability to stand on one leg, bilateral brachydactylia, axial triradius t", abnormality of length of leg	(−)	Abnormal thorn test, polycythemia vera	Convulsions
6	Left frontal osteoma	(−)	Mongolismlike symptoms	Saddle nose	Pigmentary abnormality of part of body and hypertrichosis (++)	Brachydactylia (left small finger), bent hip joint (left), accelerated tendon reflexes	(−)	(−)	Pneumonia, epilepsy ?

TABLE 9.17 *(continued)*

Group I. Severe Microcephaly (head size $\leq M-3\sigma$) with Mental Retardation

Case	Head	Mouth	Eyes	Ears and Nose	Skin	Spine and Extremities	Urogenital Organ	Viscera and Blood	Past History
7	Brachycephaly	Protrusion of lips	Myopia	Small pinna	Pigmentary abnormality of whole body (+++)	Sluggish movements, accelerated tendon reflexes, decreased equilibrium function	(−)	(−)	
8	Flat occiput, mongolism	Protrusion of lips, enamel dysplasia	?	?	Leukoplakia (++)	Short limbs, bilateral short second finger, digitus varus of fifth finger, bilateral hallux valgus, bilateral flatfoot	(−)	Anemia	Fever, stomatitis
9	Brachycephaly	Gothic palate, 6$\frac{}{}$1 malposition enamel dysplasia	Divergent strabismus, right myopia, left hyperopia	Prominence of root of nose, curved concha, low pinna, small pinna	Localized leukoplakia, nevus (+), atheroma of left lower extremities (?)	Multiple bone tumors of arms and legs, difference in anterior-posterior diameter of forearm and length of arm by left and right sides, accelerated tendon reflexes, decreased equilibrium function	(−)	(−)	Twins (one has died), fever

No.									
1	(–)	2|2 Microdont, 6⌐ Caries, 5⌐ rotated teeth	Myopia	Curved concha, small pinna	Nevi over whole body, leukoplakia of part of body (++)	Brachydactylia (short second phalanx), accelerated tendon reflexes, decreased equilibrium function	(–)	(–)	Hypotension
2	(–)	Gothic palate, odontoloxia, 2|2/3|3 tion malposition, enamel dysplasia	Myopia	Prominence of root of nose, small pinna	Left facial pigmented nevus (+)	Simian crease left insufficient, cubitus valgus, axial triradius t′, accelerated tendon reflexes, decreased equilibrium function	Urobilinuria	(–)	Gastric ulcer ?
3	Convergence of vascular grooves	Osteoma of left mandibula, enamel dysplasia	Myopia	Small pinna, chronic tonsillitus	Localized leukoplakia and nevus (++)	Second phalanx of left fifth toe (short), microdactylia, cubitus valgus, limitation of extension of right middle and ring fingers, accelerated tendon reflexes, decreased equilibrium function	Urobilinuria	(–)	Dental bleeding
4	(–)	(–)	Slight myopia	(–)	Tumor of left chest	Motor paralysis (cerebral paralysis ?), cubitus valgus, excessive extension of upper and lower extremities	(–)	(–)	

TABLE 9.17 (continued)

Group III. Exposed in Utero but without Microcephaly

Case	Head	Mouth	Eyes	Ears and Nose	Skin	Spine and Extremities	Urogenital Organ	Viscera and Blood	Past History
1	Abnormal prominence of occipital protuberance	8|8 malposition, enamel dysplasia	Vitreous opacity, latent divergent strabismus	(−)	Localized pigmentation (+), tumor of left forearm	Accelerated tendon reflexes, decreased equilibrium function	(−)	Nephritis	Fever
2	(−)	3|3 malposition 5	Pigmentation of right crystalline lens, myopia	Narrow external meatus, lop ear, curved concha	Localized leukoplakia and pigmentation (++)	Ataxic gait, accelerated tendon reflexes	(−)	(−)	
3	Brachycephaly	Enamel dysplasia	Myopia	Saddle nose	Localized pigmented nevi (+)	Convulsive paralysis of lower extremities, huge transverse process of seventh cervical vertebra, retention of fifth lumbar vertebral epiphyseal center	?	Dysfunction of adrenal gland and pituitary body ?	Pneumonia
4	(−)	(−)	Left myopia	Deviated nasal septum	(−)	X-ray showed thoracic scaliosis with convexity to right, cubitus valgus	(−)	Abnormal thorn test (dysfunction of adrenal gland and pituitary body ?)	

(−): No specific findings. ?: Examination not possible.

Source: A. Tabuchi and G. Hirai, "Studies on developmental disturbances in children exposed in utero to the atomic bomb," *Journal of the Hiroshima Obstetrical and Gynaecological Society* 4 (1965): 236. A. Tabuchi, G. Hirai, S. Nakagawa, K. Shimada, and J. Fujitô, "Clinical findings on microcephalic children exposed in utero," ABCC TR (1967) 28–67.

TABLE 9.18

Frequency of Small Head Size According to City, Gestational Age, and Radiation Dose*

Exposure Dose (rads)	Hiroshima		Nagasaki	
	0–17 Weeks†	18+ Weeks	0–17 Weeks	18+ Weeks
Not in city or far from hypocenter	31/764		10/246	
0–9	4(1)/63‡	4/65‡	0/1	0/9
10–19	6(1)/54	0/44	0/7	0/6
20–29	6/24	1/14	0/5	2/7
30–39	4/8	0/10	2/4	0/6
40–49	3/11	0/6	0/6	0/3
50–99	9(2)/20	2/24	0/9	0/11
100–149	2/4	0/10	0/2	1/5
150 or over	5(5)/13	1(1)/8‡	8(3)/9	2(1)/9
Unknown	1/7	0/3	0/0	0/0
Total (in city)	40(9)/204	8(1)/184	10(3)/43	5(1)/56

* Among persons with small head circumference some also had mental retardation (numbers in parentheses).
† Gestational week at the time of exposure.
‡ Denominator includes one person with mental retardation and normal head circumference.
Source: R. W. Miller and W. J. Blot, "Small head size after in utero exposure to atomic radiation," *Lancet* 2 (1972): 784.

of gestation bore sixteen children with microcephaly. Five children with microcephaly and mental retardation were detected among the children born to thirteen mothers who had been exposed to over 150 rads. There were forty-two mothers who had been exposed to more than 50 rads after the 18th week of gestation; three children with microcephaly appeared in this group. One child who was mentally retarded was born to a mother exposed to over 150 rads.

On the other hand, in Nagasaki the effect of exposure to low doses (30–39 rads) of radiation on the head circumference was noted in two among the four children. There were nine mothers who had been exposed to over 150 rads before the eighteenth week of gestation and to whom were born eight children with microcephaly. Three of the eight children were also mentally retarded. Among the nine children who had received this high dose during the later gestational period, there were two with microcephaly, one of whom was mentally retarded. In Hiroshima, the minimum dose producing microcephaly was 10 to 19 rads; but no mentally retarded microcephalic children were observed under 150 rads in Nagasaki. Microcephaly was frequently accompanied by mental retardation at maternal doses of more than 150 rads in both cities. From this difference between Hiroshima and Nagasaki it is reasonable to suppose that the atomic bomb dropped on Hiroshima contained more neutrons than the Nagasaki bomb.

Growth and Developmental Disturbances

Experimental studies and experiences gained from medical application of
radiation to the human body have shown that young immature organisms
are more susceptible to the effects of radiation than are mature organisms
(Kaplan 1948; Murphy 1947, pp. 87–100). It was, therefore, anticipated soon
after the explosion that the effects of exposure to the atomic bomb would
appear more prominently in those exposed in utero, in infants, and in young
children and might lead to growth and developmental disturbances.

GROWTH AND DEVELOPMENT OF EXPOSED CHILDREN

The Atomic Bomb Casualty Commission carried out investigations on the
growth and development of children in Hiroshima during a three-year period
from 1951 to 1953 (Reynolds 1959; Sutow 1957). The samples consisted of
747 boys and 684 girls who had been exposed within 2 kilometers of the
hypocenter and were five to seven years of age at the time of the survey.
The 664 boys and 649 girls of a similar age who entered the city after 1
January 1946 were observed as controls. Each child in both groups received
a physical checkup and a dental examination (Terasaki and Shiota 1953)
yearly at about the time of his or her birthday. Basic body measurements
(height, weight, sitting height), observation of maturation (body hair, development of breasts), menstrual history, and standard X-ray examination (breadth
of tibia and subcutaneous fat) were carried out. Comparison of both groups
and their relation to exposure distance and severity of radiation symptoms
were analyzed.

In 1951 the mean values of measurements covering 312 items were calculated
and compared in both groups. A higher mean value was found for 249 items,
among which 45 items differed significantly in the non-exposed group. In
the following year (1952), the mean values of 221 items among 288 were
greater in the non-exposed. The mean values of 22 items showed a statistically
significant difference. The weights of the non-exposed children were found
to be greater during the first two years. Analyses of data on height and
weight during the three-year survey revealed a lower stature in both boys
and girls of the exposed group. In the exposed group, children's physiques
tended to become larger with increasing distance from the hypocenter. Exposed children with a big physique were those with or without a history of
mild acute radiation symptoms. On the contrary, small children who had
been exposed frequently had a history of moderate or severe radiation symptoms. The mean body weight of older boys in the exposed group was small
compared with that of the non-exposed. The difference was significant, especially in those exposed at a short distance (within 1.5 kilometers of the hypo-

center). A similar tendency was also found in girls of the lower age group. The mean body weight of the children exposed at a short distance was significantly less than that of children exposed at a far distance (1.5 to 2 kilometers) from the hypocenter.

A similar survey covering a four-year period after the explosion was also carried out in Nagasaki. The samples of 2,053 exposed children revealed that they were generally short in height (brevi-type) compared with the controls (Setoguchi 1951). Other surveys were made by N. Izumi (1956, p. 1701) and by M. Yasunaka and T. Nishikawa (1956, p. 1693).

MATURATION OF EXPOSED CHILDREN

Maturation, in general, was more complete in the controls than in the exposed children. In Hiroshima, this tendency was especially evident in particular items, including mammary development and menarche. In a comparison of the mean ages of menarche in 566 exposed girls and 539 non-exposed in Hiroshima, it was noted that menarche occurred somewhat earlier in the non-exposed group, although no significant difference was found statistically (Monden 1955). The exposed girls were divided into several groups by their distance from the hypocenter and by the presence and degree of acute radiation symptoms, and the mean ages of menarche were compared; but no significant difference was found.

The ages of menarche in girl students were also examined in Nagasaki, but there was no certain evidence of influence of exposure to the atomic bomb (Yamao 1951; Mitani 1953).

DENTAL GROWTH IN EXPOSED CHILDREN

In a survey carried out between 1951 and 1952 on 1,269 exposed children at the Atomic Bomb Casualty Commission in Hiroshima (Terasaki and Shiota 1953), 292 children (23 percent) showed mild enamel hypoplasia, while only one child revealed marked hypoplasia. In the control group consisting of 1,001 children, there were 137 (13.1 percent) with enamel hypoplasia, including one serious case. A significant difference in frequency of this condition can be seen between both groups. The exposed samples were divided into two groups according to the presence or the absence of epilation during the acute stage, and it was noted that enamel hypoplasia occurred in 24 (18 percent) among 133 children who had epilation and in 267 (24 percent) among 1,134 children without epilation; thus, there was no significant difference between the two groups. The time of dentition of first and second permanent teeth was somewhat delayed in the exposed children.

Dental examination with the appliance of X-ray in exposed and non-exposed children ages eight to twelve revealed somewhat earlier completion of dental root in the exposed, but the dental root tended to be smaller, although of no significant difference (Terasaki and Shiota 1955). In 1953, measurements for 22 items of the jaw were made on 659 exposed children and on 650 controls every two years from ages eight to eighteen (Ōta 1958) and were compared by age, sex, and exposure. A significant difference between exposed and non-exposed children was confirmed for only three items. The reason for this difference was not clear but was thought not to be related to exposure.

Besides the Atomic Bomb Casualty Commission survey, there is the report made by E. Maeda et al. (1955) in Hiroshima. Changes in enamel and gingiva of children exposed between ages one and three were somewhat more frequently encountered than in the non-exposed. The exposed children with these changes had a history of acute radiation symptoms, which were more severe than in the exposed without these changes. The survey made by T. Tomisaki (1955) in Nagasaki also revealed a higher incidence of enamel hypoplasia in the exposed children but showed little difference in the dentition of permanent teeth.

THE EXPOSED CHILDREN IN ADULTHOOD

Height and weight measurements were made on approximately 3,200 adults who were under eighteen years old at the time of the bombing on Hiroshima and Nagasaki (Belsky and Blot 1975). The mean adult height in those who had received an estimated dose of over 100 rads between birth and five years of age was significantly smaller than in the other groups. As indicated in table 9.19, males in Hiroshima were 4.4 centimeters smaller, and females,

TABLE 9.19

Average Adult Heights (cm) of People Exposed under Age Eighteen at the Time of Bombing

	Sex	Age ATB*	Not in City	Exposure Dose (rads)		
				0–9	10–99	100+
Hiroshima	Male	0–5	166.4‡	166.1‡	165.9‡	161.5
		6–11	162.3	164.2	166.3†	162.2
		12–17	164.3	163.6	164.3	163.4
	Female	0–5	153.3	153.6‡	152.9†	150.4
		6–11	152.5†	153.6†	153.6†	150.5
		12–17	152.1	152.3	152.2	151.9
Nagasaki	Male	0–5	166.2	162.2		166.2
		6–11	164.0	164.1		162.7
		12–17	163.2	163.9		161.8
	Female	0–5	152.8	152.9		150.8
		6–11	152.4	151.3		151.5
		12–17	151.8	151.6		151.2

* ATB: at the time of bombing.
† ($p < 0.01$) greater than 100+ average.
‡ ($p < 0.05$) greater than 100+ average.
Source: J. L. Belsky and W. J. Blot, "Adult stature in relation to childhood exposure to the atomic bombs of Hiroshima and Nagasaki," *American Journal of Public Health* 65 (1975): 489.

2.5 centimeters. In Nagasaki, the mean height of females who had received an estimated dose of over 100 rads between birth and five years of age, appeared to be smaller than of the other groups. This difference, however, was not statistically significant.

The weight measurements in Hiroshima revealed a smaller mean weight in all age groups who had been exposed to high doses of radiation (over 100 rads). The effect of high doses of radiation could be inferred in Hiroshima but not in Nagasaki.

Aging and Life Span

Acceleration of the aging process and elevation of the mortality rate are important subjects in the study of aftereffects of the atomic bomb. Animal experiments have shown that leukemia and other malignancies are induced by radiation; and increased frequencies of specific disorders associated with radiation are accompanied by a rise in mortality rate, a shortening of life, and also indications of increased aging. A large-scale survey by the National Institute of Health, Japan, and the Atomic Bomb Casualty Commission (RERF*) on approximately 109,000 people has been in progress since 1950. This survey is called the Life Span Study.

LIFE SPAN STUDY AND METHODS

In this study, a fixed population including controls was established for long-term observation. The main group consists of 28,000 persons (exposed within 2 kilometers of the hypocenter) selected from 280,000 survivors who had been exposed to the atomic bomb, according to the national census held in 1950. As a control group, people of a similar age and the same sex were selected at random from those who either had been exposed at some distance (over 2.5 kilometers of the hypocenter) or had not been exposed. Other groups include about 16,000 survivors who had been exposed 2 to 2.5 kilometers from the hypocenter, and another 9,000 who had been exposed near the hypocenter but whose family registers ("Koseki") were not in Hiroshima or Nagasaki. The estimated dose of radiation exposure has been calculated for each person. Table 9.20 shows the number of persons studied and the exposure dose.

* Radiation Effects Research Foundation.

TABLE 9.20

Distribution of Life Span Study Sample by Exposure Doses

	Total	Nonexposed	Tentative Dose in 1965 (rads)						
			0	1–9	10–49	50–99	100–199	200+	Unknown
Hiroshima	82,085	20,176	29,943	13,787	10,707	2,665	1,677	1,460	1,670
Nagasaki	26,682	6,347	4,699	6,705	3,700	1,231	1,229	1,310	1,461
Total	108,767	26,523	34,642	20,492	14,407	3,896	2,906	2,770	3,131

Source: G. W. Beebe, H. Kato, and C. E. Land, "Life span study, Report 8, Mortality experience of atomic bomb survivors 1950–74," RER TR (1977) 1–77.

Death certificates were checked to determine whether members belonging to this fixed population were alive or dead. Vital statistics were examined periodically, and records of autopsies and biopsies were sometimes referred to in order to determine accurately the cause of death.

MORTALITY RATE

Of these approximately 109,000 persons, 25,924 have died during the twenty-four years between October 1950 and September 1974 (Beebe, Kato, and Land 1977). The mortality rate rose with increased doses of radiation exposure. Figure 9.5 shows the relative risk of those exposed to high doses (over 200 rads) and those not exposed according to mortality rate and cause of death. Since errors are included in calculating the relative risk, a confidence-interval limit of 80 percent was estimated statistically. When compared with the group that had never been exposed to radiation, the mortality rates for all diseases, leukemia, and malignancies other than leukemia in the high-dose group (over 200 rads) were 1.16, 17.6, and 1.42 times higher. There was, however, no increase in mortality from trauma, tuberculosis, cerebrovascular accidents, or disorders of the circulatory system (mainly heart disease).

LEUKEMIA

Death from leukemia among the exposed survivors has been increasing since 1947. Figure 9.6 shows the yearly change of mortality rate for leukemia in the group exposed to 100 rads or more. The peak of the mortality in this group occurred between 1950 and 1954 and then gradually declined each year. A significantly higher rate than in the control group (0–9 rads) was, however, still maintained in the year 1974. Although the mortality from leukemia rises with increased doses of radiation exposure, the shapes of the dose-response curves differ between Hiroshima and Nagasaki, with leukemia-mortality-per-radiation dose being higher in Hiroshima. On the assumption that the difference between cities was caused by the different types of radiation,

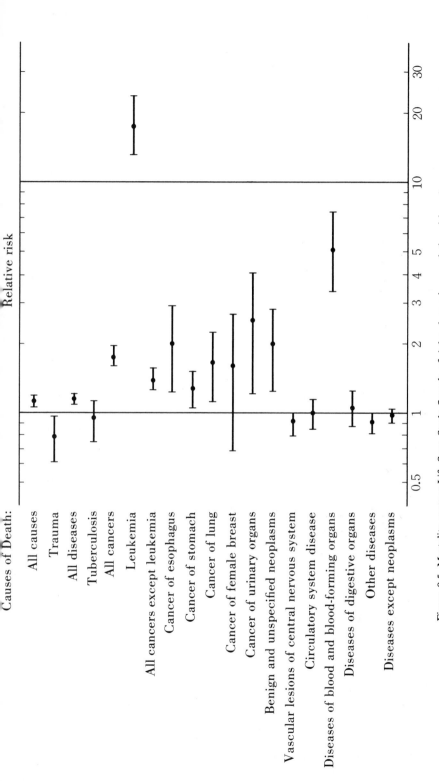

Figure 9.5. Mortality among Life Span Study Sample of A-bomb survivors; relative risk and 80% confidence intervals for major groups of causes of death, 200+ rads versus 0 rad (1950–74). (Beebe, Kato, and Land 1977).

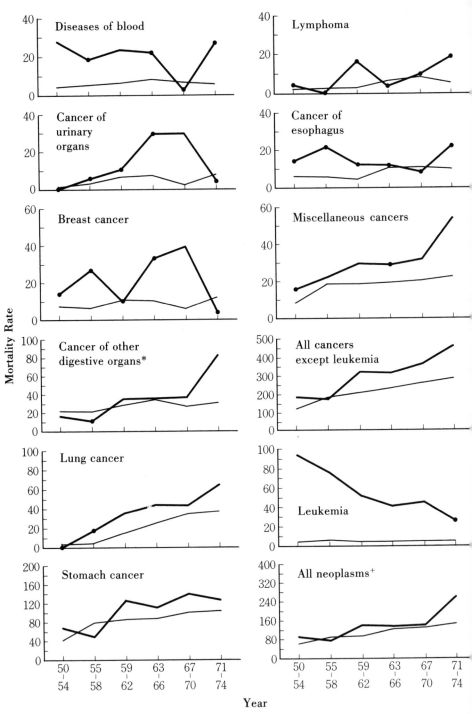

Figure 9.6. Deaths per 100,000 per year by cause of death and by calendar time, 1950–74, 100+ rads versus 0–9 rads (Beebe, Kato, and Land 1977).

the relative biological effectiveness (RBE) would be nearly 5. As shown by the dose-response curve, mortality from leukemia is proportional to neutron dose and to the square dose of gamma rays, but the RBE differs by radiation dose: RBE is larger than 5 when the radiation dose is low, while RBE is smaller than 5 when the dose is high.

MALIGNANCIES OTHER THAN LEUKEMIA

Death from malignancies other than leukemia differs according to location of the tumors but has gradually increased from about 1955 to 1960 after a latent period of ten to fifteen years after the explosion (figure 9.6); although malignancies in all locations have not necessarily increased. As can be seen in figure 9.5, the relative risk of lung, breast, stomach, esophageal, and bladder cancer, of other cancers of the urinary tract, and of malignant lymphoma has increased in the 200-rad group, as compared with the 0–9-rad group. There is also a correlation between age at exposure time and incidence of carcinogenesis. Even when the exposure dose of radiation is the same, the risk of carcinogenesis is the highest in those exposed between birth and nine years. Figure 9.7 shows the relative risk of cancer mortality in the group exposed to more than 100 rads (standardized to 0–9-rad group) by age at time of exposure (Beebe, Kato and Land 1977). It was thought that the risk of cancer was greatest to one exposed in utero (Stewart and Kneal 1970), but the mortality study (Kato 1971) on those exposed in utero has not to date revealed any signs of increased frequency of leukemia or of other malignancies in the high-dose group.

As for malignancies in general, the difference of dose-response curves in Hiroshima and Nagasaki indicates that the effect was more prominent in Hiroshima, although not so clearly as for leukemia.

OTHER CAUSES OF DEATH

If malignancies are excluded as a cause of death, the mortality of the high-dose group receiving more than 100 rads was not increased, as compared with that of the control group, either by age at exposure or by period of time (figure 9.8). No correlation between mortality and exposed dose was found for cerebral hemorrhage and heart disease (figure 9.5). In relation to the mean life span, lives were shorter by 0.3 to 1 year between 1950 and 1974, although there was some difference according to sex and exposure age in the high-dose group of over 100 rads. There was, however, no shortening of mean life span if leukemia and cancers are excluded. In other words, there are at present no data to support the hypothesis that radiation contributes to a nonspecific acceleration of aging resulting in shortening of life. Although no detectable nonspecific shortening of life expectation was seen

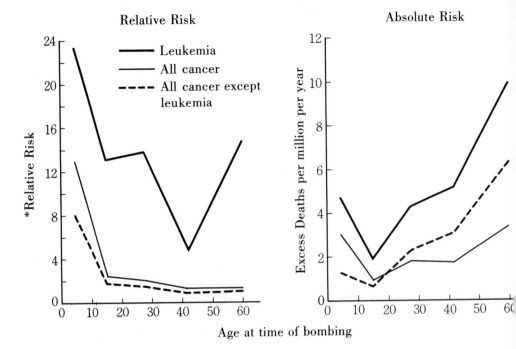

Relative Risk   Absolute Risk

*Risk of 100+ rads relative to 0–9 rads.

Figure 9.7. Comparison of leukemia, all cancer, and all cancer except leukemia, as to relative and absolute risk, by age at time of bombing. (Beebe, Kato, and Land 1977).
* Risk of 100 rads and over to 0–9 rads.

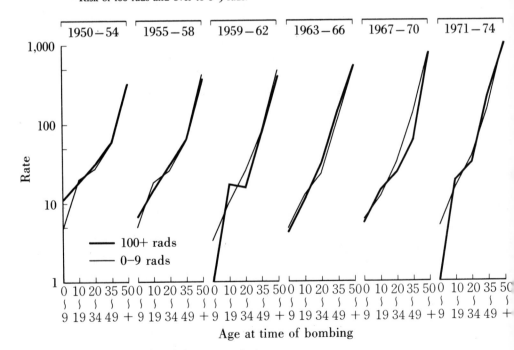

Rate standardized for sex and city

Figure 9.8. Deaths per 10,000 per year from all diseases except neoplasms by age at time of bombing, 1950–74, 100 or more rads group versus 0–9 rads group. (Beebe, Kato, and Land 1977).

in the British survey (Court-Brown and Doll 1958) on the mortality of radiologists, mortality from cancer, cardiovascular-renal disease, and other causes
combined were found to increase in a similar American survey (Seltser and
Sartwell 1965). The latter survey suggests that there is actually a nonspecific
acceleration of aging through radiation. On the other hand, however, the
surveys carried out on this subject are too few to permit any conclusions,
and the possibility of error in the results due to the way controls were selected
is open to criticism. It should also be kept in mind that the subjects of the
aforementioned survey consisted of exposed survivors who were alive in 1950
and whose mortality was followed thereafter. In other words, the deaths
during the five years immediately after the explosion up to 1950 were excluded
from this survey, since accurate data were unavailable. The possibility that
this survey included only those survivors who were in general radio-resistant
cannot be denied. From the supplementary data of deaths between 1946 and
1949, this possibility is almost negligible. It is possible that an increase in
nonspecific causes of death did not appear because of the artificial selection
of cases.

DEATHS AMONG EARLY ENTRANTS
People entering the city soon after the explosion for rescue activities were
not directly exposed to the atomic bomb, but were affected by residual radioactivity and were subject to aftereffects of radiation. In the preceding survey,
4,600 early entrants were included as non-exposed survivors; their mortality
rate was rather low compared with other non-exposed, and the effects of
residual radioactivity on their deaths could not be confirmed (Beebe, Kato,
and Land 1970).

Disorders of the Psychoneurological System

Several hundred thousands of people of different ages, sexes, living conditions,
and states of mind and body were suddenly assaulted by a hitherto unknown
catastrophe—the atomic bomb. Many were killed, wounded, or barely escaped
death. Those who survived have since grown up and become old and have
been further diversely affected by complex social life. The scars of this invidi-
ous catastrophe remain even in the children born of mothers who were exposed. With this complicated background, the mere fact of having been
exposed to the atomic bomb led to various disorders of mind and body,
symptoms, and complaints and would change psychogenic conditions. In

short, it is extremely difficult to pursue the neuropsychological aspects of this disaster.

In going through the *Bibliography of Publications Concerning Effect of Nuclear Explosions* 1945–1960 (Atomic Bomb Casualty Commission 1961) compiled by the Atomic Bomb Casualty Commission, one can find only thirty papers—or, strictly speaking, fewer than twenty—covering the psychoneurological field among the twenty-four hundred reports or papers published between 1945 and 1960. Only a few papers in this field have appeared since then. Whatever effects of exposure on the central nervous system might have been expected, they were transcended by instantaneous death on a massive scale. Although it is highly probable that many people suffered from vegetative neurosis or vegetative dystonia and various psychosomatic disorders, these were concealed as common aftereffects and did not become subjects for observation and medical care by specialists.

Since the Atomic Bomb Casualty Commission had a background in American medicine where energetic studies and practice of clinical psychology and psychoneurology were being carried on, it was expected that the commission would actively study psychoneurology during its survey of aftereffects. The ABCC, however, had no great interest in this field, and its main interests were in epidemiological and statistical analyses of a large population sample. At one time this institution was even inclined to underestimate the aftereffects of the atomic bomb. According to the ABCC report on the Joint Japanese-American Symposium held in February 1954, the delayed effects of exposure were examined in 4,231 survivors, among whom 1,435 were found to be apparently normal. In the remaining 2,796 cases, the diagnoses varied, and 4,791 different diagnoses were made. The report concluded that there were statistically no significant differences between exposed and non-exposed, except in the frequency of atomic bomb cataract and leukemia. The physical test carried out on 1,084 exposed and 1,020 non-exposed children in Hiroshima also revealed no significant difference, and there were also no significant differences in hematology and blood pressure. The report stated that mild anemia and decreased white cell count were common in both groups and could not be counted as an aftereffect of exposure. M. Konuma (1956, p. 1715), in his psychoneurological observations of the exposed who had prominent hematological changes, called attention to complaints of agony or of other symptoms. These complaints are termed *diencephalic syndrome,* and they are left out completely or mechanically negated by epidemiological statistics indifferent to mind and body correlations and to the human soul.

PSYCHONEUROLOGICAL DISORDERS IN THE ACUTE STAGE

Cerebroneuropathological Findings in the Acute Stage of Atomic Bomb Illness. The Japanese-American Joint Report on the effects of atomic radiation on the human brain has already been mentioned in chapter 8. Other reports were made by Uchimura and Shiraki (1952a; 1952b); Okada, Shimazono, and Hakamada (1953, p. 757); Shiraki (1951; 1953, p. 759), Shiraki and N. Andō (1956), and Shiraki et al. (1958); and Tamagawa et al. (1952b). Shiraki examined twenty-four cases terminating three to five weeks after exposure, and five cases, six to eight weeks after the bombing and found only a few changes of the central nervous system that were attributable to direct effects of radiation. He concluded that at this stage there was no relation between histology and clinical findings of the brain, with no cerebral deaths being confirmed.

Psychoneurological Observations of Acute Atomic Bomb Illness. Reports on the psychoneurological observations at this stage are scarce, except for those made during general clinical examination. The only report along this line seems to be that made by N. Okumura and H. Hikida (1949) at Nagasaki. They selected at random 50 survivors out of 192 who were hospitalized at the Ōmura Hospital, and psychoneurological observations were made two to three weeks after exposure (initial stage), the following one month (intermediate stage), and about one month after mid-October (late stage). The symptoms appearing immediately after exposure to atomic bomb radiation were similar to the common symptoms encountered in X-ray irradiation during daily clinical work. Okumura and Hikida, paying special attention to psychogenetic reaction, continued their study; and although there were various hearsay reports of many mental disorders occurring soon after the explosion, these researchers failed to gain accurate information on the actual facts, since many people had already died by the time of the survey. After an examination of their histories, only four cases out of fifty were found to come under the category of mental disorder.

In the intermediate stage, patients were still suffering from thermal burn and trauma, and some showed neurasthenia-like symptoms; while in the late stage, those patients with specific diathesis tended to develop neurosis. These were, however, indirect effects attributable to deterioration of environment and physical condition owing to exposure; and acute radiation illness was thought to be the only direct effect of the atomic bomb on the human psychoneurological system.

AFTEREFFECTS OF THE ATOMIC BOMB AND NEUROPSYCHIATRY

T. Nishikawa and S. Tsuiki (1961) discovered 533 patients with neurosislike symptoms among 7,297 exposed patients during the polyclinic examination of Nagasaki University in February and December 1956. The patients were divided into two groups—those with symptoms of atomic bomb radiation illness and those without them: neurosislike symptoms predominated in the former group, where they were about twice as common as in the latter. The majority showed neurasthenia-like symptoms (93 percent). Thirty patients (half severe and the other half mild) with symptoms of atomic bomb radiation illness were selected for electroencephalography, which revealed abnormal changes in three cases. Autocorrelation curves were obtained: irregular curves appeared in the severe cases and were three times more frequent. A noticeable difference from the normal was noted in the autocorrelation curve from electroencephalography. The progress was followed through questionnaires sent out to 468 survivors among 533 with neurosislike symptoms, and answers were obtained from 219. Of the 219, 16 percent recovered completely from neurosislike symptoms, 48 percent continued to suffer from the same symptoms, and 36 percent were suffering from more serious symptoms and receiving medical treatment. From these results, Nishikawa found that those exposed still suffered from a high incidence of neurosislike symptoms even fifteen years after the explosion. He pointed out that some cases were recognized as pure neurosis caused by psychogenetic factors, but that others could be caused by functional disorders of brain or body owing to radiation.

The survey carried out five years after the explosion by Tsuiki and A. Ikegami (1956, p. 1709) and Tsuiki et al. (1951; 1958) shows that the more severe were the symptoms of atomic bomb radiation illness that the victims suffered, the stronger were their neuropsychiatric aftereffects. The latter symptoms included weariness, lack of spirit, a tendency to introversion, and bad memory.

Izumi (1955a, p. 425; 1955b, p. 426) made a three-year study of the exposed children in Nagasaki seven years after the exposure. He studied the children's degree of weariness, their ability to do mental work, and their school teachers' evaluation of their intelligence and academic ability and found that children within 2 kilometers of the hypocenter had problems. Sutow, Hamada, and Kawamoto (1953) carried out neuroscientific and psychiatric tests on seventy-four children who had been exposed in utero within a distance of 2 kilometers of the hypocenter, and, as controls, on ninety-one children who had been exposed at a distance of 4 to 5 kilometers. Neurological abnormalities were encountered in nine children, with no difference being found for distance. Eight years after the explosion in Hiroshima, M. Tanaka and H. Kawahara (1954) examined intelligence and physical ability in three groups of children: children exposed in utero, and those exposed during infancy and in childhood. He pointed out that the effects of exposure were greater on the group exposed in utero than on the other groups. A similar survey eight years after the explosion was made by N. Andō (1958) on 126 children exposed within 2 kilometers of the hypocenter and on 185 exposed between 2 and 3 kilometers. These children were also divided into three groups. The decisive factor affecting the children was attributable to the difference of educational environment resulting from exposure rather than to the direct effects of the atomic bomb.

NEUROPSYCHOLOGICAL SYMPTOMS IN THE EXPOSED

In August 1953, M. Konuma et al.*—in order to study various neuropsychological problems in the exposed survivors—chose people living in conditions similar to those at the time of exposure, and carried out an analytical survey on survivors living in Ōtake City who had been exposed while working with the labor service party at Hiroshima. This survey covered 131 persons who had been exposed in groups 1.5 to 2 kilometers from the hypocenter and had quickly escaped from the area but received thermal burns. The majority had been exposed to the "black rain" that fell upon them soon after the explosion. They had, up to a certain degree, symptoms of atomic bomb radiation illness at that time, and complained of aftereffects until 1953 (table 9.21).

TABLE 9.21

Distribution of Sex and Age in the Cohort of Study

Sex	Age at Time of Study							Total
	0–10	11–20	21–30	31–40	41–50	51–60	61–70	
Male	1	2	3	4	11	21	16	58
Female	0	1	7	20	25	19	1	73
Total	1	3	10	24	36	40	17	131

N.B. This study was carried out in August 1953, 8 years after the detonation.
Source: M. Konuma, "Psychiatric atomic bomb casualties," *Journal of the Hiroshima Medical Association* (special series) 20 (1967): 231. M. Konuma, "Neuropsychiatric consideration of the atomic bomb sickness and its sequelae," in *Genbaku to Hiroshima Daigaku—"Seishi no Hi" Gakujutsuhen* [The Atomic Bomb and Hiroshima University—Science Section of "Light of Fate"] (Hiroshima: Hiroshima Daigaku Genbaku Shibotsusha Ireigyōji Iinkai, 1977), p. 96.

The complaints of aftereffects obtained by interviewing these people are shown in table 9.22. These complaints occurred after the explosion and they continued or intermittently appeared for eight years. Since 43 percent of the subjects were over fifty years old, it can be justly considered that geriatric disorders and complaints occurring in ordinary diseases may be included in these complaints. The fact that more people tended to become ill after exposure to the atomic bomb, however, cannot be disregarded. It is only natural that the victims suffered psychogenetic or neurotic effects, since an

* Konuma 1954, p. 375; 1961, 1963, p. 388; 1967; 1977, p. 96; Konuma, Furutani, and Kubo 1953; Konuma et al. 1954.

TABLE 9.22

Complaints and Symptoms Observed among Proximally Exposed A-bomb Survivors over 8 Years after the Disaster

	Male	Female	Total	Percentage	Ratio to Total Cases (percentage)
Susceptibility to fatigue	27	30	57	10.8	43.5
Impatience of mental work	19	28	47	8.9	35.9
Intolerance to environment	19	28	47	8.9	35.9
Poor health	17	27	44	8.3	33.6
Amnesic condition	17	26	43	8.1	32.8
Emotional intolerance	16	23	39	7.4	29.8
Dizziness	11	28	39	7.4	29.8
Head heavy and headache	10	28	38	7.2	29.0
Disturbances of digestive organs	11	22	33	6.2	25.2
Disturbances of circulation and vaso-motion	6	16	22	4.2	16.8
Disturbances in temperature regulation	11	20	31	5.8	23.7
Numbness	7	13	20	3.8	15.3
Psychic shock intolerance	2	8	10	1.9	7.6
Disturbances of cutaneous functions	4	3	7	1.3	5.3
Hemorrhagic tendency	1	5	6	1.1	4.6
Sexual and urinary complaints	5	0	5	0.9	3.8
Insomnia	1	4	5	0.9	3.8
Disturbances of metabolism and nutrition	1	0	1	0.2	0.8
Others	15	21	36	6.8	27.5
Total	200	330	530	100.0	

Source: M. Konuma, "Psychiatric atomic bomb casualties," *Journal of the Hiroshima Medical Association* (special series) 20 (1967): 231. M. Konuma, "Neuropsychiatric consideration of the atomic bomb sickness and its sequelae," in *Genbaku to Hiroshima Daigaku—"Seishi no Hi" Gakujutsuhen* [The Atomic Bomb and Hiroshima University—Science Section of "Light of Fate"] (Hiroshima: Hiroshima Daigaku Genbaku Shibotsusha Ireigyōji Iinkai, 1977), p. 96.

extraordinary and dreadful catastrophe had radically altered their social situation, and exposed them to atomic bomb illness and its uncertain, but undoubted aftereffects. Hence, further investigation and analysis of these complaints and symptoms must be made with reference to sex, age, education, occupation, and clinical history of each subject.

As to complaints of the digestive tract, there were nine with habitual diarrhea, four with habitual constipation, five with abdominal pain, thirteen with general gastrointestinal disturbance, three with nausea and vomiting, two with gastric convulsion, two with gastrointestinal ulcers, and two with colic pain. Although one case each of gastric contracture and abdominal pain appeared recently, the remaining complaints continued for at least several years after the explosion. Since gastrointestinal symptoms or disorders are greatly affected by psychogenetic factors, and the necessary conditions for their onset are fairly common, their etiology should be considered as unknown. Although a similar tendency was found in complaints about the circulatory system, they occurred in a high percentage (68 percent) among people in their thirties and forties. Cold hands and feet; burning sensation and cyanosis of hands and feet; numbness when placing hands into water or when raining, even during the summer; dilated veins of hands and feet, or similar changes when cold; generalized or localized edema of not only lower limbs but also of face, hands, and feet while working; and especially urticaria appearing around the scars of thermal burns—all seem to indicate the specificity of these complaints and lesions.

Twenty-three persons complained of oversweating (lower half of the body in some people) out of thirty-one persons (74 percent) with abnormal body temperature. Others complained of difficulty in sweating (1 case), of one or two yearly episodes of fever (38–39° C.) of unknown origin without a sense of fever, of mild fever when tired, of heated hands extending to the entire body, and of a sense of hotness. Some complained of gingival bleeding and petechiae of the lower limbs, and of purpura remaining after slight injury. Especially noteworthy was the general inability of the individual to endure illness or his or her immediate surroundings. This tendency was noted in 17.5 percent of the whole series. The most frequently encountered complaints were difficulty in tolerating change of weather and susceptibility to the common cold at all seasons. These people also could not endure hot weather, direct sunlight, or cold, and they complained of discomfort during a change of weather. These complaints suggest a constitutional deviation in the subjects.

The patients who are thought to have a tendency toward neurasthenia or neurosis are probably those who have generalized fatigue, poor memory, dizziness, heavy head, headache, and no tolerance for either mental work or mental shock, as mentioned in table 9.22. Patients with generalized fatigue had languid hands and feet, rested often, took two to three days off after working one whole day, and were too tired even to rest, especially during the summer season or in the sun. Many had extremely poor memory—a symptom noted in over 50 percent of those under age forty, together with emotional changes. Dizziness, headache, and heavy head became prominent during change of weather or under direct sunlight. Lack of tolerance for mental work denotes conditions such as loss of patience, inefficiency, and lack of desire to work. Among the people with no tolerance to mental shock, are those frightened by mere sound, by other people sneezing, by a flash of light, by someone turning lights on and off, by wind, lightning, and earthquake. T. Kondō et al. (1956) used various methods for examining how the A-bomb survivors would react to words related to the bombing, and noted a significant difference in excitation indices among them, as compared with the controls.

Although it has been considered that the central nervous system, with its dense covering of various tissues, is protected against radiation effects, the mental shock and stress of the atomic bomb explosion were naturally excessive and induced neurosis or psychogenetic disorders. The physical damage, however, was so great that the atomic bomb's crucial emotional implications could not be grasped separately, and it was difficult to carry out comparative studies owing to the variety of exposed conditions.

N. Okumura and H. Hikida (1949), in a survey two to three weeks to two to three months after the explosion, noted neurasthenia-like symptoms, which—in patients with specific predispositions—developed into neurosis. These symptoms were considered to be not direct effects of atomic bomb radiation but neurological and attributable to the deterioration of environmental and physical conditions after exposure. As indicated in the survey made by T. Nishikawa and S. Tsuiki (1961), the incidence of neurosislike symptoms was overwhelmingly high in the aftereffects among the exposed ten to twenty years after the explosion. Furthermore, since some victims registered abnormal waves on electroencephalography (ECG), the existence of a sort of neuropathy or psychosomatic disease attributable to organic or functional disorder following atomic bomb radiation cannot be discounted. The investigations made by M. Tanaka and H. Kawahara (1954) and by M. Konuma (1954, p. 375) support this assumption.

Hematological studies of the cases observed by M. Konuma were also made by the pathologists at Hiroshima University, and revealed marked changes in peripheral blood. From the comparison of psychoneurological symptoms and hematological changes, it can be assumed that the marked hematological damage occurring as an aftereffect of the atomic bomb reflects upon the vegetative nervous center, leading to complaints or symptoms of encephalopathy or the "diencephalonic symptoms." In order to confirm this assumption, 49 persons (23 males and 26 females) were selected at random from the aforementioned 131, and various tests were carried out on them. Pulse and blood pressure were unstable, and changes contrary to the achievement of normal function under various processes and conditions were detected. In the 18 cases with almost normal ECG at rest, one case showed abnormal ECG, and 7 cases were suspected to have an abnormal ECG under load. Further examination revealed that the disturbance was not necessarily inherent in the heart itself but was rather a generalized regulation disorder at its basis.

Contrary to expectations, the concept of neurosis is widely interpreted outside the field of psychoneurology; and those with organic ECG changes are frequently included in cardioneurosis. Strictly speaking, however, this should be called a neurosislike condition. Although Konuma's cases may include neurosis if each were separately studied, the aftereffects on the whole can be interpreted as a neurosislike condition. In other words, the atomic bomb illness, especially radiation illness and its aftereffects, reflects upon the vegetative nervous center either functionally or organically and induces a degenerative disorder of the psychoneurological system called *encephalopathy*. Furthermore, the patient is unable to disregard his or her various mental concerns; and when they are aggravated by aging or common illnesses, he or she suffers a variety of the preceding complaints and symptoms.

Malignant Tumors

RADIATION AND CARCINOGENESIS

Radiation is one of the most important factors in carcinogenesis, and the possibility that exposure to the atomic bomb in Hiroshima and Nagasaki would cause an increase in carcinogenesis has been greatly feared. This apprehension, unfortunately, was not unfounded. The high incidence of leukemia and other malignancies among the exposed remains a serious problem. Before describing the various malignancies related to exposure to the atomic bomb, we will introduce general matters concerning the relation between radiation and human cancers and then present a statistical outline of malignancies among the exposed.

Epidemiology of Carcinogenesis by Radiation. The first report on human cancer thought to have been induced by radiation was made by Frieben in 1902, and was followed by O. Hesse's general remarks (1911) on 94 cases of X-ray cancer in 1911. Attention had been paid to the relation between radiation and carcinogenesis soon after the first medical application of radiation. In 1942, C. E. Dunlap (1942), reviewing the literature, reported twenty-four cases of leukemia in people whose occupation was intimately related to radiation. P. S. Henshaw et al. (1944), examining the causes of death of American physicians during a ten-year period from 1933 to 1942, discovered the incidence of leukemia to be 1.7 times higher than in other white males. A similar survey made by H. C. March (1944) from 1929 to 1943 revealed the mortality of leukemia among radiologists to be more than ten times higher than in physicians—a significant statistical difference.

Following the report (Folley, Borges, and Yamawaki 1952) of the high incidence of leukemia among people exposed to the atomic bomb in Hiroshima and Nagasaki, the relation between radiation and leukemia again attracted the attention of many scientists. A review on the relation between therapeutic irradiation and carcinogenesis was planned in England; follow-up surveys were made by Court-Brown and Doll (1957) on patients receiving X-ray therapy for ankylosing spondylitis. This disease is similar to articular rheumatism, and X-ray irradiation had been given for therapeutic purposes. Among the 13,352 patients who had been given X-ray irradiation for this condition between 1935 and 1954 at eighty-one radiotherapy centers in England, 28 were found to have died from leukemia. Since the maximum expected mortality from leukemia in the general population in England was 2.9 during the same period, this was an extremely significant difference. Natural cancerization of ankylosing spondylitis did not occur; and since the drugs given together with X-ray therapy were not carcinogenic, the high incidence of leukemia among patients with ankylosing spondylitis receiving irradiation was considered to be due to X-ray irradiation. The latent period between irradiation and onset of leukemia was three to five years in patients receiving one course of X-ray therapy. The majority of the leukemia cases were of the myeloid type, and chronic lymphatic leukemia was encountered in only one case.

This survey was highly evaluated scientifically as corroborative evidence of radiation carcinogenesis in man. After a relatively accurate estimation of radiation dose had been made, a linear proportionate relation was confirmed between radiation dose and development of leukemia. In a selection of 2,195 cases from the whole series, the actual irradiation doses given were examined, and at the same time the radiation dose was directly measured on a life-sized model of a human being. By this process, the radiation dose to the vertebral marrow, and the integral radiation dose to the whole body, were estimated. When such a radiation dose is applied to man, the yearly incidence of leukemia among 10,000 would reach a high figure of 16 to 17, as compared with the low 0.5 per 10,000 in males who were not irradiated. The dose-response relation in this case would be linear. A linear dose-response relation between radiation dose and incidence of leukemia would indicate that the majority of leukemias occurring in patients with ankylosing spondylitis were caused by X-ray irradiation applied for therapeutic purposes. Although the linear dose-response relation may mean in one aspect that there is no "threshold" in leukemia-inducing effect of radiation, Court-Brown and Doll stated that this was not the only point that was noncontradictory to these data.

In 1955, C. L. Simpson, L. H. Hempelmann, and L. M. Fuller (1955) made a follow-up study on 1,722 children who had received X-ray for thymic enlargement between the years 1926 and 1951 and found 17 of these children developing malignant tumors, including 7 leukemias and 6 thyroid cancers. These figures were quite different from figures for those not receiving X-ray therapy. In 1956, E. E. Pochin, N. B. Myant, and B. D. Corbett (1956) reported on leukemia occurring after radioiodine treatment of hyperthyroidism; and this was followed by similar reports.

Among the surveys of malignant neoplasias developing after medical radiation in Japan, the survey made by S. Takahashi and his group (1964) is representative. The past histories of 8,923 patients and 11,556 controls were reviewed. Of the patients with skin cancer, 4.5 percent had previously received therapeutic irradiation at the site of the tumor—a significantly higher percentage than the 0.8 percent in the noncancer controls. Of the patients with thyroid cancer, 4.5 percent had a history of irradiation on the head—significantly more than the 0.6 percent in the controls. In a calculation of the relative risk by radiation doses of 1,788 cases with skin cancer, thyroid cancer, and other cancers of the neck, an almost linear relation could be found. At 2,000 to 4,000 roentgens, the risk was 4.8 times that of the controls.

Another type of medical radiation which attracted attention is thorotrast. *Thorotrast* is a colloidal thorium dioxide, which was first introduced in 1930 as a contrast medium for X-ray examination. It was first thought not to have any side effects, but thorotrast contains minimum radioactivity and is taken up by cells of the reticuloendothelial system, accumulates, and remains in the tissue for long periods of time. Its carcinogenecity was first noted by experimental study. On the other hand, the reports by F. Wohlwill (1942) on leukemia, and by H. E. MacMahon, A. S. Murphy, and M. I. Bates (1947) on endothelial cell sarcoma of liver, confirmed its carcinogenicity in human subjects. Since then follow-up studies of those who had received thorotrast injections were started in Denmark, followed by similar surveys in Sweden, Portugal, West Germany, the United States, and England. In Japan, the survey made by Takahashi and his study group (Takahashi 1977; Takahashi et al. 1965) is still in progress. According to the reports by T. Mori (1977) and Mori et al. (1966), a total of 202 people who received intravascular injections of thorotrast in the past have lived for more than three years, with a survival rate of 52 percent in 1975. This survival rate is significantly low compared with the 78 percent in 1,414 selected controls. In the thorotrast group, there were 17 with malignant liver tumors, 11 with liver cirrhosis, 1 leukemia, and 1 osteosarcoma. When these figures are compared with the expected incidence in those of the controls, the frequency of malignant liver tumor is 34 times higher, and that of liver cirrhosis 6 times higher. Autopsies of 139 cases from 1945 to 1975 confirmed malignant liver tumors in 63 percent, leukemia in 6 percent, and other malignant neoplasias in 8 percent, with the ratio reaching 78 percent when all the malignancies were included. The incidence of bile duct cancer and endothelial cell sarcoma among malignant tumors was characteristic of thorotrast.

In England, A. Stewart, J. Webb, and D. Hewitt (1958) reported the high incidence of leukemia in children exposed in utero. This survey was carried out between 1953 and 1955 and made by interviewing the mothers of 1,299 children who had died from leukemia or other cancers under age ten, and the mothers of another 1,299 children of similar sex, age, and locality, who were in good health. Past histories of X-ray irradiation were investigated to reveal deaths of children from leukemia or cancer in 13.7 percent of the mothers who had abdominal X-ray films taken during pregnancy, while only 7.2 percent of the mothers in the healthy controls had been exposed to similar irradiation. The difference between the two groups is significant, with the relative risk being twice as high as for the controls. According to the survey made by B. MacMahon (1962) in the United States, 15.3 percent of the 556 cancer deaths born of single pregnancies had been exposed to X-ray in utero. This was higher than the 10.6 percent found in 7,242 children born of single pregnancies, who were selected at random as controls. After correction for indirect associations with birth order, birth date, mother's age, and sex, the relative risk was 1.42, and the excess cancer mortality was most marked between five and seven years, at which time the relative risk was 2.0. In England, Court-Brown, Doll, and A. B. Hill (1960) examined 39,166 children whose mothers had histories of abdominal or pelvic X-ray examination. Only 9 fatal cases of leukemia were encountered, and the expected mortality of the general population was 10.5, showing no significant correlation between exposure in utero and incidence of leukemia (leukemogenesis).

Mortality Statistics of Cancer in Those Exposed to the Atomic Bomb. In order to know whether a certain disease occurs more frequently in a specific group than in the general population, the most desirable method would be to obtain the morbidity rate with the population as the denominator. This, however, was virtually impossible in Hiroshima and Nagasaki, because of the great change in the postwar population, because of individual changes in the exposed over the years, and because of difficulties in grasping the exposed groups as a whole and in detecting every malignant tumor among them. It was, therefore, necessary first to establish a fixed population including controls on a definite scale, as has been done by the Atomic Bomb Casualty Commission (RERF), and then to carry out analytic studies (Adult Health Study, Life Span Study). A data bank of the exposed is being set up in the Hiroshima University Research Institute for Nuclear Medicine and Biology. The city medical association with the cooperation of the ABCC set up a tumor registry in Hiroshima in May 1957 and in Nagasaki in April 1958. A tumor tissue registry was also started in 1975. The data obtained should prove fruitful and are of special importance. Although the analysis of the tumor registry is not yet complete, there are the reports made by Harada et al. (1963), Ide et al. (1965), and Y. Ishida (1960).

Since the statistics of cancer morbidity in the exposed are limited, mortality statistics furnish the basic data on the developmental conditions of cancer among the exposed. There are, however, not many statistical studies on cancer mortality among atomic bomb survivors in Hiroshima and Nagasaki. Reports on the Hiroshima survivors have been made by G. Oho (1956; 1959; 1960; 1961; 1963), K. Shimizu (1961), M. Watanabe (1968), and M. Munaka et al. (1975, p. 8); while studies on the Nagasaki survivors have been reported by Y. Mitani and S. Mori (1961) and Y. Mitani and A. Kidera (1967). On the other hand, the ABCC, through its Life Span Study on a fixed population, has been systematically estimating the mortality rates of the main causes of death (Jablon and Kato 1972). Table 9.23 shows the malignant tumor mortality (including leukemia) of the exposed as compared with that of the non-exposed (nationwide, Hiroshima Prefecture, Nagasaki Prefecture).

Although the malignant tumor mortality was high among those exposed to the atomic bomb, except for the reports made by Munaka et al., the difference from the mortality rate of the controls varied greatly according to year of survey and to author.

The incidence of leukemia in the exposed was extremely high compared with the general population. The mortality indicated in table 9.23 includes leukemia. It is necessary to know the malignant tumor mortality by location in order to see whether mortality from malignant tumors other than leukemia was high among those exposed to the atomic bomb. In table 9.24 are found the corrected mortalities of cancers occurring in different locations in Hiroshima from 1951 to 1960 (Oho 1963) and in Nagasaki from 1953 to 1957 (Mitani and Mori 1961). The standarized mortality ratio of cancers occurring in the main locations have been calculated in the Life Span Study by the ABCC. In regard to the effects of exposure on carcinogenesis, the relative risk calculated by distance from the hypocenter and estimated exposure dose is applied. Table 9.25 gives the standardized mortality ratio when the estimated exposure dose was over 100 rads and between 0 and 9 rads (1950–72) and the relative risk of both groups (Moriyama and Kato 1973). According to these tables, lung and breast cancers tend to occur frequently in those exposed to the atomic bomb, but this tendency was not clearly found for stomach cancers. Thyroid cancers and salivary tumors, which occurred frequently in the exposed according to other methods of survey, have not been proved so by statistical analysis owing to a deficit in the absolute number of cases.

LEUKEMIA AND RELATED DISEASES

In 1945, at the time of the Hiroshima and Nagasaki bombings, scientists were already aware of the increasing incidence of leukemia and of the mortality

TABLE 9.23

Summary of the Reports on Mortality for Malignant Neoplasms (including Leukemia) among A-Bomb Survivors

Authors	Surveyed Area	Surveyed Years	Rate	Control	Ratio to Cont Male	Fem
Oho (1)	Hiroshima City	1951–55	age-adjusted rate	Japan Hiroshima Prefecture	1.30 1.29	1.0 1.0
Oho (2)	Hiroshima City	1954–58	age-adjusted rate over 10 years of age	Japan Hiroshima Prefecture Non-exposed in Hiroshima City	1.27 1.36 1.41	1.1 1.2 1.4
Oho (3)	Hiroshima City	1951–58	age-adjusted rate over 10 years of age	Japan Hiroshima Prefecture Non-exposed in Hiroshima City	1.28 1.44 1.38	1.1 1.1 1.1
Oho (4)	Hiroshima City	1951–60	age-adjusted rate	Japan Hiroshima Prefecture Non-exposed in Hiroshima City	1.25 1.31 1.23	1.1 1.1 1.4
Mitani and Mori (5)	Nagasaki City	1953–57	age-adjusted rate	Japan Nagasaki Prefecture	1.01 1.16	1.0 1.1
Mitani and Kidera (6)	Nagasaki City	1958–64	age-adjusted rate over 10 years of age	Japan Nagasaki Prefecture	1.23 1.31	1.2 1.3
Shimizu (7)	Hiroshima City	1960	crude rate	Non-exposed in Hiroshima City	1.59	1.2
Watanabe (8)	Hiroshima City	1965	age-adjusted rate over 20 years of age	Japan	1.27	0.7
Munaka and seven co-authors (9)	Hiroshima City	1965 1972	age-adjusted rate over 25 years of age	Non-exposed in Hiroshima City	0.78 0.48	0.6 0.5
Jablon and Kato (10)	Hiroshima and Nagasaki (Life Span Study cohort*)	1950–54 1955–59 1960–64	standardized mortality ratio	Japan	1.22 1.10 1.11	1.0 1.1 1.0
Moriyama and Kato (11)	Hiroshima and Nagasaki (Life Span Study cohort*)	1965–69 1970–72 1950–72	standardized mortality ratio	Japan	1.19 1.15 1.15	1.1 0.9 1.0

* Including the non-exposed.

Source: (1) G. Oho, "Statistical observation on deaths due to malignant neoplasm in A-bomb survivors," *Nihon Iji Shinpō* [Japanese Medical Jour 1686 (1956): 8.

(2) G. Oho, "Statistical observation on deaths due to malignant neoplasm in A-bomb survivors. Third report," *Journal of the Hiroshima Medical Associa 13 (1960): 287.

(3) G. Oho, "Statistical study on the causes of death occurring among atomic bomb survivors," *Journal of the Hiroshima Medical Association* 14 (19 323.

(4) G. Oho, "Statistical observation on deaths due to malignant neoplasm in A-bomb survivors. Fourth report," *Nagasaki Medical Journal* (spe issue) 38 (1963): 117.

(5) Y. Mitani and S. Mori, "Statistical observations on mortality due to malignant tumor of the atomic bomb survivors in Nagasaki," *Nagasaki Med Journal* 36 (1961): 724.

(6) Y. Mitani and A. Kidera, "A survey on the mortality rate of Nagasaki A-bomb survivors in relation to malignant diseases," *Journal of the Hirosh Medical Association* (special series) 20 (1967): 406.

(7) K. Shimizu, "Trend of deaths due to malignant neoplasms in Hiroshima City, part 3. Comparison of those with and without survivors' he handbooks in 1960 and 1958–1960," *Journal of the Hiroshima Medical Association* 14 (1961): 578.

(8) M. Watanabe, "The crude and standardized death rate of atomic bomb survivors in Hiroshima City, 1965," *Nagasaki Medical Journal* 43 (19 852.

(9) M. Munaka, T. Watanabe, H. Sumita, H. Yamamoto, H. Ueoka, M. Kodama, M. Watanabe, and N. Okamoto, "Study on population mob among A-bomb survivors. I. Survivors residing in Hiroshima City in fiscal year 1972," in *Proceedings of Fifteenth Annual Meeting of Late Effect Atomic Bombs* (Nagasaki: Nagasaki Genshi Bakudan Kōshōgai Kenkyū-kai, 1975), p. 8.

(10) S. Jablon and H. Kato, "Studies of the mortality of A-bomb survivors. Fifth report. Relationship between radiation dose and mortality, 1950– *Radiation Research* 50 (1972): 649.

(11) I. M. Moriyama and H. Kato, "JNIH-ABCC life span study. Seventh report. Mortality rate of A-bomb survivors, 1970–72 and 1950–72," AB TR (1973) 15–73.

TABLE 9.24

Mortality for Malignant Neoplasms by Sites among A-bomb Survivors

A. Ratio of Age-adjusted Death Rate, Hiroshima City, 1951–60

Site of Malignant Neoplasm	Ratio to Japan†		Ratio to Hiroshima Prefecture†		Ratio to Non-exposed in Hiroshima City†	
	Male	Female	Male	Female	Male	Female
Buccal cavity and pharynx	1.42	2.00	1.89	3.00	8.50	1.71
Digestive organs and peritoneum	1.22	1.04	1.33	1.18	1.19	1.37
Stomach	1.16	0.99	1.23	1.11	0.97	1.26
Liver and biliary passages	1.28	1.09	1.30	1.08	1.48	1.84
Respiratory system	1.49	1.13	1.68	1.94	1.12	1.13
Trachea, bronchus, and lung	1.62	1.21	1.06	0.92	1.40	1.00
Breast and genitourinary organs	1.16	1.22	1.16	1.27	0.62	1.44
Breast	*	1.50	*	*	*	2.00
Uterus		1.11		*		1.32
Ovary		1.80		*		1.38
Other and unspecified sites	0.65	0.95	*	*	1.27	1.71
Lymphatic and hematopoietic tissues	2.21	2.66	2.88	3.08	2.88	3.08
Leukemia	2.89	3.42	2.89	2.71	3.00	3.82

* Unknown.
† Ratio is the relative value when the control value is 1.0.
Source: G. Oho, "Statistical observation on deaths due to malignant neoplasm in A-bomb survivors. Fourth report," *Nagasaki Medical Journal* (special issue) 38 (1963): 117.

B. Ratio of Age-adjusted Death Rate, Nagasaki City, 1953–57

Site of Malignant Neoplasm	Ratio to Japan	
	Male	Female
Buccal cavity and pharynx	0.89	0
Digestive organs and peritoneum	0.92	1.01
Respiratory system	0.79	1.87
Breast	*	0.89
Female genital organs		1.23
Male genital organs	1.00	
Bladder	0.87	2.00
Other and unspecified sites	0.35	0.17
Lymphatic and hematopoietic tissues	1.75	1.43

* Unknown.
† The ratio is 0.89-fold.
Source: Y. Mitani and S. Mori, "Statistical observations on mortality due to malignant tumor of the atomic bomb survivors in Nagasaki," *Nagasaki Medical Journal* 36 (1961): 724.

TABLE 9.25

Standard Mortality Ratio and Relative Risk for Malignant Neoplasms in the ABCC Life Span Study Sample in Hiroshima and Nagasaki by Radiation Dose and Sites, 1950–72

Site of Malignant Neoplasm	Sex	Standard Mortality Ratio*		Relative Risk	Test for Significance
		100+ rads	0–9 rads	100+ rads/0–9 rads	
All sites	Male	1.57	1.15	1.37	$p<0.1$
	Female	1.64	1.02	1.61	$p<0.1$
All sites except leukemia	Male	1.29	1.14	1.13	
	Female	1.39	1.01	1.38	
Digestive organs & peritoneum	Male	1.17	1.10	1.06	(−) n.s
	Female	1.14	0.92	1.23	(−) n.s
Stomach	Male	1.05	1.02	1.03	(−) n.s
	Female	1.05	0.93	1.13	(−) n.s
Respiratory system	Male	1.78	1.35	1.32	(−) n.s
	Female	2.29	1.46	1.57	(−) n.s
Lung	Male	2.20	1.28	1.71	$p<5$
	Female	2.78	1.47	1.89	$p<5$
Breast	Female	3.16	1.27	2.50	$p<1$
Uterus	Female	0.93	0.98	0.95	(−) n.s
Other disease except leukemia	Male	1.68	1.24	1.35	(−) n.s
	Female	2.42	1.23	1.96	$p<0.1$

* Ratio to the total Japanese population.

Source: I. M. Moriyama and H. Kato, "JNIH-ABCC life span study. Seventh report. Mortality rate of A-bomb survivors, 1970–72 a 1950–72," ABCC TR (1973) 15–73.

in those exposed to radiation for a long period of time. On the other hand, experimental studies on the induction of leukemia in mice following irradiation had been previously reported in the 1930s by C. Krebs, H. C. Rask-Nielsen, and A. Wagner, (1930), J. Furth and O. B. Furth (1936), and P. S. Henshaw (1944). It was thus anticipated that leukemia might occur more readily in A-bomb survivors exposed to large doses of radiation. This, unfortunately, proved true; and leukemia is now considered to be a characteristic disease following exposure to the atomic bomb.

T. Misao, Y. Haraguchi, and K. Hattori (1953, p. 1041) were the first to report on a case of leukemia in an A-bomb survivor. The case was that of a nineteen-year-old male who had been exposed to atomic radiation at a distance of 1,000 meters from the hypocenter in Nagasaki. Although he had recovered after a moderate, acute phase, three months later he again showed signs of high fever, sore throat, and subcutaneous hemorrhage and was diagnosed as suffering from acute leukemia. Among the A-bomb survivors of Hiroshima, the first acute case of leukemia was reported by E. Komiya and

S. Yamamoto (1947). The case was that of a twenty-seven-year-old male who had been exposed to the atomic bomb during his military service in Hiroshima and was diagnosed in October 1946 in Kumamoto Prefecture. It was reported that he had suffered from massive burns over the entire exposed portion of his body.

A statistical survey on the relation between the occurrence of leukemia and exposure to the atomic bomb was first made by J. H. Folley, W. Borges, and T. Yamawaki (1952). Between the end of 1948 and the summer of 1949 Yamawaki saw at the Hiroshima Red Cross Hospital two patients who were suffering from leukemia following exposure to the atomic bomb. This led him to begin a survey on the relation between A-bomb exposure and onset of leukemia in Hiroshima. Soon after, a joint survey with the Atomic Bomb Casualty Commission was carried out in both Hiroshima and Nagasaki, and a report was made on the incidence of leukemia and its mortality between 1948 and 1950. Since then a great number of survey reports on leukemia occurring in those exposed to the atomic bomb have been published.* From 1972, the Atomic Disease Institute, the Faculty of Medicine at Nagasaki University, the Research Institute for Nuclear Medicine and Biology at Hiroshima University, and the ABCC (which after 1975 became the Radiation Effects Research Foundation) have been carrying out their own surveys and studies; and when necessary, joint studies are also done.

The Incidence of Leukemia among Those Exposed to the Atomic Bomb. Up to 1975 a total of 1,838 cases diagnosed as leukemia in both Hiroshima and Nagasaki have been registered. Among these were 512 cases exposed to the atomic bomb (those exposed within 10,000 meters of the explosion), and 256 cases considered to have received more than 1 rad (figure 9.9). The yearly change in the number of leukemia cases showed a peak in 1951 and 1952 and tended to decline thereafter in both cities. However, many cases are still being followed. Figure 9.10 shows the yearly changes in number of leukemia cases among survivors who received 100 rads or more, and its distribution pattern is similar to that of figure 9.9.

A joint survey was carried out by the Atomic Bomb Casualty Commission and the National Institute of Health, Japan, on the yearly incidence of leukemia in a fixed population of 109,000 (1950) in Hiroshima and Nagasaki (table

* Bizzozero, Johnson, and Ciocco 1966; Bizzozero et al. 1966; Brill, Tomonaga, and Heyssel 1962; Heyssel et al. 1960; Hirose 1967 and 1968; Ichimaru 1968, 1979, p. 105, and 1981; Ichimaru and Ishimaru 1975, p. 89; Ichimaru et al. 1976; Ishimaru et al. 1971a, p. 216, 1971b, p. 1009, and 1977; Lange, Moloney, and Yamawaki 1954; Ohkita 1969 and 1976; Ohkita, Ohara, and Nakanishi 1969; Ohkita et al. 1976; Ohkita and Watanabe 1979, p. 85; Takahashi, Ohkita, and Enzan 1974; Tomonaga 1964, p. 704; Tomonaga et al. 1959 and 1967; Watanabe 1961, 1965 [p. 485], 1974 [p. 461]; Watanabe et al. 1972, p. 57; Watanabe and Yokoro 1964, p. 721; Yamawaki 1953 [p. 387], 1954a, and 1954b.

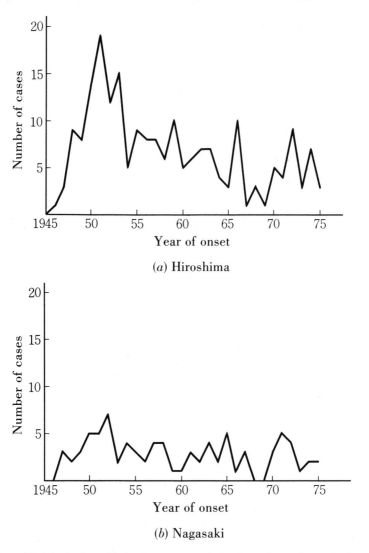

Figure 9.9. Distribution of leukemia among atomic bomb survivors who received more than 1 rad in Hiroshima and Nagasaki, according to year of onset (1946–75) (Ichimaru 1981).

9.26). Sheltered conditions and assumed exposure dose at the time of the bombing were investigated as far as possible. The incidence of leukemia was especially high in people exposed to more than 100 rads. Although the incidence in this population somewhat declined during the 1960s compared with the 1950s, the incidence between the years 1965 and 1971 was still high, at 25.35 per 100,000 population. Since the death rate of leukemia at the same period in Japan was approximately 3.3 per 100,000 population, the incidence of leukemia among those exposed to large doses of radiation is about seven times higher.

Regular physical checkups, including blood examinations, are still being

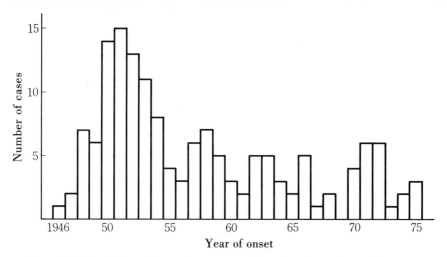

Figure 9.10. Distribution of leukemia among atomic bomb survivors who received 100 rads or more in Hiroshima and Nagasaki, according to year of onset (1946–75) (Ichimaru 1981).

TABLE 9.26

Crude Annual Incidence of Leukemia (All Types) and Comparison of Observed and Expected Numbers in the Extended Life Span Study Sample in Hiroshima and Nagasaki by Year and Month of Onset and Dose, 1950–71

	Not in City	Tentative Total Dose in 1965			
		<1	1–99	≥100	No Estimate
		October 1950–September 1955			
Person years	96,048	169,303	191,396	29,520	11,953
Observed cases (O)	1	4	12	28	1
Expected cases* (E)	9.26	15.59	17.09	2.87	1.17
O/E	0.11	0.26	0.70	9.76	0.86
Relative risk†	0.4	1.0	2.7	37.5	3.3
Rate‡	1.04	2.36	6.27	94.85	8.37
		October 1955–September 1960			
Person years	126,391	160,634	181,996	28,162	11,228
Observed cases (O)	3	7	10	15	1
Expected cases* (E)	8.93	11.45	12.84	2.01	0.77
O/E	0.34	0.61	0.78	7.46	1.30
Relative risk†	0.6	1.0	1.3	12.2	2.1
Rate‡	2.37	4.36	5.49	53.26	8.91
		October 1960–September 1965			
Person years	119,991	151,799	171,861	26,792	10,749
Observed cases (O)	2	4	12	7	2
Expected cases* (E)	6.74	8.34	9.47	1.75	0.70
O/E	0.30	0.48	1.27	4.00	2.86
Relative risk†	0.6	1.0	2.6	8.3	6.0
Rate‡	1.67	2.64	6.98	26.13	18.61
		October 1965–September 1971			
Person years	141,858	178,474	201,326	31,555	12,906
Observed cases (O)	4	8	7	8	0
Expected cases* (E)	6.80	8.27	9.66	1.61	0.67
O/E	0.59	0.97	0.73	4.97	0
Relative risk†	0.6	1.0	0.8	5.1	0
Rate‡	2.82	4.48	3.48	25.35	0

* Adjusted for sex, age at time of bombing and city.
† The ratio for O/E in those exposed to less than 1 rad as standard.
‡ Per 100,000 per year.
Source: M. Ichimaru, T. Ishimaru, J. L. Belsky, T. Tomiyasu, N. Sadamori, T. Hoshino, M. Tomonaga, N. Shimizu, and H. Okada, "Incidence of leukemia in atomic bomb survivors, Hiroshima and Nagasaki, 1950–71: By radiation dose, years after exposure, age and type of leukemia," RERF TR (1976): 10–76.

carried out on those who were exposed to the atomic bomb. The reason for the high incidence among these people is assumed by some scientists to be due to the greater chance of detection through these checkups. The mortality rate for leukemia between 1971 and 1975 in the population exposed to the atomic bomb in Hiroshima (Ohkita and Watanabe 1979, p. 85) was two to three times higher for those who had been exposed near the explosion than for those farther away—more than 2,000 meters (table 9.27).

TABLE 9.27

Death Rate of Leukemia among Hiroshima Survivors by
Exposure Distance, 1971–75

	Distance from Hypocenter (m)		
	≤1,500	≤2,000	2,001–4,000
Person years	95,588	197,022	164,512
Observed cases (O)	18	23	11
Expected cases (E)	3.5	7.2	6.1
O/E	5.1	3.2	1.8
Standardized death rate	18.8	11.7	6.7
Relative risk	2.8*	1.8	1.0

* χ^2 test: $p < 0.01$.
Source: T. Ohkita and S. Watanabe, "Epidemiology of leukemia. Prevalence of leukemia among Hiroshima atomic bomb survivors," in *Shinpan Nihon Ketsueki-gaku Zensho* [Handbook of Hematology, new ed.], vol. VI (Tokyo: Maruzen, 1979), p. 85.

Type of Leukemia in Those Exposed to the Atomic Bomb in Hiroshima and Nagasaki.   Data on the dose of radiation and type of leukemia in the exposed population registered in Hiroshima and Nagasaki from 1946 up to 1975 (Ichimaru 1981, p. 86) show that the number of cases assumed to have been exposed to more than 1 rad in Hiroshima is about two times greater than that in Nagasaki, and that chronic myeloid leukemia is much more prevalent in Hiroshima (figure 9.11). This difference in the two cities has been noticed for a long time and was assumed to reflect the difference in nature of the atomic bombs in the two cities, with neutrons predominating in the Hiroshima bombardment (Watanabe 1961; Watanabe and Yokoro 1964, p. 721). Chronic leukemia in the non-exposed and in those exposed to less than 1 rad differ somewhat in both cities. The incidence of chronic myeloid leukemia is rather higher in Hiroshima than in Nagasaki, while that of chronic lymphatic leukemia is just the opposite. From the standpoint of geographical pathology, chronic lymphatic leukemia is a relatively rare leukemia in Japan. Compared with other districts of Japan, this type is relatively higher in not only Nagasaki but also in the Kyushu district as a whole. The percentage of chronic lymphatic leukemia among those exposed to the atomic bomb

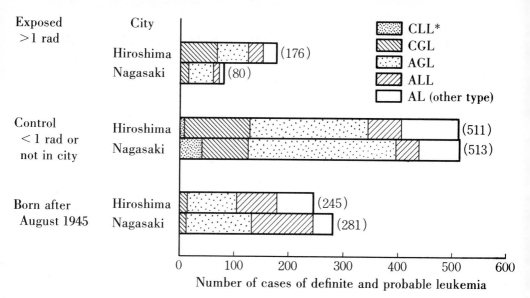

Exposed >1 rad — City — Hiroshima (176), Nagasaki (80)

Control <1 rad or not in city — Hiroshima (511), Nagasaki (513)

Born after August 1945 — Hiroshima (245), Nagasaki (281)

Legend: CLL*, CGL, AGL, ALL, AL (other type)

Number of cases of definite and probable leukemia

* CLL: Chronic lymphocytic leukemia   ALL: Acute lymphocytic leukemia
  CGL: Chronic granulocytic leukemia   AL : Acute leukemia
  AGL: Acute granulocytic leukemia

Figure 9.11. Number of leukemia cases in Hiroshima and Nagasaki, 1945–75, by city, type of leukemia, and exposure status (32 cases were excluded from this figure because of uncalculated exposure doses) (Ichimaru 1981).

was, however, low compared with the other types (Ichimaru and Ishimaru 1975; Ohkita 1976). The type of leukemia in both cities does not differ in those under age thirty who were born after the war. In Hiroshima chronic myeloid leukemia occurred relatively soon after exposure to the atomic bomb in the people who were living near the hypocenter (see figure 9.12). In recent years this type of leukemia is declining in Hiroshima and has hardly been seen since 1956 in Nagasaki.

Figure 9.12. Number of leukemia cases among Hiroshima survivors exposed within 2,000 meters of the hypocenter, according to year of onset (Ohkita 1976).

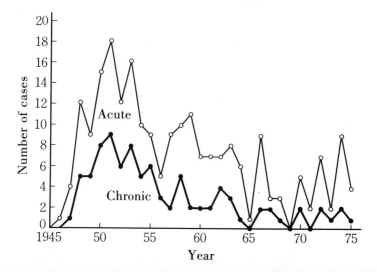

The Relation between the Occurrence of Leukemia and Dose of Radiation.
How is leukemia induced in man? This question remains unanswered. Although from past medical experience and epidemiological surveys, one cannot deny that radiation may in some cases be inducive of human leukemia, the disease is generally rarely encountered following exposure to radiation. The inducive factors are almost always obscure in cases of leukemia as well as in other malignancies that are encountered in everyday life. On the other hand, even in cases having an intimate relation to radiation exposure, one cannot expect to find characteristic clinical signs that differ from those of ordinary cases.

Investigation of the relation between distance from the site of bombardment, which is a rough indicator of exposure dose, and incidence of leukemia has revealed a higher incidence of leukemia in those exposed at shorter distances. In the fixed population up to 1971 this relation was linear in both cities (figure 9.13): incidence of leukemia increased with increased exposure dose. However, in Hiroshima and Nagasaki the incidence of leukemia differed in the fixed populations exposed to radiation of less than 100 rads. In Nagasaki there was no significant increase in cases of leukemia at this low dose level (figure 9.13). There were fewer leukemia cases among the smaller fixed popula-

Figure 9.13. Crude incidence of leukemia among A-bomb survivors and controls in the RERF Cohort Sample by dose and city (October 1950–December 1971) (Ishimaru, Otake, and Ichimaru 1977).

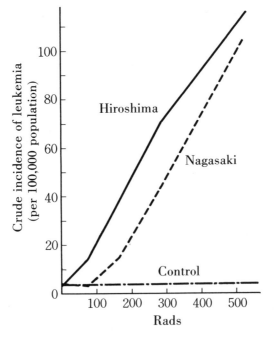

tion in Nagasaki than in Hiroshima—which may be an accidental result of
the deficit number of cases for knowing its correlation to radiation doses of
less than 100 rads. But this phenomenon was also pointed out by M. Ichimaru
(1968) in his survey on a whole population of survivors in Nagasaki. Another
possible cause of the difference in the two cities is the difference in doses
of neutrons. The nature of A-bomb radiation was not the same in each city.
Neutron rays were found at all levels of radiation dose in Hiroshima; while
in Nagasaki the rate was low, and at the level less than 100 rads, gamma
rays predominated. The incidence of leukemia among those exposed to the
A-bomb at every level of radiation dose in Hiroshima was greater than that
in Nagasaki. Chronic myeloid leukemia in Nagasaki only increased among
those exposed to more than 200 rads, while in Hiroshima its incidence increased even in those exposed to low doses over 20 rads (Ichimaru et al.
1976). With these data one must keep in mind the different nature of the
rays thought to be related to the induction of leukemia. Although the relative
biological effectiveness (RBE) of neutrons in carcinogenesis is still unknown,
it is noteworthy that RBE of neutrons is higher than that of gamma rays
in experimental breast carcinogenesis in rats, and also higher in the range
of low dosage of neutron than in those exposed to high dosage.*

According to the epidemiological survey analyzed by T. Ishimaru, M.
Otake, and M. Ichimaru (1977), the relation between incidence of leukemia
and radiation dose in those exposed to the atomic bomb in Hiroshima and
Nagasaki well agrees with these researchers' model curve (figure 9.14). The
incidence of leukemia increases with the increase of neutron rays in a linear

Figure 9.14. Schematic model for the relation of leukemia incidence to radiation dose (Ishimaru,
Otake, and Ichimaru 1977).

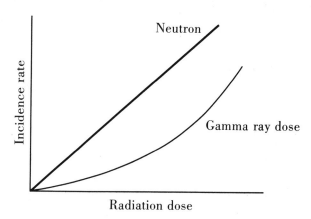

* Rossi and Kellerer 1972; Shellabarger et al. 1974, pp. 391–401; Vogel and Zaldívar 1972.

fashion, while that of gamma rays shows a quadratic function. The results of the 1977 survey made by Ishimaru et al. also suggest that both rays can induce acute leukemia, but that the incidence of chronic myeloid leukemia is mainly dependent on doses of neutron rays. On the other hand, the occurrence of chronic lymphatic leukemia is rare in those exposed to the atomic bomb.* This fact has been confirmed not only in Japan, where this type of leukemia is generally rare, but also in a survey on radiation exposure in Europe and the United States, where the general incidence of chronic lymphatic leukemia is higher. It can be said that an intimate relation does not exist betweeen chronic lymphatic leukemia and radiation exposure.† Since only a few people survived an exposure of over 500 rads during the bombing, nothing definite can be asserted about the relation between a single exposure to a high dose of rays and the occurrence of leukemia.

The Relation between Age at Exposure and Period of Onset, Incidence and Type of Leukemia. From a cellular point of view, actively dividing cells are more susceptible to radiation injuries than nondividing cells. It is not evident, however, whether leukemia and cancer develop more readily in those exposed at a young age when actively growing, or whether the exposed older generation in the so-called cancer age is more affected.

Figure 9.15 shows the incidence of leukemia per 100,000 people over twenty-one years (October 1950–December 1971) by estimated exposure dose (below 99 rads, 100–199 rads, and over 200 rads) in four age groups (at the time of exposure) (Ichimaru et al. 1976). These results reveal a high frequency of leukemia at a relatively early period in those exposed under age twenty-nine; and thereafter, it declined with the lapse of time. On the other hand, the incidence of leukemia was low at an early period among people who were exposed at an advanced age, but tended to increase as they got older. A change in incidence of leukemia was observed in the age group from thirty to forty-four years, especially in those exposed to more than 200 rads. The incidence of leukemia by age when exposed is summarized in figure 9.16, which reveals no significant difference among the various age groups. In other words, the leukemogenic effect of atomic bomb radiation appears similarly irrelevant to age at time of exposure, but occurred earlier among those exposed young than among the older group, in whom it continued for a longer time.‡

The yearly incidence of leukemia up to 1971 in the groups receiving more and less than 100 rads is shown in figure 9.17. (Ichimaru and Ishimaru 1975;

* Ichimaru 1979, p. 105; Ichimaru and Ishimaru 1975; Ohkita 1976; Ohkita and Watanabe 1979, p. 85.
† Tomonaga et al. 1976; Watanabe 1974, p. 461; Watanabe et al. 1972, p. 57.
‡ Ichimaru 1968, 1979 [p. 105]; Ichimaru and Ishimaru 1975, p. 89; Ohkita 1976; Ohkita and Watanabe 1979, p. 85.

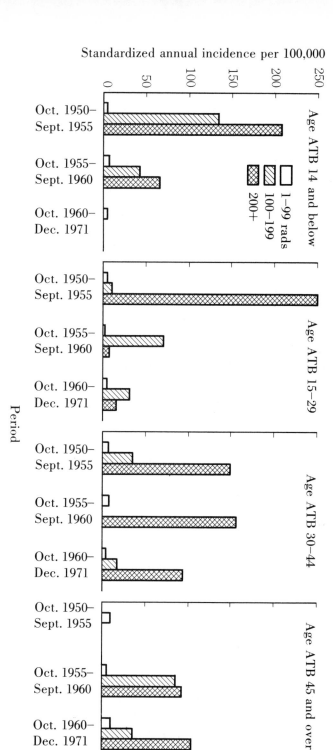

Figure 9.15. Comparison of standardized annual incidence of leukemia excluding chronic lymphocytic leukemia by dose, age at time of bombing (ATB), and calendar time after bombings (October 1950–December 1971) (Ichimaru et al. 1976).

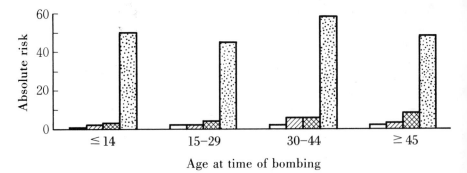

* Crude annual incidence rate per 100,000 persons.

☐ NIC (not in city at
    time of bombing)
▨ < 1 rad
▨ 1–99
▨ 100+

Figure 9.16. Comparison of absolute risk for incidence (1950–71) of leukemia in Hiroshima and Nagasaki by dose and age at time of bombing (Ichimaru et al. 1976).

Figure 9.17. Distribution (1948–71) of definite and probable leukemia in the fixed cohort of atomic bomb survivors and controls in Hiroshima and Nagasaki, according to year of onset, dose, and chronicity of leukemia (Ichimaru and Ishimaru 1975; and Ichimaru et al. 1976).

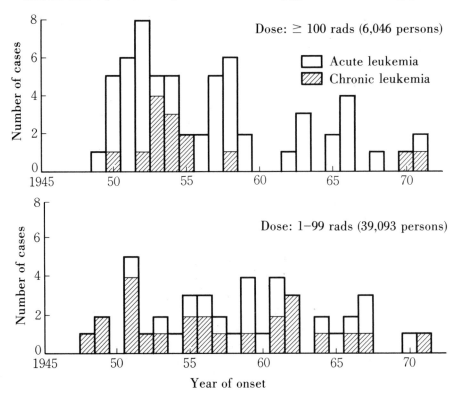

Ichimaru et al. 1976). The effects of radiation appeared at a relatively early period in the high-dose group, while they appeared continuously in the low-dose group. This tendency was especially noteworthy of chronic myeloid leukemia in Hiroshima. The standardized incidence of chronic myeloid leukemia by exposure dose, exposed age, and time period is shown in figure 9.18.

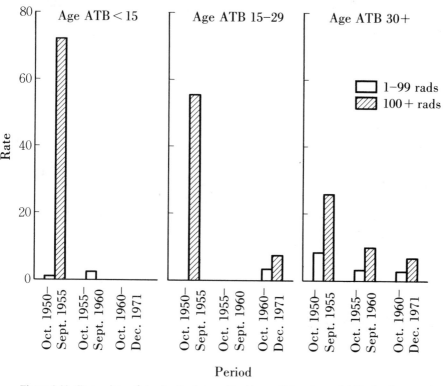

Figure 9.18. Comparison of standardized annual incidence of chronic myeloid leukemia, according to dose, age at time of bombing (ATB), and time after bombs, October 1950–December 1971 (Ichimaru and Ishimaru 1975; and Ichimaru et al. 1976).

As can be seen in this figure, this type of leukemia appears earlier in the age group exposed at a young age. In general, chronic myeloid leukemia is rare in the younger generation, but the many cases among the exposed survivors in Hiroshima and among the heavily exposed (containing neutrons) in Nagasaki may suggest an intimate correlation between this condition and exposure to neutrons.

Leukemia in Early Entrants. Leukemia occurring in early entrants has been recorded. Early entrants were people who had not been directly affected by the atomic bomb, as they were far from the hypocenter, and who had entered the city after the explosion as members of a rescue party or to search for relatives and friends. Up to 1975, the leukemia cases among entrants three days after the explosion in Hiroshima totaled sixty-nine; while in Naga-saki there were fourteen cases till 1967 (Ichimaru 1979, p. 105; Ohkita 1976). Surveys on leukemia in entrants were started from 1950 in Hiroshima and from 1953 in Nagasaki. At no time was there as high an incidence of leukemia as in the exposed cases. The entrants were assumed to be either externally exposed by residual radioactivity or internally by aspiration and swallowing of induced-radioactive material. Watanabe (1965, p. 485) and Watanabe and Yokoro (1964, p. 721) assumed that the high incidence of leukemia among early entrants in Hiroshima was attributable to high doses of neutrons which were able to induce radioactivity.

Detailed explanations have already been given of the estimated dose of gamma rays emitted from radioactivity induced in soil (pages 74–77). At the hypocenter in Hiroshima, the total radiation dose was about 100 rads from immediately after the explosion to infinite time (actually it is all but insignificant 100 hours after exposure). It was about 20 rads at 500 meters and about 1 rad at 1,000 meters. In Nagasaki, the doses were about 40 rads at the hypocenter, 7 rads at 500 meters, and 0.4 rad at 1,000 meters. One who stayed for eight hours near the hypocenter in Hiroshima on the day following the explosion would have been exposed to less than 10 rads; and in Nagasaki, to approximately 40 percent that of Hiroshima. These estimated doses do not include exposure to fallout or internal exposure, and it is at present virtually impossible to correct these values. It is difficult to follow accurately the activities of each individual in the contaminated areas and also to estimate the doses of external or internal exposure.

The actual number of early entrants remained unknown for a long time. The crude mortality rate for leukemia—according to the 1960 national cen-sus—was three times greater for those entering Hiroshima within three days after the bombing than the average crude mortality rate for leukemia in all of Japan.*

In the Nishiyama district of Nagasaki, where people did not receive initial radiation but were contaminated by radioactive fallout, the residents took food and water that were contaminated by radiation material. As a result, there were cases of leukocytosis, which continued long after exposure (chapter 8). Two cases of chronic myeloid leukemia, one in 1960 and another in 1970, were recorded among the two hundred inhabitants of this district. Although this incidence can be said to be extremely high, its relation to radiation is not necessarily evident.

The problem of leukemia as an effect of radiation fallout or induced radia-tion is complex and conflicting and remains to be clarified in the future.

---

* Hirose 1968; Watanabe 1965 [p. 485], 1974 [p. 461]; Watanabe and Yokoro 1964, p. 721.

Leukemia in Children Exposed in Utero and Children Born to Exposed Parents. B. MacMahon (1962, p. 1173), A. Stewart and G. W. Kneal (1970, p. 1185), and E. L. Diamond et al. (1973, p. 283) have reported the high risk of leukemia and of malignant neoplasia in children whose mothers had received abdominal or pelvic X-ray irradiation during pregnancy. Contrary to these reports, the data obtained by W. M. Court-Brown et al. (1960) did not show any increase of leukemia among children under similar conditions. On the other hand, there are reports on the high incidence of leukemia in children whose parents or one parent had received medical radiation prior to conception (Bross and Nataraian 1972; Graham et al. 1966). From 1970 to 1978, S. Jablon and H. Kato* carried out follow-up studies on children who had been exposed in utero in Hiroshima and Nagasaki. The number of children totaled 1,293, including the controls. In these studies, the relation between mortality after birth and exposed dose was analyzed, together with some observations on the mortality of malignant tumors. During a thirty-two-year period up to 1976, there were 203 deaths among these children; and 5 among the 148 for whom cause of death was known died of malignant neoplasia: 2 were leukemia, and the remaining 3, stomach, liver, and colon cancer. The 2 leukemia cases were from Hiroshima, and the mother of the first case was exposed in the tenth month of pregnancy. The child was born two days after exposure and died of acute myeloid leukemia at age eighteen. The estimated exposure dose of the mother was 1 rad and that of the fetus, none. The estimated exposure dose of the mother in the second case was 5 rads, and that of the fetus 1 rad. The child lived until age thirty and then died of acute myeloid leukemia. In these two cases, no direct evidence indicates that leukemia had developed from exposure in utero. The survey did not reveal an increase in malignant tumor mortality among those exposed in utero. There was also no significant difference in the children by exposure of one or both parents.

T. Hoshino et al. (1967) carried out a survey between 1946 and 1963 on the mortality of leukemia in children born to the exposed: no effects of such exposure were found. Another survey has revealed similar results (Ichimaru 1981). Thirty-four cases of leukemia were recorded between 1946 and 1977 from a master specimen consisting of 53,522 subjects, including children of exposed parents (table 9.28). There was, however, no correlation between incidence of leukemia, exposure of parents, and exposed dose.

Factors Other than Atomic Bomb Exposure and Leukemogenesis. There is no appropriate tool for distinguishing whether leukemia in the various cases was induced by radiation exposure or by other causes. It is difficult

* Jablon and Kato 1970a; Kato 1971, 1973, 1978 [p. 49].

TABLE 9.28

Crude Annual Incidence Rate and Standardized Relative Risk of Confirmed Leukemia in Children of A-Bomb Survivors and Controls in RERF Children of A-Bomb Survivors Mortality Sample by Additive Parental Dose, May 1946–December 1977

Items	Additive Parental Kerma† Dose (rads) (father's dose + mother's dose)				
	Control*	1–99	≥100	Unknown	Total
Number of subjects	34,212	12,356	4,953	2,001	53,522
Person years	837,735	304,573	119,787	48,182	1,310,277
Number of cases	23	8	3	0	34
Crude annual incidence rate (10^{-5}) (per 100,000)	2.75	2.63	2.50	0.00	2.59
95% confidence limits					
Upper	4.12	5.17	14.60	—	3.62
Lower	1.74	1.14	1.03	—	1.80
Standardized relative risk adjusted for sex and year of birth	1.00	0.96	0.91	—	—

Test of significance: x^2 (2) = 0.31. Probability: not significant
* 0 dose or not in city at time of bombing.
† *Kerma* is the acronym for "kinetic energy released in materials," whose special unit is the rad.
Source: M. Ichimaru, "Radiation and human leukemia," in *Hakketsubyō no Subete* [All of the Leukemias]. 1981.

to assume a relation between leukemia occurring a long time after exposure to the atomic bomb and that past exposure, and the participation of other causes cannot be unconditionally denied. T. Ishimaru et al. (1972) carried out an epidemiological survey on the correlation between leukemia and various environmental factors in Hiroshima and Nagasaki. This investigation revealed a significantly high risk of leukemogenesis (approximately 2.5 times higher) in those with occupational histories of handling benzene and its derivatives, or X-ray. The risk was especially high in people who had been working for more than five years. The relation between atomic bomb exposure, occupational history, and leukemogenesis was then investigated. The effect of atomic bomb radiation was conspicuous in those receiving high doses near the hypocenter, and it was impossible to verify the effects of occupational history. No conclusion was reached in the low-dose group, since only a few cases had occupational histories related to leukemogenesis.

When discussing leukemia in the exposed, one must not forget the effects of medical radiation. For instance, two cases were exposed to the atomic bomb in Hiroshima who had received postoperative radiation for breast cancer and developed acute leukemia three to four years later. Both were exposed 900 meters and 860 meters from the hypocenter, and the estimated exposure doses were 364 rads and 594 rads, respectively. In such cases it was difficult to decide which of the two radiations was more crucial to leukemogenesis.

Although W. J. Russell (1975) and S. Sawada et al. (1971) in their surveys noted that medical X-ray examinations were more frequent among atomic bomb survivors than the non-exposed by a factor of about 1.2, there was no significant difference according to distance of exposure. The cumulated bone marrow integral doses per subject of the survivors from medical X-ray exposure are increasing year by year, but when the cumulative dose to the active bone marrow was estimated from 1946 to 1970, it was found not to exceed 2.5 rads. One cannot, therefore, consider that the effect of medical irradiation contributes to the continued high incidence of leukemia in those proximally exposed.

Malignant Lymphoma and Myeloma in the Exposed. With knowledge of the high incidence of leukemia in the exposed, the frequency of tumors in other hematopoietic organs started to attract the attention of those working in this field.

R. E. Anderson and K. Ishida (1964) found in Hiroshima 91 cases of malignant lymphomas (including Hodgkin's disease, lymphosarcoma, reticulosarcoma, multiple myeloma) out of 562 extirpated lymph nodes for histological diagnosis and 2,287 autopsies at the Atomic Bomb Casualty Commission between 1949 and 1962. There was an increase in morbidity rate for Hodgkin's disease, lymphosarcoma, and multiple myeloma in those exposed within 1,400 meters of the hypocenter. Nishiyama et al. (1973) added the Nagasaki cases to Anderson's collection and extended the observation period to 1965. The compiled cases consisted of 242 cases from Hiroshima and 321 cases from Nagasaki, totaling 563; and they were reviewed by estimated exposure dose in each case. Although there were only 38 cases of malignant lymphoma in the fixed population for which exposure dose was estimated, an elevation in morbidity rate of malignant lymphoma in Hiroshima was noted in the group exposed to over 100 rads, compared with the control exposed to less than 1 rad (table 9.29). There were, however, only 12 cases in Nagasaki. At least two factors may be considered to have caused this difference in the two cities. First, one might assume a biological difference between residents of the two cities; but a host factor cannot be considered, since the morbidity rate of malignant lymphoma in Nagasaki is higher than the nationwide mean value. Second, the difference may be attributable to the difference in quality of atomic bomb radiation, with the greater radiation dose of neutrons in Hiroshima. The latter factor was assumed to be more important. The risk to the occurrence of malignant lymphoma was greater in the group that had been exposed under age twenty-five than in the group over that age.

TABLE 9.29

Period Prevalence of Malignant Lymphoma among Survivors in Extended Life Span Study Sample by Total Dose Estimate and City,* 1950–65

| | Hiroshima | | | | | Nagasaki | | | | |
	<1 (rad)	1–99 (rads)	≥100 (rads)	No Estimate Available	Total	<1 (rad)	1–99 (rads)	≥100 (rads)	No Estimate Available	Total
Number in sample	29,973	27,187	3,138	1,676	61,974	4,702	11,642	2,542	1,462	20,348
Malignant lymphoma										
Number of cases	11	7	8	0	26	3	6	2	1	12
Crude prevalence rate	3.67	2.58	25.49	0	4.19	6.38	5.15	7.86	6.84	5.93
Adjusted prevalence rate†	3.47	2.48	27.91	0	4.06	7.95	5.88	9.44	6.68	6.84
Relative risk‡	1.0	0.7	8.0	—	—	1.0	0.7	1.2	—	—

* Prevalence rates expressed per 100,000 population.
† Prevalence adjusted to standardized population; this adjustment corrects for the skewed character of the populations of Hiroshima and Nagasaki at the time of the bomb due to the paucity of civilian males of military age.
‡ Relative risk calculated from adjusted prevalence with <1 rad exposure category arbitrarily assigned value of 1.0.
Source: H. Nishiyama, R. E. Anderson, T. Ishimaru, K. Ishida, Y. Ii, and N. Okabe, "The incidence of malignant lymphoma and multiple myeloma in atomic bomb survivors, Hiroshima-Nagasaki 1945–65," Cancer, 32 (1973): 1301.

The latent period until onset of the condition tended to be shorter in the group that had received more than 100 rads when young than in either the low-dose group or those exposed at an older age.

T. Yamamoto et al. (1975) found 69 cases of malignant lymphomas among a fixed population of approximately 100,000 (Hiroshima and Nagasaki) between 1950 and 1972. The cases consisted only of those for whom the histological diagnosis was agreed upon by all members of the survey. Histologically, there were 29 reticulosarcomas, 20 lymphosarcomas, 13 Hodgkin's disease, and 7 unclassified—a distribution pattern close to that in Japan as a whole.

Although the incidence of malignant lymphoma in the fixed population was slightly higher in Nagasaki than in Hiroshima, the actual figures were 48 cases in Hiroshima and 21 cases in Nagasaki. As to the type of lymphoma, reticulosarcoma prevailed in Hiroshima, while lymphosarcoma tended to be more common in Nagasaki. Reticulosarcoma occurred more frequently in those over age sixty-one. The various types appeared at different periods, with the peak for Hodgkin's disease between 1956 and 1960; lymphosarcoma, from 1961 to 1965; and reticulosarcoma from 1966 to 1970.

M. Ichimaru et al. (1978a) confirmed 29 cases of multiple myeloma during a period of twenty-six years (1950–76) among a fixed population of 99,383 people in both cities. Their relation to estimated exposure dose was examined and revealed a crude incidence per 1,000 persons of 0.97 in the heavy exposure group of over 100 rads. This was 4.6 times that in the low-dose group of less than 1 rad (the crude incidence rate of 0.21). The standardized relative risk by city, sex, and age of exposure in the heavy-exposure group was 4.7 times that of the control, with a significant difference ($p < 0.05$) being noted statistically. When observing the incidence for age of exposure and exposed doses, the risk was significantly high in the heavy-exposure group, with the age of exposure being between forty and fifty-nine years; but no significant correlation was seen between age of exposure, exposure dose, and incidence in the heavy-exposure group under age twenty and over age sixty, since no cases came under this category in the samples. In a comparison of the annual cumulative incidence with the exposure doses, it was found that an excess risk in the heavy-exposure group became marked fifteen years after exposure, suggesting a latent period of over fifteen years in multiple myeloma related to radiation exposure. No special clinical characteristics were seen in multiple myeloma of the heavily exposed group.

The mortality rate of those exposed to the atomic bomb in Hiroshima and Nagasaki was analyzed by G. W. Beebe, Kato, and Land (1977), using death certificates from the year 1950 through 1974. Their results suggested that radiation exposure contributed to the excess mortality from malignant tumors of the lymphatic and hematopoietic tissues (200–203 and 208–209 in the International Classification of Diseases of the World Health Organization), excluding leukemia.

THYROID CANCER

After about 1950, the relation between human thyroid cancer and radiation began to draw the attention of those interested in this field. The clinical observations made by B. J. Duffy, Jr., and P. J. Fitzgerald (1950, p. 1018) constituted the first report on the subject. They investigated 430 cases of thyroid cancer occurring in the sixteen years between 1932 and 1948, and found twenty-eight patients in whom the cancer appeared before age eighteen, among whom ten had a history of therapeutic radiation for enlarged thymus between four months and sixteen months after birth. These results were then confirmed by C. L. Simpson, L. H. Hempelmann, and L. M. Fuller (1955), D. E. Clark (1955), E. L. Saenger et al. (1960), T. Winship and R. V. Rossvoll (1961), and L. H. Hempelmann (1968). It also became evident that X-ray irradiation during childhood and puberty (Morris and Creighton 1964; Albright and Allday 1967) and during the adult stage (Hanford, Quimby, and Frantz 1962; Block, Miller, and Horn 1969) can cause similar effects. The radiation dose of 200–725 roentgen was ample to induce thyroid cancer after irradiation during infancy, with a latent period of three to ten years. Although the rate of irradiation during infancy in the cases of thyroid cancer differs among the groups examined, Duffy's was the lowest, at 36 percent, while in some reports the rate was as high as 100 percent.

On the other hand, G. Burke, M. J. Levinson, and I. H. Zitman (1967); I. R. McDougall, J. S. Kennedy, and J. A. Thomson (1971); and A. M. Safa and O. P. Schumacker (1975) have reported on the occurrence of thyroid cancers following iodine-131 therapy.* The high incidence of nodular goiter and thyroid cancer found among the inhabitants of the Marshall Islands who were exposed to radioactive fallout during nuclear experimentation, has been an important subject for radiation biology. Among the 243 inhabitants of the Marshall Islands who were exposed in 1954, seven cases (5.4 percent) of thyroid cancer had been detected by the fall of 1976 (Conrad 1977, pp. 241–57).

Thyroid Cancers in Hiroshima and Nagasaki. As previously mentioned, much of the knowledge about the relation between human thyroid cancer and radiation has been gained after the atomic bombings in Hiroshima and Nagasaki, and thyroid cancer occurring after a certain latent period in the exposed became a matter of great concern. The earliest reports on thyroid cancer occurring in exposed survivors were made by N. Kaneko and

---

* *Iodine 131* is a radioactive isotope of iodine, which is used in the diagnosis of thyroid disease and to treat hyperthyroidism. (Ed.)

J. Numata (1957). They found a histologically proven thyroid cancer in a twelve-year-old leukemic girl who had been exposed to the atomic bomb 800 meters from the hypocenter in Hiroshima. Two years later in 1959, Y. Fujimoto et al. reported two cases of thyroid cancer in young children (1959*b*) and another case with leukemia (1959*a*).

In 1958–59, the Atomic Bomb Casualty Commission-National Institute of Health, Japan, Adult Health Study (Hollingsworth et al. 1963) obtained data suggesting that thyroid cancers were occurring in the exposed. The subjects for study consisted of 5,553 persons: 1,329 exposed near the hypocenter (within 2 kilometers), with acute radiation symptoms; 1,403 exposed near but without acute radiation symptoms; 1,415 exposed far from the hypocenter (3 to 3.5 kilometers); and 1,406 non-exposed (those more than 10 kilometers from the hypocenter or not in the city during the explosion). The thyroids were carefully examined to reveal twelve cases of thyroid cancer (another two cases were suspected), among whom ten had been exposed. Eight of the ten (four males and four females) were exposed near the hypocenter. Nodular goiters were seen in thirty-nine female cases, among whom nineteen were exposed near the hypocenter; and thyroid cancers were detected in eight of them. These results suggested a possible future increase of thyroid cancer among women who were exposed within 1.4 kilometers of the hypocenter. Similar results have also been reported by R. Shirabe, C. Harano, and H. Tezuka (1962) and T. Shigemitsu (1962).

Epidemiological Survey of Thyroid Cancer in the Exposed.   After the survey made by Hollingsworth et al. (1963), the incidence of thyroid disease and thyroid cancer and their relation to exposure in the fixed population of the ABCC-JNIH Adult Health Study have been repeatedly investigated at the ABCC. The reports made by E. L. Socolow et al. (1963), J. W. Wood et al. (1969), and L. N. Parker et al. (1973) are included in this study.

Socolow et al. (1963), in their survey from July 1958 to July 1961, discovered thyroid swelling in 355 persons (310 in Hiroshima and 45 in Nagasaki) among 15,319 (10,780 in Hiroshima and 4,539 in Nagasaki) selected from the ABCC-JNIH Adult Health Study samples. The incidence distribution by exposure status of the 310 cases in Hiroshima is shown in table 9.30. A significantly high incidence of single nodules can be found in those exposed within 2 kilometers of the hypocenter and showing symptoms of acute radiation illness. Approximately one half of the cases with thyroid swelling were examined histologically, revealing 21 cases of thyroid cancer. The incidence distribution by exposed distance of the 21 cases with thyroid cancer is indicated in table 9.31. The occurrence of this condition in 14 cases (12 cases in Hiroshima) exposed within 1.4 kilometers of the hypocenter was significant in confirming the correlation between thyroid cancer and exposure.

J. W. Wood et al. (1969) examined 13,000 persons belonging to the ABCC-

TABLE 9.30

Distribution of Physical Findings in Cases with
Goiter according to Exposure Group,
Hiroshima, 1958–61

Physical Findings	Exposure Group*				Totals
	1	2	3	4	
Single nodule	44†	18	16	24	102
Multinodular	18	19	14	7	58
Diffuse goiter	39	42	27	42	150
Totals	101	79	57	73	310

* Group 1. Exposed within 2,000 m of the hypocenter; with acute radiation symptoms.
   Group 2. Exposed within 2,000 m of the hypocenter; without acute radiation symptoms.
   Group 3. Exposed 3,000–3,499 m from the hypocenter.
   Group 4. Nonexposed, beyond 10,000 m or not in the city at time of bombing.
   † $0.02 > p > 0.01$.
   Source: E. L. Socolow, A. Hashizume, S. Neriishi, and R. Niitani, "Thyroid carcinoma in man after exposure to ionizing radiation. A summary of the findings in Hiroshima and Nagasaki," *New England Journal of Medicine* 268 (1963):406.

TABLE 9.31

Cases of Thyroid Cancer according to Distance from Hypocenter and
City, Adult Health Study, 1958–61

	Distance from Hypocenter			Not Exposed
	<1,399 m	1,400–2,000 m	3,000–3,500 m	
Hiroshima	12*	1	3	2
Nagasaki	2	1	0	0
Totals	14*	2	3	2

* $p < 0.001$
   Source: E. L. Socolow, A. Hashizume, S. Neriishi, and R. Niitani, "Thyroid carcinoma in man after exposure to ionizing radiation. A summary of the findings in Hiroshima and Nagasaki," *New England Journal of Medicine* 268 (1963):406.

JNIH Adult Health Study groups through 1964 to 1965 and found 39 cases of thyroid cancer. Twelve more cases were added from another group. A significant increase in the number of thyroid cancers was recognized in those receiving over 50 rads within 1.4 kilometers of the hypocenter. Although the male-to-female ratio was 1:3, there was hardly any difference between the sexes in those exposed under age twenty. Histologically, the majority showed either follicular adenocarcinoma or papillary adenocarcinoma; there were no undifferentiated carcinomas. Also, no cases took a malignant course with marked invasiveness. Although 16 cases terminated in death, none of these deaths was due to thyroid cancer.

The report made by L. N. Parker et al. (1973) is a summary of the survey made from 1958 to 1971 on the same population. There were 19,961 subjects selected from the Adult Health Study groups, and 74 cases of thyroid cancer were confirmed. Among the 74 cases, 40 were confirmed by histological examination after being detected on clinical examination. The remaining 34 cases were discovered and confirmed at autopsy. There were 17 males and 57 females indicating the high incidence among females. The confirmed number of thyroid cancers per 10,000 people per year in those exposed to less than 1 rad was 0.3 case of the *evident* type (symptoms apparent in an ordinary external

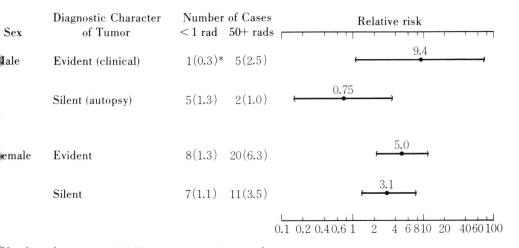

Number of cases per 10,000 person-years in parentheses.

Figure 9.19. Relative risk of thyroid cancer (Parker et al. 1973).

physical examination) and 1.3 cases of the *silent* type (as detected through operation or autopsy) in males; and of those in females, 1.3 and 1.1 cases, respectively. The confirmed rate of thyroid cancer was high in those exposed to over 50 rads, and the highest figure of 6.3 cases per 10,000 people per year was seen in the evident type in females. Figure 9.19 is a comparison of the mean relative risk of thyroid cancer in those exposed to over 50 rads, with those in the low-exposure and the non-exposed groups. The relative risk of the evident type of thyroid cancer by exposure dose and age of exposure is shown in figure 9.20. The relative risk of the evident type for those exposed to over 50 rads is thought to increase in both males and females. In females the risk in those exposed under ten years of age (risk over 14.4) and in

Sex	T65 Dose	Number of Cases		Relative risk
		<1 rad	50+ rads	
Male	1–49 rads	1(0.3)*	2(1.5)	5.5
	50–99	1(0.3)	2(4.0)	15.0
	100–199	1(0.3)	0(0.0)	Indeterminate
	200+	1(0.3)	3(3.7)	14.0
Female	1–49 rads	8(1.3)	4(1.5)	1.2
	50–99	8(1.3)	8(8.1)	6.4
	100–199	8(1.3)	3(3.0)	2.3
	200+	8(1.3)	9(7.6)	6.0

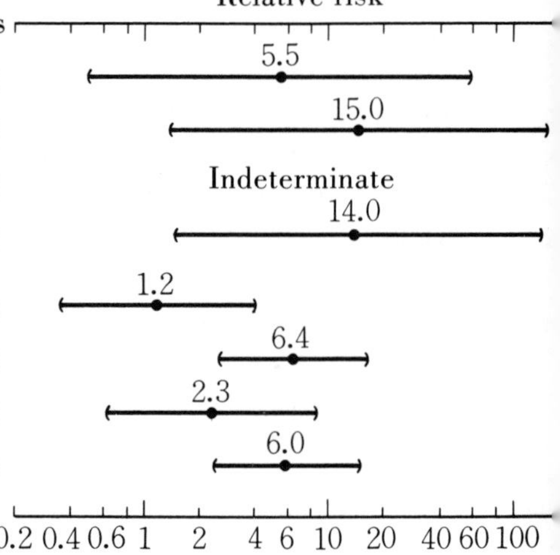

0.2 0.4 0.6 1   2   4 6 10   20   40 60 100

(a) Tentative dose in 1965 (T65D)

* Number of cases per 10,000 person-years in parentheses.

Sex	Age ATB	Number of Cases		Relative risk
		<1 rad	50+ rads	
Male	< 10 years	1(2.4)*	2(9.3)	3.8
	10–19	0(0.0)	2(3.4)	Indeterminate
	20–49	0(0.0)	0(0.0)	Indeterminate
	50+	0(0.0)	1(6.5)	Indeterminate
Female	< 10 years	0(0.0)	4(14.2)	Indeterminate
	10–19	1(0.6)	5(5.5)	8.8
	20–49	7(1.9)	10(5.5)	2.9
	50+	0(0.0)	1(5.4)	Indeterminate

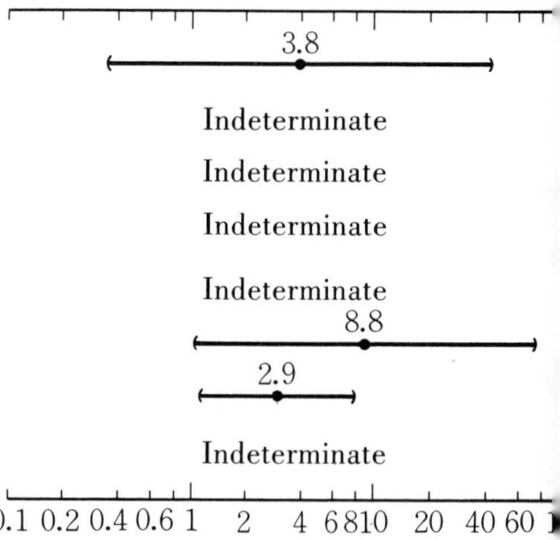

0.1 0.2 0.4 0.6 1   2   4 6 8 10   20   40 60 1

(b) Age at time of bombing (ATB)

Figure 9.20. Relative risk of clinical thyroid cancer (Parker et al. 1973).

those between ten and nineteen years (risk 8.8) is significantly higher than in the twenty-to-forty-nine-year-old group (risk 2.9). This relation could not be clearly identified in males owing to the few cases examined but there seems to be a similar tendency. From these analyses, it can be said that the morbidity rate thirteen to twenty-six years after the exposure to the atomic bomb was significantly high in those exposed to over 50 rads, especially in females exposed under age twenty. Actually, the majority of cases were females with papillary adenocarcinomas.

Clinical Observations of Thyroid Cancer in the Exposed. Aside from the epidemiological survey made by the ABCC, detailed clinical observations have been carried out by the Hiroshima University Research Institute for Nuclear Medicine and Biology (Ezaki and Shigemitsu),* and by the Department of Surgery, Nagasaki University (Shirabe, Harano, Tezuka, and Shigematsu).†

In table 9.32 are found the thyroid diseases examined by H. Ezaki and

TABLE 9.32

Occurrence of Various Thyroid Diseases and the Rate of A-Bomb Survivors in Total Cases, Hiroshima, 1951–63

Disease	Total Number of Cases	Number of Exposed Cases	Percentage of Exposed Cases to Total Cases
Thyroid carcinoma	136	38	27.9
Thyroid adenoma	332	68	20.5
Simple goiter	469	54	11.5
Thyroiditis	186	35	18.8
Hyperthyroidism	652	56	8.6
Total	1,775	251	14.1

Source: H. Ezaki and T. Shigemitsu, "Studies on thyroid cancer induced by A-bomb exposure," *Journal of the Hiroshima Medical Association* 20 (1967): 336.

T. Shigemitsu in Hiroshima between 1951 and 1963 and the ratio of those exposed by each disorder. The ratio of the exposed among the outpatients was only 10.3 percent on the average, but the ratio was extremely high in the exposed cases with thyroid cancer, benign thyroid tumors (adenoma), and thyroiditis. The incidence of thyroid cancer was 2.25 percent (34/1,509) in the exposed and 0.44 percent (58/13,211) in the non-exposed—thus, significantly high in the exposed. From the annual trend, an increase in exposed cases was seen between 1960 and 1961, and fell slightly between 1962 and 1963 but remained higher compared with 1958–59. The incidence of thyroid

* Ezaki and Shigemitsu 1967, 1970; Shigemitsu 1965.
† Harano, Tezuka, and Shirabe 1961, 1967; Shirabe et al. 1964.

cancer between 1958 and 1959 was 0.7 percent (2/270) and 2.6 percent (32/1,239) between 1960 and 1961, with the latter being 3.5 times higher than the former. This increase is statistically significant ($p < 0.01$). In the same period, incidences of 2.6 and 2 were found in benign thyroid tumors and thyroiditis, respectively. In order to know the general tendency in Hiroshima City as a whole, the incidence of thyroid cancer was examined among people on the city's national health insurance list between August 1960 and December 1961. The incidence of thyroid cancer in the exposed was about five times higher than in the non-exposed, being 6 out of 22,386 (26.80/100,000) and 6 out of 114,262 (5.25/100,000).

Of the 38 cases of thyroid cancer shown in figure 9.21, there are 6 males

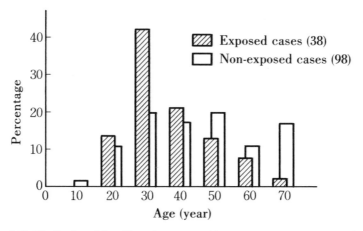

Figure 9.21. Distribution of thyroid carcinoma, according to age at time of diagnosis, Hiroshima (Ezaki and Shigemitsu 1967).

and 32 females. From age distribution at the time of diagnosis, the cancer peaked in the thirties among those exposed, while its incidence is about the same from thirty to fifty years in the non-exposed. Table 9.33 gives the distribution of thyroid diseases by distance of exposure. Six cases (15.8 percent) out of the 38 thyroid cancers occurred in those exposed within 1 kilometer of the hypocenter—an incidence about five times higher than for other thyroid disorders. Since the distribution of survivors exposed within 1 kilometer of the hypocenter is 3.6 percent, it can be said that the incidence of thyroid cancer is extremely high. As to the latent period of this condition, an analysis of 37 thyroid cancers in the exposed revealed 3 cases within five years; 8 cases, six to ten years; 15 cases, from eleven to fifteen years; with a peak between fourteen and sixteen years. No relation to exposure dose could be found.

Although detailed studies were made to see whether there were any differences in symptoms and clinical course of thyroid cancer in the exposed as

TABLE 9.33

Distribution by Distance from Hypocenter of Thyroid Disease and of A-Bomb Survivors in Hiroshima Prefecture

Distance from Hypocenter (m)	Cases with Thyroid Cancer		Cases with Thyroid Disease Other than Cancer		A-Bomb Survivors in Hiroshima Prefecture	
	Number	Percentage of Total Cases	Number	Percentage of Total Cases	Number	Percentage of Total Cases
0–999	6	15.8	7	3.3	5,555	3.6
1,000–1,999	10	26.3	75	35.2	47,120	31.0
2,000–2,999	8	21.1	61	28.6	30,459	20.0
3,000 or more	6	15.8	27	12.7	24,976	16.4
Early entrants into city	7	18.4	42	19.7	44,126	29.0
Unknown	1	2.6	1	0.5	—	—
Total	38	100	213	100	152,236	100

Source: H. Ezaki and T. Shigemitsu, "Studies on thyroid cancer induced by A-bomb exposure," *Journal of the Hiroshima Medical Association* 20 (1967): 336.

compared with the non-exposed thyroid tumors, no characteristic changes could be detected; and the histological patterns were also similar.

Up to 1965 in Nagasaki, C. Harano, H. Tezuka, and R. Shirabe (1967) examined 394 cases of thyroid diseases (96 in the exposed and 298 in the non-exposed). Thyroid cancers were found in 42 exposed survivors and in 74 non-exposed. The ratio of cancer to all thyroid diseases was 43.6 percent in the exposed and 24.8 percent in the non-exposed. The ratio of thyroid tumors other than cancer to cancer was 1:0.78 in the exposed and 0.33 in the non-exposed, showing the high frequency of thyroid cancer among the exposed. The thyroid cancer cases in the exposed consisted of 6 males and 36 females. In respect to age at the time of onset, 13 cases were found for ages thirty to thirty-nine; and the ratio to all thyroid disorders was 40.6 percent in this age group and ranks second to the 62.5 percent seen in the twenty-to-twenty-nine-year-old group. The annual trend indicated an elevation after 1960, with the peak in 1962 and 1963 (table 9.34). Seventeen were exposed under age nineteen, including 6 who were exposed under nine years of age. Twenty of the 42 cases were exposed within 2 kilometers of the hypocenter, and the incidence was significant at a risk rate below 1 percent. In thyroid cancers there were no histological changes that were characteristic of exposure.

Pathological Survey of Thyroid Cancer in the Exposed. Among thyroid cancers are included those that were discovered clinically and confirmed histologically (evident type) and those that were recognized for the first time at autopsy (silent type). There are also microcarcinomas (micropapillary ade-

INJURY TO THE HUMAN BODY

TABLE 9.34

Thyroid Cancer in Nagasaki, 1947–65

Calendar Year	Non-exposed			Exposed		
	Overall Number of Thyroid Tumors	Number of Thyroid Cancers	Percentage	Overall Number of Thyroid Tumors	Number of Thyroid Cancers	Percentage
1947	1					
1948						
1949	6					
1950	3	1	33.3			
1951	5			1		
1952	10	3	30.0	2	2	100.0
1953	7			3	2	66.7
1954	12	3	25.0			
1955	13	4	30.8	2	1	50.0
1956	2	2	100.0	7	2	28.6
1957	12	3	25.0	6	1	16.7
1958	29	7	24.1	9	2	22.2
1959	29	6	20.7	6		
1960	36	10	27.8	9	6	66.7
1961	49	15	30.6	5	3	60.0
1962	28	7	25.0	16	8	50.0
1963	19	2	10.5	19	10	52.6
1964	20	6	30.0	9	4	44.4
1965	17	5	29.4	2	1	50.0
Total	298	74	24.8	96	42	43.8

Source: C. Harano, H. Tezuka, and R. Shirabe, "Thyroid cancer in atomic bomb survivors," *Journal of the Hiroshima Medical Association* (special series) 20 (1967): 348.

nocarcinoma or latent carcinoma) that were overlooked on gross examination at autopsy but were found microscopically on step sections. There are still many opinions about the clinical significance of microcarcinoma or latent carcinoma, about their essential nature, and their relation to the usual thyroid cancers. At any rate, detailed examination at autopsy is essential for accurate information on thyroid cancer. With this object, investigations on thyroid cancer based on autopsy materials of the exposed at the ABCC and the university hospitals in Hiroshima and Nagasaki were carried out by R. J. Sampson et al. (1969*a*; 1969*b*; 1970*a*; 1970*b*; 1970*c*).

The thyroids were examined thoroughly and revealed 536 thyroid cancers from a total of 3,067 cases autopsied between 1957 and 1968 in Hiroshima (2,327 cases) and from 1951 to 1967 in Nagasaki (740 cases). The ratio was 402 out of 2,327 (17.3 percent) in Hiroshima and 134 out of 740 (18.1 percent) in Nagasaki. The incidence was high among females—282 out of 1,453 (19.4

percent); while in males, it was 254 out of 1,614 (15.7 percent). Histopathologically, the majority were papillary adenocarcinomas (525 cases, 98 percent), among which were found 518 cases of latent carcinomas with a maximum diameter of less than 1.5 centimeters. These results suggest that the majority of the cases had not been noted clinically. Thyroid cancer was the cause of death in 5 cases, with one having a diameter of 1.5 centimeters, and the remaining four, larger than that.

The morbidity rate of thyroid cancer was significantly high in those exposed to over 50 rads, compared with the non-exposed. The relative risk for those exposed to more than 50 rads was 1.41 times higher than for the non-exposed, and the excess risk was 6.7 percent. In other words, thyroid cancer can be expected in 6.7 percent of those exposed to more than 50 rads. The incidence of latent thyroid cancer in the non-exposed, however, was 16 percent, which is extremely high, compared with similar surveys made in the United States. In Japan, the silent type of thyroid cancer, which is not fatal, predominates; while the evident type is rare. On the basis of this pattern, an increase in both types of thyroid cancer was observed in females exposed near the hypocenter in Hiroshima and Nagasaki.

The question whether these micropapillary adenocarcinomas or latent carcinomas can be interpreted as true cancers must be answered. With this in mind, metastases were searched for; and it was found that, among 518 cases of latent papillary adenocarcinoma, there were 45 with metastasis to the cervical nodes. One hundred and forty-one cases of micropapillary thyroid cancer with a maximal dimension of less than 0.1 centimeter were divided into two categories according to mode of proliferation: invasive microcarcinoma and noninvasive circumscribed microcarcinoma. The incidence of the latter correlated significantly with exposure dose, while no significant relation was found between exposure dose and morbidity rate in the former.

LUNG CANCER

As to lung cancer developing after exposure to radiation, there was for centuries a high incidence of lung cancer among the miners of Schneeberg in Germany and of Joachimsthal in Czechoslovakia (Lorenz 1944), and rather recently reported cases among uranium miners in the United States (Saccomanno et al. 1971). Experimentally, tumors of the lung have been successively produced in mice, guinea pigs, and rabbits by repeated whole-body gamma radiation (Gates and Warren 1961; Lorenz 1950). Lung cancer in people exposed to the atomic bomb was reported for the first time in 1954, almost ten years after the explosion.

At the annual meeting of the Japanese Pathological Society held in 1954, T. Monzen and M. Kamimatsuse (1954) of Hiroshima University reported a case of undifferentiated lung cancer in a fifty-eight-year-old male who had been exposed to the atomic bomb in Hiroshima. Some comments were made suggesting the cause-and-effect relation of exposure and lung cancer. At this meeting, I. Hayashi of Nagasaki University added 3 cases of lung cancer seen in 37 cases of malignancy among the exposed in Nagasaki. Two years later, in 1956, G. Oho (1956; 1959; 1960) pointed out the increased incidence of malignant tumors, especially those of the digestive tract and lung cancer, among the exposed in Hiroshima, and also the increase of deaths from malignancies in an inverse proportion to distance from the hypocenter. In 1960, K. Shimizu (1960a; 1960b; 1961) and Shimizu, Watanabe, and Itō (1961) of Hiroshima University—on the basis of an investigation made from vital statistics during 1957 and 1960—indicated the increased incidence of cancer of the digestive tract (stomach and liver), and of lung cancer in males, along with an increase in leukemia and thyroid cancer in the exposed.

From 1959 to 1960, with the cooperation of the JNIH Hiroshima laboratory and the ABCC, the Research Committee on Tumor Statistics (chairman, T. Harada) of the Hiroshima City Medical Association analyzed the materials of 1,750 cases filed in the Tumor Registry from 1957 (Harada and Ishida 1960; Ishida 1959). The lung cancers among those exposed within 1.5 kilometers in Hiroshima were four times as much as the estimated number (table 9.35). A similar tendency was also seen in cancers of stomach, breast, and ovary.

TABLE 9.35

Comparison of Observed and Expected Cases of Malignant Neoplasms of Selected Sites among Individuals in Hiroshima City Population Exposed within 1,500/m of the Hypocenter, May–December 1958

Site	Observed	Expected	Ratio	Test Result
Cancer of stomach (sexes combined)	24	12.41	1.93	*
Cancer of lung (sexes combined)	10	2.32	4.31	*
Cancer of breast	5	2.49	2.00	†
Cancer of cervix uteri	8	4.99	1.60	N.S.
Cancer of ovary	4	1.01	3.96	†

Results of the chi-square test mentioned by Mantel and Haenszel show significant findings in each site of cancer except cancer of the cervix uteri.
   * Significant at the level of 1 percent.
   † Significant at the level of 5 percent.
   N.S.: Not significant.
   Source: T. Harada and M. Ishida, "Neoplasms among A-bomb survivors in Hiroshima: First report of the research committee on tumor statistics," Hiroshima City Medical Association, Hiroshima, Japan, ed. *Journal of the National Cancer Institute* 25 (1960): 1253.

Fujimoto et al. in 1962 reported the clinical findings of 31 primary lung cancers, including autopsy findings of 20 cases among 32,726 exposed patients visiting the Hiroshima Atomic Bomb Hospital through 1956 to 1961. An increase in the number of lung cancers among the exposed was also suggested from the pathological surveys carried out by L. J. Zeldis, S. Jablon, and

Ishida (1964), D. M. Angevine and Jablon (1964), and G. W. Beebe et al. (1967) in Hiroshima and Nagasaki. These were followed by the reports by C. K. Wanebo et al. (1968) mentioning the increased incidence of lung cancer in people estimated to have been exposed to more than 90 rads.

In 1967, A. Yamada of Hiroshima University described in detail the characteristic location of the lung tumors, the histological types encountered, and their prevalence in thirty-one cases of lung cancer in the exposed. Based on these findings, he attempted to gain information on the developmental mechanism of lung cancer in these subjects, and concluded that one could not disregard the effects of intrapulmonary irradiation following aspiration of radiation particles produced by the explosion. (Shohno 1967; Watanabe and Yokoro 1963, p. 287).

The primary cancer was distributed peripherally to the segmental bronchi in 75 percent of the 31 cases. The relation between distance from the hypocenter and histological type of cancer was examined in 27 of the 31 cases. Almost one half of the cases were exposed within 2 kilometers of the hypocenter; and, among the various histological types, epidermoid carcinoma (squamous cell carcinoma) was the most common, followed in order by undifferentiated carcinoma and adenocarcinoma. On the other hand, undifferentiated carcinoma and adenocarcinoma predominated in those exposed at distances of more than 2 kilometers (table 9.36).

TABLE 9.36

Lung Cancer among Hiroshima A-bomb Survivors; Histologic Type and Exposure Distance

Histologic Type	Exposure Distance					
	1–2 km		2–3 km		over 3.1 km	
	Male	Female	Male	Female	Male	Female
Epidermoid	8	1	1			
Adenocarcinoma	1				2	2
Carcinoma solidum (undifferentiated)	3		2	2	4	1
Total	13 (49%)		5 (18%)		9 (33%)	

Source: A. Yamada, "Some pathomorphological considerations on lung cancer observed in Hiroshima A-bomb survivors," *Journal of the Hiroshima Medical Association* (special series) 20 (1967): 369.

G. P. Mansur et al. in 1968 discovered 200 primary lung cancers among 1,576 cases autopsied between 1950 and 1964 at the ABCC in Hiroshima and Nagasaki. Among the 63 cases whose estimated exposure dose was known, a significant increase in incidence of lung cancer was noted in those exposed to over 128 rads. There was, however, no difference between exposure dose and incidence of lung cancer in either Hiroshima or Nagasaki.

In 1972, Cihak et al. carried out a large-scale joint survey on lung cancer in the exposed survivors (1974). The subjects belonged to a fixed population in the ABCC-JNIH Life Span Study. The groups for study consisted of an exposed group (27,800 exposed within 2 kilometers, 16,600 between 2 and 2.5 kilometers, and 27,800 between 2.5 and 10 kilometers) and a non-exposed group of 27,800 with matched sex and age. The tentative 1965 dose (T65D) was used for exposure dose in each case.

Among the 10,412 deaths occurring in the ten years from 1961 to 1970, 3,778 cases were autopsied. Lung cancer was confirmed pathologically in 204 cases (162 exposed, 42 non-exposed), with squamous cell carcinoma (epidermoid carcinoma) predominating (46/136, or 33.8 percent) in males, followed in order by adenocarcinoma (42 cases, or 30.9 percent) and small cell anaplastic carcinoma (31 cases, or 22.8 percent). In females, adenocarcinoma was most common (36/68, or 52.9 percent), followed by squamous cell carcinoma (19 cases, 27.9 percent) and small cell anaplastic carcinoma (8 cases, 11.8 percent) (table 9.37).

In regard to the correlation between the estimated exposure dose and preva-

TABLE 9.37

Distribution of 204 Lung Cancers by Histologic Type and Sex, Life Span Study Autopsy Series, Hiroshima and Nagasaki, 1961–70

Group	Histologic Type	Male		Female		Total	
		Number	Percentage	Number	Percentage	Number	Perce
I	Epidermoid	46	33.8	19	27.9	65	3
II	Small cell anaplastic	31	22.8	8	11.8	39	1
III-1	Bronchogenic adenocarcinoma	33	24.3	26	38.2	59	2
III-2	Bronchiolo-alveolar adenocarcinoma	9	6.6	10	14.7	19	
IV	Large cell anaplastic	4	2.9	3	4.4	7	
V	Combined epidermoid and adenocarcinoma	5	3.7	0		5	
VI	Unclassified*	8	5.9	2	2.9	10	
	Total	136	100.0	68	100.0	204	10

Test of significance by sex and type: $\chi^2 = 13.206$; $df = 6$; $p < 0.05$.
* This group included the following histologic types of cancer: epidermoid + large cell anaplastic—2 cases; epidermoid + small cell anaplastic— small cell anaplastic + bronchogenic adenocarcinoma—3 cases; and 2 cases of undifferentiated carcinoma which could not be classified into any of th categories. (Classification according to ICD–O [International Classification of Diseases for Oncology], adopted by the committee of the World Health Organi
Source: R. W. Cihak, T. Ishimaru, A. Steer, and A. Yamada, "Lung cancer at autopsy in A-bomb survivors and controls, Hiroshima and Na 1961–70. I. Autopsy findings and relation to radiation," *Cancer*, 33 (1974): 1580.

lence of pulmonary cancer in the 162 exposed cases, there was no significant difference in the morbidity rate of lung cancer between the 61 cases exposed to less than 1 rad and the 42 cases with lung cancer but not exposed to the atomic bomb in either Hiroshima or Nagasaki. On the contrary, there was no difference in sex, but there was a twofold increase in morbidity rate in the 13 cases of lung cancer receiving estimated exposure doses of over 200 rads as compared with the lung cancer cases exposed to less than 1 rad (table 9.38)

TABLE 9.38

evalence Rate of Lung Cancer in Life Span Study Autopsy Series by Dose, Hiroshima and Nagasaki, 1961–70

	Not Estimated (unknown)	Tentative Total Dose in 1965 (rads)					Not in City	Total
		≥200	100–199	50–99	1–49	<1		
mber of autopsies	58	127	120	182	1,271	1,196	824	3,778
mber with lung cancer	4	13	5	11	68	61	42	204
de prevalence rate per 1,000)	69.0	102.4	41.7	60.4	53.5	51.0	51.0	54.0
ndardized prevalence ate* (per 1,000)	88.9	93.9	48.4	60.2	54.3	50.2	49.8	—
ative risk†	1.8	1.9	1.0	1.2	1.1	1.0	—	—

est of significance, crude prevalence rate: ≥200 = <1; $\chi^2 = 4.800$; $df = 1$; $p < 0.05$.
est of significance, standardized prevalence rate: ≥200 = <1; $\chi^2 = 5.406$; $df = 1$; $p < 0.05$.
* Standardized prevalence rate, adjusted by sex and age at time of bombing.
† Prevalence rate of each dose group/prevalence rate of the <1 rad group.
ource: R. W. Cihak, T. Ishimaru, A. Steer, and A. Yamada, "Lung cancer at autopsy in A-bomb survivors and controls, Hiroshima and Nagasaki, –70. I. Autopsy findings and relation to radiation," *Cancer* 33 (1974): 1580.

As for the relation between exposure dose and histological type, a significant increase in small cell anaplastic carcinoma was found in the group exposed to more than 200 rads. Three cases of lung cancer exposed to more than 400 rads belonged to the small cell anaplastic type (table 9.39).

In this survey, other factors such as smoking habit and occupation causing respiratory disorders were also studied (Ishimaru et al. 1975).

To examine the correlation between smoking habits, occupation, and lung cancer during life, 180 cases (Hiroshima, 147; Nagasaki, 33) were selected from the 204 cases. At the same time, the same number of cases of matched sex, age, and period of death with no lung cancer was selected from the autopsy cases. Close relatives of these cases were interviewed to learn their smoking habits, and the smoking histories of 1,196 cases exposed to low-dose radiation (estimated under 1 rad) and another 127 cases exposed to high-dose radiation (estimated over 200 rads) were examined by going through hospital records and other available materials. As to occupation, those having

TABLE 9.39

*Crude Prevalence Rate for Lung Cancer in Life Span Study Autopsy Series by Histological Type
and Dose, Hiroshima and Nagasaki, 1961–70*

		Not Estimated (unknown)	Tentative Total Dose in 1965 (rads)			Not in City	Total	Test for Significance
			≥200	1–199	<1			
Number of autopsies		58	127	1,573	1,196	824	3,778	
Morphological Type								
Epidermoid	Number	2	3	30	17	13	65	
	Rate†	34.5	23.6	19.1	14.2	15.8	17.2	$p > 0.1$
	Relative risk	2.4	1.7	1.3	1.0	—		
Small cell anaplastic	Number	0	5	14	12	8	39	
	Rate	—	39.4	8.9	10.0	9.7	10.3	$p < 0.05$
	Relative risk		3.9	0.9	1.0	—		
Bronchogenic	Number	2	4	21	19	13	59	
adenocarcinoma	Rate	34.5	31.5	13.4	15.9	15.8	15.6	$p > 0.1$
	Relative risk	2.2	2.0	0.8	1.0	—		
Bronchioloalveolar	Number	0	0	11	6	2	19	
adenocarcinoma	Rate	—	—	7.0	5.0	2.4	5.0	—
	Relative risk	—	—	1.4	1.0	—	—	
Large cell carcinoma	Number	0	0	3	3	1	7	
	Rate	—	—	1.9	2.5	1.2	1.9	—
	Relative risk	—	—	0.8	1.0	—	—	
Combined and	Number	0	1	5	4	5	15	
unclassified	Rate	—	7.9	3.2	3.3	6.1	4.0	—
	Relative risk	—	2.4	1.0	1.0	—	—	

* Test for significance: >200 rads versus >1 rad.
† Rate per 1,000 autopsies.
Source: R. W. Cihak, T. Ishimaru, A. Steer, and A. Yamada, "Lung cancer at autopsy in A-bomb survivors and controls, Hiroshima and Nagasaki, 1961–70. I. Autopsy findings and relation to radiation," *Cancer* 33 (1974): 1580.

histories related to lung cancer were also carefully examined. The obtained results, however, indicated no evident effect of smoking or occupational factors on the occurrence of lung cancer by radiation exposure.

T. Hamada and S. Ishida (1974) reviewed the 1,037 cases (excluding those born after 1945) autopsied at the Hiroshima Atomic Bomb Hospital and the Hiroshima Red Cross Hospital between 1955 and 1972. These included 292 exposed within 2 kilometers of the hypocenter, 338 exposed at a distance of more than 2 kilometers or entering the city soon after the explosion, and 407 non-exposed. There were 197 cases of malignant neoplasias, among which lung cancer consisted of 39 cases, or 19.8 percent in those exposed near the hypocenter. The *Annual of the Pathological Autopsy Cases in Japan* (edited by the Japan Pathological Society) recorded 6,720 primary lung cancers autopsied in Japan for five years. The ratio of primary lung cancer to the total cases autopsied in Japan is 6.1 percent and to the total neoplasia cases autopsied in Japan is 10.4 percent. Therefore, the ratio of lung cancer among the exposed (19.8 percent) is almost twice as high as the national ratio. Since the incidence of lung cancer was high among those exposed near the hypocenter, exposure may well have contributed to the development of lung cancer.

When all these statistics are considered together, it must be admitted that exposure to the atomic bomb surely elevates the incidence of lung cancer, though not a few points remain unclarified. Most of the findings accumulated by the past surveys have been obtained from people who had been exposed at relatively old ages, and results of careful study in the future are awaited so as to gain a complete picture of lung cancer that includes those exposed at relatively young ages (Beebe and Kato).

BREAST CANCER

In 1965, I. Mackenzie reported the results of a survey made at the Nova Scotia Tumor Clinic on patients with breast cancer who had received repeated fluoroscopies of the chest. This survey was started when Mackenzie first saw a patient with breast cancer showing marked radiation dermatitis on the chest wall. This patient had been ill with pulmonary tuberculosis for the past ten years and had received repeated fluoroscopies during artificial pneumothorax therapy. The fluoroscopies totaled 200 in four years. Dermatitis of the anterior chest appeared during this period and was thought to have been caused by radiation. The fact that, in general, breast cancer develops in the upper inner quadrant coinciding with the area of radiation dermatitis, led Mackenzie to suspect the cause-and-effect relation of radiation and breast cancer. His later surveys have also demonstrated similar cases among tuberculous patients in the Nova Scotia district. Data supporting this survey have also been obtained in the study made on women with past histories of tuberculosis in the United States (Boice, Jr., and Monson 1977; Shore, Albert, and Pasternack 1976).

Though extremely rare, thorotrast has also been known to be related to the development of human breast cancers. In 1939, it was demonstrated that injection of thorotrast into mammary glands of guinea pigs induced breast cancer or sarcoma (Foulds 1939). The first report on the relation between thorotrast and human breast cancer was reported by H. Brody and M. Cullen (1957) in 1957. They detected thorotrast deposition in the cancer lesion where thorotrast had been injected at the time of operation for removing a benign tumor seventeen years previously. A similar description is found in the survey made by T. Mori (1966) on chronic damage by thorotrast among the Japanese. The injury to the mammary glands caused by atomic bomb radiation differs somewhat from the actions of chest X-ray radiation of localized thorotrast. The possibility of a tumor developing in the breast by whole-body exposure to radiation has been surmised through experimental study from a relatively early period. In 1950, E. Lorenz (National Cancer Institute)—through repeated whole-body irradiation of low-dose gamma rays to mice, guinea pigs, and rabbits—succeeded in inducing tumors at a higher rate and at an earlier stage in hematopoietic organs, lungs, mammary glands, and ovaries. Between 1959 and 1960, J. Furth, A. C. Upton, and A. W. Kimball (1959) (Oak Ridge National Laboratory) and A. C. Upton et al. (1960)—with the object of studying the biological effects of the atomic bomb—carried out a detailed experimental investigation using mice. An atomic bomb of a similar nature to the one dropped on Hiroshima and Nagasaki was prepared and exploded from an iron tower set about 30 meters above the ground. The mice were so shielded as to be mainly exposed to neutrons in one group and to gamma rays in another. This experiment resulted in an increased incidence of thymomas,* liver tumors, and mammary carcinomas.

Early surveys on mammary tumors among the exposed in Hiroshima and Nagasaki were made by S. Nishida (1956) and A. Tabuchi (1959) on the exposed in Hiroshima, and by R. Shirabe et al. (1964) on the exposed in Nagasaki.

The surveys by Nishida and Tabuchi, based on the death certificates of the exposed between January 1951 and August 1955, noted an increased number of deaths from breast and ovarian cancer among the exposed women in Hiroshima. On the other hand, Shirabe et al. selected 254 patients with mammary tumors who had been seen and treated at the Nagasaki University Hospital between January 1946 and October 1963, compared the incidence of malignant mammary tumors among those exposed within 5 kilometers of the hypocenter (47) and those exposed at a greater distance or with no history of exposure (207), but found no difference in incidence of breast cancer between the groups.

The death survey made at about the same time by G. Oho (1956; 1959; 1960) in Hiroshima, however, showed that mortality from breast cancer among the exposed was higher than among the non-exposed and than the national rates. Soon afterward, in 1961, K. Shimizu of Hiroshima University reported a twofold increase in mortality from breast cancer among the exposed compared with the national mean rate.

Analysis of the 1,750 cases of malignant tumor obtained from the clinical tumor registry started in 1957 by the Hiroshima City Medical Association

---

* A *thymoma* is a tumor originating in the thymus. (Ed.).

(Harada and Ishida 1960; Ishida 1959) revealed a higher incidence of malignant tumors in people near the hypocenter. The morbidity rate for malignant tumors in the exposed within 1 kilometer of the hypocenter was four times that in the non-exposed. In the exposed within 1.5 kilometers, the incidence of breast cancer was high, as was cancer of the ovary, the lung, and the stomach (table 9.35).

The survivors had received whole-body irradiation at the time of the atomic bomb explosion, and the breast was likely to have received a greater dose of radiation than other organs of the body. In light of the latent period of breast cancer as estimated by its development following fluoroscopy and thorotrast, there was the possibility that breast cancers would occur in about 1965, more than ten years after exposure to the atomic bomb. The results of the survey made by C. K. Wanebo et al. (1968, p. 667) in 1966 have actually supported this hypothesis.

The subjects for study in Wanebo's survey consisted of 12,003 exposed and non-exposed women, who were living in Hiroshima and Nagasaki in 1950. Most of these women had been seen at least once in the past at the ABCC in Hiroshima and Nagasaki, and the survey was based on their clinical records, death certificates, histopathological records, and data of tumor registry at the medical association in each city. It was found that 31 women had developed breast cancer after 1945. One fourth of the subjects were not in the city at the time of the explosion, and they were of similar age to those exposed.

Though 3 of the 31 cases with breast cancer were not in the city at the time of the explosion, the remaining 28 were all exposed to the atomic bomb. Distance from the hypocenter and estimated exposure dose were available for 27 of these cases. Twelve were estimated to have received over 90 rads.

Among the 12,003 women, 10,142 had been examined at least once up to 1966 at the ABCC in both cities. Since 16.2 percent of these women were assumed to have received over 90 rads, the finding that 12 (44.4 percent) of the 27 cases with breast cancer had been exposed to over 90 rads is a statistically significant increase in breast cancer among those exposed to over 90 rads (table 9.40). This figure is two to four times that in Miyagi Prefecture (table 9.41).

The average period from exposure to development of breast cancer in the 31 women was 14.7 years. When the 12 cases with estimated exposure dose of over 50 rads were compared with the 11 exposed to less than 50 rads, the period from exposure to development of cancer was 15.2 years and 15.5 years, or of hardly any difference. However, the mean age at the time of the explosion in the over-50-rad group was 28.1 years, while that in the under-50-rad group and in the non-exposed was 39.8 years—a significant

TABLE 9.40

Observed and Expected Cases of Breast Cancer in Women Examined in Adult Health Study, 1958–66, according to Total Estimated Dose (T65D)

Total Dose (rads)	Number of Women Examined	Women with Breast Cancer			
		Definite Only		Definite and Possible	
		Observed	Expected	Observed	Expected
Not in city	2,458	2	5.4	2	6.1
0–9	3,082	3	6.5	3	7.3
10–39	1,262	4	2.7	5	3.0
40–89	857	2	1.8	2	2.0
90–199	802	4	1.7	5	2.0
200+	841	5	2.0	6	2.3
Not estimated (unknown)	840	2	1.9	2	2.3
Totals	10,142	22	22.0	25	25.0

Source: C. K. Wanebo, K. G. Johnson, K. Sato, and T. W. Thorslund, "Breast cancer after exposure to the atomic bombings of Hiroshima and Nagasaki," *Journal of the Hiroshima Medical Association* 22 (1966): 752, *New England Journal of Medicine* 279 (1968): 667.

TABLE 9.41

Comparison of the Observed Number of Cases of Breast Cancer Found after First Examination and the Expected Number in the Fixed Population Examined More than Once

Total Dose (rads)	Women with Breast Cancer	
	Observed	Expected*
90+	6	1.53
0–89	9	10.36
Unknown	1	0.61

* Assuming Miyagi Prefecture incidence rates.
Source: C. K. Wanebo, K. G. Johnson, K. Sato, and T. W. Thorslund, "Breast cancer after exposure to the atomic bombings of Hiroshima and Nagasaki," *Journal of the Hiroshima Medical Association* 22 (1969): 752, *New England Journal of Medicine* 279 (1968): 667.

difference. Nine cases (75 percent) out of the 12 exposed to over 50 rads developed breast cancer before menopause, while only 1 (9 percent) of the 11 who were exposed to less than 50 rads developed breast cancer before menopause. It can, therefore, be said that among the exposed women, breast cancer occurred at a higher rate before menopause than among the non-exposed women.

The survey made by S. Jablon and H. Kato (1972) on the cause of death in the exposed during the twenty years from 1950 to 1970 also showed a high mortality rate for breast cancer among the exposed in both cities and thus supported the results obtained by Wanebo et al.

D. H. McGregor et al. (1977) collected the records and data on breast cancers filed at the ABCC and the tumor registry, and also gained access to other materials with the cooperation of pathologists in both cities. They discovered 231 cases with breast cancer from the subjects included in the ABCC Life Span Study between 1950 and 1969. Among the 231 cases, 192 (83 percent) were confirmed histologically, and 138 (60 percent) were reconfirmed histologically by McGregor et al.

Among the 63,275 female subjects of the ABCC Life Span Study are included the 12,003 female subjects of the Adult Health Study. Forty out of the 231 cases of breast cancer in McGregor's collection were subjects of the Adult Health Study.

Epidemiological analysis of the survey data revealed the estimated relative risk of breast cancer to be 4 cases per 1,000,000 per year per rad in those exposed at ages over ten; and hardly any difference in carcinogenic effect could be found between neutrons and gamma rays. When the expected number of breast cancer in the high dose group is compared with that expected in Miyagi Prefecture (Doll, Muir, and Waterhouse 1970), the figure is much higher in the present series. For instance, among the 1,048 women, who were exposed between the ages of ten and nineteen years and received an estimated exposure dose of over 100 rads, 10 cases of breast cancer have been confirmed up till 1969; while the expected number in Miyagi Prefecture is a mere 1.4; and the whole-life expected number after 1950 is 11.5 cases (table 9.42; figure 9.22). In other words, in the exposed women of this group, the total of breast cancer cases occurring twenty-four years after exposure is almost equal to the whole-life expected number.

A similar tendency was also seen in the older groups (ages twenty to thirty-four, thirty-five to forty-nine, fifty and over). The preceding data indicate that the period when breast cancer could occur in the exposed was no shorter, but that exposure increased its incidence.

Results showing that the young are much more susceptible to radiation than are the old have been obtained from the higher incidence of breast

TABLE 9.42

Observed and Expected Breast Cancer Cases in Women Exposed to 100+ Rads, by Age at Time of Bombing

Age	Number of Women	Number of Breast Cancer Cases		
		Observed 1950–69	Expected* 1950–69	Expected in Lifetime after 1950
0–9	429	0	0.1	4.7
10–19	1,048	10	1.4	11.5
20–34	887	13	3.8	9.5
35–49	685	7	3.5	5.2
50+	309	4	0.9	1.1
Total	3,358	34	9.7	32.0

* Based on rates of Miyagi Prefecture.
Source: D. H. McGregor, C. E. Land, K. Choi, S. Tokuoka, P. I. Liu, T. Wakabayashi, and G. W. Beebe, "Breast cancer incidence among atomic bomb survivors, Hiroshima and Nagasaki, 1950–69," *Journal of the National Cancer Institute* 59 (1977): 799.

Figure 9.22. Breast cancer incidence (1950–66), according to age at risk in Okayama (1966) and Miyagi (1962–64) prefectures versus low-dose and high-dose women in the extended Life Span Study sample (McGregor et al. 1977).

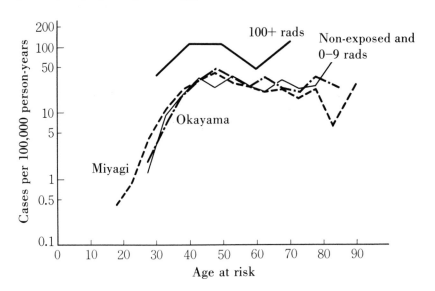

cancer in those exposed at a young age (ten to nineteen years). These results suggest the necessity of considering age and endocrinological conditions accompanying age in breast cancers from exposure to the atomic bomb.

There was a definite parallel between exposure dose and incidence of breast cancer in Hiroshima and Nagasaki, and no difference in risk rate by dose could be noted between neutrons and gamma rays. The histological type of breast cancer did not differ by exposure dose.

Recently, between 1950 and 1974, Tokunaga et al. (1977) of the Radiation Effects Research Foundation found 360 women with breast cancer, who were subjects of the ABCC Life Span Study. Thus, more material has been added to the 231 cases collected by McGregor and his collaborators. Even in this new sample, the risk of breast cancer was extremely higher for those exposed to over 100 rads at ten to nineteen years of age than for the non-exposed.

From these results, one can safely assume an evident correlation between exposure and breast cancer. Further detailed survey, however, should be continued on the development of breast cancer in the exposed women, especially in those exposed at a young age (Beebe and Hamilton 1975; Beebe and Kato 1975). As to breast cancer among exposed men, there is one description in the report made by Jablon and Kato (1972). Though detailed information concerning this phenomenon is lacking at present, it, too, should also be kept in mind.

SALIVARY GLAND NEOPLASIAS

The high incidence of salivary gland tumors occurring in persons who had received therapeutic irradiation during infancy drew the attention of many scientists, as did the thyroid tumors.* Hempelmann et al. (1967) reported benign salivary gland tumors in 4 cases among 2,878 children who had received X-ray irradiation for thymic enlargement, while no such tumors were found in the 5,006 controls. B. Modan, D. Baidatz, and H. Mart (1974) carried out a follow-up study on 10,902 children who had received X-ray therapy for tinea capitis† of the neck, and found 4 cases with malignant salivary gland tumors but detected none in the controls. Later, N. H. Harley, R. E. Albert, and R. E. Shore (1976), in a follow-up study of X-ray irradiated patients with tinea capitis, estimated the irradiation dose in the thyroid, pituitary, and salivary glands to be 39 rads. In 1976, R. E. Shore, R. E. Albert, and B. S. Pasternack found 4 cases of salivary gland tumors, including one malignant case among 2,215 children who had received X-ray therapy for tinea capitis. A crude incidence of 1.8×10^{-3} was estimated for all

---

* Hazen, Pifer, and Toyooka 1966; Jacower and Miettinen 1971; Pifer et al. 1963; Saenger et al. 1960.

† *Tinea capitis* is ringworm of the scalp.

salivary gland tumors, and this suggests a salivary gland tumor risk rate of $12(1-35) \times 10^{-6}$ per rad during a twenty-year period.

Survey of Salivary Gland Neoplasia in a Fixed Population of Exposed Subjects. The preceding confirmation of a relationship between salivary gland neoplasia and radiation led to interest in salivary gland tumors in people exposed to the atomic bomb in Hiroshima and Nagasaki. In 1971, J. L. Belsky, K. Tachikawa, and T. Yamamoto (1972) carried out a survey on the ABCC-JNIH Adult Health Study samples. As a result, 22 cases of salivery gland tumors, including 8 malignant ones, were discovered, revealing a significant relation between salivary gland neoplasia and high-dose exposure. At about the same time, a high morbidity rate for salivary gland tumors compared with the non-exposed was found among the exposed patients at the Hospital of the Hiroshima University Research Institute for Nuclear Medicine and Biology (RINMB) (Takeichi et al. 1973; 1976a). This survey was extended to other hospitals in Hiroshima City and Kure City (Takeichi et al. 1974). Since Takeichi et al. discovered 8 cases that were overlooked at the first screening made by Belsky et al., a reanalysis was made on the fixed-population samples. According to this reanalysis made by Belsky et al. in 1975, 30 cases of salivary gland neoplasia were found in the approximately 100,000 Adult Health Study samples between 1957 and 1970. They were divided by exposure dose and the expected number of cases, on the assumption that the 30 cases were distributed in proportion to the person-years, and the relative risks are shown in table 9.43. The number of cases by age at time of exposure

TABLE 9.43

Salivary Gland Tumors by Exposure Group

	Dose (rads)			
	Not in City + 0*	1–299	≧300	Total
Population	57,859	40,457	1,340	99,656
Person-years	700,552	487,669.5	16,171.5	1,204,393
All cases				
Observed	14	13	3	30
Expected	17.45	12.15	0.40	30.00
Relative risk	1.00	1.33	9.35	
Malignant cases				
Observed	4	3	2	9
Expected	5.23	3.64	0.12	8.99
Relative risk	1.00	1.08	21.8	

* People who were exposed in the city but whose exposure dose might have been 0 rad.

Source: J. L. Belsky, N. Takeichi, T. Yamamoto, R. W. Cihak, F. Hirose, H. Ezaki, S. Inoue, and W. J. Blot, "Salivary gland neoplasms following atomic radiation. Additional cases and reanalysis of combined data in a fixed population 1957–70," *Cancer* 35 (1975): 555.

TABLE 9.44

Distribution of Thirty Definite Cases of Salivary Gland Tumors by Age at Time of Bombing and Estimated Radiation Dose (T65D)

Tentative Dose in 1965 (rads)	Age ATB* (years)						Average Age ATB
	<25		25–49		≥50		
	Observed	Expected†	Observed	Expected	Observed	Expected	
≥300	2	0.23	1	0.14	0	0.03	25.7
1–299	6	6.50	7	4.49	0	1.16	25.4
Not in city + 0‡	6	9.15	3	6.63	5	1.66	33.4
Total	14	15.88	11	11.26	5	2.85	29.1

* At time of bombing.
† Based on Life Span Study population under observation at the ABCC.
‡ People who were exposed in the city but whose exposure dose might have been 0 rad.
Source: J. L. Belsky, N. Takeichi, T. Yamamoto, R. W. Cihak, F. Hirose, H. Ezaki, S. Inoue, and W. J. Blot, "Salivary gland neoplasms following atomic radiation. Additional cases and reanalysis of combined data in a fixed population 1957–70," *Cancer* 35 (1975): 555.

and year of occurrence by five-year period are indicated in tables 9.44 and 9.45. These tables confirm the correlation between salivary gland tumor and exposure, and the tumors tended to appear at a higher rate in those exposed at a young age. The highest incidence was noted between 1961 and 1965, with the mean period from exposure to detection of tumor being 19.4 years.

Salivary Gland Neoplasias in the Exposed Survivors in Hiroshima. Takeichi, Hirose, and Yamamoto (1976b) collected a total of 211 cases of salivary gland tumor recorded from 1953 to 1971 at various hospitals in Hiroshima City and Kure City, and examined their relation to exposure. Of the 211 cases, 62 were exposed and the remaining 149 non-exposed, among whom 23 were born after August 1945. The 23 were excluded, reducing the total of non-exposed to 126. Fifty percent of 62 exposed survivors and 24.6 percent

TABLE 9.45

Cases by Five-Year Interval

Interval	A-bomb Exposure (rads)		
	Not in City + 0*	≥1	Total
1957–60	3	3	6
1961–65	8	6	14
1966–70	3	7	10
Total	14	16	30

* People who were exposed in the city but whose exposure dose might have been 0 rad.

Source: J. L. Belsky, N. Takeichi, T. Yamamoto, R. W. Cihak, F. Hirose, H. Ezaki, S. Inoue, and W. J. Blot, "Salivary gland neoplasms following atomic radiation. Additional cases and reanalysis of combined data in a fixed population 1957–70," *Cancer* 35 (1975): 555.

TABLE 9.46

Histologic Classification of Salivary Gland Tumors, Hiroshima and Kure, 1953–71

Tumor	Exposed Cases		Non-exposed Cases	
Benign tumors	31		95 (22*)	
Benign mixed tumors		22		86 (20)
Papillary cystadenomata lymphomatosa		6		6 (1)
Oxyphilic adenomas		0		2
Other adenoma		1		0
Benign lymphoepithelial lesions		2		1
Cysts		0		0 (1)
Malignant tumors	31		31 (1*)	
Malignant mixed tumors		11		9
Mucoepidermoid tumors		7		9 (1)
Squamous cell carcinomas		2		2
Adenocarcinomas				
Adenoid cystic		5		4
Acinic cell		2		2
Mucous cell		0		2
Miscellaneous forms		4		3
Total	62		126 (23*)	
Malignant tumors (%)	50.0%		24.6%	

* Tumor cases in persons born after the A-bomb.
Source: N. Takeichi, F. Hirose, and T. Yamamoto, "Salivary gland tumors in atomic bomb survivors, Hiroshima, Japan. 1. Epidemiologic observation," *Cancer* 38 (1976): 2462.

of the 126 non-exposed had malignant neoplasias (histological classification of the whole series is shown in table 9.46).

Figure 9.23 gives the annual incidence of salivary gland neoplasias in Hiroshima. There were no cases before 1952, and between 1953 and 1971 there were 73 cases with neoplasias, of whom 36 were the exposed cases. Although a peak was found in 1962 among the exposed, the entire pattern is one of gradual increase. The peak of malignant salivary gland neoplasia was found in 1960, with a drop in 1967 and 1969. Among the 73 cases of salivary gland tumors in Hiroshima between 1953 and 1971, 7 non-exposed cases were excluded from this series, since they were born after August 1945. The mean annual crude incidence and the incidence standardized to the age distribution (five-year age group) in Hiroshima by the 1960 census are shown in table 9.47. The mean annual standard incidence per 100,000 is 1.8 in the exposed, or about 2.6 times greater than that in the non-exposed, with a significant difference ($p < 0.001$) between both groups. If limited to malignant tumors, the standard incidence in the exposed is 1.0 and that in the non-exposed

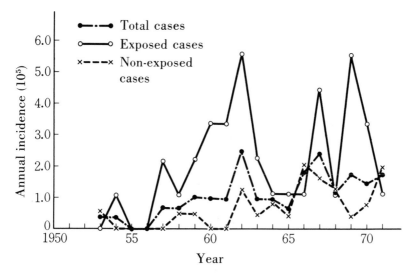

Figure 9.23. Annual incidence (1953–71) of salivary gland tumors in Hiroshima (Takeichi, Hirose, and Yamamoto 1976).

TABLE 9.47

Incidence of Salivary Gland Tumors by Exposure Status, Hiroshima, 1953–71

Group	Total Exposed	Directly Exposed	Early Entrants	Non-Exposed
Person-years	1,729,271	1,490,146	239,125	4,333,814
All tumors				
Observed cases	36	31	5	30
Expected cases	18.82	15.61	1.83	
Test*	$p < 0.001$	$p < 0.001$	$p < 0.02$	
Crude incidence†	2.1	2.1	2.1	0.7
Standardized incidence‡	1.8	1.9	1.4	0.7
Malignant tumors				
Observed cases	19	17	2	5
Expected cases	6.27	5.12	0.26	
Test*	$p < 0.001$	$p < 0.001$	$p < 0.001$	
Crude incidence†	1.1	1.1	0.8	0.1
Standardized incidence‡	1.0	1.0	0.6	0.1
Benign tumors				
Observed cases	17	14	3	25
Expected cases	11.98	9.98	1.46	
Test*	$p < 0.05$	$p < 0.05$	$p < 0.05$	
Crude incidence†	1.0	0.9	1.3	0.6
Standardized incidence‡	0.9	0.9	0.8	0.5

* Exposed versus non-exposed.
† Per 100,000 per year.
‡ Rates are standardized to the age distribution of the 1960 national census in five-year age groups.
Source: N. Takeichi, F. Hirose, and T. Yamamoto, "Salivary gland tumors in atomic bomb survivors, Hiroshima, Japan. 1. Epidemiologic observation," *Cancer* 38 (1976): 2462.

0.1—hence, ten times higher in the former. The exposed survivors were divided into a directly exposed group and an early entrant group; and in regard to the incidence of all salivary gland tumors and malignant salivary gland tumors, there was significant difference between the two groups and the non-exposed. In the exposed, the tumor occurred more frequently in males, while in the non-exposed the incidence was higher in females.

Table 9.48 shows the relations between salivary gland tumor and distance

TABLE 9.48

Incidence of Salivary Gland Tumors by Exposure Distance, Hiroshima, 1953–71

	Distance from Hypocenter (m)				
Group	0–1,500	1,501–5,000	>5,000 (nonexposed)	Total	χ^2 Test for Significance
Person-years	322,768	1,167,373	4,333,814	5,823,955	
All tumors					
Observed cases	14	17	30	61	
Expected cases	3.38	12.23	45.39	61.00	$p < 0.001$
Crude incidence*	4.3	1.5	0.7		
Standardized incidence†	3.8	1.3	0.7		
Malignant tumors					
Observed cases	7	10	5	22	
Expected cases	1.22	4.41	16.37	22.00	$p < 0.001$
Crude incidence*	2.2	0.9	0.1		
Standardized incidence†	2.2	0.7	0.1		
Benign tumors					
Observed cases	7	7	25	39	
Expected cases	2.16	7.82	29.02	39.00	$p < 0.01$
Crude incidence*	2.2	0.6	0.6		
Standardized incidence†	1.6	0.6	0.5		

* Per 100,000 per year.
† Rates are standardized to the age distribution of the 1960 national census in five-year age groups.
Source: N. Takeichi, F. Hirose, and T. Yamamoto, "Salivary gland tumors in atomic bomb survivors, Hiroshima, Japan. 1. Epidemiologic observations," *Cancer* 38 (1976): 2462.

of exposure during the years 1953 to 1971. The early entrants are not included in this table. The mean annual standard incidence per 100,000 of all salivary gland neoplasias is 3.8 in those exposed near the hypocenter (0–1.5 kilometers), 1.3 in the remotely exposed (1.5–5 kilometers), and 0.7 in the non-exposed— thus, indicating a higher incidence at shorter range or with greater radiation dose. This relation is statistically significant ($p < 0.001$). A similar relation can be found in both benign and malignant tumors.

The incidence of salivary gland tumors in those exposed between birth and age nineteen and between twenty and forty-nine rose with closeness to the hypocenter. This tendency was not evident in those over age fifty at the time of exposure, partly because of the few cases in this group. Among those exposed at near the hypocenter, the younger the age, the higher the incidence. But among the remotely exposed and the non-exposed, the incidence rose with age.

Exposure to the Atomic Bomb and Salivary Gland Neoplasias. As noted, the fact that salivary gland tumors occurred at a higher rate in those exposed in Hiroshima and Nagasaki than in the non-exposed has been confirmed by the observations made by Belsky et al. (1975) and by the large-scale survey by Takeichi, Hirose, and Yamamoto (1976*b*). At present there are no accurate data on the nationwide incidence of salivary gland neoplasias in Japan, and the incidence found in various districts is but fragmentary. Though the general background of the preceding results is not altogether clear, Takeichi et al. have calculated the mean annual standard incidence per 100,000 of salivary gland neoplasias in Hiroshima City as a whole. During the nineteen years between 1953 and 1971, the rate was 0.8 for all salivary gland tumors (malignant tumor, 0.3; benign tumor, 0.5), while that between 1962 and 1971 was 1.1 (malignant, 0.3; benign, 0.8). An unrealistically small figure may have resulted from the limited number of cases used for study. In comparison with the incidence for all salivary gland tumors of 1.0 in Selangor, Malaya (Loke 1967), and with that for malignant tumors of 0.1 in Bombay, India (1964–66), of 1.0 in the United States, of 0.2 in Miyagi Perfecture, and of 0 (male) and 0.5 (female) in Okayama Prefecture, Japan (Doll, Muir, and Waterhouse 1970), the preceding rate for Hiroshima is not altogether too high. Furthermore, the incidence of salivary gland tumors in the exposed was apparently high compared with the mean annual standard incidence per 100,000 population.

OTHER CANCERS

All the aforementioned malignant tumors have been shown to have a significant relation to atomic bomb exposure, but this relation is not necessarily evident in the tumors to be discussed in this section. With the accumulation of more cases and with the conclusion of the latent period of radiation carcinogenesis, it may be possible to find a clear correlation to exposure in some tumors in the near future.

Stomach Cancer. While there is a tendency for stomach cancer to decrease in advanced countries, its incidence is still high in both sexes among the Japanese and ranks first among all malignancies (Segi 1977). With this high incidence in Japan, it is only natural that much attention has been paid to the prevalence of this condition among people exposed to the atomic bomb. Generally speaking, the mucosal epithelia of the stomach and intestine, especially that of the small intestine, and blood cells are highly sensitive to radiation; and gastrointestinal disturbance has been actually observed in those exposed to about 100 rads after the explosion. Autopsies of early death after the explosion revealed abnormal changes of epithelial cells of both gastric and intestinal mucosae. In spite of this, delayed effects in the stomach did not take such an evident form as they did in leukemia, thyroid cancer, and breast cancer. Several reasons for this phenomenon can be considered: (1) The digestive tract is located in a relatively deep part of the body and is covered by an outer tissue. (2) Even if canceration of epithelial cells of the digestive tract were to occur, the greater part of these cells may be removed during regeneration and turnover of the mucosal epithelia. (3) The incidence of stomach cancer is high in Japan, and even if radiation were to induce this condition, it may be only one among other carcinogenic factors. In other words, its effects may not be reflected in the incidence of stomach cancer.

On investigating the incidence of stomach cancer as a delayed effect of the atomic bomb in the exposed, an epidemiological method of comparing the exposed to the non-exposed is used as for other tumors. One method is to refer to the death certificates, and another uses the data obtained from autopsies. The former method was applied in the analytical study made by G. W. Beebe, H. Kato, and C. E. Land (1977) between 1950 and 1974 on a fixed population of 109,000. Investigation using death certificates has, in general, the merit of accumulating cases throughout a wide area; but, on the other hand, sometimes the diagnoses are inaccurate. The confirmed rate (detected rate) of stomach cancer between 1951 and 1970 in Hiroshima and Nagasaki was 83.9 percent and 71.5 percent (Steer, Moriyama, and Shimizu 1973) and is quite accurate. Among the 25,924 deaths in the fixed population between 1950 and 1974, there were 1,968 deaths from stomach cancer. Since the exposure dose could be calculated in 1,479 cases, the relation between this condition and exposure dose was examined in them. Though an elevation of stomach cancer incidence was seen among the exposed survivors from about 1960, there was no evident correlation between exposure dose and incidence of stomach cancer either by annual trend or by age at the time of exposure (table 9.49).

K. Nakamura (1977), referring to death certificates, also investigated the relation of mortality rate to stomach cancer and exposure dose among a fixed population of approximately 80,000 between 1950 and 1973. Taking into account that a high-dose exposure is necessary to induce stomach cancer, a statistical analysis was made with special emphasis on high-dose level of over 200 rads. Though the many questionable points in the highly exposed cases in Nagasaki made it difficult to reach any clear conclusions, a correlation was found between mortality rate for stomach cancer and estimated exposure dose in those receiving 400 to 499 rads in Hiroshima (table 9.50, figure 9.24). In the high-dose group of 200 to 499 rads, the mortality for stomach cancer

TABLE 9.49

Relative Risk of Stomach Cancer as Determined (every five years from 1950 to 1974) from Death Certificates of People Exposed to ≥100 Rads Compared with People Exposed to 0–9 Rads at the Time of Bombing

Calendar Year	Relative Risk	Calendar Year	Relative Risk
1950–54	1.54	1963–66	1.13
1955–58	0.74	1967–70	1.17
1959–62	1.34	1971–74	1.09

Source: A. Steer, I. Moriyama, and K. Shimizu, "ABCC–JNIH pathology studies, Hiroshima and Nagasaki. Report 3," ABCC TR (1973) 16–73.

TABLE 9.50

Death Rate (per 1,000 Person-years) for Stomach Cancer by Dose and Sex in Hiroshima, 1950–73

	Exposure Dose (rads)						
	0–9	10–99	100–199	200–299	300–399	400–499	≥500
Male	1.38	1.31	1.57	1.78	1.13	3.74	1.88
Female	0.64	0.70	0.68	0.82	1.37	2.12	0
Total death rate for both sexes in each category	0.93	0.95	1.04	1.20	1.30	2.76	0.86

Source: K. Nakamura, "Stomach cancer in atomic bomb survivors," RERF TR (1977) 8–77.

Figure 9.24. Death rate (October 1950–September 1973) for all malignant neoplasms and stomach cancer by radiation dose, Hiroshima, both sexes (Nakamura 1977).

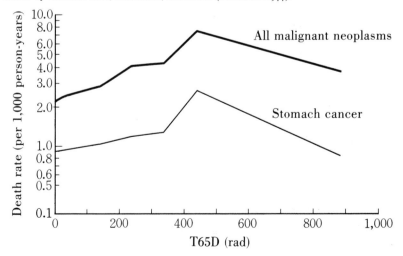

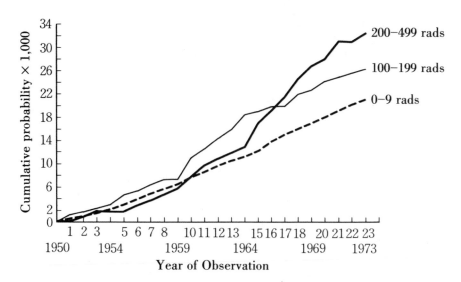

Figure 9.25. Cumulative probability of death from stomach cancer, Hiroshima, both sexes (Nakamura 1977).

increased with radiation dose fifteen years or more after exposure (figure 9.25).

The method using data obtained from autopsy provides accurate diagnoses, but the collection of cases is limited; and in a pathological survey on a fixed population, the autopsy rate and the possibility of cases being biased must be taken into account. In order to stand an epidemiological investigation, a high autopsy rate and autopsy cases not biased to radiation dose are essential. T. Yamamoto and Y. Shimizu (1978) investigated the 535 cases of stomach cancer selected from an autopsy series of 4,694 in the fixed-population samples of Hiroshima and Nagasaki between 1961 and 1974. Although the morbidity rate for stomach cancer tended to be high in the high-dose group, no evident correlation could be found between this condition and radiation. The morbidity rate of stomach cancer in the autopsy cases was corrected by the mortality rate from death certificates (Nakamura 1977) to obtain a corrected morbidity rate. This showed a high incidence of stomach cancer in the high-dose group (figure 9.26). The histological classification of stomach cancer in Japan and that of P. Laurén (1965) were applied to investigating the relation of histological type to radiation (Yamamoto and Kato 1971b), but no correlation of significant difference could be found statistically between histological type and exposure dose. Deep invasion of cancer cells and lymph node metastases, however, occurred more frequently in the high-dose group.

Other Cancers of the Digestive Tract.   The relation of mortality of esophageal carcinoma to exposure has been indicated in Beebe, Kato, and Land's survey (1977) based on death certificates. This relation, however, has not

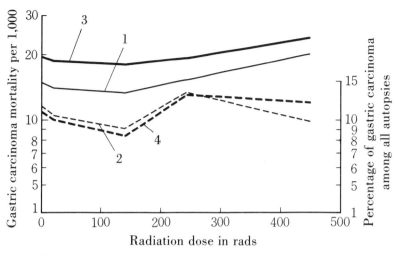

1. Gastric carcinoma mortality 1959–74.
2. Proportion of gastric carcinoma among autopsies 1961–74.
3. Corrected gastric carcinoma mortality 1959–74.
4. Corrected proportion of gastric carcinoma 1961–74.

Figure 9.26. Gastric carcinoma mortality and proportion of gastric carcinoma among autopsies (Yamamoto and Shimizu 1978).

been proved with autopsy cases. Malignant tumors of the small intestine are extremely rare, and the majority of malignant intestinal tumors are those of the large intestine, especially the ascending colon, the sigmoid, and the rectum. T. Yamamoto and H. Kato (1971a), in their study of 94 cases with intestinal cancer between 1950 and 1970, found no correlation with exposure.

Liver Cancer. W. M. Schreiber, H. Kato, and J. D. Robertson (1970) reported on 34 cases of liver cancer (28 liver cell carcinomas, 6 bile duct carcinomas) selected from 2,457 autopsies of the fixed-population sample in Hiroshima and Nagasaki between 1961 and 1967. There was a regional differ-ence in liver cancer, with the morbidity being 0.9 percent in Hiroshima and 2.6 percent in Nagasaki. Liver cancer was frequently complicated with liver cirrhosis (Hiroshima, 52.9 percent; Nagasaki, 64.7 percent). Twenty-three of the 34 with liver cancer were exposed, but its relation to exposure was not evident owing to the few cases.

Cancer in Survivors Exposed during Childhood. S. Jablon et al. (1971) surveyed the incidence of malignant tumors occurring among the 20,609 belonging to the fixed population, who had been exposed before age ten. Though there were only few cases of leukemia and cancer in the group exposed to over 100 rads, the figures were several times higher than those in the low-dose group of children or in those who had not been in either city at the time of the explosions. The number of deaths from leukemia was the

TABLE 9.51

Number of Deaths Attributed to Leuke-
mia and to Other Malignant Neoplasms,
Life Span Study Cohort Age Less than
Ten Years at Time of Bombing (all radi-
ation categories), Hiroshima and Naga-
saki, 1950–69

Years	Leukemia	Other Malignant Neoplasms
1950–54*	9	1
1955–59	5	2
1960–64	8	5
1965–69	4	15
Total	26	23

* From 1 October 1950.
Source: S. Jablon, K. Tachikawa, J. L. Belsky, and
A. Steer, "Cancer in Japanese exposed as children to the
atomic bombs, 1950–69, Hiroshima and Nagasaki," *Lancet*
1 (1971): 927.

highest until 1950–60, but between 1965 and 1969 there was an increase in
deaths from malignant neoplasias other than leukemia (table 9.51). The survivors, who had been exposed at age ten or less, are now in their forties and
reaching the reputed cancer age, so it is necessary to follow closely the trend
of incidence of malignant neoplasias in these subjects.

Double Cancer. According to S. Warren and O. Gates (1932), *double
cancer* means that two or more independent malignancies are occupying different locations, and that one malignancy is not the metastasis of the other(s).
Several theories have been proposed concerning the formation of double cancer; with one preceding cancer already existing, a second cancer grows more
easily; or a preceding cancer inhibits new growth; or both growths are altogether different and unrelated. Knowledge of the effect of atomic bomb radiation on the development of double cancer is of great interest. On examining
the 4,353 autopsy cases between 1950 and 1970 in Hiroshima and Nagasaki,
A. Steer et al. (1973) found cancer in 1,569 cases, including 1,440 where it
was the main diagnosis. Double cancer occurred in 128 cases (8.2 percent);
and if one excludes the cases from whom the first cancer had been removed
or those with intramucosal carcinoma or latent carcinoma, the cases of double
cancer confirmed through autopsy total 43. These 43 cases include 89 independent malignancies (table 9.52).

Stomach and lung cancer were the most common preceding cancer. Among
the 13 cases where lung cancer was the preceding cancer, stomach cancer
was the second cancer in 5 cases. On the other hand, there were no cases

TABLE 9.52

Multiple Primary Malignancy by Site of Origin

Site	First	Second	Third
Stomach	6	14	—
Lung	13	1	—
Colon, rectum	4	7	1
Hepatobiliary	5	1	—
Female genitals	3	2	1
Male genitals	2	2	—
Thyroid	—	5	—
Kidney	1	4	—
Leukemia	1	2	—
Esophagus	1	1	—
Pancreas	2	—	—
Larynx	1	—	—
Breast	1	1	—
Lymphoma	1	1	—
Subcutaneous	1	—	—
Thymus	—	1	—
Peritoneum	—	—	1
Undetermined	1	1	—

Source: A. Steer, T. Wakabayashi, J. D. Kirshbaum, Y. Ii, and K. Ishida, "Multiple primary malignancies and radiation exposure, Hiroshima and Nagasaki," presented at the Sixth International Congress Cancer Society, 28 June 1973, Perugia, Italy.

of primary stomach cancer (6 cases) where the second cancer was lung cancer.

Investigation of the relation between observed/expected and exposure dose ($<$ 10 rads, 100 + rads) in the various double cancers of all malignant tumors, stomach cancer, lung cancer, and malignancies excluding stomach cancer and lung cancer revealed a statistically significant correlation among three of these cancers, with the exception of stomach cancer. Double cancer tended to occur more frequently in the high-dose group exposed at a young age compared with those exposed to fewer than 10 rads. The incidence was extremely high among the aged. In other words, double cancer is related to age at death and is presumably related to exposure dose.

Carcinomas of the Urinary Bladder and Kidney. The death certificate survey on a fixed population in Hiroshima and Nagasaki (1950–74) by Beebe, Kato, and Land (1977) suggested that a relation exists between mortality from cancer of the urinary tract and exposure dose. When the researchers divided the years between 1950 and 1974 into segments of four, they found a significant increase only between 1967 and 1970 in the high-dose group. As to age at the time of exposure, an effect was evident only between thirty-five to forty-nine years and over fifty years, but this was statistically significant only when the two groups were considered together.

Cancer of the Reproductive Organ. 1. *Prostate cancer.* The mortality for prostate cancer is low among the Japanese. The incidence of prostate cancer, however, is increasing year by year, and the morbidity rate per 100,000 population of prostate cancer reported as the cause of death was 0.84 in 1954–55, and 1.82 in 1966–67 (Segi and Kurihara 1972). M. A. Bean et al. (1974) investigated the prevalence of prostate cancer in 1,357 cases between 1961 and 1969 in Hiroshima and Nagasaki. The entire morbidity rate was 8.7 percent, which included 2.1 percent of active carcinoma and 6.6 percent of occult carcinoma. Prostate cancer was the cause of death in 1.2 percent. Neither active carcinoma nor latent carcinoma was related to exposure. K. Akazaki (1969) examined the slides of latent carcinoma in Japan, Colombia, Hawaii, and the United States mainland and found the age-corrected morbidity rate of occult carcinoma to be 21.2 percent among Japanese, 31.3 percent in Colombians, 25.3 percent in Hawaiians of Japanese descent, and 30.8 percent in Americans. Bean et al. examined the prostates of 213 cases of a similar age distribution. The 213 cases were divided into three groups, 71 in each, according to their relation to exposure: not in the city during explosion, exposed to no rads, and exposed to over 100 rads. Occult carcinoma was looked for in an examination of the entire prostate cut at intervals of 5 millimeters. The morbidity rate of occult carcinoma was 27.2 percent; and morbidity, histological type, and biological activity of this condition were not found to be related to exposure.

2. *Cancer of the female reproductive organ.* Ovarian tumor in mice is an example of radiation carcinogenesis in animals. Only few reports have been made on tumors of the female reproductive organ following radiation in human subjects. In the study of a few cases examined clinically at the Atomic Bomb Casualty Commission between 1953 and 1957, no significant difference in the incidence of uterine tumor and other tumors of the female genital organ could be seen between the exposed and the non-exposed groups (Sawada 1958). From the analysis of mortality rate at the early stage of exposure and that of tumor registry, no tumorigenic effect of statistical significance was noted by radiation (Tabuchi et al. 1966).

Bone Tumors. Bone tumors have occurred in workers who paint with radium. T. Yamamoto and T. Wakabayashi (1969) made a study on 76 malignant and 87 benign bone tumors in the exposed selected from 8,179 autopsies and 65,789 surgicals between 1950 and 1965. Autopsy materials consisted of 4 cases of osteosarcoma, 1 case each of Ewing's sarcoma and reticulum cell sarcoma, while biopsy and surgicals showed 44 cases with malignant tumors (22 cases of osteosarcoma). Those of the autopsy cases were seen in the non-exposed, and only 5 cases (4 osteosarcomas, 1 ameloblastoma) in the biopsy and surgicals had been exposed to the atomic bomb. A statistical study on their relation to exposure dose could not be carried out owing to the few cases.

Other Tumors. Though the central nervous system is not sensible to radiation, and the incidence of brain tumors is low compared with tumors in other organs, the Radiation Effects Research Foundation has started studies on the relation of intracranial and pituitary tumors to radiation and also studies on tumors of the head and neck, excluding tumors of brain, salivary gland, and thyroid.

Chromosome Changes

The chromosome is known to be a carrier of genes in the nucleus of a cell, and its basic chemical constituent is called DNA (deoxyribonucleic acid). Usually the chromosomes cannot be seen because they show either an amorphous structure or a cluster of threadlike appearance within the nucleus. However, they can be observed through a microscope with high magnification as visible entities only during the period of cell proliferation, called *cell division* or *mitosis*. It is also known that the number and the shape of chromosomes are constant and specific to each species of living organism; the number of chromosomes in a human being, for example, is invariably forty-six (Tjio and Levan 1956).

Recent progress in radiation biology has firmly established the high susceptibility of chromosomes to ionizing radiation, which induces chromosome breaks and hence aberrant chromosomes owing to mismatching of broken chromosomes. The role of chromosome examination (chromosome study is also called *cytogenetics* or *cytogenetic study* in the field of genetic science) has become increasingly important for the evaluation of genetic and somatic effects of ionizing radiation in man (United Nations 1969). In this section, therefore, we shall outline the significance of radiation-induced chromosome aberrations observed in the somatic cells of people exposed in Hiroshima and Nagasaki.

RADIATION-INDUCED CHROMOSOME ABERRATIONS

A tissue culture method, by which living tissue cells removed from the body can proliferate in test tubes, is considered to be the most feasible technique for chromosome examination (Boué and Boué 1974). Since the new method for making lymphocyte cultures from peripheral blood by using phyto-hemagglutinin (PHA) was first established by P. S. Moorhead et al. in 1960, the procedure for the preparation of human chromosomes has become greatly simplified; and as a consequence, there has been an explosion in knowledge of human cytogenetics.

Chromosomes as shown in figures 9.27 and 9.28 vary in size and consist

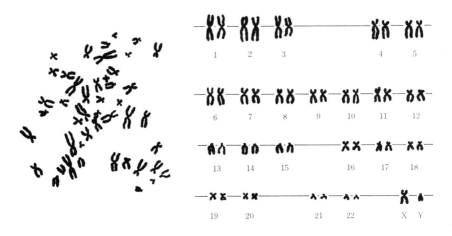

Figure 9.27. A normal male metaphase and its karyotype (46, XY).

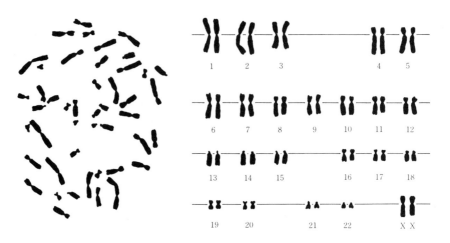

Figure 9.28. A normal female metaphase and its karyotype (46, XX).

of two common subunits *(chromatids),* paired in appearance. There is always a constriction called a *centromere* in every chromosome, where the spindle fibers are attached for the migration of chromosomes at cell division. The chromosomes on either side of the centromere are *chromosome arms:* of these arms, one is long arm, and the other is short. Each pair of chromosomes can be arranged and then numbered in descending order of size. Such an alignment of chromosome pairs is a *karyotype*.

Various types of chromosome aberration result from irradiation. When the chromosomes are broken, the majority of them rejoin identical chromosomes to reconstitute their original and undamaged state. Of the others, and especially when there are many chromosome breaks, the broken ends of two different broken chromosomes will join to make an aberrant chromosome; this process is *exchange-type* or structural chromosome aberration. If a broken chromosome does not join either an identical or a different chromosome, it is an *acentric fragment* or a *terminal deletion.* Exchange-type aberrations are divided into two basic types depending on the orientation and the combination of broken pieces for rejoining: *intrachromosome exchange* and *interchromosome exchange,* as in the diagram in figure 9.29. Figures 9.30

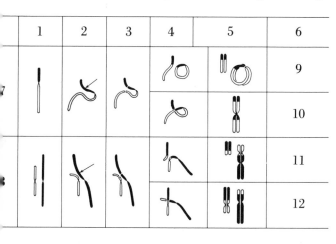

1	2	3	4	5	6
					9
					10
					11
					12

1. Before irradiation
2. Irradiation
3. Break
4. Rejoining
5. (DNA synthesis) Metaphase chromosomes
6. Type of aberration
7. Intrachromosomal exchange
8. Interchromosomal exchange
9. A ring (r) with an acentric (ace)
10. Pericentric inversion (inv)
11. A dicentric with an acentric (ace)
12. Reciprocal translocation (rep t)

Figure 9.29. Mechanism and types of radiation-induced chromosome aberration.

to 9.33 show typical chromosome aberrations. Among the four types of exchange-type aberration, both *ring* and *dicentric* chromosomes are referred to as *asymmetric* exchanges, and *pericentric inversion* and *reciprocal translocation,* as *symmetric* exchanges. Asymmetric aberrations may cause mechanical disturbances for the separation of chromosomes at cell division and thus may lead to cell death. When the chromosomes are separated into daughter cells at anaphase, cell division may proceed without any trouble as in the forms shown in *A, D,* and *G* in figure 9.34; while chromosome bridge in *B* and *E* and also the chromosome interlocking in *C* and *F* are the major cause for the error in cell division.

Among the radiation-induced chromosome aberrations, the frequency of terminal deletions is known to increase linearly with increasing radiation

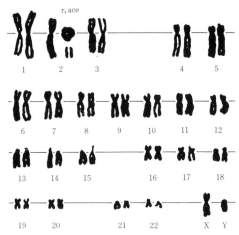

Figure 9.30. A ring chromosome (r) with an accompanying acentric (ace).

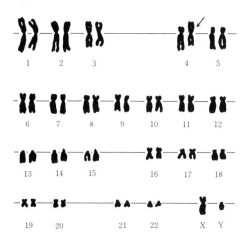

Figure 9.31. A pericentric inversion (inv).

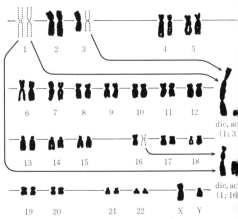

Figure 9.32. Two dicentrics (dic) and their accompanying acentrics (ace).

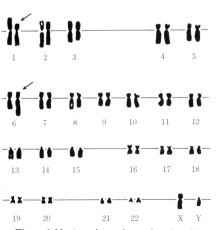

Figure 9.33. A reciprocal translocation (t).

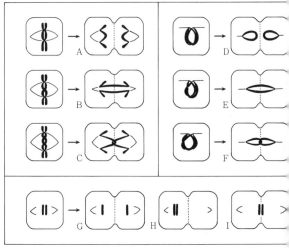

Figure 9.34. Types of mitotic error caused by asymmetric chromosome exchanges (A,D,G: Normal division; B,E: Chromosome bridge; C,F: Chromosome interlocking; H: Unequal segregation of chromosomes; I: Chromosome lagg

dose. In the case of exchange-type aberrations, when two breaks are produced by one ionizing particle (a one-hit event), their frequency increases linearly in proportion to radiation dose; while when the two breaks are produced by different particles (a two-hit event), the increase in incidence is proportional to the square of the radiation dose. By gamma rays and X-rays, known as low *linear energy transfer* (LET), yield of chromosome aberrations approximates to the square of the radiation dose; while in those with a high LET, such as neutrons, the dose-response relationship is linear, with a high frequency of chromosome aberrations.

CHROMOSOME ABERRATIONS IN LYMPHOCYTES OF PEOPLE EXPOSED TO THE ATOMIC BOMB

Chromosome aberrations observed in the peripheral blood lymphocytes of subjects receiving radiation therapy were first reported by I. M. Tough et al. in 1960. A similar type of chromosome aberration in exposed survivors in Hiroshima and Nagasaki was initially observed by T. Ishihara and T. Kumatori in 1965. They examined the lymphocyte chromosomes derived from 6 cases (2 in Hiroshima and 4 in Nagasaki), and reported a high frequency of exchange aberrations in the exposed as compared with the non-exposed. In the same year, Y. Doida, T. Sugahara, and M. Horikawa also found exchange aberrations and terminal deletions among 5 exposed in Hiroshima and among 2 in Nagasaki. In 1966, T. Iseki carried out a study on 25 Nagasaki survivors and obtained similar results. A systematic survey on chromosomes in circulating lymphocytes was carried out by A. D. Bloom et al. (1966) on 94 exposed survivors (51 in Hiroshima, 43 in Nagasaki), who were under 30 years of age at the time of the bombing, and on 94 controls (those who had been exposed to an estimated dose of less than 1 rad or were 3 to 4 kilometers from the hypocenter). The exposed group was within 1.4 kilometers of the hypocenter in both cities, and their estimated dose was over 200 rads in Hiroshima and over 220 rads in Nagasaki.

In 1967, Bloom et al. reported on a further examination on 77 exposed survivors (55 in Hiroshima, 22 in Nagasaki), who were thirty or more years old at the time of atomic bomb exposure, and on 80 controls (58 in Hiroshima, 22 in Nagasaki). Although over twenty years had elapsed since exposure, the two surveys confirmed the significantly high frequency of structural chromosome aberrations in the exposed as compared with the controls. On the other hand, no significant correlation could be found between the frequency of numerical abnormality of chromosomes and exposure dose. As to age at the time of explosion, the frequency of chromosome aberrations was slightly higher in subjects over thirty than in those under thirty. Clones of cells with identical chromosome aberrations were found to occur among the older subjects. These findings suggest that, with the lapse of time, cells with radiation-induced chromosome aberrations could have proliferated in the body to form a group of aberrant cells. Though these surveys have demonstrated that residual chromosome aberrations can be observed in peripheral blood lymphocytes for decades after radiation exposure, there remains some technical problem about the three-day-culture method which was mainly employed in these investigations. The chromosome figures thus prepared are considered to be in their second cell division in culture. Cells with asymmetric exchanges—that is, dicentric and ring chromosomes—are likely to be lost through the first cell division, so that the observed values from three-day-culture samples are estimated to be lower than the actual frequency in the body. Taking the preceding possibility into consideration, M. S. Sasaki (1971, p. 81) and Sasaki and H. Miyata (1968) have examined induced chromosome aberrations in Hiroshima survivors based on two-day-culture samples.

A detailed chromosome analysis was made by Sasaki and Miyata on 83,506 cells from 51 exposed survivors in Hiroshima and 11 non-exposed controls. The chromosome aberrations were classified by type; and attempts were made to estimate the radiation dose for individual cases. There was a positive correlation between each of the estimated doses and the frequency of dicentrics plus rings (dic + r), as well as of reciprocal translocations plus pericentric inversions (t + inv). These researchers further attempted to estimate individual absorbed doses by extrapolating the frequency of induced chromosome aberrations from each case onto the dose-response curve obtained experimentally from data by X-ray; there was a good fit between the aberration frequency and in-air dose (T65D) (Auxier et al. 1966). This finding suggests that the frequency of chromosome aberrations may prove to be a valuable tool for quantitative estimation of radiation exposure dose. Another noteworthy point was the higher frequency of chromosome aberrations in the 19 remotely exposed survivors (more than 2.4 kilometers from the hypocenter) than in the non-exposed controls. Eleven of the 19 survivors had entered the city within three days after the explosion. The remaining 8 had either entered the city after four or more days after the bombing or had not entered at all. The difference in the frequencies between the two groups was statistically significant, with higher frequency for the early entrants. Clones of cells with exchange aberrations were found in 2 of the 7 heavily exposed survivors.

A. A. Awa (1974, pp. 634–74; 1975*b*) and Awa et al. (1971, 1978) carried out chromosome analyses on about one thousand exposed and non-exposed controls selected from among the participants of the ABCC-RERF Adult Health Study samples. The exposed group consisted of those who had received an estimated dose of more than 1 rad; and the controls were those who were remotely exposed with an estimated dose of less than 1 rad, and included early entrants. So that only the effects of the atomic bomb irradiation could be examined, people receiving radiation therapy and radioisotope treatment at any time in the past were excluded. Observations were made on two-day-cultures of peripheral blood lymphocytes. The results obtained by Awa et al. are shown in table 9.53.

TABLE 9.53

Distribution of Cells with Chromosome Aberrations by Dose, Hiroshima and Nagasaki

Dose Group (rads)	Mean Total Dose (rads)	Number of Cases	Number of Cells Examined	Number of Cells with Exchange Aberrations*
Hiroshima control	—	263	24,414	210 (0.86%)
1–99	37.3	70	6,459	141 (2.18%)
100–199	142.9	137	12,634	528 (4.18%)
200–299	243.2	72	6,484	544 (8.39%)
300–399	348.4	43	3,896	433 (11.11%)
400–499	441.1	30	2,869	371 (12.93%)
≥500	—	34	3,222	489 (15.18%)
Nagasaki control	—	156	14,748	128 (0.87%)
1–99	48.5	57	5,472	77 (1.41%)
100–199	147.0	62	5,727	73 (1.27%)
200–299	249.9	58	5,443	117 (2.15%)
300–399	336.1	30	2,753	83 (3.01%)
400–499	437.2	24	2,312	147 (6.36%)
≥500	—	16	1,566	196 (12.52%)

* Figures in parentheses are percentages of cells examined.
Source: A. A. Awa, T. Sofuni, T. Honda, M. Itoh, S. Neriishi, and M. Otake, "Relationship between the radiation dose and chromosome aberrations in atomic bomb survivors of Hiroshima and Nagasaki," *Journal of Radiation Research* (Tokyo) 19 (1978): 126.

The frequency of cells with chromosome exchange aberrations increased with increasing radiation dose in both cities. Though the frequency of chromosome aberrations in the controls was about the same for the two cities, in the exposed the values were consistently higher at all dose ranges in Hiroshima than in Nagasaki. There was a linear relationship between aberration frequency and dose in Hiroshima, while in Nagasaki it appeared to show a curve by the square of the dose. This difference may be attributed to the difference in the radiation material of the two bombs.

Approximately 90 percent of the aberrations observed were symmetric in type (reciprocal translocations and pericentric inversions), and these were the major constituent for the dose-aberration relationship. Since the probability of both symmetric and asymmetric aberrations being produced is expected theoretically to be 1:1, the predominance of symmetric aberration observable at this moment suggests that cells with asymmetric aberrations were eliminated from the body with the lapse of time. On the other hand, the presence of cells carrying a dicentric (or a ring) with an accompanying acentric fragment is evidence that cells with such aberrations induced at the time of exposure have survived to date in a dormant state without cell division. While some lymphocytes have a long life span, it is important to note that clones of cells with identical chromosome aberrations were produced through repeated cell divisions in the body among heavily exposed subjects.

Lymphocytes consist of T-cells (thymus-derived) and B-cells (bone-marrow–derived). Since the T-cells are known to respond to the stimulation of PHA* to initiate cell division, the foregoing results are based on T-cells. Recently N. Kamada et al. (1979) isolated the B-cells and cultured by adding a *mitogen* (a substance that causes cell division); and he has succeeded in establishing twelve cell culture strains of the B-cells from the proximally exposed subjects. Of these, six cell strains showed chromosome aberrations.

Somatic chromosomes have been examined by A. D. Bloom, S. Neriishi, and P. G. Archer (1968) for 38 cases exposed in utero (an estimated dose to each mother of over 100 rads) and for 48 controls; and a significantly increased frequency of chromosome aberrations was noted among the exposed in comparison with the controls.

As already mentioned elsewhere (pages 150–51 and 270), leukocytosis was noted among the residents exposed to the radioactive fallout of the explosion in the Nishiyama district of Nagasaki; and later leukemia developed in a couple of the residents. The chromosomes among the Nishiyama residents were investigated by S. Okajima et al. (1972). The frequency of chromosome aberrations in the 50 Nishiyama residents was slightly higher than that in the 50 non-exposed controls, but the difference was not statistically significant. The aberration frequency was obviously lower than that found among 38 Nagasaki survivors exposed to radiation dose of more than 200 rads.

CHROMOSOME ABERRATIONS IN BONE MARROW CELLS OF PEOPLE EXPOSED TO THE ATOMIC BOMB

Some reports concerning the chromosomes of bone marrow cells are derived from atomic bomb survivors. N. Ozono (1965) examined the chromosomes in bone marrow cells of 39 exposed survivors in Hiroshima (14 within 1.5 kilometers, 11 between 1.5 and 2 kilometers, and 14 over 2 kilometers), and N. Kamada (1969) continued an examination on 47 survivors (16 within 1.5 kilometers, 14 between 1.5 and 2 kilometers, 17 between 2 and 3 kilometers) and found no abnormalities. Further studies in the bone marrow cells from heavily exposed survivors with the improved method by N. Kamada, T. Tsuchimoto, and H. Uchino (1970) have found, in one of the G-group

---

* *Phytohemagglutinin* is an extract of red kidney beans which acts to stimulate mitosis of white blood cells in tissue culture. (Trans.)

chromosomes, a long-arm deletion that resembles the Philadelphia chromosome* characteristic of chronic myeloid leukemia. H. Uchino and N. Kamada (1972) observed chromosome aberrations in the marrow cells of 5 survivors exposed within 1 kilometer of the hypocenter. To summarize the data from the bone marrow study of the exposed in Hiroshima by N. Oguma et al. (1975, p. 75): chromosome aberrations were found in 7 of the 9 cases (78 percent) exposed within 0.5 kilometers, in 7 of the 17 (41 percent) exposed between 0.5 and 1 kilometer, and in none of the 59 exposed between 1 and 3 kilometers.

In Nagasaki, Y. Tomonaga, et al. (1976) examined the chromosomes of bone marrow cells in 30 exposed cases, but failed to demonstrate any radiation-induced aberrations.

FUTURE CYTOGENETIC STUDIES

Exposure to atomic bomb radiation induced chromosome aberrations in the somatic cells; and even now, more than thirty years after the explosion, these aberrations can persist in the lymphocytes and marrow cells among exposed survivors in Hiroshima and Nagasaki; the aberration frequency is closely associated with the increase in radiation dose. It is obvious that these aberrations are the consequence of radiation injury, and that the "casualties" from radiation exposure at a cellular level have not yet healed. The implication of chromosome aberrations of somatic cells for the health of the exposed is still unclear, and no correlation to any specific diseases or symptoms can be found. Chromosome aberration exists as if it were unrelated to health but is closely related only to radiation dose. It remains to be elucidated in the future whether any association exists between chromosome aberrations and possible etiology for somatic, especially malignant, diseases. In this connection, careful follow-up studies must be continued. It is also necessary to apply new cytogenetic methods—called "banding technique"—currently in use (Sofuni et al. 1977), for detailed chromosome analysis, in order to determine any specific fragile sites on the chromosomes and to search for their biological and medical significance.

Genetic Effects

H. J. Muller, in 1927, first discovered abnormal offspring born to X-irradiated parents of fruit flies (Drosophila).

---

* A *Philadelphia chromosome* is a deficient number 22 chromosome and is found in the blood cells of many patients with chronic granulocytic leukemia. (Ed.)

This experiment was epoch-making in the field of medicine and biology and threw light on how mutation is induced artificially by irradiation. In light of this knowledge, there was great concern about possible genetic effects in the offspring of people exposed to atomic bomb radiation in Hiroshima and Nagasaki. Careful genetic surveys have thus been carried out over the years since then; but, fortunately, no harmful genetic effects have yet been confirmed to date.

Genetic effects on offspring following irradiation are manifested by injury to the parental germ cells (sperm, ova, and their precursor cells) in the gonads. The degree of injury varies according to radiation dose. With high radiation doses, the germ cells die and lose their ability to produce gametes (either sperm or ovum), and thus bring about sterility with no genetic effects. With a moderate degree of radiation, injuries are induced to the chromosomes as well as to the genes, and it is possible that genetic effects may appear only if damaged germ cells retain their normal reproductive capacity. Of the various types of induced chromosome aberration, if the cells with asymmetric exchanges (dicentrics and rings) are produced by ionizing radiation, cells are likely to die—as a result of mechanical disturbance at cell division—before becoming sperm and ova. Production of chromosome imbalance at fertilization would result in an abnormal fetus. Nondisjunction due to abnormalities of centromeres and spindle fibers would also result in numerical abnormality of chromosomes in the fetus. According to the degree of gene injury, abnormalities in the fetus vary from death (dominant lethal mutations) to congenital malformations in the fetus. Detailed studies on specific gene locus in mice have been carried out extensively and systematically by W. L. Russell (1963, p. 205).

Abnormalities in germ cells may be caused by factors other than radiation, and also many congenital malformations can be produced without genetic factors. In the human being, the generation time is long, and the abortion rate, high. Furthermore, socio-economic factors have made human genetic analysis difficult and complex. Consequently, we have inaccurate data on the natural incidence of genetic abnormalities as a basis for understanding the genetic effect of radiation. A large-scale survey has been conducted on the incidence of congenital malformations at birth in a population of about two million residents in British Columbia in Canada (Trimble and Daughty 1974), and another on the estimation of the frequency of chromosome anomalies in liveborn babies in Europe and North America (Evans 1977). However, no such basic data are available in Japan. In spite of the many difficulties, estimations of the genetic risks to man from radiation are being attempted on an international scale through comparison of various congenital malformations and of chromosome abnormalities among the general human population and also from various experimental data. Details of these studies have been described in the Report of the United Nations Scientific Committee on the Effects of Atomic Radiation (United Nations 1972), an outline of which is given in table 9.54.

TABLE 9.54

Estimated Effect of 1 Rad per Generation of Low-dose, Low Dose-rate, Low Radiation on a Population of One Million Individuals Born Alive

Disease Classification	Current Incidence	First Generation
Autosomal dominant and X–linked diseases	10,000	20
Recessive diseases	1,100	relatively slight
Chromosomal diseases	6,000	40
Congenital anomalies, anomalies ex-pressed later, constitutional and degenerative diseases	90,100	5
Total	107,200	65 (0.06%*)

* Percentage of current incidence.
Source: United Nations, *Report of the United Nations Scientific Committee on the Effects of Atomic Radiation, Ionizing Radiation: Levels and Effects* (1972).

EARLY GENETIC STUDY IN HIROSHIMA AND NAGASAKI

The following items were investigated as indices for detecting genetic effects of atomic radiation: spontaneous abortions and stillbirths due to lethal muta-tions, infantile deaths resulting from harmful effects during the fetal stage, decrease in birth weight, increased frequency of congenital malformations among children born to exposed parents, and change in sex ratio of children. If the sex ratio is altered as a genetic effect, theoretically there would be a decrease in the number of males from exposed mothers, and a relative increase in males from exposed fathers.

A survey on pregnancy termination in Hiroshima and Nagasaki was carried out between 1948 and 1953 by J. V. Neel and W. J. Schull (1956). Follow-up studies included sex ratio, body weight, frequency of malformations and stillbirths. About one third of these subjects were selected randomly, and both mothers and children were examined nine months after birth. Informa-tion concerning mortality of infants, growth and development, and any malfor-mations that might have been overlooked at birth, was collected and analyzed. Table 9.55 gives the number of subjects; and table 9.56, a summary of the statistical analysis.

Considering the sample size in this survey, a genetic effect of parental radiation exposure may be explained with the confidence limits at 90 percent under the following conditions: (1) absolute decrease of over 1.6 percent in

TABLE 9.55

Distribution of Registered Births by Parental Exposure

Father's Exposure	Mother's Exposure				
	1	2	3	4 + 5	Total
1 Hiroshima	18,723	5,721	2,320	1,208	27,972
Nagasaki	16,338	10,141	823	596	27,898
2 Hiroshima	1,611	1,993	451	217	4,272
Nagasaki	2,420	4,483	298	129	7,330
3 Hiroshima	648	416	545	116	1,725
Nagasaki	258	301	109	35	703
4 + 5 Hiroshima	422	264	161	127	974
Nagasaki	149	188	39	30	406
Total Hiroshima	21,404	8,394	3,477	1,668	34,943
Nagasaki	19,165	15,113	1,269	790	36,337

1. Not present in Hiroshima or Nagasaki at the time of the bombing.
2. Present in Hiroshima or Nagasaki but at a distance from the hypocenter *(a)* greater than 3,000 m, or *(b)* less than 3,000 m and heavily shielded, or *(c)* 1,500–3,000 m and moderately shielded, or *(d)* 2,000–3,000 m and lightly shielded.
3. Present at a distance of *(a)* 2,000–3,000 m and unshielded, or *(b)* 1,000–2,000 m and lightly shielded, or *(c)* less than 1,000 m and moderately shielded.
4. Present at a distance of *(a)* less than 2,000 m and unshielded, or *(b)* less than 1,000 m and lightly shielded.
5. Present at a distance of less than 3,000 m from the hypocenter and exhibiting one or more of the following three symptoms of radiation sickness: epilation, petechiae, gingivitis.

Exposure doses approximately correspond to: (1) 0 roentgen, (2) 5–10 roentgen, (3) 50–100 roentgen, (4) 100–150 roentgen, (5) 200–300 roentgen.
Source: H. Kato, "Review of thirty years' study of Hiroshima and Nagasaki atomic bomb survivors. II. Biological effects, B. Genetic effects, 1. Early genetic surveys and mortality study," *Journal of Radiation Research* (Tokyo) 16 (1975, supplement): 67. J. V. Neel and W. J. Schull, "The effect of exposure to the atomic bombs on pregnancy termination in Hiroshima and Nagasaki," National Academy of Sciences, National Research Council, United States (1956), no. 491.

TABLE 9.56

Summary of the Comparisons of the Various Indicators with Parental Exposure When (a) All Exposure Cells Are Considered (the 4 × 4 case), and (b) Only Those Cells Where Both Parents Were Exposed Are Considered (the 3 × 3 case)

Indicator	Parental Exposure			
	Fathers		Mothers	
	4 × 4 case	3 × 3 case	4 × 4 case	3 × 3 case
Sex ratio	0.30–0.50 ↑	0.90–0.95 ↑	0.10–0.20 ↓	0.95–0.98 ↓
Malformation:				
at birth	0.50–0.70 ↑	0.80–0.90 ↓	0.50–0.70 ↑	0.99 ↑
at 9 months		0.30–0.50 ↓		0.02–0.05 ↓
Stillbirth*	0.20–0.30 ↑	0.80–0.90 ↑	0.001–0.01 ↑	0.30–0.50 ↓
Neonatal death*		0.20–0.30 ↓		0.02–0.05 ↓
Death in 9 months		0.95–0.98 ↑		0.50–0.70 ↓
Birthweight means:				
males-Hiroshima	0.10–0.25 ↓		>0.25 ↓	
females-Hiroshima	>0.25 ↓		>0.25 ↓	
males-Nagasaki	>0.25 ↑		0.10–0.25 ↓	
females-Nagasaki	>0.25 ↑		0.10–0.25 ↑	
Anthropometrics: generalized means	<0.001	0.25–0.50	0.02–0.05	0.05–0.10

Note: The figures in the columns refer to probability levels. The arrows indicate the direction of the difference between heavily and lightly irradiated groups.
* *Stillbirth* is fetal death in utero; *neonatal* refers to the period immediately after birth and continuing through the first month of life.
Source: H. Kato, "Review of thirty years' study of Hiroshima and Nagasaki atomic bomb survivors. II. Biological effects. B. Genetic effects. 1. Early genetic surveys and mortality study," *Journal of Radiation Research* (Tokyo) 16 (1975, supplement): 67. J. V. Neel and W. J. Schull, "The effect of exposure to the atomic bombs on pregnancy termination in Hiroshima and Nagasaki," National Academy of Sciences, National Research Council, United States (1956), no. 491.

number of males born to exposed mothers; (2) absolute increase of over 4 percent in number of males born to exposed fathers; (3) stillbirths over 80 percent of normal value and increase in mortality of newborn babies; and (4) increased incidence of malformations by more than 100 percent of normal value. The analysis, however, revealed no significant trends—except for altered sex ratio—indicating genetic effects by radiation exposure to the atomic bombs. Though the change in sex ratio was seen to be significant at the beginning of the study, the follow-up survey supplemented by newborn infants between the years 1954 and 1958 (Schull, Neel, and Hashizume 1966) failed to demonstrate any positive results beyond those in the previous findings.

MORTALITY OF CHILDREN BORN TO THE EXPOSED

Following the early survey, the ABCC (and later the Radiation Effects Research Foundation) has undertaken the follow-up studies on the mortality of children (first filial generation, F_1) born to the exposed (Kato 1975; Kato, Schull, and Neel 1966; Neel, Kato, and Schull 1974). A sample of 54,000 children, who were born to parents whose history at the time of explosion was known, was divided into the following three groups: (1) one or both parents exposed within 2 kilometers of the hypocenter; (2) one or both parents exposed at a distance of more than 2.5 kilometers, or neither parent exposed within 2 kilometers; and (3) neither parent exposed. All cases in group 1 were the subjects for study; and those matched by sex and age were selected at random from groups 2 and 3 to serve as controls. Causes of death were confirmed by family registry and death certificates. On the basis of the reported evidence to date, the mortality of children (three to fifteen years, average nine years after birth) in the exposed has not been affected by parental radiation dose. Though the age and the order of birth are different between the two groups, this difference is expected to act toward an increase in the mortality of those in group 1. No increase in mortality, however, was confirmed in group 1. Consequently, no evidence verifying genetic effects by parental radiation exposure has been obtained.

HEIGHT OF CHILDREN BORN TO THE EXPOSED

In 1965 the height of 200,000 children in primary schools, junior high schools, and senior high schools was measured in Hiroshima and Nagasaki. In this study T. Furushō (1976) analyzed the relation between the parental radiation exposure and the growth of children. Height is controlled by polygenes; and since these are easily influenced by environmental factors and other variables, genetic effects of irradiation on height have not been demonstrated to date.

CYTOGENETIC SURVEY

It has already been mentioned that a genetic effect can be manifested by chromosome abnormalities induced in parental germ cells. There are a variety of experimental data using mice on chromosome abnormalities induced in germ cells by irradiation (United Nations 1972). Since chromosome abnormalities similar to those found in mice are expected to occur in human beings, it is possible to estimate their genetic risk on the basis of these experimental data. Obviously, experimenting on human beings is impractical even for the evaluation of genetic risk; thus, such evaluation is feasible only through indirect methods, such as the comparison of the rates of fetal and newborn abnormalities and of spontaneous abortions and stillbirths for normal and affected populations.

Another way of evaluating genetic effects of irradiation on parental germ cells in humans is to see if there is any increase in the frequency of children with chromosome aberrations that might be ascribed to parental radiation exposure, when compared with non-exposed controls.

The rate of abortions under natural conditions is known to be high. Approximately one half of such abortions are due to chromosome anomalies (Boué and Boué 1974, pp. 317–42). Further, one half of these chromosome anomalies consists of *trisomies* (having one more than the normal two chromosomes); and one fourth, of *monosomies* (having one fewer than the normal two chromosomes). Most numerical chromosome abnormalities result in fetal death, and hence spontaneous abortion. Only fetuses with chromosome anomalies—like trisomic conditions such as XXY, XYY, XXX, and 21 trisomy, known as "Down's syndrome"—can survive to term. The problem is to clarify the elevated rate of offspring with chromosome anomalies in addition to the value derived from the general human population. A. A. Awa (1975*a;* 1975*c;* 1976) has undertaken to answer to this question through chromosome analysis of somatic cells in children of the exposed.

Table 9.57 gives the interim results of the cytogenetic study on children born to exposed parents by comparing the results of the controls and of newborn screening surveys carried out in Europe and North America, as reported by H. J. Evans (1977). The exposed group in this table consists of children born to either one or both parents receiving an estimated dose of over 1 rad; and the controls are the children whose parents were either exposed to an estimated dose of less than 1 rad or not exposed. The frequency of children with chromosome anomaly was slightly higher among the exposed than among the controls, but the difference was not statistically significant. There was also no statistical difference between the newborn and the exposed. In other words, the frequency of chromosome abnormalities in the exposed group is within the normal limits of variation.

TABLE 9.57

Comparison of Cytogenetic Data on Children of A-Bomb Survivors and Newborn Infants in European Countries

	First Filial Generation of Survivors*		Newborn Infants in Europe*
	Control	Exposed	
Total examined	2,202	4,230	43,558
Males examined	1,026	1,960	28,582
Females examined	1,176	2,270	14,976
I. Sex anomaly*			
Male: XYY	1(0.10%)	3(0.15%)	26(0.09%)
XXY	2(0.19%)	3(0.15%)	30(0.10%)
Other	—	—.	17(0.06%)
Subtotal	3(0.29%)	6(0.31%)	73(0.26%)
Female: XO	—	—	2(0.01%)
XXX	—	2(0.09%)	13(0.09%)
Other	1(0.09%)†	2(0.09%)‡	5(0.03%)
Subtotal	1(0.09%)	4(0.18%)	20(0.13%)
Total**	4(0.18%)	10(0.24%)	93(0.21%)
II. Structural anomaly			
A. Balanced			
D/D***	—	3(0.07%)	31(0.07%)
D/G***	—	2(0.05%)	8(0.02%)
Other	3(0.14%)	5(0.12%)	42(0.10%)
Subtotal	3(0.14%)	10(0.24%)	81(0.19%)
B. Unbalanced			
D/D + D/G***	—	—	2(0.0045%)
Other	—	—	19(0.04%)
Subtotal	—	—	21(0.05%)
III. Autosomal trisomy			
+G	—	—	45(0.10%)
Other	—	—	9(0.02%)
Total	—	—	54(0.12%)
Grand total	7(0.32)	20(0.47)	249(0.57)
(I + IIA.) Total	7(0.32)	20(0.47)	174(0.40)

* The percentages for sex anomaly apply only to the affected sex—not to the total studied, except for the total in I as indicated by the double asterisks (**), where the percentages are expressed as the total number of cases examined for each column.

** See preceding note.

*** Robertsonian translocations.

† One case with mosaicism (X/XXX).

‡ Two cases with mosaicism (X/XXX, XX/XXX).

Source: H. J. Evans, "Chromosome anomalies among live births," *Journal of Medicine and Genetics* 14 (1977): 309.

The difference between newborn babies and the exposed group is the lack of cases with autosomal trisomies and the structural rearrangements of unbalanced type in the latter. Since these chromosome anomalies are associated with severe congenital malformations with a high neonatal mortality rate, there is a possibility that children with these abnormalities had already died prior to the cytogenetic survey, when considering their average age of twenty and over at the time of this survey. Or, alternatively, had they been alive, they might have been institutionalized, and thus excluded from this survey.

To date, it is unclear whether there is any difference in frequency of chromosome aberration between different human races. Consequently, it is still difficult to make a direct comparison of data for F_1 children with data from newborn screening undertaken in other countries.

BIOCHEMICAL GENETICS STUDY

Protein consists of amino acids that are determined by a gene (or genes). A gene mutation produces a change in the amino acid sequence within polypeptide chains and finally leads to a protein variant. A change in the amino acid sequence is often associated with an alteration of the electric charge of the protein molecule, which is easily detectable by electrophoretic techniques currently in use. Hence, this is one of the practical ways to detect gene mutations. Biochemical genetics study includes examination of various proteins in which variants are detectable among many samples at a time, and the observed protein variants are confirmed through family studies whether they are inherited from generation to generation. The frequency of gene mutations can thus be estimated accurately by electrophoresis; any increase in the rate of gene mutations by parental radiation exposure would also be reflected with certainty in this study.

The RERF has recently started an electrophoretic analysis of twenty-six proteins (serum proteins and red blood cell enzymes) obtained from 10,000 children born to exposed parents and from another 10,000 controls (Satoh 1976). When this survey is completed, it will become possible to investigate the gene mutation frequency among the 260,000 protein determinants in each group, and thus to evaluate in detail the genetic effects of ionizing radiation on the human being.

Results of the preliminary study, however, have revealed no increased mutation rates among the proteins studied in the children born to the exposed.

FUTURE PROBLEMS IN GENETIC STUDIES

Genetic surveys undertaken to date have yielded no positive evidence for a genetic hazard due to atomic bomb radiation. As already pointed out, it is possible that genetic effects do not show up so distinctly in human beings, since they have fewer pregnancies as well as fewer fetuses per pregnancy than do experimental animals. Furthermore, human population is thought to be heterogeneous, with an exceptionally low rate in consanguinity. The chances of producing recessive homozygotes would be extremely low. In this regard, the human is again markedly different from various experimental animals. Even if harmful genetic injuries were to occur from radiation exposure, they would have been eliminated through spontaneous abortion or, most likely, through the elimination as in the form of unrecognized abortions. In other words, through the mechanism of natural selection, most genetic damage may disappear before it is recognized.

Even though remarkable progress has been achieved in methodology for studying human genetics, they are at present not perfect; and all of the variations at a gene level have not been thoroughly verified. Over thirty years—only two generations—have passed since the explosion of the atomic bombs. This seems, in a sense, to be a very short interval in view of human genetics; and there is much to be done in the future.

From the theoretical aspects of radiation genetics, Y. Tajima (1972) estimated the number of children born to the exposed, between 1946 and 1980, to be 63,000 in Hiroshima and 42,000 in Nagasaki. Based on individual radiation doses and relative biological effectiveness (RBE) of neutron to gamma ray, the estimated number of affected offspring of the exposed would be increased by 11 percent to 16 percent in Hiroshima and by 5 percent to 7 percent in Nagasaki, when compared with the rate of abnormal offspring born to non-exposed controls. Tajima also pointed out the possibility of spreading recessive traits in the heterozygous condition in subsequent generations. Further studies are obviously needed to test his hypothesis.

Other Disorders

The various injuries and disorders occurring in the human body following exposure to the atomic bomb in Hiroshima and Nagasaki have been outlined. In the acute stage, thermal injuries, trauma, and radiation illness were seen. Keloid, leukemia, anemia, other blood disorders, cataract, thyroid cancer, lung cancer, breast cancer, salivary gland cancer, and other cancers as delayed effects were found to be significantly higher in the exposed compared with the non-exposed. It has become evident that exposure in utero and during infancy affects growth and development. Surveys and studies are also being made on chromosome abnormality and genetic effect.

Aside from the obvious disorders and abnormalities of exposure, the health of the exposed must be investigated from various medical points of view. Not only is it impossible to forecast when and what kind of disease will appear in the exposed, but it is also an important responsibility of medical care to manage the health of the gradually aging exposed people. Besides the aforementioned aftereffects, no other specific diseases have appeared in the exposed; but it may be said that no one who has been exposed to the atomic bomb will ever be relieved from its consequences.

ADULT HEALTH STUDY AT THE ATOMIC BOMB CASUALTY COMMISSION

Since 1958, the ABCC with the cooperation of the JNIH has been continuing adult health studies* with special emphasis on obtaining answers to the following problems: (1) Do the effects of exposure reflect upon the incidence of disease? (2) Can changes attributable to exposure be seen during the course of a disease in the exposed? (3) Do minimal physiological and biochemical changes not confirmable as a disease occur in the exposed? (4) Are there any new disorders having a cause-and-effect relation to exposure? These studies are being made by annual long-term observations on a fixed population consisting of both exposed and control subjects. The fixed population was selected from the residents of Hiroshima and Nagasaki, whose permanent domiciles, moreover, were in either city or in certain districts adjacent to each city according to the national census of October 1950. The studies were especially focused on the 5,000 subjects exposed within 2 kilometers of the hypocenter and showing symptoms of acute radiation illness (epilation, bleeding, oropharyngeal changes) as a result of exposure. The controls consisted of subjects of similar sex and age. These samples were divided equally into the following three groups: (1) those exposed within 2 kilometers but with no symptoms of acute radiation illness; (2) those exposed at a greater distance (3 to 3.5 kilometers in Hiroshima, 3.5 to 4 kilometers in Nagasaki); and (3) the non-exposed (those residing in neither city at the time of the explosion). The entire study consisted of four groups totaling approximately 20,000 subjects. Since 700 had died by the end of 1958, and about 2,000 had left the two cities by mid-1959, approximately 17,000 subjects were seen at the first examination. Twenty years later, the number was slightly over 12,000. The mean age at the time of exposure in Hiroshima was 32.1 years in males and 30.6 years in females; and that in Nagasaki, 25 years and 23.6 years, respectively. Thus, the mean age is now over 60 years. All the subjects were divided into twenty-four groups, and one group was examined each month;

* Belsky, Tachikawa, and Jablon 1971; Finch and Anderson 1963; Freedman, Fukushima, and Seigel 1963; Hamilton and Brody 1975; Hollingsworth and Anderson 1961; Sagan and Seigel 1963.

it took two years to examine all twenty-four. The investigation consists of history taking, physical examination, and general tests, with specific tests added whenever necessary.

Results of the ABCC-JNIH Adult Health Study. By 1972, there were about 30 reports under Adult Health Study and a total of about 120 reports including other related studies. Not a few reports have been made on hematological changes, cataract, growth and development disturbance, thyroid cancer, breast cancer, chromosome abnormality, exposure dose, and aging. Since so many papers have already been published, each report will not be mentioned separately, but a summary based on the introductory studies by J. L. Belsky, K. Tachikawa, and S. Jablon (1971) and by H. B. Hamilton and J. A. Brody (1975) will be given here. Aside from the preceding aftereffects, tuberculosis, diseases of the ear and mastoid, hypochromia,* and abnormal blood pressure in relation to exposure became subjects for discussion in the adult health study carried out between 1958 and 1968. The systolic blood pressure in males exposed under the age of fifty in Hiroshima and under the age of twenty in Nagasaki was low in the group receiving over 100 rads. The systolic pressure in females, especially those exposed between birth and age nineteen in Nagasaki, tended to drop somewhat with radiation dose. These results were, however, of no significance statistically. Later studies showed an increase in incidence of apoplexy and ischemic heart disorders with increased radiation dose among females in Hiroshima. Hitherto unknown diseases related to exposure have not yet been discovered, and no definite signs of accelerated aging have been found in subjects exposed to high doses. There were also no special changes in the functions of white blood cells and lymphocytes pertaining to immunity and defense of the living body.

The adult health studies also investigated cardiovascular diseases, diabetes, rheumatic arthritis, gastric and liver disorders, and—in relation to these disorders—various aspects of blood chemistry, immunoglobulins, rare diseases, and vital materials. Relatively recently, therapeutic radiation exposure has also attracted much attention. As to studies on cardiovascular diseases, the method used for studying these diseases in Framingham, Massachusetts, was first employed. Later a joint study by the ABCC, the Honolulu Heart Association, and the University of California began and is being carried out on the Japanese living in Hiroshima, Nagasaki, Hawaii, and San Francisco (Tripartite Cardiovascular Disease Study, or Nihon-San). Emphasis is being placed on comparative studies of diabetes and rheumatic arthritis with Americans. To date, however, the incidence of the majority of these diseases has not been found to be obviously related to exposure.

ABCC-JNIH Adult Health Study and Its Problems. The ABCC-JNIH

---

* *Hypochromia* is an abnormal decrease in the hemoglobin content of erythrocytes. (Ed.)

Adult Health Study has been following the health of the exposed through long-term physical examinations on the same fixed-population samples in order to clarify the effects of exposure by statistical means. The data accumulated during a twenty-year period are of great value for studying the delayed effects of exposure and also for medical investigation in general. There are, however, many problems in the surveys themselves and also in their results. First of all, there is still some doubt whether the fixed population for study is appropriate. To begin with, the number of subjects exposed to high doses included in this population is too small; and changes have occurred in the total number, in the number of subjects in each group, with the lapse of time. These people are now becoming inappropriate as subjects in whom to detect the effects of exposure. Thus, as the detection of the effects of exposure on aging and geriatric disease is about to take an important turn in the near future, it is time to reorganize the population used for this study. Second, an interval of two years is too long between examinations of each subject when aging and the chances of cancer occurring in this population are considered. Furthermore, renewal and revision of methods and categories of examination are of special importance. People exposed at a distance and the non-exposed were frequently used together in a control group for the statistical examination of exposure effects in the population. The assumption was that it was possible to discount the effects of different living conditions, aside from exposure dose, after the explosion, and that radiation effects of the atomic bomb were negligible in people who were far away. There remain, however, the problems of early entrants and secondary radioactivity; and the problem of low-dose exposure especially is becoming important.

ACTUAL CONDITIONS OF DISEASES IN THE MEDICAL CARE OF THE EXPOSED

Health management and medical care of the exposed will be described in detail in chapter 13. A brief description of the condition of the "sick exposed survivors" will be made here based on various data of health management and medical care of the exposed.* Even from the somewhat negative data of the Adult Health Study, it is clear that, with the process of aging, at least a portion of the exposed survivors are still actually ill owing to the influence of exposure on various disorders connected with aging.

The exposed survivors in Hiroshima and Nagasaki are being examined under the Atomic Bomb Victims Medical Care Law. According to the report made by Kumazawa, Matsusaka, and Teragami (1974) at the symposium of the fourteenth meeting of the Atomic Bomb Aftereffect Study Group held in 1974 in Hiroshima, 7,141 people out of 93,001 were found to need treatment

---

* Misao et al. 1967; Kumazawa et al. 1974; Shigeto 1967; Shimizu et al. 1970; Shimizu 1976; Yasuhi and Yokouchi 1967; Yokota 1967.

TABLE 9.58

Main Disorders Detected by the Periodical
Health Examination of Ambulatory A-bomb
Survivors, Hiroshima, 1971

Disorder	Number of Cases*
Hematological disorders	2,154 (18.8)
Cardiovascular disorders	3,382 (29.5)
Liver dysfunction	2,314 (20.2)
Endocrinological diseases	1,861 (16.2)
Nephropathy	233 (2.0)
Gastrointestinal diseases	156 (1.4)
Respiratory diseases	196 (1.7)
Pulmonary tuberculosis	121 (1.1)
Motor dysfunction	330 (2.9)
Ophthalmological diseases	259 (2.3)
Malignant neoplasms	32 (0.3)
Cerebrovascular diseases	21 (0.2)
Others	411 (3.6)
Total number of persons who needed medical care	11,470

* Figures in parentheses are percentages of total number of persons.
Source: T. Kumazawa, Y. Matsusaka, and M. Teragami, "Investigation of a regular mass examination of atomic bomb survivors," *Journal of the Hiroshima Medical Association* 27 (1974): 626.

at the time of examination at the Hiroshima Atomic Bomb Casualty Council Health Control Clinic for Atomic Bomb Survivors (table 9.58). Disturbance of hematopoietic function still showed a high incidence, and this was followed by disorders of the circulatory system and of liver and endocrinological functions.

Table 9.59 gives the various diseases and their incidence in the hospitalized patients between 1956 and 1974 at the Hiroshima Atomic Bomb Hospital (reported at the symposium of the sixteenth meeting of the Atomic Bomb Aftereffect Study Group by S. Ishida (Shimizu et al. 1976). The patients had all been exposed to the atomic bomb. The incidence of malignant tumors had the highest annual average, at 19.7 percent, and was followed in order by diseases of the digestive tract, anemia, hypertension, cerebrovascular disease, heart disease, and arthritis-rheumatism. From the annual trend, an increase was noted in diabetes, liver cirrhosis, hypertension, heart disease, cerebrovascular disease, and diseases of the bile tract and the pancreas. It should also be noted that survivors are still suffering from thermal burn scars, contracture, and residue of foreign bodies.

TABLE 9.59

Number of Patients with Malignant Neoplasms and Other Diseases among Survivors Hospitalized i Hiroshima Atomic Bomb Hospital, 1956–74

Classification of Diseases	Calendar Year										Total*	Ave Y
	1956–65	1966	1967	1968	1969	1970	1971	1972	1973	1974		
Malignant neoplasms	468	72	69	78	79	95	103	88	89	81	1,222 (19.7)	
Blood diseases												
Aplastic anemia	49	2	2	2	3	4	5	6	4	2	79 (1.3)	
Other types of anemia	304	6	13	1	6	9	5	9	6	11	370 (6.0)	
Leukopenia	23	1	1	0	1	0	0	0	0	0	26 (0.4)	
Others	8	1	0	0	0	3	1	0	3	1	17 (0.3)	
Endocrinological diseases												
Thyroid	27	1	0	2	1	1	7	4	5	2	50 (0.8)	
Diabetes mellitus	50	7	12	15	13	16	12	26	26	29	206 (3.3)	
Others	4	0	1	2	5	5	3	2	5	1	28 (0.5)	
Diseases of the digestive system												
Liver cirrhosis	103	3	5	6	19	13	10	36	29	23	247 (4.0)	
Other types of liver diseases	97	9	21	13	17	21	11	12	16	9	226 (3.6)	
Gallbladder, bile ducts, and pancreas	237	42	32	7	6	11	20	25	23	15	147 (2.3)	
Others				45	40	38	36	55	44	42	571 (9.2)	
Cardiovascular diseases												
Heart	64	2	16	22	19	16	19	38	42	32	270 (4.3)	
Hypertension	101	15	13	15	30	26	28	37	32	25	322 (5.2)	
Cerebrovascular diseases	83	12	11	15	18	11	29	41	42	52	314 (5.1)	
Respiratory diseases	100	12	12	21	18	10	15	19	22	21	250 (4.0)	
Neurological diseases	59	6	10	16	17	23	29	34	29	12	235 (3.8)	
Renal diseases	40	6	8	3	7	8	9	13	14	9	117 (1.9)	
Sequelae due to burns scar	179	3	1	1	1	7	0	3	2	1	198 (3.2)	
Motor dysfunction												
Arthritis	103	15	8	37	32	22	12	9	23	13	274 (4.4)	
Fracture of the spine and other bone fracture	63	3	7	8	19	17	10	5	13	13	158 (2.5)	
Arthrosis deformans and others	43	7	11	1	2	2	7	7	23	19	64 (1.0)	
				22	12	14	17	11	20	12	166 (2.7)	
Sequelae due to foreign bodies	21	2	0	0	2	1	1	3	0	0	30 (0.5)	
Other diseases not always related to *sequelae*	158	38	37	32	31	40	67	77	63	78	621 (10.0)	
Total of hospitalized patients†	2,259	277	301	330	382	366	390	381	334	330	5,350	

* Figures in parentheses are percentages of the total number of diseases (6,208).
† Since one patient could have had more than two diseases, the number of patients are not equal to the number of diseases.

(10 August, near Nagasaki Station.) (Photograph by Yōsuke Yamahata.)

PART III

THE IMPACT ON SOCIETY AND DAILY LIFE

Chapter 10

A Society Laid Waste

Special Features of A-bomb Damage

An atomic bomb, because of the enormous energy it releases in the multiple forms of heat, blast, and radiation, is capable of unprecedented physical destruction, killing, and maiming. It is a weapon of mass slaughter. The first special feature of this bomb, then, is its capability for massive devastation and death.

Besides the awesome physical, medical, and biological threats of the bomb, we are especially concerned that in 1945 it was dropped directly on cities whose people had no way to anticipate, or to protect themselves from, its enormous destructive powers. From the course of events that led to its development and use,* it is clear that from the outset this new weapon was not intended for use in war theaters where opposing armies were locked in battle; rather, it was to be dropped on densely populated centers that contained military facilities and industries as well as a high concentration of houses and other buildings. Moreover, the A-bomb attacks were needed not so much against Japan—already on the brink of surrender and no longer capable of mounting an effective counteroffensive—as to establish clearly America's postwar international position and strategic supremacy in the anticipated cold war setting. One tragedy of Hiroshima and Nagasaki is that this historically unprecedented devastation of human society stemmed from essentially experimental and political aims.

---

* The American A-bomb, developed under the code name "Manhattan Project," was judged operationally feasible in May 1945 by the project's Interim Committee (chaired by Secretary of War Henry L. Stimson) which oversaw the project's overall political, military, and scientific requirements. On 6 June this committee made the following decisions regarding its use: (1) the bomb should be used against Japan as soon as possible; (2) it should be used against targets that had both military facilities and war plants and also high density of easily destroyed houses and other buildings; and (3) no advance warning of the bomb's special destructive potential should be given (Freed and Giovannitti 1965; Groves and Groves 1962; Knebel and Bailey II 1960; Stimson 1947).

The two cities were, indeed, dense with houses and people. They were developed communities with families, neighborhood associations, stores, schools, hospitals, prefectural and municipal offices, courts, banks, companies, and industries—that is, organizations and personnel with many social relations and functions, many life styles and activities, all integrated into traditional corporate societies. The atomic bombs reduced to dismal ruins these centers of human life and livelihood.

The second feature of an atomic bombing is that its massive destruction occurs instantaneously and sweepingly without discrimination—young and old, men and women, combatants and noncombatants, residents and visitors— none is exempt from its death-dealing fury. In Hiroshima and Nagasaki, not just personal lives, families, and neighborhood groups but the entire network of community life, all the social systems, structures, and functional organs built up over many years, were burned and blasted into oblivion. Countless people lost parents, friends, and neighbors; their households and places of work were reduced to rubble; and all human relationships were ruptured as the whole of society was laid waste to its very foundations.

In the overall breakdown of the cities, their administrative organs also were subjected to confusion and collapse. The civil defense and first-aid systems* for dealing with air raids and other emergencies were destroyed and, thus, unable to give the aid urgently needed by the seriously injured who barely survived the atomic holocaust.† As Hiroshima and Nagasaki were in designated air defense zones, they therefore had special military police garrisons, civil police and civil defense systems, and government-conscripted workers teams, as well as many well-trained local neighborhood associations and relief, first-aid, and sanitation teams, along with emergency hospitals, first-aid stations, and refuge shelters. All townships and factories and firms had emergency evacuation plans; evacuation shelters had food, clothing, and medical supplies; and routes for evacuation by railway, streetcar, and truck had been established. The A-bomb damages, however, far exceeded all levels of preparedness; as both cities were almost totally destroyed, all these agencies were rendered virtually useless. Consequently, countless A-bomb victims huddled in bombed-out buildings and, unable to move due to serious injuries, died in an inferno. Of those who managed somehow to escape the blazing cities, most could not get needed treatment at the evacuation shelters and thus died in harsh circumstances.

Most crucial of all was the enormous amount of radioactivity released by the atomic bombs; it penetrated deeply into the victims' bodies and caused

---

* Hiroshima A-bomb Medical Care History Editorial Committee 1961; Hiroshima Shiyakusho 1946, p. 48.
　† Hiroshima Prefectural Office 1973; Hiroshima Prefectural Police History Editorial Committee 1954; Nagasaki Shiyakusho 1977.

a variety of serious diseases. Massive radiation doubled the gravity of the situation and greatly increased the number of casualties.

People who had been evacuated, or who for other reasons had left the cities, not only lost family members and friends but were also deprived of places to live and work. Dispossessed of all means of livelihood, theirs, too, was a desperate situation.

An atomic bomb's massive destruction and indiscriminate slaughter involves the sweeping breakdown of all order and existence—in a word, the collapse of society itself. The destruction of the social and environmental systems that support human life, combined with the A-bomb victims' own loss of health and resources for living, brought about a "total disintegration of human life" (Yuzaki 1976b, p. 287).

The problems of atomic destruction were not, of course, confined to Hiroshima and Nagasaki. At the time of the bombings there were in the two cities people from nearby towns and villages, from other prefectures, and even from foreign countries—many of whom were among the dead and injured. Their families, too, experienced great shock and loss. Moreover, persons who came into the two cities immediately after the bombings to look for family members and friends or as part of civil defense and relief teams were subjected to direct or residual radiation, as were people in outlying areas where wind currents carried the radioactive "black rain." The effects of radiation did not, of course, end with the bombings but have continued to plague the A-bomb victims and cause grave anxieties among their children and grandchildren.

Third among the special features of A-bomb damage, in addition to social and economic loss, are the aftereffects of both heat and radiation injuries, which seriously handicapped the A-bomb victims' efforts to restore their health and livelihood. This handicap includes both real impairment and the constant fear of its striking. The damages of conventional war are generally temporary or one-time affairs; A-bomb damages continue indefinitely. The long delay in extending aid to the victims aggravated their initial hardships, and many victims remained in serious difficulty (Japan National Preparatory Committee 1977, p. 67).

The main points of these several special features of A-bomb damage (T. Itō 1975; Japan Confederation of A-bomb and H-bomb Sufferers Organizations 1966; Yuzaki and S. Yamate 1978, pp. 157–85) are outlined in figure 10.1 (Yuzaki 1978).

A-bomb damage, then, is so complex and extensive that it cannot be reduced to any single characteristic or problem. It must be seen overall, as an interrelated array—massive physical and human loss, social disintegration, and psychological and spiritual shock—that affects all life and society (see figure 10.2) (Yuzaki 1978). Only then can one grasp the seriousness of its total

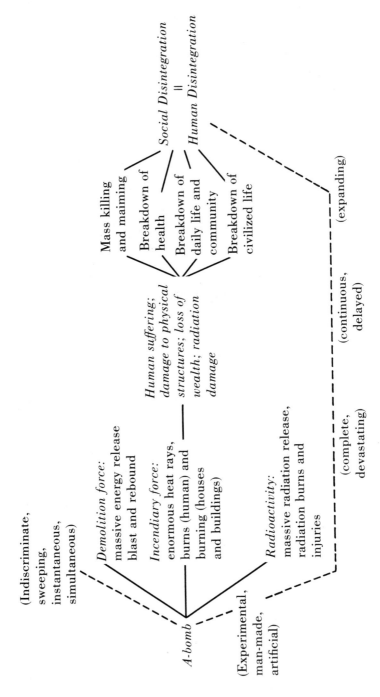

Figure 10.1. Special features of atomic bomb damage (Yuzaki 1978).

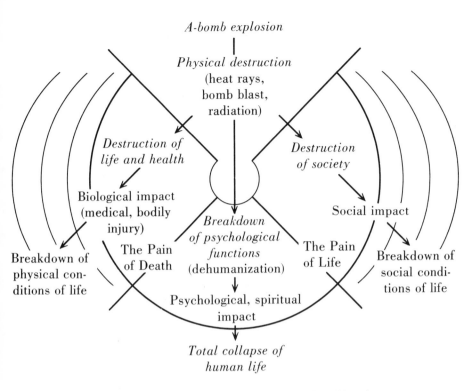

Figure 10.2. The total breakdown of human life (Yuzaki 1978).

impact on the biological systems that sustain life and health, on the social systems that enable people to live and work together, and on the mental functions that hold these two dimensions in integrated unity. The essence of atomic destruction lies in the totality of its impact on man and society and on all the systems that affect their mutual continuation.

The functional breakdown caused by the loss of key household members and by the drastic decline in manpower, the consequent inability of corporate groups (families, relatives, community organizations) to give aid to each other, and the added aggravation of radiation injuries and the constant anxiety over them—these together inflicted great distress on A-bomb victims and their families. The bodily, social, and psychological handicaps have continued to exert heavy pressures that, in time, have led to further loss of livelihood, to disintegration of families, and, worse, to personality breakdown.

Despite the desolation of the cities and the sufferings of the A-bomb victims, the response of the Japanese government was exceedingly passive. From the time of the bombings to the end of the war—when the victims' needs were most urgent—the government gave neither any reports on radiation casualties nor the help the people desperately needed. It simply left them to fend for themselves (Yuzaki and Yamate 1978, pp. 157–85). Afterward, demands were made for surveys of the A-bomb victims, including the dead, and responsible organizations publicly advised the government to conduct surveys,* but the government ignored all advice and appeals.

This attitude is not unrelated to the fact that, even to this day, the government has consistently rejected the demand for an "A-bomb Victims Relief Law" that would require it to extend aid to A-bomb victims who suffered bodily injury or loss of livelihood, on the premise that the government should assume responsibility for and give compensation to those victimized by the war and the atomic bombings. The aid extended through the General Plan for Relief to A-bomb Victims by the cities of Hiroshima and Nagasaki† has not been able, due to limited financial and political resources, to match what national policies could have achieved. Given this situation, the A-bomb victims have had to grow old and then die in social isolation. Thus, the A-bomb victims' initial suffering has been exacerbated by social and political circumstances ever since.

Out of their own experiences, therefore, the A-bomb victims have persistently appealed for the eradication of all nuclear weapons; and to this end they have compiled countless diaries and testimonies, for they feel strongly that there must never be another victim of an atomic bomb. Their own cruel fate came not, as was claimed soon after the bombings, from the Allies' desire to end the war quickly and restore peace; it came, as we know now, from the United States's expectation of a postwar confrontation with the Soviet Union and its wish to make a show of force by demonstrating the bomb's incredible might.‡ Moreover, the superpowers have continued to escalate their nuclear capabilities, in both mass and might; and the danger of nuclear war mounts daily. All this creates an intolerable spiritual burden for the world's first A-bomb victims.

The total disintegration of society and the unmitigated and indiscriminate killing of people in Hiroshima and Nagasaki cannot be dismissed as just another hazard of war. The magnitude of the killing is, in essence, better termed *genocide*—if not also *sociocide, ecocide, biocide,* and *earthocide*—for it is a complete negation of human existence. The experience of these two cities was the opening chapter to the possible annihilation of mankind. To

---

* The Science Council of Japan, a body authorized to advise the government on matters of scientific and scholarly research, at its 59th General Assembly in October 1971 passed a resolution on "Counsel concerning Basic Surveys of Records of the A-bomb Damages," advising the government to conduct a supplementary survey of the A-bomb victims as part of its 1975 national census (dated 9 November 1971). Memorandum from Fujio Egami, President of the Science Council of Japan, to Prime Minister Eisaku Satō (Proceedings of the Council, no. 1687) (Yuzaki 1977b, pp. 279–313).

† Hiroshima Shiyakusho 1978a, pp. 62–68; and Nagasaki Shiyakusho 1978, pp. 54–61.

‡ Allen 1952; Blackett 1948; and Nishijima 1968.

all peoples of the world, it poses the crucial question of human existence (S. Shibata 1978, pp. iii–xi; and Yuzaki 1976*b*, p. 287). With the wide range of modern scientific knowledge and military technology at his disposal, man at last can devise the means for ending all human life. Such is the dilemma of modern civilization: Will we choose the way of self-destruction? Or will we, by abolishing all nuclear weapons, choose to preserve life on this earth? We stand today at the crossroads of that choice. This life-or-death question was put clearly in the preamble of the declaration adopted by the first International Symposium on the Damage and Aftereffects of the Atomic Bombing of Hiroshima and Nagasaki (21 July–9 August 1977), sponsored by nongovernmental organizations (NGO) related to the United Nations (Japan National Preparatory Committee 1977, pp. iv–v).

What has the atomic bomb done to man and society? And what have people done about the death and destruction it wrought? Providing a comprehensive answer to these questions is a colossal task, and many complex factors await further clarification.

The Breakdown of Community

DAMAGED BUILDINGS

Determining the layout of the streets and the numbers of buildings and people of Hiroshima and Nagasaki is a prerequisite to assessing A-bomb damage. Because of the frequency of U.S. air raids in the late phase of the war, particularly in 1945, many heavy industries, buildings, and personnel were moved out of the cities. This precautionary measure altered the shape of the cities considerably.

As Hiroshima was excluded from the list of target cities (see p. 461), it was not subjected to heavy (conventional) bombing. Even so, by April 1945 some 2,500 households, involving 7,500 people, were evacuated from the city (Hiroshima Prefectural Office 1973, pp. 45–46); and on several occasions thereafter (Hiroshima Shiyakusho 1946, p. 4), many buildings were torn down in various places to create firebreaks. Hence the building count is difficult to determine. The city plan of Hiroshima at bombing time is shown in figure 1, and the general distribution and density of streets as of 1943 is shown in figure 10.3. Owing to the evacuation of industries and other facilities, however, the situation is thought to have changed considerably in particular places, though not overall, by the bombing date. The area in and around the hypocenter, in any case, remained densely developed.

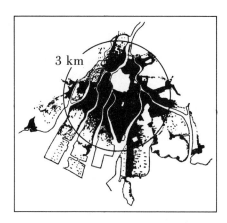

Figure 10.3. Street distribution and density in Hiroshima (excluding military facilities) in 1943; circle of 3-kilometer radius from hypocenter added (Kitagawa 1963).

In contrast to the virtually flat expanse of Hiroshima's delta, Nagasaki is situated in an elongated north-south basin through which flow two rivers from the north and the northeast. Its houses stand on various levels formed by valleys and mountainsides.

As there are no records of the number of buildings in either city immediately before the bombings, a detailed calculation is difficult to make. Concerning the number of buildings damaged by the atomic bombs, however, each city has two (though dissimilar) kinds of records (table 10.3).*

Hiroshima City in August 1946, one year after the bombing, requested all local township councils to report on damaged buildings. It found that there were 76,000 buildings, 85 percent of which were residences (table 10.1). Approximately 60 percent of the buildings were within 2 kilometers of the hypocenter, 85 percent within 3 kilometers (table 10.2). These two records show a high concentration of buildings in the city's center.

In Nagasaki, the City Almanac (Nagasaki Shiyakusho, Investigation Section 1949, p. 167) gave a prewar house estimate of 51,000, of which 2,050 were torn down shortly before the bombing. Details on distribution by district and distance from the hypocenter are not given. Judging from the population distribution (as explained later), roughly half of the city's buildings were within 3 kilometers of the hypocenter.

As for the number of damaged buildings (table 10.3), police reports of 30 November 1945 list 67,860 in Hiroshima; a survey of A-bomb damages a year later reported 70,147 (in each case, buildings that were more than half-burned or half-destroyed were counted) (Hiroshima Shiyakusho 1947, pp. 55–60).

* *United States Strategic Bombing Survey Report* 1946a; Hiroshima Shiyakusho 1947, pp. 55–60; Nagasaki Shiyakusho, Investigation Section 1949, pp. 96, 167.

TABLE 10.1

Types of Buildings in Hiroshima prior to the Atomic Bombing, according to Use (Hiroshima City Survey of A-bomb Damages, August 1946)

Type (use) of Building	Number	Percentage of Total
Dwellings	64,521	84.5
Stores	8,712	11.4
Restaurants	701	0.9
Factories	625	0.8
Banks and companies	348	0.5
Cooperative associations	140	0.2
Public offices	87	0.1
Inns	249	0.3
Schools	69	0.1
Entertainment facilities	76	0.1
Others	799	1.0
Totals	76,327	100.0

Source: Hiroshima Shiyakusho, *Hiroshima Shisei Yōran,* First-anniversary-of-reconstruction issue, 1946 ed. (Hiroshima, 1947), pp. 56–62.

TABLE 10.2

Buildings in Hiroshima prior to the A-Bombing, according to Distance from the Hypocenter (Hiroshima City Survey of A-bomb Damages, August 1946)

Distance from Hypocenter (km)	Number	Percentage of Total		
0–1	19,667	25.8	} 59.2	} 84.8
1–2	25,526	33.4		
2–3	19,551	25.6		
3–4	6,160	8.1		
4–5	2,737	3.6		
5 and more	2,686	3.5		
Totals	76,327	100.0		

Source: Hiroshima Shiyakusho, *Hiroshima Shisei Yōran,* First-anniversary-of-reconstruction issue, 1946 ed. (Hiroshima, 1947), pp. 56–62.

TABLE 10.3

Number of A-Bomb Damaged Buildings in Hiroshima and Nagasaki

	Total Number of Buildings	Damaged Buildings*					Partially Damaged
		Totally Burned	Totally Demolished	Half-burned	Half-demolished	Subtotal	
Hiroshima							
Hiroshima Prefecture Police Report,[1] 30 November 1945	—	55,000 (72.1)	6,820 (8.9)	2,290 (3.0)	3,750 (4.9)	67,860 (88.9)	—
Hiroshima City Survey of A-bomb Damages,[1] August 1946	76,327 (100.0)	47,969 (62.8)	3,818 (5.0)	253 (0.3)	18,107 (23.7)	70,147 (91.9)	6,180 (8.1)
Nagasaki							
Nagasaki Prefecture Security Report,[2] November 1945	—	11,494 (23.5)	2,652 (5.4)	150 (0.3)	5,291 (10.8)	19,587† (40.0)	29,363‡ (60.0)
Nagasaki City Survey of Population and Social Conditions[3]	48,950[4] (100.0)	11,574 (23.6)	1,326 (2.7)	5.509§ (11.3)		18,409 (37.6)	—

* Figures in parentheses are percentages based on the building totals of 76,327 in Hiroshima and 48,950 in Nagasaki.
† In another place, the same document gives the number of damaged buildings as 21,174 (43.3%).
‡ Estimated figure, assuming a total of 48,950 buildings.
§ Recorded as "seriously damaged."
Source: (1) Hiroshima Shiyakusho, *Hiroshima Shisei Yōran,* First-anniversary-of-reconstruction issue, 1946 ed. (Hiroshima, 1947), pp. 55–60.
(2) *United States Strategic Bombing Survey Report.* Pacific War Reports, no. 3. (1946), "Report of the third survey team, Morale Division" (by Lt. sserson, dated 5 November 1945).
(3) Nagasaki Shiyakusho, *Nagasaki Shisei Yōran,* 1949 ed. (Nagasaki, 1949), pp. 96, 167.
(4) Nagasaki Shiyakusho, *Nagasaki Shisei Yōran,* 1949 ed. (Nagasaki, 1949), p. 167.

As is clear from figure 10.5, the central area of Hiroshima was completely destroyed—all buildings within 2 kilometers of the hypocenter were burned or leveled by the blast, and over 90 percent of those within 3 kilometers were burned or demolished. Two out of three buildings within a 4-to-5-kilometer radius were heavily damaged. Of all buildings, 68 percent were completely burned or demolished, and 24 percent were more than half-damaged. Of buildings that could still be used, there were only 6,180, or 8 percent (table 10.3).

The hypocenter in Nagasaki was north of the city's center, but over one third of all buildings were severely damaged. Figure 10.6 compares the totally burned-out areas of the two cities (Kiuchi 1953, p. 158).

THE NUMBER OF A-BOMB VICTIMS

Determining the numbers of those killed and wounded in the atomic bombings is most difficult. Populations are by nature fluid in any case, and there are no accurate population records for Hiroshima and Nagasaki immediately before the bombings—without which casualties are difficult to estimate.

A thoroughgoing military conscription, along with evacuation of young schoolchildren and the elderly, caused a heavy exodus of people; while the mobilization of older students and conscripted workers for tearing down buildings to make firebreaks brought many other people into the two cities. In Hiroshima there were several army facilities with both uniformed personnel

Figure 10.4. Smoldering ruins of central Hiroshima, looking west along Hondōri Street toward the bank district (7 August 1945). (Photograph by Mitsugi Kishida.)

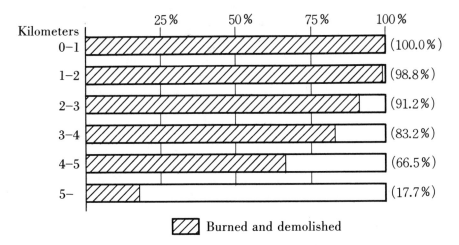

Figure 10.5. Buildings damaged by the atomic bombing of Hiroshima (Hiroshima City Survey of A-bomb Damages, August 1946 [Hiroshima Shiyakusho 1947, pp. 56–62]).

Figure 10.6. Comparison of damaged areas in Hiroshima and Nagasaki (Kiuchi 1953, p. 158).

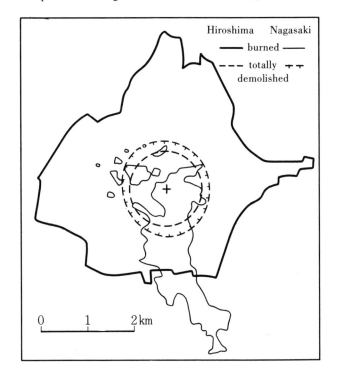

and civilian workers. And, against possible invasion of Japan's main island, the Second Army headquarters in Hiroshima was at the time enlarging its forces. In Nagasaki, even greater numbers—Student Service Corps, Girls Volunteer Corps, conscripted workers, and even prisoners of war and ordinary prisoners, as well as many Korean workers brought over forcibly from their homeland—were mobilized to increase munitions production.

Both Hiroshima and Nagasaki, as seats of prefectural government, drew in many daytime workers and students from neighboring towns and villages. Most of those sent to outlying evacuation sites commuted daily to jobs or schools in the cities. And many people visited the two cities on government, military, and commercial business. On the other hand, many people moved or commuted to outlying districts to work in factories or to purchase supplies. Moreover, the "number of A-bomb victims" includes those entering the two cities soon after the bombings and, thus, subjected to residual radiation. Many of these early entrants came for personal reasons, to check on the fate of family, relatives, and friends; many were ordered to come as part of military, police, relief, first-aid, and inspection teams. Concerning these people, crucial questions arise: When did they come? Where did they go? And how long did they stay?

Various estimates of the number of A-bomb victims have been made. To assess these, it is necessary to distinguish among three population groups: *resident* (those living in the bombed areas); *physically present* (all those physically present in the bombed areas at bombing times); and *secondary* (those affected soon after the bombings).

The Resident Group.   As shown in table 10.4, records of rice ration registra-

TABLE 10.4

Resident Populations of Hiroshima and
Nagasaki before the Bombings

	Survey Date	Population
Hiroshima	late June 1945*	245,423
	August 1946†	320,081
Nagasaki	May 1945*	206,996
	July 1945*	195,290

* Records of rice ration registrations.[1]
† Hiroshima City Survey of A-bomb Damages (estimate).[2]

Source: (1) Hiroshima Shiyakusho, *Hiroshima Shisei Yōran*, First-anniversary-of-reconstruction issue, 1946 ed. (Hiroshima, 1947), pp. 54–55. Nagasaki Shiyakusho, *Nagasaki Shisei Yōran*, 1949 ed. (Nagasaki, 1949), p. 96. A. W. Oughterson and S. Warren, *Medical Effects of the Atomic Bomb in Japan* (New York: McGraw-Hill, 1956), pp. 449–50.

(2) Hiroshima Shiyakusho, *Hiroshima Genbaku Sensai-shi* [RHAWD], (Hiroshima, 1971), vol. I, p. 165.

tions in Hiroshima indicate a resident population of 245,423 in late June 1945; similar records for a resident population in Nagasaki give 206,996 in May and 195,290 in July of 1945.* A 1946 survey of A-bomb damages in Hiroshima provides an additional report of a resident population of 320,081 (Hiroshima Shiyakusho 1971a, p. 165).

The "rice ration" population data is closest in time to the bombings. These data were used by the Joint Commission (Japan–United States) survey team in its effort to evaluate the effect of the A-bombs on men and matter, as a basis for computing the number of people in each city on the bombing dates; they have been used since then to analyze the extent of human losses.† But these data, after all, cover only persons "registered for rationing"; and thus, there were doubtless more residents and transients actually in the cities at bombing times.

For its own estimate, Hiroshima conducted the Survey of Damages Resulting from the 6 August 1945 Atomic Bombing, with help from the medical faculty of Tokyo Imperial University (Shimizu et al. 1969, pp. 174–76), and also gathered data on households through its local town council heads. The methods used for calculating these data are not clear, however; and, in any case, many of the town council heads and officials had died in the bombing. From the survey's content, it appears that lists of households include some that were later evacuated outside the city, so closer scrutiny of this survey is needed.

Even so, the population distribution revealed by the preceding report indicates, as shown in table 10.5, that 57 percent to 61 percent of Hiroshima's population was within 2 kilometers, and 81 percent to 87 percent were within 3 kilometers, of the hypocenter. Like buildings, people were densely concentrated in the targeted central area of the city. Population distribution in Nagasaki was 24 percent to 25 percent within 2 kilometers and 48 percent to 50 percent within 3 kilometers of the hypocenter (Yuzaki and Yamate 1978, pp. 157–85).

Although available records vary somewhat, it is nonetheless clear that over 80 percent of Hiroshima's resident population and about half of Nagasaki's resident population lived within 3 kilometers of their respective hypocenters.

Death rates computed according to distance from the hypocenters (table 10.6) show that over 90 percent of those within 0.5 kilometer, and over 80 percent in the 0.5-to-1-kilometer zone, died instantly or soon after the bombing. Even within 1 to 1.5 kilometers, the death rate exceeded 50 percent. Figure 10.7, drawing from the same sources, indicates the relation of deaths to injuries

---

* Hiroshima Shiyakusho 1947, pp. 54–55; Nagasaki Shiyakusho, Investigation Section 1949, p. 96; Oughterson and Warren 1956, pp. 449–50.
† Oughterson et al. 1951, pp. 82, 83; Oughterson and Warren 1956, pp. 449–50.

TABLE 10.5

Population Distribution by Distance from Hypocenter in Hiroshima and Nagasaki before the Bombing

Distance from Hypocenter (km)	Hiroshima			Nagasaki	
	June 1945* Rice Ration Registrations[1]	*November 1945* Joint Commission (estimates)[2]	*August 1946* Survey of A-bomb Damages (estimates)[3]	*May 1945* Rice Ration Registrations[4]	*July 1945* Rice Ration Registrations[2]†
0–1	19.5	12.2	23.3	11.8	12.0
1–2	41.8	44.3	34.3	13.2	12.0
2–3	25.4	24.0	26.1	25.3	24.1
3–4	⎫	11.5	8.9	23.6	24.6
4–5	⎬ 13.3	⎫ 8.0	3.6	17.2	16.6
5 and more	⎭	⎭	3.8	9.3‡	11.0
Totals§	100.0 (245,423)	100.0 (255,260)	100.0 (320,081)	100.0 (206,996)	100.0 (195,290)

* Figures are percentages of total population.
† Computed by comparing reports of Oughterson and Warren (1956)[2] with zonal distribution by distance from hypocenter in Nagasaki City Survey of Population and Social Conditions (1949).[4]
‡ Includes those living on board vessels.
§ Total population in parentheses.
Source: (1) Hiroshima Shiyakusho, *Hiroshima Shisei Yōran*, First-anniversary-of-reconstruction issue, 1946 ed. (Hiroshima, 1947), pp. 54–55.
(2) A. W. Oughterson and S. Warren. *Medical Effects of the Atomic Bomb in Japan* (New York: McGraw-Hill, 1956), pp. 449–50.
(3) Hiroshima Shiyakusho, *Hiroshima Genbaku Sensaishi* [RHAWD] (Hiroshima, 1971), vol. I, p. 165.
(4) Nagasaki Shiyakusho, *Nagasaki Shisei Yōran*, 1949 edition. (Nagasaki, 1949), p. 96.

TABLE 10.6

Death Rates by Distance from Hypocenter, Hiroshima and Nagasaki, November 1945

Distance from Hypocenter (km)	Death Rates (percentage)	
	Hiroshima	Nagasaki
0–0.5	96.5	⎫ 88.4
0.5–1.0	83.0	⎭
1.0–1.5	51.6	51.5
1.5–2.0	21.9	28.4
2.0–2.5	4.9	6.4
2.5–3.0	2.7	2.1
3.0–4.0	2.5	1.2
4.0–5.0	1.1	0.7
Average	25.3	17.0

Source: A. W. Oughterson and S. Warren. *Medical Effects of the Atomic Bomb in Japan* (New York: McGraw-Hill, 1956), p. 84.

TABLE 10.7

Populations of Hiroshima and Nagasaki according to the 1944 National Census and Estimated Values for August 1945

	1944 National Census*	Estimated Population for August 1945†
Hiroshima	343,034	327,457
Nagasaki	272,312	286,702

* Prime Minister's Bureau of Statistics, *Shōwa Jūkyūnen jinkō chō* [1944 National Census, conducted 22 February] (military personnel included).
† Based on population trends of 1920–45.
Source: M. Yuzaki and H. Ueoka. "Study of the population exposed to the atomic bomb and of the number of deaths from the viewpoint of population changes," Report 1: "The methodology and general condition of Hiroshima," *Journal of the Hiroshima Medical Association* 29(1976): 193–203; and Report 2: "The general condition in Nagasaki," *Nagasaki Medical Journal* 51(1976):135–39.

in the resident group according to distance from hypocenter. That the casualties were very heavy is clear.

The government took a census in February 1944—a year and a half before
the bombing—that showed populations of 343,034 in Hiroshima and 272,312
in Nagasaki (excluding military personnel). If one begins with the first national
census in 1920 and checks each subsequent national census for the next twenty-
five years, the population trends for the two cities' areas as of August 1945
yield estimated values for "expected populations" to be plus or minus 327,000
in Hiroshima and plus or minus 286,000 in Nagasaki (table 10.7) (Yuzaki
and Ueoka 1976a; 1976b). These estimates, of course, are hypothetical values
that assume no significant change. In the year and a half after February
1944, however, critical turns in the war provoked great changes.

With the advent of 1945 the Second Army headquarters and the Chūgoku
Regional Governor-General's office were established in Hiroshima, bringing
an influx of related personnel and their families into the city. Some people
escaping Tokyo and other heavily bombed cities also came to Hiroshima.
Hence, there was a notable increase in the city's population. At the same
time, the population decrease resulted from the conscription of army recruits
and other causes. On 18 November 1944, the Ministry of Home Affairs issued
a directive that required the enforced removal of certain buildings, and hence,
the evacuation of the people in them; 133 places were emptied out in the
initial phase.* Evacuation measures were strengthened from the spring of
1945, and 23,500 children were evacuated from the city (Hiroshima
Shiyakusho 1958, p. 701).

As shown in table 10.8, six evacuation schedules were carried out in Hiroshima from late 1944 to August 1945 (the A-bombing interrupted the sixth).†
The actual number of persons evacuated is not clear, but the number of
households alone suggests that it was a large-scale operation. Not all households, however, were necessarily moved outside the city. According to a
"reconstruction survey" that, with the cooperation of pre-bombing residents
or their survivors, reconstructed the former situation in the bombed area
(generally, within a 2-kilometer radius) and inquired, household by household,
into conditions of the A-bomb victims, 22 percent to 28 percent of the households were removed just before the bombing, as shown in figure 10.8. This
is a rather high percentage, but those moved outside the city amounted to
a mere 8 percent.‡ These estimates cover only the central bombed area, but
the percentages should be somewhat higher, it is thought, as the survey
could not deal with households for which data were lacking or unclear. If

* Hiroshima Prefectural Police History Editorial Committee 1954, p. 397.
† Hiroshima Prefectural Police History Editorial Committee 1954, pp. 398–99.
‡ Hiroshima Shiyakusho, A-bomb Survivors Measures Department 1978b, p. 26; Yuzaki 1975b,
p. 2.

TABLE 10.8

Compulsory Evacuation from Hiroshima City

Evacuation Plans	Kind	Number of Households Involved	Number of Persons Involved
1 (late 1944)	buildings	400	—
	personnel	1,029	4,210
2 (February–March 1945)	buildings	2,454	—
	personnel	5,532	21,710
	aged, young, pregnant women, etc.	6,561	25,920
3 (April 1945)	personnel	1,550	—
4 (May 1945)	personnel	2,380	—
5 (June–July 1945)	personnel	4,000	—
6 (July–August 1945)	personnel	6,000 (2,500 cases completed)	—

Source: Hiroshima Prefectural Police History Editorial Committee, *Shinpen Hiroshimaken Keisatsushi* [History of Hiroshima Prefectural Police, New Edition], (Hiroshima: Hiroshimaken Keisatsu Renraku Kyōgikai, 1954), pp. 398–99.

the exodus rate is applied as a provisional coefficient to the population since the 1944 national census, then 8 percent of the population, or 27,000, were drafted into military service or were evacuated from the city. If the number of evacuated students is added to this exodus, then it appears that approximately 50,000 left the city. As some aged persons and young children, along with pregnant women, were evacuated from resident households, the overall

Figure 10.7. A-bomb casualties by distance from hypocenter in Hiroshima and Nagasaki (Oughterson and Warren 1956, p. 84).

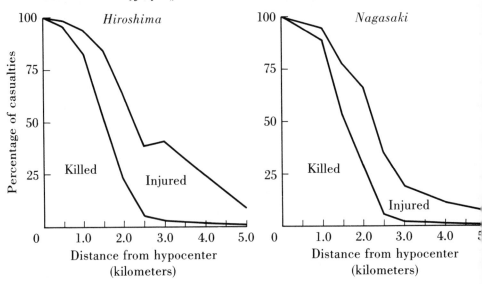

TABLE 10.9

Compulsory Evacuation from Nagasaki City

Evacuation Period	Kind (No.) of Plan	Number of Households Involved	Number of Persons Involved
November 1944	Buildings (1st)	1,129	4,906
April 1945	Buildings (2nd)	6,926	26,494
	Personnel (1st)	4,773	14,198
June–July 1945	Buildings (3rd) Buildings (4th)	} 874	3,648
	Personnel (2nd)	766	2,515
Totals*		14,468	51,761

* Of the totals, 8,310 households, involving 27,005 persons, are regarded as having moved outside the city.

Source: Owing to inaccuracies in the report in *Nagasaki Shisei Rokujūgonenshi* [Sixty-five-year History of the Municipality of Nagasaki] (Nagasaki Shiyakusho 1959, vol. 3, pp. 414–16), this table is based on RNAWD (Nagasaki Shiyakusho 1977, vol. 1, pp. 60–63) as well as basic materials for *Nagasaki Shisei Rokujūgonenshi* (owned by Nagasaki International Cultural Hall) and memorandum written by Tomosuke Takeda, chief of Nagasaki City's Civil Defense Section at the time of bombing—neither of which has been published.

population outflow can be set at 50,000 to 60,000 persons. Accordingly, the resident population of Hiroshima at the time of the bombing is estimated to have been 280,000 to 290,000.

Similarly, in Nagasaki four building removal plans and two personnel evacuation plans were carried out from November 1944 to the bombing date (table 10.9). Approximately 50,000 people were moved, of whom 27,000 are recorded as going outside the city.* According to a memorandum of the U.S. Strategic Bombing Survey, a report was received from the Nagasaki Prefectural Security Section that the police issued permits to move outside the city to 29,313 persons (of whom 11,700 moved outside Nagasaki Prefecture).† Accordingly, the 1944 national census population of 272,000 was reduced by 30,000 departures, leaving a bombing-date population estimated at approximately 240,000.

The Physically Present Group. The most important calculation, in assessing the number of people affected by the atomic bombs, is that of all those physically present in Hiroshima on 6 August and in Nagasaki on 9 August— not just the resident populations in each city.

In Hiroshima, the reconstruction survey indicates that an average of one out of four persons in the surveyed households was outside the city, for military duty or other long-term purposes, at the time of the bombing.‡ As the surveyed area coincides with the bombed area, many of the evacuated

* Nagasaki Shiyakusho 1977, pp. 60–63; Nagasaki Shiyakusho, Investigation and Statistics Section 1959, vol. 3, pp. 414–16.
† *United States Strategic Bombing Survey Report 1946a.*
‡ Hiroshima Shiyakusho, A-bomb Survivors Measures Department 1978*b*, pp. 82–83.

children and aged people must also be included among those not present in the city at the time. While the city's total situation is not completely clear, it is estimated that a considerable number of citizens were outside the city on the bombing date.

The day before the atomic bombing of Hiroshima, 5 August, was a Sunday; and many people who had gone outside the city to visit children and family members at evacuation sites, to take refuge, or to purchase supplies in outlying districts, had not yet returned home. Moreover, many had gone to their jobs in factories in the suburbs or outlying districts. The actual number of those temporarily away from the city on that day, however, is not known.

A city's daytime population normally exceeds its nighttime population, and large numbers of students and workers had in fact come into the city on that day. On the other hand, not a few people sought nightly refuge outside the city to escape possible air raids at night. And there is at present no way of estimating how many people might, just before the bombing, have been on trains leaving Hiroshima or, conversely, just arriving on incoming trains. Because these various movements cannot be quantified, the numbers of people involved are intentionally discounted here.

Among other contingencies, some 10,000 conscripted workers from rural districts are said to have been on duty in the sixth building removal plan (Hiroshima Shiyakusho 1958, p. 703); defense mobilization had brought many soldiers and their dependents into the city; and for strengthening army facilities, many construction workers were present. Between 2,000 and 3,000 Korean workers, brought over forcibly in groups from Korea and from temporary internment camps in Japan, were working at Mitsubishi Heavy Industries' Hiroshima shipbuilding docks and machine manufacturing plant and at some other factories and shops in Hiroshima.* All these together amounted to about 20,000, which, added to the resident population of 280,000 to 290,000, gives a physically present population of 300,000 to 310,000.

Among the extensive documents of the U.S. Strategic Bombing Survey there is a report provided by the Second Army headquarters which lists

---

* According to one estimate, 2,800 to 3,000 conscripted Korean workers were forcibly brought to work in the shipbuilding and machine manufacturing sites of Mitsubishi Heavy Industries in Hiroshima, but a steady flow of desertions had reduced their numbers to approximately 1,000 by bombing time. Statistical documents of the Ministry of Home Affairs' security section (*Kokumin dōin keikaku ni motozuku inyū Chōsenjin rōdōsha no jōkyō* [The Situation of Korean Workers Imported under the National Mobilization Plan]) show that there was large-scale migration of conscripted workers from Korea late in the war, and desertions and disappearances among them also occurred on a large scale. Besides the Mitsubishi plants, the Korean workers were also assigned to Ujina shipyard, to the army's marine transport base, to Nishimatsu construction group, to Nippon Express, and to other places; but the actual number of conscripted Korean workers is not known (Fukagawa 1974, pp. 108–10; Pak 1976; Twenty-year History Compilation Committee 1964).

23,158 troops in Hiroshima (United States Strategic Bombing Survey Report 1946b). But this report did not include special units, such as the special military police, and army units undergoing reorganization, or the smaller number of naval personnel such as supervisors assigned to war plants and research institutes. Besides these, new troop replacements had arrived in Hiroshima as late as the day before and even the day of the bombing. These additional personnel amounted to about 20,000 men; and this count, added to that for Second Army troops based in Hiroshima, gives a total of 43,000. The population physically present in Hiroshima on 6 August, then, was between 343,000 and 353,000. The estimate of those directly affected by the atomic bombing of Hiroshima is put at plus or minus 350,000.

Heretofore it has been common to peg the military count at 90,000 and, thus, Hiroshima's A-bomb-victim population at 400,000 to 420,000. But 90,000 was simply the number of troops under Hiroshima headquarters' command; at a time when men were needed at the front, it is inconceivable that they were all in Hiroshima. As the popular view ignores this fact, we do not adopt the figure here, just as we would not accept estimates that ignore the exodus of civilians from the city.

In the case of Nagasaki, there were no war plants outside the city, and so no large-scale exodus (apart from military units dispatched elsewhere); rather, there was probably a large influx of people into the city from surrounding areas on the day of the bombing. How many entered cannot be accurately determined, due to lack of relevant documents. Air defense and naval reports included in the U.S. Strategic Bombing Survey give 6,291 men of the 122nd Brigade and 2,700 of the 134th Anti-aircraft Regiment, plus a few army personnel and sixty-three navy personnel.*

Prison camps in the city are said to have had 350 POWs (Tajima 1976, p. 124); and about 2,500 conscripted Korean workers (the precise number is not known) (Ikeda 1968, p. 261) were assigned to Mitsubishi's Nagasaki Shipyard. A fairly large number of foreigners are estimated to have been present in Nagasaki.

Jukichi Okada, then mayor of Nagasaki, reported (September 1945) (Oughterson et al. 1951, pp. 82, 83) a bombing-date population of 270,000 to the survey team of the U.S. Manhattan Project. Professor I. Bronowsky, a mathematician and member of the British Mission that participated in the U.S. Strategic Bombing Survey, reached an estimate of 260,000 after making allowances for persons not included in the May 1945 rice ration population of 233,935.† When these estimates are taken into account and to them added

---

* United States Strategic Bombing Survey Report 1946c.
† Report of the British Mission to Japan on an Investigation of the Effects of the Atomic Bombs dropped at Hiroshima and Nagasaki (n.d.), p. 15.

those of military personnel and conscripted workers, the population physically present in Nagasaki at the time of the bombing can be set at approximately 270,000.

Secondary A-bomb Victims. The A-bomb damage was not confined to those directly affected by the explosions; large numbers of secondary victims were indirectly affected by the fallout of radioactive materials and irradiation by neutron rays (see chapter 5).

Secondary A-bomb victims can be divided into three groups: (1) early entrants into the cities—those looking for families, relatives, and friends, and relief and clean-up workers; (2) relief teams, working at hastily set-up first-aid stations and relief stations to treat the wounded and dispose of corpses; and (3) victims of the "ashes of death" (radioactive fallout) carried by "black rain."

Only rarely did secondary victims suffer greater effects than did primary victims, so they are regarded as a low-radiation-dose group. Nonetheless, no one yet knows fully how long radiation remains in the human body and what damage it does, so that these people must be carefully watched for a long time in case of further developments.

It is of first importance to determine the kind and the dose of radiation exposure; but dosage varies greatly according to a victim's activity and surroundings. As these circumstances were infinitely diverse, it is extremely difficult to assess each individual exposure. Moreover, victims without medically confirmed abnormalities are themselves, nonetheless, aware of certain symptoms; this, along with the uncertainty about which symptoms call for what treatment, arouses anxieties over health that simply cannot be dismissed. Such a condition is a special characteristic of A-bomb illness.

The great number of secondary victims was due to the extent of the unprecedented devastation suffered by Hiroshima and Nagasaki. As the official 1945 report of Hiroshima City *(Shōwa Nijūnen Hiroshima-shi Jimu Hōkoku)* put it:

As part of our defense preparations, leaders and staff were appointed for medical care and disposal of corpses; medical supplies and materials for corpse disposal were stored; and other steps, learned from past wars, were taken. But on 6 August thirty-two first-aid stations and eighteen field hospitals throughout the city, along with all leaders and staff personnel, were rendered wholly incapable of caring for the dead and wounded, though we did our best in cooperation with the army and prefectural agencies. (Hiroshima Shiyakusho 1946, p. 48)

In an instant all key functions of prefectural and municipal agencies, all means of defense, relief, medical care, police protection, and firefighting, were destroyed or thrown into confusion. For example, there were six desig-

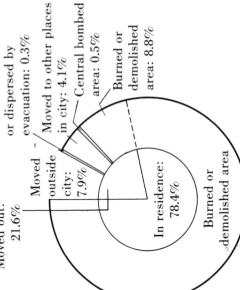

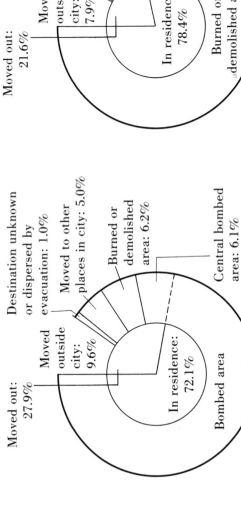

Destination unknown
or dispersed by
evacuation: 0.3%

Moved to other places
in city: 4.1%

Central bombed
area: 0.5%

Burned or
demolished
area: 8.8%

Moved
outside
city:
7.9%

Moved out:
21.6%

In residence:
78.4%

Burned or
demolished area

B. Results of March 1977 survey (Hiroshima
Shiyakusho, A-bomb Survivors Measures
Department 1978b, p. 26). "Burned-out area"
9,625 households and work places

Destination unknown
or dispersed by
evacuation: 1.0%

Moved to other
places in city: 5.0%

Burned or
demolished
area: 6.2%

Central bombed
area: 6.1%

Moved
outside
city:
9.6%

Moved out:
27.9%

In residence:
72.1%

Bombed area

A. Results of March 1975 survey (Yuzaki 1975b,
p. 2). "Central bombed area" 2,431 households
and work places

Figure 10.8. Reconstructed conditions of households residing in Hiroshima at bombing time
(a) Yuzaki 1975b, p. 2; (b) Hiroshima Shiyakusho, A-bomb Survivors Department 1978b, p.
26.

nated refugee shelters in the solid buildings of the city hall, Honkawa Primary School, Fukuya Department Store, the Chamber of Commerce, and, at some remove from the city center, Aki Higher Girls School, and Tamon'in temple at the foot of Hijiyama hill. Most of these were burned or demolished and could not be used. Only after some difficulty, by the evening of the sixth, was the sixth shelter (Tamon'in temple) made the temporary air defense headquarters (Hiroshima Prefectural Office 1973, pp. 99–166).

Help from outside the city was the only hope. Appeals were directed through the army and the police to all districts of the prefecture; but the communications network inside and outside the city was virtually disrupted, and initial contacts had to be made on foot. Relief teams were hurriedly formed at police stations in nearby districts; and one after another, squads of policemen, firemen, and relief workers came into the city. Some craft of the army's marine transport unit based in Ujina were relatively undamaged; these and others stationed at nearby islands came quickly to take on board and transport the many victims, giving first aid to the wounded and helping dispose of the dead.

In time, various relief, first-aid, and inspection teams were formed by medical associations, medical schools, and other health care agencies in Hiroshima Prefecture's districts and nearby prefectures. While these teams began working in the first-aid stations and emergency clinics in Hiroshima City's less-damaged sections, suburbs, and outlying districts, the town and village offices mobilized doctors, nurses, and women's societies to help receive the overflow of wounded who came streaming to clinics and stations.

To cope with conditions caused by the new bomb, army headquarters in Tokyo dispatched "relief and survey teams" composed of doctors from the army's medical school and its Tokyo First Army Hospital and also from the Institute of Physical and Chemical Research. Army hospitals and sanatoriums close to Hiroshima sent security guards and medical relief teams; they helped not only in the care of the wounded but also in reopening cluttered roads and cleaning up the ubiquitous ashes and debris. On orders from Kure Naval Base, relief and first-aid teams came from Kure Naval Hospital, Kamo Medical School, and the Ōtake Marine Corps Base.

Besides all these, neighboring towns and villages sent teams of relief workers, who also helped cook and serve emergency rice rations. As word spread of the awesome destruction of Hiroshima, countless numbers of friends and relatives streamed into Hiroshima to search for family members and colleagues at former homes and places of work, despite police orders prohibiting entry into the city by anyone without official business.

Inside the city, the wounded were driven by conflagrations and fierce fire-fueled wind storms to flee, if they could move at all, to refuge shelters and evacuation sites, or to homes of friends and relatives in the countryside—usually without being able to look after the safety of their own homes and families. Thousands fell along the way, unable to go on, and were carried by unknown farmers to open fields, schools, town halls, and temples for treatment. Even so, untold numbers lost their lives.

Figure 10.9 shows the routes taken by those fleeing and by relief groups going into the city (Hiroshima A-bomb Medical Care History Editorial Committee 1961, p. 106). From the latter group emerged the mass of secondary victims.

Because of the great confusion at that time, it is impossible to know just how many people entered the city or engaged in the various relief activities outside it. According to *Hiroshima Genbaku Iryōshi* [Hiroshima A-bomb Medical Care History], in which relief efforts of medical personnel from Hiroshima Prefecture are carefully examined:

An aggregate of 21,145 persons from the prefecture assisted the citizens of devastated Hiroshima during the initial two months of greatest medical need, and by 20 August 1,043 policemen and 13,646 volunteer guards had helped with the transport of the wounded and the disposal of corpses, as well as the clearing of roads. (Hiroshima A-bomb Medical Care History Editorial Committee 1961, p. 108)

And the 1946 edition of *Hiroshima Shisei Yōran* [Hiroshima City Almanac] indicates that some 150,000 A-bomb victims fled to the towns, villages, and countryside in the prefecture (Hiroshima Shiyakusho 1947, pp. 66–68).

As chapter 6 explains in detail, a huge mushroom cloud billowed over the A-bomb explosion point. A lower stratum of the cloud began shortly to move in a north-northwest direction and, twenty or thirty minutes later, dropped heavy rain over a wide area (figure 6.1) (Uda, Sugahara, and Kita 1953, p. 98). This "black rain" was filled not only with dust and rubble swept up by the bomb's blast but also with large amounts of radioactive matter. The rain gradually spread out over an even wider area to the northwest (figure 6.2) (Uda, Sugahara, and Kita 1953, p. 98) and dropped its deadly load on the people living and engaged in relief work there, and thus created many secondary victims.

Similar conditions created innumerable secondary victims in Nagasaki. Early entrants into the city came from nearby and more distant places. They included relief and first-aid teams from naval hospitals in Ōmura, Sasebo, Isahaya, and Takeo, from Hario marine base, and from naval arsenals in Sasebo and Kawatana; a first-aid team from Obama sanatorium; police and volunteer guards from police stations throughout the prefecture; relief teams from towns, villages, and schools in the prefecture; first-aid teams from army units stationed nearby; as well as police first-aid teams from Saga, Fukuoka,

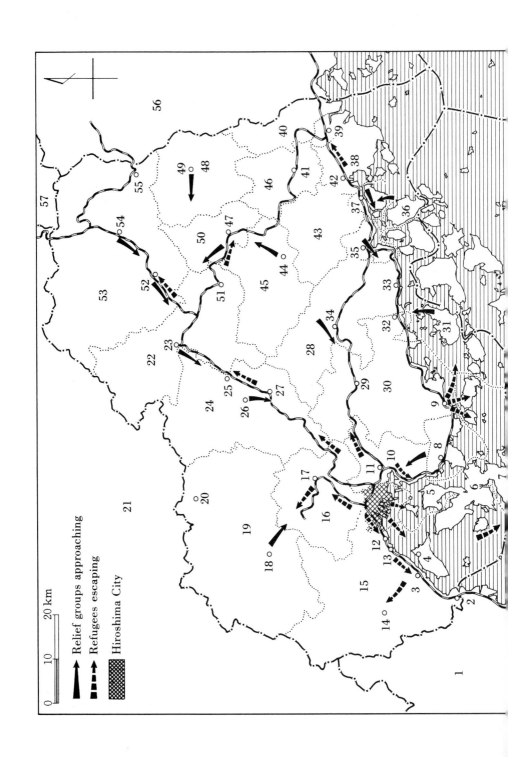

Relief groups approaching

Refugees escaping

Hiroshima City

0   10   20 km

Kumamoto, Ōita, Miyazaki, and Kagoshima prefectures. Relief centers for the burned and wounded were set up in nearby towns and villages and in cities such as Saga and Kurume (Nagasaki Shiyakusho 1977, pp. 408–576). The atomic cloud, bearing dust, rubble, and "ashes of death," was carried by winds from the southwest to the area northeast of the city, where the "black rain" fell on the local people (see pages 354–357).

The secondary A-bomb victims are today living not only in Hiroshima and Nagasaki but also in other places throughout Japan. As they have never been the subject of a national survey, it is not known how many such victims resulted from the atomic bombings. But the 1957 A-bomb Victims Medical Care Law regards as A-bomb victims anyone exposed to radioactivity, not just those directly affected by the explosions. Accordingly, under the law, many secondary victims have been issued "A-bomb health books." The bombed and the related areas of Hiroshima and Nagasaki to which the A-bomb Victims Medical Care Law applies are shown in figures 10.10 and 10.11, respectively.*

According to this law, there were, in all Japan as of March 1978, 106,186 A-bomb victims who qualified as postbombing early entrants into Hiroshima or Nagasaki. Of this number 16,915 had engaged in corpse disposal and relief

* Hiroshima Shiyakusho, A-bomb Survivors Measures Department 1978a, p. 30; Nagasaki Shiyakusho, A-bomb Survivors Measures Department 1978, p. 21.

Figure 10.9. Routes of refugees escaping and relief groups approaching Hiroshima (Hiroshima A-bomb Medical Care History Editorial Committee 1961, p. 106).

1. Yamaguchi Prefecture	20. Ōasa Town	39. Fukuyama City
2. Ōtake Town	21. Shimane Prefecture	40. Fukayasu County
3. Ono Town	22. Futami County	41. Shin'ichi Town
4. Miyajima Town	23. Miyoshi Town	42. Matsunaga Town
5. Etajima Town	24. Takata County	43. Mitsugi County
6. Ondo Town	25. Kōtachi Town	44. Kōzan Town
7. Kurahashijima Village	26. Yoshida Town	45. Sera County
8. Kure City	27. Mukaihara Town	46. Ashina County
9. Kawajiri Town	28. Toyota County	47. Jōge Town
10. Aki County	29. Saijō Town	48. Jinseki County
11. Kaitaichi Town	30. Kamo County	49. Yuki Town
12. Itsukaichi Town	31. Kinoe Town	50. Kōnu County
13. Hatsukaichi Town	32. Takehara Town	51. Kisa Town
14. Tsuta Town	33. Tadanoumi Town	52. Shōbara Town
15. Saeki County	34. Kouchi Town	53. Hiba County
16. Asa County	35. Mihara City	54. Saijō Town
17. Kabe Town	36. Innoshima Town	55. Tōjō Town
18. Kake Town	37. Onomichi City	56. Okayama Prefecture
19. Yamagata County	38. Numakuma County	57. Tottori Prefecture

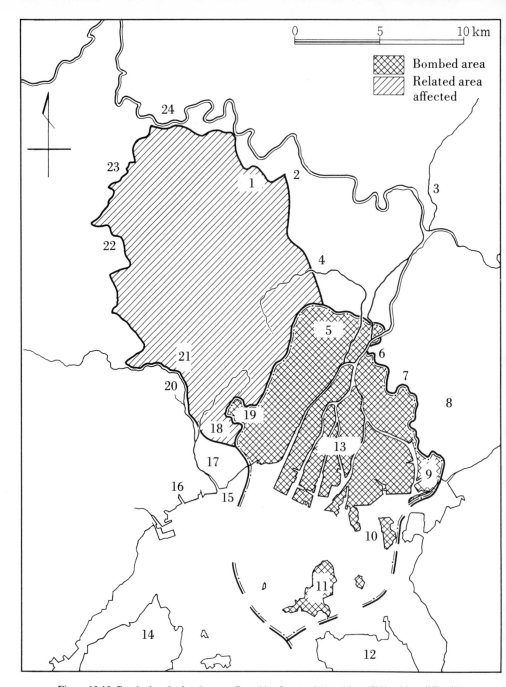

Figure 10.10. Bombed and related areas affected by the atomic bombing of Hiroshima (Hiroshima Shiyakusho, A-bomb Survivors Measures Department 1978a, p. 30).

1. Kuchi	9. Mukainada	17. Inokuchi Village
2. Kegi	10. Kanawajima Island	18. Toshimatsu
3. Kabe Town	11. Ninoshima Island	19. Yamada
4. Chōrakuji	12. Etajima Island	20. Nakagō
5. Gion Town	13. Hiroshima City	21. Uokiri
6. Hesaka Village	14. Itsukushima Island	22. Ege
7. Nakayama Village	15. Yahata River	23. Yanagare
8. Fuchū Town	16. Itsukaichi Town	24. Usa

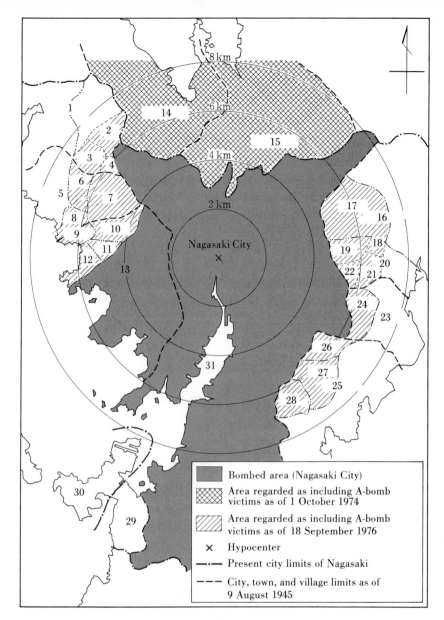

Figure 10.11. Bombed and related areas affected by the atomic bombing of Nagasaki (Nagasaki Shiyakusho, A-bomb Survivors Measures Department 1978, p. 21).

Bombed area (Nagasaki City)
Area regarded as including A-bomb victims as of 1 October 1974
Area regarded as including A-bomb victims as of 18 September 1976
× Hypocenter
—·— Present city limits of Nagasaki
– – – City, town, and village limits as of 9 August 1945

Place names*
1. Mie Village
2. Tōnokoba
3. Tsumenouchi
4. Shiraga
5. Shikimi Village
6. Makino
7. Koba
8. Mukai
9. Teguma
10. Kamiura
11. Nakaura

12. Kakidomari
13. Fukuda Village
14. Togitsu Village
15. Nagayo Village
16. Yagami Village
17. Utsutsugawa
18. Satsumajiro
19. Tanokōchi
20. Tanaka
21. Nakao
22. Yahazu
23. Himi Village

24. Kawachi
25. Mogi Town
26. Tadewara
27. Koba
28. Tagami
29. Fukahori Village
30. Kōyagi Village
31. Nagasaki Port

*Place names are those in use as of 9 August 1945.

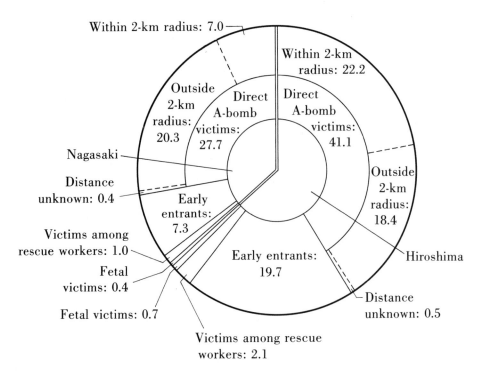

Figure 10.12. Distribution of A-bomb victims by place and circumstance (percentages of total)
(Ministry of Health and Welfare 1977a, p. 4).

TABLE 10.10

*Comparison of Conditions Causing Secondary A-Bomb Victims,
Hiroshima and Nagasaki*

Source of Data	Kind of Victim	Hiroshima*	Nagasaki	Total
Ministry of Health and Welfare survey, 1975	early entrants	57,839 (73.07)	21,315 (26.93)	79,154 (100.0)
	relief, first-aid, and other workers	6,184 (67.08)	3,035 (32.92)	9,219 (100.0)
Number of A-bomb health book holders, March 1978	early entrants	77,590†	28,596†	106,186
	relief, first-aid, and other workers	11,347†	5,568†	16,915

* Figures in parentheses are percentages of the total numbers of secondary victims.
† Values reached by applying 1975 percentages to 1978 totals.
  Source: Ministry of Health and Welfare, Public Health Bureau, Planning Section, *Shōwa Gojūnen Genshibakudan Hibakusha Jittai Chōsa* [1975 Actual Status Survey of Atomic Bomb Survivors] (Tokyo: Kōseishō Kōshūeiseikyoku Kikakuka, 1977c), p. 1.

activity or were subjected to the "black rains" (Hiroshima Shiyakusho 1978a, p. 41). In some cases, however, the records are not clear about which of the two cities these people had entered. The distribution of early entrants, according to the Ministry of Health and Welfare's 1975 Survey of A-bomb Victims' Conditions, is shown in figure 10.12 (Ministry of Health and Welfare 1977a, p. 4). Computations for Hiroshima and Nagasaki based on actual counts in this report are given in table 10.10 (Ministry of Health and Welfare 1977c, p. 1). When these are reconciled with the 1978 figure, early entrants among secondary victims number approximately 77,600 for Hiroshima and 28,600 for Nagasaki. Those related to rescue activity or "black rain" fallout number about 11,300 for Hiroshima (a ratio of 3:1) and 5,500 for Nagasaki (2:1).

The 1975 survey also indicates that males among early entrants slightly outnumbered females in Hiroshima; male-female distribution was roughly the same in Nagasaki. Among those related to rescue activity and "black rain" fallout, however, females were six times more numerous than males in Hiroshima and 2.5 times more in Nagasaki.

These figures for secondary victims are only rough estimates and should, therefore, be viewed cautiously. There are potentially many secondary victims who never applied for A-bomb health books; and by 1978 some thirty-three years had elapsed, and not a few of these people had already died.

THE NUMBER KILLED

The number of people killed by the atomic bombings is even more obscure than the total number of A-bomb victims. Many estimates have been made in the past; and of those published, table 10.11 shows the most important (Yuzaki and Ueoka 1976a; 1976b).

Even disregarding figures from the confused period soon after the bombings, counts of the dead that also include missing persons vary greatly—as much as several tens of thousands for Nagasaki and a hundred thousand for Hiroshima. The scope of A-bomb damage was so extensive that public agencies responsible for surveys were demolished; and there was no one and no way to check individually the thousands who were burned to death instantly or buried under the ruins, or who plunged into rivers and were carried away to death. Many more thousands who got as far as evacuation centers, and even received some treatment, later died; and records for estimating their numbers are insufficient. Later estimates also vary because different premises and source materials were used.

In evaluating the number of A-bomb deaths, one must keep in mind that deaths from radiation damage kept on and are still occurring. Hence, it is necessary to qualify all death counts by some time limit—that is, as occurring before some definite date.

TABLE 10.11

Main Estimates of A-Bomb Deaths, Including Missing Persons*

Source	Dead	Missing	Total
HIROSHIMA			
I. Hiroshima Prefecture, Governor's report, 20 August 1945	32,959	9,591	42,550
II. Hiroshima Prefecture, public health section report, 25 August 1945	46,185	17,429	63,614
III. Hiroshima Prefecture, police department report, 30 November 1945	78,150	13,983	92,133
IV. Hiroshima City, "official report," 8 March 1946	47,185	17,425	64,610
V. Hiroshima City, survey section report, 10 August 1946	118,661	3,677 (fate unknown)	122,338†
VI. Joint Japan–United States survey report, 1951	64,602	—	64,602
VII. Japan Council against A- and H-bombs: "White paper on A-bomb damages," 1961	119,000–133,000 (32,900 military personnel not included)	—	(151,900–165,900)
NAGASAKI			
I. Nagasaki Prefecture, report, 31 August 1945	19,748	1,924	21,672
II. Nagasaki Prefecture, external affairs section, 23 October 1945	23,753	1,924	25,677
III. Private estimate by Motosaburō Masuyama, January 1946 survey	29,398–37,507	—	29,398–37,507
IV. British Mission report‡	39,500	—	39,500
V. Nagasaki City, A-bomb Records Preservation Committee, 1949	73,884	—	73,884
VI. Joint Japan–United States survey report, 1951	29,570–37,997 –39,214	—	29,570–39,214
VII. Joint Japan–United States survey report, 1956	39,000	—	39,000

* All estimates are of civilian deaths (military personnel excluded).
† Estimated one year after the bombing.
‡ The British Mission participated in the United States Strategic Bombing Survey but compiled an independent report, which is thought to have been done prior to 1947.

Acute and subacute illnesses due to atomic bombs developed most notably in the first five months after the bombings; the three months to the end of October were the worst. According to the Reconstruction Survey conducted in Hiroshima, the death rate ran highest to the end of September (table 10.12).* Except for the Hiroshima estimate indicated by item V of table 10.11, other estimates generally are limited to the first few months (at the latest, to the end of November) after the bombing. But their sources and methods of calculation are not always clear, and thus it is difficult to ascertain how close they are to the real count.

* Hiroshima Shiyakusho, A-bomb Survivors Measures Department 1978*b*, pp. 130–31.

TABLE 10.12

Distribution of Deaths of 16,007 Persons Physically
Present in Hiroshima on the Bombing Date, by Date
or Period of Death, with Cumulative Percentages

Date of Death	Percentage of Total	Cumulative Percentage
6 August 1945 (bombing date)	28.9	28.9
Date unknown	9.4	38.3
Missing	11.1	49.4
7–13 August 1945	7.8	57.2
14–20 August 1945	4.0	61.2
By end of August 1945	5.0	66.2
By end of September 1945	6.4	72.6
By end of October 1945	0.8	73.4
By end of December 1945	0.6	74.0
By 5 August 1946	1.3	75.3
By end of December 1946	0.5	75.8
1947–49	2.1	77.9
1950–end of March 1957	6.1	84.0
By end of October 1965	7.2	91.2
November 1965 to survey date	8.8	100.0

Source: Hiroshima Shiyakusho, Public Health Bureau, A-bomb Survivors Mea-
sures Department, *Genbaku Higai Zentaizō Chōsa Jigyō Hōkokusho* [A-bomb
Disaster Overall Picture Survey Report] (Hiroshima: Hiroshimashi Eiseikyoku
Genbaku Higai Taisakubu, 1978*b*), pp. 130–31.

Figure 10.13. Population changes in Hiroshima City, Hiroshima Prefecture, and other prefectures
in Chūgoku region (Yuzaki and Ueoka 1976*a*).

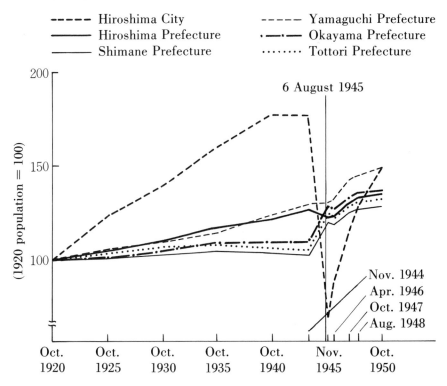

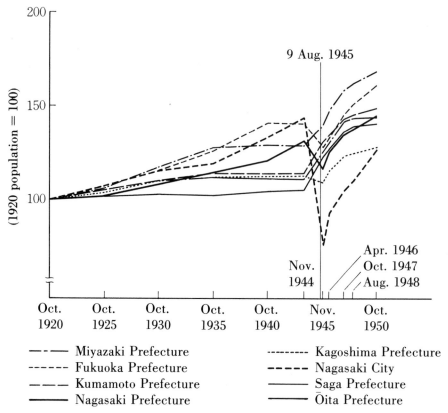

Figure 10.14. Population changes in Nagasaki City, Nagasaki Prefecture, and other prefectures in Kyushu (Yuzaki and Ueoka 1976*b*).

On the other hand, the national census conducted on 1 November 1945 determined the populations of both cities about three months after the bombings. Using this census and other prewar population data, population fluctuations and movements before and after the war in Hiroshima and Nagasaki, surrounding towns and villages, and districts of their respective prefectures, yield rates of population decline from which a loss of approximately 105,000 to 108,000 in Hiroshima due to the bombing can be estimated (as of 1 November 1945; military personnel excluded) (Yuzaki and Ueoka 1976*a*).

As for military personnel, the 10 December 1945 report of Second Army headquarters (United States Strategic Bombing Survey Report 1946*b*) lists 6,082 dead, 687 missing, and 3,353 injured. Records compiled by the Hiroshima chapter of the Mid-Japan Veterans Association list 9,242 dead and 889 missing as of November 1947 (Hiroshima Shiyakusho 1958, p. 736). From these two sources it is clear that the count had not greatly exceeded 10,000 by the end of 1945. The Veterans Association figures do not clearly specify the military units and bases involved; and the Second Army report does not cover some 20,000 men in special units or certain units undergoing reorganization. Under the circumstances of the time, these units were most probably close to the central bombed area. Assuming that half of them died then, the number of military deaths rises to 20,000—thus increasing the estimate of A-bomb deaths in Hiroshima to about 130,000 by the beginning of November 1945.

The estimate of 110,000 civilian deaths in Hiroshima covers daytime population, including conscripted workers, within commuting range of the city. A considerable number of people from other prefectures were among the dead, though precise figures are not available. Details on Korean workers and other foreigners in the city at the time are given in chapter 11 (pages 461–83).

For Nagasaki, similar survey reports yield an estimate of 80,000 to 90,000 killed in the bombing. In the city at the time, however, were many students and volunteer corps members from other prefectures (figure 10.15), many of whom returned home during immediate postwar demobilization. How many returned home is not clear; but by the reckoning of some of those involved, the number would not fall below 20,000. Taking this into account, A-bomb deaths in Nagasaki are estimated at 60,000 to 70,000 (Yuzaki and Ueoka 1976b).

Military personnel in Nagasaki were mostly anti-aircraft units and special military police. Casualties among army personnel and employees were 62 killed, 103 seriously wounded (of whom 31 died), and 93 with light injuries (Nagasaki Shiyakusho 1977, p. 369). Of 250 troops at the Mt. Konpira camp, 48 were reported killed (Konpira War Comrades Association 1977, p. 3). A naval unit was assigned to the Mitsubishi Munitions plant, but casualties were few. Altogether, there were about 150 deaths among military personnel.

In addition to 1,500 to 2,000 Koreans killed in Nagasaki, a number of Chinese students, workers, merchants, and others, as well as some Allied POWs, died in the bombing (see chapter 11, pages 472–83) (Kamata 1978, pp. 52–74).

In 1949 the government revealed the number of "citizens on the home front" sacrificed in the war. But for Hiroshima and Nagasaki it failed to conduct its own survey; it merely quoted figures, given in table 10.11, of the Hiroshima Prefectural Police Department (30 November 1945) and the Nagasaki Prefectural Office of External Affairs (23 October 1945) (Economic Stabilization Board 1949). Although, as noted, these estimates are clearly too low, they nonetheless constitute one third of the reported nationwide total of 323,495 killed. Not only has the government subsequently regarded these figures as the official count of deaths in the two cities, but the figures were also the basis for the first official United Nations report on the "Effects of the Possible Use of Nuclear Weapons and on the Security and Economic

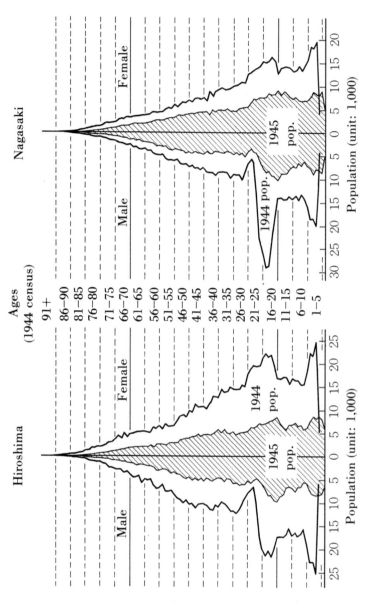

Figure 10.15. Population changes by sex and age in Hiroshima and Nagasaki, 1944–45. Based on provisional tabulations of 1944 and 1945 censuses. N.B. As these censuses were 1 year and 8 months apart, the intervening period is counted as two years for comparing ages.

Implications for States of the Acquisition and Further Development of These Weapons" (United Nations 1967) by U.N. Secretary-General U Thant, which listed 78,000 dead in Hiroshima and 27,000 in Nagasaki.

Details of deaths since November 1945 remain unclear, but the death rate of A-bomb victims is easily inferred to be higher than that of the general Japanese populace. The October 1950 national census, supplemented by the Atomic Bomb Casualty Commission survey, for the first time clarified the number of A-bomb survivors throughout the nation: 158,597 plus 10 from the Hiroshima bombing, 124,901 plus 10 from the Nagasaki bombing (the "10" are those who experienced both bombings).* Measured against the numbers physically present in the two cities on bombing dates, deaths in the five years from the bombings to 1950 amount to some 200,000 for Hiroshima and over 140,000 for Nagasaki.

Although fewer in number, it should be remembered that some of the early entrants into the two cities later died from residual radiation.

Unprecedented population loss like that wrought by the A-bombs has an enormous influence on population curves (figures 10.13, 10.14) (Yuzaki and Ueoka 1976a; 1976b). With the exodus to outlying districts and other prefectures already under way in the 1944–45 period, Hiroshima's population fell suddenly to 199,472 (58.1 percent decline), Nagasaki's to 128,143 (47.1 percent decline), as shown in table 10.13. The impact on population composition is

TABLE 10.13

*Populations and Decline Rates in Hiroshima and Nagasaki between 22 February 1944 and 1 November 1945**

City	Total	1944 Census	1945 Census	Rate of Decline (percentage)
Hiroshima	Total	343,034	143,562	58.1
	Male	164,271	73,642	55.2
	Female	178,763	69,920	60.9
Nagasaki	Total	272,312	144,169	47.1
	Male	139,210	70,898	49.1
	Female	133,102	73,271	45.0

* Figures for both cities were taken from provisional tabulations; hence, figures differ from those officially reported in 1977.

Source: Prime Minister's Office, Statistics Bureau, *Shōwa Jūkyūnen Jinkō Chōsa Shūkei Kekka Tekiyō* [Summary of the Tabulated Results of the 1944 Census] (Tokyo: Nihon Tōkei Kyōkai, 1977a). Prime Minister's Office, Statistics Bureau, *Shōwa Nijūnen Jinkō Chōsa Shūkei Kekka Tekiyō* [Summary of the Tabulated Results of the 1945 Census] (Tokyo: Nihon Tōkei Kyōkai, 1977b).

likewise great, especially as seen in Hiroshima's female and in Nagasaki's male populations; and distortions appear at all age levels (figure 10.15). It took nearly ten years to recover the prebombing population levels of 1944 (figure 10.16) (Hiroshimashi-Nagasakishi 1976, p. 52).

* Hiroshima A-bomb Medical Care History Editorial Committee 1961, pp. 462–63.

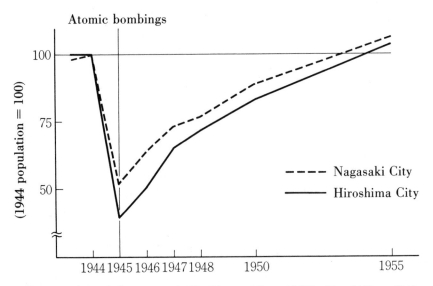

Figure 10.16. Population recovery in Hiroshima and Nagasaki (Hiroshimashi-Nagasakishi 1976, p. 52).

THE BREAKDOWN OF FAMILIES

The massive human damage caused by atomic bombs is not a matter of mere numbers: the lives of breadwinners along with wives, the aged, youth, children, and babies are swept away without distinction, or they are left maimed for life. Whole families are wiped out, while others are deprived of key members. The normal bonds of family life are so ruptured that innumerable households are doomed to serious breakdown, if not to total disintegration.

Due to the bombings, how many families lost a father and husband, a wife and mother, a wife and children, both parents, all children? Such family losses are largely beyond measure because whole families have moved elsewhere to seek a living.

Investigations that have taken households as units and tried to determine how much damage was suffered by each member are extremely rare. One early effort was made in Hiroshima in August 1946 to assess the damages suffered by approximately 34,900 households (with an aggregate of 143,000 members); but it covered only the number of A-bomb victims and the death rate, leaving analysis of the details of family losses to future study (Hiroshima Shiyakusho 1947; Ishida and Matsubayashi 1961).

From 1968 the social medicine section of Hiroshima University's Research Institute for Nuclear Medicine and Biology carried out a reconstruction survey focused on the central bombed area;* then both Hiroshima and Nagasaki

* Survey Committee for the Map Restoration of A-bombed Areas 1968.

cities conducted reconstruction surveys of areas within 2 kilometers of their hypocenters.* Through such broad reconstruction efforts, the kinds of and the extent of damage suffered by families in each township, not just overall population loss, are gradually becoming clear. Here we wish to focus on the results of reconstruction research in Hiroshima in order to summarize what has been found out to date about the actual damage sustained by families.†

As table 10.14 shows, 84.2 percent of the resident households in the central bombed area lost at least one member; in the other three target districts, the proportions ran 78.9 percent, 57 percent, and 48.5 percent (column B). And, although outside the focal target area of this particular survey, it was discovered in the course of investigations that even in "half-burned or half-demolished areas" between 2 and 3 kilometers from the hypocenter, 39.9 percent of the resident households lost at least one family member. Similarly, the rate was 41.6 percent for households in city areas outside the 3-kilometer radius.

While the percentages refer only to surveyed households, it is striking that the central area households losing a member constitute nearly nine tenths of all households that experienced some damage directly or indirectly (column C). The relation between the number of members per household and the households losing members is shown in figure 10.18 (Yuzaki et al. 1974, p. 10).

Cases where the lost member was the household head constituted a majority of 57.7 percent in the central area; in the other three target areas, 44.7 percent, 22.3 percent, and 18.2 percent; in the 2-to-3-kilometer zone, the rate was 11.2 percent; and in areas beyond 3 kilometers, 13.5 percent—all above one tenth.

The incidence of A-bomb deaths was also high among spouses and heirs, especially in the central area. Many people were in their own homes, or somewhere close by, on the day of the bombing; thus, the instantaneous impact was crushingly fatal—all the more so the closer to the hypocenter they were.

The ratio of deaths among household members in relation to the total of all household members in zones of varying distance from the hypocenter is shown in table 10.15. Of all household members in the bombed area, including those absent for long periods due to military service or evacuation, 65.8 percent suffered direct A-bomb damage, 47.3 percent were killed. Of those in the central bombed area, 84.7 percent died on the bombing date, though

* Committee for the Restoration of A-bombed Areas 1970–1976; Nagasaki Municipal International Cultural Hall 1975; Shirabe, Yazaki, and Matsuo 1972.
† Hiroshima Shiyakusho, A-bomb Survivors Measures Department 1978b; Yuzaki 1978.

TABLE 10.14

Losses and Injuries Sustained by Households, by Residential District and Distance from Hypocenter, Hiroshima

Residential District	Distance from Hypocenter (km)	Number of Households Surveyed	(Percentages)						
			A Some Direct‡ Damage	B Lost Member§	C Percentage $\frac{B}{A} \times 100$	D Head Directly Injured	E Head Lost	F Spouse or Heir Lost‖	G Eldest Son Lost‖,**
Central bombed area*	0–0.5	842	94.3	84.2	89.2	77.1	57.7	—	—
Burned and demolished areas†	0.5–1.0	3,491	97.9	78.9	80.6	77.5	44.7	49.8	22.3
	1.0–1.5	4,452	98.8	57.0	57.6	78.9	22.3	19.4	13.8
	1.5–2.0	472	97.9	48.5	48.9	80.9	18.2	16.1	15.8
Half-burned and demolished areas	2.0–3.0	268	99.3	39.9	40.2	81.3	11.2	10.4	5.9
Other urban areas	3.0–	89	96.6	41.6	43.0	82.0	13.5	8.6	8.7

* Reconstruction survey conducted by Hiroshima University's Research Institute for Nuclear Medicine and Biology (results as of March 1975).
† Reconstruction survey conducted by the Committee for the Map Restoration of A-bombed Areas (results as of March 1976). Includes households that moved outside burned areas.
‡ Includes those indirectly exposed, such as early entrants into bombed areas.
§ Includes those who died soon after (by the end of October 1945), those bombed to death but date of death unknown, and missing persons among those directly killed.
‖ Households with spouse or eldest sons used as parameters.
** Includes resident husbands of eldest daughters.

Source: Hiroshima Shiyakusho, Public Health Bureau, A-bomb Survivors Measures Department, *Genbaku Higai Zentaizō Chōsa Jigyō Hōkokusho* [A-bomb Disaster Overall Picture Survey Report] (Hiroshima: Hiroshimashi Eiseikyoku Genbaku Higai Taisakubu, 1978b). M. Yuzaki, "From the restoration survey of the A-bomb disaster—For the reinstatement of man," in *Hiroshima-Nagasaki Sanjūnen no Shōgen* [Testimony of Hiroshima and Nagasaki on the Thirty Years after the Atomic Bombings] (Tokyo: Miraisha, 1976), vol. II, p. 287.

Figure 10.17. Remains of Shima Hospital at the hypocenter in Hiroshima (October 1945). Boards like this one, with messages asking about someone's fate or welfare, were seen standing everywhere following the bombing. (Photograph by Shigeo Hayashi.)

Figure 10.18. Relation of number of members in households (total 842) to number of households losing members (total 709) in Hiroshima (Reconstruction survey of central bombed area [Yuzaki et al. 1974, p. 10]).

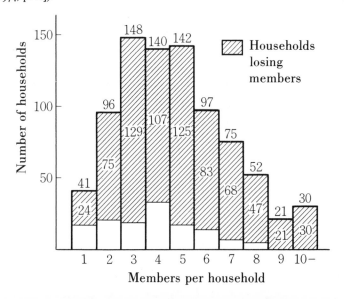

TABLE 10.15

Deaths and Injuries to Household Members, by Residential District and Distance from Hypocenter, in Hiroshima

Residential District	Distance from Hypocenter (km)	(Percentages)		Number of Deaths§
		Direct Injuries	Other Injuries‡	
Central bombed area*	0–0.5	65.8	—	47.3 (64.5)
Burned and demolished areas†	0.5–1.0	65.6	8.8	38.2 (51.8)
	1.0–1.5	70.6	9.3	20.5 (23.5)
	1.5–2.0	72.8	6.0	18.5 (18.6)
Half-burned and demolished areas	2.0–3.0	75.1	6.8	12.7 (11.2)
Other urban areas	3.0–	76.2	4.5	11.9 (12.9)

* Reconstruction survey conducted by Hiroshima University's Research Institute for Nuclear Medicine and Biology for 1,659 households. Data on deaths of household members through September 1945.

† Reconstruction survey conducted by the Committee for the Map Restoration of A-bombed Areas (results as of March 1976). Includes households that moved out of burned areas. Data on deaths through October 1945.

‡ Refers to indirect (secondary) injuries to early entrants into the city, those engaged in rescue activity outside the city, and those affected by "black rain."

§ Includes those who died soon after (by the end of October 1945), those bombed to death but date of death unknown, and missing persons, among those directly killed. Figures in parentheses are percentages of the total number of household members regularly resident at bombing time.

Source: Committee for the Restoration of A-bombed Areas, *Genbaku Hisai Zentaizō Chōsa Jigyō Hōkokusho* [Atomic Bomb Disaster Overall Picture Survey Reports], Reports for each year, 1969–75 (Hiroshima: Genbaku Hisai Fukugen Iinkai, 1970–76). M. Yuzaki, "Facts of the Hiroshima A-bomb disaster," *Rekishi Hyōron* [Historical Review 336 (1978): 12–18.

the rate exceeds 90 percent for the three districts located directly below the explosion (figure 10.19) (Yuzaki 1975*a*, p. 3).

For the three concentric zones within the larger burned-demolished area within a 2-kilometer radius, the rates of direct damage to household members were 65.6 percent, 70.6 percent, and 72.8 percent; death rates were 38.2 percent, 20.5 percent, and 18.5 percent. As is clear from table 10.15, the ratio of A-bomb casualties among household members rises with distance from the hypocenter—probably because evacuations and other departures had reduced the number of persons physically present in the closer zone; while the ratio of damage rises for the closer zones—probably because of the increase of entrants into the city. On the other hand, if long-term absentee members are discounted, then over half of the regularly resident household members died—64.5 percent in the central bombed area (by the end of September), and 51.8 percent in the next closest district, 0.5 to 1 kilometer from the hypocenter (by the end of October). And even in city districts outside the 2-kilometer radius, over one tenth of the households lost at least one member (table 10.15).

In Nagasaki, also, similar reconstruction surveys were made, the results of which appear in table 10.16. In Nagasaki's central bombed area, 61.5 percent

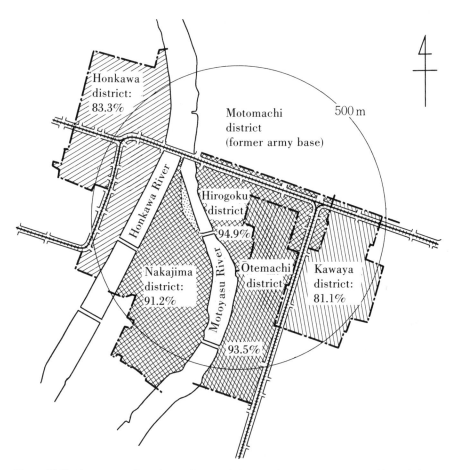

Figure 10.19. Percentage of deaths on the day of the bombing among members of households residing in the central bombed area of Hiroshima; these deaths include the dead and missing on 6 August, 1945, plus those burned to death but whose date of death is unknown (Reconstruction survey of central bombed area, results as of March 1975 [Yuzaki 1975a, p. 3]).

TABLE 10.16

Death Rates of Household Members, by Residential Districts, Nagasaki*

Residential District	Number of Households Surveyed	Death Rates	
		Percentage of all Household Members, Including Long-term Absentees	Percentage of Regularly Resident Household Members
Central bombed area	1,507	61.5	68.3
Burned and demolished areas	5,413	39.0	42.6

* Source: Reconstruction survey (results as of March 1975). Data includes both deaths through September 1945, and missing persons. Hiroshimashi-Nagasakishi, Expert Committee for Compilation of Data to Appeal to the United Nations, *To the United Nations* (1976), p. 49.

of resident household members (counting also long-term absentee members) died; the death rate for regularly resident members was 68.3 percent. In the larger burned-demolished area, the respective ratios were 39 percent and 42.6 percent (Hiroshimashi-Nagasakishi 1976, p. 49). These figures run somewhat higher than comparable rates in Hiroshima (table 10.15).

If the A-bomb injuries and deaths involving household members of various residential districts in Hiroshima are further differentiated by household heads and other family relationships, the results are as shown in figure 10.20 (Yuzaki 1977a, p. 3). Loss of life among spouses, parents, live-in relatives, and others sharing the same domicile stands out; and among children, girls suffered more than boys.

The death rate per average number of household members in each district is shown in table 10.17. In the central bombed area, there were 2.31 deaths per 4.88 persons (average household); in the larger burned-demolished area, 1.85 deaths per 4.85 persons within a 1-kilometer radius, and 0.98 deaths per 4.78 persons within a 1.5-kilometer radius. Among regularly resident members, the ratio was 2.28 per 3.54 persons in the central bombed area, or roughly 2 out of 3 persons. Deaths in the 1-kilometer, the 1.5-kilometer, and the 2-kilometer zones were, respectively, 1.82 per 3.51 (roughly 1 out of 2) persons, 0.86 per 3.65 (1 out of 4) persons, and 0.72 per 3.89 (1 out of 5) persons.

In addition to these reconstruction surveys, a separate sociological survey shows that in the Kan'on district, about 1 kilometer west of the hypocenter, the death rate was 54 percent of all household members, 2 percent of regularly resident members; in the Fukushima district (1.5 kilometers) the rates were 42 percent and 12 percent. The average number of deaths per household in these districts was 1.58 and 1.67, respectively.*

The preceding death rates alone reveal how severe and fateful was the A-bomb impact on families. All the death counts given, however, cover only the first month or two after the bombings; the full counts are thought to be much higher. So many families were obliterated, and the dead and the missing so numerous, that reconstruction efforts leave many households unaccounted for.

Post-bombing population and map-restoration studies indicate that direct explosion-time injuries were heavier among women than among men; and also that among men in the cities, the effects were heaviest in the forty-to-fifty age bracket.

Reconstruction studies show that the A-bomb damages to households within the 1-kilometer radius were conspicuously heavy, as might be expected; but damages to households in other city areas and even in towns and villages outside the city were far from light. Such damage is related to the commuting

* Kawai, Harada, and Tanaka 1969; Yoneyama, Kawai, and Harada 1968.

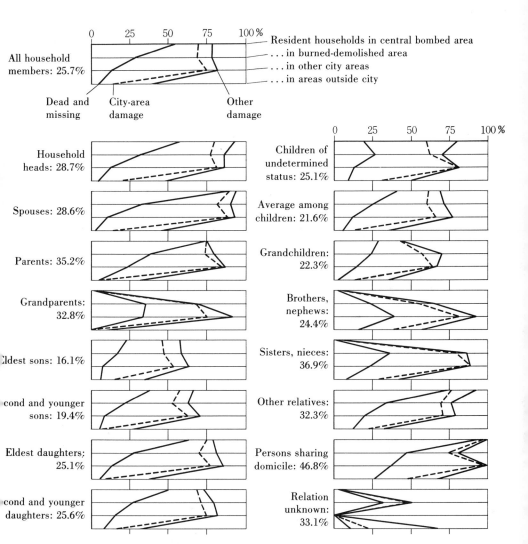

Figure 10.20. Family status differentiations in A-bomb damage and deaths among household members in residential districts of Hiroshima; data include households that moved out of the survey area and also related households; figures in parentheses are percentages of the status group out of the total of all household members (Reconstruction survey of burned-demolished area; results as of March 1976 [Hiroshima Shiyakusho, A-bomb Survivors Measures Department 1978*b*; and Yuzaki 1977*a*, p. 3]).

TABLE 10.17

Death Rates per Household in Hiroshima by Residential Districts and Distance from Hypocenter

Residential District	Residential District Distance from Hypocenter (km)	Deaths per Average Household Membership			
		Average Total Household (including long-term absentees)	Number of Deaths	Average Household (those actually resident)	Numbe Deat
Central bombed area*	0–1.0	4.88	2.31	3.54	2.2
Burned and demolished areas†	0.5–1.0	4.85	1.85	3.51	1.8
	1.0–1.5	4.78	0.98	3.65	0.8
	1.5–2.0	4.83	0.89	3.89	0.7
Half-burned and demolished	2.0–3.0	4.69	0.60	3.74	0.4
Other urban areas	3.0 and beyond	4.53	0.54	3.56	0.4
	City averages‡	4.81	1.31	3.61	1.2

* Reconstruction survey conducted by Hiroshima University's Research Institute for Nuclear Medicine and Biology for 1,659 households. Da deaths of household members through September 1945.

† Reconstruction survey conducted by the Committee for the Map Restoration of A-bombed Areas (results as of March 1976). Data on house that moved out of burned areas also included. Data on deaths through October 1945.

‡ From results of the Map Restoration of A-bombed Areas survey of burned and demolished areas (8,820 households)—that is, excluding the c bombed area survey (1,659 households).

Source: Hiroshima Prefectural Office, *Genbaku Sanjūnen-Hiroshimaken no Sengoshi* [Thirty Years Since the Atomic Bombing—Postwar Histc Hiroshima Prefecture] (Hiroshima: Hiroshimaken, 1976), p. 90. Hiroshima Shiyakusho, Public Health Bureau, A-bomb Survivors Measures Depart *Genbaku Higai Zentaizō Chōsa Jigyō Hōkokusho* [A-bomb Disaster Overall Picture Survey Report] (Hiroshima: Hiroshimashi Eiseikyoku Genbaku Taisakubu, 1978).

patterns of workers and students and to the mobilization of work forces, as well as to the presence of Koreans, military personnel, and transient visitors. Many of these people were key members of their households, and the impact on their households was serious.

A survey of the neighboring community of Nakayama village (present-day Nakayama township of Hiroshima City) in Aki-gun (county) to the east of Hiroshima shows that, as in the city, an average of 1.13 deaths occurred per household (Shimizu et al. 1967, p. 4). Of the 1,000 population of Kawauchi village (present-day Satō-chō township of Hiroshima City) in Asa-gun, 186 died as laborers conscripted to work in Hiroshima or in other capacities. Many of them were household heads or wives, and their loss led to family breakdowns. (Yuzaki 1972; Yuzaki and Watanabe 1972, p. 4)

THE COLLAPSE OF SOCIAL ORGANIZATIONS AND FUNCTIONS

Hiroshima and Nagasaki made it unmistakably clear that an A-bomb assault on urban society means the liquidation of an integrated entity consisting of people in communities. This dissolution extends to the relations of the city and its surrounding districts, for the wrecking of livelihood spreads as people from these districts flow into the ruined city. The overall destruction and its diffused effects render survivors unable to help each other, making rehabilitation tortuous and leaving deep psychological scars.

Compared with Hiroshima's total loss of its central functions, Nagasaki narrowly got by with very heavy damage to, but not total loss of, its key capabilities. The industrial structures of the two cities, in particular, were different; Hiroshima's city area was full of small- and medium-sized commercial and industrial enterprises, and had a large army installation in its center; but heavy industries were dispersed outside the city. Nagasaki was studded from north to south with large industries such as Mitsubishi Steel, Mitsubishi Munitions, and Mitsubishi Shipbuilding.

In Hiroshima many major facilities—prefectural office, city hall, fire departments, police stations, national railroad stations, post offices, telegram and telephone offices, broadcasting station, and schools—were totally demolished and burned. Streetcars, roads, and electricity, gas, water, and sewage facilities were ruined beyond use. Eighteen emergency hospitals and thirty-two first-aid clinics were destroyed; and most of the personnel needed to restore them to use were killed or injured. As approximately 90 percent of all medical personnel in the city were dead or disabled, and the hospitals were destroyed or damaged, all medical care was thrown into confusion (table 10.18). It

TABLE 10.18
Number of Medical Personnel Killed or
Injured in Hiroshima

Profession	Number of Casualties	Percentage of Total Profession
Physicians	270	90
Dentists	132	86
Pharmacists	112	80
Nurses	1,650	93

Source: Hiroshima A-bomb Medical Care History Editorial Committee (HAMCH), *Hiroshima Genbaku Iryōshi* (Hiroshima: Hiroshima Genbaku Shōgai Taisaku Kyōgikai, 1961), p. 10.

was the same with the army's Chūgoku Regional headquarters and various units under the Second Army's command in Hiroshima. The only units still functioning were the army marine transport headquarters, barracks, training center, and artillery facilities in Ujina; several units of the navy's training center at Kōnoura on Etajima island; and the quarantine and medical units on Ninoshima island. For rescue work in the city, the naval training center at Kōnoura sent not a full-fledged medical unit but 1,500 men (nonmedical) with only 1 doctor, 1 intern, 2 noncommissioned medical officers, and 12 medical corpsmen. From Ninoshima 20 army doctors and 350 officers, noncommissioned officers, and medical corpsmen, plus four veterinarians, came to treat countless victims brought to relief stations.*

On the day of the bombing, first-aid teams from the army sanatorium for wounded soldiers in Saijō, the naval base in Kure, and medical associations in Onomichi City and Toyota and Yamagata counties in Hiroshima Prefecture reached Hiroshima; on the following day, first-aid teams from districts in Hiroshima Prefecture and from the Okayama Prefectural Medical Association arrived. But because the wounded were so numerous, and because there was no "rear base" for full-scale treatment, all that could be done was to put dressings on their burns. First-aid stations were set up in schools and hospitals at least 1.2 kilometers, but generally 1.5 to 2 kilometers, from the hypocenter. Fifty-three stations were recorded for the initial period.†

On 7 August the commander of the army's marine transport base was made the acting police chief of Hiroshima, with authority to restore order to the city.‡ Cleaning up the streets and disposal of corpses were begun; but due to transportation difficulties, the corpses could only be burned or buried where found. On this same day, first-aid teams arrived from army hospitals in Yamaguchi, Hamada, Kakogawa, Fukuchiyama, and Okayama; on 11 August, a group of 200 special air defense medics came from army hospitals in Kokura and Fukuoka (Toda 1945), and at last long-term care of patients could begin (Nishina Memorial Foundation 1973, pp. 26–28). In this period most of the first-aid stations in the smoldering ruins and nearby places were manned by teams sent by the medical associations of cities, towns, and villages in Hiroshima Prefecture. Help from within the prefecture is estimated to have daily averaged 300 first-aid personnel, 200 volunteer workers, 150 police, and 130 trucks (Nishina Memorial Foundation 1973, p. 35).

The training and transport units in Ujina were ordered on 10 August to reorganize as a field hospital. By the time systematic care of patients finally began, the war had ended; but on the twenty-fifth, this field hospital became the Ujina branch of Hiroshima First Army Hospital. In this period it received 18,153 patients, of whom 2,623 (14.4 percent) died. The army medical school in Tokyo formed a special 144-man medical team which was sent to work in the Ujina branch hospital (Imahori 1959–60, vol. 1, p. 100). Other hospitals that helped treat A-bomb victims include Hiroshima First Army Hospital's Eba branch, a field hospital set up in school buildings north of Hiroshima by the First and Second Army hospitals, and the Hiroshima Red Cross Hospital. For example, about fifty personnel, including eight army doctors, one commissioned and twenty noncommissioned medics, and eight nurses, of the Eba branch hospital gave emergency treatment to over ten thousand

---

* Hiroshima Shiyakusho 1971, pp. 86–125; Nishina Memorial Foundation 1973, pp. 22, 29.

† Hiroshima A-bomb Medical Care History Editorial Committee 1961, p. 107; Nishina Memorial Foundation 1973, pp. 23–24.

‡ Hiroshima A-bomb Medical Care History Editorial Committee 1961, p. 78; Hiroshima Prefectural Office 1973, pp. 99–166.

Figure 10.21. Street corner in Nishi Tōkaichi township of Hiroshima, about 700 meters from the hypocenter, on 18 August 1945. (Photograph by Yūichirō Sasaki.)

persons.* After 10 August, most of the patient care was done at facilities some 20 kilometers from Hiroshima.

Then, on 17 September, the Makurazaki typhoon hit Hiroshima, washing away most of its bridges and leaving railroads unusable until November—and thus administered another severe jolt to the already miserable life of the A-bomb victims.

Total destruction in Nagasaki extended 2 kilometers in every direction from the hypocenter in the city's northern sector, and in the 2–3 kilometer zone, some places were completely burned and demolished, others only partially so. Located within the 2-kilometer zone of total destruction were the Nagasaki plants of Mitsubishi Munitions, Mitsubishi Steel, Mitsubishi Electrical Machinery, and their many subcontract factories, as well as Kyushu Power's thermoelectric plant, Saibu Gas's Ōhashi plant, and Nagasaki Electric Railway's Ōhashi shop—that is, various enterprises related to the city's key functions. Also in this zone were the chief medical facilities: Nagasaki Medical University and its related hospital, the Urakami branch of Mitsubishi Hospital, Urakami First Hospital, and others. Even 3.3 kilometers from the hypocenter, the Nagasaki Prefectural Office building smoldered awhile, then burst into flames and was consumed. Urakami, the central bombed area, had been incorporated into Nagasaki City in 1919. Public housing had earlier been erected in its Shiroyama section; but as air raids and firebreak demolition

* Hiroshima Shiyakusho 1971, pp. 348, 358, 359, 363; Nishina Memorial Foundation 1973, p. 36.

emptied parts of the old city center, more and more families moved into this section, as did many commuters' families. There was also the Urakami Cathedral (Roman Catholic); and of the city's 20,000 Catholics, some 15,000 are said to have been concentrated in this area. About 10,000 of them are thought to have been sacrificed to the atomic bomb. (Nagasaki Shiyakusho 1977, p. 258).

Of the city's firefighting capabilities, seven of thirty-six automatic pump trucks were lost, and two badly damaged; fourteen of sixty-four hand-cranked, gasoline-powered pumps and two of forty-two manually-operated pumps were destroyed. Soon after the bombing, two hose companies under the direct control of the Nagasaki Fire Department began fighting fires near Nagasaki Railroad Station; but as new fires broke out one after another, both companies retreated and, by evening, were able to establish a final fire-defense line near the city hall, the fire department, and Shinkōzen Primary School (Nagasaki Shiyakusho 1977, pp. 202–4).

Nagasaki Broadcasting Station also ceased to function with the bombing; afterward, broadcasting stations in the neighboring prefectures of Kumamoto, Fukuoka, and Saga became the only sources of news. Sasebo Naval Base first got a report on Nagasaki and ordered the formation of rescue teams by naval units in Isahaya, Ōmura, and Hario (Nagasaki Shiyakusho 1977, pp. 180, 185).

Most of the hospitals, so desperately needed, had been burned or demolished. Of seventy or so doctors in private practice in the city, twenty were dead and about twenty more seriously wounded, leaving hardly thirty to help (Nagasaki Shiyakusho 1977, p. 378). Apart from the small-scale Nagasaki Army Hospital in the old city quarter, there were no facilities to serve as bases for emergency care. First-aid stations set up in primary schools were the main places for emergency treatment of people in the vicinities soon after the bombing. A team from the city's medical association quickly assembled at Katsuyama Primary School northeast of the city hall; and by evening of the first day, a first-aid team of thirteen (two doctors, two noncommissioned medical corpsmen, eight nurses, and a noncommissioned bus driver) from Isahaya Naval Hospital arrived at the school. Fear of spreading fires forced them to move to Irabayashi Primary School; but by evening the number of patients exceeded a thousand, and available medical supplies were exhausted. Requests for more supplies and personnel were sent to Isahaya Naval Hospital, but it was already crowded with a thousand patients transported by emergency train; so the naval medical team returned to Isahaya on the following day (10 August) and was replaced by doctors sent to the school by the city's medical association (Nishina Memorial Foundation 1973, p. 87).

Katsuyama Primary School fortunately escaped the fires, and a medical team from Obama Medical Association came to help. On 10 August an advance party of doctors from the Takeo branch of Sasebo Naval Hospital reached Shinkōzen Primary School, nearby to the west; and a 249-man rescue team from Hario arrived that evening, followed by the main Takeo staff on the twelfth.* The Hario group used the office of Mitsubishi Steel in Urakami as its base for relief activity; and on the eleventh, three trucks loaded with drugs and medical supplies arrived. These trucks made it possible to begin mobile operations. Shinkōzen Primary School also served as sleeping quarters for the medical teams, so people seeking care also gathered there. On 15 August medical supplies were brought in from Takeo, and the school soon became a center for emergency care. A team from Fukuoka Army Hospital came on or around 12 August to help at the first-aid station run by the city's medical association at Nagasaki College of Economics; and on 17 August patients sent from the Mitsubishi Steel office and Nagasaki Medical University were received there (Nagasaki Shiyakusho 1977, p. 501). These were among the twenty-nine places where emergency care was given to A-bomb victims in the city during the first several days of urgent need.†

Mitsubishi Steel office handled not only the plant's workers but also many citizens. At its request a team of three doctors and five nurses was sent from the main Mitsubishi Hospital located at Mitsubishi Shipbuilding in Akunoura (3.5 kilometers from the hypocenter) (Nishina Memorial Foundation 1973, pp. 94–5). A team from Ōmura Naval Hospital gave emergency treatment at Ibinokuchi, near Mitsubishi Shipbuilding's plant in Saiwai-machi township. Meantime, four Nagasaki-bound trains had been put into service as carrier coaches for patients, and some 3,500 seriously wounded victims were transported to Isahaya, Ōmura, Kawatana, and Haiki for treatment at various hospitals and first-aid stations.‡

Food for the sufferers, of course, was a major problem. Some hardtack rations were finally distributed in the central city area in the evening of the first day; but even this was extremely difficult, as most of the local officials and volunteers were themselves dead or injured. Women's groups in some townships apparently cooked some emergency rations. Relief from nearby towns and villages came early in the morning of the following day (10 August), and the ration was two balls of cooked rice per person. The peak period for food distribution ran four days from the tenth (about 200,000 servings) to the thirteenth (almost 80,000 servings), after which rations changed to

* Aihara 1978; Relief Squad dispatched by Hario Marine Corps 1973, pp. 211–14; Kenmyō 1975, pp. 234–43.

† Nagasaki Shiyakusho 1977, pp. 408–576; Nishina Memorial Foundation 1973, pp. 88, 96, 104–6.

‡ Nagasaki Shiyakusho 1977, pp. 263, 281, 457; Nishina Memorial Foundation 1973, pp. 99–100.

uncooked rice and canned foods. Distribution of cooked food was stopped on the eighteenth, ending a ten-day effort that provided some 650,000 servings (Nagasaki Shiyakusho 1977, pp. 201, 391–94). Ration cards had been issued from 11 or 12 August (Nagasaki Shiyakusho 1977, pp. 396–98). Some sections near the city's center were cut off from relief activities—the streetcars were not running, and town associations were wiped out—so people sometimes died in air-raid shelters, not infrequently with symptoms that appeared after the bombing (Nishina Memorial Foundation 1973, p. 228).

Telephone service for the army and the main government agencies was restored the first day and, by the twenty-first, for 559 important subscribers. Lights came on throughout the city on 14 August, as electricity was restored to all but the bombed area. Train service was resumed with the last-scheduled train out of Nagasaki Station (10:15 P.M.) on 11 August, but streetcar service was not revived until the following year.

The army began demobilization from 15 August when the war ended, and its relief activity ceased or diminished. Most of the A-bomb victims left the bombed area for relatives' homes; but as late as September some 700 households were reportedly still living in air-raid shelters amid the scorched ruins. Their life was made doubly miserable by heavy rains on 2 and 3 September. In October electricity became available in the Urakami district, but not to those still in the shelters. Soon after, emergency housing construction was begun in the Iwakawa township by the public housing agency, and 332 units were soon completed (Nagasaki Shiyakusho 1977, pp. 401, 583, 594).

The Loss of Wealth

WHAT IS "WEALTH"?

Wars kill and maim mercilessly, but they also rob nations of immeasurable wealth. It has always been assumed that the A-bombs dropped on Hiroshima and Nagasaki caused immense losses of wealth, but heretofore no detailed assessments have been made. Indeed, as explained below, source materials are extremely scarce. For the early post-bombing period, three sources are of special importance:

1. City surveys of damages in Hiroshima and Nagasaki. The "Hiroshima City Almanac" of 1946 (first-anniversary-of-reconstruction issue) (Hiroshima Shiyakusho 1947, pp. 63–64) gives estimated values of lost wealth based on an October 1945 investigation; though no estimate of total loss was made for Nagasaki, volume I of "Record of the Nagasaki A-bomb War Disaster" (Nagasaki Shiya-

kusho 1977) and the "Sixty-five-year History of the Municipality of Nagasaki" (Nagasaki Shiyakusho 1959) give detailed explanations of physical damages.

2. Report of the United States Strategic Bombing Survey, Urban Areas Division (1947a; 1947b).

3. Economic Stabilization Board, "A Comprehensive Report on the Damages to Our Country Due to the Pacific War" (Economic Stabilization Board 1949). This report does not specifically investigate Hiroshima and Nagasaki and thus only roughly evaluates A-bomb damages. It is useful, however, as a general guide to the national loss of wealth.

Defining the scope of "wealth" is of first importance. Our own assessment considers all losses of physical property caused directly by the atomic bombings. For individual households or business enterprises, property includes both material assets and financial assets (cash, bank deposits, corporation stocks and bonds, and government securities). Therefore, loss of both physical and financial assets enters into our calculations. Stocks, bonds, and deposits of individual households and enterprises are converted through various channels into material assets of large corporations and the government, so a simple tally of physical and material assets results in some overlap. But when credits exceed liabilities in Hiroshima and Nagasaki in relation to other districts, the surplus may be considered the wealth of the two cities. The families and the enterprises of the two cities possessed considerable financial assets, and their losses were considerable. The actual losses, however, are shrouded in obscurity, and full evaluation awaits future clarification.

The practical difficulty of counting losses is the method of appraisal. First of all, it is extremely difficult to assess the value of all kinds of physical property as of bombing times. The main reason is that registered values in most cases are no longer known. Because Hiroshima's city hall was completely burned, the tax ledgers were lost (the U.S. Strategic Bombing Survey also stresses this point); and while Nagasaki's city hall was not burned, no effort was made to check each loss carefully against the tax ledgers. Second, even when registered values are known, what index should be used to convert acquisition values at acquisition time to 1945 values? If the wholesale price index is used, it is only natural that different indices be applied according to the kind of material asset (the recent National Wealth and National Income Survey devised a table of values for each kind of property). And third, any effort to assess property values should take into account depreciation due to the lapse of time. But there is no way to determine the age of each of the more than 120,000 houses in question in Hiroshima and Nagasaki together, or even the average for the total. As production of all wealth not directly or indirectly related to military programs was severely restricted, as were all renovations, real residual values are thought to have been less than August 1945 values reached by conversion rates.

The range of properties is wide. The categories in the government's National Wealth Survey include buildings, attached facilities, structures, machinery, equipment, vessels, vehicles, transport equipment, tools, furnishings and fixtures, reclaimed land, animals, plants, construction expense accounts, and all other tangible fixed assets and inventories. Using the last prewar (1935) survey of national wealth, the Economic Stabilization Board (1949) ventures estimates of the amounts and percentages of losses for each category (Prime Minister's Office, Statistics Bureau, 1948). The Hiroshima data, however, are not accommodated to so many separate categories. To break down the data at this time would be next to impossible.

The Economic Stabilization Board's report (1949) made rather careful nationwide estimates of direct and indirect war damages; and, though perfection is impossible due to loss of vital records in the wartime and postwar confusion, the estimate of total loss of nonmilitary wealth is 65,000,000,000 yen (49.6 billion in direct losses). This report acknowledges that detailed estimates for Hiroshima and Nagasaki are not possible, but puts their aggregate share of the total loss at about 2 percent (Hiroshima alone, 1.4 percent)—that is a loss of 695,000,000 yen for Hiroshima and of 281,000,000 yen for Nagasaki (August 1945 values). The Hiroshima City Almanac (Hiroshima Shiyakusho 1947, pp. 63–64) estimates the city's losses at 763,430,000 yen (October 1945 survey), a figure fairly close to that of the Economic Stabilization Board. The Hiroshima survey, however, estimated losses in only six categories— private houses (440,000,000 yen), buildings (250,000,000 yen), bridges (8,000,000 yen), roads (1,500,000 yen), household effects (33,930,000 yen), and communications facilities (30,000,000 yen), and the criteria of assessment are not clarified. Accordingly, it is not certain how accurately the estimates reflect the real losses.

Here we shall limit ourselves to correlating the few existing records and making rough summations of the losses incurred.

LOSSES IN HIROSHIMA

Buildings were the primary targets of material damage. By a Hiroshima City count, those more than half-burned or half-demolished numbered 70,147 (August 1946 survey [Hiroshima Shiyakusho 1947, pp. 57–58]). The U.S. Strategic Bombing Survey, Urban Areas Division (1947a) counted only 50,160; but here we use the Hiroshima City figure. The buildings counted include everything—residences, commercial stores, factories, offices, government agencies, schools, and the like. How many of the destroyed buildings were residences is not clear; but 64,521 residences existed before the war. Taking into account the U.S. Strategic Bombing Survey and a separate estimate that 92 percent of these were destroyed, the number of residences more than

half-burned or half-demolished is put at roughly 59,000. The overall loss is
then calculated as follows:

1. The 1934–36 net value per *tsubo* (3.3 sq. meters) is set at 59 yen (after depreciation).
2. If the 1934–36 value is 100, the August 1945 index is 353; hence, the net value
   per *tsubo* in 1945 is 208 yen.
3. At an average of 18 *tsubo* per house, net worth of a residence is 3,744 yen.
4. Of 59,000 residences, 90 percent were totally burned or demolished; the rest
   were half-destroyed.
5. The total estimated loss, therefore, is 214,000,000 yen.

In step 1, estimated values for "capital stock" (Ōkawa et al. 1966) were
used. In step 3, the Hiroshima City Almanac (Hiroshima Shiyakusho 1947,
p. 6) estimate (August 1946) of prebombing population of 312,277 and the
estimated 59,000 residences were used to reach an estimate of 4.8 persons
per household—a figure that was multiplied by Tokyo's average of 3.76 *tsubo*
per person. We have already estimated Hiroshima's resident population at
280,000 to 290,000 (p. 351). The 1940 national census put average family
size at 5.1 persons; the 1945 census, at 4.9 persons. Given the estimated population, the estimates of family and house size are considered proper. Losses
for some of the "half-burned or half-demolished" districts were calculated
at 0.7 × 3,744 yen.

These losses, as already noted, are net values. If the gross or reacquisition
values were estimated, the figures would be much higher. The rate should
be at least 1.5 times higher, so gross loss would be 321,000,000 yen.

Buildings other than homes and factories included government agencies,
schools, stores, offices, and so on. They were some 10,500 in number (among
these were many retail stores with combined living quarters). The U.S. Strategic Bombing Survey, Urban Areas Division (1947a) estimated completely
and heavily damaged building losses for nonresidential structures at 5.5 times
(per structure) that of residences. At this rate, the average loss per building
was 21,000 yen. Assuming 80 percent were completely destroyed and 20
percent were half-destroyed, the total loss was 210,000,000 yen.

Factories constituted a third class of building. In Hiroshima the large,
important factories, which accounted for 76 percent of industrial production,
were located outside the destruction zone and, thus, reportedly sustained
only light damage. The vast majority of damaged buildings were residences
and other non-industrial structures; the 600-plus damaged factories were
chiefly small- and medium-sized plants. These losses may be estimated as
follows:

1. Following the U.S. Strategic Bombing Survey report, an average factory loss was 2.3 times that of a residence, or 8,600 yen. Supposing 90 percent were totally destroyed and 10 percent were half-destroyed, the total loss was 5,000,000 yen.
2. For assessing losses of machinery and tools, the guidelines are estimated "capital stock" (Ōkawa et al. 1966) and the estimate in the 1935 National Wealth and National Income Survey (Prime Minister's Office, Statistics Bureau 1948) that the value of existing equipment then was 2.1 times that of buildings. This estimated loss was 10,500,000 yen. (In the "Comprehensive Report on the Damages to Our Country Due to the Pacific War" [Economic Stabilization Board 1949], the value of existing equipment is 2.5 times that of buildings.)
3. Loss of industrial products is estimated at about 10,000,000 yen (following nationwide estimates [Economic Stabilization Board 1949] that loss of equipment and loss of product are roughly equal).

In accordance with these estimates, total losses of medium, small, and petty industries are appraised at 25,500,000 yen.

According to the National Wealth and National Income Survey (Prime Minister's Office, Statistics Bureau 1948), losses of household effects and furnishings were 54 percent of estimated nonindustrial building loss. Lacking other relevant data, this rate may be applied to yield an estimated total loss of 286,000,000 yen (for all Japan, the loss of household effects and furnishings was 62 percent of nonindustrial building loss).

Other major properties include roads, bridges, railroads, ships, and electricity, gas, telegraph, telephone facilities, and water supply. As there is no way to make an estimate for each of these categories, the only option is to adopt estimates made by each city and by the U.S. Strategic Bombing Survey. In any case, the losses are regarded as much less than building losses, so underestimation would not greatly affect the overall estimate of losses.

A summation of the preceding categories is given in table 10.19. Since

TABLE 10.19

Property Losses in Hiroshima

	Estimated Loss (millions of yen)
Buildings	536.0
Bridges	8.0
Roads	1.5
Industrial machinery and tools	10.5
Railroads and rolling stock	15.8
Electric and gas facilities	10.3
Water and sewage facilities	6.0
Household effects and furnishings	286.0
Industrial products	10.0
Total	884.1

Source: Hiroshima Shiyakusho, *Hiroshima Shisei Yōran* [Hiroshima City Almanac], First-anniversary-of-reconstruction issue, 1946 ed. (Hiroshima: Hiroshima Shiyakusho, 1947), pp. 63–64. The United States Strategic Bombing Survey, Urban Areas Division, *The Effects of Air Attack on the City of Hiroshima* (Washington, D.C.: U.S. Government Printing Office, 1947).

large factories, ships, coins, gold and silver, precious metals, and some other categories are not included, the overall estimate of losses is conservative. Even so, the almost 900,000,000 yen exceeds the Economic Stabilization Board's total of 695,000,000 yen and Hiroshima City's total of 760,000,000 yen.

Hiroshima's initial budget for 1946 (both operating and contingency funds) was 9,610,000 yen, and the national per capital annual income in 1944 (estimated by Yūzō Yamada [Economic Planning Agency 1978, p. 72]) was 1,044 yen. Taking these figures at face value, the total loss of 884,100,000 yen was equal to what nearly 850,000 people would earn in a year if they spent nothing—or roughly three times the earning power of Hiroshima's estimated population of 280,000 to 290,000. Converted to August 1945 values, the minimal estimated loss was 1,100,000,000 yen, or the equivalent of the annual incomes of 1,100,000 people. The magnitude of the A-bomb damage, seen in these terms, is almost beyond comprehension.

LOSSES IN NAGASAKI

Nagasaki City's own survey gives only the number of destroyed buildings and a list of the most important ones, but provides no monetary estimates, thus making impossible the kinds and the extent of estimates available for Hiroshima.

Nagasaki's population before the bombing was about 240,000; the number of buildings approximately 49,000. Among the reports on damages to dwellings, the highest estimate (from records of Nagasaki's civil defense bureau [Nagasaki Shiyakusho 1959, vol. 3, p. 477]) lists 14,146 totally burned or demolished houses and 5,441 half-destroyed—a total of 19,587. Clear distinctions between residences, factories, and other buildings are not available, although the U.S. Strategic Bombing Survey, Urban Areas Division (1947b) records 8,700 residences as totally destroyed and 3,373 residences as heavily damaged (the USSBS figures probably do not include stores and factories with live-in quarters).

Even if these figures are more or less accurate, it remains problematic whether the average loss per house can be projected on Hiroshima standards. Nagasaki was a regional center with rather highly developed commercial and industrial enterprises; there is, accordingly, little basis for assuming that its standards were below Hiroshima's (indeed, the National Wealth and National Income Survey of 1935 puts the two cities' wealth-per-kilometer on the same level). If, for these reasons, the rates of Hiroshima are applied to Nagasaki, then the net loss in residences was 41,400,000 million yen. It should be remembered, though, that "the destruction affected all parts of the city; and 21,174 households lost their homes, which were made unusable by broken glass and rain-soaked flooring [thick woven-straw mats]; it would take a year to restore these homes to use" (records of Nagasaki City's civil defense bureau [Nagasaki Shiyakusho, Investigation and Statistics Section 1959, vol. 3, p. 477]).

While careful lists were made of important nonresidential buildings such as factories, offices, stores, government agencies, and schools, these lists have not been subsequently ordered so as to make loss estimates possible. One estimate of the extent of "damages to industry" is found in the U.S. Strategic Bombing Survey, Urban Areas Division (1947*b*): "Relatively reliable figures received from the various Mitsubishi enterprises permit an assessment of material damages to industry, and the figures represent over 90 percent of Nagasaki's industrial capacity—a reliable index to damages suffered by the rest of industry." As Mitsubishi losses are estimated at 80,610,000 yen, the total loss of industrial buildings and equipment in Nagasaki may be put at 90,000,000 yen. This figure includes raw materials and semifinished and finished products—that is, the entire manufacturing industry—but does not include raw materials and finished products stored in warehouses. If, as in Hiroshima's case, these are included, then the total industrial loss may be set as high as 150,000,000 yen.

Records for assessing losses of nonindustrial and nonresidential buildings have not been found. But if Hiroshima's unit-loss rate for offices, government agencies, schools, and stores (in most cases, with live-in quarters) is applied, the estimated loss was 108,000,000 yen. And if Hiroshima's 54 percent rate for losses of household effects and furnishings is used, the figure is approximately 80,700,000 yen.

Descriptions of damage to electricity, gas, transportation, telegraph, telephone, water, and shipping facilities are available but do not permit financial assessments to be made. On the other hand, as we have explained, the damage to residences, factories, and other buildings represent the major losses and, thus, a close approximation to the city's total loss. Table 10.20 summarizes the main conclusions. These results admittedly involve more omissions and

TABLE 10.20

Property Losses in Nagasaki

	Estimated Loss (millions of yen)
Residences	41.4
Nonresidential, nonindustrial buildings	108.0
Household effects and furnishings	80.7
Factories	150.0
Total	380.1

Source: Nagasaki Shiyakusho, *Nagasaki Genbaku Sensaishi* [Record of the Nagasaki A-bomb War Disaster], vol. 1. Nagasaki: *Nagasaki Kokusai Bunka Kaikan* [Nagasaki International Cultural Hall], 1977. The United States Strategic Bombing Survey, Urban Areas Division, *The Effects of Air Attack on the City of Nagasaki* (Washington, D.C.: U.S. Government Printing Office, 1947). The figures in this table were estimated on the basis of these sources.

uncertainties than Hiroshima's calculations; yet it is not unreasonable to estimate total losses in Nagasaki as close to 400,000,000 yen.

The 380,100,000-yen total given in the table represents the annual earning power of 365,000 people at that time—far more than Nagasaki's prebombing population. The gross or reacquisition value would be 480,000,000, or the annual incomes of 460,000 people.

LOSSES CALCULATED AT CURRENT VALUES

How much Hiroshima's property loss of 884,100,000 yen and Nagasaki's 380,100,000 yen would be at today's values is an intriguing question. The conventional method of conversion uses price indices. If wholesale prices are used, then August 1945 = 1 becomes 1977 = 200. Since building damages constituted major losses, the building materials indices may be used to yield a ratio of August 1945 = 1 as against 1977 = 292 (both figures are from wholesale price indices of the Bank of Japan [Statistics Bureau 1964]) based on 1960 determinations of prewar and postwar levels). Losses of wealth at 1977 rates, based on costs of construction materials, for Hiroshima run to 258,000,000,000 yen, for Nagasaki to 110,900,000,000 yen.* Concrete substantiation of these amounts, of course, is not possible at this late date; but the converted values are thought to fall below actual ones.

As we have just explained, Hiroshima's loss was equivalent to the annual incomes of 850,000 people, and Nagasaki's loss represented the annual incomes of 365,000 people. These hypothetical figures are 1.1 percent and 0.5 percent, respectively, of Japan's population of 74,430,000 as of 22 February 1944 (national census, 1944). As Hiroshima's average per capita income in 1977 was about 1,400,000 yen, Hiroshima's loss for 850,000 people would be 1,200,000,000,000 yen; and Nagasaki's loss for 370,000 people would be 510,000,000,000 yen. Per capita income in Hiroshima, however, ranks 126 in relation to the national average (100) (*Asahi Shimbun* 1978); on this basis, Hiroshima's loss would be that for 670,000 people, or about 80 percent of the city's 1977 population of 850,000, but 1.3 times that for the 510,000 people in the former city area. The 1977 per capita income in Nagasaki was 0.96 of the national average (100) (*Asahi Shimbun* 1978), making its loss that of 390,000 people, or 89 percent of its present population of 440,000.

Converted at reacquisition rates, Hiroshima then registers 1,540,000,000,000

* Although desirable, it is difficult to convert these yen figures into, for example, precise U.S. dollar amounts, owing to postwar fluctuations in yen-dollar parity. In December 1948 the yen-dollar exchange rate was fixed at ¥360/$1.00. In December 1971 this fixed rate was adjusted to ¥308/$1.00 (by finance ministers of ten nations, based on the Smithsonian monetary system); this fixed rate lasted till 9 February 1973, when a floating rate was adopted. Under the floating-rate system, parity has fluctuated between ¥306/$1.00 (8–9 December 1975) and ¥176/$1.00 (31 October 1978).

yen, or the equivalent of 870,000 people's annual incomes; for Nagasaki, the converted figures are 640,000,000,000 yen and 480,000 people.

These manipulations of figures are, of course, nothing more than convenient means for indicating the magnitude of material losses in easily appreciated current values. As we cautioned at the outset of this section, precise calculation of the wealth losses are virtually impossible; but the estimates we have offered are, even in the strictest economic terms, modest, if not conservative.

In assessing unit costs of buildings, one should never forget that cities do not consist merely of a collection of buildings. The personal dimensions of even a single street or township remind us that each and every structure represents the immeasurable efforts of many citizens over long periods of time. And estimates of material losses by no means convey the total destruction of the social fabric of a city reduced to ruins by a single atomic bomb.

Chapter 11

Life and Livelihood of the A-bomb Victims

The horrors of an atomic bomb do not end with the massive destruction caused when one is dropped; they continue to haunt and handicap people and communities for succeeding generations and spread far beyond those individuals initially assaulted by its awesome power.

The special features of an atomic bomb's continuing impact are residual radiation and the eruption of radiation symptoms, fetal damage, and hereditary problems, to mention a few. The physical and medical aspects of atomic destruction and their aftereffects have been treated in parts I and II. Chapter 10 of part III has shown the extensive damage done to whole cities that were nearly wiped out. In this chapter we turn to the lives of the A-bomb victims and others affected by the bombs, and focus on some of the critical difficulties they have struggled to overcome from 1946 to the present. In the process we shall see that the problems of the A-bomb victims today are not theirs alone but are issues faced by the whole society.

A-bomb Survivors and Other Affected Persons

The scope and the substance of the damage suffered by A-bomb victims are complex and diverse. In the past it was commonplace to regard as

A-bomb victims those who, directly or indirectly, were affected by the bomb's blast, heat, and especially its radiation. Owing to the comprehensive nature of the damage and the changes it wrought, however, many more people than these suffered from the bombings (Yuzaki 1978). There were, thus, two distinct groups of sufferers (table 11.1):

TABLE 11.1

Categories of Persons Affected by the Atomic Bomb

I. A-bomb Victims		II. Others Affected	
A. Directly exposed	residents of the city or of neighboring towns at bombing time	A. family members of A-bomb victims	away from city at the time of bombing, but lost family member(s)
B. Indirectly exposed	*early entrants* into the city were affected by residual radiation or other causes; *other victims* were affected by radioactivity at the time of or after the bombing—for instance, people who were caught in the "black rain" or who engaged in rescue activities of the directly exposed or in the disposal of corpses outside the city limits	B. new members of affected households	joined a household with an A-bomb victim (as defined I: A, B, C) or one that had lost a family member (II: A)
C. Exposed in utero	radiation in mother's womb	C. later generations	children and grandchildren of all other groups

(1) *A-bomb victims*—that is, persons who themselves were damaged; and (2) *Others affected,* those persons who were not personally damaged but had family members or close relatives who were.

Group 1 includes people damaged directly by the bomb, and also those damaged indirectly, such as those entering the two cities shortly after the bombings as well as damaged fetuses (those exposed in utero). Group 2 includes people who were away from either city (for example, evacuees or soldiers serving elsewhere) and who did not sustain residual radiation injury, but who lost parents, spouses, children, brothers, and sisters; and, thus, it includes also children and aged persons orphaned by family losses—in short, all those whose lives were seriously affected by such losses. This second group must be broadly interpreted to include persons who initially had no connection with A-bomb damage but later, through marriage, became members of households that had, as well as children and grandchildren of such households.

The others affected, especially those related to victims' households, have in common with victims of conventional wars the loss of family members, homes, property, and places of work. But an atomic bombing also involves the collapse of all the community functions that sustain life and livelihood, and particularly the loss of people in the prime of life who are essential to home and work.

Because of radiation injuries, A-bomb victims were often handicapped or limited in the kinds of work they could do. Not only did this condition inflict actual hardships on spouses and families, but it also was a continuing source of anxiety to them all that latent problems might bring new crises.

It is crucial to grasp the full picture of what an atomic explosion inflicts on human beings, though there is no certainty about what may yet develop, because the aftereffects continue to permeate the warp and woof of society (Yuzaki 1978). Such a picture is necessarily incomplete because no comprehensive survey has yet been conducted by Japan's national government; and relevant records have yet to be fully compiled and analyzed. Within the limited scope of what is known at present, we propose to review the processes and the changes in the lives of A-bomb survivors.

One of the earliest documents on survivors who were residents in one of the two cities on the bombing dates is a "supplementary survey" of the October 1950 national census. This survey was done at the request, channeled through the Occupation GHQ, of the Atomic Bomb Casualty Commission (ABCC), which had been established earlier to investigate the effectiveness of the atomic bomb, and particularly the long-term biological effects of radiation. The survey was designed to determine the number of A-bomb survivors as an epidemiological group, classified by name, age, sex, and residence at both bombing and survey times (Yuzaki 1976a, p. 243); but it actually focused on people directly affected by the bombings and omitted those indirectly affected (such as early entrants and fetal victims).

This supplementary survey was not included in the national census report prepared by the Prime Minister's Office, Statistics Bureau (1951a), and owing to methodological inadequacies, the results have never been officially publicized. The ABCC, however, did make the nationwide results available in July 1952 in response to a request by Hiroshima City (Chūgoku Shinbunsha 1966, pp. 64, 67). Figure 11.1 gives aggregate totals, as of August 1960, for major regions, prefectures, and the two A-bombed cities.*

As of October 1950, the nationwide total of A-bomb survivors was 283,498 + 10 (283,508). Of this total, 158,597 + 10 (55.9 percent) survived the Hiroshima bombing; 124,901 + 10 (44.1 percent) the Nagasaki bombing. The "+10" indicates survivors who experienced both bombings. The total of Hiroshima survi-

* Hiroshima A-bomb Medical Care History Editorial Committee 1961, pp. 462–63; Maki 1959.

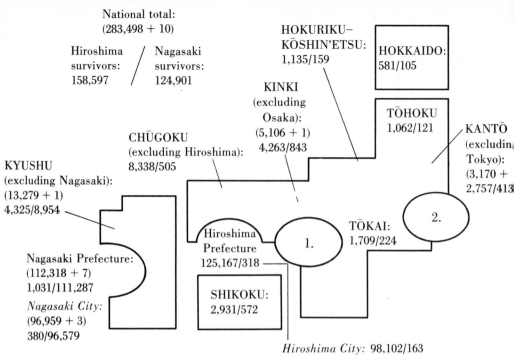

National total:
(283,498 + 10)

Hiroshima survivors: 158,597 / Nagasaki survivors: 124,901

HOKURIKU–KŌSHIN'ETSU: 1,135/159

HOKKAIDO: 581/105

KINKI (excluding Osaka): (5,106 + 1) 4,263/843

CHŪGOKU (excluding Hiroshima): 8,338/505

TŌHOKU 1,062/121

KANTŌ (excluding Tokyo): (3,170 + 2,757/413

KYUSHU (excluding Nagasaki): (13,279 + 1) 4,325/8,954

Hiroshima Prefecture 125,167/318

1.

TŌKAI: 1,709/224

2.

Nagasaki Prefecture: (112,318 + 7) 1,031/111,287

Nagasaki City: (96,959 + 3) 380/96,579

SHIKOKU: 2,931/572

Hiroshima City: 98,102/163

1. *Osaka Urban Prefecture*: 2,362/634
2. *Tokyo Metropolitan Prefecture*: 2,936/766

KEY: CAPITALS = regions
italics = cities, metropolitan prefecture, and urban prefecture

Figure 11.1. Distribution of atomic bomb survivors in major regions, prefectures, and the cities of Hiroshima and Nagasaki in 1950 (National Census, ABCC Supplementary Survey, 1 October 1950 [Hiroshima A-bomb Medical Care History Editorial Committee 1961, pp. 462–63; and Maki 1959]). Left-hand totals are for survivors of the Hiroshima bombing; right-hand totals, for survivors of the Nagasaki bombing. Numbers plus an additional number in parentheses indicate survivors of both bombings. Hiroshima and Nagasaki prefectural counts include totals for their respective cities.

vors (at survey time) throughout the nation was 158,607; of Nagasaki survivors, 124,911.

Nationwide sex distribution of survivors was 138,465 males (48.8 percent) and 145,043 females (51.2 percent). The male/female percentages for Hiroshima were 50.1/49.9; for Nagasaki, 47.2/52.8.

There were 125,167 residential locations of survivors (57,232 males, 67,935 females) at survey time in Hiroshima Prefecture, of whom 98,102 (61.8 percent) lived in Hiroshima City; among Nagasaki survivors, 111,294 (89 percent) lived in Nagasaki Prefecture, 96,582 (77.3 percent) of them in Nagasaki City.

A total of 47,057 survivors (including the ten who experienced both bombings) lived outside the prefectures of Hiroshima and Nagasaki; they were 16.6 percent of the nationwide total. Males were 66 percent of this national total. Hiroshima's survivors in this group numbered 33,440 (21.1 percent) against Nagasaki's 13,617 (10.9 percent). (See table 11.2.)

Ten years later, on the occasion of the October 1960 national census, the two prefectures of Hiroshima and Nagasaki conducted their own joint survey

TABLE 11.2
Residential A-bomb Survivors, by Sex, 1950

Group Totals (percentage total)	Residence at Survey Time (subgroups)	Males (percentage of subgroup)	(percentage of group)	Females (percentage of subgroup)	(percentage of group)
Nationwide 283,498 + 10* (100)		138,456 + 9	(48.8)	145,042 + 1	(51.2)
Hiroshima survivors 158,597 + 10* (55.9)	subgroup total	79,536 + 9 (100)	(50.1)	79,061 + 1 (100)	(49.9)
	Hiroshima City	42,591 (53.5)	(43.4)	55,511 (70.2)	(56.6)
	Hiroshima Prefecture (excluding Hiroshima City)	14,641 (18.4)	(54.1)	12,424 (15.7)	(45.9)
	other prefectures	22,304 + 9 (28.1)	(66.7)	11,126 + 1 (14.1)	(33.3)
Nagasaki survivors 124,901 + 10* (44.1)	subgroup total	58,920 + 9 (100)	(47.2)	65,981 + 1 (100)	(52.8)
	Nagasaki City	42,251 + 3 (71.7)	(43.7)	54,328 (82.4)	(56.3)
	Nagasaki Prefecture (excluding Nagasaki City)	7,895 + 3 (13.4)	(53.7)	6,813 + 1 (10.3)	(46.3)
	other prefectures	8,774 + 3 (14.9)	(64.4)	4,840 (7.3)	(35.6)

* "+ 10" denotes people who were in both cities at bombing times.

Source: Hiroshima A-bomb Medical Care History Editorial Committee (HAMCH), *Hiroshima Genbaku Iryōshi* (Hiroshima: Hiroshima Genbaku Shōgai Taisaku Kyōgikai, 1961), pp. 462–63. H. Maki, *Kōsei no Shihyō* [Index of Health and Welfare Statistics], ABCC studies (1959) 6(1):14. National Census, ABCC supplementary survey (1 October 1950).

TABLE 11.3

Number of A-bomb Survivors, according to Joint Hiroshima-Nagasaki Prefectures' Survey,
1 October 1960*

Bombed Area	Resident of Hiroshima at Survey Time			Resident of Nagasaki at Survey Time		
	Total	Hiroshima City	Nearby	Total	Nagasaki City	Nearb
Hiroshima:						
Directly damaged in the city	108,110	79,835	28,275	826	417	40
Others affected†	55,514	13,005	42,509	184	59	12
Totals	163,624	92,840	70,784	1,010	476	53
Nagasaki:						
Directly damaged in the city	384	239	145	84,894	72,658	12,23
Others affected†	54	29	25	16,707	6,675	10,03
Totals	438	268	170	101,601	79,333	22,26

* Survey limited to residents of Hiroshima and Nagasaki prefectures.
† Indirectly affected persons: early entrants, fetal victims, and so on.
Source: Hiroshima Prefectural Office and Hiroshima City Office, *Hiroshimaken Genbaku Hibakusha Jittai Chōsa Hōkoku* [Hiroshima Prefectu
A-bomb Survivors Actual Status Survey Report], 1960 (Hiroshima: Hiroshimaken-Hiroshimashi, 1964a). Nagasaki Prefectural Office and Nagasa
City Office, *Nagasakiken Genbaku Hibakusha Jittai Chōsa Kekkahyō* [Table of Results of Nagasaki Prefecture A-bomb Survivors Actual Stat
Survey], 1960 (Nagasaki: Nagasakiken-Nagasakishi, 1964).

to determine the situation of A-bomb survivors within their respective borders. The results of this joint survey appear in table 11.3. Of survivors directly affected in Hiroshima City, 108,110 were living in Hiroshima Prefecture, 826 in Nagasaki Prefecture—a total of 108,936. Of Nagasaki's directly affected survivors, 84,894 lived in Nagasaki Prefecture, 384 in Hiroshima Prefecture— a total of 85,278. This survey dealt only with those living in the two prefectures, but it nonetheless produced detailed counts of directly affected victims as well as early entrants and others affected, whether or not they held health books issued under the 1957 A-bomb Victims Medical Care Law.*

In regard to sex distribution and bombing-time circumstances of both directly and indirectly affected A-bomb survivors, one should first note that the total number of A-bomb victims surviving in Hiroshima's case was 164,634, in Nagasaki's 102,039 (figure 11.2)—an overall total of 266,673. Notably large groups among Hiroshima survivors were directly affected females (37 percent) and indirectly affected males who were early entrants (18 percent); among Nagasaki survivors, the large groups were directly affected males (28 percent) and females (39 percent) who had been 2 kilometers or more from the hypo-center.*

The 1960 joint Hiroshima-Nagasaki prefectural survey and the 1950 ABCC supplementary survey were both conducted in conjunction with the national

* Hiroshima Prefectural Office and Hiroshima City Office 1964a; Nagasaki Prefectural Office and Nagasaki City Office 1964.

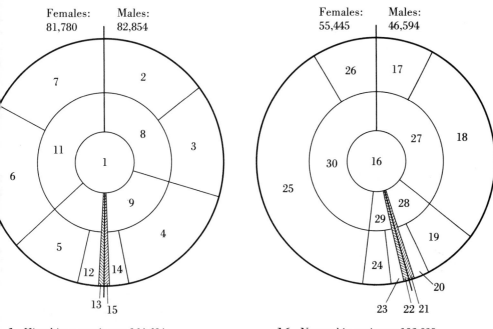

Females: Males:
81,780   82,854

Females: Males:
55,445   46,594

1. Hiroshima survivors: 164,634
2. Within 2-km range: 24,253
3. Outside 2-km range: 24,300
4. Early entrants into burned-demolished
   area: 28,839
5. Early entrants into burned-demolished
   area: 15,408
6. Outside 2-km range: 31,699
7. Within 2-km range: 28,684
8. Directly affected: 48,553
9. Others affected: 33,175
10. Others affected: 20,207
11. Directly affected: 60,383
12. Others affected: 4,799
13. Fetal victims: 1,190
14. Others affected: 4,336
15. Fetal victims: 1,126

16. Nagasaki survivors: 102,039
17. Within 2-km range: 7,938
18. Outside 2-km range: 28,311
19. Early entrants into burned-demolished
    area: 7,424
20. Others affected: 2,128
21. Fetal victims: 793
22. Fetal victims: 778
23. Others affected: 1,750
24. Early entrants into burned-demolished
    area: 3,888
25. Outside 2-km range: 40,050
26. Within 2-km range: 8,979
27. Directly affected: 36,249
28. Others affected: 9,552
29. Others affected: 5,638
30. Directly affected: 49,029

Figure 11.2. Sex distribution and bombing-time circumstances of A-bomb survivors in Hiroshima and Nagasaki (Joint Hiroshima-Nagasaki prefectures' survey, 1 October 1960 [Hiroshima Prefectural Office and Hiroshima City Office 1964a; and Nagasaki Prefectural Office and Nagasaki City Office 1964]).

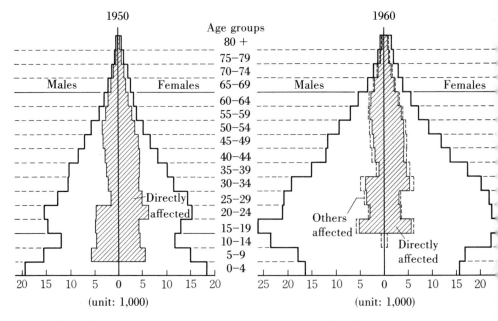

Figure 11.3. Relation of A-bomb survivors to population in Hiroshima in 1950 and 1960, by age group and sex (1950 data from ABCC Supplementary Survey [Hiroshima Prefectural Office and Hiroshima City Office 1964a; Lange, Moloney, and Yamawaki 1954; Prime Minister's Office, Statistics Bureau 1954; and Prime Minister's Office, Statistics Bureau 1963]).

Figure 11.4. Relation of A-bomb survivors to population in Nagasaki in 1950 and 1960, by age and sex (1950 data from ABCC Supplementary Survey [Nagasaki Prefectural Office and Nagasaki City Office 1964; Prime Minister's Office, Statistics Bureau 1953; and Prime Minister's Office, Statistics Bureau 1962]).

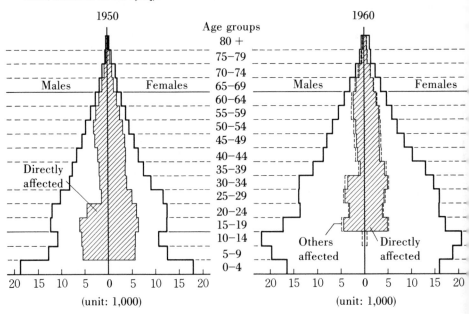

census made in those years. When the two surveys are compared with the populations of the two cities, graphs showing the relation of A-bomb survivors to population by five-year age groups for each city can be drawn, as in figures 11.3 and 11.4.*

In both cities the percentage of A-bomb victims in the upper age brackets is high. The percentage of males in the twenty-five-to-thirty-nine age range is distinctly low—indeed, less than the population between fifty and sixty (see figure 10.15). The reason presumably is that many younger men were absent from the city for military service or compulsory work in the 1944–45 period, and others migrated from the cities in the first five years following the war. Details of the postwar migration, however, remain unclear. Figure 11.5 compares age-group changes in the ten-year interval between the 1950 and the 1960 surveys.

In 1950 both Hiroshima and Nagasaki show increases in their youth populations but significant decreases in A-bomb survivors between ten and twenty-four years of age (between twenty and thirty-four in 1960) as well as in survivors who were forty-five and over (fifty-five and over in 1960). The rates of decrease among A-bomb survivors in Hiroshima and Nagasaki are clearly higher than the nationwide rates for the same age groups (table 11.4) (Prime

* Hiroshima Prefectural Office and Hiroshima City Office 1964a; Lange, Moloney, and Yamawaki 1954; Nagasaki Prefectural Office and Nagasaki City Office 1964; Prime Minister's Office, Statistics Bureau 1953; 1954; 1962; 1963.

Figure 11.5. Comparison of changes in relation of A-bomb survivors to population of Hiroshima and Nagasaki during the 1950–60 period, by age group and sex (directly affected survivors only) (1950 data from ABCC Supplementary Survey [Hiroshima Prefectural Office and Hiroshima City Office 1964a; Nagasaki Prefectural Office and Nagasaki City Office 1964; Prime Minister's Office, Statistics Bureau 1953; Prime Minister's Office, Statistics Bureau 1962; and Prime Minister's Office, Statistics Bureau 1963]).

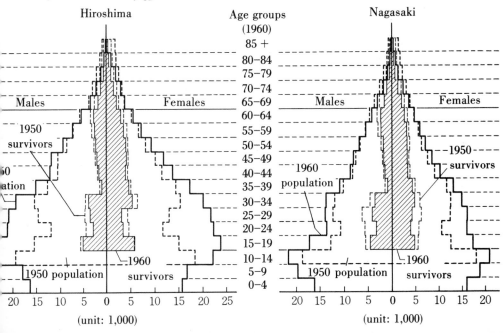

TABLE 11.4

Changes in the Number of Hiroshima's and Nagasaki's Directly Affected A-Bomb Survivors in Relation to NonVictims, by Age and Sex

Age Groups (survey time, 1950)	Males					Females				
	Nationwide	Hiroshima City		Nagasaki City		Nationwide	Hiroshima City		Nagasaki City	
		A-bomb Victims	Non-Victims	A-bomb Victims	Non-Victims		A-bomb Victims	Non-Victims	A-bomb Victims	Non-Victims
0–14	−3.5	−18.8	67.6	−29.8	32.2	−1.8	−10.3	65.2	−20.7	37.8
15–29	−3.4	−19.0	42.7	−29.5	25.5	−3.0	−16.0	65.2	−19.6	40.5
30–49	−6.5	−11.8	17.4	−15.5	5.7	−4.9	−8.8	32.6	−12.2	21.1
50–64	−24.9	−27.5	4.9	−32.9	−4.0	−17.4	−19.2	32.3	−23.8	8.1
65 and over	−65.1	−64.9	−39.1	−67.1	−51.1	−57.0	−56.2	30.4	−61.9	−44.9
All ages	−8.9	−22.0	42.4	−29.4	20.9	−7.5	−16.1	27.1	−21.1	30.9

N.B. Because Hiroshima and Nagasaki each absorbed three neighboring towns between 1950 and 1960, the 1950 nonvictim populations of both cities were adjusted by the 1960 national census for these areas.

1950 data are taken from the ABCC Supplementary Survey.

Source: Hiroshima Prefectural Office and Hiroshima City Office. *Hiroshimaken Genbaku Hibakusha Jittai Chōsa Hōkoku* [Hiroshima Prefecture A-bomb Survivors Actual Status Survey Report], 1960 (Hiroshima: Hiroshimaken-Hiroshimashi, 1964a). Nagasaki Prefectural Office and Nagasaki City Office. *Nagasakiken Genbaku Hibakusha Jittai Chōsa Kekkahyō* [Table of Results of Nagasaki Prefecture A-bomb Survivors Actual Status Survey], 1960 (Nagasaki: Nagasakiken-Nagasakishi, 1964). Prime Minister's Office, Statistics Bureau, *Shōwa Nijūgonen Kokusei Chōsa Hōkoku* [1950 National Census Report], vol. 6: Settled Population and Present Population (Tokyo: Nihon Tōkei Kyōkai, 1951). Prime Minister's Office, Statistics Bureau, *Shōwa Nijūgonen Kokusei Chōsa Hōkoku* [1950 National Census Report], vol. 7: Region and Prefectures Section—34: Hiroshima Prefecture (Tokyo: Nihon Tōkei Kyōkai, 1951). Prime Minister's Office, Statistics Bureau, *Shōwa Nijūgonen Kokusei Chōsa Hōkoku* [1950 National Census Report], vol. 7: Region and Prefectures Section—42: Nagasaki Prefecture (Tokyo: Nihon Tōkei Kyōkai, 1953). Prime Minister's Office, Statistics Bureau, *Shōwa Sanjūgonen Kokusei Chōsa Hōkoku* [1960 National Census Report], vol. 4:—34: Hiroshima Prefecture. (Tokyo: Sōrifu Tōkeikyoku, 1962). Prime Minister's Office, Statistics Bureau, *Shōwa Sanjūgonen Kokusei Chōsa Hōkoku* [1960 National Census Report], vol. 4:—42: Nagasaki Prefecture. (Tokyo: Sōrifu Tōkeikyoku, 1963). Prime Minister's Office, Statistics Bureau, *Shōwa Sanjūgonen Kokusei Chōsa Hōkoku* [1960 National Census Report], vol. 1: Total Number of Population (Tokyo: Sōrifu Tōkeikyoku, 1966).

Minister's Office, Statistics Bureau 1951*b*; 1966). Indeed, for all ages the rates of decrease among males in Hiroshima (22 percent) and Nagasaki (29.4 percent) greatly exceed the nationwide rate (8.9 percent), as do those rates for females in Hiroshima (16.1 percent) and Nagasaki (21.1 percent) compared with the nationwide rate (7.5 percent).

The Hiroshima and Nagasaki decreases in A-bomb survivors are regarded as resulting more from moves to other places for work and marriage than from deaths, particularly among teenagers and young adults of working age. The decline in survivors between fifty and sixty-four years of age—though their migration to other places is thought to have been comparatively low— still exceeds the national rate; while that among survivors sixty-five and over is only slightly less than the national rate. In the 1950–60 decade, however, Hiroshima and Nagasaki each absorbed three neighboring towns, thereby presumably adding to their populations directly affected survivors of relatively older ages who resided in these towns. Although details of A-bomb victims resident in these towns in 1950 are not known, and thus adjustments for the comparable city sections in 1960 cannot be made, death probably accounted for much of the decline.

Another source of information on the number of A-bomb survivors is the health-book system of the A-bomb Victims Medical Care Law passed in 1957, though the data is incomplete as not all A-bomb victims are included in the law's scope.* The range of A-bomb victims covered by this law is outlined in table 11.5. Moreover, when the law went into effect, quite a few

* The health book is a passport-size booklet that certifies its holder as an A-bomb victim. A written application for the book must be accompanied by one of the following certificates:
  1. A certificate of disaster or some other certificate issued by a public office at the time of the bombing;
  2. In the absence of either of the above certificates, any recorded document such as a letter with the date of the bombing or a photograph taken at that time;
  3. For an applicant lacking such a recorded document, any certificate issued by a mayor or head of village;
  4. For an applicant lacking any document to satisfy the preceding requirements, a certificate drawn up by two or more persons, excluding blood relatives to the third degree; or
  5. If an applicant does not have any of the preceding documents or certificates, a certificate written by someone other than the applicant, or the applicant's own statement about

TABLE 11.5

A-Bomb Victims Covered by the A-Bomb Victims Medical Care Law, 1957

Legal Source	Category	Definition
·ticle 2, Section 1	directly damaged	persons who, at the time of bombing, were residing within the city limits of Hiroshima or Nagasaki, or within definite areas adjacent to these cities
·ticle 2, Section 2	early entrants into burned areas	persons who, within two weeks of the time of bombing, entered areas within 2 km of the hypocenter of either city
·ticle 2, Section 3	rescue workers and others affected	persons other than the above who, at the time of bombing or after, were bodily affected by radiation (e.g., when aiding A-bomb victims, disposing of corpses, or aboard uncovered vessels outside burned areas mentioned above)
·ticle 2, Section 4	fetal victims	fetuses of mothers who qualify as any one of the above

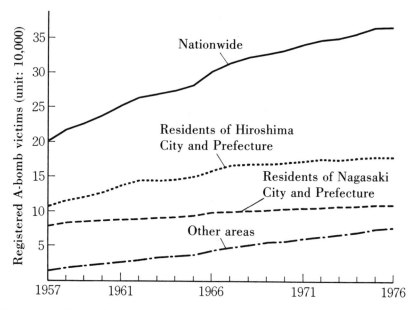

Figure 11.6A. Increase in the number of A-bomb survivors under the A-bomb Victims Medical Care Law, 1957–76.

Figure 11.6B. Percentage of increase/decrease of atomic bomb survivors by region (1957–76).

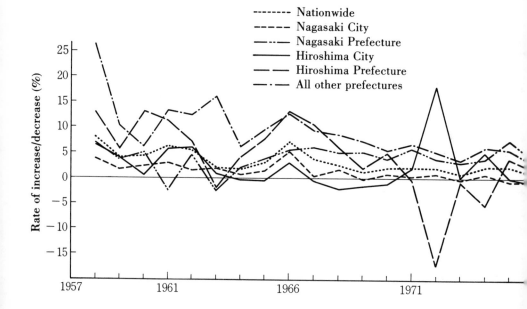

A-bomb victims did not apply for health books. Among reasons for not applying were: (1) the law provided only medical care without sufficient aid of other kinds; (2) excessive difficulty in locating witnesses to confirm one's eligibility; and (3) reluctance to be identified as an A-bomb victim due to the prejudice toward and the lack of understanding of victims and because the aid was inadequate. There was also strong feeling against receiving aid unless it came as *compensation* from the state; consequently, many who applied, and qualified, refused to accept aid.

The A-bomb Victims Medical Care Law was subsequently revised several times to widen the scope of eligibility (see pages 549–51). The resultant increases from 1957 to 1976 in the number of registered A-bomb survivors, and the rates of increase by prefecture and city, are shown in figures 11.6A and 11.6B. The total number of registered A-bomb victims at the end of the first year (31 March 1958) was 200,984. Of these, 106,952 (53.2 percent) lived in Hiroshima Prefecture, 79,065 (39.3 percent) in Nagasaki Prefecture,

---

the actual condition of the bombing and a written oath of his or her own, together with a deposition of some person who actually met the applicant somewhere in the city, or saw him or her at a relief station inside or outside the city, or fled with him or her to a safer place immediately after the bombing.

TABLE 11.6

Residential Locations (31 March 1977) of A-bomb Survivors Registered Under the A-bomb Victims Medical Care Law, according to Situation at the Time of Bombing *

Residence		People Directly Affected	Early Entrants	Rescue Workers and Others	Fetal Victims	Total
Hiroshima Prefecture	Hiroshima City	82,518 (34.2)	25,797 (24.4)	3,040 (20.8)	2,029 (40.7)	113,384 (30.9)
	other cities, towns, and villages nearby	27,888 (11.6)	32,307 (30.5)	5,350 (36.5)	708 (14.2)	66,253 (18.1)
	total	110,406 (45.8)	58,104 (54.9)	8,390 (57.3)	2,737 (54.9)	179,637 (49.0)
Nagasaki Prefecture	Nagasaki City	58,292 (24.2)	21,321 (20.1)	1,341 (9.2)	1,038 (20.8)	81,992 (22.4)
	other cities, towns, and villages nearby	14,298 (5.9)	9,671 (9.1)	3,844 (26.2)	131 (2.6)	27,944 (7.6)
	total	72,590 (30.1)	30,992 (29.3)	5,185 (35.4)	1,169 (23.4)	109,936 (30.0)
Other prefectures		58,026 (24.1)	16,770 (15.8)	1,071 (7.3)	1,083 (21.7)	76,950 (21.0)
Total		241,022 (100.0)	105,866 (100.0)	14,646 (100.0)	4,989 (100.0)	366,523 (100.0)

* Figures in parentheses are percentages.
    Source: Ministry of Health and Welfare, Public Health Bureau, Planning Section, *Shōwa Gojūnendo Genshibakudan Hibakusha Taisaku no Gaiyō* [Summary of Measures for Atomic Bomb Survivors in 1976]. (Tokyo: Kōseishō Kōshūeiseikyoku Kikakuka, 1977).

and 14,967 (7.5 percent) in other prefectures. Ten years later, the registrations for fiscal year 1966 (ending 31 March 1967) had grown to 301,695 (Hiroshima Prefecture, 160,395, or 53.2 percent; Nagasaki Prefecture, 98,253, or 32.5 percent; and other prefectures, 43,047, or 14.3 percent). The number of registered A-bomb victims living outside Hiroshima and Nagasaki prefectures had almost doubled. By the end of fiscal year 1976 (31 March 1977), the total number of registrations had climbed to 366,523, or 1.8 times the initial 1957 count. In Hiroshima Prefecture the count was 179,637 (49 percent), and in Nagasaki Prefecture, 109,936 (30 percent), or 1.7 and 1.4 times, respectively, the initial numbers. Registrations in other prefectures had jumped 5.1 times, to 76,950 (21 percent). Breakdown of the 1976 registrations is given in table 11.6.

Increases of registered A-bomb survivors in the major prefectures and big city areas (metropolitan and urban prefectures*) are indicated in figure 11.7. Because of inadequacies in the initial legislation, applicants for health books in the early stage were scarce; and therefore registrations in the first year probably should not be used as a base. Taking, rather, the number of

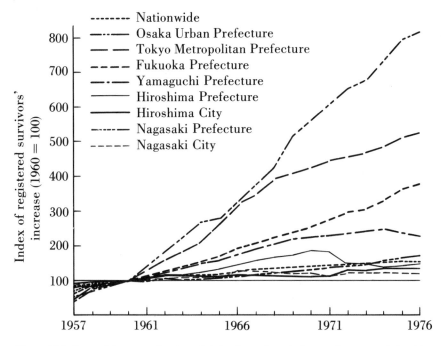

Figure 11.7. Rates of increase of registered A-bomb survivors in key prefectures, and the cities of Hiroshima and Nagasaki (1957–76).

* Administrative units in Japan include, in addition to one region *(dō)* and prefectures *(ken)*, two special categories for the larger cities: one is *to,* here rendered "metropolitan prefecture" (Tokyo is the only instance); and the other is *fu,* here rendered "urban prefecture" (Osaka and Kyoto).

registrations in 1960—when the first revision of the law created a "Special A-bomb Victims" category, and medical aid funds for general symptoms were greatly increased—we find that registrations in Osaka (urban prefecture) had risen by 1976 to eight times the 1960 base, in Tokyo (metropolitan prefecture) to five times that base. On the other hand, A-bomb survivors in Yamaguchi Prefecture, once numerous, have recently been decreasing.

While registered A-bomb survivors increased greatly in the two decades, the rate of increase has slackened recently; all areas show decreases in 1975 and 1976, and Hiroshima and Nagasaki cities registered losses (figure 11.6B). The marked fluctuations for Hiroshima Prefecture and Hiroshima City in 1972 stemmed from the latter's incorporation of neighboring towns.

These data on registered A-bomb survivors, compiled by the Ministry of Health and Welfare, tell us only how many registered survivors are in which prefecture or city; it has not been organized into tables on the overall or prefecture/city situations in regard to age and sex distribution, new registrations, mobility, deaths, and other vital statistics necessary to analyzing the A-bomb survivors' conditions.

First of all, subgroups of the Hiroshima and Nagasaki numbers, as defined, for instance, by sex and age distribution, have not been made known. Second, even as late as 1974 there was no definition of the "Special A-bomb Victims" category, nor were any details given that would permit subdivision of mothers of fetal victims. The data, in a word, were not useful for further analysis of the survivors' situations, especially as no distinctions were made between the first survivors and later generations.

Finally, in September 1975 the Ministry of Health and Welfare carried out a survey of the actual conditions of registered A-bomb survivors throughout the country. The results of this survey make it possible to clarify some of the vital statistics of the survivors (Ministry of Health and Welfare 1977c).

Graphs drawn from the 1975 survey to show male-female ratios of survivors according to individual situations at bombing times and age distribution are presented in figures 11.8 and 11.9. Survivors of the Hiroshima bombing predominate in all categories and are 64 percent of the total. Females outnumber males in most age groups and are 55.5 percent of the total (males, 44.5 percent). Females are particularly numerous among survivors in the "rescue workers and others" group, a startling 81.6 percent (males, 18.4 percent), and also in the fifty-to-fifty-nine age group (age at survey time). In the early entrants group, females under forty and between fifty and fifty-nine years old are slightly more numerous; but males dominate the group as a whole, especially in the forty-to-forty-nine and the sixty-to-sixty-nine age groups, and are nearly double the women for age seventy and above. Age differentiation totals for Hiroshima and Nagasaki are not available.

The Ministry of Health and Welfare has published data on the residential

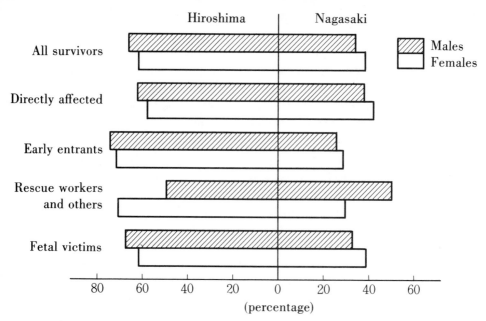

Figure 11.8. Sex distribution in 1975 of Hiroshima and Nagasaki survivors, by situation at bombing times (Ministry of Health and Welfare, Public Health Bureau, Planning Section, 1977c).

Figure 11.9. Age distribution in 1975 of A-bomb survivors, by situation at bombing times (Ministry of Health and Welfare, Public Health Bureau, Planning Section, 1977c).

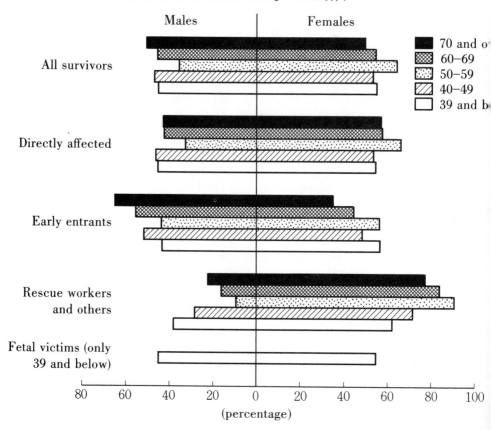

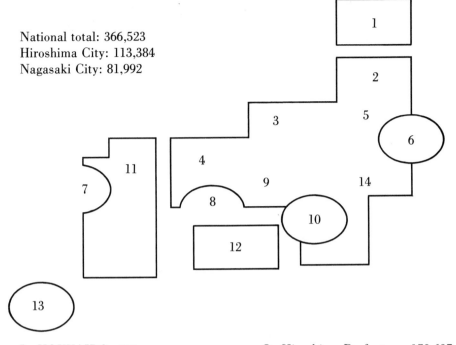

National total: 366,523
Hiroshima City: 113,384
Nagasaki City: 81,992

1. HOKKAIDO: 612
2. TŌHOKU: 754
3. HOKURIKU-KŌSHIN'ETSU: 1,020
4. CHŪGOKU: 192,533
5. KANTŌ: 18,921
6. Tokyo Metropolitan Prefecture: 9,397
7. Nagasaki Prefecture: 109,936

8. Hiroshima Prefecture: 179,637
9. KINKI: 18,247
10. Osaka Urban Prefecture: 9,525
11. KYŪSHŪ: 126,254
12. SHIKOKU: 3,511
13. Okinawa Prefecture: 327
14. TŌKAI: 4,344

Figure 11.10. Regional distribution (31 March 1977) of A-bomb survivors registered under the A-bomb Victims Medical Care Law [Ministry of Health and Welfare 1977*d*]. Totals for Hiroshima and Nagasaki prefectures include totals for Hiroshima and Nagasaki cities.

locations, as of 31 March 1977, of A-bomb survivors registered under the A-bomb Victims Medical Care Law (table 11.6 and figure 11.10). Of a total of 366,523, directly affected A-bomb survivors number 241,022 (65.7 percent); early entrants number 105,866 (28.9 percent); others affected, 14,646 (4 percent); and fetal victims, 4,989 (1.4 percent). Half of the survivors live in Hiroshima Prefecture; three tenths, in Nagasaki Prefecture.

These figures do not, of course, account for A-bomb victims outside the law's scope, such as households with A-bomb victims and second- and third-generation descendants. Only when we have a complete account of these households and persons can we adequately evaluate the full social and psychological impact of atomic destruction and, thus, the damage done to all family, community, and social organizations; and only then as well can proper policies and measures for governmental and community care of all victims be systematically planned and executed. The coordinated efforts of all sectors of society are needed to provide such a full and accurate account.

Occupational Factors

Hiroshima in 1945 had many light industries as well as commercial and service enterprises. In Nagasaki, heavy industries dominated, particularly Mitsubishi Shipbuilding. Even in Hiroshima, though, five major firms—Nippon Steel, Tōyō Kōgyō (motor vehicles), Mitsubishi Shipbuilding, Mitsubishi Machinery, and the army clothing depot—employed 46 percent of the city's total workforce. The top ten firms employed an estimated 64 percent of the workforce. As these larger industries were dispersed in Hiroshima's suburbs, however, they suffered little direct damage and few casualties. The heaviest damages befell the medium- and small-sized enterprises in the city's center (United States Strategic Bombing Survey, Urban Areas Division, 1947a, pp. 25, 26, 28). In Nagasaki, however, the four major firms—Mitsubishi Shipbuilding, Mitsubishi Electrical Machinery, Mitsubishi Munitions, and Mitsubishi Steel—employed 85 percent to 90 percent of the total workforce; and of these, major plants of Mitsubishi Munitions and Mitsubishi Steel were located in the central bombed area (United States Strategic Bombing Survey, Urban Areas Division 1947b).

A comparison of the February 1944 and November 1945 censuses shows that the bombings and defeat in the Second World War brought about population declines of 58 percent and 47 percent in Hiroshima and Nagasaki, respectively. It took the two cities about ten years to recover their former population levels. Hiroshima lost only 55 percent of its male population, but 61 percent of its female population; while Nagasaki lost 49 percent of its male but only 45 percent of its female population. The decline was especially heavy among males and females around age twenty (pages 369–403). These population decreases include both deaths and migration. The 1950 Atomic Bomb Casualty Commission survey indicates that male and female victims were about equal in Hiroshima; but in Nagasaki, female (53 percent) outnumbered male (47 percent) victims (see table 11.2).

As for the occupational picture, a Hiroshima Prefecture sampling (10 percent) of Hiroshima City's population in 1958 showed fewer A-bomb victims than nonvictims in service, transport, communications, and specialized-skill-related jobs, but more victims than nonvictims in skilled manufacturing, nonskilled work, retail trade, and forestry, farming, and fishing (table 11.7) (Hiroshima Prefectural Office and Hiroshima City Office 1960, pp. 18–19). Similar 1960 surveys in Hiroshima and Nagasaki (cities and prefectures) showed increases in farming and fishing, as the surveys were extended to include towns and villages. Those with manufacturing and nonskilled jobs, accounted for more than half of the victims' occupations (table 11.8).*

---

* Hiroshima Prefectural Office and Hiroshima City Office 1969a, pp. 23–25; Nagasaki Shiyakusho 1964, pp. 80–81.

TABLE 11.7

Occupational Distribution, by Sex, of A-bomb Victims and Nonvictims in Hiroshima, 1958*

Occupation	Total		Males		Females	
	A-bomb Victims	Non-Victims	A-bomb Victims	Non-Victims	A-bomb Victims	Non-Victims
Specialized skills	5.9	9.0	6.5	9.0	4.8	8.8
Administrative	4.6	4.4	7.0	5.9	0.3	0.6
Office	16.5	19.5	14.6	18.6	19.9	19.7
Retail	22.1	19.7	19.8	18.7	26.3	22.0
Farming, forestry, and fishing	6.4	1.9	5.8	1.8	7.6	2.1
Mining and quarrying	0.0	0.2	0.1	0.2	—	0.2
Transport and communications	3.3	4.7	5.0	6.6	0.2	0.3
Skilled and nonskilled manufacturing jobs	33.2	28.2	36.3	32.0	27.7	19.1
Services	7.9	13.0	5.0	7.1	13.2	27.2
Unspecified	0.0	—	0.1	—	—	—

* Figures are percentages of all employees in Hiroshima.
Source: Hiroshima Prefectural Office and Hiroshima City Office, *Shōwa Sanjūsannen Jūgatsu Ichijitsu Hiroshima Shinai Genshibaku-dan Hibakusha Tōkei Hōkoku* [Report on Statistics of Atomic Bomb Survivors in Hiroshima City as of 1 October 1958] (Hiroshima: Hiroshimaken Tōkeika, 1960), pp. 18–19.

TABLE 11.8

Occupational Distribution of A-bomb Victims in Hiroshima and Nagasaki, 1960*

Occupation	Hiroshima[1]			Nagasaki[2]
	Total	Males	Females	Total
Specialized skills	5.7	5.9	5.3	6.8
Administrative	3.2	4.6	0.5	2.1
Office	13.4	12.9	14.3	14.1
Retail	13.1	10.9	17.2	13.9
Farming, forestry, and fishing	28.0	26.9	30.0	23.5
Mining and quarrying	0.1	0.2	0.1	0.7
Transport and communications	3.4	4.7	0.8	3.6
Skilled manufacturing	20.9	24.0	15.1	23.5
Nonskilled manufacturing	6.7	5.9	8.2	5.8
Services	4.6	3.2	7.2	6.0
Unspecified	0.9	0.8	1.3	—

* Figures are percentages of all employees in Hiroshima and Nagasaki.
Source: (1) Hiroshima Prefectural Office and Hiroshima City Office, *Hiroshimaken Genbaku Hi-bakusha Jittai Chōsa Hōkoku* [Hiroshima Prefecture A-bomb Survivors Actual Status Survey Report], 1960 (Hiroshima: Hiroshimaken-Hiroshimashi, 1964a), pp. 23–25.
(2) Nagasaki Shiyakusho, Civil Welfare Department, Social Affairs Section, *Nagasakishi o Shutosuru Genbaku Hibakusha Jittai Chōsa no Kenkyū* [Study of A-bomb Survivors Actual Status Survey Mainly with Reference to Nagasaki City] (Nagasaki, 1964), pp. 80–81.

The first nationwide survey was made in 1965, by which time the number of A-bomb victims engaged in farming and fishing had decreased; and these, with skilled and nonskilled workers, had dropped below half of all victims and even below national levels. A-bomb victims' employment in specialized skills, office, retail, and administrative jobs had, rather, risen above national levels (table 11.9) (Ministry of Health and Welfare 1967b, p. 28). The shifts

TABLE 11.9

Nationwide Occupational Distribution of A-bomb Victims, by Sex, in Relation to National Averages, 1965*

	Males		Females	
Occupation	A-bomb Victims	National Average	A-bomb Victims	National Average
Specialized skills	8.2	5.9	6.8	5.2
Administrative	5.0	4.6	0.8	0.4
Office	14.6	12.0	20.0	14.6
Retail	11.9	10.8	20.5	13.1
Farming, forestry, and fishing	17.5	19.5	19.5	32.4
Mining and quarrying	0.5	0.7	0.1	0.1
Transport and communications	5.2	6.3	1.2	1.4
Skilled and nonskilled manufacturing jobs	32.5	35.3	20.1	22.0
Services	4.6	4.9	11.0	10.8

* Figures are percentages of all employees.
Source: Ministry of Health and Welfare, Public Health Bureau. *Shōwa Yonjūnendo Genshibakudan Hibakusha Jittai Chōsa* [1965 Actual Status Survey of Atomic Bomb Survivors. Summary of Health Survey and Living Survey], (Tokyo: Kōseishō Kōshūeiseikyoku, 1967b), p. 28.

in employment probably reflect the influence of Japan's rapid economic growth on the A-bomb victims, who were largely concentrated in major cities, including Hiroshima and Nagasaki.

The 1965 survey had three parts: the Basic Survey, the Health Survey, and the Living Survey. In the Basic Survey, the Ministry of Health and Welfare added 45,543 new applicants for A-bomb health books, making a total of 277,955 persons surveyed. But the totals reported did not include all the late applicants. The Health Survey covered 9,042 persons; the Living Survey, 13,593 (9,070 households). The employment rate shown by the Basic Survey was 82 percent; that by the Living Survey, 86.5 percent—both lower than the national rate of 88.5 percent (if the national rate equals 100, then 92.7 and 97.7, respectively). The gap is most notable for the twenty-to-twenty-nine and fifty-five-to-sixty-four age groups, though the rate for those age seventy and over exceeded the national rate. For females, the rates were 38.3 percent in the Basic Survey, 36.5 percent in the Living Survey—both above the national rate of 34.5 percent, a trend most notable for females aged sixty and over (table 11.10) (Ministry of Health and Welfare 1967b, p.

TABLE 11.10

Employment Rates of A-bomb Victims, by Sex, 1965

Age Group	Males			Females		
	All A-bomb Victims	A-bomb Health-book Holders	National Average*	All A-bomb Victims	A-bomb Health-book Holders	National Average*
20–24	73.8%	73.4%	81.7%	60.3%	60.9%	60.3%
25–29	88.0%	87.9%	96.5%	33.9%	34.5%	32.9%
30–34	91.6%	91.7%	97.3%	33.3%	33.6%	31.5%
35–39	91.7%	91.6%	97.5%	40.5%	40.7%	36.7%
40–44	90.4%	90.3%	97.2%	41.6%	41.6%	39.2%
45–49	89.8%	89.6%	96.7%	44.4%	44.0%	39.0%
50–54	88.2%	87.8%	95.2%	40.5%	40.6%	33.5%
55–59	80.1%	80.2%	89.5%	33.8%	33.6%	27.4%
60–64	71.0%	70.8%	78.9%	27.2%	27.0%	18.0%
65–69	60.6%	60.2%	65.3%	22.0%	21.9%	12.6%
70 and over	40.4%	40.4%	32.8%	10.5%	10.7%	4.7%
Gross rate	79.2%	78.8%	88.5%	37.2%	36.9%	34.5%
Adjusted rate†	82.2%	82.0%	88.5%	38.1%	38.3%	34.5%

* National figures are from the 1965 Basic Employment Survey.
† Adjusted to national age composition.
Source: Ministry of Health and Welfare, Public Health Bureau, *Shōwa Yonjūnendo Genshibakudan Hibakusha Jittai Chōsa* [1965 Actual Status Survey of Atomic Bomb Survivors. Summary of Basic Survey] (Tokyo: Kōseishō Kōshūeiseikyoku, 1967*a* [p. 7]; 1967*b* [p. 23]).

23; 1967*a*, p. 7). A 1960 Hiroshima Prefecture/City survey yielded employment rates of 85 percent for males and 45 percent for females, or roughly the same as the results of the 1965 Living Survey, though rates of a similar Nagasaki Prefecture/City survey were slightly lower.

Layoffs among A-bomb victims affected 2.8 percent of males (over twice the national rate of 1.1 percent) and 0.8 percent of females (60 percent more than the national 0.5 percent). Unemployed male victims were 46 percent more than the national level (Ministry of Health and Welfare 1967*b*, p. 23). Day laborers among victims amounted to 5.8 percent (national, 3.8 percent) for males and 10.1 percent (national, 5.5 percent) for females (Ministry of Health and Welfare 1967*b*, p. 26).

A 4.4-percent job-change rate for both male and female victims exceeded the national rate of 3.1 percent by two fifths, and job mobility among males in their forties and over was especially high (table 11.11). Among reasons for changing jobs, low wages and resultant hardships, sickness, and aging stand out. These causes, as well as personnel adjustments, company failures, and dismissals, affected female victims more severely than was true nationally. Personal and family reasons, illness, aging, and compulsory retirement seriously affected job changes for both males and females (table 11.12). High death rates and lowered work capacity in A-bomb-affected households pre-

TABLE 11.11

Job-change Rates for Three Age Groups of A-bomb Victims,
by Sex, 1965*

A. Rates for A-bomb Victims

	Totals		Age Group		
	Gross Rate†	Adjusted Rate‡	20–39	40–64	65 and over
Total	4.2	4.4	4.9	4.0	2.0
Males	4.9	5.1	5.5	4.8	2.4
Females	3.0	3.2	3.7	2.8	0.5

B. National Rates

	Total§	Age Group		
		20–39	40–64	65 and over
Total	3.1	4.1	1.9	0.7
Males	3.3	4.2	2.2	0.9
Females	2.7	3.8	1.3	0.4

$$* \text{ Job-change rate} = \frac{\text{Number of changes within one year}}{\text{Total of employed persons}} \times 100.$$

† Gross rate includes 19-year-olds.

‡ Adjusted rate was revised to cover only employees age 20 and over, according to the 1965 Basic Employment Survey.

§ Rates are from 1965 Basic Survey for employed persons age 20 and over.

Source: Ministry of Health and Welfare, Public Health Bureau, *Shōwa Yonjūnendo Genshibakudan Hibakusha Jittai Chōsa* [1965 Actual Status Survey of Atomic Bomb Survivors. Summary of Health Survey and Living Survey] (Tokyo: Kōseishō Kōshūeisei-kyoku, 1967b), p. 30.

TABLE 11.12

Job-change Rates by Sex and Reason for Change among A-bomb Victims, 1965

	Nationwide A-bomb Victims*				National Rates§	
	Gross Rates†		Adjusted Rates‡			
Reason for Change	Males	Females	Males	Females	Males	Females
Personnel adjustments, dismissals, and company bankruptcies	9.3	12.5	8.6	12.6	12.5	8.2
Inadequate income	9.7	19.8	10.3	18.1	11.9	6.6
Temporary work, job insecurity	10.8	4.2	11.7	5.5	12.8	7.8
Better working conditions	9.7	9.4	9.6	4.7	14.8	11.9
Personal or family reasons	45.5	49.0	50.5	57.0	40.1	61.7
Sickness, aging, compulsory retirement	14.9	5.2	9.3	2.2	7.9	3.9

* Figures are percentages of all job changes.

† Gross rate includes 19-year-olds.

‡ Adjusted rate was revised to cover only employees age 20 and over, according to the 1965 Basic Survey.

§ National rates are for employees age 15 and over, from the 1965 Basic Survey.

Source: Ministry of Health and Welfare, Public Health Bureau, *Shōwa Yonjūnendo Genshibakudan Hibakusha Jittai Chōsa* [1965 Actual Status Survey of Atomic Bomb Survivors. Summary of Health Survey and Living Survey] (Tokyo: Kōseishō Kōshūeisei-kyoku, 1967b), p. 31.

sumably made it necessary for females to take jobs—as is evident in the fact that among those who gave such responses to the Health Survey as "weak," "inclined to illness," and "frequently must stay in bed," 16 percent of female victims, as well as 47 percent of male victims, were obliged to work (Ministry of Health and Welfare 1967*b*, p. 24).

Many victims, in fact, had infirmities that made it impossible for them to hold regular jobs. Employment was low among males, particularly the young and elderly; job changes, layoffs, and unemployment were high; and many were day laborers. Given widespread family losses and low wages, many older men and women were forced to find work; the fact that they could find jobs indicates the manpower loss in the young adult generation. In the 1965 Basic Survey, 2.2 percent of the A-bomb victims claimed to have experienced some "adverse discrimination," but the rate rose to 6.2 percent for discrimination experienced when seeking jobs (Ministry of Health and Welfare 1967*a*, pp. 2–3). Average annual income for salaried laborers was 390,000 yen among A-bomb victims, or only 90 percent of the national average of 430,000 yen; income of a worker's household (excluding farmers and fishermen) was slightly less than 88 percent of the national level (Ministry of Health and Welfare 1967*b*, p. 32).

In the second (1975) nationwide Survey of A-bomb Victims Conditions (Basic, Health, and Living surveys) conducted by the Ministry of Health and Welfare, 293,693 (82.2 percent) of the A-bomb health-book holders responded. For the Living Survey, methods similar to the 1965 survey were used to select 16,192 persons (12,822 households) and conduct case studies beginning with initial damages and tracing living conditions to the present (survey time). The data on these A-bomb victims' households were compared with corresponding nonvictims' households of persons thirty and older throughout the nation.

Results of the 1975 survey showed a lower percentage of workers' households among victims than among nonvictims, though farming households had increased among victims. Moreover, A-bomb victims without paying jobs now amounted to 10.6 percent, against 6.2 percent for nonvictims. This trend was especially strong in Hiroshima, where many victims' households ran their own small businesses without hiring other workers (table 11.13). If conditions of employment and occupational status are investigated, a striking difference is found between the employment rates of both victims (56.4 percent) and nonvictims (66.9 percent) (table 11.14), and thus between their unemployment rates. Among males alone, there were more than twice as many unemployed victims (21.7 percent) as unemployed nonvictims (9.3 percent). That A-bomb victims had a lower employment rate than nonvictims was due not to layoffs or dismissals but simply to their inability to do work,

TABLE 11.13

Comparison of Job Distribution among A-bomb Victim and Nonvictim Households, November 1975*

| | All Employed, Self-employed, or Employable Households | | | | | | | | | | | | | All Farm Households | | | |
| | Salaried Households | | | | | | | Self-Employed Households | | | Other Households with Paying Jobs | Others without Paying Jobs | Total | | | | |
	Executive Positions	Small Firms of Fewer than 30 Employees	Firms with 30-999 Employees	Firms or Public Agencies with 1,000 or More Employees	Tempo-rary Workers	Day Labor-ers	Total	Employing Others	Employing No Others	Total				Full-time	Part-time	Other	Total
Nationwide:																	
A-bomb victims	3.2	11.6	21.1	18.9	1.3	1.3	57.4	5.8	11.2	17.0	3.9	10.6	88.9	3.4	6.8	0.9	11.1
Nonvictims	2.8	15.5	24.3	20.7	1.1	1.4	65.7	6.4	9.8	16.2	3.3	6.2	91.4	2.6	5.1	0.9	8.6
Hiroshima City:																	
A-bomb victims	4.3	14.7	22.3	18.3	1.2	1.3	62.1	7.2	12.2	19.3	3.2	11.8	96.5	0.8	2.5	0.2	3.5
Nonvictims	4.1	19.7	26.6	23.6	0.7	0.7	75.4	7.0	8.4	15.4	1.5	5.3	97.6	0.2	2.0	0.2	2.4
Nagasaki City:																	
A-bomb victims	2.5	11.4	24.7	21.0	1.9	1.1	62.7	5.4	10.6	16.0	5.0	14.8	98.5	0.4	0.9	0.2	1.5
Nonvictims	2.6	14.0	27.8	20.8	2.1	1.2	68.5	7.2	10.9	18.1	3.2	8.0	97.8	1.0	0.7	0.5	2.2

* Figures are percentages of all employed, self-employed, or employable households and all farm households.

Source: Ministry of Health and Welfare, Public Health Bureau, Planning Section, *Shōwa Gojūnen Genshibakudan Hibakusha Jittai Chōsa* [1975 Actual Status Survey of Atomic Bomb Survivors], Data Section (Tokyo: Kōseishō Kōshūeiseikyoku Kikakuka, 1977c), p. 6.

TABLE 11.14

Employment and Occupational Conditions among A-bomb Victims and Nonvictims, 1975

Workers with Income*

	Self-Employed			House-hold Employee	Official of Company or Organization	Regular Salaried Worker				Tempo-rary Workers	Day Laborers	Other	Total of Workers with Income
	Employing Others	Employing No Others	Total			Firm with Fewer than 30 Workers	Firm with 30–999 Workers	Firm or Public Agency with 1,000 or More Workers	Total				
Nationwide:													
A-bomb victims	3.6	11.2	14.8	5.5	2.0	8.8	11.1	8.6	28.5	1.8	1.2	2.6	56.4
Nonvictims	3.8	8.9	12.7	1.8	1.8	11.1	16.1	12.4	39.7	1.5	1.4	3.1	66.9
Hiroshima City:													
A-bomb victims	4.3	9.6	13.8	5.9	2.7	10.2	10.7	8.4	29.4	1.9	1.1	2.3	57.2
Nonvictims	4.2	6.2	10.4	4.0	2.5	14.5	18.2	14.6	47.3	1.7	0.7	2.4	69.0
Nagasaki City:													
A-bomb victims	2.8	7.2	10.1	3.7	1.5	7.8	10.7	7.1	25.6	1.9	1.0	2.2	45.9
Nonvictims	4.1	7.7	11.9	5.9	1.6	9.2	16.5	11.6	37.3	2.2	1.1	2.0	62.0

* Figures are percentages of either total A-bomb victims or total nonvictims in Hiroshima, in Nagasaki, or nationally.
Source: Ministry of Health and Welfare, Public Health Bureau, Planning Section, *Shōwa Gojūnen Genshibakudan Hibakusha Jittai Chōsa* [1975 Actual Status Survey of Atomic Bomb Survivors], Data Section (Tokyo: Kōseishō Kōshūeiseikyoku Kikakuka, 1977c), p. 17.

even housework; and this condition increased from 1965 to 1975 (tables 11.15 and 11.16).

The numbers of day laborers, however, declined to approximately the same level as that of nonvictims, because aging and illness rendered more people unable to work. In terms of financial support roles in households, nonvictims were the main income earners in half of their households on a nationwide basis, and 88.6 percent of male nonvictims were the principal income earners in their households. A-bomb victims, however, were the main income earners in only 47.7 percent of their households; and only 80 percent of male victims were the principal breadwinners in their households. Females were the primary earners in only 14.9 percent of nonvictims' households but in 22.3 percent of victims' households. Thus, the level of secondary earners in victims' households was lower (17.9 percent) than in nonvictims' households (20.3 percent). Female dependents were about the same in both groups, but male dependents (12.1 percent) were twice their nonvictim (5.8 percent) counterparts (table 11.17).

Actual expenditures of A-bomb victims' households fell below that of non-victims' households by a monthly rate of 2.2 percent (2,690 yen less than the nonvictim average of 121,300 yen), though the gap was greater in Hiroshima (5.8 percent) and Nagasaki (5.3 percent) (Ministry of Health and Welfare

TABLE 11.15

Comparison of Work Situations of A-bomb Victims and Nonvictims Able and Not Able to Do Productive Work, by City and Sex, 1975

City	Sex	Status	Able to Work				Unable to Work		
			Em-ployed	Laid-off	Unem-ployed	Total	House-work	Other	Total
Hiroshima	total	A-bomb victims	55.5	1.4	0.6	57.5	23.5	18.9	42.5
		nonvictims	68.5	1.1	0.6	70.3	23.3	6.7	29.7
	males	A-bomb victims	78.5	2.4	1.1	81.9	0.7	17.3	18.1
		nonvictims	93.4	1.6	1.0	96.1	0.0	3.8	3.9
	females	A-bomb victims	40.4	0.8	0.3	41.5	38.5	20.0	58.5
		nonvictims	44.3	0.6	0.2	45.1	45.9	9.0	54.9
Nagasaki	total	A-bomb victims	45.0	1.0	0.7	46.7	32.5	20.8	53.3
		nonvictims	61.3	1.4	0.9	63.6	26.2	10.2	36.4
	males	A-bomb victims	70.7	2.1	1.8	74.6	0.9	24.5	25.4
		nonvictims	87.2	2.4	1.7	91.3	0.1	8.6	8.7
	females	A-bomb victims	31.2	0.4	0.2	31.7	49.4	18.8	68.3
		nonvictims	38.3	0.4	0.3	39.0	49.3	11.7	61.0

Source: Ministry of Health and Welfare, Public Health Bureau, Planning Section, *Shōwa Gojūnen Genshibakudan Hibakusha Jittai Chōsa* [1975 Actual Status Survey of Atomic Bomb Survivors], Data Section (Tokyo: Kōseishō Kōshūeiseikyoko Kikakuka, 1977c), pp. 19–20.

TABLE 11.16
Nationwide Changes in Work Situations of A-bomb Victims Able and Unable to Work, 1965–75

Sex	Date of Survey	Able to Work (%)				Unable to Work (%)		
		Em-ployed	Temporarily Laid-off	Unem-ployed	Total	House-work	Other	Total
Males	1965	82.7	3.3	1.6	87.6	0.7	11.7	12.4
	1975	57.4*	3.1	1.2	79.8	0.8	19.4	20.2
Females	1965	43.1	0.9	0.4	44.3	47.7	8.0	55.7
	1975	38.2	0.9	0.3	39.4	42.2	18.5	60.6
Totals	1965	61.6	2.0	1.0	64.6	25.4	10.0	35.4
(male and female)	1975	54.6	1.9	0.7	57.2	24.0	18.9	42.8

* Quoted as given in source; presumably this figure should be 75.4.
Source: Ministry of Health and Welfare, Public Health Bureau, Planning Section, *Shōwa Gojūnen Genshibakudan Hibakusha Jittai Chōsa* [1975 Actual Status Survey of Atomic Bomb Survivors], Data Section (Tokyo: Kōseishō Kōshūeiseikyoku Kikakuka, 1977c), p. 21.

TABLE 11.17
Financial Support Roles in Households of A-bomb Victims and Nonvictims, 1975

	Primary Earner of Income	Secondary Earner of Income	Dependents	Totals
Nationwide:				
A-bomb victims	47.7	17.9	34.4	100
Nonvictims	50.1	20.3	29.6	100
Hiroshima:				
A-bomb victims	46.2	19.8	34.0	100
Nonvictims	53.6	18.5	27.9	100
Nagasaki:				
A-bomb victims	44.7	13.7	41.6	100
Nonvictims	52.4	14.4	33.2	100
Males:				
A-bomb victims	80.0	7.8	12.1	100
Nonvictims	88.6	5.7	5.8	100
Females:				
A-bomb victims	22.3	25.8	51.9	100
Nonvictims	14.9	33.6	51.5	100

Source: Ministry of Health and Welfare, Public Health Bureau, Planning Section, *Shōwa Gojūnen Genshibakudan Hibakusha Jittai Chōsa* [1975 Actual Status Survey of Atomic Bomb Survivors], Data Section (Tokyo: Kōseishō Kōshūeiseikyoku Kikakuka, 1977c), pp. 15–16.

1977*a*, p. 24). The 1965 survey had shown a 12-percent discrepancy in annual incomes and, thus, a 1-percent gap in monthly expenditures for salaried A-bomb victims (excluding those engaged in agriculture and forestry); but the methods used for measuring groups varied, so comparisons with the 1975 survey cannot be readily made. As already observed, employment of A-bomb victims rose in connection with rapid economic growth, but in time victims turned to farming and self-employment—and some lost the ability to work altogether. Hence, it is reasonable to suspect that their average income dropped below the national level. The fact that a commensurate drop in expenditures did not appear may be attributed to the nonvictims who were primary or secondary wage earners in victims' households, if not also to the law providing aid to victims. Compared with nonvictim households, expenditures were notably less for victim households of one-member (15.5 percent) or of two members (6 percent), as well as for households of husband and wife alone (7.5 percent) (Ministry of Health and Welfare 1977*c*, p. 11).

Finally, victims reporting "adverse discrimination" in the 1975 survey amounted to 2 percent; among males, the rate was 3 percent, and for those in their forties, 4 percent (Ministry of Health and Welfare 1977*c*, p. 4).

Marriage among A-bomb Victims

Marriage possibilities for A-bomb victims are seriously affected by their other problems—losses at the time of bombing, aftereffects on health and livelihood, and fear of hereditary effects of radiation. Surveys made in the 1950s, however, disclosed a higher marital rate among victims than among nonvictims, and an ABCC health survey showed a slightly higher than normal marriage rate among males more severely injured by radiation. On the other hand, the Ministry of Health and Welfare's 1965 survey concluded that marriages among male and female A-bomb victims were less than normal for nonvictims when the data were adjusted to comparable age groupings. In fact, adequate research has yet to be done on the relations of various damages and marital status, especially in statistical terms, or on the effects on reproductivity in various generations of the A-bomb victim population.

To recall previous data, Hiroshima's A-bomb victims numbered approximately 350,000 and its dead by November 1945 some 130,000, or 37 percent, of the victims. Similar data for Nagasaki are 270,000 victims, with 60,000 to 70,000 dead, or 24 percent (pages 353–54, 367). The supplementary survey of the 1950 national census, however, recorded 160,000 A-bomb survivors for Hiroshima and 125,000 for Nagasaki. When these totals are deducted the death rate for both cities is 54 percent—close to the proportion in reconstruction surveys for Hiroshima (48.9 percent) and Nagasaki (48 percent). In the heavy bombing of Tokyo on 9 March 1945, for example, there were 100,000 deaths among about 1,000,000 casualties—a death rate of 10 percent; and in the city's Fukagawa ward, where damages were heaviest, 30,000 of the 150,000 casualties died—a rate of 20 percent. The death rates in the A-bombed cities, therefore, were abnormally high (War Disaster Editorial Committee 1973, pp. 26, 28, 284).

The extraordinarily high death rates imposed heavy losses on the households in the cities at bombing times (pages 370–78). Reconstruction surveys of Hiroshima revealed that deaths of household heads ran to 57.7 percent within 0.5 kilometer of the hypocenter and to 44.7 percent between 0.5 and 1 kilometer; among spouses, 49.8 percent died. Although these rates decreased with distance from the hypocenter, the death rates of spouses remained higher than those of household heads. A supplement to the 1975 reconstruction survey showed that deaths of female victims exceeded those of male victims in all districts within a 1-kilometer radius; and the reverse was true beyond that distance. Within the city limits, male deaths were 37.5 percent; female deaths, 29.8 percent (table 11.18). Losses such as these caused extensive ruptures in marital relationships and, thus, great hardship and insecurity in all efforts to reorganize households or to establish new marital relationships.

A 1958 interim census by Hiroshima Prefecture disclosed that, thirteen years after the bombing, the marriage rate for male A-bomb victims was 57.9 percent and for female victims 51.1 percent, both higher than for nonvictim males (49.2 percent) and females (46.4 percent). By age group, however, the rate was especially high for male victims in their twenties and those age sixty and over, and for female victims age sixty and over; it was low for male victims in their thirties and for female victims between ages twenty to fifty-nine. Hence, the relatively high marriage rate for all A-bomb victims resulted from the higher rates in the upper age brackets. That the formation of new households was in fact difficult seems clear from the noticeably low marriage rates for males aged thirty to thirty-nine (seventeen to twenty-six at bombing time) and females aged twenty to twenty-nine (seven to sixteen at bombing time). And, of course, death rates were high for the forty-to-fifty-nine age groups, male and female (table 11.19).

In a 1958 ABCC-conducted health survey of adult A-bomb victims resident in Hiroshima, 70.45 percent of the males and 58.78 percent of the females were already married; of these, 73.13 percent of the males and 57.31 percent of the females had been within 2 kilometers of the hypocenter at bombing

TABLE 11.18

Percentages of Deaths of A-bomb Victims in Hiroshima, by Distance from Hypocenter (Supplement to Ministry of Health and Welfare Reconstruction Survey, 1975)

Distance from Hypocenter (km)	A-bomb Victims			Deaths			Death Rates			
	Males	Females	Sex Unknown	Males	Females	Sex Unknown	Total	Males	Females	Sex Unknown
0–0.5	44.8	54.7	0.5	44.8	54.6	0.6	57.3	57.3	57.2	70.0
0.5–1.0	46.7	53.0	0.3	46.1	53.6	0.3	48.6	48.0	49.1	55.8
1.0–1.5	44.4	55.4	0.2	50.6	49.2	0.2	37.6	42.9	33.5	34.5
1.5–2.0	46.1	53.7	0.2	53.3	46.5	0.2	31.7	36.7	27.4	38.8
Subtotal	45.5	54.3	0.2	50.0	49.8	0.2	38.3	42.1	35.2	45.2
2.0–3.0	46.6	53.3	0.1	54.9	44.9	0.2	28.4	33.5	23.9	36.8
3.0–	47.2	52.7	0.1	54.0	45.9	0.1	28.2	32.2	24.6	52.2
Total for city	46.2	53.7	0.1	51.9	47.9	0.2	33.4	37.5	29.8	43.6

(Left margin label spanning the first five distance rows: Bombed area)

Source: Hiroshima Shiyakusho, Public Health Bureau, A-bomb Survivors Measures Department, *Genbaku Hibakusha Taisaku Jigyō Gaiyō* [Summary of A-bomb Survivors Measures Projects], 1978 (Hiroshima, 1978a), pp. 126–27.

TABLE 11.19

Comparison of Marriage Distribution by Sex and Age among A-bomb Victims and Nonvictims, Hiroshima*

(Hiroshima Prefecture Survey, 1958)

Age Group	Unmarried		Married		Widowed		Separated		Age Distribution	
	Non-victims	A-bomb Victims	Non-victims	A-bomb Victims	Non-victims	A-bomb Victims	Non-victims	A-bomb Victims	Non-victims	A-bomb Victims
Males										
10†–19	99.8	99.7	0.1	0.1	—	—	—	0.1	28.8	19.7
20–29	72.1	64.5	27.1	34.0	0.1	0.1	0.6	1.4	23.7	21.5
30–39‡	7.7	13.1	89.9	84.9	0.2	0.2	2.2	1.8	21.6	12.5
40–49	1.4	0.9	93.8	94.2	1.9	2.7	2.8	2.2	15.1	13.7
50–59	0.5	0.6	89.5	90.2	6.2	6.3	3.8	2.9	7.3	15.5
60 and over	1.3	0.3	73.8	76.1	23.3	22.4	1.8	1.2	3.5	17.1
Total	47.8	35.4	49.2	57.9	1.6	5.2	1.4	1.5	100.0	100.0
Females										
10†–19	99.0	98.9	0.9	1.0	—	—	0.1	0.1	29.3	15.4
20–29	44.0	49.0	54.3	48.6	0.6	1.0	1.2	1.4	27.2	16.0
30–39‡	5.7	8.1	84.6	81.9	5.2	5.8	4.4	4.2	20.2	20.3
40–49	2.2	2.1	77.2	72.5	16.3	20.9	4.3	4.4	12.3	17.1
50–59	1.8	1.1	63.4	62.6	31.2	33.9	3.6	2.4	5.5	15.4
60 and over	2.6	0.2	23.4	28.3	71.1	68.6	3.0	2.9	5.5	15.8
Total	42.7	25.3	46.4	51.1	8.8	21.0	2.1	2.7	100.0	100.0

* Figures are percentages either of total nonvictims or of total A-bomb victims.
† For A-bomb victims, age 12 and over.
‡ At bombing time, ages 17–26.
Source: Hiroshima Prefectural Office and Hiroshima City Office, *Shōwa Sanjūsannen Jūgatsu Ichijitsu Hiroshima Shinai Genshi-bakudan Hibakusha Tōkei Hōkoku* [Report on Statistics of Atomic Bomb Survivors in Hiroshima City as of 1 October 1958] (Hiroshima: Hiroshimaken Tōkeika, 1960), pp. 16–17.

time and showed major symptoms of acute radiation. The 1960 national census recorded marriage rates of 60.8 percent for males and 56.7 percent for females; the rate for married A-bomb victims, especially males, was higher than national levels; and among these, those severely affected by the bombings stand out. According to R. J. Lifton's assessment of these records, "A-bomb victims show a high rate of marriage and must be assumed to have given birth to many children" (Lifton 1967). J. W. Hollingsworth and P. S. Anderson (1961) note that "the ABCC survey results indicate a high marriage rate for males and females who received the highest levels of radiation," but at the same time register some concern whether "an adequate explanation perhaps lies in the disparities of actual age composition." That this attitude is proper should be clear from the preceding figures, and similar trends are evident in the independent surveys made by Hiroshima and Nagasaki cities and their respective prefectures in connection with the 1960 national census (table 11.20).

If the results of the Ministry of Health and Welfare's 1965 nationwide survey and national census figures for the same year are combined and adjusted for age composition, the nationwide rate for males is 73 percent against

TABLE 11.20

*Marital Status of A-bomb Victims according to the 1960 National Census**

	Age Group									Averaɡ
	15–19	20–24	25–29	30–39	40–49	50–59	60–69	70–79	80 and over	
Unmarried:										
Nationwide	99.3	79.9	33.6	7.5	2.1	1.2	0.9	0.9	0.4	30.6
Hiroshima	98.7	84.0	31.9	7.9	1.8	0.9	0.6		0.8	17.8
Nagasaki	99.1	83.7	37.7	10.3	3.3	1.7	1.0		1.1	27.7
Married:										
Nationwide	0.7	19.8	65.0	88.3	86.8	80.6	65.7	41.2	44.0	58.8
Hiroshima	1.1	15.5	66.3	87.0	84.0	78.3	68.7		46.0	66.8
Nagasaki	0.8	15.9	60.6	84.8	83.8	78.2	66.8		41.4	61.7
Widowed:										
Nationwide	0.0	0.0	0.3	1.7	8.4	16.0	31.6	56.5	80.4	9.1
Hiroshima	0.1	0.1	0.3	2.0	10.6	18.1	29.0		51.6	13.1
Nagasaki	0.0	0.0	0.4	1.9	9.9	18.1	30.5		55.7	11.0
Separated:										
Nationwide	0.0	0.2	1.1	2.4	2.6	2.2	1.7	1.4	1.0	1.5
Hiroshima	0.1	0.4	1.5	3.1	3.0	2.3	1.6		1.6	2.1
Nagasaki†	0.1	0.4	1.3	2.9	3.0	2.1	1.7		1.8	1.7
Age distribution:										
Nationwide	14.3	12.8	12.7	20.7	15.0	12.0	7.8	3.9	1.0	100.0
Hiroshima	8.9	5.2	7.0	22.0	17.7	18.2	14.3		6.7	100.0
Nagasaki	10.7	8.2	10.6	22.2	14.4	15.5	12.7		5.7	100.0

* Figures are percentages of total A-bomb victims either nationally or in Hiroshima or Nagasaki.
† Table 9 in the source document inadvertently reversed, we believe, the Nagasaki figures for "widowed" and "separated."
Source: Hiroshima Prefectural Office and Hiroshima City Office, *Hiroshimaken Genbaku Hibakusha Jittai Chōsa Hōkoku* [Hiroshima Prefecture A-bomb Survivors Actual Status Survey Report], 1960 (Hiroshima, Hiroshimaken-Hiroshimashi, 1964a, p. 26). Nagasaki Shiyakusho, Civil Welfare Department, Social Affairs Section, *Nagasakishi o Shutosuru Genbaku Hibakusha Jittai Chōsa no Kenkyū* [Study of A-bomb Survivors Actual Status Survey Mainly with Reference to Nagasaki City] (Nagasaki, 1964), pp. 50–51.

72.8 percent for male A-bomb victims; comparable figures for females are 67.4 percent against 62.7 percent. Victims' rates are lower generally than national rates, and particularly for males aged twenty-five to twenty-nine (aged five to nine at bombing time) and for females aged twenty to thirty-four (birth to fourteen at bombing time) and fifty-five to sixty-four (thirty-five to forty-four at bombing time). The unmarried rate is high for males aged twenty-five to twenty-nine and for females aged twenty to thirty-four; while the rate of women aged forty-five to sixty-nine (aged twenty-five to forty-nine at bombing) who were widowed exceeds the national level (Ministry of Health and Welfare 1967a, p. 8).

Data on marital status from the Ministry of Health and Welfare's 1975 Survey of A-bomb Victims' Conditions has not been reported, but national census figures for that year show that, for males under age forty, the marriage rate for A-bomb victims falls below the national rate, and for female victims the gap is about 7 percent (table 11.21).

The Living Survey part of this larger 1975 survey deals with "households including nonvictims age thirty and above," and thus reflects some of the distinctive features of "A-bomb-related" households (pages 415–20). Of households with three to four persons—that is, typical nuclear families—there were fewer among A-bomb victims than among nonvictims, although there were relatively more A-bomb-victim households with only two persons and with six or more persons. Some 40 percent of the smaller two-person households included an elderly wife, and the larger households generally included three generations (Ministry of Health and Welfare 1977c, p. 5). Households of elderly A-bomb victims were nearly twice those of elderly nonvictims, but 60 percent of the former were one-person units (Ministry of Health and Welfare 1977a, p. 6). Household heads among nonvictims peaked at ages thirty to thirty-nine, among victims at age forty and over, and especially at age sixty and over (Ministry of Health and Welfare 1977a, p. 9). Of households including elderly members, those with two elderly persons were more numerous among victims' households (Ministry of Health and Welfare 1977a, p. 8).

These statistics provide further evidence of the rapid growth of elderly A-bomb survivors as a population group. This growth cannot be explained in terms of lengthening of the average life span of A-bomb victims, or of a higher death rate among children than among the parental generation. The effect of aging on the health of A-bomb survivors is, of course, of medical interest; and as for younger persons, young men in their twenties were away on military duty, while infants and children were evacuated; and thus the percentage of younger victims was in fact low. Consequently, older persons made up the bulk of the A-bomb victims. The aging of the survivors as a

TABLE 11.21
Marital Status of A-bomb Victims by Age and Sex, 1975*

	Age Group	Unmarried		Married		Widowed		Separated		Age Distribution	
		Nation-wide	A-bomb Victims	Nation-wide	A-bomb Victims	Nation-wide	A-bomb Victims	Nation-wide	A-bomb Victims	Nation-wide	A-bomb Victims
Males	30–39	10.4	10.9	88.4	87.4	0.2	0.4	1.0	1.3	32.6	18.3
	40–49	3.1	2.4	94.6	95.4	0.8	0.8	1.5	1.4	28.8	28.8
	50–59	1.5	1.2	94.7	95.1	2.3	2.3	1.5	1.4	17.3	16.1
	60–69	1.1	0.5	89.8	91.4	7.7	6.5	1.4	1.6	13.0	18.2
	70 and over	0.9	0.4	71.8	75.8	26.0	22.6	1.3	1.2	8.4	17.3
	Totals	4.8	3.1	90.0	89.8	3.9	5.7	1.3	1.4	100.0	100.0
Females	30–39	6.6	9.7	90.1	86.3	1.1	1.4	2.2	2.6	29.7	17.9
	40–49	5.0	6.0	87.0	84.0	4.6	5.1	3.4	4.9	26.2	26.1
	50–59	3.3	3.6	75.0	73.0	17.9	18.1	3.8	5.3	19.3	23.3
	60–69	1.9	2.1	54.8	50.3	40.7	43.8	2.6	3.8	14.2	17.5
	70 and over	1.6	1.1	24.1	23.2	72.7	73.3	1.6	2.4	10.6	13.6
	Totals	4.3	4.7	74.4	67.6	18.5	23.7	2.8	4.0	100.0	100.0

* Figures are percentages either of the national population or of A-bomb victims.

Source: 1975 National Census and Ministry of Health and Welfare Survey of A-bomb Victims' Conditions (1975). Prime Minister's Office, Statistics Bureau, *Shōwa Gojūnen Kokusei Chōsa Hōkoku* [1975 National Census Report], vol. 3: Region and Prefectures Section—86: Hiroshima Prefecture (Tokyo: Nihon Tōkei Kyōkai, 1977). Ministry of Health and Welfare, Public Health Bureau, Planning Section, *Shōwa Gojūnen Genshibakudan Hibakusha Jittai Chōsa* [1975 Actual Status Survey of Atomic Bomb Survivors], Data Section (Tokyo: Kōseishō Kōshūeiseikyoku Kikakuka, 1977c), p. 3.

group is also related to the heavy losses suffered through the deaths of house-hold heads and spouses, to the long delays in remarrying and reorganizing households, and to the insecurity experienced by spouses afterward, not to mention the inability of some to remarry or establish new households, the fears of hereditary effects of radiation, and other perceived risks. Contrary to Lifton's expectation (1967), in the life cycle of thirty years since the bombing there has been, rather, a relative decrease in the second generation of the A-bomb survivors' community; and this decrease is the principal cause of the aging of that community as a whole.

Of all respondents to the 1965 Survey of A-bomb Victims' Conditions, 2.6 percent experienced "adverse discrimination" in relation to marriages; but the rate was higher for specific groups—4.1 percent of unmarried victims (11.4 percent in the thirty-five-to-thirty-nine age group) and 5.7 percent of those separated (12.5 percent in the thirty-to-thirty-four age group). This experience was especially common among males between thirty-five and thirty-nine who were unmarried (12.1 percent) or widowed (17.2 percent), and among separated males (18.7 percent) between thirty and thirty-four (Ministry of Health and Welfare 1967a, pp. 3, 9). Of the 3.8 percent of survivors reporting adverse discrimination in the later 1975 survey, 7.1 percent were males and 8.5 percent females below age forty. The pervasive impact of A-bomb damages is further seen in the extent of directly affected victims within 2 kilometers (6.8 percent) and fetal victims (5.6 percent) who reported later discrimination (female respondents were slightly higher in both cases, being 7.3 percent and 6.6 percent, respectively) (Ministry of Health and Welfare 1977c, p. 4).

Hardships of Making a Living

In Hiroshima, it will be remembered, the death rate was higher for wives than for husbands within the 1-kilometer radius, and the reverse was true outside that radius. This was because many husbands living within that radius had gone to work that morning in major industries in the city's suburbs, while many husbands living beyond that radius had commuted from the suburbs into the city's center to work in the many small and medium-sized enterprises clustered there. More wives were killed and damages to whole families were heavier, though, in the city's inner sector. In Nagasaki, the main plants of Mitsubishi Shipbuilding were outside the range of heaviest damage, and some household heads had left Urakami district to work in these plants. But the factories of Mitsubishi Munitions, Mitsubishi Steel, and Mitsubishi Electrical Machinery were in the most heavily burned and demolished parts of the city, and consequently large numbers of household heads and young men workers are thought to have been killed in this city's bombed area.

In fifteen years after the bombings, more A-bomb victims than nonvictims found unskilled manufacturing, forestry, farming, and fishing employment, and fewer found specialized skills, service, office, transport, and communications jobs. Immediately after the bombings, many people fled the bombed cities. Due to this exodus and the deaths from war and the atomic bombings during the 1944–45 period, Hiroshima's population dropped 58.1 percent; Nagasaki's, 47.1 percent. Not a few of those people leaving the cities sought out relatives in forestry, farming, and fishing households and, eventually, took up these occupations themselves. People who returned to the cities and sought there to rebuild their shattered lives between 1945 and 1950 found that they had lost their wealth and social bases and thus became salaried workers. As such, they had many handicaps, among which was their late entry into the now-rebuilding economy.

Nonetheless, by 1965 fewer A-bomb victims were engaged in forestry, farming, and fishing. Indeed, more than half the employed victims were working in manufacturing and low-skilled jobs—but their numbers were less than the national level of those in such jobs. Conversely, A-bomb victims employed in specialized skills, office, retail, and administrative jobs exceeded national levels in these fields (table 11.9). From 1955, and especially from 1960, Japan's rapid economic growth increasingly affected cities other than Tokyo, Osaka, and Kobe. And the A-bomb victims themselves were getting older. It is understandable, therefore, that the employment and compensation levels of the rather large concentration of victims in Hiroshima and Nagasaki slightly exceeded nationwide levels. On the other hand, because many injured household heads could no longer work at all, many women and the elderly and infirm in A-bomb victims' households were forced to seek jobs. The work of all women workers, however, was insecure: 5.8 percent of them were engaged as day laborers, in contrast to the national proportion of 2.7 percent. Given the low wage scales common among certain A-bomb victims, the average annual income of salaried A-bomb victims was 10 percent below the national average.

By 1975 the percentage of A-bomb victim households depending on salaried jobs dropped below the national level, while the percentage of victims engaged in farming rose; and victims without paying jobs exceeded their nonvictim counterparts by 70 percent. There were 2.3 times as many male victims without paying jobs as their nonvictim counterparts. These trends were due more to the victims' inability to work than to loss or lack of jobs, along with their advancing age and A-bomb-inflicted injuries. In the 1975 survey it was found that cash expenditures of A-bomb victim households were slightly less than those of nonvictims, and that this gap had widened since 1965. As victims became increasingly incapable of working, the burden of meeting necessary expenses shifted to nonvictims in the victims' households. In only 47.7 percent of all households were A-bomb victims the main income earners (80 percent of them males), against 50.1 percent nonvictim primary breadwinners (males, 88.6 percent); and among male dependents, victims (12.1 percent) exceeded nonvictims (5.8 percent) (Ministry of Health and Welfare 1977c, pp. 15–16). The gap in cash expenditures averaged 2.2 percent but was 15.5 percent for one-person victim households (Ministry of Health and Welfare 1977a, p. 24).

Given the rapid aging of the A-bomb victims group, their losing the ability to work, the initial family losses followed by the diminishing marriage rate and difficulties in marital relations, a relative decline in second-generation offspring of A-bomb victims was not unnatural.

Many A-bomb victim households consist of only an elderly couple, or even a single aged member; other larger households include the aged and infirm. In still other households, second-generation nonvictims have had to support dependent victims. Clearly, life has been more difficult for these than for ordinary households.

The burden of caring for dependents is made harsher by the injuries and infirmities of some of them. The 1965 Survey of A-bomb Victims' Conditions revealed that 44 percent of their households had one member "receiving medical care"—nearly twice the national count. Victims' households with "medical costs" were 2.5 times the national count; households purchasing medicines, 3.5 times; and households having members with physical handicaps, 3.5 times the respective national levels (Ministry of Health and Welfare 1967b, pp. 7–9). In the 1975 survey, 58.8 percent of the A-bomb victims reported "infirmities," as against 29.4 percent for nonvictims; 2.9 percent of the victims were "hospitalized" against 1.5 of the nonvictims. There were 1.34 times as many victim households with an injured member as such nonvictim households; and twice as many victims' households had a hospitalized member. Despite some assistance with medical costs under the A-bomb Victims Medical Care Law, far more victims' households had monthly medical expenses in excess of 2,000 yen than did nonvictims' households. And victims with physical handicap certification were about twice their nonvictim counterparts (Ministry of Health and Welfare 1977a, pp. 26, 35, 38).

The preceding paragraphs give both general and statistical outlines of the hardships encountered by A-bomb victims during the three postwar decades. The specific and qualitative details are to be found only in individual case histories of the victims' daily lives. The case studies in the 1975 Survey of

Figure 11.11. A street scene near Nagasaki Railroad Station, late August 1945. (Photograph by Eiichi Matsumoto.)

A-bomb Victims' Conditions were made for just that purpose. Subjects were selected from among persons interviewed earlier in 1966 by Hiroshima and Nagasaki officials in projects commissioned by the Ministry of Health and Welfare. Of the 156 cases investigated in Hiroshima, both husband and wife were victims in 36 percent of the cases; husband only in 17 percent; wife only in 21 percent. Among households, 3 percent had a victim husband; 22 percent a victim wife. Of all victims, 37 percent had been within 1.5 kilometers of the hypocenter; 39 percent of the households (within a 2–3-kilometer radius) had lost a family member; 36 percent of the victims experienced a delay of a year or more in recovering their livelihood; and roughly one third of the victims had sustained heavy damages or serious injuries (table 11.22) (Blackett 1948).

A comparison of the occupational standings and standards of living before and after the bombings (table 11.23) shows that those in the upper classes down to the mid-middle classes were by 1949 still below their prebombing

TABLE 11.22

Deaths and Injuries Due to the Atomic Bomb, by Household

	Death or Injury	Death Suffered		Injury Suffered		Other Households	Total*
		Head of Household or Primary Supporter	Other Employed Members	Head of Household or Primary Supporter	Other Employed Members		
All household members are A-bomb victims	death and injury	5	5	4	0	8	22 (14.1)
	death only	3	3	—	—	5	11 (7.1)
	injury only	—	—	14	0	21	35 (22.4)
	neither death nor injury	—	—	—	—	18	18 (11.6)
Some household members are A-bomb victims	death and injury	3	0	5	1	7	16 (10.3)
	death only	3	1	—	—	8	12 (7.7)
	injury only	—	—	5	3	9	17 (10.9)
	neither death nor injury	—	—	—	—	25	25 (16.0)
	Total*	14 (9.0)	9 (5.8)	28 (17.9)	4 (2.6)	101 (64.8)	156 (100.0)

* Figures in parentheses are percentages of total interviews.
Source: M. Chūbachi, "Structural relationship of life conditions of atomic bomb sufferers: As revealed through the interviews conducted in shima area [1966]," *Mita Gakkai Zasshi* [Mita Journal of Economics] (Keio University, Tokyo), 61 (December 1968): 1221.

TABLE 11.23

Changes in Economic Status of Households of A-bomb Victims*

Occupational Rank	Standard of Living	Pre-bombing*	1945–49	1950–54	1955–66
Upper	upper	2.6	0.6	1.9	2.6
	middle	3.8	3.8	2.6	1.9
	lower	5.1	3.8	4.5	5.8
Subtotal		11.5	8.2	9.0	10.3
Middle	upper	9.0	5.1	5.1	7.1
	middle	16.7	7.7	12.2	14.1
	lower	23.1	19.9	17.3	14.1
Subtotal		48.7	32.7	34.6	35.3
Lower	upper	30.8	25.0	32.1	35.3
	middle	7.7	30.8	20.5	17.9
	lower	1.3	3.2	3.8	1.3
Subtotal		39.7	59.0	56.4	54.5
Total		100.0	100.0	100.0	100.0

* Figures are percentages of all households in each time span.
Source: M. Chūbachi, "Structural relationship of life conditions of atomic bomb sufferers: As revealed through interviews conducted in Hiroshima area [1966]," *Mita Gakkai Zasshi* [Mita Journal of Economics] (Keio University, Tokyo) 61 (December 1968): 1221.

levels; and though their lot had improved by 1954 and continued to do so afterward, they had not altogether reclaimed their prebombing positions by 1966. Those in the lower-middle class experienced a gradual but persistent decline, in contrast to the gradual upgrading of the upper-lower class. The two lowest classes rose threefold and fourfold by 1949, but have since declined.

Personal and family standings before the bombings had virtually no relation to the extent of loss and injury suffered: A-bomb damages were suffered by all classes in the two cities. But the time needed to recover and the level attained were definitely related to prebombing classes and standards of living: the higher the former class, the speedier the recovery; and the lower the former class, the slower and more difficult the recovery (Chūbachi 1968).

Of the original 156 cases, the 1975 Hiroshima case studies focused on 47 city households that were burned out. The residential distribution of these particular cases at bombing time was 64 percent within 1 to 1.5 kilometers, 28 percent within 1.5 to 2 kilometers, and 8 percent within 2 to 2.5 kilometers of the hypocenter (Ministry of Health and Welfare 1977b, p. 4). The age distribution of the persons involved (at bombing time) was 36 percent for ages twenty-five and below, 15 percent for ages twenty-five to thirty-four, 28 percent for ages thirty-five to forty-four, and 21 percent for age forty-five and over. Household heads aged forty-five and over were 51 percent of the total; and of these, 43 percent had eldest children who had completed middle school or above, or were employed or married. These household heads were most likely to be self-employed; there were also many salaried household heads aged twenty-five to thirty-four whose eldest children had not started school (Ministry of Health and Welfare 1977b, pp. 1–2). The same pattern among household heads in Nagasaki is evident from the many published testimonies and records (T. Ishida 1973; 1974).

Turning first to the self-employed, let us assume a typical case where the father was age forty-five or over (in some cases, thirty-five to forty-four) and the eldest child was already employed or married, while younger children were still in school. If the father survived the bombing, as did his son (perhaps returned from military service), then in the first postwar decade the family business probably suffered a slump, or perhaps a different trade was tried, but business somehow continued. From 1955 things would have begun to improve. Even where the father died or was injured in the bombing, if the son remained healthy or regained lost health, the family was able gradually to recover its prebombing standing. To effect such recovery, the aid of a relative or some friend in the same line of business was often crucial. If, however, the father and his male heir were lost in the bombing (or the son was but an infant then), then the mother and daughter(s) would have had to work in order to support the family. Were they to experience symptoms of aftereffects of the bombings, then they would have been forced to seek aid under relief measures as administered at the time. Single women survivors in their thirties might have had some chance of remarrying; but those age forty and over had great difficulty in recovering their former standard of living, and simply grew old alone. Some self-employed workers who were late in re-establishing their businesses were forced into gradual decline by occupational changes brought on by the country's rapid economic growth.

Among salaried workers, a typical case might have been a father aged thirty-five or younger (some cases, thirty-five to forty-four) with an eldest child in school or possibly not yet in school. If the father survived the bombing (or perhaps returned from military service), as did his son, he still faced the problem of unemployment, given the stagnation or closing of industries and the personnel adjustments provoked by the atomic bombing and the defeat in war. If the father's discharge from the military and, thus, his re-entry into the job market were delayed, he may have been forced to use his savings or sell his possessions just to live; or the whole family may have been forced to work at temporary and insecure jobs. The situation of the salaried worker was in some respects more vulnerable than that of the self-employed. But a salaried worker, once settled in a job, especially in public administration or as a regular employee of a large enterprise, could then, barring ill-health, expect to recover financially in due time. Still, job fluctuations caused by postwar economic changes were common among small- and medium-sized enterprises; and if job mobility were also accompanied by A-bomb aftereffects affecting the father or other family members, then salaried household heads more often faced crippling circumstances than did the self-employed. An able-bodied son was more helpful to a father who was self-employed than to one who was salaried; and circumstances were harder still on daughters working to help make ends meet, for their marriages were often delayed. And thus was postponed the birth of—and eventual assistance from—the next generation. As children matured and left home for work and marriage, salaried couples more frequently were left alone than were self-employed parents—though the advantages of retirement bonuses and pensions for salaried persons should not be overlooked. Unskilled workers and day laborers, even those who had suffered little or no direct A-bomb damage, generally experienced great difficulty in recovering and sustaining their means of livelihood (Ministry of Health and Welfare 1977*b*, pp. 2–3).

A-bomb Orphans

Particularly tragic among all the losses of life, property, and means of livelihood caused by atomic destruction were the countless children who lost both parents and older brothers and sisters as well. In Hiroshima and Nagasaki, many "war orphans" had been created by the war itself, but the problem was intensely aggravated by the atomic bombings in which adults of all ages were killed, and which brought the added damage of radiation.

Strictly speaking, an orphan is a child separated from its parents by death and must therefore depend on someone else. In Hiroshima and Nagasaki, thousands of children instantly lost only one parent in the bombings, but the remaining parent suffered such damage as to be incapable of caring for a child; such a child therefore clearly suffered an orphan's distress. The surviving children of mothers killed while the fathers were elsewhere in military service, may have had grandparents or other relatives and family friends among the survivors but could not always depend upon them; such a child, too, was orphaned, was a waif. All such children came to be called "A-bomb orphans." According to Ichirō Moritaki, who got involved with the problem of A-bomb orphans through the Hiroshima Society for the Care of Children, "children with only one surviving parent, or only grandparents, naturally came to be called A-bomb orphans because of their extreme distress, and that was the main concern" (Moritaki 1954, pp. 40–51).

On 3 March 1944—when Japan's main island was being subjected to incessant air raids, and the overall war situation was uncertain—the government hurriedly issued the Plan to Promote General Evacuation: it urged the evacuation of children in the third grade and above in primary schools to relatives' homes in remote rural places (and, at the same time, demolition of inner-city buildings to create firebreaks). As the war situation subsequently became even more critical, the School Children Evacuation Plan was issued on 30 June; and stronger measures were initiated to move children in groups to the countryside. Other measures followed, such as the 7 November plan for evacuation of children, aged persons, and pregnant women, and the 15 March 1945 program to speed up evacuation from the major cities. Throughout the nation, steps were taken to prepare the principal cities for the defense of the Japanese homeland.

The evacuation measures applied, of course, to Hiroshima and Nagasaki as well. In Hiroshima, 15,000 children were evacuated to distant relatives' homes. Group evacuation of schoolchildren began on 3 April 1945 with 91 children from the Ōtemachi Primary School in the city's central district; and by July, some 8,500 children had been moved out of the city. Thus, a total of 23,500 children were reportedly sent to various places in the prefecture (Hiroshima Shiyakusho 1958, p. 701).

Thanks to the evacuations, many children escaped the direct horrors of atomic destruction. Even so, the massive devastation robbed countless children of parents and guardians and, in an instant, added them to the tragic ranks of "A-bomb orphans." Some children could not be evacuated because they had neither family nor relatives in the countryside or were below school age, and many of these were orphaned. And a great many children who did not get along with relatives in remote rural places, ran away and became vagrant waifs; these, too, were counted among the orphans.

It is not clear how many such unfortunate children there were. Records on all who were, or were not, evacuated are no longer available, due to the burning of school buildings and the death of many school officials. Group evacuations were well organized at the time of departure. But after the bombings, chaos reigned; and custody of the children passed from official to private hands. What actually became of all the children is beyond confirmation now. People earliest involved in the care of these youngsters in Hiroshima after the bombing said that "there were over 6,500 orphans" (Osada 1953, p. 17); but, on the basis of the number of evacuated children and of some data on children after the bombing, it is estimated that there were between 4,000 and 5,000 orphans.* Although accurate counts are lacking, the losses of husbands and wives revealed by the reconstruction surveys indicate a considerable number of parentless children. Data on damages sustained by parents of evacuated children who in April 1945 had been enrolled in schools that were located in Hiroshima's central bombed area show that, of 886 children, some 600 (third grade and above) had been sent from Fukuromachi Primary School to Futami county, and 96 (60 boys, 36 girls)† to Kamisugi village (presently Kamisugi district of Miyoshi City). The whereabouts of 51 of the 96 had been determined by August 1976; and of 44 respondents (involving 37 households) to inquiries, 28 (24 households) had lost both parents, 5 (4 households) had lost fathers, and 3 (3 households) had lost mothers— a total of 36 (31 households), or 82 percent (84 percent of the households) (*Asahi Shimbun* 1976). In the collection of 105 memoirs compiled in *Genbaku no Ko* [Children of the Atomic Bomb] (Osada 1951), published in 1951 and edited by Arata Osada, 19 memoirs are taken as indicating the loss of one or both parents in the explosion; 16 others reveal loss of a father; 18, loss of a mother; and 21, loss of brothers, sisters, and other close relatives. Altogether, 53 memoirs disclose lost parents—half of all the published memoirs.

Genbaku no Ko is an excellent record of the bitter experiences of children

* Moritaki 1954, pp. 40–51; Kozumi 1956, p. 70; Hiroshima Promoters Group 1955, p. 44.
† Kamisugi Primary School Centennial Bulletin Editorial Committee 1975, p. 54.

subjected to the horrors of atomic war. A second-grade girl who lost six family members writes of those tragic days:

My older brother went off to do compulsory labor and was never seen again. My younger brother was burned all over his body and died the following day at Koi Primary School. . . . Mother said she was going into town, as there was no good doctor in the country; the day after she got there, she suddenly became much worse. By evening word came from Uncle for us to come, so Father and I and my younger sister set out for town early the next morning. "At last we made it," I thought when we got there, only to find out that Mother had breathed her last a little earlier. Mother's body was burned in an open field by the river. That evening, just as we reached Uncle's house in the country, my older sister died. The day after her funeral, my lovable younger sister also passed away. Father managed to attend my older sister's funeral, but he just didn't have the strength to go to my younger sister's funeral. The temple priest who conducted my sisters' rites must have breathed some poison, for he wasn't present for Father's funeral. . . .

Father left this world on the morning of 10 September, worrying all the while about leaving me alone. Before dying, he often said, "I don't want to die. The bomb may have burned our home and our clothes; but even if we have to wear rags, let's stay in the country, just the two of us, and farm for a living."

(Osada 1951, pp. 133–34)

A third-grade girl who lost both parents and was left alone with her grandmother related her wretched situation thus:

When I learned that Father and Mother had died, no tears came into my eyes, no sound from my throat. But later, when I would think about it, the tears just flowed.

To make things even sadder, the friends I had been living with were gradually taken back to Hiroshima—today one, the next day two—by their fathers and brothers. It was saddest when the time came for my best friend to go. Just before she left, when I should have been there to share her joy, I hid instead in the shadow of the old temple and wept. I didn't even have a chance to say goodbye.

Gradually all my friends were taken back home. But no one came for me. Not even after a month had passed.   (Osada 1951, pp. 145–46)

And a sixth-grade girl who lost both parents, while she was at an evacuation site, wrote:

In the farmhouse of an acquaintance where I stayed, I was thrown in among all the adults. I would just sit on a straw mat and cry to myself. Because it was out in the country, I could not study although I wanted to; but I was scolded for not helping with the farm work. It was not a life I cared for. . . . Gradually I became quite gloomy, a cold-hearted person who rarely laughed. The sunsets in the country were beautiful. Everything was so fresh. Looking at so much beauty made me cry. I was starved for affection.

Death. I could think of nothing but death.   (Osada 1951, p. 242)

Many such children were orphaned at a time when the mutual relationships between families and communities were shattered, community functions had ceased in a defeated nation, and the social service agencies intended to deal with such situations were rendered weak, if not useless. The children thus turned to grandparents, relatives, or some close or distant friend as foster parents; and if they had no such recourse, they were committed to facilities hastily established to care for them. Some older children who tried to manage independently, but without any place to go or settle down, drifted aimlessly amid the brutal realities of postwar society and inevitably became delinquent and antisocial. In the rough-and-tumble conditions that prevailed after the bombings and defeat, they were continuously pressed down by the doubly harsh conditions of being orphans in a disabled and disorderly society.

The first opportunity, after thirty years (August 1975), for reunion of the Fukuromachi Primary School evacuation group proved that they were no exception. The few children who found custody somewhere had managed to live in peace thereafter. The rest confronted shifting circumstances and complications at every turn, and most of them had moved from one relative's house to another and from one place or region to another.

One youth had run away from a relative's home in Ishikawa Prefecture, fallen in with delinquents and gangsters, and, to eke out a living, had drifted from job to job; his long ordeal ended only after he was finally able to open a shop of his own. A young girl, who had been the last to leave her evacuation site, subsequently managed to eat by traveling around the country with a theatrical troupe. A brother and sister were separated and taken care of at different places. The sister was cared for by the chief priest of a Buddhist temple at her evacuation site; the brother passed from place to place until, at the last stop in Nagoya, he died from malnutrition (*Asahi Shimbun* 1976).

In July 1955, the Hiroshima Society for the Care of Children solicited testimonies from the A-bomb orphans on "How I Have Managed since Then." Twenty persons responded. One was a second-year student in middle school at bombing time who had lost both parents and whose grandmother and younger brother had died from A-bomb injuries. Cared for first by relatives who eventually sent him away like a stray dog, he wandered about doing odd jobs as farm hand, day laborer, and shop clerk, and later tried to commit suicide by taking an overdose of sleeping pills. When, at last, he was about to establish himself as a confectioner, he came down with tuberculosis of the lungs; and then, when he was able to return to work, his business failed. A young girl whom evacuation had saved from the atomic bombing, lost her father on the battlefield and her mother in that bombing. Two brothers survived with her, but both were diagnosed as having tuberculosis and thoracic empyema, and had no money to pay for medical care. One night she awoke

Figure 11.12. Atomic bomb orphans receiving encouragement from the elderly Catholic priest Zeno in front of Hiroshima Railroad Station, 10 January 1949. (Photograph by Chūgoku Shinbunsha.)

to discover her bedridden elder brother weeping; the next morning he died. She later got a telephone operator's job, but then contracted tuberculosis herself. What she wanted most for herself now, she wrote, was "a house with running water," and her fervent wish for the world was "peace" (Imahori 1960).

Care for the A-bomb orphans naturally began with those found alone in the smoldering ruins who did not even know their own names, whose parents were missing or dead, and many of whom were wounded or badly burned. In Hiroshima a "lost children's center" was opened in the Hijiyama Primary School which had escaped destruction; beginning on 10 August, it admitted children ranging from infants to first- and second-graders; at one time the number exceeded 150 (Hiroshima Shiyakusho 1958, p. 791). School personnel and neighborhood mothers took turns caring for them day and night, but child after child died while calling out for his or her mother.

The situation was much the same in Nagasaki. The city first opened a center for 30 orphans in Togiya Primary School, and later another for 28 orphans of ages between one month and one year in the Kanayama School classroom annex in Tairamachi town on the Shimabara Peninsula. Operations beyond the first ten to fifteen days, however, are not clear (Nagasaki Shiyakusho 1977, pp. 402–5).

In September attention extended to care of orphans wandering and loitering in the city as well as to those still left at evacuation sites. Through the compassionate efforts of some of the city's teachers and Buddhist leaders, the Hiroshima War Orphans Foster Home was founded in Itsukaichi town of Saeki county late in the year to accommodate 87 orphans left at evacuation sites, such as Tōkaichi and Mirasaka towns and in the Hijiyama center, whom no one had yet taken into custody. In October 1945 the Hiroshima Prefecture Foundation for Relief of Fellowcountrymen opened a facility named Shinsei Gakuen [New Life School] for orphans brought back from formerly occupied Southeast Asian territories. Another facility was established in September 1946 in the former army quarantine station on the offshore island of Ninoshima in Hiroshima Bay; and the House of Providence of the Roman Catholic Garden of Light school was opened in August 1948 in Gion town of Asa county. These, along with prebombing foster homes, such as Hiroshima Shūdōin and Roppō Gakuen, undertook the long-range care and rearing of orphans (Hiroshima Prefectural Office 1976, pp. 260–62).

In Nagasaki, the Knights of the Holy Mother, a Roman Catholic religious order, initiated relief for orphans and had at one time as many as one hundred orphans in its care. Other facilities for orphans were opened in the city by various philanthropists, but details of these activities are unclear (Nagasaki Shiyakusho 1977, pp. 406–7).

Thus, a number of facilities for the immediate relief and long-term rearing of A-bomb orphans were started in the two cities—most of them by private social service groups. The combined capacity of these facilities (about 300) was far below the need at the time, so most of the children in fact depended on the goodwill and charity of individuals, whether relatives, family friends, or completely unrelated people. In April 1948, Japanese residents in Hawaii who were originally from Hiroshima Prefecture formed the Hawaii Society for Relief of Hiroshima War Victims. The following year, this society sent a contribution of $45,000 (about 16,000,000 yen), part of which went to 101 orphans in facilities and to 518 orphans in the care of foster parents (Hiroshima Shiyakusho 1958, pp. 793–95). The figures given here show clearly that individuals' care of orphans was predominant, but the two modes of care still fell far short of actual need.

In August 1953, the Hiroshima Society for the Care of Children conducted a survey of public schools and confirmed the enrollment of 423 A-bomb orphans in the city's primary and middle schools. Of these, 28 percent were kept in homes that faced hardships in providing adequate food and clothing (Moritaki 1954, pp. 40–51). Even though enrolled in schools for compulsory education, the orphans could rarely devote themselves to study; they were often required to tend to younger children and assist with work and, thus, were absent from school for extended periods.

In October of the following year, the same society carried out a second survey to ascertain the number of A-bomb orphans. Tables 11.24 and 11.25 are drawn from Ichirō Moritaki's report (1954) of this survey (pp. 40–51). The number of A-bomb orphans enrolled in primary and middle schools was 1,810, though in May 1954 the previously noted facilities had only 106 orphans.

TABLE 11.24

*Number of A-bomb Orphans in
Primary and Middle Schools in
Hiroshima, October 1954*

Schools	Males	Females	Total
Primary	415	387	802
Middle	469	539	1,008
Total	884	926	1,810

Source: Survey by the Hiroshima Society for the Care of Children: I. Moritaki, "A-bomb Orphans," in *Genbaku to Hiroshima* [The Atomic Bomb and Hiroshima], University Group to Protect Peace and Learning, ed. (Collection of research papers of University Group, 1) (Hiroshima: Hiroshima Kyōshokuin Kumiai Jigyōbu, 1954), p. 40.

Sociologists at Hiroshima University conducted successive surveys in 1951–53 and 1958–60 and found 1,780 orphans in Hiroshima Prefecture as well as approximately 1,300 outside the prefecture. Of the latter group, one third (450) were living in distant places, such as Osaka, Tokyo, and Hokkaido (Hiroshima Shiyakusho 1961, pp. 655–56).

If, as noted earlier, the number of A-bomb orphans is estimated at 4,000 to 5,000, one naturally wonders about the fate of the remaining 1,000 to 2,000. Did they perhaps starve to death or succumb to illness during the difficult postwar days? The answer at present is not known.

Meanwhile, in August 1949, New York's *Saturday Review of Literature* editor Norman Cousins visited the Hiroshima War Orphans Foster Home in Itsukaichi town and was deeply impressed by their situation. After returning to the United States, he appealed for understanding of the orphans' plight and campaigned for a "moral adoption" movement in which "spiritual parents" would contribute $2.50 (1949 value: 900 yen) per month toward the care and upbringing of an orphan. His appeal had a wide impact, and the initial contribution, sent to the mayor of Hiroshima in January 1950, amounted to $2,000. This was used for 71 "adopted" orphans at the foster

TABLE 11.25

Number of A-bomb Orphans in Foster Home Facilities in Hiroshima and Suburbs, May 1954

Facility	A-bomb Orphans			Other Orphans			Total in Facility			Orphans with "Moral Adoption"		
	Males	Females	Total	Males	Females	Total	Males	Females	Total	Males	Females	Total
Hiroshima War Orphans Foster Home	16	9	25	20	7	27	36	16	52	50	20	70
Ninoshima Gakuen	35	6	41	115	39	154	150	45	195	101	29	130
Shinsei Gakuen	7	3	10	49	22	71	56	25	81	37	20	57
Hiroshima Shū-dōin Orphanage	7	4	11	52	36	88	59	40	99	22	18	40
Garden of Light's House of Providence	1	4	5	44	30	74	45	34	79	6	11	17
Roppō Gakuen	10	4	14	57	31	88	67	35	102	1	1	2
Total	76	30	106	337	165	502	413	195	608	217	99	316

Source: I. Moritaki, "A-bomb Orphans," in *Genbaku to Hiroshima* [The Atomic Bomb and Hiroshima]. University Group to Protect Peace and Learning, ed. (Collection of research papers of University Group, 1) (Hiroshima: Hiroshima Kyōshokuin Kumiai Jigyōbu, 1954), p. 40.

home Cousins had earlier visited. This adoption network spread to other facilities; by April 1959, after the first decade of effort, an overall amount of 20,000,000 yen had been contributed to the support of approximately 500 orphans.

Stirred by the American effort, Arata Osada in Hiroshima appealed in December 1952 to the Japanese to undertake a foster child movement of their own. On this occasion, the Hiroshima Society for the Care of Children and a similar group in a branch school of Hiroshima University were formed anew to engage in assistance for, and to compile records on, the A-bomb orphans. These groups remained active for a decade until May 1964, by which time all orphans had reached age eighteen (Hiroshima Prefectural Office 1976, pp. 263–65). During this period, 85 "moral adoption" arrangements were made.

Some Hiroshima orphans, who by the end of the first postwar decade had become young adults, formed their own group in October 1955, with the support of Professor and Mrs. Seiichi Nakano* who had frequently counseled and encouraged many of them. This spontaneous effort was widely noted, though the driving force behind it—that the orphans had all been forced to break through rigid barriers—was not always recognized. In Japanese society, family and educational backgrounds are weighty factors affecting employment; thus, the A-bomb orphans faced discrimination from the outset. As their families were scattered or dead, they lacked personal identification, and many grew up in poverty; when seeking jobs, they were especially disadvantaged. So they often wound up in jobs where background was less important—in places of entertainment, small stores, and workshops. Such adverse factors influenced the frequent changes in job or residence by A-bomb orphans. Because such precarious conditions deepened their already considerable distress, some attempted suicide. It was to find friends in a common cause of mutual help and support that the group was formed.

The group was formally named the Youth Section of the Hiroshima Society for the Care of Children, but it was known popularly as the "Ayumi Group," from the name of its newsletter, *Ayumi* [Moving on]. It met regularly on the third Sunday of each month and organized ping-pong, baseball, chorus, and cooking activities. Almost daily some of the members looked in on the Nakano couple, who were like parents and whose house was like home to

---

* Professor Seiichi Nakano already enjoyed a nationwide reputation as one of Japan's most prominent sociologists before he was invited to teach at Hiroshima University in 1949 (he later became dean of the university's department of politics and economics). In 1949, he was elected to the board of directors of the Japan Sociological Society, a position he held till 1961.

After the "Ayumi" group was organized in 1955, he devoted all his spare time to welfare problems of A-bomb orphans for a decade until he retired from Hiroshima University and moved to Uji City to teach at Ritsumeikan University. His long-time devoted service to young orphans raised his personal reputation but, at the same time, ruined him as a scholar—the ten years away from study were too long and could not be compensated for later.

the orphans. Out of the group, four couples married and began new families (Professor Seiichi Nakano Commemorative Projects Society 1965, pp. 113–15).

The Ayumi group was also active in sharing experiences of the A-bomb damage, and its members received invitations from all over Japan and from New York and Moscow as well. The Mongolian Peace Committee awarded it 250,000 yen in 1957 and later a second gift—a total of 500,000 yen (Yamaguchi 1964, p. 73). Visitors came from East Germany, China, India, and elsewhere. Membership exceeded one hundred. And accessories made at its own leather goods shop not only sold well but were acclaimed for their artistic quality.

In 1965 the Nakano couple moved to Uji City. The time had also come when the Ayumi members themselves were no longer concentrated in Hiroshima; they were growing up and moving elsewhere. In the fall of 1976, Ayumi members born between 1931 and 1944 held a reunion to reminisce and renew old ties; and they brought their own children, ranging in age from five to thirteen (Nakano 1978).

The obstacles that stood in the way of the A-bomb orphans were many and large. There were human barriers, social barriers, and, not least, the barriers within themselves. The Ayumi members faced all these barriers head on and, knitting a bond of mutual solidarity, overcame the obstacles one by one. And there are many others who also overcame many trials to attain maturity and self-reliance, who today are making their own personal contributions to society.

Even so, most of the A-bomb orphans were outside the pale of government services to A-bomb victims, as these services were largely related to radiation damage. The orphans were socially alienated and spent their younger years in circumstances they would never have freely chosen. What impact and what harm the hardships and rapid changes of postwar society—and these orphans' estrangement from that society—had on their daily lives and their sense of identity and self-reliance is a sociohistorical question that needs to be systematically studied in order to promote the welfare of these A-bomb victims.

The Orphaned Elderly

The extensive family losses caused by the atomic bombings created yet another special problem—the large number of orphaned elderly people.

The "orphaned elderly" were older persons who, whether or not they themselves were A-bomb victims, lost their spouses and children and thus were completely without anyone on whom to depend. Some of them had one or more grandchildren but no one else to rely upon; others had some surviving family members but were forced, for some reason, to live apart in the same conditions as the fully orphaned elderly. Both the quasi-orphaned and the fully orphaned came to be called the "orphaned elderly."

From time to time the news media have called attention to elderly persons* orphaned by the atomic bombs who have committed suicide or died in utter loneliness. But scientific studies of the conditions under which these people actually lived are extremely scarce. It is not even clear how many aged persons were so orphaned in Hiroshima and Nagasaki, much less what has happened to them since. It is an urgent social task to discover how they have fared throughout the postwar years of rapid social change and economic growth, with the swift transition to the nuclear family and the aging of all A-bomb victims.

An October 1960 survey of A-bomb victims in Hiroshima and Nagasaki cities and prefectures showed that victims age seventy and over were 6.6 percent in Hiroshima and 5.8 percent in Nagasaki. National census figures for the same time put nonvictims of the same age group at 1.4 percent in Hiroshima and 1.3 percent in Nagasaki, or one fourth the victims in that age bracket (table 11.26).†

A further survey of A-bomb victims age seventy and over in Hiroshima was conducted in 1963. According to Kiyoshi Shimizu's report (1964), the survey group of 1,889 persons (853 males, 1,036 females) included 30 elderly males (3.5 percent) and 75 elderly females (7.2 percent)—a total of 105 (5.6 percent). Of the 105 aged victims, 94 (89.5 percent) were below the middle-level standard of living. Factors determining livelihood distress were low incomes for 30 persons (31.9 percent); sickness, 7 persons (7.4 percent); and debts, 4 persons (4.3 percent). For living expenses, the majority depended on meager relief and pension payments from public sources, while 15 percent of the total relied on funds from other people or on day-labor wages. In addition to financial strain, 34.3 percent had health problems, especially high blood pressure and heart ailments; geriatric diseases constituted 44.5 percent of all health problems. Most of these elderly persons reported that, if forced to bed by illness, they would look to some friend for help rather than to public agencies; but they were not sure who that friend would be. These

* In Japan (under Chinese influence), "elderly" starts at age sixty; even now, age fifty-five is the common retirement age; and the life span was shorter in 1945.

† Hiroshima Prefectural Office and Hiroshima City Office 1964*b*; Nagasaki Prefectural Office and Nagasaki City Office 1964; Prime Minister's Office, Statistics Bureau 1963, pp. 58–61; Prime Minister's Office, Statistics Bureau 1962, pp. 56–59.

TABLE 11.26

Percentages of A-bomb Victims and Nonvictims Age 70 and Over in Hiroshima and Nagasaki,
1 October 1960*

		Hiroshima			Nagasaki		
		Males	Females	Total	Males	Females	Total
A-bomb victims	Age 70 and over	2,499 (6.3)	3,615 (6.8)	6,114 (6.6)	1,922 (5.7)	2,689 (5.9)	4,611 (5.8)
	Total in survey group	39,754	53,119	92,873	33,605	45,728	79,333
Nonvictims	Age 70 and over	1,537 (0.9)	3,125 (1.9)	4,662 (1.4)	1,205 (0.9)	2,359 (1.8)	3,564 (1.3)
	Total in survey group	173,153	165,310	338,463	133,108	131,712	264,820

* Figures in parentheses are percentages of total in each survey group.
Source: Hiroshima Prefectural Office and Hiroshima City Office. *Hiroshimaken Genbaku Hibakusha Jittai Chōsa Kekkahyō* [Table of Results of Hiroshima Prefecture A-bomb Survivors Actual Status Survey], 1960 (Hiroshima: Hiroshimaken-Hiroshimashi, 1964). Nagasaki Prefectural Office and Nagasaki City Office, *Nagasakiken Genbaku Hibakusha Jittai Chōsa Kekkahyō* [Table of Results of Nagasaki Prefecture A-bomb Survivors Actual Status Survey], 1960 (Nagasaki: Nagasakiken-Nagasakishi, 1964). Prime Minister's Office, Statistics Bureau, *Shōwa Sanjūgonen Kokusei Chōsa Hōkoku* [1960 National Census Report], vol. 4: Region and Prefectures Section—42: Nagasaki Prefecture (Tokyo: Sōrifu Tōkeikyoku, 1962), pp. 56–59. Prime Minister's Office, Statistics Bureau, *Shōwa Sanjūgonen Kokusei Chōsa Hōkoku* [1960 National Census Report], vol. 4: Region and Prefectures Section—34: Hiroshima Prefecture (Tokyo: Sōrifu Tōkeikyoku, 1963), pp. 58–61.

findings throw into tragic relief the image of pitiful old people living out their days in utter loneliness, hardship, and fear of sickness.

On the other hand, as discussed earlier (page 412), the employment rates for men victims age seventy and over and for women victims of all ages are well above national levels (see table 11.10). Here, then, is a countervailing image of some elderly A-bomb victims getting up each day and forcing their aged and sometimes infirm bodies to work in order to support themselves.

Day laborer jobs constituted a large part of the employment of A-bomb victims, including the elderly, who complained, "If it weren't for the atomic bombings, we wouldn't have had such a hard time." Those working at publicly provided jobs designed to relieve unemployment would reply, when urged by friends to seek government aid, "I'd rather do government work." They saw government aid for living expenses as relief, and resisted such aid vigorously, saying, "I'm in no mood to accept relief money." Had the government, however, acknowledged A-bomb damage as part of its own war responsibility and offered to pay compensation to all victims, they would have gladly accepted it, even if the amount were less than relief payments. Such was the attitude of most A-bomb victims.

The elderly victims lost almost everything in an unprecedented experience, and it takes all their energy to keep body and soul together; but they prefer to manage by themselves and not become a burden to others. Still, more than thirty years have passed, and they are getting even older and are haunted daily by health worries, especially by the fear of becoming bedridden.

The first official survey of the elderly orphaned by the atomic bombings was done by Hiroshima City on 1 January 1972. It covered persons aged sixty and over as of 3 June 1971. Using the basic residence registers, volunteer home workers sought interviews with the 4,266 single-member households in the city; excepting those who had died or moved away, 3,394 persons were surveyed (Hiroshima Shiyakusho, A-bomb Survivors Measures Section 1972). There were 347 (57 males, 290 females), or 10.2 percent, without any relatives whatsoever. Those who lived alone because any relatives with some responsibility for their support had moved elsewhere (the quasi-orphaned elderly), numbered 801 (145 males, 656 females), or 23.6 percent.

The preceding 10.2 percent of elderly orphans is, because of differences in survey time and age limits, much higher than the 3.8 percent for those age sixty-five and over without any relatives, as determined by the 1 August 1973 survey of elderly victims conducted by Hiroshima Prefecture (Hiroshima Prefectural Office, Civil Welfare Department 1973).

Of the 347 elderly persons without relatives (1972 survey), 127 (36.6 percent) reported normal health; 38 (11 percent), poor health; 136 (39.2 percent), physical weakness; 41 (11.8 percent), some illness; 5 (1.4 percent) were bedridden; and 234 (67.4 percent) were regular outpatients at some hospital. As for distribution of various forms of public support, 247 (71.2 percent) received allowances under the A-bomb Victims Special Measures Law; of these, 243 (70 percent) were getting health care allowances. Other allowances included: welfare for the aged, 111 (32 percent); public relief, 36 (10.4 percent); pensions, 24 (6.9 percent); and welfare pensions, 21 (6.1 percent).

Of the same 347 elderly orphans, 85 (24.5 percent) were employed: 55 (15.9 percent) as salaried workers, and 30 (8.6 percent) self-employed. The reasons they gave for working were "necessary to meet expenses," 65 (76.5 percent of the 85 employed); "good for one's health," 10 (11.8 percent); "for pocket money," 8 (9.4 percent). Public pensions represented the major source of income, accounting for 141 persons (40.6 percent); other income sources were jobs and work at home, 85 (24.5 percent); property gains (mostly interest on savings deposits), 42 (12.1 percent); allowances, 11 (3.2 percent); public relief, 50 (14.4 percent). Monthly living-expense budgets fell below 20,000 yen for 251 persons (72.3 percent), and less than 10 percent budgeted over 30,000 yen.

Aged persons unable to manage by themselves at that time were relatively few, or only 17 (4.9 percent). Apparently reflecting this fact, 270 (77.8 percent) showed no desire for assistance from a home volunteer, as against 19 (5.5 percent) who did. Only 213 (61.4 percent), however, knew of the home volunteer system. The A-bomb Victims Nursing Home (a joint prefecture-city project with national support) was known to 216 (62.2 percent), but only 28 (8.1 percent) indicated a desire to enter this home, as against 233 (67.1 percent) who had no such desire. These figures suggest a need to reconsider the policies and the facilities intended to help aged A-bomb victims. In this connection, the nursing home on 1 January 1978 had 146 persons in regular care, of whom only 8 (5.5 percent) were orphaned elderly A-bomb victims and 24 (16.4 percent) were quasi-orphaned elderly; and 99 persons were in special care, of whom there were 10 each (10.1 percent) of the orphaned elderly and quasi-orphaned elderly (Hiroshima A-bomb Survivors Relief Projects Group 1978).

Some 123 persons (35.4 percent) were burdened by worries; but only 19 (5.5 percent) consulted public welfare officers, and only 16 (4.6 percent) turned to home volunteers. The vast majority (105, or 30.3 percent) turned to relatives, friends (59, or 17 percent), or neighbors (46, or 13.3 percent). Thus, among the 123, there was a distinct preference for kin and community.

Of the 347 elderly persons without relatives, 158 (45.5 percent), felt their daily lives lacked any joy or pleasure; and a startling 250 (72 percent) had come to feel their lives were not worth living. Their spiritual props had fallen away, and they faced their remaining days without purpose.

From these survey results, it is clear that the orphaned elderly, despite their loneliness, have little interest in the measures and facilities intended

Figure 11.13. An elderly couple living in a shack, November 1952. (Photograph by Yūichirō Sasaki.)

for their well-being. Their feelings of wanting to avoid the friction and bother of relating to other persons cannot be ignored; but neither can the obvious deficiencies in policies and facilities, as suggested by the 72 percent who find life not worth living and the bare 5 percent willing to turn to a public welfare worker or a home volunteer.

The 1975 Survey of A-bomb Victims' Conditions conducted by the Ministry of Health and Welfare put the victims' average age at 53.7 (54.1 for males, 53.4 for females) (1977a, p. 3). The Living part of that survey indicated an extremely high percentage of households with aged members (table 11.27).

TABLE 11.27

Distribution of Households with Elderly A-bomb Victims, 1 November 1975

Area	Households	Survey Total	Households with Elderly (percentage)	Households with Only Elderly (percentage)	Elderly Single Person (percentage)	Elderly Couple (percentage)
Nationwide	A-bomb victims	12,822	46.4	12.2	6.1	6.5
	Nonvictims	234,151	30.6	6.9	4.3	3.3
Hiroshima City	A-bomb victims	3,720	48.0	14.5	8.1	7.0
	Nonvictims	2,254	20.7	5.3	3.7	2.3
Nagasaki City	A-bomb victims	2,938	44.6	14.2	8.2	6.2
	Nonvictims	2,334	27.0	6.9	4.7	2.9

Source: Ministry of Health and Welfare, Public Health Bureau, Planning section, *Shōwa Gōjūnen Genshibakudan Hibakusha Jittai Chōsa* [1975 Actual Status Survey of Atomic Bomb Survivors], Data Section (Tokyo: Kōseishō Kōshūeiseikyoku Kikakuka, 1977), pp. 6–8.

Households of only one aged person were 8.1 percent in Hiroshima and 8.2 percent in Nagasaki (nationally, 6.1 percent); those of an elderly couple sixty or over were 7 percent in Hiroshima, 6.2 percent in Nagasaki (nationally, 6.5 percent), or twice that of nonvictims in the same age group (Ministry of Health and Welfare 1977c, pp. 6–8). Moreover, 85 percent of the households with elderly A-bomb victims (1,561 nationwide, 541 in Hiroshima, 418 in Nagasaki) also reported members who were ill (Ministry of Health and Welfare 1977c, p. 13).

Given the progressive aging among A-bomb victims and the rapid trend toward the nuclear family in Japan, there is an urgent need to see that the elderly living at home have proper provision for medical care, food, bathing, and laundry. Besides the heavy spiritual burdens of grief over family losses and anxiety over A-bomb injuries, the A-bomb victims have experienced the added burdens of impaired health as well as discrimination and other social barriers to marriage and employment. And the loss of working family members, the breakdown of community, and the rupture of human relationships have wrought permanent damage to the lives of these elderly persons.

For them to lose all hope in life, and even to end their own lives, pushes the tragedy to its limits. Only a few suicides among A-bomb victims are reported each year; but behind these reports, the actual circumstances of the elderly are grave.

In June 1975, the Federation of A-bomb Victims Associations reported that, in the five years from 1 January 1970 to 30 April 1975, there were 31 suicides among A-bomb victims. Hiroshima Prefecture claimed 25 of these (17 resident in Hiroshima City); and 8 were orphaned elderly victims, for whom suffering from illness was the major motive. In the twelve years from January 1965 to December 1976, 60 suicides among A-bomb victims were reported nationally; and, again, suffering from illness was the motive in 45 cases (75 percent) (Kawaguchi 1977, p. 225). To overcome the psychological handicaps of loneliness and anxiety spawned by human alienation in modern society, every effort must be made, and with all haste, to provide adequate policies and care fully integrated with spiritual support.

Victims of Exposure in Utero (Fetal Victims)

All the problems of social disruption and day-to-day hardships made life extremely difficult for women who were pregnant at the times of the atomic bombings; and things only got worse, for mother and infant, from the moment of birth.

Following the bombings there were few obstetricians or midwives in the bombed cities. One mother who went into labor was put in a baby carriage and carried 4 kilometers outside the city to a relative's house, where a midwife was found to deliver her baby. For those who remained in the cities, living conditions were dismal: burned houses were patched up with pieces of board and tin sheeting, and many people lived in simple dugout shelters with a triangular roof to keep out the rain and dew. In such makeshift dwellings babies were born and reared. Food was extremely scarce, and some infants had to depend on synthetic formulas. Malnutrition was an ever-present danger. Expectant mothers could sign up for monthly rations of one to six cans of powdered milk (each can contained about 400 grams) and approximately 600 grams of sugar, though deliveries were not guaranteed. In the context of hardship and deprivation, severely retarded physical and mental growth was not uncommon among the A-bomb fetal victims—especially in the form of microcephaly. *Microcephaly* generally refers to a condition wherein an individual's head size develops small in proportion to body size, and symptoms of mental abnormality appear. Among the various causes of this condition, one is irradiation of the fetus in the womb (see pages 222–33). Most parents of microcephalic infants believed the tragic underdevelopment of head size had been caused by the dire conditions under which these babies were born and nurtured—only to learn later, that the intense radiation of the atomic bombs was the real cause.

Retarded head growth among A-bomb fetal victims was an object of medical research from an early stage, when such symptoms were observed in infants born to mothers who were A-bomb victims (pages 222–33). The shocking truth was finally made public on 17 October 1965 when an overall academic review of A-bomb damages was presented to the Seventh Research Council on A-bomb Damages meeting in Hiroshima. That presentation (by Akira Tabuchi [1967]) was reported by the Kinoko-kai (Mushroom Club), an association of parents with microcephalic children, in the 1966 issue of the association's news organ, *Kinoko-kai Kaihō* (no. 1). A part of this report reads as follows:

> Regarding the survey of A-bomb fetal victims, we shall confine ourselves here to cases of microcephaly. Definition of microcephaly is a problem; our reference is to head sizes of 2 or more degrees below the average of 473 nonvictim infants of the same age studied in 1963 by Gō Hirai and others. Cases of 3 or more degrees are regarded as severe microcephaly. . . .
>
> We formed our association this year [1966] and appealed for new studies of our children. Publication of the reports of microcephalic symptoms among A-bomb fetal victims issued by the Atomic Bomb Casualty Commission and by Toshinori Funahashi, Gō Hirai, and others, added to this appeal; so we have put our children in hospitals where, with the cooperation of psychiatrists and physicians who specialize in A-bomb diseases, new examinations have been made. Here we wish to report the major findings as of this date. Severe microcephaly has been confirmed in twelve children—seven girls and five boys—of whom ten were affected by the A-bomb during the first three months of pregnancy. Half of the mothers (six) were age twenty-nine at bombing time, and their unborn infants are all thought to have received radiation doses of 100 rads or more. . . .
>
> The ABCC and Dr. Funahashi have examined twelve other cases of microcephaly, one of whom has since died. . . .
>
> At present we have twelve cases of A-bomb-caused microcephaly in Hiroshima— thirteen if the case of Fumio Shigetō (currently residing in Atami City) is included. Altogether there are, in broad terms, forty-five such cases.
>
> (Kinoko-kai 1966)

The reason that the Kinoko-kai requested new examinations was that the earlier examinations by R. W. Miller of the ABCC were made when the A-bomb fetal victims were all age nine or younger; of those examined, two boys later developed normal-size heads but showed no improvement in earlier symptoms of mental retardation. On the other hand, a boy who at age eight was judged microcephalic by the ABCC showed no growth in head size by age nineteen; but his mental development was remarkable, and he was then enrolled in university. Indeed, his family was not affiliated with the Kinoko-kai. Clearly, A-bomb damages to fetal victims could not be determined by head measurements alone; broader criteria for observations were needed.

One serious handicap was that the A-bomb Victims Medical Care Law, intended to protect and improve the health of A-bomb victims, did not recognize microcephaly as an A-bomb-related condition. But it would have violated the spirit of this law simply to neglect persons so obviously damaged by the atomic bombs. So, in 1966, in response to strong demands of the affected families and to an aroused public, the Ministry of Health and Welfare arranged for a team to conduct "epidemiological research of microcephaly and other functional damages." The team's principal findings on microcephalic fetal victims (Nakaizumi et al. 1967) are as follows:

1. In fetal victims, development of head size, height, and weight was poor from birth. It is inferred that the embryo's organs were damaged in the early developmental stage.

2. Microcephaly, mental deficiencies, and poor physical development are all found in general cases of mentally retarded patients; but in A-bomb fetal victims, the incidence has been higher, and there have been abnormalities in skin pigmentation, bone hypoplasia, and benign tumors as well.

3. Among symptoms to be treated, there was a high incidence of anemia and susceptibility to infectious diseases, as is common in severe cases of mental retardation; but factors thought closely related to A-bomb damages to fetuses include (a) epileptic symptoms and behavioral abnormalities related to damage to the central nervous system, (b) eye problems such as strabismus and abnormalities of refraction, (c) orthopedic problems such as bone tumors and deficiencies in motor functions related to bone deformities or loss, and (d) skin problems such as skin tumors.

4. The chief problem is lack of ability to make social adjustments, due to serious deficiencies in psychological development. The worst cases are classified as severely mentally retarded, and most suffer imbecility: these cases should be admitted to and cared for in proper institutions. Lighter cases are capable of doing work under proper supervision and can take care of their daily needs if a suitable social environment is provided.

Acting on the research team's report, the Ministry of Health and Welfare issued a notice to all prefectural governors. This notice, dated 23 October 1967, announced its intention of certifying A-bomb fetal victims with severe microcephaly as authorized A-bomb victims (*Eihatsu* [Health report], no. 788). The first group of six persons to apply for official certification, some twenty-two years after the bombings, were authorized as eligible for national assistance as a special class defined as a "group of fetal victims

Figure 11.14. Microcephalic fetal victim Yuriko Hatanaka (born February 1946) and her mother Yoshie in 1975. The mother was 800 meters from the hypocenter at bombing time in Hiroshima and died December 1978. (Photograph by Yomiuri Shinbunsha.)

with symptoms of A-bomb damage sustained close to the hypocenter in the initial period." As this definition indicates, certification was not limited to microcephalic conditions but covered all kinds of damage to the entire body. At present twenty-two patients are certified in this group—thirteen in Hiroshima Prefecture (nine in Hiroshima City), four in Nagasaki Prefecture (two in Nagasaki City), two each in Yamaguchi Prefecture and Osaka Urban Prefecture, and one in Miyazaki Prefecture.

Certification alone, however, did not solve all problems. It only made fetal victims eligible for government payment of medical costs, and these people's problems were more than medical. Finally, in May 1968, the A-bomb Victims Special Measures Law was passed; it provided funds for "special treatment," and real relief for the fetal victims could begin.

Today, more than thirty years since the bombings, the fetal victims are confronted by a new and equally serious problem: the people upon whom they depend for support are getting old. What will victims who cannot manage by themselves do when their supporters die? Some victims have already lost one or both parents. All who presently care for fetal victims feel a growing uneasiness and wonder, "How can I die and leave this child alone?"

As of 1978 the fetal victims, at age thirty-three, belong to the adult generation. Seventeen are affiliated with the Kinoko-kai; unaffiliated fetal victims include two in Hiroshima Prefecture and three in Nagasaki Prefecture (Shimizu 1978). According to reports of the Kinoko-kai, the social environment of A-bomb fetal victims is not favorable. Only four have both parents, two have neither parent, three have only their fathers, and eight have only their mothers. Of the seven surviving fathers, three are age seventy or older; and of these, only three had monthly incomes exceeding 100,000 yen as of June 1977. Of the twelve surviving mothers, three suffered radiation exceeding 400 rads; two sustained radiation of 200 to 400 rads, and two, of 100 to 200 rads. Half are age sixty-five or older. Many are infirm; and only five earn some income, though the amounts are quite small. Not a few mothers of microcephalics depend solely on their own relief or health payments as A-bomb victims. Among the fetal victims, six (boys) are employed, but not at regular jobs, and certainly not at what would be expected of men aged thirty-three. They barely manage to serve as workers' helpers or do odd jobs for sympathetic employers. They tend to be slow-moving and short on understanding and judgment; and as they can hardly perform normal duties, their pay is extremely low.

Ten years have passed since certification of fetal victims began in 1967, but early expectations have not all been fulfilled. Of those needing but unable to qualify for help under the Special Measures Law, two need special treatment, seven need medical care, and fifteen need relief. In March 1976 the regulation requiring reapplication every three years for certification as a microcephalic victim was dropped. Even so, the procedures of applying for and receiving the various kinds of assistance are a burden to the victims and their aging supporters.

For over ten years these victims and their families have appealed and petitioned repeatedly for reforms in treatment and provisions; but they are too few in number compared to all A-bomb victims, so the laws have remained virtually unchanged. In April 1978 the aid programs for microcephalic victims started by Hiroshima and Nagasaki prefectures and cities were accepted as projects for national subsidy, and the microcephalic victims became eligible for monthly 30,000-yen payments. Even that subsidy, however, goes only to certified victims.

The relative needs of the seventeen victims affiliated with the Kinoko-kai are ranked as severe (twelve), moderate (four), and light (one). Two of the victims are married; marriage is considered impossible for eleven, difficult for two, and possible for the remaining two (though considerable help from the surrounding community and society would be needed). Two victims are in mental hospitals, and three more are in institutions for the mentally retarded.

The outlook is not bright for maintaining the present livelihood of microcephalic victims, and certainly not after their present supporters die. Some thirteen are hoping to rely on brothers or close relatives when their parents or guardians are gone. But over half of the homes involved have conditions that would make it difficult to accommodate a microcephalic victim, and in fact the victims need to be admitted eventually to specialized institutions.

The impact of the atomic bombs on fetal victims was permanent; they were robbed for life of the ability to look after themselves, and they have been virtually shut out of normal social life. The state, then, as a matter of national responsibility, must establish a system of adequate social support for these victims and their families who must bear the burden of their infirmities all the days of their lives.

Changes in the Lives of the A-bomb Victims

With the passage of over three decades since the atomic bombings, those born then have now become the parents of yet another generation. A full generational cycle has brought the parents of the bombing era to their fifties and sixties; the children of that time are in their forties; the grandchildren are now forming their own families; and great-grandchildren are being born and raised. The life changes of the A-bomb victims throughout this time can be grouped into three general periods.

FIRST PERIOD (1945–54)

The first period can be defined as the time when the A-bomb victims, as members of their community groups, shared in the physical, social, and spiritual devastation of their cities and then in the tasks of rebuilding them. In the latter half of this period various literary expressions of the bombing experience appeared, mainly as a way of sharing that experience among young people. Surveys of the victims' conditions were also made, and demands for medical care were directed to the national government. The year 1949 saw the passage of the Hiroshima Peace Memorial City Reconstruction Law and the Nagasaki International Culture City Reconstruction Law. Hiroshima in the same year and Nagasaki in the following year held conferences where young people could share their experiences. The mayors and the municipal assemblies of both cities in 1953 appealed to the national government for medical expense aid to the victims of the bombings.

Although, by late 1946, people who had earlier fled to the outskirts of Hiroshima or to other places were returning to the edges of the burned-out area, resettlement of the central zone destroyed by the bombing took much longer (see table 11.28). Those who suffered little family loss or injury, or

TABLE 11.28

*Population Resettlement, by Distance from Hypocenter, Hiroshima**

Distance from Hypocenter (km)	1 November 1945	26 April 1946	20 August 1946	10 December 1946	August 1947	August 1948
0–1.0	3.1	6.8	23.4	28.9	33.2	52.8
1.0–1.5	11.5	18.4	27.8	32.8	34.1	51.2
1.5–2.0	22.5	32.5	36.7	39.7	47.8	60.1
2.0–2.5	75.5	101.0	114.3	117.7	119.1	132.4
2.5–3.0	128.5	139.2	146.7	152.5	173.4	176.6
3.0–	181.6	216.7	201.3	211.8	209.7	213.5
Average	55.6	67.8	76.7	81.9	86.4	100.2

* Figures are percentages of the prebombing population; prebombing population based on rice ration registrations of June 1945.
Source: K. Yoneyama and T. Kawai. 1965. "The atomic bomb and social changes (I)—A socio-demographic review of atomic bomb sufferers and atomic bomb experience of occupational and work groups," *Hōgaku Kenkyū* [Journal of Law, Politics, and Sociology] 38:1163.

whose houses—at some distance from the hypocenter—suffered only light damage, reorganized their households, resettled in the city, and recovered their economic stability early in the resettlement process. The population increased as people gradually moved back into the city from the outskirts (places 3 kilometers or more from the hypocenter) and set up makeshift communities near Hiroshima and Koi stations on the national railway line (Kōno 1958, pp. 24–25).

Various official restrictions were imposed on the population flow into Hiroshima after the bombing, and were continued into 1946. But the reopening of, and recruitment of workers by, one of the major industries (Tōyō Kōgyō) sparked economic recovery; and enactment of the Special Cities Planning Law led to erection of 200 emergency housing units in Motomachi township. Gradually a mood of recovery spread among the citizens. By August 1948 the area within 1 kilometer of the hypocenter had reached 52.8 percent of the prebombing population (based on rice ration registrations), and the city as a whole had recovered its prebombing population level. As production got under way at Tōyō Kōgyō (a government-designated manufacturer of small three-wheeled motor vehicles), and laborers were hired for construction work under the Hiroshima Peace Memorial City Reconstruction Law, the city's population continued to grow. Then the city felt the impact of the

Occupation's "Dodge line"* deflationary policies; and industrial plants and places of business, numbering 3,840 at the start of 1949, had dropped to 1,317 by the year's end.

With the outbreak of the Korean War, the economy of western Japan gradually recovered, and the influx of people into the city drove the population up to its first postwar peak. This trend continued until 1954, when it reached the 1944 population level. During this time Hiroshima changed in character from a "city of A-bomb victims" to a postwar regional center. A supplementary survey of the 1950 national census showed that persons who had been in Hiroshima and Nagasaki at bombing times now constituted 34 percent of Hiroshima's population; a 1958 sample survey indicated that proportion had dropped to 24 percent (Hiroshima Prefectural Office and Hiroshima City Office 1960, p. 8). At the same time a wide gap had appeared between people who had managed to take advantage of the growth and recovery trends, and those whose status had declined due to losses and injuries sustained in the bombings. It was gradually recognized by knowledgeable civilians that special relief measures were needed to help the more disadvantaged; but during this first period virtually no concrete steps were taken.

Nagasaki's immediate population decline due to the bombing was 48 percent in 1945—compared to Hiroshima's 58 percent. Resettlement in parts of the burned-out area began gradually in the following year, though recovery in Urakami, center of the bombed area, was much slower. In the latter half of 1946 some simple emergency housing units were erected in Iwakawa township by the municipal housing corporation; later other public housing projects were completed in Iwakawa (66 units), Aburagi (16), and Shiroyama (180) townships (Nagasaki Shiyakusho 1977, pp. 594–95). By 25 November 1945, streetcar services were restored on the Hotarujaya–Nishihamanomachi–Nagasaki Station line (beyond the 2-kilometer limit of the worst damage), but alterations in the Nagasaki Station–Urakami line delayed its opening till early February 1946; and services on the Urakami–Ōhashi section began finally in late May 1947 (Nagasaki Shiyakusho 1977, p. 401). Gas service was restored to 760 households by June 1946, and Mitsubishi Shipbuilding launched its

---

* The *Dodge line* was a series of economic and financial policies executed by the Yoshida Cabinet under the guidance of Joseph M. Dodge, president of the National Bank of Detroit, who visited Japan in February 1949 as the GHQ's financial adviser.

Basically, this line was to make concrete an economic stabilization plan of nine principles—stringent measures of balanced budget, increased taxation and controlled financing, the establishment of a single exchange rate of ¥360 to a dollar, and so on—that the United States Government issued in December 1948.

This line resulted in the bankruptcy of many small and medium enterprises because of money stringency, created many jobless workers due to the rationalization of management, and intensified social unrest. However, it managed to help check inflation, thus enabling the Japanese economy to recover.

first postwar vessel, the *Daiichi Nisshin Maru*, in October of that year. Still, restoration of the city was limited to the old city district outside the zone of the worst destruction. Rebuilding of the suburbs began the following year with the construction by the municipal housing corporation of units in Shiro-yama (200) and Sumiyoshi (20), and was continued in 1948 with units in Sumiyoshi (66), Akasako (34), and Takenokubo (56). Public housing units for war victims and returned military personnel were erected in Shiroyama (66) and Aburagi (34) townships (Nagasaki Shiyakusho 1977, pp. 594–95). By 1948, the number of telephone subscribers had reached the prewar level; shipbuilding was into a five-year plan; and the Nagasaki branch of the Ministry of Labor's Women and Minors Bureau had embarked on a survey of women wounded and disabled by the atomic bomb. In 1949, the Nagasaki International Culture City Reconstruction Law was expedited; and in 1950, activities to exchange A-bomb experiences and to preserve peace were initiated.

Retail shops in the city's old district were generally reopened by this time, though business in front of Nagasaki Station had recovered to only one fourth of its prewar level.* Meantime, a new streetcar line had been laid between Ōhashi and Sumiyoshi in 1949, and the hospital attached to Nagasaki Medical University was moved from Shinkōzen to Urakami near the heart of the bombed area. Around 1952–53 housing construction in the Urakami district increased rapidly, and the city's population reached the 1944 level about one year earlier than Hiroshima's did.

SECOND PERIOD (1955-64)

The second period was a time of rapid growth in the Japanese economy and of changes in the lives of the A-bomb victims. Most people who, after the bombings, had left the cities of Hiroshima and Nagasaki returned during the first period. As explained earlier (page 349), the prebombing 1944 populations were 340,000 in Hiroshima and 270,000 in Nagasaki. Drafting of men for military service and evacuation of women and children had reduced these figures by 50,000 and 30,000, respectively. The A-bombs killed 110,000 in Hiroshima and 60,000 to 70,000 in Nagasaki, leaving postbombing populations of approximately 180,000 in each city. The 1945 census, however, listed populations of 140,000 in each city, indicating that some 40,000 people had fled each city after the bombings. The maximum estimates of the populations by the end of the first period, after the return of evacuees and discharged military personnel, are 90,000 in Hiroshima and 60,000 to 70,000 in Nagasaki. Among the A-bomb victims of both cities, some settled permanently else-where, and others left after having once returned; and most victims experi-

* Nagasaki Shiyakusho, General Affairs Department Investigation and Statistics Section, 1959, vol. 2, pp. 561–62.

enced some loss of status and delay in regrouping their families and in finding employment due to losses and injuries suffered. But, on the whole, during the second period the A-bomb victims managed, despite various setbacks, to resettle in the cities, to find jobs, and generally to improve their economic conditions.

A 1958 interim census of Hiroshima Prefecture shows that more A-bomb victims than nonvictims worked in the farming, fishing, forestry, and low-skill industrial sectors; fewer victims had service, office, transport, and high-skilled industrial jobs than did nonvictims. However, in the 1965 survey by the Ministry of Health and Welfare, fewer A-bomb victims were engaged in farming, fishing, and forestry, and more were involved in low-skill industrial sectors. In total, A-bomb victims' employment in both of the preceding categories had fallen below national levels. These comparisons are not wholly precise, since the 1958 census compares A-bomb victims with nonvictims in the same prefectures, while the 1965 survey makes adjustments according to nationwide age groups. Even so, this reversal in employment patterns indicates that the A-bomb victims' livelihood improved along with the nation's rapid economic recovery. On the other hand, the employment rate, especially in day-labor jobs, was high for women victims, while unemployment and layoff rates for men victims remained higher than national levels. Job changes constituted a key factor in victims' status decline, especially for middle-aged persons, even in this era of high growth. Employment of disabled persons was high, as there was no overt job discrimination; but the average annual income of A-bomb victims fell 10 percent below the national average.

People who had been teenagers at the time of the bombings, like their parents, generally sought employment in this second period. In addition to losing one or both parents, more of these young people remained unmarried than was the case nationwide. As loss of nearly 30 percent of married couples in the bombings hindered the recovery of livelihood in the first period, so loss of about 20 percent of the younger generation contributed to the lack of manpower in the second period of economic growth; while in the third period (1965–74) there appeared the special aftereffects of the aging of the A-bomb victims. The aging process added to the difficulties of the many victims who remained unmarried.

In the early half of the first period, people left and then returned to the A-bombed cities; then in the latter half of that period an influx of nonvictims exceeding that of victims swelled the populations of both cities. In the second period the influx of nonvictims continued; while many victims, particularly the young, began leaving the two cities once again. As noted earlier (pages 401–3), the population of young people in both Hiroshima and Nagasaki expanded, but that of boys and girls aged five to nineteen at bombing times (aged ten to twenty-four in 1950, twenty to thirty-four in 1960) declined, as did that of people forty and older (forty-five and older in 1950, fifty-five and older in 1960). That the population decrease in the two cities stemmed from the departure of A-bomb victims is clearly evident from the marked increase of such victims in Tokyo, Osaka, Fukuoka, and other large urban areas (figure 11.7), as reflected in the distribution of people holding A-bomb health books. The A-bomb victims could no longer be regarded as regional social groups located in Hiroshima and Nagasaki; they had become a national population group of "A-bomb-related people" who, while still centered in the two cities, were now involved in the full spectrum of social, economic, and political changes occurring throughout the nation.

These trends were evident in the patterns of participation by A-bomb victims in the antinuclear movement's first world rally held in August 1955 in Hiroshima and in the administration of the nation's A-bomb health program, as well as in the antinuclear movement's subsequent split, in the campaign to compile a white paper on A-bomb damages, and in the efforts to preserve records of the bombings spurred by the white paper campaign.

THIRD PERIOD (1965–74)

Despite inadequacies in aid provided the A-bomb victims, the third period marks the eventual restoration of their livelihood and, at the same time, the emergence of grave anxieties over the aftereffects of the A-bombs. The passage of two or three decades has by no means lessened or lightened the sufferings of the A-bomb victims. While the physical restoration of society has now exceeded prewar levels, the victims and those related to them face not only the nagging fear of medical aftereffects but also the burdens of aging and underlying spiritual distress. Such problems were already apparent in the second period; as one source put it, "The cities may be outwardly restored, but the wounds of our inner world are not yet healed." (Nagasaki Shiyakusho, General Affairs Department, Investigation and Statistics Section, 1959, vol. 3, p. 694.)

The mobility of the A-bomb victims, already notable in the second period, was even greater in the third. Victims were only 24 percent of Hiroshima's population according to a 1958 survey; but the 1960 count, though expanded to include all A-bomb health-book holders, was only 21 percent; and the 1965 figure dropped to 16 percent (or 20 percent even if those without health books are included). By way of contrast, A-bomb victims constituted only 5.8 percent of the 1965 populations in the nine prefectures encompassed by the Tokyo capital region and the Kyoto-Osaka-Kobe region; but they made up 10.3 percent of these populations in 1975, according to the Ministry of Health and Welfare surveys (1977a, p. 3).

Comparison of the 1965 and 1975 surveys clearly indicates the problems of natural aging and the loss of productivity due to illness among the A-bomb victims themselves, as well as the symptoms of "regressive reproductivity" contingent upon the aging of the A-bomb victims and their relatives. The former problem is seen, for example, in declining employment and income; the latter, in low rates of marriage among those aged thirty and older. The causes, as already assessed, are to be found in losses suffered in the bombings, in subsequent hardships in making a living, and in various anxieties, including the finding of suitable mates. As one example, household expenditures of A-bomb victims are not notably different from those of nonvictims (though a 1965 survey showed a widening gap), but there are indications of considerably greater dependence on the incomes of nonvictims in A-bomb victims' households.

Thus, the parental generation of those forty and older at bombing times was active in the first period's rebuilding of communities, and these people are now in their seventies. People who were in their teenage youth at bombing times have since rebuilt their lives despite the burdens of a rapidly changing society and, in many instances, are supporting their parents. A significant feature of this third period is that, out of all the diversities and complexities of their lives, the members of each generation have tended to objectify, and gain an overall perspective of, their experiences, of which, through sharing them, they seek some historical understanding. All this has led to the compilation of personal testimonies, the preservation of records, and efforts to reconstruct the actual situation at the time of and following the bombings.

Meantime, A-bomb victims' associations and the cities of Hiroshima and Nagasaki have pressed for government policies of assistance to the victims beyond the scope of medical care. In this connection the Ministry of Health and Welfare began investigations that in 1965 led to the A-bomb Victims Special Measures Law and, at the same time, to the realization that the health and the livelihood of the victims no longer differed much from those of the general populace. This view, however, spurred further research to produce a fuller, more complete picture of the A-bomb victims' actual situation. Also, in Hiroshima a movement arose to reconstruct conditions at the time of the bombing. Similar efforts in Nagasaki produced ten volumes of testimonies in the decade from 1968 to 1978.

These trends became especially marked in the latter part of the third period, as many people of different generations and social classes, including nonvictims, endeavored through mutual exchange and activities to compile records and evaluate the historical significance of the whole A-bomb experience. The increased activity stemmed largely from the conviction on the part of survivors of the atomic bombings that they have an invaluable lesson to pass on to the next generation. The base for the heightened activity was not only the municipalities of Hiroshima and Nagasaki, as important regional centers, but also a wide range of independent associations of A-bomb victims and · their supporters. And these associations, because of the nationwide dispersion of A-bomb victims typical of this period, are national in the scope of their organization and activities.

Foreigners among the A-bomb Victims

The primary concern of the American military authorities who decided to drop the atomic bomb on Japan was to confirm its immense destructive power.* The targets chosen for this purpose were cities large enough to allow the bombs to demonstrate their full powers. Such reasoning may have been natural in wartime, but the confirmed presence of American and other Allied prisoners of war in the targeted cities† was not allowed to deter the bombing plans.‡ Prisoners in the POW camps of the two cities were American, British, Australian, and Dutch (mostly born in Java, then a Dutch colony), but their lives were essentially ignored. Hiroshima was not thought to have POWs; but, in fact, over ten American POWs were interned directly under the targeted spot.

More important, several thousand noncombatant foreigners were victims of the same assault. Besides Americans of Japanese descent (born in the United States) who were living in Hiroshima, there were clergy, students, and other citizens from Germany, Russia, China, Mongolia, Korea, and several Southeast Asian countries residing in the city at the time (Hiroshima Shiyakusho 1971a, pp. 168–81). In Nagasaki there were many Chinese residents as well as missionaries, including nuns, of foreign nations (Kamata 1978, p. 52; NGO International Symposium 1977b, pp. 89–90). As far as the records show, however, the welfare of these citizens of the United States and other countries was never, from the outset of planning, considered.

* Blackett 1948; Freed and Giovannitti 1965; Groves and Groves 1962; Knebel and Bailey II 1960; A. Nishijima 1968.

† To demonstrate the might of the A-bombs, the cities of Kokura, Hiroshima, Niigata, and Kyoto were initially chosen, and orders prohibiting the bombing of these cities with conventional bombs were issued prior to the atomic bombings (Freed and Giovannitti 1965; Groves and Groves 1962; and Knebel and Bailey II 1960). The "target committee" is said to have drawn up an initial list of seventeen cities, including Tokyo, Kawasaki, Yokohama, Nagoya, Osaka, Fukuoka, and Nagasaki, in addition to the above four cities (*Asahi Shimbun,* 3 June 1979, Yokohama edition).

‡ Freed and Giovannitti 1965; Knebel and Bailey II 1960; Sodei 1978.

The many foreign nationals among the A-bomb victims posed a variety of serious problems. It was bad enough that foreigners in wartime Japan were subject to abusive treatment at the hands of militaristic and colonialistic Japanese; but even after the atomic bombings, aid to foreign survivors and disposal of their dead took second place to the care of Japanese victims. Most of the surviving foreign A-bomb victims returned to their homelands after the war; but for them or those remaining in Japan, the Japanese government undertook neither relief nor diplomatic measures, then or later. Indeed, people returning to Korea faced very poor living conditions. Many sources have reported on their daily troubles;* and their death rate is reported to be high (Cheong et al. 1978).

A-bomb victims in the United States today include not only Americans of Japanese descent but also Japanese who have emigrated there in the postwar years. Other victims have settled in Canada, Australia, Brazil, Argentina, Peru, and elsewhere. The existence of these victims in various places around the world must not be ignored.

The whole gamut of A-bomb problems—anxiety over radiation aftereffects, hardships in making a living, social estrangement due to lack of understanding of their plight, and concern for their children and grandchildren—all weigh heavily on the foreign victims remaining in Japan, on their compatriots who returned to homes abroad, and on the Japanese victims who emigrated. For these groups the long-term problems of A-bomb victims are greatly magnified.

KOREAN A-BOMB VICTIMS

To understand why the vast majority of foreign A-bomb victims in Hiroshima and Nagasaki were Koreans—said to number in the tens of thousands, although precise figures are not known—it is important to recall that Japan annexed Korea in August 1910 and that a Japanese governor-general ruled there until Japan's defeat in 1945. Japanese colonial policy during these thirty-five years was not limited to political control: it deprived the Koreans of their lands, their natural resources, and even their language, and forced them to engage in Shinto shrine worship as well as to bow reverently toward the distant imperial palace in Tokyo. They even had to change their names in the thoroughgoing "assimilation" policies designed to render them "imperial subjects." Of particular importance were the land survey (1910–18) and the campaign to increase rice production (from 1920) through which Korea's farm communities were plundered and eventually destroyed. Most of the farmers whom these measures had deprived of their land and, thus, of their means of livelihood, abandoned their villages and headed overseas, often in

---

* Hiraoka 1966, pp. 229–35; Hiraoka 1969, p. 48; S. Pak, Kwak, and Sin 1975, p. 296.

groups (Korean History Research Society 1974; Miyata 1977). The Japanese economy prospered during, and because of, World War I; and cheap Korean labor was rapidly introduced into Japan's coal mines, manufacturing plants, and civil engineering works.

Japan's manpower needs rose rapidly following its takeover of Manchuria in 1931 and the outbreak of war with China in 1937; and the influx of Korean laborers also accelerated. Implementation of the National Mobilization Plan in 1939 sparked the first phase of official recruitment of young able-bodied Korean men to work in Japanese mines. Depletion of Japan's own manpower by military conscription led in 1942 to the second phase of recruitment, in which government agents from the Japanese governor-general's office dispatched labor gangs to Japan. Finally, under the National Compulsory Work Order of 1944, Korean workers were forcibly rounded up and shipped to Japan.

Various reports, based on statistics of the security bureau of the Ministry of Home Affairs and on other sources, have been made on the influx and settlement of Koreans in Japan;* although there are discrepancies in the figures among the sources. There are errors in the recently reissued records (G. Pak 1976, pp. 563–64) of the Ministry of Home Affairs' security bureau (and this source should be scrutinized anew). For this book we have compared and coordinated data in the security bureau's reissued records, the rather voluminous records on forcible dispatching of Korean workers compiled by various bureaus related to the Ministry of Justice (Morita 1955), and documents produced through other energetic efforts to study the problem of forced labor among Koreans (G. Pak 1965). The resultant figures on population trends of Koreans resident in Japan appear in table 11.29.

The Korean resident count for the year of annexation (1910) is not clear, but Koreans in Japan in the previous year numbered only 790. A decade later, in 1920, this figure had jumped to 30,189, and had multiplied tenfold by 1930, to 298,091. Security bureau records (Ministry of Home Affairs 1976, p. 499) show that the National Mobilization Plan had pushed the count by 1940 to 1,190,444; by the end of December 1944, a peak of 1,936,843 had been reached. Pak Gyeung-sik—a specialist in contemporary Korean history who was educated in Japan—gives the even higher figure of 2,365,263 as of the war's end in 1945 (G. Pak 1965). This figure suggests that labor mobilization for the final defense of Japan brought in 400,000 more Korean workers in half a year. In any case, the 1945 war's-end figure is not based on authoritative sources. Moreover, according to security bureau documents (Ministry of Home Affairs 1976, p. 499), the heavy Allied bombing of Japan in 1945 pro-

* Korean History Research Society 1974; Miyata 1977; Morita 1955; Nakatsuka 1978; C. Pak 1957; G. Pak 1965; S. Pak 1969, p. 290.

TABLE 11.29

Population Trends among Koreans Resident in Japan, 1900–34

Year	Resident Population*	Increase	Remarks
1900	196	—	
1905	303	107	Treaty ended Russo-Japanese War (1904–1905)
1907	459	156	
1909	790	331	
1910	—	—	Japan annexed Korea
1911	2,527	1,737	
1912	3,171	644	Land survey announced
1913	3,635	464	
1914	3,542	− 93	First World War began
1915	3,917	375	
1916	5,624	1,707	
1917	14,502	8,878	
1918	22,411	7,909	Land survey completed
1919	26,605	4,194	March First Movement for Independence; travel permit system introduced
1920	30,189	3,584	Campaign to increase rice production
1921	38,651	8,462	
1922	59,722	21,071	Regulations on voyages rescinded
1923	80,415	20,693	Great Kantō earthquake
1924	118,152	37,737	
1925	129,870	11,718	Restrictions on voyages imposed
1926	143,796	13,926	
1927	165,286	21,490	Depression of Japanese economy and currency
1928	238,102	72,816	
1929	275,206	37,104	Depression of world economy
1930	298,091	22,885	
1931	311,247	13,156	Manchurian incident
1932	390,543	79,296	
1933	456,217	65,674	
1934	537,695	81,478	

* Year-end figures.

Source: Y. Morita, "Changes and present status of treatment of Koreans in Japan," *Hōmu Kenkyū Hōkokusho* [Ministry of Justice Research Reports] 43rd Collection, no. 3 (Tokyo: Hōmu Kēnshūsho, 1955). G. Pak, *Chōsenjin Kyōsei Renkō no Kiroku* [Record of Forced Arrest of Koreans] (Tokyo: Miraisha, 1965), pp. 64–66, 122, 168–69.

voked considerable agitation among Korean residents, and they undertook to return home or to escape elsewhere. Thus, increase in population was offset by some decrease; and it is reasonable to assume that there were approximately 2,000,000 Koreans resident in Japan when the war ended. In the same source, the security bureau's report on "the security situation at the time of the Cabinet's decision to end the war" (dated 1 September 1945) states, "Koreans resident in this country number 1,930,000 . . . of whom 280,000 were brought in as groups of laborers." The 280,000 figure must be regarded as too low; for, as table 11.30 shows, plans were approved for the compulsory introduction of 710,000 workers, and some 600,000 are thought to have been forcibly mobilized. Moreover, passage on the national railways and shipping between Shimonoseki and Pusan (two of the closest major cities in the two countries) were strictly controlled to prevent desertions.*

The total number of Koreans resident in Japan includes not only laborers recruited or forced to come to Japan but also ordinary immigrants and their families, as well as students. This background explains the many Koreans among the A-bomb victims of Hiroshima and Nagasaki. But all Korean A-bomb victims—whether voluntary or involuntary immigrants—are distinguished from Japanese victims in that they were long victims of repressive policies before falling victim to the atomic bombs (Ri 1977, p. 105).

How many Koreans, then, were in Hiroshima and Nagasaki? Table 11.31 lists the Korean populations in Hiroshima and Nagasaki prefectures for the years 1935–45. The increase of Koreans in the two prefectures, especially Nagasaki, was much greater than in the rest of the nation. By the end of 1944, Hiroshima Prefecture had 81,863 Koreans (5,944 of them brought over in forced-labor groups), and Nagasaki had 59,573 (20,474 in forced-labor groups). How many of them lived in the cities of Hiroshima and Nagasaki, however, is not clear. As the security bureau records indicate, Koreans were subject to surveillance and, in 1940, to enforced adoption of Japanese names as they were converted into "imperial subjects" and integrated into the national populace; and full public records were not kept. Today it is impossible to determine how many Koreans were living in the bombed areas or how many were among early entrants affected by residual radiation. Hence, it is extremely difficult to ascertain the real situation regarding Korean A-bomb victims.

As the Japanese government had not previously conducted a full-scale

* The regular steamship line between Shimonoseki (Yamaguchi Prefecture) and Pusan (Korea) was inaugurated in 1905, enabling the Japanese to reach Korea in the most time-saving way. Only Koreans with authorized entry permission were allowed to get on board the ship. Japanese policemen were also on board to keep a sharp eye out for Korean stowaways.

TABLE 11.30
Korean Resident Population in Japan, 1935–45[1]

Year	Resident Population	Increase	Workers Imported under "National Mobilization Plan"			Remarks
			Approved (Immigrants)	Actual Immigrants	Immigrants Actually Present*	
1935	625,678	87,983	—	—	—	
1936	690,501	64,823	—	—	—	"Cooperative project," strengthening of assimilation policy
1937	735,689	45,188	—	—	—	war with China proclaimed
1938	799,878	64,189	—	—	—	National Mobilization Plan proclaimed; also applied to Korea
1939	961,591	161,713	(38,959)	19,135	18,626	National Mobilization Plan implemented; workers recruited and exported to Korea
1940	1,190,444	228,853	(120,780)	86,765	63,038	Koreans forced to take Japanese names
1941	1,469,230	278,786	(184,773)	126,092	77,086	Pacific War proclaimed
1942	1,625,054	155,824	(307,043)	248,521	124,097	compulsory labor enforced in Korea; labor groups recruited and exported to Japan
1943	1,882,456	257,402	(438,130)	366,464	167,215	labor groups rounded up and forcibly exported to Japan; military conscription implemented in Korea
1944	1,936,843	54,387	(655,483)	551,674[3]	270,660	
1945 (31 March) (end of war)	2,365,263[2]		(711,505)	604,429[3]	288,488 264,030[1]	A-bombs dropped
1946 (1 January)	1,155,594[4]					

* Excluding those who completed compulsory work and returned home, escaped, or were sent home.

Source: (1) Ministry of Home Affairs, Security Bureau, "Status of movements of resident Koreans—Special Secret Service Police Monthly Report' manuscript 1945," in *Zainichi Chōsenjin Kankeishiryō Shūsei* [Collection of Data on Koreans in Japan], Pak Gyeung-sik, ed. (Tokyo: San-ichi Shobō, 1976); vol. V, p. 499.

(2) G. Pak, *Chōsenjin Kyōsei Renkō no Kiroku* [Record of Forced Arrest of Koreans] (Tokyo: Miraisha, 1965), pp. 64–66, 122, 168–69.

(3) S. Pak, "Forced arrest of Koreans—as told from personal experience," in *Dokumento Nihonjin 8—Anchihyūman* [Document Japanese 8—Antihuman], Ken'ichi Tanigawa, Shunsuke Tsurumi, and Ichirō Murakami, eds. (Tokyo: Gakugei Shorin, 1969), p. 290.

TABLE 11.31

Korean Populations in Hiroshima and Nagasaki Prefectures, 1935–45[1]

Year	Hiroshima Prefecture Resident Population	Imported Workers* Approved (Immigrants)	Actual Immigrants†	Immigrants Actually Present‡	Nagasaki Prefecture Resident Population	Imported Workers* Approved (Immigrants)	Actual Immigrants†	Immigrants Actually Present‡
1935	17,385				7,229			
1936	19,491				7,046			
1937	19,525				7,625			
1938	24,878				8,852			
1939	30,864	—	—	—	11,343	(2,920)	657	652
1940	38,221	—	—	—	18,144	(9,715)	6,308	4,692
1941	48,746	(1,700)	1,421	721	22,408	(13,865)	8,967	5,322
1942	53,951	(2,500)	2,332	936	34,515	(21,784)	17,471	9,551
1943	68,274	(—)	—	5,944	—	(27,546)	24,294	11,483
1944	81,863				59,573	(—)	—	20,474
1945	60,000[2]	—	—	—	—			—

* Included in resident population count.

† Includes a small number of workers brought from other prefectures in Japan.

‡ Excluding those who completed compulsory work and returned home, escaped, or were sent home.

Source: (1) Ministry of Home Affairs, Security Bureau. 1976. "Status of movements of resident Koreans—'Special Secret Service Police Monthly Report' manuscript 1945," in *Zainichi Chōsenjin Kankeishiryō Shūsei* [Collection of Data on Koreans in Japan] vol. V, p. 499. Pak Gyeung-sik, ed. San-ichi Shobō, Tokyo.
(2) Hiroshima Prefectural Police History Editorial Committee, *Shinpen Hiroshimaken Keisatsushi* [History of Hiroshima Prefectural Police, New Edition] (Hiroshima: Hiroshimaken Keisatsu Renraku Kyōgikai, 1954), p. 895.

survey of this situation, the Seoul-based Association for the Relief of Korean A-bomb Victims (now the Korean A-bomb Victims Association) estimated the number of Koreans who were A-bomb victims (table 11.32) (Pak, Kwak,

TABLE 11.32

Korean A-bomb Victims

City	Total	Deaths	Survivors	Returned to Korea	Remained Temporarily in Japan
Hiroshima	50,000	30,000	20,000	15,000	5,000
Nagasaki	20,000	10,000	10,000	8,000	2,000
Total	70,000	40,000	30,000	23,000	7,000

Source: April 1972 report in S. Pak, K. Kwak, and W. Sin, *Hibaku Kankokujin* [A-bomb Exposed Koreans] (Tokyo: Asahi Shimbunsha, 1975), p. 296.

and Sin 1975, p. 296). According to these estimates, there were 50,000 in Hiroshima and 20,000 in Nagasaki; but still unclear are the scope of the bombed area considered, the date up to which deaths were counted, and whether survivors who returned to Korea were included in the calculations.

Korean A-bomb Victims in Hiroshima. The estimated numbers of Hiroshima and Nagasaki A-bomb victims given in chapter 10 naturally include countless Koreans who migrated to Japan with the help of relatives and settled into Japanese communities in the cities and their environs.

Koreans also were presumably among the young male workers, the women's volunteer corps, the students' service corps, and other groups brought into the cities by the nationwide mobilization plan. Given the army's voluntary enlistment program started in Korea in 1938, the conscription of laborers for army-related work in 1939, and the military conscription conducted in Korea in 1944, a small number of Korean soldiers and workers were certainly billeted in army camps in Hiroshima.

Moreover, groups of workers brought over in forced-labor programs to work in Hiroshima's industries were housed in dormitories in the city. Table 11.31 shows 5,944 Korean residents of Hiroshima Prefecture in 1944. The number of Korean residents at bombing time is not certain, for there were deaths and desertions among them; but Koreans were definitely working in the Mitsubishi shipbuilding and machinery plants, on the construction of an electrical generating plant at Yasuno village in Yamagata county, in the shipyards at Kure and Innoshima, and elsewhere. About one thousand were working at Mitsubishi Shipbuilding inside the city, and police records show about eight hundred at the Yasuno generating plant site (G. Pak 1976, vol.

V, pp. 563–64). While the number of other Korean labor groups is unclear, various estimates have been made, of which the most important follow:*

1. Immediately after the war there were approximately 60,000 Koreans in Hiroshima Prefecture, of whom *30,000–40,000 were subjected to the atomic bombing of Hiroshima City.* (Hiroshima Shiyakusho 1971a, pp. 168–81)

2. Of the 81,000 [Korean] residents of the prefecture, *at least 50,000 were concentrated in Hiroshima* with all its war plants. . . . At the time, construction of an airport was under way, and temporary quarters for imported Koreans working on the airport were clustered in the Higashi Kan'on, Tenmachō, and Funairi townships. Between Yokogawa bridge and Kōhei bridge alone, there were 300 [Korean] households. *All were near the central bombed area in Hiroshima's western sector, and all were destroyed.* There were 700 [Koreans] in the Ujina shipyard, 1,000 in the Mitsubishi machinery plant, and *an estimated 20,000–30,000 other compulsory [Korean] workers.* Including their families, at least 20,000 of the Koreans were killed in the atomic bombing. (Kanai 1970, pp. 308–09)

3. In 1944 there were 81,863 Koreans living in the [Hiroshima] prefecture, and it is estimated that *roughly 30,000 of these resided in Hiroshima City.* . . . Koreans entering Hiroshima Prefecture were mainly farmers or laborers working in factories in Hiroshima's suburbs. They worked at Mitsubishi Shipbuilding in the city, and as factory hands or longshoremen at Ujina port, Tōyō Kōgyō, Hiroshima Precision Machines (Gion town, Asa county), Nippon Steel (Funakoshi town, Aki county), the Kure shipyard, and other factories, and as common laborers for harbor and river projects. The number at all places is uncertain; but nearly 500 Koreans are said to have worked at the "Dawn Patrol" (Akatsuki) military transport base in Ujina port, and close to 3,000 Koreans were forced to work at the Kan'on munitions plant of Mitsubishi Heavy Industries under construction on reclaimed land. They lived in nearby shantytowns, and *most of the Korean workers had been forcibly brought over under compulsory labor plans.* (Uehara 1972, pp. 11–17)

4. When the atomic bomb hit Hiroshima, there were between 84,000 and 85,000 Koreans in Hiroshima Prefecture. Some 20,000 were forced to work in tunnel construction at the naval arsenal and powder dump in Kure, and many others worked at Hitachi Shipbuilding on Innoshima Island, the naval facility at Ōtake, the Kōbo dam project in Hiba county (northern Hiroshima Prefecture); so it is estimated that *approximately 50,000 were in Hiroshima City,* most of whom suffered A-bomb damage. (Nakatsuka 1978)

5. Korean labor groups were forcibly imported to work at Mitsubishi's Kan'on plant and the army clothing depot in Ujina, as well as at the Akatsuki military transport facility and Nippon Steel's Hiroshima plant. It is also known that many Koreans worked directly for the army. Their families lived mainly in the townships of Fukushima, Kan'on, Ujina, Hirose, Tenma, and Onaga—all within 1 to 4 kilometers of the A-bomb's hypocenter. Thus, *most of the approximately 50,000 Koreans living and working in Hiroshima City are thought to have sustained A-bomb damage.* . . . Our estimate is that there are well over 2,000 A-bomb victims in the Democratic

---

* Italics added to all the following quotations.

People's Republic of Korea [North Korea] and some 15,000 in the Republic of Korea [South Korea]. (Ri 1977, p. 105)

To summarize the preceding sources, almost 50,000 Koreans lived in Hiroshima City at the time of the atomic bombing, and roughly 20,000 of these died. As most of the survivors returned to their homeland, there are more than 17,000 A-bomb victims on the Korean peninsula. These figures generally match the foregoing estimates of the Association for the Relief of Korean A-bomb Victims.

Because of discrepancies in the definition of Korean immigrants and residents in Japan, however, estimates of the resident Korean population in Hiroshima City are not necessarily accurate. Koreans brought over forcibly in labor groups are sometimes confused with other Korean residents who were subjected to general mobilization.

Places of residence and work are sometimes quantified without regard to distance from bombed areas, as when less-affected places like the Ujina shipyard, Tōyō Kōgyō, and Nippon Steel are lumped together with plants in the central area. Takashi Hiraoka, for instance, records testimony that Koreans living in the city were conscripted for work in the suburban Nippon Steel factory (Fukagawa 1974, pp. 108–11). Along with other errors or misconceptions in assessing A-bomb victims and deaths among Korean residents, Munetoshi Fukagawa points out that, in May and June of 1945, many conscripted Korean workers in Mitsubishi Shipbuilding in the city escaped—reducing their number by a thousand by late July—and that some Koreans were employed by the Hiroshima branch of Nippon Tsūun (Nippon Express) and the Nishimatsu construction group (Fukagawa 1974, pp. 108–11). On the other hand, however, the areas where the aforementioned Koreans lived and those where they were subject to A-bomb damage are of great importance. As is clear from the recent report (Cheong et al. 1978) on Korea's Hyopchong-gun district where many victims of the Hiroshima atomic bombing now live, most of them were living on Hiroshima's west side within 1 to 3 kilometers of the hypocenter; and their compulsory work was in factories inside the city limits and beyond, within 3 to 6 kilometers of the hypocenter. (There were, of course, other Koreans engaged in military and public projects who lived and worked among the Japanese.)

Accurate records and documents concerning Koreans, then, are scarce. Relating what is known of them to what is known generally about the bombing, we offer the following general estimates of Koreans in Hiroshima.

Under late wartime mobilization, a relative majority of the increased Korean population in Hiroshima Prefecture was mobilized for work in military and industrial facilities in Hiroshima City's suburbs. If the Korean population in the city and its environs is set tentatively at 40,000 to 50,000, half of them lived in the burned-out area (1 to 3 kilometers); the other half lived in suburban districts near factories. If one applies the November 1945 death rates in Hiroshima published by the Joint Commission (table 10.6), in which 40,555 died out of the 174,370 people within 1 to 3 kilometers of the hypocenter—a death rate of 23.3 percent—(Oughterson and Warren 1956, pp. 84, 457–58), then of the estimated 20,000 to 30,000 Koreans within the same range, between 4,700 and 7,000 died. The death rate for the 3-to-5-kilometer range was 1.9 percent (958 deaths out of 49,710 people), so there would have been approximately 400 deaths among the estimated 20,000 Koreans in that same range. In the intermediate range, 2.5 to 4 kilometers, the death rate was 2.6 percent—indicating 78 deaths among the 3,000 Koreans estimated for that range. Even if several thousand Koreans were among early entrants into the city, the death rate would not change noticeably. To sum up, if the number of Korean A-bomb victims is set at 40,000 to 50,000, then those who died during or soon after the bombing numbered between 5,000 and 8,000.

The Association for the Relief of Korean A-bomb Victims estimated 20,000 Korean survivors of the Hiroshima bombing (15,000 returned home; 5,000 stayed in Japan); on the basis of the city's average death rate of 25.3 percent, 5,060 of these survivors died. Reckoning back from this figure, the total number of Korean A-bomb victims becomes 27,000. This death count of 5,060 is close to that reached above (5,000–8,000), but there is a sharp discrepancy between these figures (27,000 victims, 5,060 dead) and the association's estimates of 50,000 victims and 30,000 dead. Because there were many Koreans among early entrants into the city, the total number of victims can be reasonably raised to 32,000, but that would require a commensurate number of survivors. Hence, the 50,000 figure is thought also to include nonvictim Koreans living in towns and villages outside Hiroshima City.

Finally, it is not clear how many Koreans were among the 40,000 A-bomb victims and 20,000 deaths estimated for military personnel and civilian employees of the military (pages 353, 366–67). There were some Koreans conscripted to work as civilian employees for the army transport facility at Ujina (Akatsuki Unit), and one unit is recorded to have had 500 such workers. Conscription of Korean workers for military use began in 1939 and escalated rapidly to 16,000 in 1941, 22,000 in 1942, 12,000 in 1943, 45,000 in 1944, and 48,000 in 1945. Moreover, the army's voluntary enlistment order of 1938, the navy's similar order of 1943, and universal military conscription in Korea in 1944 brought many Koreans into uniform. Consequently, they numbered 186,980 in the Japanese army, 22,290 in the navy, and 154,907 in military-related jobs (G. Pak, 1965, pp. 64–66, 122, 168–69). Li Wu-gong, an educational officer in the Second Army, has confirmed a number of these cases (Hiroshima Shiyakusho 1971*a*, pp. 168–81); but altogether they do not greatly alter the total number of Korean A-bomb victims or deaths.

Korean A-bomb Victims in Nagasaki. As table 11.31 shows, the Korean population increase in Nagasaki Prefecture was remarkable, and the influx of conscripted Korean workers far exceeded that in Hiroshima Prefecture. The primary factor behind conscription was labor needs in the prefecture's coal mines, and thus most of the conscripted workers were located outside Nagasaki City. Other Koreans are thought to have been engaged in construction of military facilities in Nagasaki's environs (Kyushu Regional Group 1974, pp. 32–41; Taura 1971, p. 44).

According to reconstruction surveys, quarters for Korean workers within 2.5 kilometers of the hypocenter included housing for some 300 conscripted Koreans working at Mitsubishi Steel (600 meters from the hypocenter) and five other quarters for workers at Mitsubishi Munitions' Ōhashi plant, its underground plant, and the Sumiyoshi tunnel project, all within a range of 1.5 to 2.5 kilometers. About 2,500 conscripted Koreans worked at Mitsubishi Shipbuilding's Nagasaki shipyard (Ikeda 1968, p. 261); their housing was in Kibachi, 5 kilometers southwest of the hypocenter (Kanamaru 1970, p. 140). Other quarters were in Nishidomari, Kosedo, and other places within 5 to 6 kilometers.

Several sources that refer to Koreans in Nagasaki follow:*

1. When the war ended, there were at Kawanami Shipyard 500 to 2,000 conscripted workers, 1,500 to 4,000 prisoners, and *300 Korean laborers.*

At Mitsubishi Shipbuilding there were, as of January 1945, 250 prisoners, 443 POWs, *3,474 Koreans,* 3,485 students, 1,627 women, 566 volunteer corpsmen, and 586 national service corpsmen—a total of 10,431. (Nagasaki Shiyakusho, General Affairs Department, Investigation and Statistics Section, 1959, vol. 3, p. 431)

2. According to reports of a dozen or so fellow countrymen, *several thousand Koreans who had been forced to work at Mitsubishi Shipbuilding and the Nagasaki Arsenal, as well as 300 Korean girl students, were killed instantly by the bomb.* The vast majority of the remains of 150 Koreans found at Jōkōin temple in Ōura Motomachi were killed by the A-bomb. (*Chōsen Shinpō* 1965)

3. *About 300 Koreans were working at the main and branch plants of Mitsubishi Munitions,* and there were many shanties along the banks of Urakami river. Some 3,000 [Koreans] paid dues to a community organization, according to a 1943 record; but *were there not actually more than 10,000 of them?* Of 120 in one dormitory when the bomb was dropped, only two survived. Most Koreans in the Urakami district were wiped out. (*Asahi Shimbun,* 16 April 1974)

4. They worked on the Kawanami landfill between Kosedo and Kaminoshima. At that time, the Uemura construction group maintained over ten housing quarters in Kosedo, Kaminoshima, Kamiyama, Shimayama, Nishio, Tanaka, Nakamura, Arai,

---

* Italics added to the following quotations.

and elsewhere. Each housing unit had a boss and 200 to 300 occupants. Laborers were assembled from here and there until *altogether 2,000 to 3,000 Koreans were mobilized. Over 3,000 conscripted Mitsubishi workers were housed in the Kibachi dormitory, and as many as 3,000 were assigned to jobs related to Mitsubishi Munitions.* Considerable numbers of Koreans also worked in the somewhat distant coal mining districts of Kōyagijima, Hashima, Takashima, Iōjima, and elsewhere. (M. Pak 1978, p. 158)

As was the case in Hiroshima, of the 3,000 conscripted workers at Mitsubishi Shipbuilding, there were only 2,400 to 2,500 by bombing time (Ikeda 1968, p. 261; Kanamaru 1970, p. 140).

The preceding sources indicate three principal zones where Koreans lived and worked: *(a)* the Ōhashi dormitory of Mitsubishi Steel and temporary quarters for workers in projects related to Mitsubishi Munitions, within 2.5 kilometers of the hypocenter in northern Nagasaki; *(b)* Mitsubishi Shipbuilding's main plant in the 3.5-to-4-kilometer range; *(c)* Kibachi dormitory and quarters in Nishidomari and Kosedo, within 4 to 6 kilometers. Precise counts of the Koreans in each zone are not possible; but if the number of Korean workers in the three zones is tentatively estimated at 3,500, and the number of their family members the same, and if the number of workers and family members scattered in other parts of the city is set at 1,000 to 2,000, then the total number of Koreans in Nagasaki City was 11,500 to 12,500. If early entrant estimates are added, the total becomes 12,000 to 14,000.

On the basis of death rates calculated by the Joint Commission's survey team (November 1945), the 63.1 percent for zone *(a)* at 2.5 kilometers yields 2,200 deaths among the 3,500 Koreans there.

But a closer look at zone *(a)* shows that there were two quarters with many Korean inhabitants, as was described earlier: Mitsubishi Steel's Ōhashi dormitory with about 300 Korean residents (600 meters) and Mitsubishi Munition's bunkhouses for Korean workers (within a range of 1.5 to 2.5 kilometers). Thus, if the average death rate for everywhere up to 2.5 kilometers is used in this case, the result is probably a little higher than the actual average death rate. The death rate for the 1.5-to-2.5-kilometer zone was only 17.2 percent; for the 1-to-2.5-kilometer zone, 34.9 percent. Given the proximity to the hypocenter of the Ōhashi dormitory, it and its occupants probably were completely destroyed. The Mitsubishi Munitions workers were working in open fields, and their quarters were shanties; so, again, damages were probably very heavy. If we assume that all 300 close to the hypocenter died, and apply the average death rate of 34.9 percent to the rest of zone *(a)*, there were more than 1,100 deaths—a total of about 1,500 deaths.

For Mitsubishi Shipbuilding workers in zone *(b)*, we refer to *Nagasaki Genbaku Sensaishi* [Record of the Nagasaki A-bomb War Disaster] (Nagasaki Shiyakusho 1977, pp. 295–311). Within the 2-kilometer range this enterprise had a vessel-testing facility, a sawmill, plants in Saiwaimachi for casting, machines, and boilermaking, a parts plant in Ōhashi, and two dormitories; damages were heavy in all these places. Mitsubishi's main plants were farther away in Akunoura, Mukōjima, and Tategami on the western shore of Nagasaki Bay, where human damages were much lighter. It was one of Japan's largest enterprises, with almost daily movements of personnel; hence, worker counts are not easily confirmed. Mitsubishi Shipbuilding itself reported A-bomb deaths among its employees, including Japanese, as 1,815 by June 1951. As a survey at that late date probably overlooked some deaths, the actual count is believed to have been higher. Given the location of its major plants, the death rate is assumed to be low (1.2 percent within 3 to 4 kilometers in the Joint Commission's survey), or more than 2,000 deaths.

Since work was done in three shifts during wartime, and the Kibachi dormitory was 5 kilometers away in the mountains, deaths among conscripted laborers and other Korean workers are put at 150 to 200 of the 3,500 total. Nishidomari and Kosedo of zone (c) were within 3 to 5 kilometers and topographically protected, so fatal damages were few. Deaths in zone (c), then, were limited.

To sum up, there were 12,000 to 14,000 Koreans in the damaged areas of Nagasaki, and deaths are estimated at 1,500 to 2,000. Survivors in zones (a), (b), and (c) are taken to be in general agreement with estimates of the Association for the Relief of Korean A-bomb Victims (approximately 10,000; see table 11.32), but there is a considerable discrepancy in estimated deaths.

In Nagasaki, as elsewhere, Koreans were forced to adopt Japanese names, and it is quite possible that Koreans were among the deaths recorded for the student service corps, the women's volunteer corps, and so on. As for military personnel, 4 Koreans were among the 48 soldiers killed at the Mount Konpira base (Nagasaki Shiyakusho 1977, pp. 295–311). But these cases are too few to affect noticeably the preceding death counts.

Problems of Korean A-bomb Victims. Having outlined the historical situation of Koreans in Japan and ventured estimates of the number of deaths among Korean A-bomb victims, we turn now to the survivors. The Association for the Relief of Korean A-bomb Victims estimates that there were 20,000 Korean A-bomb survivors in Hiroshima and 10,000 in Nagasaki. A calculation of 5,000 to 8,000 Korean deaths in Hiroshima indicates that there were 25,000 to 28,000 Korean survivors in that city; in Nagasaki, 1,500 to 2,000 deaths indicate 11,500 to 12,000 Korean survivors there.

Measured against population estimates (table 11.31), it appears that between 1 of 3 and 2 of 5 of the estimated 60,000 to 80,000 Koreans living in Hiroshima Prefecture were A-bomb victims, of whom 20 percent to 28 percent died. Korean A-bomb victims accounted for 1 of 5 of the estimated 60,000 Koreans living in Nagasaki Prefecture, the dead amounting to 13 percent to 16 percent.

Most of the Korean A-bomb survivors in Japan have suffered—besides physical, psychological, and economic difficulties—the added burden of ethnic discrimination. Most of those who returned to Korea experienced even greater difficulties in making a living and securing medical care. But within these general outlines, details are not always easily available.

Many reports, from many different points of view, have been issued on the problems of Korean A-bomb victims. Even so, much remains unknown about the number of victims, the kind and extent of their injuries or deaths, how many returned home, stayed in Japan, or moved elsewhere, and how they fare today. Scientifically confirmed answers to these questions are still wanting.

In the 1951 San Francisco Peace Treaty, Japanese A-bomb victims lost all rights to claim compensation for A-bomb damages from the United States. Likewise, in the 1965 Japan–Republic of Korea Normalization Treaty, the South Korean government surrendered the right to press such claims against the Japanese government—a great loss to the Korean A-bomb victims. To date, compensatory actions have been limited to movements, backed mostly by private citizens' organizations in Japan, to secure medical care for the victims in Japan and Korea and to restore claim rights. One step in that direction was taken by Japan's Supreme Court, on the basis of national indemnity, in a March 1978 ruling in support of Son Jin-doo, that Koreans are to be treated equally with Japanese and issued A-bomb health books.

CHINESE A-BOMB VICTIMS

While the number of Chinese A-bomb victims has not yet been ascertained, they were clearly fewer than Korean victims. The reasons the Chinese were in Japan and the problems they have faced, however, bear great similarities to their Korean counterparts.

Hiroshima. A major point of Hiroshima's cultural contact with China was the presence of several dozen foreign students from China and the former Manchurian territory; they were enrolled in Hiroshima University of Literature and Science and Hiroshima Higher Normal School (and its preparatory school). Once the Pacific War began, however, many of them returned home to escape repression by the military police and the Special Higher ["thought control"] Police. By the time of the atomic bombing, at least 37 are said to have remained,* and only a few deaths among them (one a Mongolian) have been confirmed. Names of only 5 survivors have been ascertained.† The total number of A-bomb victims among Chinese students is regarded as approxi-

* Hiroshima University A-bomb Dead Memorial Functions Committee 1975, pp. 339–42.
† Ibid.; Hiroshima Shiyakusho 1971a, pp. 168–81; and You 1950.

mately 20. Because of wartime educational directives in March and May of 1945, all Japanese students were required to engage in production, literature classes were suspended, and science classes met only irregularly. Also, some Chinese students had gone back home for summer vacation and thus escaped the atomic bombings.

Many Taiwanese were serving in, or employed by, the Japanese armed forces, and a few civilians and students were in Japan, though accurate counts of all these groups are unknown. Two clinical charts for Taiwanese military employees were found in the Hiroshima First Army Hospital. By the time of the bombing, the First Army Hospital had built twenty-two branches, to which 37,559 A-bomb victims, mostly military personnel and employees, were sent. Two Taiwanese military employees were among 60 persons sent to the Yanai Branch Hospital. Military personnel and employees among the A-bomb victims in Hiroshima are estimated at 40,000, among whom were presumably many Taiwanese, but estimating the latter's number is most difficult (Hiroshima Shiyakusho 1971a, pp. 168–81, 329–428). Nonmilitary victims include foreign students, women volunteers, and some commercial and industrial workers and their families; but the total number of Taiwanese victims is thought to have been only a dozen or so. Some of these have come to the Hiroshima A-bomb Hospital for treatment after having once returned to Taiwan.

Nagasaki. Prewar shipping between Nagasaki and Shanghai was a major link between Japan and China. Even after the Chinese consulate in Nagasaki was closed on 31 January 1938, the overseas Chinese merchants remained in the city's Shinchi district. It is said they numbered 600 (Huany 1972), and many of them presumably became A-bomb victims. The Chinese Merchants Association of Japan in 1970 reported that the Nagasaki Chinese residents indeed numbered slightly over 600, most of them from Fukien and others from Chiangsu, Chekiang, Kwangtung, and Chianghsi provinces and from Taiwan. Discounting postwar second- and third-generation descendants, there were about 200 resident Chinese in Nagasaki from prewar days, and many of these probably suffered A-bomb damages.

As Taiwan was then a Japanese colony, Taiwanese were employed and enrolled in schools as Japanese citizens. At Nagasaki Medical University, many Taiwanese teachers and students became A-bomb victims. Deaths among them included Assistant Professor Lu Yun-lung, 3 medical assistants, 11 students, and 3 doctoral candidates with their 6 family members—a total of 24 (Shirabe 1971, appendix; Hayashi 1970, p. 27). Taiwan-born Dr. Lin Chung-shih, of the university's obstetrics department, reports, "Late in 1945, when over sixty of the surviving medical staff, students, and family members gathered to return home, we held a joint memorial service for our dead colleagues" (Hayashi 1970, p. 27). Some of the Taiwanese in the university sought to remain in Japan, as did quite a few Taiwanese merchants, both victims and nonvictims. As of March 1970, Taiwanese holders of A-bomb health books numbered 101; of these, 5 had been within 1.5 kilometers of the hypocenter, 6 within 1.5 to 2 kilometers, and 27 within 2 to 3 kilometers at bombing time. By March 1978 there were 124 with A-bomb health books. These facts suggest that there were no more than 10 deaths among Taiwanese not related to the Medical University.

A-bomb Victims among Chinese Forcibly Brought to Japan. A-bomb victims among Chinese forcibly brought to Hiroshima and Nagasaki merit special attention (*Sekai* 1960, p. 131; Usami 1963). The wartime cabinet decided on 27 November 1942 to round up Chinese workers for heavy labor in Japan; these included some already being so used in China. The transfer of 208 Chinese workers from the Dairen Fuchang Company to the Hiroshima Harbor Transport Company in Yano town on the outskirts of Hiroshima City is regarded as such a case (Hiroshima Prefectural Police History Editorial Committee 1954, pp. 594–96). (They served as longshoremen for military transport ships in Ujina port; the Chinese company provided these laborers in Dairen.) The shipping lanes of the Inland Sea serving Hiroshima were closed by American mines in early 1945, so the Chinese longshoremen were transferred to Fushiki port in Toyama Prefecture. Thus, all escaped the atomic bombing.

Some 40,000 were forcibly taken to Japan, and about 30,000 of them were able to go back home after the war (Usami 1963). Those brought to Hiroshima were put to work on the Nippon Hydroelectric Generating Plant project in Yasuno village.* There were 360 of these Chinese workers; and on 13 July 1945, 13 of them clubbed to death two pro-Japanese fellow workers. At bombing time, one Chinese was being held in Hiroshima Prison (Hiroshima Prefectural Police History Editorial Committee 1954, pp. 594–96)—possibly one of the workers involved in this case. Anyone in the prison surely suffered A-bomb damage but probably escaped death. Five other Chinese workers were detained in the West Hiroshima Police Station and are said to have died in the bombing (Hiroshima Shiyakusho 1971a, pp. 168–81). After the war there was a story among Chinese students in Japan that six Chinese prisoners had died in Hiroshima Prison during the bombing (Hiroshima Shiyakusho 1971a, pp. 168–81), but it is not clear that these were the same six prisoners.

Chinese workers were also taken to Nagasaki. According to one record: "To the Makimine mine of Mitsubishi Mining, 244 were taken, and 70 of them died; 15 of the 204 taken to Takashima and Hashima mines died; 15

* Hiroshima Prefectural Police History Editorial Committee 1954, pp. 594–96; Ishitobi 1973, p. 56.

of the 205 taken to the new mine at Takashima died; 64 of the 436 taken to the Sakito mine died; and 21 of the 196 taken to the Shikamachi coal mine of Nippon Steel died" (Editorial Committee of Data on the Case of Forced Arrest of Chinese 1964). These mines were outside the range of the A-bomb; but a Liu Yu-hai and 27 others from the Sakito mine and a Chao Wen-chang and 6 others from the Shikamachi mine, along with one Korean, were detained in the Urakami Prison at bombing time, and all are known to have been killed instantly (Editorial Committee of Data on the Case of Forced Arrest of Chinese 1964).

To sum up, Chinese A-bomb victims in Hiroshima ranged from several score to several hundred, and in Nagasaki numbered approximately 650. If Japanese A-bomb death rates are applied (table 11.18), in Hiroshima (37 percent) there were between 20 and 240 deaths, and in Nagasaki (24 percent) possibly 156 deaths. For both cities together, fewer than 100 deaths can be confirmed because surveys were not carried out.

FOREIGN STUDENTS AND PRISONERS OF WAR

In order to cultivate human potential for the future of what it called the "Greater East Asia Co-Prosperity Sphere,"* the Japanese government in 1943 decided to invite promising young men from influential families in Southeast Asian countries to study in Japan. In April of the following year, twenty or so young men from the Philippines, Java, Sumatra, Borneo, Malaysia, and Burma were enrolled as special students in Hiroshima Higher Normal School and housed in Kōnan dormitory. Heavy American bombing led to a cabinet decision on 29 December 1944 to evacuate the foreign students. Only nine foreign students were left in Hiroshima after April 1945. Excepting one who on the bombing day had gone to a hospital outside the city (the name of the hospital and the student's fate are unknown), the other eight received A-bomb injuries in the school or dormitory, and two Malayan students died (Hiroshima University A-bomb Dead Memorial Functions Committee 1975, pp. 339–42).

Prisoners of war from Java and elsewhere became victims in Nagasaki. The Fukuoka POW Camp No. 14 was located in Saiwaimachi, 1,650 meters from the hypocenter. Another, POW Camp No. 2, was 10 kilometers away at Kōyagi Shipyard. Camp No. 14 in Saiwaimachi was opened in January 1943 and had 480 POWs brought from Southeast Asia, mostly Javanese but including a few British and Dutch captives. The POWs were put to work at Nagasaki Shipyard (280), its machine shop (100), and its casting shop

* The *Greater East Asia Co-Prosperity Sphere* refers to the new order that Japan hoped to establish under its leadership in East Asia to further coexistence and co-prosperity among the peoples of Asia, and was part of Japan's national policy during the Pacific War. Its slogan was "Down with the United States and Great Britain."

(100) in Saiwaimachi. Because they did heavy labor and were poorly fed, bronchitis was prevalent, and malaria and malnutrition were not uncommon. By the time of the atomic bombing, 110 had already died. On 1 August 1945, an American carrier-based plane dropped a 500-kilogram bomb on the air-raid shelter of POW Camp No. 14 at Saiwaimachi Shipyard, killing 1 Japanese soldier and 3 POWs. The air-raid shelter was marked with a red cross, and the POWs were shocked that the plane had headed directly for that cross and had come in so low that they could make out the pilot's figure. The air raid heavily damaged the shipyard, and afterward the POWs worked at repairing the prison camp. Thus, on 9 August all the POWs sustained A-bomb damage, and POW Camp No. 14 was completely destroyed (Tajima 1976, p. 124). Between 60 and 80 died; and of the 300 survivors, over 200 sustained heavy or light injuries (Nagasaki Shiyakusho 1977, pp. 316–17). According to the official POW report (Prisoners of War Information Bureau 1955), there were 4 dead and 57 injured, and a total of 161 POWs were released by occupying Allied forces—a considerable discrepancy in numbers. Reporter W. H. Laurence wrote in the *New York Times* (10 September 1945) that, among Allied POWs, 8 died and 38 were injured in the atomic bombing of Nagasaki. At that time some 200 prisoners from Nagasaki Prison were working at the Saiwaimachi site; 29 died instantly, and 20 received serious injuries (Nagasaki Shiyakusho 1977, pp. 311–12). Had the same death and injury rates occurred among POWs, the counts would have been 53 dead and 37 injured. Lance Corporal Jidayū Tajima of POW Camp No. 14, however, on 13 August entrusted the bones of 50 POWs to Taiheiji temple and says that the number subsequently rose to possibly 150 (Tajima 1976, p. 124). British POW R. E. Bryer reports that every evening for several days about 20 POW corpses were cremated (H. Hirose 1970, p. 196). These various reports, along with 161 POWs finally released from the POW camps, lead then to the conclusion, as indicated, that 60 to 80 died, and that no less than 200 received injuries, heavy or light.

In Fukuoka POW Camp No. 14 in Nagasaki, there were, from its opening in 1943, a few Dutch and British POWs, and between 30 and 40 American and Australian POWs were added in May 1944; all became A-bomb victims (Nagasaki Shiyakusho 1977, pp. 316–17). According to a letter by POW Bryer, who was at Nagasaki Shipyard for three years, there were 20 British POWs at Camp No. 14, of whom 6 were released after the war (H. Hirose 1970, p. 196). Other POWs freed from Camp No. 2 at Kōyagi Shipyard were: American, 5; British, 160; Dutch, 324 (by Thomas H. Evans' account [which follows], mainly Javanese with Dutch citizenship); Australian, 3; and 5 others (Prisoners of War Information Bureau 1955). One of them, British sailor Thomas H. Evans, explains that the camp initially had 2,000 POWs, half of whom were later sent to Hokkaido, and that approximately 400 of the remaining 1,000 had died at the camp before the atomic bombing. There were only a few American and British POWs, according to Evans; most were Dutch and Javanese. His recollection appears mistaken on the number of British POWs, and he gives no concrete data on A-bomb damages at Kōyagi POW Camp No. 2. Evans himself does not appear to have suffered any effects from the atomic bomb. Because of its distance (10 kilometers) from the bomb's hypocenter, casualties at the camp were probably slight; though, of course, there is the possibility of subsequent secondary injuries if the POWs were taken into the city. At Britain's A-bomb Medical Center, 8 Britishers are being treated for leukemia, and Evans himself is examined once each year for symptoms of leukemia (T. H. Evans 1973, p. 120). Former American POWs affected by the atomic bomb are hospitalized in an army hospital in Houston, Texas (Sodei 1978, pp. 210–12). At Australia's Cancer Research Center in Melbourne, a cytogenetical survey of 21 survivors of the Nagasaki bombing is reportedly being conducted (Chee and Ilbery 1977).

In Hiroshima Prefecture, a POW camp was first opened in Miyoshi town and two more at shipyards on Innoshima and Mukaishima islands (Hiroshima Prefectural Police History Editorial Committee 1954, pp. 600–604). There was no POW camp in Hiroshima City proper, but some captured American bomber crews were turned over to the military police and kept there. Of the POWs who had parachuted from the B-24 *Lonesome Lady*—which left Okinawa on 28 July 1945 to bomb the battleship *Haruna* at Kure—6 were taken to Hiroshima where all died in the atomic bombing (according to NHK-Hiroshima telecast, 7 August 1978).

Concerning A-bomb victims among American POWs, a document in the diplomatic archives of Japan's Ministry of Foreign Affairs entitled "One Condition of Acceptance of the Potsdam Declaration—Allied POWs and Detained Personnel," includes a list of POWs kept in western Japan. It records the names, ranks, serial numbers, and other relevant data on U.S. servicemen killed in the atomic bombing of Hiroshima. Twenty persons appear on this list, though the names of 2 are unknown and particular data in some cases are questionable. Reliable data show that of B-24 crewmen of the 494th bomber squadron based in Okinawa, 2 were taken prisoner in Saeki county of Hiroshima Prefecture on 28 July 1945; 6 were taken prisoner in Kuga county of Yamaguchi Prefecture the same day, and their names, ranks, and serial numbers are clearly recorded. They all suffered the atomic bombing in Hiroshima; and 6 died on 6 August; one each on 8 and 19 August. In the Saeki county case, Private First Class Masumoto of the First Infantry Reserves (former Eleventh Regiment), who was sent to Yahata village to take the POWs into custody, says that the two Americans exclaimed fearfully, "A bomb will be dropped soon that will completely destroy Hiroshima" (Hiraoka 1969, p. 48). Two crewmen (one named, one unidentified) from planes based on the aircraft carrier *Ticonderoga,* who were taken prisoner in Yamaguchi Prefecture on 28 July, were escorted to Hiroshima and killed by the atomic bomb— one on 6 August, the other dying on 19 August. One crewman from the carrier *Randolph,* captured in Yoshiki county of Yamaguchi Prefecture, died instantly on 6 August.

Besides these, the Ministry of Foreign Affairs document also lists 6 prisoners captured in early May in Aso-gun of Kumamoto Prefecture and 3 taken in Yame-gun of Fukuoka Prefecture on 27 July. Both groups were B-29 crewmen, but their units are not identified. There is no explanation why personnel captured in Kyushu were taken to Hiroshima, and their serial numbers are not recorded. And while the POW list gives place (Hiroshima), cause (atomic bombing), and date of death of each prisoner, these two groups are simply recorded as such, with the notation that all personnel died on 6 August. Whether these 9 were in fact A-bomb victims awaits further confirmation.

Various observations and stories concerning American servicemen who were A-bomb victims are also recorded in *Hiroshima Genbaku Sensaishi* [Record of the Hiroshima A-bomb War Disaster (RHAWD)]. Whatever the truth or falsehood of these stories, it is certain that the lives of more than ten American servicemen were lost in the atomic bombing of Hiroshima.

JAPANESE-AMERICAN A-BOMB VICTIMS

More Japanese have emigrated from Hiroshima Prefecture to foreign countries than from any other prefecture in Japan. By the end of 1936, 26,403 had gone to Hawaii and 20,260 to the United States mainland from Hiroshima Prefecture. The large majority of these people emigrated originally from Hiroshima City and three neighboring counties—Asa-gun, Aki-gun, and Saeki-gun. These three counties, of course, included many of the prewar city's nearby towns and villages, over half of which are today incorporated into Hiroshima City. Descendants of the Japanese emigrants naturally were American citizens; but in 1935 about 20,000 of them came to Japan for educational purposes; and as many as 3,200 second-generation Japanese-Americans were reportedly in Hiroshima (Sodei 1978, pp. 8–19). They were proud of their American citizenship and tried to justify the United States and its policies to the Japanese; but with the onset of the Pacific War, they accommodated themselves to Japanese militarism for fear of being looked upon as spies. But when the atomic bombing of Hiroshima was planned, no one in the U.S. military command raised any questions about killing or wounding these American citizens in the city.

After the war, the Japanese-American A-bomb victims one after another returned to the United States; and Japanese women A-bomb victims have married Americans and gone there as well. Today there are reported to be some 1,000 A-bomb victims in the United States; but names and addresses have been confirmed for only 299, mostly in California. Of this confirmed group, 150 were within 2.5 kilometers of the hypocenter, 120 within 2.5 to 10 kilometers, and 29 beyond 10 kilometers. Those born in the United States before the war number 131; 48 are Japan-born naturalized U.S. citizens. Altogether, 60 percent of the Japanese-American A-bomb victims are American citizens, and the rest are Japanese citizens who have permanent resident status. The male-female ratio of 84:215 indicates a high incidence of international marriages. Of the total group, only 11 are Nagasaki A-bomb victims; all the rest were in Hiroshima (Sodei 1978, pp. 106–7, 210–12, 256).

On 13 October 1971, with the support of Los Angeles chief examiner-coroner Thomas Noguchi, the Japanese-American A-bomb victims formed the American A-bomb Victims Association, which has held national and regional conferences to press for legislation to provide aid for the victims. Through their efforts, many people have learned for the first time that American citizens also became A-bomb victims in Hiroshima and Nagasaki, and some have sympathized with their plight. But at public hearings, other people have asserted, "These people were our enemies"; and the proposed legislation was voted down (Sodei 1978, pp. 148–96).

OTHER FOREIGN A-BOMB VICTIMS

Because of its long tradition as a center of Roman Catholic activity and as an international trading center, Nagasaki had many priests and nuns as well as merchants, overseas traders, and consular personnel among its residents. As the Second World War expanded and the Pacific War got under way, most of these foreigners were regarded as citizens of enemy, or at least hostile, nations and thus were put under detention in St. Mary's School and elsewhere. Eventually, the Convent of Immaculate Mary was forced to close, and virtually all priests, monks, nuns, and people of American, Canadian, Dutch, and other nationalities were interned there and kept under surveillance by the local police and the military police.

On 31 July, just prior to the atomic bombing, over ten foreigners, including the French proconsul and two other Frenchmen, were moved to Saga Prefecture and interned in an inn in Ogi town. Two Polish priests of the Convent of Immaculate Mary were interned at Tochinoki spa in Kumamoto Prefecture. Canadian priests and nuns of the St. Francis Abbey were moved and interned in Den'enchōfu district of Tokyo and the Futatabisan section of Kobe, where they lived to see the war end. Thus, by the time of the 9 August bombing, the only foreigners left in Nagasaki were twenty to thirty monks and nuns and a Polish priest who were interned in the Convent of Immaculate Mary. Within a week after the bombing, however, most of those interned in Ōita and Kumamoto prefectures began returning to Nagasaki and engaged as soon as possible in relief and rebuilding. Particularly remarkable were the monk Zeno Zebrowski's efforts to help orphans and the medical care extended by the Franciscans' Urakami First Hospital (Kamata 1978, p. 52).

Other foreign A-bomb victims in Hiroshima included two German priests of the Roman Catholic Church in Noborichō township, and three White Russians (with a total of seven family members, three of whom died) who were engaged in the clothing and the bread businesses and in teaching music in Kyōbashi, Kamiyanagi, and elsewhere (Hiroshima Shiyakusho 1971a, pp. 168–81).

Chapter 12

Psychological Trends among A-bomb Victims

Overcoming Psychological Shock

The 370,000 A-bomb victims living today in Japan and the several thousands in other countries naturally have different personalities as well as, in some cases, different nationalities. Thus, it is impossible to make sweeping generalizations about their psychological makeups. This is not to say, however, that they have nothing in common psychologically. The numerous articles, surveys, and other literature on the A-bomb victims, not to mention their own diaries and testimonies, all bear witness to shared psychological traits. More precisely, some psychological conditions are common to most, if not all, A-bomb victims, while others may be shared by only a few. Certain psychological problems are evident in connection with government policies toward the bombings and subsequent conditions, and the importance of these problems cannot be ignored simply because they may concern only one group of A-bomb victims. For this reason, the many questionnaires and surveys are rarely adequate for assessing the gravity of psychological problems; case studies are usually more effective. And the novelist's keen perception at times is more helpful than the scientist's survey.

Certainly the most sweeping and searing destruction ever visited upon mankind left an enormous, abhorrent, and lifelong impression in the minds and memories of all its victims. Even today, over thirty years after the bomb-ings, there is no end to the hundreds of diaries, testimonies, and drawings that annually come from the hands of victims, some of which gain the attention of the mass media. Despite the passage of time, the memories of these survivors are strikingly vivid and concrete. An exhibition of their drawings in major cities throughout the nation, for example, drew surprisingly large crowds; and the artless forthrightness of the pictures caused many viewers literally to swoon. The startling lucidity of the A-bomb victims' memories is surely one proof of the enormity of the psychological shock they suffered.

The severity of this shock, along with other disabling conditions, has robbed the victims of their psychological equilibrium; indeed, the psychological dam-age was so great that it may be said that they were deprived of their "human-ity." At the same time, the victims have struggled to overcome psychological disintegration and to recover their humanity. Such psychological breakdown, continuing and growing in severity, and the efforts to surmount it have been shared by all A-bomb victims.

PSYCHOLOGICAL SHOCK OF THE ATOMIC BOMBINGS

On the psychological condition of the victims following the atomic bomb-ings, Yoshitoshi Kubo's (1952) "Study of Human Behavior Immediately after the Atomic Bombing of Hiroshima" is one of the most reliable sources. According to his research design, the explosion of the bomb was an external stimulus to which the victims made various responses. In this scheme, the bomb's flash and blast and the initial collapse of buildings are termed the first set of stimuli. The moment people became aware of the flash, they were "startled and, depending on their distance from the hypocenter, fell down and covered their heads or eyes with their hands; they turned their bodies away from the flash or sometimes began to stand up, facing the illumi-nated area." Kubo calls this "instinctive behavior."

In the explosion's split-second sequence, the flash was swiftly followed by the blast, which blew people down and completely demolished buildings, glass, furniture, and the like. For the affected people, it was "something never before experienced, and for an instant they were so stunned that their minds were blank." Some people, of course, lost consciousness; but upon awakening, they experienced the same blankness, the same mental emptiness. Then they had a "vague awareness" of "Hey! I'm alive." But they had been thrown off balance psychologically and, to cope with this feeling, wondered, "Did something fall on me?" Many at once concluded, "It was a direct [bomb] hit!" They feared for their lives and started to protect themselves, to get away from the bombed area. At this point people began to see themselves and their immediate surroundings more objectively. Even those who themselves were not wounded or burned observed those who were severely burned and injured, as well as the utter devastation on all sides, with flames leaping everywhere. These phenomena Kubo calls the second set of stimuli.

With awareness of these stimuli, the initial judgment of a "direct hit" gave way at once to a consciousness of "utter chaos" beyond comprehension, and the only option was instinctive movement to escape the danger to one's life. Having lost the capacity to make clear judgments, people were unable to select clear objectives for action or to determine how to attain their objectives. They engaged in the blind action of a "crisis mentality"—a state of mind that led to all kinds of mistakes which, in turn, provoked panic. Increasing awareness of their surroundings further stimulated fearful bewilderment. "It was like hell." "It was beyond words." "All those wounds and burns!" Blown about by raging hot winds, they sensed "the rapidly spreading fires," "the roar of reconnaissance planes," "the repeated explosions caused by the fires," and the deafening, mystifying "thunder of the mushroom cloud"— all this was accompanied by the unprecedented "black rain"; and successive waves of maimed and burned people were leaving the city, shouting, "That way's dangerous," and "Another air raid's coming." All these together constituted the third set of stimuli, which intensified the sense of panic. Not a few people lost all ability to cope with the overwhelming array of stimuli and simply followed along aimlessly with the fleeing crowds. People eventually reached some place they felt to be safe, where they rested and slept and also received food and treatment—there at last they began gradually to recover their psychological functions.

Kubo conducted his research in Hiroshima from 1949 to 1952 on fifty-four A-bomb victims, most of whom were within 1 to 3 kilometers of the hypocenter at bombing time. Because his survey was made relatively soon after the bombing, the victims' memories were still vivid and immediate, with virtually no subsequent revision. Hence, his report is accorded high credibility. And because 80 percent of Hiroshima's population is estimated to have been within the 3-kilometer radius, the experiences of his target group may be regarded as representative of many A-bomb victims.

As is clear from Kubo's study, the experiences of the A-bomb victims are similar because they all had one unique source—the explosion of the atomic bomb. People temporarily lost their normal mental capacities and, thus reduced to the lowest level of animal behavior, were dominated by their physical functions. Kubo's scheme of stimulus → response involves some methodological problems because it omits the mediating function of human subjectivity; but, on the other hand, it may well reflect the reality of people reacting directly without benefit of normal psychological functions. In his explanations of the A-bomb victims' behavior, Kubo does not imply that

Figure 12.1. A mother and child holding rice balls provided by relief agencies (Ibinokuchi section of Nagasaki, 10 August 1945). (Photograph by Yōsuke Yamahata.)

their reactions to the sets of stimuli were entirely autonomous, for in countless cases the physical organs that play a part in human subjectivity were lost or impaired by multiple burns and injuries. And the magnitude of the various external stimuli was enormous: tremendous confusion and chaos were imposed on each individual's powers of discernment and judgment. From the currently more common psychological scheme of stimulus → subject → response, the middle function was blocked out by a dehumanizing impact that robbed the victims of their psychological functions.

LOSS AND RECOVERY OF PSYCHOLOGICAL EQUILIBRIUM

The severe psychological shock that A-bomb victims experienced immediately after the bombings had continuing effects on them, which will be described later. Most victims, however, began soon to recover their mental capacities, especially as they got out of the city temporarily and received treatment for their wounds and burns. Kubo notes a degree of recovery even by the second day. From a week to three weeks after the bombing, however, symptoms of acute radiation illness appeared among those who had been close to the hypocenter. Among these symptoms of an unknown illness that no one had ever suffered before, were high fever; hemorrhaging of the gums, throat, nose, and womb; loss of hair; and general malaise (including both physical fatigue and psychological numbness). A sense that one hovered between life and death greatly disturbed the recovery process. When people who had only light symptoms and were well on the way to recovery would see and hear of the many dying with severe symptoms, they would suffer extreme anxiety over what might yet happen to themselves.

Shirō Nakayama, who received burns on the head and half his body, wrote of his personal experiences in a novel entitled *Shi no Kage* [The Shadow of Death]. One excerpt reads:

I took Kazuo home and let him lie down in a hastily constructed hut in one corner of the garden. The sun beat down upon the low sheet-metal roof, making it intolerably hot inside. The hut's ovenlike temperature and Kazuo's own high fever occasionally caused him to lose consciousness. He lay still, his eyes almost closed, and caught fragments of conversation with the ear not burned.

After lying there a long time, even he was not sure whether he was awake or sleeping, until his head would ache with a pain that seemed to permeate his whole body, and he would regain consciousness. He would think it day when it was really midnight; morning he confused with evening.

Then he would wail, "It hurts so, please kill me!" Anything that would let him escape such pain seemed worthwhile. I wanted to kill him for his own sake. (Nakayama 1968, p. 38)

This is a portrait of a person so thoroughly incapacitated psychologically as to prefer death over life, one whose survival instinct no longer functions. A "loss of humanity" no less than that experienced by some people right after the bombing befell others a month later.

Those with symptoms less severe than Nakayama depicted, who were beginning to recover their normal psychological functions and, thus, were able to discern and assess more of what had happened around them, became thereby and in the purest sense—that is, without impairment of physical organs—overcome anew with psychological stress. Some A-bomb victims experienced directly the death of family members, the loss of home, wealth, and work place, and even the breakdown of group and community functions. But most victims did not; only later were they hit with the realization and confirmation of all these losses. As Robert J. Lifton in his *Death in Life* (1967) reports one victim's testimony:

I heard [from my uncle] that my mother was killed . . . that she died in the house . . . when the house was burning . . . that she was asphyxiated by the smoke and died. . . . He explained it that way. . . . But I think it was his imagination . . . because my grandfather told us that my mother was out buying things at the store . . . so she must have been killed on the way to the market and not at home . . . somewhere around the center of the city. Well, this too is imagination . . . but since we couldn't find any remnant of her body or bones, we could only imagine. . . . Rather than a feeling of sorrow [what I experienced] was shock, strong shock. . . . It must have been shock that I felt. . . . (Lifton 1967, p. 87)

In coping with a particular situation, one usually first grasps the situation, then reaches some understanding and judgment of how one fits into that situation, and finally makes some move designed to cope with it. In extreme cases, however, this process is aborted: then one must be led, or find a way, to accept the loss of the most decisive elements in one's life—that is, one's most intimate human relations and the basic means by which one lives. Thus, instead of rational coping, there is only "shock" and the loss of judgment— or what Lifton calls a "vacuum state" and Kubo calls "blankness" or "emptiness." Here another excerpt from Lifton is pertinent.

In those days we were in a vacuum state. . . . We lost hope entirely. In prewar times we thought in terms of getting ahead in the world. . . . Then suddenly we lost these hopes. . . . And I lost all other kinds of hope as well. . . . (Lifton 1967, p. 88)

And as another witness [in Lifton's study] put it:

But my feeling was, there was no place to go . . . so if I were to die, it was all right, I would die here where the bomb fell. . . . A feeling of not caring—not a feeling based on understanding but just not caring. . . . (Lifton 1967, p. 88)

Takeshi Itō (1975) in his *Hibaku no Shisō to Undō* [The Thought and Actions of A-bomb Victims] speaks of "total collapse": that is, "for individuals it means, after all, that 'the setting in which I have lived my life has suddenly disappeared.' " It is a situation beyond coping, where "chaos" rules the spirit.

The injured, as they recover their health, and with it their psychological functions and livelihood, move from an awareness of "void" and "emptiness" to a realization of "breakdown," especially of the burned victims whose suffering and distress are intensified by the appearance of keloid scars. As one who experienced this, Shirō Nakayama writes:

I hated for people to stare at me.
Yet, every nerve in my body was attuned to the outside world; and to avoid even the slightest sinister look, I walked with a rigid [on guard] posture.
Even so, I secluded myself at home and spent hours before the mirror looking at my own face. What I saw was ugly hunks of flesh, like lava oozing from a crater

wall, covering the left half of my face, with the eyebrow burned off and my eye and lips pulled out of shape. My neck was pulled over to one side, and however much I tried to straighten it, it wouldn't move back to the normal position. (Nakayama 1968, p. 153)

So it was for this fourteen-year-old youth whose keloid-scarred face was a painful psychological cross to be borne day and night.

In his *Zoku Hangenbaku* [More against A-bombs], Tadashi Ishida tells of Tsutomu Fujishima, an A-bomb victim whose six-year-old son was burned to death in the bombing, and whose wife and nine-year-old son died two weeks later from acute radiation illness. Fujishima says of his experience:

Well, I was left all alone, like it or not. And after awhile I didn't even care any more. At first it was pretty rough . . . lost my home and everything. I just wanted to forget, so I'd get drunk, just so I could forget for a while, even for a little bit. That's how I felt. I got to feeling so miserable, I thought maybe I'd be better off dead. (1974, pp. 198–230)

In a "total collapse" situation, survival can seem unnatural. When devastation is so thorough that an overwhelming majority of the people around one die, it seems only natural for oneself to succumb, too. As Kenzaburō Ōe wrote of the A-bomb victims in his *Hiroshima Nōto* [Hiroshima Notes], "they are people who, despite all, didn't commit suicide" (1965, p. 76).

But time was on their side. For with the passage of time they gradually recovered from their wounds and diseases. They returned to work and began putting their lives back together again. Having lost homes and all possessions, they could now rely only on their ability to work. Since family members and old community ties were gone, they remarried or joined with others also left alone, and found ways to rebuild their personal lives and communities. Recovery and rebuilding depended, at root, on what Lifton calls "the sense of life-energy and movement," (p. 90) and just as surely on the revival of a sense of "connection to other human beings" (p. 90). It was this sense of solidarity with others that enabled survivors to shed the feeling that survival was somehow "conspicuous" and, indeed, unnatural in a world where "death and desolation" reigned; a sense of solidarity with other survivors helped them believe again that *life* is the ruling principle of a properly ordered world. To recognize that others, too, had survived, and to begin sharing life with them, cast a new ray of light to help the survivors out of the darkness that locked them in with only their departed dead.

Tsutomu Fujishima, in Tadashi Ishida's account, expressed this transitional experience succinctly:

If I died, then who would there be to look after our [family's] dead? My two children are dead. So is my wife. If I'm not around to pay respect to them, then there's no one . . . to look after them. That thought alone makes me feel like I just can't die. (Ishida 1974, pp. 198–230)

Fujishima is among the living, but his heart is with the dead. For him, there is no positive reason for living—only a negative reason for not dying.

In his article "The A-bomb Victims' Situation and Their 'Negation' Mentality," Takeshi Itō (1960, pp. 422–31) says that A-bomb victims feel isolated from other people and that their "negation" mentality stems from a pessimism about their own futures; thus, they tend to be passive and withdrawn. The cause for this he finds in the loss or, at least, in the serious depletion of the physical strength and energy needed for living. In *Hangenbaku*, Ishida speaks of such victims as "drifters," but sympathetically, for he also pleads their case: "What hope is there for a body ruined by the atomic bomb? What purpose is there in such a life?" (p. 23). They are "drifters" because they "cannot believe the future holds any potential" (p. 23) for them, and thus they give themselves up to a life of spiritual desolation that "negates" any future possibility.

Even so, after half a year's slump, says Fujishima, "I was told by Mother that I couldn't go on like that forever," and so he returned to his old job, found a new place to live, and a year later remarried (Ishida 1974, pp. 198–230). The crucial factor here was, first of all, being "told by Mother." Second, the chance to break out of his inability and get moving on his own came through an encounter with other living people. And, third, the admonition provoking that effort came from someone he could trust, from his own mother.

Likewise, many A-bomb victims made their passage from "death and desolation" to "life and hope" through encounters with others who survived. Often the crucial helping hand was that of a mother with whom there already existed a strong human bond.

PRECARIOUS LIVELIHOOD AND PSYCHOLOGICAL STRESS

The rebuilt lives of A-bomb victims remained precarious for several reasons. First of all, there was always the threat to their health from delayed radiation effects. Second, there was the fear that their children would be unhealthy or deformed. Third, economic instability threatened if delayed radiation effects decreased their ability to work or care for themselves and also required increased medical expenses. Fourth, death, sickness, and decline or loss of ability to work and manage could further accelerate the disintegration of A-bomb victims' families. Fifth, discrimination against them by nonvictims added to life's difficulties. These multiple effects on health, life, and livelihood imposed a great psychological burden on the A-bomb victims. Their efforts to rebuild were extremely vulnerable to setbacks from external factors, and not a few survivors saw their efforts collapse two, three, or more times.

The fragility of the victims' existence is particularly marked in the following cases of microcephalic fetal victims.

Yukiko Ōta was nineteen when she experienced the atomic bombing of Nagasaki. In January of the following year she gave birth to her son Masanobu. Even as late as 1948 she suffered bleeding of the gums (gingival hemorrhaging) and feared, "So many others are dying from A-bomb effects, will I too die?" At age seven Masanobu was enrolled in the first grade of primary school; but his I.Q. was so low that he was withdrawn and re-enrolled a year later. His mother wrote of this time, "I bowed deeply before his teacher and implored, 'He is a retarded child, so please help him.' I would leave the morning dishes and our baby for grandmother to care for and go with Masanobu to school. While I waited for him, I would help clean the classroom and take other inexperienced first-graders to the toilet." The mother did her best to get the other children to like Masanobu. Then, "one day his teacher said, 'Our school field day is coming up, but please refrain from participating.' Having never before missed a day of school, Masanobu and I stayed home that day, and I entertained him with all the games and songs I could remember. He said, 'It's nice to be a baby, so you get held and carried on Mommie's back. I want to be a baby.' " Finally, Masanobu was enrolled in a special school for retarded children. After graduating, he got a job; but after a week his attitude worsened. " 'What happened?' I asked one day when he came home with tears welling up in his eyes. 'Mommie, I made a mistake, a mistake.' He was supposed to work with concrete blocks, but he could not grasp them properly, so he dropped and broke many. We would get more blocks, and every evening he and his father would practice till dark." At age nineteen this mother had a burden imposed upon her that she must bear till she dies, a burden for which no words suffice (Y. Ōta 1977, pp. 24–28).

Tomie Yoshimoto, a microcephalic victim who is now married, writes of herself in her diary:

I was born in Hiroshima during the cold winter of 1946 when, because of the A-bomb and Japan's defeat, we had nothing. Misfortune was my lot from birth, for my right foot was deformed. . . . It hurt so much during the rainy season, I don't know how often I've thought I'd just like to cut off this old foot.

Her father worked in a bakery, but began "a long, long period of hospitalization" about the time Tomie was in third grade. Mother, Tomie, and a younger sister were taken into an uncle's home, but after a while were forced to leave. "After that, there was nothing to do but build a riverside shanty for ourselves in Hiroshima's Motomachi district." They lived there without electricity or running water. "Mother worked from early in the morning till late at night. I took my younger sister to a nursery school in the Nakajima district before going on to Kanzaki Primary School. At school I was teased and made fun of because of my bad foot." Then, "when I was in fifth grade, father came home from the hospital. At last, I thought, the four of us could enjoy living together; but in vain, for younger sister died suddenly." Tomie's sister had gone swimming but "came home sooner than expected, complaining, 'My head hurts,' and went to bed. If we had taken her to a doctor, she might have been saved. But we did not have the money, so her young life was ended." After that,

Father changed completely. He would get drunk and become violent. When I was only half a year short of completing middle school, Mother and Father had a heated argument, and she left home forever. As if that were not enough, soon after I graduated our house burned down, and we lost everything. So I decided to go to work.

Eventually Tomie went to Osaka to work.

In Osaka I had no dreams, no hope. Every day was filled with despair. Then I met Mr. Y. He gave me courage, and I experienced a new desire to make a go of it. In time I became attracted to him, but kept telling myself that I could not, indeed, I should not expect to marry him.

Their love, however, was strong, and they did in fact marry. But Tomie was not always able to manage the routines of daily life well. "Perhaps I was too careless, or because of frequent moves I was too careful, but one misfortune after another befell me. And the biggest shock came when I had a miscarriage, and the bond of our love was ruptured." Later, Tomie had a second miscarriage. "After that my husband thought I was unable to bear children, so he avoided me. Also, I became sick and had to visit the hospital frequently." Of course, there were provocations enough from her husband, and their marital relations soured. But Tomie had this to say: "I'm stupid, but I want to be loved. That's all. So, as long as I can stand it I'll just listen to my husband's cutting remarks, if it will only salvage our happiness. . . ." (Yoshimoto 1977, pp. 53–57.)

In the diary of this woman, a fetal victim suffering from microcephaly, we see the tragic misfortunes of the A-bomb victims in a concentrated form: born with a "damaged body" and a "low I.Q.," reared in "poverty" and a "broken family," and the marriage she finally gained threatened by "miscarriage," "sickness," and "poor ability to cope with daily life." Precisely because her affliction is less severe, she reacted all the more sensitively to "human betrayal" and "discrimination" and tasted the bitter fruits of "loneliness" and "despair."

The precarious existence of the A-bomb victims cannot, of course, be considered apart from the many kinds of mental distress they have suffered. Moreover, the various factors that make their lives vulnerable have remained operative, in greater or lesser degree depending on the individual, throughout the postwar years. And those factors have intensified the psychological pain.

The existence of almost purely psychological phenomena, however, cannot be denied. Such are closely connected with what Lifton (1967, p. 87) terms the "taint of death" and "death guilt," or what Ishida explains as a "sense of guilt and shame."

Lifton's "taint of death" refers to a consciousness deeply imprinted in the minds of the A-bomb victims "by three aspects of their ordeal: the suddenness and totality of their death saturation, the permanent taint of death associated with radiation aftereffects, and their continuing group relationship to world fears of nuclear extermination" (p. 482). The "death guilt" he describes as stemming from the "profoundly inappropriate . . . premature death" of many people, which provoked in the survivors the virtually insurmountable feeling that their "survival was made possible by others' deaths" (p. 487).

T. Ishida's "sense of guilt and shame" refers to the victims' self-condemnation with respect to the inhuman behavior they inevitably engaged in immediately following the bombings; the "guilt and shame" emerged later, after the victims had recovered their psychological functions, as self-condemnation. Ishida's concepts, like Lifton's, focus on the meaning the victims gave to all their impressions, conduct, and experiences following the bombings.

It is possible to comprehend these concepts from another perspective. The "taint of death" falls within what we call that perception of reality as ruled by "death and desolation," which has as its basis an overwhelming awareness of "total collapse." The "death guilt" and the "sense of guilt and shame" stem from realization that to be "alive" now is a deviation from an order in which "death and desolation" are the norms. Even after one moves through human contact and solidarity to an affirmation of reality where "life and hope" are the norms, the initial shock of the bombing remains so powerful, and the precariousness of continued existence so threatening, that the ghost of "death and desolation" returns again and again to haunt the A-bomb victims.

Yet another heavy psychological burden that the A-bomb victims must bear, is their inability to accept fully the factual reality of A-bomb illness. They cannot go on living without squarely facing this reality as a condition of their lives, but it nonetheless darkens all future prospects, erodes all their hopes, and fills them with insecurity. The uncertainties of A-bomb illness pervade their lives not only because of its broad scope—which expands with time—but also because of the great complexity of its afflictions. Moreover, because the A-bomb victims were the first human beings to suffer the repercussions of an atomic bomb, they had no past experiences or accumulated wisdom to fall back upon. They had to fend for themselves, and they made one mistake after another each step along the way. For example, immediately after the explosion some thought it was a "direct hit" [of a conventional bomb]; some believed that symptoms of acute radiation were the result of "breathing poisonous gas"; others that bloody stools indicated dysentery. Virtually all A-bomb victims later learned that these attempts to comprehend an unprecedented experience in conventional terms were, in fact, mistaken. Forced subsequently to cope with one trouble after another in their fragile existence, they were afraid they would continue to make mistakes. The uncertainties of the future, therefore, often turned their hopes into despair. "Death and desolation" stalks from the past as "uncertainty" rises from the future to assault and spoil their present "life."

Evolution of the A-bomb Victims' Attitudes toward Their Experience

Caught between the specters of past and future, the A-bomb victims had to wrest some meaning from, and attempt some evaluation of, the A-bomb experience and the afflictions they suffered, if they were to go on living in the present. Without some such meaning and perspective they could not muster up the necessary inner strength and resolve to cope with the difficulties their various sufferings imposed on daily life. Options ranging from the "resignation" commonly adopted in the face of natural calamities to the "self-condemnation" felt in instances of personal loss emerged as the victims sought to regain the spiritual vitality needed to make their way back into the land of the living where "life and hope" prevail.

INITIAL ATTITUDES AND CONVICTIONS OF THE A-BOMB VICTIMS

As they overcame their initial confusion, emptiness, and panic and recovered their psychological functions, most A-bomb victims first interpreted their sufferings in the context of the war effort and the then prevailing commitment to victory: that is, they first saw their personal damages as necessary sacrifices for the success of Japan's vision of hegemony in East Asia, and the proper response was to seek revenge against the enemy. For several days it was rumored in Hiroshima that "this makes it possible for our planes to attack America with atomic bombs." This rumor was perhaps only a pathetic attempt to retain some psychological equilibrium despite the massive destruction. Then, suddenly, came the Emperor's declaration of Japan's defeat on 15 August 1945. This news was far more shocking to the A-bomb victims than to the general public, for it undermined all mental balance they had somehow retained.

Imperial proclamation of the war's end exposed, first of all, the seriousness of atomic destruction as well as the overall futility of the war itself. Until then the Japanese government had endeavored to control and to discount reports of A-bomb injuries. Police authorities in Hiroshima, for example, on 7 August had issued a statement advising, "All burns should first be bathed in solutions of half sea water and half fresh water; this way we can fully defend ourselves against this kind of attack" (Hiroshima Prefectural Office 1972, p. 116). The real truth of the A-bomb disaster, not to mention the overall situation, was concealed from the victims. Thus, not only were their personal responses mistaken; they also had no way of knowing that the A-bombs had wrought a decisive reversal in the war itself. The proclamation ending the war stated:

> The enemy has for the first time used cruel bombs to kill and maim extremely large numbers of the innocent, and the heavy casualties are beyond measure; if the war were continued, it would lead not only to the downfall of our nation but also to the destruction of all human civilization.

This statement confirmed both the magnitude of atomic destruction and its decisive effect on the war effort. Moreover, the atomic bombings were given as the reason that the war had to end. Once the American occupation got under way, a new interpretation was propagated: Japan's war effort was a great folly, the end of the war a great good; the public was released from allegiance to the state, and defeat became the gateway to peace—a totally different, and confusing, point of view for the A-bomb victims. Since U.S. President Truman had made a statement on 7 August to the effect that "the A-bomb was dropped in order to end the Pacific War," the attitude that the Allied forces had "liberated" the Japanese people gradually spread. Accordingly, the idea that the A-bomb damages were "a sacrifice that Japan simply had to accept" began to gain currency among the Japanese people. On the first anniversary of the atomic bombings, the Hiroshima Citizens' Rally for the Restoration of Peace passed a resolution asserting, "We should be the cornerstone to build a peaceful Japan." In a public atmosphere of "corporate penitence by a hundred million souls," the A-bomb victims were lumped together with all other war victims and, indeed, with the leaders of Japan's war effort, on the premise that all Japanese shared equally in war guilt. This resolution implied that even the afflictions of the A-bomb victims were punishment for their part in a sinful war. Hence, no matter how painful, their sufferings were viewed as strictly "their own responsibility." This view led to the conclusion, then, that the A-bomb victims should undertake a penetrating self-examination so that the same mistakes would never again be repeated—and should, of course, submit meekly to their predicament. In this rationale, the ultimate responsibilty fell on those who were "at fault," even if the other side had perhaps used rather extreme measures to bring them to judgment. Responsibility for ascertaining the truth about A-bomb damage, therefore, fell into limbo.

For its part, the United States stuck to the policy of strict secrecy it had imposed on the A-bomb project from the very beginning. On 19 September 1945, the Occupation authorities issued a press code intended to suppress and play down the full story of the A-bomb damages. The A-bomb victims were thereby obstructed in their efforts to understand and cope with the full range of damage they had suffered and were still suffering; they were left with no choice but to accept their misfortunes as tragic but inevitable. Of course, there were, among the A-bomb victims and the general public, people whose new commitments to peace were genuine and positive. Even the Japanese government made similarly positive statements each year in public ceremonies. On the international scene, however, the United States held a nuclear monopoly and continued nuclear tests in order to build more and bigger A-bombs. In 1949 Russia entered the competition with the development of its own atomic bomb. Thus, nuclear arsenals expanded. Nuclear weapons were declared essential to preserve peace, and a worldwide "rationale of peace" was promoted to support nuclear defense strategies. Moreover, the Japanese government supported this view. In other words, "atomic bombs and nuclear weapons are symbols of peace; those who are victimized by these weapons are disturbers of the peace," according to this bizarre rationale.

This view of the atomic bombs, championed mainly by the superpowers, caused confusion and mistakes in, and often obstructed, the A-bomb victims' efforts to interpret their A-bomb losses and injuries. Nevertheless, in contrast to the prevailing public orthodoxy, the A-bomb victims harbored private dissenting views based on their own initial and continuing experiences of horror and hardship. Their view was rooted in the conviction that "no matter what anyone says, we absolutely will not approve of atomic bombs as long as we live." This was an absolute and decisive condition for preserving the passage they had made from the old order of death and desolation to their present affirmation of life. Hatred of those who had dropped the bomb naturally accompanied this view. The "sacrifices for the sake of peace" rationale not only provided a cover-up for the victimizers but also, with its affirmation of atomic bombs and nuclear weapons, was, in the victims' eyes, a retrogression to the old rule of death. Far from comforting and pacifying the A-bomb victims, the orthodox view was psychologically oppressive.

Starting with the Bikini hydrogen bomb test in 1954 and gathering public support by 1960, the movement against nuclear bombs provided the opportunity for forging a completely different interpretation of the A-bomb experience. This movement clearly rejected the notion that damages from nuclear bombs are for the sake of peace, and thus questioned anew whether the Japanese people should, for the sake of peace, submit obligingly to the victimization of Hiroshima and Nagasaki.

Heretofore hemmed in by the orthodox view of personal responsibility and long hindered by nonvictims' difficulty in understanding their hardships and suffering, the A-bomb victims at last had an opportunity to break out of their painful isolation. The "drifters" who had abandoned themselves to spiritual wastelands had needed help from others in order to rise up again and become actively engaged in living their own lives. Until the emergence of the antinuclear movement, however, the only others available were usually groups of relatives and friends. The antinuclear movement greatly expanded the scope of group support and helped convert the "private dissenting interpretation" of the victims into a "publicly accepted view." Their personal passage from death to life was now strengthened by public recognition of their heterodoxy as both reasonable and responsible.

Unfortunately the Japanese antibomb movement subsequently became divided just as the movement was beginning to gain wide support among national organizations for the A-bomb victims' own interpretation of their experiences—and this schism was deeply discouraging to many victims. Having once set out, however, some A-bomb victims refused to turn back; and they have gone on to produce an authentic interpretation of their experiences. Many victims have even developed this interpretation into a body of thought to form a basis for their own self-determined and self-supported movement. And their efforts show signs of durability and promise for the possible reunification of the antinuclear movement and for its promotion worldwide.

EMERGING CONVICTIONS

Thus far we have dealt with the general characteristics of psychological disintegration, the continuing spiritual malaise, and the eventual recovery of humanity among the A-bomb victims. As noted earlier, not all victims have yet broken out of the drifter phase; indeed, in terms of numbers, more have settled into that phase. But some have definitely overcome it and have undergone the spiritual exercises needed to internalize the lessons of the A-bomb experience and, at the same time, to objectify these lessons in order to produce interpretations that have, in turn, become convictions. Now it is possible to outline some basic tenets of the emerging convictions of the A-bomb experience.

1. *Rejection of the rule of death and desolation and affirmation of the rule of life.* The overpowering situation of "total collapse" left the A-bomb victims incapable of affirming life—their world was completely ruled by "death and desolation." The bombing and its continuing effects constantly pulled them back into that world. But these victims were surrounded daily by other people whose silent testimony was that mankind still lives; that babies are being born; and that the victims too are, in fact, a part of that living community. Passage from death to life became a matter of pressing necessity, and most victims chose life. It was not an easy choice, but one reached through painful trials and tribulations and made in basic, ultimate terms. The affirmation of life embraces those now living and those yet to be born, and it originates with recognition that each A-bomb victim is one survivor among the many living. In that sense, it is a perspective that sees "human beings as holding the future within themselves."

2. *Rejection of nuclear weapons and removal of the uncertainties of the future.* Nuclear weapons and those who use them are, for the A-bomb victims, symbols of death and desolation. This is so not merely because they reflect the tragic past but even more because they make the future uncertain and may drag us all back into the old order of death and desolation.

For A-bomb victims who have broken with that old order to affirm a new order of life, it is only natural that they should strive to assure and to preserve the promise of the new order. But nuclear weapons, and the rationale used to legitimize them, oppose the new order; they make the future uncertain and insecure. The rejection of nuclear weapons and of the power structures they symbolize is an integrated part of the A-bomb victims' vision of life; it is for them the way to promote a safe and secure future. Such a stance helps remove uncertainty from the future for all mankind, not just for the A-bomb victims.

3. *The social position and functions of A-bomb victims.* Because the A-bomb victims affirm life over death and thus reject the nuclear weapons which both symbolize and threaten to thrust us back into death and desolation, they envisage a unique role for themselves. Their affirmation of life is not merely an expression of their instinct for survival. It is a conviction won at the cost of repeatedly overcoming the temptation to revert to the old order; it is truly the fruit of a sustained spiritual pursuit. Theirs is a vision confirmed

by years of testing; they alone, among all mankind, have experienced the death and desolation that they reject in favor of life. This experience instills in them confidence to give warning and counsel to people whose only experience is to be alive. In a time when that old order of death and desolation could very well rob us of our future, initiatives by those who affirm life after experiencing the realities of death and desolation contribute to the stability of human existence and strengthen their own convictions. Thus, the A-bomb victims see themselves as a "chosen people"—hence, their sense of mission.

The ideology of the A-bomb victims outlined here is not merely an expression of "restored" and "recovered" psychological functions. It represents a higher level of consciousness attained through the strenuous processes of recovering those functions.

For the A-bomb victims, the forging of this ideology has changed the vague and remote concept of "mankind" into a real and close feeling for actual people. The view of human life held by most people is constricted, if not microscopic. Life in the A-bomb victims' ideology has expanded spatially to embrace all the living and chronologically to include all yet to be born. Furthermore, each victim is a "very important member" of the whole human community and has something unique to contribute to it and to our common future. Not often are a few chosen people challenged to fulfill so crucial a role in human history. But the A-bomb victims, though they may lack superior intelligence or stamina, can fulfill their vision as they strive with all their might to overcome hardships and opposition. And their lessons, the A-bomb victims believe, can and should be learned by all peoples who wish to live on into the twenty-first century.

Atomic bomb victim Chieko Watanabe, held by her mother, appeals to the World Conference against Atomic and Hydrogen Bombs (Nagasaki, August 1969). (Photograph by Sakae Murazato.)

PART IV

TOWARD THE ABOLITION OF NUCLEAR ARMS

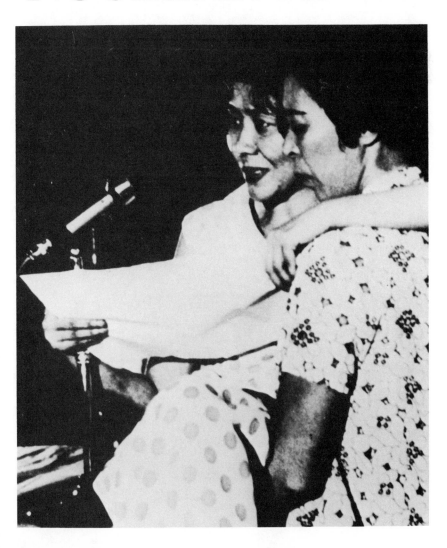

Chapter 13

Relief and Medical Care for A-bomb Victims

Surveys and Studies of Atomic Bomb Casualties

IMMEDIATE POSTBOMBING SURVEYS*

Surveys and studies of A-bomb casualties were begun soon after the 6 August 1945 bombing of Hiroshima. The first surveys were planned by administrative and military agencies in cooperation with scientists of various universities and institutes. Their main objective was to determine the essential nature and the actual conditions of the damages caused by the bomb. The Kure Naval Base's survey team first entered Hiroshima on 6 August; it was followed by survey teams dispatched by the Technology Agency, the Imperial Headquarters, the War Department, and the navy command in Hiroshima on 8 August, by the Western Japan Army Command on 9 August, by Kyoto and Osaka imperial universities on 10 August, and by a second team of the War Department on 14 August. Survey teams entering early into Nagasaki were those dispatched by the Nagasaki District Military Police on 10 August and the Kure Naval Base on 14 August. The scientist Ken'ichi Shinohara reached the city on 13 August, followed by Yoshio Nishina (Japan's leading atomic physicist at the time) on the fourteenth.

* Chūgoku Shinbunsha 1966; HAMCH 1961; Hiroshima Prefectural Office 1972; Hiroshima Shiyakusho 1971, vols. I and V; Nagasaki Shiyakusho 1977, 1959; Science Council of Japan 1951, 1953; Nishina Memorial Foundation 1973; Shirabe, Yazaki, and Matsuo 1972.

The survey teams in Hiroshima worked energetically, and on 10 August a joint army-navy meeting was held under the auspices of the Imperial Headquarters' survey team. It was at this meeting that the bomb was first confirmed to be an atomic bomb, and the epicenter was estimated to be 300 meters south of the Gokoku Shrine at an altitude of about 550 meters. On 11 August the Technology Agency's survey team reported its findings to a liaison meeting of the government, the army, and the navy in Tokyo. It was Yoshio Nishina who, by inspecting the conditions of the casualties and the exposure of stored photographic films, confirmed that the bomb was an atomic bomb. He sent materials to the Institute of Physical and Chemical Research to be measured for radioactivity (10 August). H. Tamaki, M. Kimura, and K. Murachi of this institute arrived in Hiroshima on 14 August, together with the War Department's second survey team, and until 17 August measured the radioactivity at different locations inside the city. On the afternoon of 10 August, B. Arakatsu and others of Kyoto Imperial University's survey team collected soil samples from the Western Drill Ground (500 meters northeast of the hypocenter) and its vicinity and left Hiroshima at night. Arriving in Kyoto the following day, they measured the radioactivity in their samples at the university. The need for further systematic measurement was confirmed, and Sakae Shimizu and others re-entered Hiroshima on 12 August to collect soil and other materials from over one hundred sites within the city during a two-day period (13–14 August). On 10 and 11 August, T. Asada and others of Osaka Imperial University's survey team had measured the radioactivity detected at several locations in Hiroshima City. Although Ken'ichi Shinohara detected radioactivity in Nagasaki on 14 August, systematic measurement was not begun until September.

Early pathological autopsies, essential for clarifying radiation effects on the human body, were performed by Kiyoshi Yamashina (10–15 August; twelve cases) and Shigeteru Sugiyama (11–12 August; three cases) at the Ninoshima Quarantine Station. Besides these fifteen cases, there were two cases at the Iwakuni Naval Hospital, three at the Hiroshima Sanatorium for Disabled Veterans, and five at the Hario Marine relief station—a total of twenty-five cases. Autopsies were performed on all cases within two weeks after the explosion (Kinoshita and Miyake 1951, p. 79).

EARLY SURVEYS BY UNIVERSITIES AND INSTITUTES*

Many changes occurred in the domestic situation after Japan was occupied by the Allied forces soon after surrender on 15 August. But from late August to early September, before these changes took place, various universities and

* Hiroshima Prefectural Office 1976; Imahori 1959–60; Kikuchi 1970; and Japanese Pathological Society 1965.

institutes were active in conducting surveys and sending relief teams to Hiroshima and Nagasaki. Masao Tsuzuki and others at Tokyo Imperial University,
with the cooperation of the Army Medical School and the Institute of Physical
and Chemical Research, sent a survey team to Hiroshima. Led by Tsuzuki,
its participants were Y. Ishibashi (surgery); K. Nakao (internal medicine);
M. Miyake, Z. Ishii and others (pathology); K. Misonou, K. Yamashina,
H. Motohashi, and others (Army Medical School); and A. Sugimoto, F.
Yamasaki, and others (Institute of Physical and Chemical Research). They
left Tokyo on 29 August and arrived in Hiroshima on the following day.
Miyake and others performed twenty-six autopsies between 30 August and
8 September. During the same period, hematological surveys and surgical
surveys on thermal burns and trauma were being made by Nakao, Ishibashi,
and other doctors.

On 27 August the Chūgoku Regional Military Headquarters sent Yuzuru
Imachi to Kyoto Imperial University to request cooperation in a survey to
be conducted in Hiroshima. A study team was organized by the end of the
month; it consisted of forty members, among whom were Seigo Funaoka
(anatomy), Shigeteru Sugiyama (pathology), Takehiko Kikuchi and Shun'ichi
Mashimo (internal medicine). They were divided into two groups and entered
Hiroshima on 3 and 4 September. The Kyoto Imperial University team met
with grievous misfortune on 17 September when the Hiroshima area was
hit by the Makurazaki typhoon; and the Ōno Army Hospital was destroyed
by an avalanche that killed eleven Japanese scientists, among whom were

Figure 13.1. Pathological autopsy of an exposed victim (Hiroshima, October 1945). (Photograph
by Shunkichi Kikuchi.)

Mashimo and Sugiyama. The large-scale, comprehensive survey planned by Kyoto Imperial University was thus thwarted.

With the cooperation of Hiroshima Communications Hospital (Michihiko Hachiya, director), Chūta Tamagawa of Hiroshima Prefectural Medical College performed nineteen autopsies between 29 August and mid-October. The Okayama University Medical School relief team, headed by M. Hayashi, entered Hiroshima on 11 September; in addition to giving first-aid to exposed victims, it also helped Tamagawa with his pathological survey (Hachiya 1955, pp. 189–90; Sugihara and Takahashi 1960, 1961).

Hiroshima Prefecture requested the Institute of Infectious Diseases of Tokyo Imperial University for support in a survey being conducted in Hiroshima, and Nobuo Kusano and others were dispatched to Hiroshima. Arriving on 29 August, Kusano and his colleagues performed an autopsy at Miyajima and then went to the Hiroshima Sanatorium for Disabled Veterans at Saijō (Minoru Fujii, director). The sanatorium's staff had actively engaged in first-aid service from 16 August, and with the arrival of Kusano's team a pathological survey was undertaken, with twenty-one autopsies being recorded by the end of November (Kusano 1953a).

Hiroshima University of Literature and Science, Hiroshima Higher Normal School, and other schools inside the city were greatly damaged, and almost all research ceased with the explosion. Takeo Fujiwara (physics), Haruo Takeyama, and other members of Hiroshima University of Literature and Science, however, organized a small party for estimating radioactivity, and measurements were made on residual radioactivity at the hypocenter (13 to 14 September). Between 21 August and 7 September, Eiji Hirahara (physics) of Hiroshima City Technical College also measured the radioactivity at different locations in the city and prepared a chart indicating the distribution of radiation intensity (Hiroshima University A-Bomb Dead Memorial Functions Committee 1977).

Survey and relief teams from Kyushu Imperial University, Kumamoto Medical College, and Yamaguchi Prefectural Medical College were sent to Nagasaki between late August and early September. At the request of Fukuoka prefectural government, Kyushu Imperial University sent to Nagasaki on 11 August its first relief team, composed of twenty-eight members including Nobuyoshi Takita, to help at the first-aid stations in Shinkōzen and Yamazato primary schools from 12 to 16 August. This team was relieved by a second one consisting of approximately thirty persons. From late August to late September, the Kyushu Imperial University team carried out investigations from its base in Shinkōzen.

The Kumamoto Medical College's A-bomb casualties survey team was organized mainly by radiologists and pathologists; it was in Nagasaki from 3 to 8 September. The first-aid team from Yamaguchi Prefectural Medical

College reached Nagasaki on 12 September and engaged in survey and treatment of victims until 20 September.

The facilities of Nagasaki Medical University, located close to the hypocenter, were heavily damaged, and many of the personnel were killed or wounded. The few remaining doctors, nurses, and medical students, who had barely escaped death, organized small medical squads and gave treatment to victims. The Shinkōzen first-aid station was moved to this school on 6 October (Shirabe 1968–74; 1979).

A-BOMB CASUALTIES SURVEY OF THE SCIENTIFIC RESEARCH COUNCIL OF JAPAN*

While university and institute teams made their surveys, the research scope and criteria for dealing with A-bomb casualties were vigorously discussed by Yoshio Nishina and members of the Ministry of Education's Science and Education Bureau and the Scientific Research Council of Japan. Finally, on 14 September, they decided to establish the Special Committee for the Investigation of A-bomb Damages within the Scientific Research Council of Japan. This Special Committee, headed by Haruo Hayashi (chairman) and Kyōsuke Yamazaki and Yoshio Tanaka (vice-chairmen), had nine sections: physics, chemistry and geology, biological science, mechanical engineering and metallurgy, civil engineering, electrical and telecommunication engineering, medicine, agriculture and fishery, forestry, and veterinary and livestock science.

Meanwhile, the Nippon Eiga-sha (Japan Film Corporation) laid plans for producing a documentary film of A-bomb casualties and damages, and organized a film crew to cooperate with the scientists of the Special Committee.†

Data from surveys made by universities, institutes, and hospitals were received and compiled by the Special Committee for the Investigation of A-bomb Damages, and funds were distributed for surveys to be continued until 1947. During this period the Special Committee held three meetings in which the collected data were discussed by the various sections. The first and second were held in Tokyo on 30 November 1945 and 28 February 1946, respectively; the third was held in Osaka on 7 April 1947.

The main data of the surveys of the Special Committee were arranged and compiled by the Publication Committee of the Atomic Bomb Casualty Investigation Report, headed by Naoto Kameyama of the Science Council of Japan. The Japan Society for the Promotion of Science published a summary report in August 1951, and two volumes of the full report were published in May 1953 (Science Council of Japan 1951; 1953). These two volumes contained 1,642 pages, with 38 sections on science and engineerng, 6 on biology, and 130 on medicine.

* Science Council of Japan 1951, 1953; Tsuzuki ca. 1945.
† Nishina Memorial Foundation 1973; Kanō and Mizuno 1965.

The history of A-bomb casualty surveys would have been completely different if this kind of systematic study had been supported and continued thereafter. As it was, the project was actively pursued for only a year and a half. One reason for the halt in systematic study was the revision of the educational and scientific system, but the most serious factor was Occupation policy. On 19 September 1945 the General Headquarters (GHQ) of the Allied Forces issued a press code restricting speech, reporting, and publication. At the first meeting of the Special Committee for the Investigation of A-bomb Damages, the person in charge of the GHQ's Economic and Scientific Bureau served notice that further surveys and study of A-bomb matters by the Japanese would require permission from GHQ, and publication of A-bomb data was thenceforth prohibited. The study and publication by Japanese scientists of A-bomb casualties and damages were therefore greatly restricted until the Occupation ended with the San Francisco Peace Treaty of 1951.

FORMATION AND ACTIVITY OF THE JAPAN–U.S. JOINT COMMISSION

One specific phase in the study of A-bomb casualties stemmed from the formation of the Japan–U.S. Joint Commission for the Investigation of the Effects of the Atomic Bomb in Japan (Brues 1968; Liebow 1965). During the American occupation, the Special Manhattan Engineer District Investigating Group, headed by Thomas Farrel and with some thirty members from medical and engineering fields, was dispatched from the United States to Japan. The group's mission was to carry out a preliminary study on the effects of the atomic bombings and to determine, for the safety of the occupying troops, the levels of residual radioactivity. The team was divided into two parties, one of thirteen members that entered Hiroshima on 8 September 1945; the other entered Nagasaki on the ninth. Marcel Junod of the International Red Cross joined the first party (Junod 1945). Ashley Oughterson, GHQ Consultant Surgeon, prepared a survey plan on the medical effects of the atomic bombings and submitted it to the GHQ Chief Surgeon, Guy Denit, on 28 August. The plan was approved by GHQ, and a U.S. Army Surgeons Investigation Team was organized. On 4 September, Oughterson, Farrel, and Stafford Warren met in Tokyo and agreed to coordinate data of the medical study and then prepare a joint report of the two survey teams. Since the Japanese scientists had already been actively investigating the effects of the A-bombs and their cooperation was in fact indispensable for this study, the Americans came into contact with Masao Tsuzuki. This is the background of the formation of the Joint Commission.

Headed by Oughterson, the Joint Commission was composed of the GHQ Army Surgeons team, the Manhattan Project team, and the Japanese government team. They were divided into two groups, with one entering Nagasaki on 28 September and the other entering Hiroshima on 12 October. A joint survey was commenced at once and was completed by late December of the same year (1945). Mimeographed copies of the Japanese data were distributed to the Japanese participants but, by American decision, were not made public. The Japanese survey data were later compiled in the "Collection of the Reports on the Investigation of the Atomic Bomb Casualties," edited by the Science Council of Japan (1953). In September 1946 the American data were compiled by Oughterson, Shields Warren, A. A. Liebow, G. V. LeRoy, C. Hammond, and H. Barnett in the "Medical Report of the Joint Commission for the Investigation of the Effects of the Atomic Bomb in Japan—Atomic Energy Commission Classified Document." The greater part of this report was made public in 1951 by the Atomic Energy Commission's Public and Technical Information Service. Parts of this report were published from time to time by Shields Warren, Liebow, LeRoy, and E. DeCoursey between 1946 and 1948.*

According to the report made by Oughterson and Warren (1956), the activities of the Joint Commission included the following: (1) reappraisal of the Japanese records, autopsy materials, and clinical histories; (2) examination of survivors and those dying later; (3) clinical examination of hospitalized patients; (4) examination of survivors, with or without injuries, who had not been treated at the time of initial exposure; (5) investigation of survivors with known exposed conditions; (6) collection of examined cases and autopsy materials; (7) collection of materials for numerical surveys of population and injuries; (8) collection of materials of structural damage and shielding conditions; and (9) collection of photographs and films. The cases examined totaled 13,500; autopsies, 217; and photographs, 1,500. Most of these materials and data had been obtained through the efforts of Japanese doctors and scientists, either independently or under the auspices of the Special Committee of the Scientific Research Council of Japan, and in the joint project had been presented to the Americans.

One incident that was symbolic of Japanese-American relations during the joint A-bomb casualty survey was the experience of Nippon Eiga-sha, which had participated in the documentation of A-bomb damages as a supporting agency of the Scientific Research Council's Special Committee (Kanō and Mizuno 1965). This company had organized a documentary film crew, and an advance party had already left Tokyo on 7 September 1945; the main crew began operations on 25 September. They took films in both Hiroshima

* Beck and Meissner 1946, 1947; Cogan, Martin, and Kimura 1949; DeCoursey 1948, 1949; Harris and Stevens 1945; Larkin 1946; LeRoy 1947; Liebow, Warren, and DeCoursey 1949; Looney 1949; Lyon 1947; Schlaegel 1947; Timmes 1946; Warren 1946, 1948; Warren and Draeger 1946.

and Nagasaki, and the first phase of their work was completed by 29 October. On 17 October in Nagasaki an assistant cameraman was arrested by American military police while shooting film near the hypocenter. On 19 October the GHQ prohibited the filming of A-bomb scenes (H. Nakayama, unpublished). An official prohibition on taking films was issued by the GHQ Civil Information and Education Section on 12 December, and an order was given on 17 December to submit all films concerning the atomic bombs to the General Headquarters. Since filming, developing, and cutting of the documentary film were not completed, and as a result of negotiations with GHQ, the Nippon Eiga-sha was engaged to produce and complete the atomic bomb casualty documentary film at the request of the U.S. Strategic Bombing Survey (USSBS). Accordingly, the second filming was done between 22 December and 26 January of the following year, and a third filming was done from 27 January to 15 February. This 15,000-foot-long film, entitled *The Effects of the Atomic Bombs on Hiroshima and Nagasaki,* was completed by the end of April. All films, including 30,000 feet of negatives and other data, were requisitioned by the American authorities and sent to the United States in mid-May. Only ten reels of film, secretly stored by Akira Iwasaki, Ryūichi Kanō, Sueo Itō, and others, were left in Japan. In a similar incident, two cyclotrons at the Institute of Physical and Chemical Research were ordered dismantled by the GHQ on 24 November.

The U.S. Strategic Bombing Survey had been organized by the U.S. Army in November 1944 to investigate the bombing effects in Germany. On 15 August 1945, the day of surrender, President Harry S. Truman ordered the USSBS to investigate all effects of the atomic bombings on Japan and to report the findings to the United States departments of War and of the Navy. This survey staff was headed by T. D'Oliver, assisted by Paul M. Nitze and Henry Alexander, and was composed of 1,150 personnel (300 civilians, 350 officers, and 500 noncommissioned officers). The head office was set up in Tokyo, with branch offices in Nagoya, Osaka, Hiroshima, and Nagasaki. This survey was programmed to cover all Japan, the Pacific islands, and part of continental Asia, and a thorough investigation was conducted on a large scale from September to the early part of 1946 (United States Strategic Bombing Survey 1946).

FORMATION AND HISTORY OF THE ATOMIC BOMB CASUALTY COMMISSION*

As analysis of various data obtained by the Japan–U.S. Joint Commission and the U.S. Strategic Bombing Survey progressed, the Americans felt it was necessary to continue the investigations of the A-bomb effects in Japan. On 18 November 1946, Secretary of the Navy James Forrestal advised President

* Atomic Bomb Casualty Commission 1958, 1968, 1975.

Truman of the need to follow up the aftereffects of A-bomb injuries. The President agreed and on 26 November issued a supporting directive to the National Academy of Sciences' National Research Council (NAS-NRC), leading to the establishment of the Atomic Bomb Casualty Commission (ABCC).

The NAS-NRC dispatched a survey team, headed by Austin M. Brues and Paul Henshaw, to Japan in December 1946 (Brues 1968). The team's leaders recommended that the ABCC should study the following subjects in Japan: cancer, leukemia, shortening of life, loss of vigor, growth and developmental disorders, sterility, genetic alteration, visual alteration, abnormal pigmentation, epilation, and epidemiological changes. The hematological study of exposed patients at the Hiroshima Red Cross Hospital by James V. Neel in April 1947 was the first investigation carried out by the ABCC in Japan. In June 1947, Shields Warren, Carl F. Tessmer, and Neel of the ABCC, together with Masao Tsuzuki, visited the Disease Prevention Bureau of the Ministry of Health and Welfare and requested the cooperation of the Japan National Institute of Health (JNIH) in the medical survey of A-bomb effects. The Health and Welfare Ministry and the JNIH arranged for funds, personnel, and research planning, and in January 1948 the ABCC office was set up temporarily in a former army facility in Hiroshima's Ujina township. Tessmer took office as the first director of the ABCC in March 1948; and in June, Hiroshi Maki became the head of the JNIH's Hiroshima branch laboratory and associate director of the ABCC. A temporary research institute was opened in July 1949 adjacent to the ABCC office. A permanent ABCC building was completed in November 1950 atop Hijiyama hill, and the office and research institute moved there from Ujina in early January of the following year. The ABCC in Nagasaki started its activity in July 1948 at the Nagasaki Health Center, and its permanent facilities were set up in July 1950. The successive directors of the ABCC until 1975, when the ABCC was succeeded by the Radiation Effects Research Foundation, were Grant H. Taylor (1951–53), John J. Morton (1953–54), Robert H. Holmes (1954–57), George B. Darling (1957–72), and LeRoy R. Allen (1972–75). The associate directors during this period in Hiroshima and Nagasaki were Hiroshi Maki and Isamu Nagai, respectively; they also served as the directors of JNIH's branch laboratories in the two cities, respectively.

From the earlier studies of Neel and others, it was clear that major attention should be given to abstracting survey samples, to establishing a fixed population that accurately reflected the actual conditions of exposed victims, and to fixing a systematic screening program based on this population. The ABCC in 1949 carried out a survey of the exposed population; and on 1 October 1950, in conjunction with the national census, a nationwide survey of the exposed population was conducted. The adult and child subjects to be periodically examined by the ABCC were selected from the survey materials. This was significant progress in the investigation of the exposed, but there remained many difficulties in securing the survey samples. Furthermore, many negative results were obtained from the examination of adults, and the validity of the sampling came to be doubted. By 1955 it was clear that the survey activities of the ABCC were seriously hampered by the closed character of this Occupation-era agency, by the frequent turnover among the American specialists, and by the general feelings of the citizens of Hiroshima and Nagasaki toward the ABCC. The U.S. National Academy of Sciences recognized the necessity of reassessing the ABCC's operations; and an Inquiry Commission headed by R. K. Cannon was sent to Japan to appraise the ABCC's results and reactivate its work. The Francis Committee (headed by Thomas Francis) of this commission, after thoroughly reviewing the ABCC program, recommended major restructuring (Francis, Jablon, and Moore 1955); that there should be a systematic epidemiological study, a continued morbidity survey, clinical and pathological investigations, and a death certificate study; and that these efforts should be based on a well-established fixed population. It was also decided that studies to estimate exposure doses would be continued in collaboration with the Oak Ridge National Laboratory.

In 1957, George B. Darling became director of the ABCC. In the following year the Adult Health Study on 20,000 subjects was reactivated, as were the Life Span Study on 100,000 subjects in 1959 and the Pathology Program in 1961. A better understanding between the two countries was awakened by that time, and strong efforts were being made for the establishment of a Japanese Advisory Committee, cooperation with Japanese universities and institutes, improvement of relations with local communities of Hiroshima and Nagasaki, and publication of the *ABCC Technical Report* (1975) as well as its distribution to concerned organizations.

END OF THE OCCUPATION AND REVIVAL OF JAPANESE RESEARCH

Research on atomic bomb casualties and publication of the results by Japanese scientists were greatly restricted during the Occupation period. After oral reports (by Takehiko Kikuchi, Seiji Kimoto, Masanori Nakaizumi, Ryōjun Kinoshita, and others) were given at the twelfth annual meeting of the Japanese Association of Medical Sciences in April 1947, reports on A-bomb casualties at scientific meetings were discontinued until 1951. Although some reports on A-bomb matters were in fact written, their publication was, in principle, prohibited.

Conditions improved in 1951 when the San Francisco Peace Treaty was signed, and restrictions came to an end the following year when the treaty went into effect. On 9 December 1951 a meeting on studies of A-bomb effects was held under the auspices of the ABCC and the Hiroshima Association of Medical Sciences at the hall of the Hiroshima Prefectural Medical Association (*Journal of the Hiroshima Medical Association* 1952). In January of the following year, with the cooperation of the Science Council of Japan, a report was given in Tokyo by the ABCC, and informal talks were held between personnel of the ABCC-JNIH and the Science Council. It was not until the fourth annual meeting of the Hiroshima Association of Medical Sciences in February 1952 that Japanese academic societies were able to engage freely and independently in investigations of A-bomb injuries (*Journal of the Hiroshima Medical Association* 1952). A symposium on radiation and A-bomb injuries was held at the annual meeting of the Japan Hematological Society in April of that year in Osaka (Japan Hematological Society 1953).

With the end of the Occupation, reorganization of comprehensive research on A-bomb casualties was discussed by Masao Tsuzuki and the seventh section of the Science Council of Japan.* These discussions led to the formation of the Atomic Bomb Casualty Research Group, which was supported by scientific research funds from the Ministry of Education in 1952. This composite research group worked together for six years until it was reorganized as the Comprehensive Research Group on Atomic and Hydrogen Bomb Injuries in 1958, with some personnel changes and the addition of Bikini H-bomb injuries to its program. This group worked actively till 1967.

On 12 November 1953 the government established the A-bomb Aftereffects Research Council in the National Institute of Health (JNIH). The mission of this council was to plan surveys on exposed survivors and set up guidelines for the treatment of A-bomb illnesses in Hiroshima and Nagasaki. A symposium on the latter task was held in February 1954. The Atomic Bomb Casualty Councils of Hiroshima and Nagasaki (see pages 540–42) had been formed in January and May, respectively, of the previous year. The new Research Council cooperated with medical associations, universities, hospitals, local governments, and citizens' groups, especially in promoting physical checkups of exposed survivors. At the local level, its work was implemented by the two cities' Casualty Councils, which in 1959 took the initative in founding the Research Society for the Late-effects of the Atomic Bombs. This society was composed of people throughout the country who were interested in A-bomb aftereffects, though the leading members were physicians and scientists in Hiroshima and Nagasaki. Annual meetings of the society have been held since in Hiroshima and Nagasaki alternately.

DEVELOPMENTS SINCE THE BIKINI INCIDENT

The hydrogen bomb test conducted by the United States in March 1954 at Bikini atoll and the consequent exposure of Japanese crewmen of the *Fukuryū Maru No. 5* fishing vessel restimulated research on, and countermea-

* Hiyama 1971; Education Ministry Scientific Research Grant 1965; and Tsuzuki 1954a.

sures to prevent, A-bomb casualties. This incident made clear not only the increasing danger of nuclear weapons but also the fact that the A-bomb injuries in Hiroshima and Nagasaki were not mere accidents.

At its seventeenth annual meeting in April 1954, soon after the Bikini incident, the Science Council of Japan issued statements calling for "abolition of atomic weapons and effective international control of atomic energy" and for "open, democratic, and independent research and use of atomic energy." It also decided to establish a liaison committee for the scientific investigation of A-bomb injuries (Science Council of Japan 1974). The resulting Special Research Committee on Radiation Effects had a comprehensive scope, with survey groups in the fields of basic science, medicine, biology, geophysics, fishery, agriculture, and social effects. Investigations of aftereffects in Hiroshima, Nagasaki, and Bikini were included. In order to cope with the pressures arising from the Bikini incident, the government decided to organize the Liaison Council for the Investigation of A-bomb Aftereffects. The council held its inaugural meeting on 15 October 1954, and the A-bomb Aftereffects Research Council, established a year earlier in the JNIH, was disbanded. Research data obtained by both councils, along with those from observations made in the Southern Pacific area by Hiroshi Yabe and others between 15 May and 4 July 1954, were compiled by the Japan Scientific Council [Science Council of Japan], Special Research Committee on Radiation Effects in 1956 and published by the Japan Society for the Promotion of Science under the title *Research in the Effects and Influences of the Nuclear Bomb Test Explosions* (two volumes containing 1,824 pages) (Japan Scientific Council 1956).

One noteworthy effort of the Special Research Committee during its early stage was the holding of a joint Japan–U.S. conference on the use and effects of radioactive materials (15–19 November 1954), specifically in regard to the Bikini incident. Seven scientists from the American side and fifteen from Japan participated in the five-day proceedings held in the hall of the Science Council of Japan. Closed discussions were held on tolerable radiation dose, elimination of contamination, dosimetry, food contamination, and the use of radioisotopes. In March 1956 the Special Research Committee participated in the selection of Japanese delegates to the United Nations Scientific Committee. This committee is formally called the United Nations Scientific Committee for Effects of Atomic Radiation (UNSCEAR) and was established by the U.N. General Assembly on 3 December 1955; its members represented fifteen nations—Argentina, Austria, Belgium, Brazil, Canada, Czechoslovakia, France, India, Japan, Mexico, the Soviet Union, Sweden, the United Arab Republic, the United Kingdom, and the United States of America. Although Japan had not yet joined the United Nations, it was admitted to the committee because it was one of the countries with advanced research in radiation effects and had experienced the misfortune of radiation exposure at Hiroshima, Nagasaki, and Bikini. UNSCEAR's first meeting was held in March 1956 in New York, with Masao Tsuzuki and Masanori Nakaizumi representing Japan. Japan has since then made many important contributions to the work of this committee.

At its eighteenth annual meeting in October 1954, the Science Council of Japan adopted a resolution calling for establishment of an institute for nuclear radiation research. After much effort, the National Institute of Radiological Sciences was founded in July 1957 under the jurisdiction of the Science and Technology Agency. In 1962 a radiation research group was organized in this institute; and in August, T. Hashizume was sent to the Oak Ridge National Laboratory in Tennessee to explore requirements for making experimental studies. The thermoflourescent method was used to measure gamma rays contained in bricks and tiles of the buildings remaining after the atomic bombings, and neutrons were measured by induced activity of cobalt in reinforced concrete buildings (Hashizume 1967; Hashizume et al. 1967). Other achievements made at the National Institute of Radiological Sciences include estimation of exposure dosage from induced radioactivity by using radiation sources similar to those of the atomic bombs, estimation of absorbed dosage of atomic bomb radiation in the main organs of the human body, extensive surveys of residual radioactivity, and estimation of exposure dosage due to residual radiation materials taken into the body.

In April 1958 the Institute for Nuclear Radiation Research was founded in the School of Medicine of Hiroshima University and led to the establishment of the Research Institute for Nuclear Medicine and Biology in April 1961. The Atomic Disease Institute was established in Nagasaki University's School of Medicine in the following year.

After reorganization of the ABCC was discussed among Japanese and United States government officials, both the ABCC and the JNIH branch offices were disbanded in June 1974. The governments of Japan and the United States reached an agreement that a foundation under Japanese law should be established in Japan, and that this new research organization that was to replace the ABCC and the JNIH should be managed by the two nations on an equal footing. As a result, the Radiation Effects Research Foundation was established in April 1975.

Hiroshima in 1945*

The Air Defense Law was enacted in October 1937 and subsequently revised in 1941 and 1943. The Wartime Casualties Care Law was passed in February

* Hiroshima A-bomb Medical Care History Editorial Committee 1961; Hiroshima Prefectural Office 1972; Hiroshima Shiyakusho 1971; and Nishimaru 1960.

1942 and enforced from late April of that year. These two laws symbolized the way the war directly affected the daily lives of the people. Prior to August 1945 the city and prefecture of Hiroshima had, under these laws, established an air defense headquarters, evacuated people and demolished certain buildings, organized a medical rescue system, and stocked medical supplies. These precautions, however, were designed to cope with the repeated U.S. air raids, using conventional bombs, that the cities of Japan were experiencing at the time. The atomic bombing of Hiroshima on the morning of 6 August, therefore, left the entire city momentarily immobilized. A 1943 directive by the governor of Hiroshima Prefecture had authorized an "air defense medical rescue plan," which forbade evacuation of medical doctors and ordered formation of medical rescue squads consisting of one physician, one dentist, one pharmacist, three nurses, and one clerk. Township councils and civil defense teams worked with these medical squads for the protection and relief of each local district. Of the 298 mobilized doctors in Hiroshima City, 270 became A-bomb victims. Casualty rates among pharmacists and nurses ranged between 80 percent and 93 percent. Death rates among all medical personnel were high. For all practical purposes, the well-prepared medical care system was rendered totally useless. Prefectural and municipal agencies, where the air defense headquarters were located, also suffered heavy damages to personnel and buildings.

By the evening of 6 August the Hiroshima Prefectural Office managed to gather thirty surviving officials, including Governor Genshin Takano, to set up a temporary air defense headquarters in Tamon'in temple at the foot of Hijiyama hill. During the night, requests were sent to the national Ministry of Home Affairs and to neighboring prefectures for doctors, medicines, and food supplies, and orders went out to all police stations in the prefecture for assistance by relief squads, police officers, and civil defense teams, as well as for food supplies. As the prefectural office was completely burned down, the headquarters was moved to the East Police Station early in the morning of 7 August. From 10:00 A.M. the Relief Measures Council was convened, with national and municipal agencies as well as army and navy units based in the Hiroshima area cooperating. There were a number of major military commands concentrated in Hiroshima at the time—Western Japan Commandant, Second Army Headquarters, Chūgoku Regional Military Headquarters, Fifty-ninth Corps Headquarters, Western Japan Military Police Headquarters, Marine Transport Headquarters, and Hiroshima Supply Corps (Hiroshima Shiyakusho 1958, p. 709). Most of these, except for the Marine Transport unit, had been destroyed. The Second Army was given general command over Hiroshima following the atomic bombing; but actual overall supervision of postbombing operations fell to Marine Transport Commander

Fumio Saeki (1977, pp. 221–47). His command made care of the injured the top priority and set up relief stations in eleven places: Hijiri Bridge, Miyuki Bridge, Sumiyoshi Bridge, Kan'onmachi intersection, Eastern Drill Ground, Dobashi-chō, Yokogawa Railroad Station, Koi Bridge, East Police Station, City Hall, and Sentei. Units from the Marine Transport base, safety crews from the Army Fuel Depot, and various navy reinforcements serviced these relief stations. In this immediate postbombing period, military units played a major role in securing food and drinking water, disposal of corpses and epidemic control, removal of debris, and restoration of communications and transport services (Nishina Memorial Foundation 1973, pp. 18–28). Of special importance were the command, training, education, sanitation, and other service units from the Marine Transport base; Kamo naval medical school; and the army and navy hospitals in and near Hiroshima City. Military leadership in coping with the desperate conditions came to an end, however, when surrender was announced on 15 August.

The Hiroshima Prefectural Office was moved on 17 August to the Tōyō Kōgyō plant in Fuchū town of neighboring Aki county, though its public health section (Takemaro Kitajima, chief) went to the city's Fukuromachi Primary School to supervise medical relief work.* Mayor Senkichi Awaya was among 280 city officials lost in the bombing. When fire broke out in City Hall, the remaining staff (under Vice-mayor Shigeteru Shibata) moved into the provisional prefectural headquarters. By mid-August about eighty surviving city officials gathered to undertake the tasks of food rationing and medical relief and to ascertain the extent of suffering and damage.† The number of relief stations increased from the original eleven to fifty-three within the city limits alone. The new sites were simply places where the injured victims congregated. Medical teams sent to these sites, apart from military units, consisted of surviving medical personnel in the city assisted by medical relief teams from medical associations, hospitals, and universities outside the city (Hiroshima Prefectural Office 1972, pp. 166–67). Sixty members of Hiroshima City Medical Association died instantly in the bombing; and its president, Kan'ichi Yoshida, died several days later from A-bomb injuries. On 14 August about thirty surviving members gathered and elected his successor, Kazuhisa Kyōgoku. From then till medical relief was transferred on 5 October to the Japan Medical Service, the members devoted themselves to medical relief work. Many of these medical workers carried on valiantly despite the fact that they themselves were suffering from A-bomb injuries. Members of the Dental Association and the Pharmacists Association were also actively engaged in relief efforts.

* Hiroshima A-bomb Medical Care History Editorial Committee 1961, pp. 126–41.
† Hiroshima A-bomb Medical Care History Editorial Committee 1961, pp. 149–61.

Figure 13.2. Relief station in Fukuromachi Primary School (Hiroshima, 6 October 1945). (Photograph by Shunkichi Kikuchi.)

Medical personnel who came from elsewhere in the prefecture to assist in medical relief, apart from military personnel, included Minoru Fujii and Hirotsugu Sawazaki from Hiroshima Sanatorium for Disabled Veterans, and doctors from medical associations in Onomichi, Kure, and Mihara cities, as well as those from medical associations in Toyota, Takata, Futami, Kamo, Kōnu, Jinseki, Asa, Sera, and Hiba counties. Other medical help came from Kure Sanatorium Hospital and public health centers in Onomichi, Takehara, Kure, Mihara, Fukuyama, Fuchū, and Saijō.* By the end of September, 2,557 medical personnel had put in 21,145 work days (table 13.1).

The first medical relief team to reach Hiroshima City from outside the prefecture was one sent by the Okayama Prefectural Medical Association; it served from 7 to 9 August at Hiroshima Communications Hospital. A second team from this association served from 14 to 15 August at various relief stations in the city. Other medical relief teams arriving early included those from medical associations in Shimane and Yamaguchi prefectures (8 August), Tottori Prefecture (9 August), Hyōgo Prefecture (10 August), and Osaka Urban Prefecture (21 August) (tables 13.2A, 13.2B). Medical teams also came from Red Cross hospitals (which, at the time, were branches of

* Hiroshima A-bomb Medical Care History Editorial Committee 1961, pp. 205–308.

military hospitals) in Yamaguchi, Okayama, and Tottori. A medical survey team was sent on 8 August by the Army Medical School and the Tokyo First Army Hospital (provisional); subsequently Seiichi Ōhashi and 143 other medical personnel under the command of Colonel Chikayama provided medical care for nearly a month (12 September–10 October) at the Ujina branch of Hiroshima Army Hospital.

The number of relief stations in the city, after reaching a peak of fifty-three on 9 August, gradually decreased to eleven by 5 October. Between 11 August and 5 October (there are no records for 6–10 August), 105,861 persons were admitted to the relief stations, and 210,048 more were given outpatient clinical treatment (table 13.3). Meanwhile, streams of A-bomb victims were

Figure 13.3. Relief station in Ōshiba Primary School, Hiroshima. At center is Dr. Gorō Nagasaki (11 October 1945). (Photograph by Shunkichi Kikuchi.)

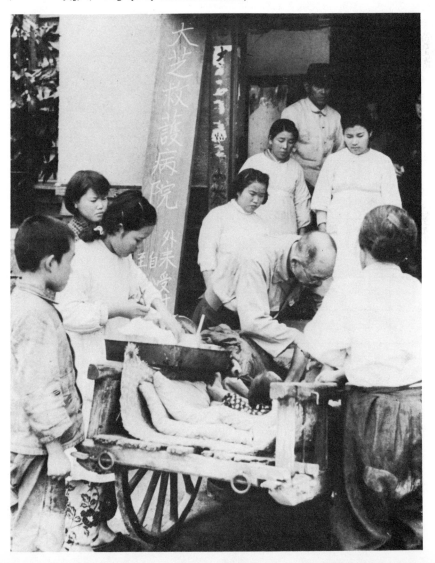

TABLE 13.1

Medical Relief Team Personnel from Hiroshima Prefecture Who Served in Hiroshima

Relief Team (place)	Physicians A	Physicians B	Dentists A	Dentists B	Pharmacists A	Pharmacists B	Public Health Nurses A	Public Health Nurses B	Registered Nurses A	Registered Nurses B	Midwives A	Midwives B	Clinical Assistants A	Clinical Assistants B	Totals A	Totals B
Yoshida	33	65	10	18			33	72	17	38					93	193
Tadanoumi	27	75	10	24	2	4	12	30	34	94	3	8			88	235
Shōbara	21	130	3	12	1	50	19	97	13	55			2	71	59	415
Kinoe	7	7	1	1	1	1			12	12			6	6	27	27
Matsunaga	7	22	2	6	4	12	1	4	6	18					20	62
Kaita	6	112													6	112
Fuchū	16	72	4	13	1	3			28	102			1	4	50	194
Mihara	49	127	21	52	18	43			132	323			10	56	230	601
Onomichi	75	174	21	49	23	55	17	54	134	319	5	10	13	110	288	771
Hiro	16	31					1	4	8	12	5	27	1	3	31	77
Yuki	11	80	2	12	1	6	12	142	8	60	3	18	1	20	38	338
Innoshima	12	36	4	12	3	9	3	9	40	120	5	15			67	201
Miyoshi	56	157	20	60	26	74	33	103	43	113			2	40	180	547
Kake	19	84	2	4	2	8			45	168			4	16	72	280
Jōge	12	72	2	12					25	132			10	40	49	256
Kouchi	23	69			1	3			27	81					51	153
Kure	32	96			1	3			61	183			5	15	99	297
Saijō	61	146	3	3	9	9			279	328			60	60	412	546
Takehara	27	54	11	22	3	6			41	82					82	164
Kabe	32	992	12	372	13	403			160	4,960			40	1,242	257	7,969
Ōtake	25	775	8	248	7	217			125	3,875			38	1,178	203	6,293
Kure branch	3	43					17	385					8	203	28	631
Sera branch	11	24	1	2	1	2	6	14	6	14	3	8	3	25	31	89
Fuchū branch							13	103					5	43	18	146
Onomichi branch	4	20					14	63	7	26			8	99	33	208
Obata branch	1	7					7	86					2	41	10	134
Oku branch					1	7			11	90			3	19	15	116
Etajima	1	4	1	5					3	13	4	18			9	40
Fukuyama branch	1	6					10	44							11	50
Totals	588	3,480	138	927	118	915	198	1,210	1,265	11,218	28	104	222	3,291	2,557	21,145

N.B. Branches belong to larger medical associations.

A: Actual working number

Date	Relief Teams (place)	Doctors	Dentists	Pharmacists	Nurses	Clerks	Totals	Relief Stations Served
August								
7	Okayama	4		1	8		13	East Police Station
7	Okayama	6			15		21	Prefectural Office
8	Okayama	5			11		16	Misasa Trust Bank
8	Okayama	5			11		16	Communications Hospital
8	Shimane	3	1		10	3	17	Ōshiba township
8	Shimane	5	1	1	8		15	Number 2 Primary School
8	Yamaguchi	3		1	11	4	19	Tōshōgū temple
9	Tottori	11	3	4	49	5	72	City Hall, Nakayama Primary School, Communications Hospital, Kurashiki Airfield (Yoshijima township)
9	Yamaguchi	2			10	1	13	Eba Ordnance School
10	Okayama	7		2	15	2	24	Kōseikan Crematory (east side)
10	Hyōgo	2			2		4	Ōshiba township
11	Shimane	2	1	1	4		8	Kanzaki Primary School, Funairi Honmachi township
15	Shimane	5		1	10		16	
17	Tottori	12	2	6	32	2	54	Eba, Funairi, Kanzaki, and Koi townships
17	Okayama, Disabled Veterans Hospital	2			16		18	Fuchū Primary School (Aki county)
17	Okayama	6		1	13	2	22	Number 2 Primary School
21	Hyōgo	41		10	38	2	91	Itsukaichi town (Saeki county); Hera and Inokuchi villages (Saeki county); Kan'on, Koi, and Kusatsu townships
21	Osaka	27			29	6	62	Fuchū and Funakoshi towns (Aki county); Nukushina and Nakayama villages (Aki county); Fukuromachi township; Number 2 Primary School
25	Tottori	1			5	1	7	Hesaka village (Aki county)
27	Hyōgo	14	11	2	5		32	Clothing Depot, Hijiyama hill, Kurashiki Airfield, Funakoshi town
30	Hyōgo	3	2		5		10	Funakoshi town
September								
1	Hyōgo	2			5		7	Number 1 Primary School
5	Osaka	15		11	25		51	Hatsukaichi and Itsukushima towns (Saeki county); Nukushina village; Aosaki and Yaga townships
6	Shimane	3		1	5		9	Teachers Sanatorium at Jigozen village (Saeki county)
October								
3	Tottori	1		1	5		7	Niho township

Source: Hiroshima A-bomb Medical Care History Editorial Committee (HAMCH), *Hiroshima Genbakuiryōshi* (Hiroshima: Hiroshima Genbaku Shōgai Taisaku Kyōgikai, 1961), pp. 124–25.

TABLE 13.2B
Medical Relief Workers from Outside Hiroshima Prefecture

Pre-fecture	Doctors		Dentists		Pharma-cists		Public Health Nurses		Registered Nurses		Midwives		Clinical Assist-ants		Totals	
	A	B	A	B	A	B	A	B	A	B	A	B	A	B	A	B
Osaka	38	389	7	71	12	79	54	567	49	315	2	14	16	117	115	1,144
Hyōgo	49	305	26	163	9	36	5	20	77	320			7	56	150	952
Tottori	27	112	5	20	3	25	11	51	45	242			10	49	139	588
Shimane	23	127	5	24			9	47					7	35	92	500
Yamaguchi	7	41							79	1,631			3	21	89	1,693
Okayama	35	140			2	8			89	356			4	16	130	520
Totals	179	1,114	43	278	26	148	79	685	339	2,864	2	14	47	294	715	5,397

A: Actual working number.
B: Aggregate working days.
Source: Hiroshima A-bomb Medical Care History Editorial Committee (HAMCH), *Hiroshima Genbakuiryōshi.* (Hiroshima: Hiroshima Genbaku Shōgai Taisaku Kyōgikai, 1961), p. 125.

Relief Stations and Patients Treated in Hiroshima

Date	Number of Relief Stations	Patients Treated		
		Inpatients	Outpatients	Total
6 August	53			
7	53			
8	53			
9	53			
10	52			
11	52	3,985	4,224	8,209
12	50	3,880	4,112	7,992
13	50	3,733	4,021	7,754
14	50	3,651	3,969	7,620
15	48	3,540	7,550	11,090
16	47	3,493	7,186	10,679
17	45	3,293	6,996	10,289
18	40	3,122	6,580	9,702
19	40	2,906	7,396	10,302
20	40	3,674	7,076	10,750
21	30	3,767	6,676	10,443
22	30	3,242	6,274	9,516
23	30	3,220	6,210	9,430
24	30	3,153	6,114	9,267
25	30	2,954	5,756	8,710
26	30	2,716	5,774	8,490
27	30	2,700	5,566	8,266
28	30	2,596	5,696	8,292
29	30	2,410	5,536	7,946
30	29	2,159	4,318	6,477
31	27	2,193	4,386	6,579
1 September	27	2,010	4,410	6,420
2	26	2,005	4,378	6,383
3	25	2,008	4,124	6,132
4	25	1,909	4,046	5,955
5	24	1,809	4,078	5,887
6	23	1,762	4,202	5,964
7	22	1,711	4,184	5,895
8	20	1,595	3,740	5,335
9	20	1,528	3,442	4,970
10	19	1,426	3,252	4,678
11	17	1,369	3,188	4,557
12	17	1,299	3,126	4,425
13	16	1,235	2,876	4,111
14	17	1,224	2,584	3,808
15	17	1,172	2,544	3,716
16	16	1,057	2,294	3,351
17	16	1,050	2,286	3,336
18	16	1,029	2,056	3,085
19	15	1,009	2,304	3,313
20	13	990	2,028	3,018
21	13	981	2,036	3,017
22	13	904	1,810	2,714
23	13	855	1,724	2,579
24	13	823	1,808	2,631
25	13	786	1,904	2,690
26	13	727	1,802	2,529
27	13	725	1,524	2,249
28	13	685	1,526	2,211
29	12	653	1,444	2,097
30	12	621	1,358	1,979
1 October	11	545	1,324	1,869
2	11	513	1,292	1,805
3	11	500	1,324	1,824
4	11	480	1,366	1,846
5	11	479	1,248	1,727
Total		105,861	210,048	315,909

Source: Hiroshima A-bomb Medical Care History Editorial Committee (HAMCH), *Hiroshima Genbakuiryōshi*. [Hiroshima A-bomb Medical Care History] (Hiroshima: Hiroshima Genbaku Shōgai Taisaku Kyōgikai, 1961), p. 148.

flowing out of Hiroshima to the towns and villages of the adjacent Aki, Saeki, and Asa counties. Approximate numbers of those fleeing to these counties were: Aki, 45,000; Saeki, 20,000; and Asa, 52,000. When those escaping to Futami, Hiba, Kamo, Takata, Toyota, and Yamagata counties are added, the total number of people who left Hiroshima is estimated at 150,000.*

Faced with this sudden influx, the surrounding towns and villages had, like Hiroshima, an urgent need of medical care. For example, in the Nakayama district 3 to 5.4 kilometers northeast of Hiroshima, 85 percent of the 246 households (1,812 people) were half-destroyed by the bombing, and about 30 percent of its 1,812 people were injured (Hiroshima Shiyakusho 1971*b*, vol. 2, p. 380). Then, from mid-morning on 6 August, A-bomb victims from Hiroshima began to pour in. As this district had no doctor, most of the refugees were sent to the relief station at Hesaka Primary School in the neighboring village. As that station could not meet the demand for help, approximately 2,500 injured persons were taken into private homes, and another 1,000 or so were accommodated in the Nakayama Primary School. A doctor came to this district on 7 August; but as necessary supplies were not available, he could only apply oil to patients' burns. The situation on subsequent days was briefly as follows:

8 August, medical team from Hiroshima Sanatorium for Disabled Veterans in Saijō
9 to 12 August, medical team from Tottori Prefecture
13 August, doctors from Kure
14 August, doctors from Kurahashi island
15 August, doctors from Kamagari and Etajima islands, and Shōbara
16–20 August, no medical relief came
21 to 25 August, medical team from Osaka

The wounded were looked after by village officials and local women. Early on, the doctors urged the local people to collect all available medical supplies, but the results were very disappointing. The situation got so bad that the prefectural health office transferred the remaining patients to the relief station in Yaga and closed the Nakayama relief station on 2 September. This is only one example, but sufficient perhaps to suggest conditions elsewhere at the time (Chen 1967; Egawa 1971).

Public hospitals in Hiroshima at bombing time included Hiroshima Red Cross Hospital, Hiroshima Communications Hospital, two hospitals of Mitsubishi Heavy Industries, Hiroshima Army Welfare Hospital, and Hiroshima Prefectural Hospital. All of these sustained damages to personnel and facilities but, even so, played major roles in caring for the casualties (Hiroshima Shiyakusho 1971*a*, vol. 1, pp. 434–500). Hiroshima Red Cross Hospital (Ken Take-

* Hiroshima A-bomb Medical Care History Editorial Committee 1961, pp. 108–9.

uchi, director; Fumio Shigetō, vice-director) was located in Sendamachi about 1.6 kilometers from the hypocenter; its main building was heavily damaged, and secondary buildings were burned down. About 85 percent of its staff, including 408 student nurses, and roughly half of the patients (army-related) were killed or wounded. Following the bombing, injured persons poured in, and through its efforts to cope with the emergency it gradually assumed a central role in treating ailments related to the atomic bomb. Hiroshima Communications Hospital (Michihiko Hachiya, director) was in Motomachi about 1.3 kilometers from the hypocenter. This hospital, too, was heavily damaged, and the majority of its forty staff present at the time were wounded. Injured persons began gathering there by the afternoon of 6 August; and by the following morning 200 persons had been treated for light injuries and 2,560 serious cases admitted. Until mid-September this hospital had about 2,300 inpatients.

Mitsubishi Heavy Industries had two hospitals—one in Minami Kan'on (4.3 kilometers from the hypocenter; Tanzō Kusakabe, director) and the other in Eba (4.5 kilometers from the hypocenter; Yasumasa Tamaki, director)— both of which sustained only light damage. From the morning of 6 August, each hospital admitted about 1,000 injured persons, and another 1,000 were placed in nearby homes. The hospital staffs also treated several thousand people who filled a nearby athletic field. During these early days Akira Masaoka performed two pathological autopsies but left no records.* The Hiroshima Army Welfare Hospital in Ujina (3.2 kilometers from the hypocenter; Tomoo Komiyama, director), under the Marine Transport command, also attended to A-bomb victims. In October it became Japan Medical Service's Ujina Hospital, and later a Hiroshima prefectural hospital. From 30 August some ten persons (including Masao Tsuzuki) from Tokyo Imperial University spent about twenty days treating patients and doing a survey; this care-survey effort was continued by Takehiko Kikuchi and others from Kyoto Imperial University. Hiroshima Prefectural Hospital (Shūzō, Ishibashi, director) at the time was in Kakomachi (800 meters from the hypocenter). Its 26,000-square-meter facility with 250 beds was totally demolished and burned, and most of the staff on duty at bombing time were killed instantly or died within a few days. The few surviving staff members opened a medical relief station in Furuta Primary School on 9 August. In September the relief station was moved to Kusatsu Primary School, and injured director Shūzō Ishibashi was replaced by Iwao Kurokawa. Part of the Kyoto Imperial University survey and autopsy work was done at the Kusatsu station. In March 1946 the Prefectural Hospital was closed, so staff and patients were transferred to the Japan Medical Service hospitals.

* Hiroshima A-bomb Medical Care History Editorial Committee 1961, pp. 308–94.

Among army hospitals, those close to the hypocenter and thus severely damaged included Hiroshima First Army Hospital (Motomachi), First Branch Hospital (Western Drill Ground), and Hiroshima Second Army Hospital (Motomachi). Those that engaged in medical relief immediately after the bombing included the Eba and the Hesaka branches of the First Army Hospital. The surviving staff of the Second Army Hospital and its Mitaki branch treated injured soldiers and citizens who gathered in their vicinities. Branch hospitals of the First and Second army hospitals (which had been evacuated to Hiroshima's environs) organized twelve medical relief teams that served from 6 to 10 August at the Hesaka branch hospital, the ruins of the Second Army Hospital, and the Marine Transport drill ground. Relief workers dispatched by Ōno Army Hospital gave first aid to some 300 afflicted persons; and this hospital admitted 1,400 casualties to its facilities and nearby Ōnonishi Primary School. Afterward, army hospitals in Hiroshima admitted over 45,000 injured persons. Navy facilities,* with dates and numbers treated, included:

Iwakuni Naval Hospital	6–18 August	51 admitted, all of whom died
Kure Naval Hospital	6 August–19 October	73 admitted
Tozuka Medical School and Koyaura Relief Station of the Naval Medical School	12 August–18 September	269 admitted, 130 died
Kure Seamen's Hospital	19 August–5 September	8 admitted
A temporary infirmary of Kure Naval Hospital	6–30 September	79 admitted

Nagasaki in 1945†

In August 1945 strict air defense conditions prevailed in Nagasaki. As a key defense zone, patrols had been strengthened since 1941. Beginning 11 August 1944, the city had been subjected to repeated air raids in 1945 on 26 April, 29 and 31 July, and 1 August. Thus, air defense measures had been intensified. The Nagasaki defense headquarters had been established in September 1944, and the Nagasaki Prefecture Defense Mobilization Council in February 1945. Rescue and relief precautions centered on the city's medical association. There were twenty-two designated relief stations, including pri-

---

* Hiroshima A-bomb Medical Care History Editorial Committee 1961, p. 98.

† Nagasaki Shiyakusho 1977; Nagasaki Shiyakusho, General Affairs Department, Investigation and Statistics Section, 1959; Shirabe 1972, 1979.

mary schools in Shinkōzen, Katsuyama, Irabayashi, Togiya, and Inasa, as well as the Japan Red Cross Nagasaki branch; and 327 persons were organized to service these stations. Nagasaki Medical University and Mitsubishi Hospital were also expected to serve as key relief centers (Nagasaki Shiyakusho 1977, pp. 77, 78–80).

But the destructive power of the atomic bomb dropped on 9 August—greater than that exploded over Hiroshima—far exceeded Nagasaki's defense and relief capabilities. Given Nagasaki's topography, devastation in the bombed area was enormous, and the initial destruction was followed by the delayed outbreak of fires in the old city area. The defense command experienced great difficulty in grasping the scope of damage. Even though prefectural police and special rescue squads, local policemen, firemen, and civil defense teams in the old city area were mobilized, they found "the situation completely beyond our capacity to cope with it" (Nagasaki Shiyakusho 1977, p. 377). "The main medical relief center—Nagasaki Medical University and its hospital—was hit hard, with many dead and wounded among its doctors and nurses," and "many private doctors in the city were killed or injured" (ibid.). The city's preparations for medical relief were wrecked from top to bottom.

In the central bombed area, "except for the few who were in air-raid shelters, every human being and animal within 400 meters of the hypocenter died instantly; even the strongest buildings were blown to bits, and nothing is now left intact" (Okada 1977, pp. 255–58). The main buildings and classrooms of Nagasaki Medical University, 700 meters southeast of the hypocenter, were demolished and burned (figure 13.4), and almost all teaching staff either died instantly or a few days later (Shirabe 1968–74; Asahi Shimbunsha 1970). Of 580 first- and second-year students who were attending general and special medical classes at bombing time, 414 died. The outer shell of the university's hospital, a reinforced concrete structure with a basement and three floors aboveground, still stood; but the interior was reduced to rubble and ashes. There were many dead, but "those with some strength left in them crawled up Anakōbō hill, crying out the names of friends and seeking water; some 300 spent the night there, but at daybreak half of them were only lifeless corpses" (Nagasaki Shiyakusho 1977, pp. 324–31). Deaths among teachers, administrative staff, and students at Nagasaki Medical University are shown in table 13.4. The injured were cared for in the school's ruins by staff and students who, themselves, barely survived. Professor of surgery Raisuke Shirabe began giving first aid to the injured from the afternoon of 9 August, but felt the need for a place to move them for treatment. He borrowed two buildings at Nameshi, his own evacuation site, where on 12 August he set up a temporary relief station to which he moved university president Susumu Tsunoo and other injured university personnel. From 12

Figure 13.4. Nagasaki Medical University in ruins (mid-October 1945). (Photograph by Shigeo Hayashi.)

to 17 August, Professor Shirabe and fifteen others (doctors, nurses, and students) treated and nursed over one hundred casualties at the Nameshi provisional relief station. On 18 August patients still alive were moved to Shinkōzen relief station, Ōmura Naval Hospital, and other places; and the provisional relief station at Nameshi was closed (Shirabe 1979). Takashi Nagai and eleven others of the university department of radiology conducted itinerant medical care in the Mitsuyama district outside Nagasaki City from 12 August to 8 October (Nagasaki Shiyakusho 1977, pp. 503–9).

Urakami First Hospital was located atop Motohara hill, about 1.4 kilometers from the hypocenter. Founded and operated by the Franciscan order, it had some seventy tubercular patients at bombing time. The hospital's interior was ruined by the bomb's blast, and a delayed fire finished off the medical equipment and supplies. But as the only hospital left in the Urakami area, it bore the burden of caring for the area's injured. Dr. Tatsuichirō Akizuki and others of the hospital staff began treating casualties on 10 August. On

TABLE 13.4

Deaths among Nagasaki Medical University Personnel

Staff	Teaching:	President; professors	17 ⎫	
		Assistant professors, lecturers	10 ⎬ 42	
		Assistants, others	15 ⎭	
	Administrative:	Supervisors, secretaries	206	206
	Nursing:	Nurses, midwives	51 ⎫	
			⎬ 109	
	Nursing:	Student nurses, midwives	58 ⎭	
Students	Medicine:	Medical students	194 ⎫	
		Special medical students	305 ⎬ 535	
	Pharmacy:	Special pharmacy students	36 ⎭	
		Total	892	

Source: Nagasaki Shiyakusho, *Nagasaki Genbaku Sensaishi* [Record of the Nagasaki A-bomb War Disaster] (Nagasaki: Nagasaki Kokusai Bunka Kaikan, 1977), vol. I, pp. 324–31. R. Shirabe, ed., *Wasurenagusa* (FMN) (Nagasaki: Kyū Nagasaki Ikadaigaku Genbaku Gisei Gakuto Izokukai, 1974), vol. V, p. 196.

12 August prefectural police and volunteers from Kawanami Industries came to clear up the debris so that the Motohara relief station could be opened there (Akizuki 1966). A relief station functioned for one day at Yamazato Primary School, but most of the injured in the Motohara district remained, without treatment, in air-raid shelters. Akizuki and others kept on giving treatment at the Motohara relief station until December 1945 when the St. Francis Medical Clinic (Father M. Prudent, director) was rebuilt. The four Mitsubishi companies (shipbuilding, munitions, steel, and electrical machinery) located in Nagasaki had three hospitals: the main hospital in Akunoura (3.5 kilometers from the hypocenter), a branch in Funatsumachi (3 kilometers), and the Urakami branch in Morimachi (1.1 kilometers). The two branch hospitals were completely destroyed; but the main hospital, though somewhat damaged, did its best to care for the wounded in its own facilities and by turning the nearby Akunoura Primary School into a temporary hospital (Nagasaki Shiyakusho 1977, pp. 476–82).

Wounded citizens naturally gathered at places designated prior to the bombing as relief stations, such as Shinkōzen, Katsuyama, Irabayashi, and Togiya primary schools and Nagasaki Commercial College; relief work was also begun in places close to the central bombed area, such as primary schools in Shiroyama and Yamazato, the Municipal Commercial High School, and Michinoo Railroad Station. In addition to surviving members of the Nagasaki Medical Association, others active in relief work included medical teams from naval hospitals in Isahaya, Takeo, and Ōmura; medical associations in Isahaya, Saga, Obama, and Shimabara; army hospitals in Nagasaki, Kurume, and Fukuoka; the Hario Marine base; and the Mitsubishi main hospital.* On 16 August, Nagasaki Commercial College was made a temporary hospital (Yoshitaka Sasaki, director) of the 216th Army Supply Company (provisional), with almost two hundred military and medical personnel; by 2 September it had admitted 395 casualties (161 died). The first to reach the relief station at Shinkōzen Primary School was a team from Hario Marine base (led by Takeshi Shima); it arrived on 10 August but moved on to Urakami the next day. It was followed, at Shinkōzen, on the eleventh by a team (Yoshimichi Harada, leader) from the Takeo branch of Sasebo Naval Hospital, with another group (Kenzō Ikemoto, leader) from the Takeo branch hospital arriving on the twelfth; and medicines and equipment from Takeo reached Shinkōzen on 15 August. A second team from Hario came on the sixteenth, and the Shinkōzen relief station could then function as an emergency hospital. After the Hario team left on 31 August and the Takeo personnel on 5 September, the Nagasaki City Medical Association maintained the emergency hospital at Shinkōzen. As this facility became the main center for medical relief, it was decided on 6 October, with influence from Occupation authorities, to transfer control of the facility to Nagasaki Medical University. Following interior remodeling, it officially became on 23 October a branch hospital (Raisuke Shirabe, director) of the university. According to the Hario Marine relief team's report, the hospital had, in the period from 17 to 31 August, an aggregate outpatient load of 3,991 and an aggregate inpatient load of 3,936, having admitted 370 and released 33 patients (154 died). Relief and research teams from Tokyo Imperial University, Kyushu Imperial University, Kumamoto Medical College, and Yamaguchi Medical College were also active at the Shinkōzen emergency hospital.

Large numbers of A-bomb victims, of course, left the city. Of vital importance to the wounded and others fleeing the city was the so-called Relief Train (figure 13.5) (Nagasaki Shiyakusho 1977, pp. 457–67). From 1:50 in the afternoon till midnight of 9 August (bombing day), the train ran four times. From its starting point midway between Michinoo and Urakami railroad stations, it transported approximately 3,500 injured persons to Isahaya, Ōmura, Kawatana, Haiki, and other points along the line. Neighboring towns that received the streams of wounded victims that came by foot, truck, and train included Togitsu village (to 18 August: 521 received at Togitsu Primary School, 62 died; 358 received at Mangyōji temple, 45 died), Nagayo village (782 received at Nagayo Primary School, 96 died), Mogi town (80 received at Kangetsu and Bōyōsō inns), Yagami village (about 200 received at Mori Clinic); and several thousand casualties poured into Isahaya city (Nagasaki

* Nishina Memorial Foundation 1973, pp. 104–8; Shirabe 1972.

Figure 13.5. "Relief Train" in the Urakami district of Nagasaki (mid-October 1945). (Photograph by Shigeo Hayashi.)

Shiyakusho 1977, pp. 509–13). Hospitals in the Nagasaki area that received injured victims included naval hospitals in Sasebo, Ōmura, Kawatana, Hario, and Isahaya. Outside Nagasaki Prefecture, receiving hospitals included army hospitals in Saga and Kurume, a naval hospital in Ureshino, university hospitals in Fukuoka and Kumamoto, and a center set up for A-bomb victims in Kagoshima. The Isahaya branch of Sasebo Naval Hospital, for example, by 1 September treated 521 patients, of whom 156 died (Nagasaki Shiyakusho 1977, pp. 513–17). Surviving patients in this hospital on 20 September were transferred to naval hospitals in Ōmura and Ureshino. The Ōmura Naval Hospital (Kōdō Yasuyama, director) on the day of the bombing admitted 758 wounded, and afterward well over a thousand more (Nagasaki Shiyakusho 1977, pp. 518–25). In addition to medical care, it is recorded that pathological autopsies were performed there by Masao Shiotsuki and others (1945; 1978). Records of these autopsies were offered by Shiotsuki to Tohoku Imperial University, but the autopsies are not included in Hitoshi Miyake's summary of pathological autopsies done on A-bomb victims. Ōmura Naval Hospital was not requisitioned by the Occupation forces; from early October, surviving personnel from Nagasaki Medical University came to assist in its medical services. Indeed, the university resumed its postwar instruction in the Ōmura hospital. The city of Ōmura had, besides the naval hospital, an army hospital and a convalescent hospital; and the number of wounded victims received by these various facilities in Ōmura is said to have reached 4,000. Kawatana Naval Hospital was in the town of that name, 60 kilometers northeast of Nagasaki; this hospital, together with a training center at the naval arsenal and Jōzaiji temple in Kawatana, received 234 casualties, of whom 73 died by the latter part of September. The Haiki branch of Sasebo Naval Hospital took in between 400 and 500 injured persons.

*Medical Care Soon after the Bombings**

Medical care in the early days after the atomic bombings was extremely handicapped by the huge numbers of casualties and severe shortages in both medical personnel and medical supplies (Ōuchi 1967). The main problem in the early stage was burns, and application of zinc oxide oil or ointment was about the only treatment. Zinc oxide oil was often not available, so in many cases rapeseed oil, cooking oil, castor oil, and even machine oil were used. For disinfecting burns and wounds, whatever was at hand—iodine tincture, mercurochrome, rivanol, boric acid solution or ointment—was used. Among traumas, the most difficult to cope with was the removal of countless glass splinters embedded in the skin and muscles. Furthermore, it was especially hard to stop A-bomb wounds from bleeding; the application of compresses moistened with adrenaline proved only slightly effective. Open wounds easily festered, and often gangrene set in. Before long, diarrhea and bloody stools became common complaints; because these could have been symptoms of dysentery, a temporary quarantine hospital was hurriedly set up in the still-standing Fukuya Department Store. But all attempts to obtain cultures of dysentery bacilli from the stools yielded negative results. Antibacterial drugs also were ineffective in relieving the symptoms. And to make things worse, it was summertime; so flies swarmed on open wounds, laid eggs, and then maggots appeared in the wounds to complicate treatment.

As hospital personnel and research teams began to detect decreases in blood cells, they gradually recognized the possibility of radioactive injury. On 26 August the director of Hiroshima Communications Hospital, Michihiko Hachiya, posted the following notice at the Communications Agency and all its offices:

* Hiroshima A-bomb Medical Care History Editorial Committee 1961; Shirabe 1979.

1. The following persons may continue working without further concern: those who on 6 August at bombing time were outside Hiroshima but subsequently entered the city for whatever reason, and have had blood tests with no indication of abnormality; and those who at bombing time were in the basement of the Communications Agency and suffered no effects of the bomb's blast or flash, and whose blood tests indicate no abnormality.

2. Persons known to have low white cell counts are generally those who work in the telephone, telegraph, and transmitter offices located close to the hypocenter. White cell counts for agency personnel are generally only slightly below, if not quite close to, normal (5,000–8,000).

3. The degree of burns seems to have no relation to decrease in white blood cells. Epilation does not necessarily indicate serious illness.

4. As persons with decreased white cell counts have low resistance to infection, they should avoid accidents and injury.

5. Persons with traumas should take care to prevent suppuration; if the wounds do become infected, treatment should be promptly received so as to prevent septicemia.

6. Experts from Tokyo Imperial University have investigated the situation in Hiroshima, and their findings indicate no residual uranium radioactivity at the present time. (Hachiya 1955, pp. 189–90)

Distinct decreases in white blood cells were also detected early by Tsurayuki Asakawa of Hiroshima Red Cross Hospital and by Ichirō Maya of the hospital at Mitsubishi Shipyard.*

On 3 September in Hiroshima, Masao Tsuzuki gave a lecture advising the following measures for treating symptoms resulting from the atomic bombing:

I. Treatment for patients with epilation, stomatitis, hemorrhage, fever, and other complaints.
　　1. *Serious cases* (patients with severe general symptoms and a white cell count of less than 1,000, with poor prognosis).
　　　　(a) Symptomatic treatment.
　　　　(b) Apply therapeutic measures as in moderate cases when possible.
　　2. *Moderate cases* (patients with epilation, stomatitis, diarrhea, but general symptoms not yet serious and a white cell count of over 1,000).
　　　　(a) Symptomatic treatment, rest, and fresh food of high nutritional value.
　　　　(b) Intramuscular injection of autogenous blood (inject 20–30 cc of venous blood into muscle of thigh) or transfuse 100 cc of fresh blood of same type once daily. Serious side effects may occur if care is not taken to carry out the transfusion slowly.
　　　　(c) Administration of large doses of vitamins B and C or fresh vegetables and fruits.
　　　　(d) Administration of calcium-containing drugs; intravenous injection of 20 cc, once or twice daily.
　　　　(e) Oral administration of fresh, roasted, or powdered liver.

* Hiroshima A-bomb Medical Care History Editorial Committee 1961.

(f) Daily subcutaneous injection of more than 500 cc of physiologic saline solution, Ringer's solution, 5 percent glucose solution. Care should be taken not to administer these solutions intravenously in severe cases.

3. *Mild cases* (patients with mild epilation, temporary epilation, or very mild gingivitis, and diarrhea, or those whose symptoms have improved and who have white cell counts of less than 3,000 and over 1,000). Therapeutic measures as in moderate cases. Rest is essential, since a trifling cause may aggravate these symptoms even after they have improved.

II. Treatment for patients without symptoms.

1. Those who were within 2 kilometers of the hypocenter (within the circle of Hiroshima Station, Hijiyama hill, Miyuki Bridge, Tenma Bridge, Yokogawa Station) and escaped thermal burns or functional injury, but with the following conditions, should immediately get a physical checkup. These people are in a latent phase of injury, and, since any trifling cause might make them ill within a month or two, they should be placed under the care of a doctor.

(a) Those who vomited within a few days after the explosion or experienced loss of appetite for several days.

(b) Those with marked malaise or who tire easily.

(c) Those who had mucus or bloody diarrhea like that in dysentery, though of a milder degree.

(d) Those with intraoral or pharyngeal pain.

(e) Those who noted slight temporary epilation ten to fourteen days after the explosion.

2. Those who were in the area 2–4 kilometers from the hypocenter and either received mild thermal burns, cut wounds from glass splinters, or sustained no apparent injury. Since such persons are likely to have received a certain degree of radioactivity, they should visit their doctors and receive advice at the first opportunity. In the meantime, they should have ample rest, eat fresh vegetables and fruits, and take special care not to catch cold. Precautions should be taken for one to two months. (Tsuzuki 1951, pp. 40–45; 1973, pp. 66–68)

Widely used, and to some extent effective, methods included autogenous blood transfusion, fresh blood transfusion, large doses of vitamins B_1 and C, and injections of calcium chloride and glucose. Somewhat unusual measures included doses of table salt (mineral dietetics—Dr. Tatsuichirō Akizuki) and broth of boiled persimmon leaves (vitamin C—Dr. Naomi Kageura). Dr. Raisuke Shirabe experienced rather rapid relief from radiation symptoms by drinking alcoholic beverages after passage of a certain amount of time (Shirabe 1978). Some other doctors had similar experiences, including therapeutic effects from injections of 40 percent alcohol solution. Tomiichi Masuya found that intramuscular injections of cattle liver abstract solution yielded rapid increase of white blood cells. Since everyone agreed about the value of nutrition and rest, it cannot be denied that postwar food shortages had a deleterious effect on A-bomb illnesses. From observations made in Hiroshima, the death rate was low among patients received at the clothing depot relief station, where food supplies were plentiful, but high at other relief stations where food supplies were scarce and environmental conditions poor (Hiroshima A-bomb Medical Care History Editorial Committee 1961, pp. 126–426).

Once the American forces occupied Japan, medical supplies were provided by the U.S. Army, the International Red Cross, and the American Red Cross. Many of the medicines provided were not at that time widely used in Japan—such as penicillin, sulfadiazine, sulfaguanidine, and plasma; and these proved extremely effective for infections after the subacute phase. Relief goods from the International Red Cross owed much to Marcel Junod.

Conditions after Expiration of the Wartime Casualties Care Law*

The Wartime Casualties Care Law included the stipulation that "relief is to be carried out for a period of two months (temporary housing may be loaned for a period of up to six months)." As there was no extension of this limit for the sake of A-bomb victims, the relief measures of the national and local governments were discontinued in early October 1945. Accordingly, the relief stations were closed. The A-bomb casualties who had not yet recovered had thenceforth to seek treatment at medical institutions at their own expense. In the ensuing period, owing to nationwide poverty as well as to the severe controls imposed by the Occupation authorities on the publishing of both research and news reports of A-bomb affairs, the A-bomb victims suffered great distress. The medical institutions strained toward recovery of their former capacities; but they, too, encountered many difficulties.

As of 5 October the eleven relief stations in Hiroshima had 479 inpatients and 1,248 outpatients. While Hiroshima Prefecture complied with the closing of the relief stations, at the same time it designated a number of facilities as Japan Medical Service hospitals (according to Article 70 of the National Medical Care Law, 1942) to continue caring for the A-bomb victims. These facilities were:

Misasa Hospital (Gorō Nagasaki, director) in Ōshiba Primary School
Kusatsu Hospital (Iwao Kurokawa, director) in Kusatsu Primary School
Eba Hospital (Yasumasa Tamaki, director) in Eba Primary School
Niho Hospital (Kazuhisa Kyōgoku, director) in Niho Primary School
Yaga Hospital (Yoshimasa Matsusaka, director) in Yaga Primary School
Fukushima Clinic (Katsumi Kodama, director) in Fukushima township

* Hiroshima A-bomb Medical Care History Editorial Committee 1961; Shirabe 1972; and Shirabe 1979.

In actuality, these hospitals carried on the work of the former relief stations; but, of course, they were unable to go beyond relief care. As evacuated schoolchildren returned to the city, and the city itself began rebuilding, the hospitals faced the necessity for reorganizing in some way. The prefecture wanted to construct a new hospital but lacked the funds to do so. The Misasa and Niho hospitals were closed soon after the number of their patients decreased. Through the efforts of Iwao Kurokawa, Kusatsu Hospital was able to move to Ujina and take over the former Hiroshima Army Welfare Hospital; it later became the Hiroshima Prefecture Central Hospital (under Japan Medical Service). Yoshimasa Matsusaka of Yaga Hospital arranged to rent a tract of land and then acquired the building of Eba branch of the Army Hospital, which he moved and remodeled to establish Hiroshima Welfare Hospital (under Japan Medical Service). In a November 1947 revision of the National Medical Care Law, Japan Medical Service was dissolved; the Central Hospital and the Welfare Hospital were therefore transferred to prefectural administration, as were Inokuchi Hospital (Saeki county), Akitsu Hospital (Kamo county), Setoda Hospital (Toyota county), and Obata Hospital (Hiba county). In the city, Hiroshima Red Cross Hospital, Hiroshima Communications Hospital, and the hospital at Mitsubishi Shipyard were gradually rebuilt. By the end of 1950 the city had thirty-five hospitals (with an aggregate of 1,551 beds) and 174 medical clinics.*

In Nagasaki, the Ōmura Naval Hospital and the Shinkōzen emergency hospital became branch hospitals of Nagasaki Medical University and continued to care for A-bomb casualties. The Ōmura facility, however, was designated solely for wounded navy personnel, so the branch hospital of Nagasaki Medical University was moved to the former Isahaya branch of Kawatana Naval Hospital in May 1946. Meantime, the need for a general hospital for A-bomb casualties in the city came to be recognized. A certain Captain Hohne, the Occupation's officer in charge of administering medical care in Nagasaki City, had the former army hospital in Tokiwamachi (requisitioned by the Occupation) outfitted and donated it to Nagasaki on 24 December 1945, with a new name, Blair Hospital.† Some of the staff and equipment of Shinkōzen emergency hospital were transferred to Blair Hospital, medical equipment was collected from various army hospitals, and medical supplies came from America. This hospital thus became a new medical center for the city; it was renamed Nagasaki Citizens Hospital (charity hospital), with Katsumi Takao as director. Meanwhile, in an administrative reform Nagasaki Medical University was made the School of Medicine of Nagasaki University

---

* Hiroshima A-bomb Medical Care History Editorial Committee 1961, pp. 427–30; Hiroshima Prefectural Office 1976, pp. 246–49.

† Akizuki 1966; NGO International Symposium 1977b, p. 73.

(May 1949), and the educational facilities and the attached hospital were rebuilt and reopened on the old site of the former medical university (1954). In addition to all the hard work needed to revive medical research and education, Raisuke Shirabe and others found time to conduct a detailed survey of about 8,000 A-bomb casualties from late October to the end of November in 1945, and from the results compiled a series of four articles, "Medical survey of atomic bomb casualties" (Shirabe 1953).

From Keloid Treatment to A-bomb Disease Treatment

The more acute illnesses and injuries among A-bomb casualties appeared within the first two months after the bombings; then the third and fourth months were a time of healing and recovery. Some patients died during this time from various multiple, severe conditions, but by the end of the fourth month—that is, by early December 1945—most patients had recovered from conditions directly related to the atomic bombings (Masao Tsuzuki, 1954a).

The primary effects of A-bomb illness and injury had largely improved within four to six months after the bombings; but this initial improvement was deceptive and shortlived, because secondary aftereffects lay deep in the victims' bodies all the while they seemed to be getting better. In the period between recovery from primary effects and clear-cut realization of the presence of secondary aftereffects, the initial aftereffect that aroused both medical and social concern was the abnormal scar tissue that formed on burns caused by the atomic bombings. This tissue was the notorious keloid, as explained in chapter 9, and was, by the end of 1945, already a serious problem in the treatment of victims. At this stage, even when keloid scars had been surgically removed, the keloid tissue tended to grow back again. In December 1945, Yoshio Itō of Hiroshima Red Cross Hospital's department of dermatology wrote a newspaper article on A-bomb burns and keloid scars. For treatment he recommended the recuperation and strengthening of physical stamina, application of medicinal ointments, local injections, massaging, and hot spring treatment; but he warned, "premature orthopedic surgery may be dangerous" (*Chūgoku Shinbun* 1945). By May 1946, Masao Tsuzuki concluded that "orthopedic surgery is now permissible in cases where the symptoms are stable" (*Chūgoku Shinbun* 1946a) and again in December of that year newspapers reported his views to the effect that "keloid scars appear to have passed their growth peak and, from October, began receding; if this is the case, victims may now receive orthopedic surgery without undue concern" (*Chūgoku Shinbun* 1946b).

With such clearances, many patients with keloid and other severe scar conditions undertook remedial surgery; but in other cases such treatment was difficult, and not a few patients were left with the abnormal scars. In particular, young girls with disfiguring scars on face, head, hands, or limbs suffered both physical and mental distress: these came to be called "A-bomb maidens." From the summer of 1951 the Reverend Kiyoshi Tanimoto of the Nagarekawa Church (United Church of Christ in Japan) in Hiroshima organized a Bible study group for such girls to give them spiritual encouragement. He was also deeply concerned to find ways for providing them with remedial surgery. With the cooperation of volunteers in the Japan P.E.N. Club such as Shizue Masugi and Tatsuzō Ishikawa, as well as with support from the Tokyo Supporters Association of the Hiroshima Peace Center, Tanimoto was able in June 1952 to send eight girls from Hiroshima and two from Nagasaki to Tokyo for treatment at the Koishikawa branch of the University of Tokyo Hospital. Other girls were sent to Osaka University's medical school and to Osaka Municipal Medical College. These beginnings led to a broader movement to help provide treatment for the A-bomb victims.

Gorō Ōuchi, Tōmin Harada, and others of the Hiroshima City Association of Surgeons conferred with Tatsuo Yoshida, chief of Hiroshima City's Social Affairs Section, about the need to provide free surgery to persons with A-bomb disabilities; and a survey of needs was made in July 1952. Of a total of 864 diagnosed cases (339 males, 525 females), it was determined that excellent results could be expected in 66 cases and relatively good results in 374 cases. To expedite the plan, the Hiroshima A-bomb Casualty Council (Shinzō Hamai, president; Yoshimasa Matsusaka, vice-president) was formed in January 1953 with the cooperation of Hiroshima City and its assembly, Hiroshima Prefecture, medical associations of the city and the prefecture, Hiroshima Women's Federation, Hiroshima Youth Federation, Hiroshima Peace Center, and other groups. The plan included not only surgery but also internal medicine and other necessary therapies. On 18 January, examinations were carried out at Hiroshima Citizens Hospital on 75 persons: 13 were found to have internal medical problems, 33 had extensive scars and possible blood complications, and 63 were judged to have good chances for improvement through surgery.*

The A-bomb Casualty Council set up a research section to work with the city's medical institutions and locate candidates for medical care. Candidates were examined and consulted as to their need for treatment. Procedures were established to determine what part of the medical expenses a patient could pay, depending on his or her family situation. Treatment was to be

* Hiroshima A-bomb Medical Care History Committee 1961, pp. 468–521; Hiroshima Shiya-kusho, A-bomb Survivors Measures Department 1977; Matsusaka 1978.

free for the financially distressed; 5 percent to 10 percent of the costs would be borne by those with average incomes; and 11 percent to 30 percent by those with higher incomes. In fact, payments were received from only nine patients; expenses thereafter were borne by the Casualty Council. Sources of funds included a gift of 200,000 yen ($556) from Japanese-Americans in Hawaii, and was followed by, later, a grant of 500,000 yen ($1,389) (fiscal year* 1953) from Hiroshima City.

About the same time, concern for the A-bomb victims' plight was aroused in Nagasaki. Raisuke Shirabe arranged for diagnosis and treatment of A-bomb patients at the medical school of Nagasaki University.† It is estimated that in Nagasaki City over 800 victims were at the time afflicted with keloid scars and other aftereffects. Shirabe examined 277 persons and found 165 with keloid scars, 74 with deeply embedded glass splinters, 25 with contusions, and 15 with fractured bones. Of these, 64 were judged as having a chance for full recovery if treated; but only one third of them actually received the needed treatment—the main reason being that the patients simply could not afford the costs. In May 1953 the Nagasaki A-bomb Casualty Council (Tsutomu Tagawa, president; Katsumi Takao, vice-president) was formed by university, prefectural and municipal representatives, medical associations, and social service, cultural, women's, and youth groups. Procedures were more or less the same as in Hiroshima. The hospital of Nagasaki University's medical school administered the treatments.

The criteria of the Casualty Councils of both Hiroshima and Nagasaki for determining need for treatment of A-bomb disabilities were as follows:

1. *Surgery:* radiation injury, or external injury (bone fractures, dislocations, burn scars, and so on) resulting from collapsed buildings or fires, if not yet healed.

2. *Internal medicine:* persons within 2 kilometers of the hypocenter at bombing time, or who entered that zone after the bombing, and who were found at the time to have white cell counts below 4,000 or red cell counts below 3 million; or persons who did not at the time have blood tests but have since experienced generally poor health, who tire easily, and who suffer anemia of undetermined cause. Also, persons who since the bombings have abnormally high white cell counts (above 12,000) but low red cell counts (below 3 million), feel weak all over (general debility), bleed easily from mucuous membranes, and are occasionally feverish.

3. *Ophthalmology:* persons with deformed eyelids (ectropion of the eyelid), lagophthalmus, and white plague; and those requiring artificial eyes and plastic surgery. (Hiroshima A-bomb Medical Care History Editorial Committee 1961, pp. 493–98)

In accordance with these criteria, 227 persons were examined in Hiroshima

---

* In Japan, the fiscal year begins 1 April and ends 31 March of the following year.
† *Nagasaki Minyū Shinbun* 1952; Nagasaki Shiyakusho, A-bomb Survivors Measures Department 1978.

by December 1953; of these, 103 needed treatment. From January to March of the following year, 270 were examined, of whom 124 needed treatment. Raising funds for all such cases was more than the two cities' councils could manage. The councils' chairmen were the mayors of the two cities; with the cooperation of the Central Community Chest of Japan and Japan Broadcasting Corporation (NHK), they set up in June 1953 a Central Campaign Committee to canvass the nation for contributions (Hamai and Tagawa 1961, p. 501). The campaign council and NHK co-sponsored a "Help the A-bomb Victims Campaign" from 1 to 10 August, and gifts totaling 5,088,279 yen ($14,134) poured in from all over the country. The total was divided (3,587,404 yen [$9,965] to Hiroshima, 1,500,874 yen [$4,169] to Nagasaki) to cover the costs of medical treatment for the selected persons.* Also in this year, the two mayors sent to the National Diet a petition, jointly signed by the speakers of the two municipal assemblies, appealing for "medical care for those injured in the atomic bombings." This petition was adopted by the Lower House on 3 August and by the Upper House on 6 August.

Guidelines for Medical Treatment of A-bomb Aftereffects

In response to the achievement in Hiroshima and Nagasaki of organized medical care for A-bomb victims, the Ministry of Health and Welfare in November 1953 formed the A-bomb Aftereffects Research Council (see page 513). The mandate of this body (Rokuzō Kobayashi, chairman) was to make a comprehensive assessment of the efficacy of medical treatment of A-bomb aftereffects and to formulate an initial set of guidelines for a medical care law. The council conducted a survey of the health conditions of 3,000 surviving A-bomb casualties in Hiroshima and Nagasaki; drafted guidelines for medical treatment of A-bomb patients; and laid plans for a symposium to consider therapies for A-bomb aftereffects. These efforts were carried out with the cooperation of the Casualty Councils of Hiroshima and Nagasaki. Masao Tsuzuki, Takehiko Kikuchi, Tandō Misao, and Jirō Uraki participated in the drafting of the guidelines; after consideration by the research council, with Kunio Kawaishi and Raisuke Shirabe cooperating, the first version of the guidelines was published in the August 1954 issue of *Nihon Ishikai Zasshi* (The Journal of Japan Medical Association). The general introduction dealt with (1) A-bomb injuries, (2) health administration, (3) prevention of nervous

* Hiroshima A-bomb Medical Care History Editorial Committee 1961, pp. 498–513.

disorders, (4) strengthening physical stamina, and (5) prevention and cure of infection. Specific sections dealt with treatment of (1) injury to hematopoietic organs, (2) endocrine dysfunction, (3) liver dysfunction, and (4) abnormal scar tissue.

One portion of the general introduction reads as follows:

The first phase of A-bomb injury lasted about four to five months. Investigation of the health conditions of A-bomb casualties at the end of this initial phase (and especially of those within 2 kilometers of the hypocenter at bombing times who showed symptoms of acute radiation illness but eventually recovered) reveals a high incidence of anemia. At the same time, many victims complained of various vague and obscure subjective symptoms. These indeterminate symptoms may have been related to the poor postwar living conditions; for with the passage of one or two years and the improvement of diets, many victims recovered their health and stamina and became more socially active than the average person. But among the survivors there were also many whose subjective symptoms have not abated, despite the passage of several years. They complain of generally poor health and insufficient mental energy to carry on their work. This latter group seems to fall somewhere between the healthy and the sick. Physicians who have examined them find no objective confirmation of abnormality; but, as these victims share many symptoms with those who have leukemia and aplastic anemia, it is important to keep them under careful observation and protective care so as to prevent more deleterious conditions from occurring.

The complaints of vague suffering without any characteristic disease should be regarded as one kind of chronic A-bomb illness. While there is in such cases no particular hindrance to leading a normal life, there is nonetheless a lack of energy reserves needed for life, as well as some abnormality in dealing with all kinds of stress. As explained earlier, it is a distinctive feature of all chronic A-bomb health problems, with subjective or objective symptoms, that there is no clearly distinguishable illness. Taking into account the patient's situation at bombing time and the extent of damage suffered—in particular, the exposure dose—chronic cases should be examined with three things in mind: (1) the effects of primary injuries in the early stage, (2) the condition of initial radiation illness, and (3) the effects of secondary injuries. Cases where confirmed effects are relatively severe should be diagnosed, for the time being, as due to aftereffects of the atomic bombings. Whenever the less clearly defined complaints are accompanied by some other clearly explicable disease or symptoms, immediate attention should be given to the known conditions. Specific efficacious therapies for chronic A-bomb illnesses are not yet known. Indeed, if the main cause of illness is taken to be the aftereffects of radiation injury, then there is no known therapy. Persons with chronic complaints should receive guidance to help avoid loss of livelihood; they should be encouraged to do everything possible to protect their health and, above all, to prevent the eruption of severe symptoms of aftereffects. If any abnormalities are discerned in those who suffer chronic A-bomb ailments, is it not the duty of clinical medicine to do its best, even if symptomatic relief is all that can be done? We must not stand by as spectators with folded arms merely because the patients' conditions have not yet been scientifically explained. (A-bomb Aftereffects Research Council 1954)

This emphasis on "chronic A-bomb illnesses" (Tsuzuki 1954*b*) had great merit, but they were not subsequently subjected to epidemiological or clinical analysis.

The initial guidelines for treatment of A-bomb aftereffects also went to great lengths in dealing with abnormal scars. "Today, eight years since they first appeared, abnormal scar tissues may be regarded as having reached a stable condition; therefore, treatment may in practice follow procedures applicable to abnormal scars resulting from other causes," the guidelines advised. At the same time, therapeutic principles are discussed in detail for the careful selection of methods for the complete removal of keloid and other abnormal scar tissues, and for the transplantation of the patient's skin, with respect to specific parts of the body. Available methods of treatment were also indicated for leukemia, aplastic anemia, granulocytopenia, abnormal blood coagulation, and functional disturbances of adrenal cortex, gonads, and liver.

Following the Bikini hydrogen bomb test, a new Liaison Council for Investigation of A-bomb Damages was formed, and the earlier A-bomb Aftereffects Research Council became its Hiroshima-Nagasaki branch (Saburō Kojima, chairman). This branch continued, after reorganization, to work for revisions of the guidelines for treating A-bomb aftereffects ailments. In the December 1955 issue of the Journal of Japan Medical Association, new material was published, with the cooperation of Kinnosuke Hirose and Shigenori Sugimoto, on "Treatment of Eye Injuries" (A-bomb Aftereffects Research Council 1955).

Enactment of the A-bomb Victims Medical Care Law

In 1954, when the movement by A-bomb victims associations and citizens' groups to win government medical care for the victims got under way, concern for this problem was also intensified at the level of the Casualty Councils and at the top levels of government in both Hiroshima and Nagasaki. Soon after the national government in March of that year took official positions on the "Lucky Dragon No. 5" incident (Bikini hydrogen bomb test), the Hiroshima City Casualty Council held an emergency session on 16 April and decided to send a petition to the National Diet and government, calling for (1) all medical costs for treatment of A-bomb diseases to be paid from the national treasury, (2) enactment of a special law to provide relief for the livelihood of A-bomb victims, (3) provision of more hospital beds and equipment for the medical care and health administration of A-bomb victims, and (4) transfer to Japan of all Atomic Bomb Casualty Commission facilities. The Nagasaki City Casualty Council responded in September 1954 by presenting a petition, signed by the mayors and assembly speakers of both Hiroshima and Nagasaki as well as by the Diet members from both places, calling for "payment by the national government of all medical costs of the A-bomb victims" (Honda et al. 1961, pp. 532–33). This petition estimated that, as of 27 August 1954, the number of victims needing medical care was 6,000 in Hiroshima and 3,000 in Nagasaki. Of the aggregate total, cases needing surgery numbered 3,900; internal medicine, 4,200; and eye or other treatment, 900. Anticipated medical expenses totaled 301,500,000 yen ($837,500); livelihood subsidies during treatment, 24,300,000 yen ($67,500)—a grand total of 325,800,000 yen ($905,000). To support the petition, citizens in Hiroshima and Nagasaki conducted a signature campaign, and a public exhibition of atomic bomb materials from the two cities was held in Tokyo.*

In response to these efforts, the government decided to take 3,522,000 yen ($9,783) from contingency funds in its 1954 budget and, through the Ministry of Health and Welfare, to distribute the money to medical institutions in the two cities (in Hiroshima, to Citizens Hospital, Red Cross Hospital, Prefectural Hospital, Communications Hospital, Hiroshima University's medical school, and Hiroshima Prefectural Medical Association; in Nagasaki, to Nagasaki University's medical school). The Hiroshima funds totaled 2,349,000 yen ($6,525); the Nagasaki funds, 1,173,000 yen ($3,258). Budget allocations were made in 1955 for a total of 12,442,000 yen ($34,561) (Hiroshima, 8,303,100 yen [$23,064]; Nagasaki, 4,138,900 yen [$11,497]) and again in 1956 for 25,682,000 yen ($71,339) (Hiroshima, 16,750,000 yen [$46,528]; Nagasaki, 8,932,000 yen [$24,811]). The breakdown of expenses covered in the 1955 allocation included detailed surveys, medical care research, publications, communications, travel to Liaison Council meetings, and so on. Expenses covered in the 1956 allocation included detailed surveys, medical care, autopsies, printing, communications, travel, and so on. Thus, medical care expenses were accepted as a government responsibility for the first time in the 1956 budget.

Enactment of a law for medical care of A-bomb victims was fervently desired by A-bomb victims and related persons. The Second World Conference against Nuclear Weapons was held for three days beginning 9 August 1956,

---

* The success of this exhibition owed much to Professor Masao Tsuzuki's painstaking efforts. The exhibition was held two months after Aikichi Kuboyama died, and at a time when the American scientists were strongly disputing Japanese views that his death was due solely to his exposure to radioactive fallout from the U.S. hydrogen bomb test on Bikini atoll. Accordingly, it was intended not only to illustrate scientifically the grim realities of the atomic bombings of Hiroshima and Nagasaki but also to justify the Japanese scientists' conclusion based on medical specimens and data as well as on such material evidence as roof tiles exposed to radiation.

in Nagasaki. The problem of relief for victims was taken up by a discussion group on the second day. At a separate gathering of A-bomb victims, the Japan Confederation of A-bomb and H-bomb Sufferers Organizations was formed; this organization passed resolutions appealing for enactment of a victims relief law as well as health administration for victims (Imahori 1971). These movements for medical care provided by law took concrete form in the 9 August decision by the Socialist Party of Japan (JSP) to sponsor in the Diet's next extraordinary session a suprapartisan bill that included an allocation of 230,000,000 yen ($638,889) for medical care and livelihood relief for A-bomb victims (*Chūgoku Shinbun* 1956). The people of Hiroshima and Nagasaki welcomed the JSP's action and increased their efforts to get the government to enact such a law with adequate financing. To that end, a new petition for an A-bomb victims relief law, jointly signed by the mayors and the assembly speakers of both cities, was sent in November to the national government, the National Diet, and each political party—and with the petition, a summary draft of the desired law (Watanabe et al. 1961, pp. 644–48). The Ministry of Health and Welfare responded by drafting a "Law concerning Medical Care for A-bomb Victims" for the government to sponsor in the Diet's next regular session and, in January 1957, requested the Ministry of Finance to budget 267,493,000 yen ($743,036) to implement this law. The budget request was trimmed to 174,589,000 yen ($484,969), but Diet deliberations yielded passage of the bill on 31 March 1957.

The Law concerning Medical Care for Atomic Bomb Victims (or, the A-bomb Victims Medical Care Law) had five sections: general regulations, health administration, medical care, an inquiry commission for medical care of A-bomb victims, and miscellaneous regulations. A-bomb victims covered by the law were those who at bombing times had been within approximately 4 kilometers of the hypocenter, early entrants into the two A-bombed cities, and fetuses of victim mothers. Under the law, A-bomb victims received health books (for certification and records) and annual health checkups. In case of illness, necessary expenses were, upon confirmation, paid by the government. At the time of enactment, the Diet also approved three supplementary resolutions:

1. The government should loan funds to A-bomb victims with low incomes when needed for rehabilitation of their household finances, and adequate funds for this purpose should be allocated.
2. To make sure that no one needing medical care will fail to receive it, the government should take appropriate steps to see that not only fetal victims but other children of A-bomb victims are checked as soon as possible for chronic illness.

3. The government should take positive steps to promote both research and medical care to deal with radiation injuries resulting from the atomic bombs and other causes.

While fostering the preceding causes and policies, the Hiroshima A-bomb Casualty Council faced a need to strengthen its organization structure, so it was incorporated as a foundation in April 1956, and the Nagasaki Casualty Council likewise was incorporated in September 1958. The original names of both councils had included the term "medical care" [omitted heretofore in this translation]; but upon incorporation as foundations, both councils dropped this term in recognition of the fact that they were also committed to a wider range of needs—livelihood relief, welfare measures, travel aid to "A-bomb maidens" going to America for treatment, support for research on A-bomb aftereffects, and promotion of hot spring therapy. Through New Year's postal card lotteries,* Nagasaki was able to erect its A-bomb Victims Welfare Center in 1960; Hiroshima, likewise, built its welfare center in 1961. Nagasaki in 1961 assumed responsibility for health administration under the Medical Care Law; Hiroshima followed suit in 1962. Both councils had in 1959 begun holding research meetings on A-bomb aftereffects. Hiroshima's first meeting (June 1959) was a symposium on "prevention and treatment of abnormal functioning of internal organs." Reports presented at this symposium included those by Susumu Hibino (leukemia), Gyōichi Wakisaka (anemia), Fumio Shigetō (general therapy), and Soichirō Yokota (internal organs, especially liver damage).

Comprehensive summaries of the two Casualty Councils' work in promoting health administration and medical care for A-bomb victims were presented at the Seventh Seminar on A-bomb Aftereffects (1965) by Kiyoshi Shimizu (1967) and Chiyota Fukuda (1967). From enactment of the A-bomb Victims Medical Care Law in 1957 through 1964, the aggregate number of health

* The New Year's postal card lotteries are government-sponsored, and there are two types: one with a 1-yen contribution; the other, without it. In both types, however, there are lottery numbers of six figures at the bottom of each card. Winning numbers are published in the newspapers some days later, and winning cards can be exchanged at local post offices for such New Year's gifts as, for 1980:

First prize	Compact camera
Second prize	Pocket camera
Third prize	Letter pad and envelope set
Fourth prize	Sheet of memorial stamps

Contributions collected this way are used as follows:

1. To promote social welfare (70.6 percent of the total);
2. To conduct medical research (17.8 percent);
3. For the medical treatment of the A-bomb victims (6.2 percent);
4. As relief goods to the sufferers in emergencies (3.1 percent);
5. For other purposes.

checkups given in Hiroshima was 367,413; of these, 70,309 were given complete examinations. According to Fukuda's report, health checkups in Nagasaki numbered 214,387; of these, 40,684 were complete examinations. In both cities the numbers have increased annually. More recently, the fourteenth research meeting held in 1973 was a symposium on "problems of A-bomb health administration."

A-bomb Hospitals and Other Specialized Institutions

With funds raised through New Year's postal card lotteries, the Japanese Red Cross Society in September 1956 founded the Hiroshima A-bomb Hospital (120 beds) next to the Hiroshima Red Cross Hospital. Fumio Shigetō, director of the latter, served concurrently as director of the A-bomb Hospital. In May 1958 the Japanese Red Cross Society established the Nagasaki A-bomb Hospital (81 beds) in the Katafuchi district, with Soichirō Yokota as director. Both hospitals subsequently increased their number of beds and equipment. On the twentieth anniversary of the bombings, the two directors presented, to the Seventh Seminar on A-bomb Aftereffects, reports on the general situation of the two hospitals (Shigetō 1967; Yokota 1967). According to these reports, the Hiroshima A-bomb Hospital from September 1956 to August 1965 had had 210,954 outpatients; this count included 40,256 new patients for internal medicine and 3,988 for surgery. The number of inpatients had reached 2,248, of whom 404 (17.9 percent) had died. Autopsies were performed in 275 cases. At the Nagasaki A-bomb Hospital from May 1958 to September 1965, there had been 41,858 outpatients (of whom 7,654 received complete examinations) and 2,646 inpatients (343 autopsies performed, representing 81 percent of the dead). Major diseases among inpatients in Hiroshima were leukemia and malignant tumors (17.5 percent), anemia (13 percent), cardiovascular disorders (9.7 percent), and cirrhosis of the liver and other liver disorders (8 percent). There were 76 leukemia cases. At the Nagasaki hospital, major diseases were cardiovascular disorders (17.3 percent), leukemia and malignant tumors (17 percent), cirrhosis of the liver and other liver disorders (14 percent), endrocrinological disorders (7 percent), and anemia (4 percent). Forty-six cases of leukemia were recorded.

These two hospitals were the first specialized hospitals for A-bomb diseases. Hiroshima University in 1961 founded its Research Institute for Nuclear Medicine and Biology; Nagasaki University in 1962 established its Atomic Disease Institute. In 1966, Hiroshima opened the Funairi A-bomb Victims Health Clinic (later Funairi Municipal Hospital); Nagasaki, the A-bomb Victims Central Clinic in 1967. Other principal institutions included Hiroshima's Arifuku A-bomb Victims Spa (1967), Hiroshima A-bomb Victims Nursing Home (1970), Hiroshima A-bomb Victims Convalescent Research Center (1968); and in Nagasaki, the Obama A-bomb Victims Spa (1965), the Megumi no Oka (Hill of Grace) A-bomb Victims Nursing Home founded (1970) and run by Junshin Seibokai (Holy Mother of Immaculate Conception Order), and Nagasaki A-bomb Victims Convalescent Center (1976).

The A-bomb Victims Medical Care Law (1957) was expanded in 1960 to include a number of special measures (table 13.5A), and the law was subsequently revised several times (table 13.5B) (Hiroshima Prefectural Office 1976). Then, in 1968 the A-bomb Victims Special Measures Law was passed "for the purpose of extending welfare through special allowances to those who

TABLE 13.5A

Classification of "Special A-bomb Victims" under the A-bomb Victims Medical Care Law

Item	Classification	Explanation
1	Directly-affected persons within a radius of 3 km	Persons (including fetuses) who were within 3 km of either hypocenter at the time of bombing
2	Certified victims	Persons certified as victims by the Minister of Health and Welfare
3	Persons with specific diseases	Persons with specific diseases confirmed by the Minister of Health and Welfare as a result of medical examination according to the items in Article 2 of the law
4	Early entrants within three days	Persons (including fetuses) who, within three days of the bombings, entered bombed areas within 2 km of either hypocenter
5	Persons (including fetuses) directly affected in "special bombed areas" with heavy residual radiation.	The scope of these "special areas" was extended by later revisions made in May 1972 (Hiroshima) and April 1973 (Nagasaki)

N.B. Reference above is to the A-bomb Victims Medical Care Law before revision, according to classifications in article 6 (old ordinance).
Source: Hiroshima Prefectural Office, *Genbaku Sanjūnen—Hiroshimaken no Sengoshi* [In the Thirty Years after the Atomic Bomb—Postwar History of Hiroshima Prefecture] (Hiroshima: Hiroshimaken, 1976), p. 275.

not only were injured in the atomic bombings but today live under special conditions" (Art. 1).* This law included the former "medical allowance" along with "special," "health maintenance," and "nursing" allowances. The "health maintenance" allowance was for certified victims with one or more of eleven designated illnesses. A "health protection allowance" was added later for certified victims, with or without any illness, who were within 2 kilometers of the hypocenter at bombing times and thus needed to take precautions against possible illness. The Special Measures Law, too, underwent later revisions (table 13.6).

---

* Law Concerning Special Measures for Atomic Bomb Survivors 1968.

TABLE 13.5B
Successive Revisions of the A-bomb Victims Medical Care Law

Date of Revision	Major Details of Revision
March 1957	Promulgation of the law (effective from 1 April 1957)
August 1960	1. "Special A-bomb Victims" classification added; payment of medical care expenses for general treatment added. 2. Payment of "medical care allowances" to "certified victims."
March 1962	1. Area for "Special A-bomb Victims" extended from 2 km to 3 km. 2. "Special A-bomb Victims" requirement relaxed. *Old:* "Directly affected A-bomb victims who also entered 2-km areas within two weeks." *New:* "Directly affected A-bomb victims and early entrants (those who entered 2-km areas within two weeks)."
March 1963	1. "Special A-bomb Victims" requirements relaxed. *Old:* "Directly affected A-bomb victims and early entrants (those who entered 2-km areas within two weeks)." *New:* "Pertains to all A-bomb victims." 2. "Medical allowances" income requirements relaxed. *Old:* "Victims who paid no income tax in the previous year, and whose main supporter paid no more than a 5,660-yen income tax." *New:* "Victims who paid no more than a 1,640-yen income tax in the previous year, and whose main supporter paid no more than a 5,660-yen income tax."
April 1965	1. "Medical allowances" increased (two categories). *Old:* "2,000 yen" and "1,000 yen." *New:* "3,000 yen" and "1,500 yen." 2. "Medical allowances" income tax requirements relaxed. *Old:* Previous year's tax for victim, "1,640 yen"; for main supporter, "5,660 yen." *New:* Previous year's tax for victim, "17,200 yen"; for main supporter, "17,200 yen." 3. Health administration broadened to provide "health checkups for those desiring them," with a limit of two yearly per person beyond regularly scheduled checkups.
October 1965	1. Reduction of time requirement for "Special A-bomb Victims" entering either city after the bombings from "two weeks" to "three days." 2. Addition of new districts in Hiroshima and Nagasaki for persons (including fetuses) at bombing times.
April 1971	Redefinition of Nagasaki's central bombed area.
May 1972	Extension of "special bombed areas" in Hiroshima.
April 1973	Extension of "special bombed areas" in Nagasaki.
June 1974	Cancellation of distinction between "Ordinary A-bomb Victims" and "Special A-bomb Victims."

Source: Hiroshima Prefectural Office, *Genbaku Sanjūnen—Hiroshimaken no Sengoshi* [In the Thirty Years after the Atomic Bomb—Postwar History of Hiroshima Prefecture] (Hiroshima: Hiroshimaken, 1976), pp. 275–76.

TABLE 13.6

Successive Revisions of the "A-bomb Victims Special Measures Law"

Date of Revision	Special Allowance	Health Maintenance Allowance	Nursing Allowance	Medical Care Allowance	Other Allowances
May 1968 (Promulgation of law)	10,000 yen monthly	3,000 yen monthly	300 yen daily	5,000 and 3,000 yen monthly; Income tax limit: less than 17,200 yen	
March 1969	Income tax limit: less than 22,700 yen Payment: 5,000 yen	Eligibility extended to include vision disorders			
July 1969					Burial allowance introduced: payment of 10,000 yen
May 1970	Income tax limit: less than 37,200 yen	Income tax limit: less than 29,200 yen	Income tax limit: less than 29,200 yen Changed to monthly: 10,000, 7,500, and 5,000 yen	Income tax limit: less than 29,200 yen	
March 1971		Age limit reduced from 65 to 60 years			
May 1972	Income tax limit: less than 54,700 yen	Income tax limit: less than 48,400 yen Age limit reduced from 60 to 55 years Payment: 4,000	Income tax limit: less than 48,400 yen	Income tax limit: less than 48,400 yen Payments raised to 6,000 and 4,000 yen	Burial allowance increase to 16,000 yen

Date					
April 1973	Income tax limit: less than 77,330 yen	Income tax limit: less than 71,070 yen	Income tax limit: less than 71,070 yen	Income tax limit: less than 71,070 yen	
July 1973	Payment increase to 11,000 yen, 5,500 yen	Age limit reduced from 55 to 50 years. Payment increase to 5,000 yen		Payments increased to 7,000 and 5,000 yen	
April 1974	Income tax limit: less than 86,500 yen	Income tax limit: less than 80,000 yen	Income tax limit: less than 80,000 yen	Income tax limit: less than 80,000 yen	
June 1974	Payments increased to 15,000 yen, 7,500 yen. Payment when "certified disease" cured: 7,500 yen monthly	Payment increase to 7,500 yen; age limit relaxed; eligibility extended to include motor functions and respiratory problems	Payments increased to 18,000, 13,500, and 9,000 yen monthly	Payments increased to 9,500 and 7,500 yen	Burial allowance increase to 22,000 yen
May 1975	Income tax limit: less than 125,000 yen	Income tax limit: less than 117,500 yen	Income tax limit: less than 117,500 yen	Income tax limit: less than 117,500 yen	
July 1975	Payment increase to 24,000 yen; 12,000 yen when "certified disease" cured.	Payment increase to 12,000 yen. Age limit abolished	Eligibility extended to "home nurses" (4,000 yen). Payments increased to 23,000, 17,250, and 11,500 yen	Payments increased to 14,000 and 12,000 yen	Burial allowance increase to 33,000 yen. Health Protection Allowance introduced; payment of 6,000 yen to victims within 2 km of hypocenter

Source: Hiroshima Prefectural Office, *Genbaku Sanjūnen—Hiroshimaken no Sengoshi* [In the Thirty Years after the Atomic Bomb—Postwar History of Hiroshima Prefecture] (Hiroshima: Hiroshimaken, 1976), pp. 277–79.

Chapter 14

Government Administration and Citizens' Movements

National Government Policies toward A-bomb Victims

Not until 1954 did the Japanese government adopt any official policies to help the A-bomb victims. The immediate cause was the groundswell of public concern and activity provoked by the damages to crewmen of the Japanese fishing vessel caused by the hydrogen bomb test at Bikini atoll in March of that year. Because the public demanded that the state assume responsibility for care of the A-bomb victims, the Ministry of Health and Welfare for the first time asserted the need, "as demonstrated by the Bikini incident, for the state to make all haste in providing compensation to the victims of atomic bombings" (Hiroshima Prefectural Office 1976, p. 268). Accordingly, the government in 1954 began making its first disbursements of living expenses to A-bomb victims, after having consulted proper authorities in Hiroshima and Nagasaki.

Afterward, government care of A-bomb victims was gradually expanded and systematized, though always in response to the victims, the nationwide peace movement, and various Hiroshima- and Nagasaki-based organizations. Even today, however, the government policies cannot be judged adequate, and the A-bomb victims remain dissatisfied. The evolution of the various policies in relation to accompanying conditions are traced below.

The Immediate Postbombing Period. By the day after Hiroshima was bombed, the Japanese government had learned from American announcements (President Truman, 6 August 1945)* that an atomic bomb had been used. The government decided, therefore, "to appeal to world opinion through an all-out international propaganda effort against the use of this inhuman weapon," and domestically "to inform the people of the A-bomb's use and urge upon them a new awareness needed to carry out the war" (Hiroshima Prefectural Office 1976, p. 93). The military authorities, however, vigorously opposed this plan, fearing such announcements would cause the people to lose their will to fight. The public, therefore, was consistently kept ignorant of the truth about the A-bomb damages. Meantime, on 10 August the Japanese government sent the following official protest against use of the new weapon to the United States government through the Swiss government:

To employ this new weapon of unprecedented and indiscriminate destructiveness compared with any existing weapons and projectiles is a crime against human nature. Our Imperial government, in its own name and, indeed, in the name of all mankind and civilization, censures the United States government in the strictest terms, and at the same time demands that it renounce further use of this inhuman weapon. (Hiroshima Prefectural Office 1976, pp. 99, 406; 1972, p. 724)

Following this lead, Japanese newspapers embarked on an all-out campaign against atomic bombs. But this was the extent of the Japanese government's initial response to the atomic bombings.

Administration of the Wartime Casualties Care Law. The Wartime Casualties Care Law, enacted in February 1942, provided for the rescue, relief, and allowances for war victims, their families and survivors. These three kinds of assistance were administered by governors of prefectures where the victims lived. For an emergency that occurred outside the home prefectures, relief was handled by the governor of the prefecture concerned. All funds came from the national treasury.

How the law was applied to the victims of the Hiroshima and Nagasaki atomic bombings is not altogether clear. According to an office memorandum by Kisaburō Takeuchi, chief of Hiroshima Prefecture's personnel section, who headed the prefecture's relief and rehabilitation efforts for A-bomb victims, an article in the *Bōei Kaihō* [Civil Defense Bulletin] reported "rescue and relief carried out in accordance with the Wartime Casualties Care Law" (Takeuchi 1971, pp. 569–632). Authorities in the prefectures and cities of Hiroshima and Nagasaki presumably did their best to carry out the provisions of the law; but as government agencies also were heavily damaged in the bombings, it is unlikely that they were able to do very much.

* 6 August 1945 in the United States was already 7 August 1945 ("the day after") in Japan.

According to "Record of the Hiroshima A-bomb War Disaster" *(Hiroshima Genbaku Sensaishi),* "the Wartime Casualties Care Law expired on 5 October [1945], and the emergency care centers were closed. . . . Thereafter, patients had to obtain medical care at their own expense" (Hiroshima Shiyakusho 1971a, p. 217). A report on the Eleventh Medical Care Unit (Takashi Nagai, leader) of Nagasaki Medical University indicates a similar situation in Nagasaki: "The law was in effect for two months; we carried out our responsibilities and then phased out on 8 October" (*Genshi Bakudan Kyūgo Hōkoku* [Report of A-bomb Emergency Care], chapter 3, section 3; August–October 1945) (*Asahi Shimbun* 1970, p. 76). Rescue work in Hiroshima and Nagasaki under this law lasted only two months because article 3 of the law stipulated a sixty-day period for relief activity, although a proviso was included that permitted "extension in case of special need" by prefectural governors, if approved by the Ministry of Health and Welfare. Whether the prefectural governors never sought an extension or whether, if they did, approval was not given, remains uncertain.

The Occupation Period. A reconstruction plan for Hiroshima City was announced by the War Damages Rehabilitation Agency in November 1946, but no government measures for A-bomb victims were included. The Occupation ended with the signing of the Treaty of Peace with Japan (San Francisco Peace Treaty) on 8 September 1951; in article 19 of the treaty, Japan relinquished all rights to press claims on the United States. The Japanese government later interpreted the article's conditions as including any claims made by A-bomb victims.

Enactment of the Law for Relief of the War Wounded and for Survivors of the War Dead. On 30 April 1952, two days after the San Francisco Peace Treaty went into effect, the Law for Relief of the War Wounded and for Survivors of the War Dead was promulgated. This law opened the way for government compensation to be paid not only to wounded military personnel and to survivors of those killed while serving in the armed forces but also to quasi-military casualties such as mobilized student workers, compulsory workers, and women volunteer workers. But the A-bomb victims among ordinary citizens—though they were certainly war victims—were not included in the law's scope. Hence, promulgation of the law served to provoke "intensified demands for measures to care for the A-bomb victims" (Chūgoku Shinbunsha 1966, pp. 64–67).

The Bikini Hydrogen Bomb Test and Enactment of the A-bomb Victims Medical Care Law. The movement to ban all nuclear weapons swelled to new strength when crewmen on the "Lucky Dragon No. 5" fishing vessel suffered damages (one died) from the hydrogen bomb test on Bikini atoll on 1 March 1954. Responding to the heightened public outcry that care of

A-bomb victims is unquestionably a state responsibility, 3,520,000 yen ($9,778) for a survey of the A-bomb victims was allotted in the fall of 1954 from contingency funds in the government's general budget. And in the following year the first specific budget allocation (12,440,000 yen [$34,556]) for a survey commission was put into the general budget.

At the August 1955 World Conference against Atomic and Hydrogen Bombs, the realities of A-bomb damages and the needs of the A-bomb victims were made clear to the people of the entire nation; thus, in both the 1955 and the 1956 budgets the government set aside funds for the medical care of A-bomb victims. There followed demands for enactment of a law guaranteeing such medical care. Accordingly, a bill to that effect was passed by the Lower House of the National Diet in plenary session on 12 December 1956. Vigorous efforts by the Japan Council against Atomic and Hydrogen Bombs and the Japan Confederation of A-bomb and H-bomb Sufferers Organizations (JCSO) subsequently led to enactment in 1957 by the Twenty-sixth Diet of the government-sponsored bill for the A-bomb Victims Medical Care Law (pages 542–46). The law as initially designed, however, was limited to registration, examination, guidance, and treatment of A-bomb victims with symptoms meeting specific standards set by the Ministry of Health and Welfare. No provisions for help with living expenses were included. The law was revised in August 1960 to distinguish between "ordinary" and "special" victims and, accordingly, to provide allowances for living expenses to the "special" victims, as well as to extend medical care to all certified A-bomb victims (pages 547–51).

Court Rulings and Enactment of the A-bomb Victims Special Measures Law. The Japan Confederation of A-bomb and H-bomb Sufferers Organizations, at its sixth general assembly in 1961, had pressed its demand for enactment of a "relief law based on national compensation." But the major stimulus to passage of such a law was the Tokyo District Court's ruling of 7 December 1963 on an A-bomb-related lawsuit. In this case three A-bomb victims brought a joint suit against the state, demanding compensation for damages resulting from the atomic bombings. The court ruled that "neither international nor domestic law upholds the right to claim compensation from the governments of either the United States of America or Japan, so the plaintiffs cannot legally hold the state responsible" (Hiroshima Prefectural Office 1972, pp. 857–901). Even so, the court also held that, in dropping the atomic bombs on Hiroshima and Nagasaki, the United States had violated international codes of war and, further, that

the question naturally arises of the state's responsibility to compensate for damages that were the outcome of a war that the state by its own authority and responsibility initiated, a war that led many citizens to their deaths and imposed great injury and anxiety upon many others. Because the magnitude of the damages was far beyond the ordinary, it is not excessive to say that the accused [the state] should learn its lesson and take steps to provide adequate relief. (Hiroshima Prefectural Office 1972, pp. 857–901)

Following this ruling, both the upper and lower houses of the Forty-sixth Diet in 1964 passed bills to strengthen relief for the A-bomb victims. The JCSO in 1966 published a detailed account of its position and claims under the title "Demand for Recognition of the A-bomb Victims' Special Needs and for an 'A-bomb Victims Relief Law.'" The government at this time was busy settling various other war claims. Landowners were compensated for losses experienced during the postwar land reform, and in 1967 compensation was paid to returnees from overseas territories for their losses of overseas assets—in stark contrast to the neglect of the A-bomb victims' needs. Indeed, when compensation for overseas losses was approved by the Diet, a supplementary resolution was passed to the effect that relief for the A-bomb victims *ought* to be considered. To counter this sluggishness, the Committee of Seven to Appeal for World Peace (including Nobel Prize winner Hideki Yukawa and others) in June 1967 held an interview with then Prime Minister Eisaku Satō and presented him with a petition for an A-bomb victims relief law. A similar petition, co-signed by the governors of Hiroshima and Nagasaki prefectures and the mayors of Hiroshima and Nagasaki cities, was submitted in September of the same year. Many other similar petitions came from other groups and localities.

The government, however, honored none of these petitions. The A-bomb victims all wanted a relief law, and for many years subsequently they have pressed their case, mainly through the JSCO, by various means—including sit-ins before the Ministry of Health and Welfare. But the government's position remains unchanged to this very day.

The main reason for the government's opposition to a relief law for A-bomb victims seems to have been its belief that the victims could not be extended special administrative treatment. Incendiary bombs, for example, are less destructive than atomic bombs; but people killed and wounded in the extensive fire bombing of Tokyo are no less victims than the A-bomb victims of Hiroshima and Nagasaki. If the A-bomb victims were accorded special treatment, then all casualties and their survivors must be given compensation. A-bomb victims who suffer hardships are therefore advised to turn to the government's various social service and welfare agencies. Such are the opinions repeated by spokesmen for the Ministry of Health and Welfare (*Sekai* 1974, p. 123). While showing an understanding of the A-bomb victims' difficulties, Health and Welfare Minister Kunikichi Saitō said (9 November

1973), "Relief in the form of government compensation is limited to military personnel and dependents, so it would be impossible to make a law providing government compensation to A-bomb victims" (*Sekai* 1974, p. 123). Such a view, however, is far removed from the feelings of those who experienced the tragedy of the atomic bombings.

Putting aside the campaign for government compensation for the time being, the Hiroshima and Nagasaki prefectural and municipal authorities, along with JSCO, then pressed for strengthening of the A-bomb Victims Medical Care Law. The government-sponsored A-bomb Victims Special Measures Law was passed in May 1968 and went into effect in September of that year. In the initial stage, this law provided, from the national treasury, special allowances and allowances for health maintenance, medical care, and nursing care (for the latter, the national government paid 80 percent, and the relevant prefectures and cities paid 20 percent).

Synopsis of National Administration of A-bomb Victims Measures. Government policies for A-bomb victims are based on the Medical Care Law and the Special Measures Law. Since their enactment, these two laws have been revised bit by bit in response to demands made by A-bomb victims and others. The major revision was the abolition in 1974 of the distinction between "ordinary" and "special" A-bomb victims; henceforth all A-bomb victims' health books became uniform, and all health-book holders were eligible for payment of medical expenses. In a 1975 revision of the Special Measures Law, health insurance allowances were instituted, with payments going to victims directly affected within 2 kilometers of the hypocenters and to their children exposed in utero. Table 14.1 shows the current situation regarding various government allowances to A-bomb victims.

The cases of the three Hiroshima A-bomb victims, who were encouraged by the 7 December 1963 court ruling to petition for application of the two A-bomb victims laws as state compensation, are well known. Two of them, Tadao Kuwabara and Akira Ishida, sought certification of their illnesses as related to the atomic bomb. Son Jin-doo sought issuance of an A-bomb victim's health book. As all three appeals were rejected, these three victims fought to have the dismissals overturned. The state's defense distinguished between relief as social security for those with specific needs at specific times, and relief as compensation for wartime sacrifices; it argued that the two A-bomb victims laws fall within social security legislation and, thus, were not to be treated as government compensation, which is limited to military personnel, their dependents, and other quasi-military personnel—that is, to those having some official relationship to the state. Although the A-bomb victims were equally war-related victims, they did not, the state's defense held, have any official government relationship. The two A-bomb victims laws could not, therefore, be treated as state compensation (to be given, that is, to *all* victims of atomic bombings irrespective of particular need, as in social security laws). This interpretation is reflected not only in the initial writing of the two laws but in subsequent revisions as well. This position gives rise to the following problems:

1. In principle the two laws should be applied without regard to whether victims are poor or have any income; but, in fact, income limits are set for all allowances under the Special Measures Law except that for funeral expenses.
2. If the standards of government compensation were applied, there would be condolence payments and annual pensions for victims' surviving family; but there are no such provisions in the two A-bomb victims laws.
3. Allowances under the two laws are regarded as "benefits," not as "rights" of the A-bomb victims. Thus, the Ministry of Health and Welfare's Commission of Inquiry that administers the A-bomb Victims Medical Care Law does not include democratic representation from among the A-bomb victims. The deliberative process for dealing with complaints also needs to be democratized.
4. The administrative procedures for determining causal relations between the atomic bombings and the victims' injuries and illnesses are unduly strict.

Thus, while it is clear that government policies toward the A-bomb victims have come a long way from the initial postwar neglect, it cannot be said that the state has yet fully met its responsibility toward the victims.

When compared with all that has been done for A-bomb victims by the victims themselves as well as by individual citizens, private organizations, and public agencies in Hiroshima and Nagasaki—despite the debilitating burdens of massive destruction and psychological disorientation—it is manifestly clear that the national government's policies and actions have been woefully inadequate. Criticism is particularly strong in Hiroshima and Nagasaki toward the government's complete lack of relief efforts during the initial decade when the A-bomb victims and citizens of the two cities were in such great distress.

From the time of the bombings to the present, the government has emphasized the inhuman nature of atomic weapons; yet it has refused to enact an A-bomb victims relief law that would accord any special relief to the victims of atomic destruction. The call for the government to adopt a positive stance toward victim relief and nuclear disarmament is not, however, for the benefit of the A-bomb victims alone. It is the cause of all who live daily under the threat of a nuclear holocaust.

Local Government Policies toward A-bomb Victims

The enormous A-bomb destruction left the prefectural and municipal agencies of Hiroshima and Nagasaki in such ruins that for a while they could do little or nothing for the victims. Delay in relief for the victims is seen even in the fact that the 1949 laws establishing Hiroshima as the Peace Memorial City and Nagasaki as the City of International Culture included no plans for relief facilities for the victims. Again, after the San Francisco Peace Treaty went into effect in April 1952, the Reverend Kiyoshi Tanimoto in a 6 August letter to John Hersey explained that he (Tanimoto) had discussed the matter of help for the "Hiroshima maidens" with Hiroshima City officials, but the city was unable to accept the proposal at the time because of limited funds (Matsusaka 1969, p. 136).

In the immediate postwar years the local governments of Japan were so financially impoverished, and the prefectures and municipalities of Hiroshima and Nagasaki had suffered such heavy losses in both personnel and organization—and faced such desperate need to begin rebuilding the cities—that it is little wonder that relief measures for the A-bomb victims were so long delayed at the local level as well. Indeed, the organized relief activities mounted by medical personnel, the victims themselves, and other citizens' groups in the two cities and prefectures, despite great adversity, stand in marked contrast to the national government's poor record.

In January 1952, Hiroshima City examined 4,038 A-bomb victims with the worst external injuries and, in July of that year, assessed means of treating 864 of these cases (Matsusaka 1969, pp. 137–38). The members of the Hiroshima City Association of Surgeons put forth a strenuous effort and by January of the following year formed the Hiroshima Atomic Bomb Casualty Council (Mayor Shinzō Hamai, chairman), and began to offer free treatment to victims. The City of Hiroshima provided some funds to support this effort.* Treatment for A-bomb victims in Nagasaki had up to this time been provided by the vigorous efforts of the hospital attached to Nagasaki University's medical school. But in May 1953 the Nagasaki Atomic Bomb Casualty Council (Mayor Tsutomu Tagawa, chairman) was formed; and, in addition to free treatment, this council undertook surveys of the A-bomb victims as well as research of A-bomb diseases (Nagasaki Shiyakusho, A-bomb Survivors Measures Department 1978, pp. 97–104).

The A-bomb Victims Medical Care Law of 1957, though woefully inadequate, served to promote local efforts to help the victims. In fact, the measures

* Hiroshima A-bomb Medical Care History Editorial Committee 1961, pp. 468–521.

projected by the Medical Care Law were actually implemented through local municipal organs and voluntary organizations. Under this law, supervision of the victims' health was a national responsibility; but few victims were examined under national auspices because the national government was not prepared to conduct examinations. This responsibility was thus delegated to the two cities' Casualty Councils, which were ready and willing to work. The councils also disbursed relief funds to the impoverished and began research on the aftereffects of the bombings. A similar Hiroshima Prefecture council in 1961 opened the A-bomb Victims Welfare Center, which had an office for supervision of victims' health. In that year, fewer than 20,000 A-bomb victims were given examinations; but the office's work was so successful that three years later its clients exceeded 70,000.* The Nagasaki Casualty Council had erected the A-bomb Victims Welfare Center in 1960 that, in addition to health supervision, provided occupational guidance and temporary lodging. To make medical examinations more accessible, the Nagasaki council even undertook to cover transportation costs and, from 1970, made examinations available on Sundays and during evening hours for the benefit of laborers.

Two decades after the bombings, local government activities were further escalated—again, in contrast to the national government's stubborn refusal to undertake relief activity. In Nagasaki, the Daiwasō Sanatorium was built in 1965 at Obama Spa to promote hot springs treatment of A-bomb victims. It was followed in 1967 by the Central A-bomb Victims Health Clinic and in 1971 by the A-bomb Victims Health Screening Center and the Tateyamasō Sanatorium. These agencies—all projects of the Nagasaki Casualty Council—helped to improve the accuracy of examinations and, in cooperation with the Nagasaki A-bomb Victims Welfare Center, to offer counsel and aid for daily life. Nagasaki City founded its own Health Supervision Center in 1970 to give thorough examinations to victims, and, in 1973, a Consultation Center to offer counsel on health, medical care, and livelihood problems. In 1975 the city began a project in which "home volunteers" twice weekly visited homes of disabled victims to help with meals, laundry, and other household chores.

Projects undertaken by the Hiroshima Casualty Council were similar to those in Nagasaki. From 1961 vocational guidance and livelihood counsel were offered by the A-bomb Victims Welfare Center. In 1967 the Arifuku Spa Sanatorium and Research Center was opened, as hot springs treatment was found effective in treating anemia and hemorrhaging in the victims. Under the city's direct administration, the Funairi Health Center was founded in 1966 to give medical examinations; this center was upgraded in 1971 to

---

* Hiroshima A-bomb Medical Care History Editorial Committee 1961, pp. 676–91; and Matsusaka 1969, pp. 180–83.

become Funairi Municipal Hospital and, thereafter, served as the city's princi-pal facility for the early detection and prevention of A-bomb diseases, as well as for medical care and counsel. Because many older victims had no place to go upon release from the hospital, a nursing home was erected in 1970, in cooperation with the prefecture, for patients needing continued care. Then, in 1977 changes were made in the regulations governing municipal housing facilities to give priority to A-bomb victims—another of the many efforts extended to A-bomb victims in need.*

For a long time after the bombings, the Hiroshima and Nagasaki prefectural and municipal budgets included no allocations for A-bomb victims, and there were no administrative units for victims' affairs. With enactment of the A-bomb Victims Medical Care Law in 1957, however, Hiroshima City estab-lished the A-bomb Survivors Measures Section. This section was elevated to department status in 1974, with survey and aid sections. The City of Naga-saki in April 1957 introduced the A-bomb Survivors Measures Desk in the Social Section of its Public Health Department; this desk became a section in 1967, then a department in 1977, with survey and aid sections. Both cities in 1967 instituted general aid plans to supplement the deficiencies in the na-tional Medical Care Law. Although there were minor differences, both cities undertook a wide range of services including, besides examinations and treat-ment, allowances for hospital visitation by families, nursing care, aid to micro-cephalic victims, and funerals, as well as dispatching of home volunteers, counseling, aid to aged victims, vocational training, and even preparation for entering employment—thus responding to a wide variety of specific needs not covered by the Medical Care Law. In 1973, Hiroshima City announced a new program of providing medical examinations of A-bomb victims' children at its A-bomb Victims Welfare Center. Both Hiroshima and Naga-saki prefectures in 1972 adopted general aid policies providing for allowances to A-bomb victims residing outside the two cities and also assumed partial responsibility for the allowances given to the two cities' residents.†

In both Hiroshima and Nagasaki there were many organizations and agen-cies, such as the A-bomb hospitals, facilities for medical examinations and care established by the two cities' Casualty Councils, and the Friends of A-bomb Health-book Holders founded by victims' groups. Private citizens devoted to helping the victims founded many facilities, such as the Hiroshima War Orphans Home and the New Life School for orphans, and the Hill of Grace Home for aged victims in Nagasaki. These various agencies and organi-

* Hiroshima Prefectural Office and Hiroshima City Office 1975, pp. 67–68; Hiroshima Shiya-kusho 1970, p. 20; 1972, pp. 27–28; Hiroshima Shiyakusho, A-bomb Survivors Measures Section 1967, pp. 12–16; 1968, pp. 12–14.
† Hiroshima Prefectural Office and Hiroshima City Office 1975, pp. 35–40; Hiroshima Shiya-kusho, A-bomb Survivors Measures Department 1976, pp. 109–110; 1977, pp. 14–27, 62–67.

zations played a vital role in providing health, livelihood, and spiritual services to the A-bomb victims. Many of these received subsidies from their respective municipal and prefectural governments; but most of the private agencies experienced financial difficulties and could not fully perform their functions. The extensive needs of the A-bomb victims, after all, far surpassed the resources of local governments and private organizations.

In April 1961 groups of Hiroshima A-bomb victims who were dispersed in various regions banded together to form the Hiroshima A-bomb Victims Association. Chapters of this association were organized in forty-nine of the city's elementary school districts, and A-bomb victims in the various areas were enrolled in these chapters to form something akin to township associations *(chōnaikai)*. Initially the chapters resembled welfare agencies, distributing money and needed articles to hospitalized or impoverished victims and their children. In time they also became active in pressing demands that Hiroshima and Nagasaki cities and prefectures and, of course, the national Ministry of Health and Welfare "adopt stronger measures for the adequate care" of all A-bomb victims. Their activities led to the opening of Kandasansō, a nursing home and research center for victims in Hiroshima and, further, to the formation of the Council of Eight (governors of Hiroshima and Nagasaki prefectures, mayors of Hiroshima and Nagasaki cities, and the four speakers of the municipal and prefectural assemblies)—a body charged with promoting better administration of A-bomb victims' affairs on the part of the national government.*

Activities of local governments outside Hiroshima and Nagasaki naturally varied in scope and kind according to the number of A-bomb victims needing care. Of particular interest are the positive measures adopted by the Tokyo Metropolitan Prefecture government in 1975. From 1962 the Tokyo administration had supported the capital city's A-bomb victims supporters organization (Tokyo Friends Association) in its efforts to provide counseling services for health, medical, and livelihood needs. From the late 1960s the Tokyo government became especially active, initiating such A-bomb victims' programs as health examinations (1971), nursing allowances (1973), and health checkups for victims' children (1974). Moreover, the Tokyo measures included use of X-ray and electrocardiogram (ECG) tests—important items missing from the national health care laws for victims. Currently, the Tokyo government estimates the number of A-bomb victims in the metropolitan prefecture at 10,000 (actually, probably about 9,600) and budgets some 35,000,000 yen

---

* Hiroshima Shiyakusho 1970, p. 27; 1973, pp. 38–39; Hiroshima Shiyakusho, A-bomb Survivors Measures Department 1977, pp. 74–75, III.

($159,381) (in 1978, 34,570,000 [$157,423]) for services to A-bomb victims. Of this amount, 2,400,000 yen ($10,929) goes to the Tokyo Friends Association for its activities. Other subsidies include grants for representatives of surviving families to visit graves in Hiroshima and Nagasaki and a grant (800,000 yen in 1977) to support a survey of A-bomb victims' conditions in preparation for the NGO-sponsored International Symposium on the Damage and Aftereffects of the Atomic Bombing of Hiroshima and Nagasaki (21 July–9 August 1977).

Directly administered facilities and subsidies for A-bomb groups are found in thirty-five other prefectural governments, such as Kyoto and Osaka, Kanagawa, Toyama, Yamaguchi, and Hokkaidō. The Ōita Prefectural Casualty Council took responsibility for constructing a sanatorium-research center at Beppu Spa (1960) that stresses rehabilitation through hot springs treatment, and citizens' efforts moved the Yamaguchi prefectural government to found the Yudaen facility for A-bomb victims (see page 569).

Funding of local government measures, however—with the exception of Tokyo, Osaka, and Kyoto—is in fact limited and hardly meets the requests of the A-bomb victims in the various places. Moreover, the aging of the victims poses a special problem in all places. Limitations faced by all local governments are the same in kind as those faced in Hiroshima and Nagasaki, but the scarcity of facilities and organizations makes the problems more severe elsewhere. Care of the A-bomb victims should, of course, have been undertaken from the very beginning by the national government in an adequate and consistent way. The necessity for the government's doing so now is stronger than ever.

Movements Advocating Medical Care and Relief for A-bomb Victims*

If the A-bomb victims' movements are viewed in terms of organizational activity and the nature of their appeals and demands, and if their strength is measured by success in getting laws enacted and budgets allocated, then there appear to be three major periods.

* Hiroshima-Nagasaki Testimony Association 1975–76; Itō 1975; NGO International Symposium 1977b, pp. 89–90.

1945–56

The first period extends from the atomic bombings to the formation of the Japan Confederation of A-bomb and H-bomb Sufferers Organizations (JCSO). Immediately following Japan's defeat, A-bomb victims in Hiroshima and Nagasaki engaged in small-scale activities to help each other. In December 1945 associations of war victims were formed in both cities to supply the war-ravaged peoples' general needs for food, clothing, and shelter. These activities continued to 1948 without any particular consciousness of having been specifically victimized by the atomic bombings.

Then, in 1948 the assistant chief of the Hiroshima workers section of the Ministry of Labor's Women and Minors Bureau, a woman named Toshiko Kobayashi, made a survey of female A-bomb victims as part of a larger project on women's problems. What she discovered was so wretched and pathetic that it could not be looked upon dispassionately. Hence, the investigators wrote their report in oblique, indirect language. Even so, the report provoked vigorous opposition from the Occupation GHQ, and publication of the report was prohibited. The women involved then decided that the least they could do was to arrange a meeting of women A-bomb victims; and on 10 August of that year the Cooperative Assembly of Wounded Women in Hiroshima Prefecture was held in the Honkawa Primary School. The assembly's moderator was Akie Tazaki, a primary schoolteacher who, during wartime demolition activities, was leading some pupils to an evacuation site when almost all of the children were killed by the atomic bomb, and she herself was injured. She was forced by her husband to leave home and give up her own children. Thinking that she might be of some service to other victims in like circumstances, she had decided to attend the assembly.

The following resolution was passed by the assembly and sent to then Prime Minister Hitoshi Ashida:

1. We appeal for a national study of medical care and for every effort to be made [to treat the A-bomb victims].
2. We appeal for treatment to be provided at cost and for free health examinations every six months.
3. We appeal for economic and spiritual stability to be restored through vocational training and religious education.
4. We appeal especially for relief measures for those in desperate need.
5. We appeal for understanding, especially from society's leaders.
6. We appeal for a foundation to be built for world peace.

Because, under GHQ directives, any mention of the atomic bomb was taboo, the two Chinese characters generally used to refer to it in Japanese—*genbaku* 原爆—did not appear in the assembly's name or anywhere in the resolution. Moreover, the real meaning of the resolution's first article was for "the state to study medical care of A-bomb injuries" and for "every effort to be made to treat the A-bomb victims." The resolution called for national assistance in restoring the "body, spirit, and livelihood" of each A-bomb victim. Today, each article in the resolution has been realized to some extent. Historically, it was the earliest statement of the victims' needs and aspirations. By joining their demand for relief with an appeal for world peace, these women became the first in a long line of citizens' movements against atomic bombs.

On 23 March 1949, the Hiroshima Peace Center was founded in New York through the leadership of Pearl S. Buck, Norman Cousins, and others. In 1950, the Reverend Kiyoshi Tanimoto founded a similar organization in Hiroshima; in addition to arranging for the "moral adoption" of A-bomb orphans by American persons, the Hiroshima center undertook a wide range of welfare services for A-bomb victims, such as organizing young female victims in the Association of Hiroshima Maidens, placement of widows in a women's home, and founding the Myōseien facility for sightless children and a boys' home for delinquent youth. Shizue Masugi in 1952 organized the Tokyo Association of Supporters of the Hiroshima Peace Center, which brought "Hiroshima maidens" to the University of Tokyo's Hospital for treatment. Rika Nishiwaki helped bring victims to the hospitals of Osaka and Osaka City universities. Appealing for the Japanese to become "spiritual parents," Arata Osada in the same year formed in Hiroshima University's attached Shinonome School the Society for the Care of Children; it became the Hiroshima Society for the Care of Children in 1953. Osada remained active until 1964. In both of these associations it was relatively poor people of good will who became "spiritual parents." In 1955, Norman Cousins arranged for some "Hiroshima maidens" to go to Mt. Sinai Hospital in New York City for treatment.

Autonomous movements among the A-bomb victims first arose after the signing of the San Francisco Peace Treaty in 1951. In that year, after over five years of hospitalization, Kiyoshi Kikkawa organized the Hiroshima A-bomb Victims Rehabilitation Society to promote self-rehabilitation, and through it many "A-bomb maidens" were treated for keloid scars.

In 1952, Ken Kawate, Kiyoshi Kikkawa, Sankichi Tōge, and others formed the A-bomb Victims Association to appeal widely for the medical care and livelihood needs of A-bomb victims. In 1953 an "A-bomb maidens" association was also formed in Nagasaki.

Then, in 1954, A-bomb victims in Hyōgo Prefecture took the lead in forming the League for Claiming Compensation for A-bomb Damages. This effort from 1953 had the active cooperation of Shōichi Okamoto of the Osaka Bar Association.

With growing support from many quarters, the A-bomb victims rapidly acquired a new consciousness of themselves, and from 1954 associations of A-bomb victims were formed throughout the nation. The Nagasaki A-bomb Victims Association held its first organizing meeting in June 1955. The year 1956 saw the founding of the Hiroshima Prefecture Federation of A-bomb Victims Associations and the Nagasaki Federation of A-bomb Victims Associations, as well as the Liaison Council of A-bomb Victims Associations covering the four prefectures of Hiroshima, Nagasaki, Nagano, and Ehime. Following the Second World Conference against Atomic and Hydrogen Bombs, the nationwide Japan Confederation of A-bomb and H-bomb Sufferers Organizations (JCSO) was born on 10 August 1956.

1956–66

At its inception the Japan Confederation of A-bomb and H-bomb Sufferers Organizations proclaimed its organizational goals: "To appeal what should be appealed to the whole world, to claim what we should claim against the state, and to rise up and together work out our own way." In addition to an international agreement to ban all nuclear weapons, the goals it set included "establishment of an A-bomb victims relief law and a system of health supervision for the victims" and "promotion of vocational training to foster self-rehabilitation, as well as priority loans for jobs and schooling needs." The legacy of earlier claims for "self-rehabilitation," "mutual help," and "medical care" remained strong in this new statement, but the claims for "state compensation" and "livelihood support" also stood out. The proposals were not sufficiently specific and concrete, but the insistence on the enactment of a "relief law" was historically significant (Hiroshima Prefectural Office 1972, pp. 792–95).

This JCSO effort led the Socialist Party of Japan (JSP) in September 1956 to set up a special committee for a "Relief Law for A-bomb Casualties"; and in November of that year, the two cities of Hiroshima and Nagasaki petitioned the national government to pass a relief law for A-bomb victims. In December the Lower House of the National Diet passed the resolution on medical care for A-bomb victims; and in March 1957—twelve years after the war's end—the A-bomb Victims Medical Care Law became a reality. This law, however, provided mainly for medical examinations; provisions for medical treatment were narrowly confined to certain designated illnesses. Moreover, the law did not take into account the various psychological damages and livelihood losses people had suffered. The A-bomb victims, and especially those in the JCSO, along with the opposition parties, criticized these deficiencies; and in 1959 the JSP introduced a relief bill that included pensions for the A-bomb disabled and grants for burial expenses, while the Democratic Socialist Party (DSP) announced its own relief measures bill designed gradually to improve the existing Medical Care Law. In 1960 the government carried out revisions of the Medical Care Law, though not fully meeting opposition demands. The Japan Council against Atomic and Hydrogen Bombs compiled the "White Paper on Damages by Atomic and Hydrogen Bombs— The Hidden Truth," which summarized the victims' demands thus: (1) medical care, (2) livelihood support, (3) state compensation, and (4) peace and the banning of nuclear weapons. With this build-up of support, the JSCO at its sixth assembly renewed its demand for "enactment of a relief law based on state compensation." The governing party, however, was not willing to pass such a law (see pages 555–57).

Meantime, the antinuclear movement, a major source of support for a relief law for A-bomb victims, experienced two disabling schisms in the five years from 1959 to 1964—just when it appeared to be reaching new heights of influence. The first split came in the 1959–61 period and resulted in the formation of the Japan Council against Atomic and Hydrogen Bombs (Nihon Gensuikyō) and the National Council for Peace and against Nuclear Weapons (Kakkin Kaigi). The second split occurred in the years 1963–64, and out of it came the Japan Council against Atomic and Hydrogen Bombs (Gensuikyō) and the Japan Congress against Atomic and Hydrogen Bombs (Gensuikin). (For details, see pages 580–81.) The A-bomb victims' movement could not escape the impact of these splits, and new organizations appeared in Hiroshima and Nagasaki. The JSCO retained enough autonomy to avoid a rupture but could not forestall stagnation of its activities. With the favorable 1963 court ruling on an A-bomb appeal, it became clear that relief for A-bomb victims was indeed a state responsibility (pages 555–56), so in 1964 the National Diet approved a bill for A-bomb victims relief. Meantime, in the midst of schism and confusion, efforts to revive the basic commitments of the antinuclear movement enlarged the overall perspective to embrace the relief needs of A-bomb victims living in Okinawa as well as of Korean A-bomb victims. The year 1965 thus marked the end of the first twenty-year season of struggle to win relief for the A-bomb victims, though this period was also marked by the unfortunate slump in both the overall antinuclear and the A-bomb victims' movements.

1966–78

The main occasion for the Japan Confederation of A-bomb and H-bomb Sufferers Organizations to overcome its slump was the 1966 publication of a pamphlet entitled "Special Features of the A-bomb and the 'A-bomb Victims Relief Law' " (the pamphlet's cover had a picture of a folded paper crane and so came to be called the "Crane pamphlet"). The "Crane pamphlet" had a great impact because it focused squarely on the realities of the A-bomb damages and of the victims. It stressed the complex difficulties the victims faced in maintaining all aspects of health, spirit, and livelihood, and insisted that adequate government care of A-bomb victims could not be limited, as in the Medical Care Law, to health problems alone but must be comprehensive for all aspects of life. The JCSO embarked on a strenuous campaign for such a relief law, sending appeals through its chapters to local governments throughout the nation. The national government's response was to enact the A-bomb Victims Special Measures Law (1968). But this law was based on a social welfare approach, not on state compensation; and even its social welfare provisions were far from satisfactory.

In 1973 the JCSO brought out a revised form of the "Crane pamphlet," updated to take account of the Special Measures Law and its subsequent revisions. In the new document the A-bomb victims' demands were refined and restated in the form of "three basic *hoshō*."* These were:

1. That America should assume responsibility for dropping the A-bombs, for concealing the damages and suppressing reports of them during the Occupation, and for opening up the era of nuclear competition and proliferation; and that the Japanese government should assume responsibility for engaging in military aggression before and during the Pacific War and for the total neglect of the A-bomb victims after the war; and thus that the A-bomb victims be compensated by the state for damages suffered in the past—that is, *compensation for the past.*
2. That measures be adopted to guarantee comprehensive relief from the health, livelihood, and spiritual hardships currently experienced—*relief for the present.*
3. That the government declare its commitment, to the A-bomb victims and the Japanese people, that there never be another "Hiroshima" or "Nagasaki"— a *pledge for the future.*

In the spirit of these three *hoshō,* concrete demands were made for pensions to be paid to all A-bomb victims and their survivors.

The JCSO campaigned in 1973 to get all political parties to study this new statement of "essentials" and to introduce bills to meet its stated goals. All opposition parties supported the statement and, in fact, drew up bills to implement it. In 1974 the opposition parties presented a joint bill to the National Diet. Due to the majority party's resistance, the bill was defeated. Despite this setback, the opposition parties have since continued to put forth supportive bills. Meantime, the JCSO endeavored to make full use of existing laws to relieve the daily hardships suffered by the A-bomb victims. In a parallel effort to provide aid and counsel to A-bomb victims in every locality, the JCSO in 1978 founded its A-bomb Victims Central Counseling Center.

As already noted, many citizens' organizations have cooperated in providing

* A play on three words, written differently in Chinese characters but pronounced similarly: the first one means "compensation"; the second, "relief"; and the third, "guarantee" or "pledge." (Trans.)

relief for A-bomb victims. The many A-bomb victims associations throughout the country have received local government support and funds, especially to help administer the provisions of the A-bomb Victims Medical Care Law. Of particular note in this connection is the work of the A-bomb Victims Welfare Center in Yamaguchi Prefecture.

The Yamaguchi Welfare Center was incorporated as the Yudaen facility and opened in May 1968. It has 900 square meters of land and a three-story building with rooms for counseling, overnight lodging, baths, and a library. Its program embraces (1) administrative counseling and guidance for making application for A-bomb health books, receiving allowances, and utilizing the Medical Care and Special Measures laws; (2) mobile units to extend medical examinations and counseling services to A-bomb victims on holidays; (3) surveys of A-bomb survivors' conditions and of circumstances of those who have died; (4) seminars on problems of A-bomb victims; and (5) travel allowances to promote thorough health examinations.

The impetus for the establishment of the Yudaen was the 1963–64 split in the antinuclear movement. Because of its proximity to Hiroshima, Yamaguchi Prefecture has many resident A-bomb victims, and they have played key roles in its active peace movement. While the national schism affected all local antinuclear movements, the Yamaguchi movement exerted great efforts to assert its local autonomy by focusing interest on relief for A-bomb victims. In August 1965 it organized a peace march from Shimonoseki to Hiroshima, with two slogans—unity in the antinuclear movement and construction of the welfare center for A-bomb victims. With this start, a building committee was formed late in the year. Many organizations and citizens from all walks of life participated in the building-fund campaign—the JCSO, labor unions, women's societies, university and high school teachers and students, and Christians—but raising the needed 43,700,000 yen ($121,389) was not easy. The vigorous campaign, however, moved prefectural and municipal authorities to contribute to the center's construction and maintenance. Thus, the Yamaguchi case is noteworthy for demonstrating the autonomy of a citizens' movement rooted in its own locality; it also showed that such a movement can influence government policies in positive directions.

For convenience, the three periods of A-bomb victims' movements are outlined in table 14.2.

TABLE 14.1

A-Bomb Health-book Holders Receiving Allowances, 31 March 1977

Area	Health-book Holders	Certified Patients*	Health Care Allowances	Health Insurance Allowances	Special Allowances	Total Health Care, Health Insurance, and Special Allowances	Nursing Allowances	Funeral Expenses
Nationwide	366,523	4,285 (1.2)	101,116 (27.5)	38,646 (10.5)	3,425 (0.9)	143,187 (39.0)	1,464	4,568
Hiroshima City	113,384	1,671 (1.4)	29,743 (26.2)	16,709 (14.7)	1,226 (1.0)	47,678 (42.0)	199	1,624
Nagasaki City	81,992	748 (0.9)	29,245 (35.6)	2,791 (3.4)	668 (0.8)	32,704 (39.8)	773	1,006

* Figures in parentheses are percentages of health-book holders in each area.

Source: Survey by Japan Confederation of A-bomb and H-bomb Sufferers Organizations. Ministry of Health and Welfare, Public Health Bureau, Planning Section, *Shōwa Gojūichinendo Hibakusha Taisaku no Gaiyō* [Summary of Measures for Atomic Bomb Survivors in 1976] (Tokyo: Kōseishō Kōshūeiseikyoku Kikakuka, 1977). This table was compiled by the Japan Confederation of Atomic and Hydrogen Bomb Sufferers Organizations, on the basis of the summary above (copyright © by Japan Confederation of Atomic and Hydrogen Bomb Sufferers Organizations).

TABLE 14.2

Three Periods of A-Bomb Victims' Organizations

Period	Dates	Organization	Demands	Focus and Scope	Government Funds for A-bomb Victims (unit: 100 million yen)
e-organizational ivity	1945 1956	small groups organize in bombed areas	medical care	mutual help	0.4 (1954) 2.5 (1956)
rmation of or- nizations	1956 1966	local associations of A-bomb victims; Japan Confederation of A-bomb and H-bomb Sufferers Organizations; decline: new bodies formed	livelihood and vocational aid; state compensation	campaigns to press demands on national government; increasing dependence on small-scale pacifist organizations	2.5 (1956) 23.9 (1966)
owth of organi- ions	1966 1978	growth of Japan Confederation of A-bomb and H-bomb Sufferers Organizations local chapters	comprehensive relief law based on state compensation	escalation of demands on national government; establishment of autonomous mass movements	23.9 (1966) 539.4 (1978)

Citizens' Movements against Atomic Weapons *

EARLY LOCAL MOVEMENTS

As defeat brought many externally imposed reforms, Japan's former system of rule gave way to rapid democratization. Socialist political parties were legalized or newly formed, and labor unions experienced rapid expansion at a rate unprecedented in world history.† As social conditions improved, various cultural and citizens' movements appeared and gradually exerted influence. Even Hiroshima, once laid waste, was no exception. Most of the movements in that city naturally were those that sought an enduring peace. Sadako Kurihara, who even in wartime had penned antiwar poems, in December 1945 formed the Chūgoku Cultural League with a monthly publication

---

* Society to Transmit the Atomic Bomb Experience 1975; Hiroshima Prefectural Office 1972, 1976; Hiroshima-Nagasaki Testimony Association 1975–76; Kurihara 1970; Nagaoka 1977.

† Japan Political Science Society 1953, p. 90; Oka 1959, p. 389.

entitled *Chūgoku Bunka* [Culture of Chūgoku]. The first issue of this monthly was a special edition on the A-bomb damages. Youth movements, such as the Hiroshima Youth Culture League, also flourished, as did the Council of Cultural Circles based mainly in labor unions. Many A-bomb victims were active in the various movements. The Hiroshima Peace Culture Association, founded by Tatsuo Morito, Arata Osada, and other intellectuals, publicly solicited "poems of peace" and received over ten thousand contributions. Women in the labor unions joined with housewives to form the Hiroshima Democratic Women's Council to engage in peace activities. Although these were only a few of the countless movements begun in those days, they were in large part the source of the later antinuclear and the A-bomb victims relief movements, and of the wider stream of antinuclear thought among the Japanese people.

While the causes of democratization and demilitarization were thus gaining broad popular support in Japan, on the international scene tension was gradually escalating between the U.S.-centered and the Soviet blocs of nations. With the March 1947 proclamation of the Truman Doctrine,* that confrontation reached a decisive stage. Soviet moves to counter the Truman Doctrine and the Marshall Plan† included the October 1947 formation of the Cominform and the Berlin blockade of February 1948. Then followed establishment of East and West Germany, in September and October of 1949, respectively, and formation of the North Atlantic Treaty Organization in 1949. The Soviet Union developed its own atomic bomb in 1949, and the United States responded by moving ahead with production of a hydrogen bomb. Escalation of the cold war came to dominate both international politics and the political dynamics in each country.

In Asia the Truman Doctrine was essentially already in force prior to its proclamation—in efforts to set up and support anticommunist regimes in the Philippines, China, and the southern part of Korea. Japan, too, was drawn into the cold war network as the early Occupation objectives of democratization and demilitarization were reversed, under General Douglas MacArthur's continuing command, to promotion of Japan's rearmament (1950) in a strategy that would make Japan a "bulwark against communism" in Asia.

* The Truman Doctrine was U.S. President Harry S. Truman's policy of giving U.S. economic and military aid to various nations in order to "contain" Communist expansion.

† In his speech of 5 June 1947 at Harvard University, U.S. Secretary of State George C. Marshall proposed that the United States Government should extend financial aid to any European countries for their smooth recovery from war's havoc. This proposal later came to be known as the Marshall Plan.

The plan was favored by the sixteen Western European countries. The Soviet Union and the eight socialist states in Eastern Europe, however, showed no interest in the plan and later united to form the Cominform.

The United States Government spent, in the next three and one-half years, $12,200,000,000 on Marshall Plan aid.

Fearing that escalation of the cold war could lead to the outbreak of a third world war, people in countries throughout the world engaged actively in peace movements. In August 1948 intellectuals from East and West met in Poland for the World Congress of Intellectuals to Protect the Peace; and in April 1949 the First World Assembly to Protect the Peace was held in Paris and Prague. The assembly committee called for "an absolute ban on atomic weapons" and "establishment of international supervision to guarantee its observance." The committee further asserted, in the famous Stockholm Appeal of May 1950, that "the first government to use atomic weapons is guilty of a crime against mankind and should be treated as a war criminal," and called for a worldwide signature campaign.

Japanese delegates who tried to attend the World Assembly were prevented from doing so by the Occupation authorities. In October 1949, however, ten organizations—including the Hiroshima City Federation of Youth Associations, the Y.M.C.A., the Hiroshima Prefecture Council of Labor Unions, and the Hiroshima Democratic Women's Council—sponsored the Hiroshima Assembly to Protect the Peace. Some two hundred Korean residents in Japan were among the broad range of citizens who participated in this assembly. The assembly's declaration stated, "As citizens of the first city in world history to experience the horrors of an atomic bombing, we demand the total abolition of atomic weapons."

Support for the Stockholm Appeal naturally was vigorous in Hiroshima. "We pledge to stand in the front lines of support [for this appeal]. To do so is a solemn responsibility laid upon us, who first experienced an atomic bombing. It is also our right to do so" (from "An Appeal for Peace," issued by the Organizing Committee for the Hiroshima Assembly to Protect the Peace). Such declarations and resolutions were issued by many cultural groups, youth and women's movements, labor unions, workshops, and high school and university groups. Thus, the signature campaign spread rapidly. In Nagasaki, too, signatures were collected, often in theaters, on the streets, and by knocking on doors of homes. With the outbreak of war in Korea in June 1950, however, the Occupation GHQ began to suppress peace movements in Japan and carried out its "Red Purge." Even so, signature collection continued, and unauthorized peace rallies were held in Hiroshima and Nagasaki on 6 and 9 August, respectively. In reporting these unauthorized rallies, the Soviet news agency Tass attracted international attention to them. Peace rallies were also held elsewhere throughout the world on 6 August. In New York City, fifteen thousand people participated in a peace march through Union Square, and at this rally was read a message from the Hiroshima rally's preparation committee. Large rallies were held in Finland, West Germany, Austria, Tunisia, and France on the same day (Hiroshima Prefectural Office 1976).

As the Korean War intensified, General MacArthur's advocacy of assaults into Chinese territory provoked fears that the conflict would escalate into all-out war. President Truman opposed MacArthur's position but, on the other hand, made it clear that the atomic bomb could be used in Korea (30 November 1950). Britain and France protested strongly against this possibility, but it was probably the strength of gathering world opinion that most effectively suppressed the use of the atomic bomb in Korea.

Political parties and labor unions held separate 6 August peace rallies in 1951. Afterward, though, the Hiroshima Colloquium on Peace Problems was held on 16 October, with Mayor Shinzō Hamai participating. In 1952 this colloquium was held on 6 August, as a mass citizens' meeting with forty-two organizations participating in it: it issued an appeal for a ban on the production and use of atomic weapons. In 1953 seventy-five hundred persons, representing forty-four organizations from Hokkaido in the north to Kyushu in the south, joined in the People's Peace Rally in Hiroshima; they marched and demanded that use of the atomic bomb be prohibited and that the A-bomb victims be guaranteed an adequate livelihood. Even all this activity, however, was in fact the work of only a small segment of the total population.

In Nagasaki, the First Kyushu District Peace Rally was held at a public athletic field on 9 August. On that same day, the Youth Peace Statue was unveiled in a ceremony at Shiroyama Primary School, where children, parents, and teachers spoke in clear and moving words addressed to the spirits of people lost in the bombing. In 1953 an exhibition of "A-bomb drawings," which had been shown throughout the country since 1950 by Iri Maruki and Toshiko Akamatsu, was held in Nagasaki. Of the 17,500 attendants at this exhibition, 1,238 proposed to form a "Gathering for Peace"; 585 of them joined the Society to Protect the A-bomb Victims, and the Nagasaki Society to Preserve Peace was formed. It was about this time that Misako Yamaguchi gathered the "A-bomb maidens" for discussion and group activities, including making artificial flowers and knitting to help earn a living.

Meantime, Ken Kawate, Kiyoshi Kikkawa, and Sankichi Tōge were busy in Hiroshima trying to organize A-bomb victims. Their appeal at the 6 August 1952 peace rally led to formation on the tenth of the A-bomb Victims Association and inaugurated the movement to form such associations. This group negotiated with national, city, and Atomic Bomb Casualty Commission officials for health and livelihood assistance; it set up a library, and, with the help of local women's groups, distributed food to A-bomb victims suffering hardships. It also sent witnesses to testify in the A-bomb compensation appeal of Shōichi Okamoto (see page 565). Besides these many ways of promoting friendship among the A-bomb victims, the most significant activity of the group was the compiling of the A-bomb victims' memoirs of their own experiences. Visiting their homes one by one, even in the remotest hills, Ken Kawate and Tomoe Yamashiro spoke with the victims about their sufferings and their passion for peace. These itinerant inquirers in no way imposed their own feelings on the victims; rather, by discussing things together, they helped prod each victim's memory. The victim then recorded, simply and directly, the many recollections of his or her actual experience. The many memoirs were then compiled in three sections—"Living," "Walking," and "Crying Out"—and published under the title "Life after the Atomic Bombing—Notes of Atomic Bomb Victims."* The result was a moving record of the victims' own postwar history in which they revealed their sufferings and the stand they took against atomic bombs. Unfortunately these memoirs did not influence many of their fellow citizens.

TOWARD A NATIONWIDE MOVEMENT

While movements up to 1953 were forward-looking, they were not able to become popular mass movements. The casualties resulting from the 1954 Bikini hydrogen bomb test provided the stimulus for the evolution of a nationwide movement.

In the hydrogen bomb test conducted by the United States on Bikini atoll in the Marshall Islands on 1 March 1954, 267 islanders received heavy doses of radiation. Both ocean and atmosphere were contaminated by radioactivity, traces of which remain to this day. Three hours later the "ashes of death" also fell on the *Fukuryū Maru No. 5* ("Lucky Dragon No. 5"), a tuna fishing vessel out of Yaizu in Shizuoka Prefecture which was operating 160 kilometers east of Bikini. The ashes kept falling for six hours, and soon afterward crew members complained of headaches and nausea. When the vessel returned to Yaizu on 14 March, all twenty-three members of the crew were diagnosed as suffering from radiation symptoms, such as skin blisters and falling hair. Then, on 23 September, crewman Aikichi Kuboyama died. Heavy radiation doses were also detected in the cargo of fish.†

This incident shocked the Japanese public and inflamed sentiment against nuclear weapons. On 27 March the Yaizu municipal assembly, "representing the people's fears," passed a resolution calling for "a ban on all military use of nuclear energy." Almost all local assemblies throughout the nation passed similar antinuclear resolutions. Both houses of the National Diet

---

* Atomic Bomb Victims' Written Notes Editorial Committee 1953.
† Hiroshima Prefectural Office 1976.

(1 and 5 April) approved resolutions calling for international controls on nuclear energy. Declarations and protests issued from many sections of society. One of the most significant movements to emerge from this groundswell of public opinion was the "Suginami Appeal." The source of this appeal was an ordinary citizens' group—a reading circle for women formed in 1953 in Tokyo's Suginami district, under the leadership of Kaoru Yasui, director of the local community center. This group participated in the Suginami Council for the Signature Campaign against Hydrogen Bombs, not because any one person urged them to do so but because they all, spontaneously, felt it important. The shopping baskets of the women of Suginami, it is said, always included a well-thumbed notebook for collecting signatures. Their zeal elicited such widespread response that, by November, eighteen million signatures had been collected—a figure representing by now, of course, the efforts of many similar citizens' groups throughout the nation.

The "Suginami Appeal," issued 9 May by the Suginami Council for the Signature Campaign, urged three main actions: for all Japanese to sign the appeal to ban the bomb; to spread the appeal to peoples and governments throughout the world; and to work for the preservation of life and happiness of all mankind. The appeal was based on humanism, not on partisan politics. As the campaign progressed, it was realized that the focus was singularly on the fresh facts and fears of the Bikini incident, and overlooked the older but nearer problems of Hiroshima and Nagasaki. After two months the attack on "hydrogen bombs" was expanded to cover "atomic and hydrogen bombs." To the name of the movement and its appeal was added the one word "atomic." Direct solidarity with the Hiroshima and Nagasaki A-bomb victims was missing from this movement, but the crucial thing is that a group of ordinary citizens—the Suginami women—had not only given new vigor to the antinuclear effort but also gained for it a genuine nationwide mass character.

What remained was to link up the new vigor and antinuclear commitment of the larger public to the continuing struggle being waged in and on behalf of Hiroshima and Nagasaki.

That linking process got under way when the Hiroshima Prefecture Regional Women's Organizations, which had previously collaborated with the Democratic Women's Council to sponsor the Women's Peace Rally in August 1949, now worked with the Colloquium on Peace Problems and the Society for the Care of Children to sponsor the Hiroshima Citizens' Conference against Atomic and Hydrogen Bombs on 15 May 1954. This conference not only approved a declaration against the production, testing, and use of nuclear weapons but also decided to campaign for a million signatures and to plan a peace rally for the coming 6 August anniversary of the Hiroshima bombing.

At the same time it called for enactment of a relief law for the A-bomb victims. These actions constituted the general format of all subsequent antinuclear movements. By the end of August the signature campaign had gathered 1,013,472 names—roughly half the total population of Hiroshima Prefecture. The list was sent to the United Nations headquarters. In September the Hiroshima Prefecture Council for the Antinuclear Signature Campaign began lobbying at the U.N. General Assembly to spread the signature campaign around the world, and simultaneously it worked to bring together all movements in Japan in planning for a major peace conference in Hiroshima in 1955 on the tenth anniversary of the atomic bombings.

Meantime, the "Suginami Appeal" campaign led to the formation in August 1954 of the National Council for an Antinuclear Signature Campaign, and its planning committee was convened in October. By that time, 14,000,000 signatures had been collected (the count would later swell to 32,000,000), but there were as yet no concrete plans for the movement's continuation. A proposal from Hiroshima moved it to join in plans for a worldwide rally against nuclear weapons the following year. Already in Hiroshima the University Group to Protect Peace and Learning (represented by Tsugimaro Imanaka, and later by Kiyoshi Sakuma) was working with the Prefecture Women's Council and the labor unions to prepare for the world rally.

The World Conference against Atomic and Hydrogen Bombs was held 6 August 1955 in Hiroshima, with fifty-four persons from twelve foreign countries also attending. The conference's demand for a ban on nuclear weapons was backed by the signatures of 32,000,000—more than half the registered voters in Japan! It was likewise strengthened by the 660,000,000 signatures gathered for the "Vienna Appeal"* against nuclear weapons. The Hiroshima City Auditorium, where the conference was scheduled, could hold only 1,900 people, so most participants followed the proceedings through loudspeakers hung outside the auditorium. The conference's first evening session in Hiroshima Peace Memorial Park drew 30,000 participants, who were all deeply moved by singing together the song "We will not tolerate atomic bombs." What moved the participants most of all, however, were the testimonies of Akihiro Takahashi of Hiroshima and Misako Yamaguchi of Nagasaki. Count-

---

* To appeal against preparations for an atomic war, the Enlarged Committee of the World Peace Council in Vienna on 19 January 1955 issued the following appeal:
   Some national governments are preparing for an atomic war.
   They are attempting to persuade their peoples that an atomic war is inevitable.
   The use of atomic weapons will result in a war of extermination of the entire human race. This we assert positively. Any government that provokes atomic war will lose public confidence; it will be condemned by all the peoples of the world. From this moment on, we will oppose any government that prepares for atomic war. We demand that the nuclear powers abolish all the atomic weapons they have in their possession and cease to produce them immediately.

less people whose fears had been aroused by the Bikini casualties now heard firsthand of the Hiroshima and Nagasaki horrors, and thus sensed in themselves the painful responsibility of living in the nuclear age. They responded with thunderous applause to the proclamation of the Hiroshima Appeal for aid to A-bomb victims and abolition of nuclear weapons (figure 14.1).

Figure 14.1. Peace memorial ceremony at Hiroshima Peace Memorial Park, 6 August 1955. (Photograph by Chūgoku Shinbunsha.)

The 1955 mass rally gave birth to a new nationwide citizens' movement against nuclear weapons. In September the Japan Council against Atomic and Hydrogen Bombs was formed, and antinuclear councils and other organizations sprang up in all prefectures and countless cities and towns throughout the nation. A citizens' group called the Hiroshima Society for the Care of Children (Yūko Yamaguchi, director), formed in 1953 to help care for orphans, had solicited short written compositions from the children to present at the conference; in September it formed a youth group called "Ayumi" ["Moving on"], whose young members traveled throughout Japan and overseas to share their A-bomb experiences (pages 442–43).* Scores of other citizens' groups,

* Professor Seiichi Nakano Commemorative Projects Society 1965, pp. 113–15.

including the Paper Crane Club formed by high school girls, were organized in Hiroshima.

The Nagasaki Atomic Bomb Young Men's Group was started in October 1955 to deal with problems of health care and jobs. It worked vigorously to duplicate survey and research data on the bombings and the victims for use in its "speakers bureau" *(kataribe)*. It merged with the A-bomb Maidens Association the following year to form a larger fellowship of both sexes. About this time A-bomb victims associations were organized in cities throughout Nagasaki Prefecture, and local district groups such as the Nishimachi ("West Township") A-bomb Victims Association were also formed. Through these activities the, local and regional base for holding the Second World Conference against Atomic and Hydrogen Bombs in Nagasaki was being established. Because of a global thawing of cold war tensions, the efforts of the Japan Council against Atomic and Hydrogen Bombs and other groups were stimulating opposition to nuclear weapons in Britain, the Soviet Union, Indonesia, Australia, and elsewhere. Hence, expectations rose rapidly for the world conference in Nagasaki.

When the Second World Conference against Atomic and Hydrogen Bombs opened in Nagasaki on 9 August 1956, victim Chieko Watanabe was carried to the conference platform in her mother's arms to relate her A-bomb experiences—and the hearts of all participants were filled with a sense of solidarity with the A-bomb victims. Conversations with A-bomb victims in each of the various discussion groups led to consideration of future tasks. A report from Okinawa on the problem of U.S. military bases and of life under an occupation government presented by Kamejirō Senaga won recognition of the Okinawan problem* as part of the larger antinuclear movement. Likewise, the A-bomb victims were prompted to overcome tendencies to focus only on themselves and their problems and, thus, were concerned with the wider questions of peace. It was a conference with many lessons for the A-bomb victims. Following this great conference, the Japan Confederation of A-bomb and H-bomb Sufferers Organizations was born; the Nagasaki Peace Colloquium was begun in October 1957, and it became, in cooperation with many groups, a principal forum for promoting the peace movement.

---

* Okinawa was occupied by U.S. forces toward the end of the Pacific War, after one of the bloodiest battles of that war. Although many Okinawans felt they had been sacrificed to save Japan's main islands, the San Francisco Peace Treaty left Okinawa under U.S. rule, which lasted until May 1972 when Okinawa reverted to Japanese administration—a two-decade period during which Okinawans suffered many unpleasant experiences. Senaga reflected the long pent-up grievances of the Okinawans toward the Americans.

Even after reversion, however, Okinawa has remained (to the present day) a U.S. military bastion in the Far East; and occasional reports (denied by both the Japanese and the American governments) of U.S. nuclear weapons on the island make the Okinawans fear their land will again be the target of attack, possibly by nuclear weapons.

Huge antinuclear rallies were held in Tokyo in 1957 and 1958. In international politics, however, the reality was the rapid proliferation of nuclear arms. Despite warnings by scientists and other scholars—as in Bertrand Russell and Albert Einstein's joint proclamation and the Göttingen Statement*—Britain betrayed worldwide antinuclear sentiment by testing a hydrogen bomb on Christmas Island.† Nuclear capabilities rapidly escalated in both number and power, as did the capacity of delivery systems for nuclear warheads such as ICBMs.

To counter this global trend, the Third World Conference against Atomic and Hydrogen Bombs (1957) did not stop at urging a ban on the development and use of nuclear weapons; it called for all-out joint action to eradicate war itself (Tokyo Declaration). Toward this end, it insisted on

an international agreement on the immediate and unconditional cessation of nuclear tests; a ban on all production, stockpiling, and use of nuclear weapons; opposition to the introduction of nuclear weapons into nonnuclear areas; a demand for complete disarmament; opposition to military bases; simultaneous dissolution of all military blocs; and the withdrawal of all military forces from foreign soil. (Japan Council against Atomic and Hydrogen Bombs 1975, p. 14)

The antinuclear movement thus could not avoid acquiring a stronger political color—especially as the Japan Council against Atomic and Hydrogen Bombs (Nihon Gensuikyō) viewed the scheduled 1960 revision of the Japan–U.S. Security Treaty as a move toward strengthening the military system linking the two nations. Nihon Gensuikyō joined with the Socialist Party of Japan and its major supporting group, the General Council of Trade Unions of Japan (Sōhyō), to organize the People's Congress to Block the Security Treaty Revision. Hence, confrontation between Nihon Gensuikyō and the Japanese government intensified in 1959 and 1960. One background factor of this confrontation lay in the concrete efforts of the cabinet of then Prime Minister Nobusuke Kishi to revise Japan's peace constitution.‡ One wing of the antinuclear movement that rejected Nihon Gensuikyō's line in

---

* The *Göttingen Statement* was issued by eighteen West German atomic energy scientists (including Otto Hahn, discoverer of nuclear fission) on 12 April 1957 to oppose their country's possession of nuclear weapons.

The statement said that West Germany should not go nuclear, and that "none who wrote their signatures on it would in any way participate in the development, testing, and disposition of nuclear weapons."

† Britain became a member of the world's nuclear club in 1952 by testing an atomic bomb on Monte Bello Islands off the west coast of Australia.

‡ The Constitution of Japan (1947) states in Article 9: "Aspiring sincerely to an international peace based on justice and order, the Japanese people forever renounce war as a sovereign right of the nation and the threat or use of force as means of settling international disputes.

"In order to accomplish the aim of the preceding paragraph, land, sea, and air forces, as well as other war potential, will never be maintained. The right of belligerency of the state will not be recognized."

November 1961 formed a separate organization, the National Council for Peace and against Nuclear Weapons (Kakkin Kaigi). Throughout the world a cleavage was emerging between peace movements that supported people's liberation struggles in Asia and Africa, on the one hand, and Western European-style movements that opposed nuclear weapons irrespective of political systems, on the other. This rift began appearing in the world conferences against nuclear weapons from 1958 on.

From 1960 the antinuclear conferences also began to reflect the China–Soviet Union confrontation as well as the struggle for power within Nihon Gensuikyō between the JSP-Sōhyō alliance and the Communist Party of Japan. No longer capable of maintaining its autonomy as a national movement, Nihon Gensuikyō in 1964 split into the Japan Council against Atomic and Hydrogen Bombs (Gensuikyō) and the Japan Congress against Atomic and Hydrogen Bombs (Gensuikin). The immediate cause of the split was differences over whether nuclear tests by any country, capitalist or socialist, should be opposed, and over the value of the Limited Test-ban Treaty (1963).

DEEPENING AND DIVERSIFICATION OF THE MOVEMENT

As outlined in the preceding section, the once-unified antinuclear movement in Japan split into three competing movements: the Kakkin Kaigi allied with the Liberal Democratic Party, the Japan Democratic Socialist Party, and the Japanese Confederation of Labor (Dōmei); the Gensuikin allied with

Figure 14.2. Peace march in Hiroshima, 4 August 1959. (Photographs by Chūgoku Shinbunsha.)

the Socialist Party of Japan and the General Council of Trade Unions of Japan (Sōhyō); and the Gensuikyō allied with the Communist Party of Japan. People in the former unified movement who lacked ties to any of these bodies had, thus, no place to go. And not a few people lost their zeal for the antinuclear movement due to this three-way split.

The fracture of the old Nihon Gensuikyō did not, however, mean the end of all citizens' movements against nuclear weapons. Because of the break-up, many citizens' groups also split, became weak, or disbanded. But Nihon Gensuikyō had begun as a general deliberative council and headquarters for a constellation of citizens' movements, and its break-up did not necessarily mean that all citizens' movements went out of existence. For instance, the Hiroshima Mothers' Group against Nuclear Weapons, formed in 1960, continued to publish its magazine *Hiroshima no Kawa* [Rivers of Hiroshima] to relate A-bomb victims' experiences. In 1966 the Hiroshima Report Group published *Hiroshima Tsūshin* [Hiroshima Report] for the enlightenment of the public. The League of Okinawan A-bomb Victims, organized in 1964, attracted attention to the easily forgotten A-bomb victims in Okinawa; a medical care law for victims in Okinawa was enacted in 1966—ten years after such a law was passed for victims on the main islands of Japan. The Korean A-bomb Victims Relief Association was formed in 1967. The American A-bomb Victims Association, for Japanese-Americans, appeared in 1971, though Japanese appreciation of and cooperation with its relief activity was less than adequate. Parents of microcephalic child victims started the Kinoko-kai (Mushroom Club) in 1965; and because children continued to die from leukemia, the Hiroshima Society for the Care of Fetal Victims and Second-generation A-bomb Victims was organized in 1966, followed by the similar Nagasaki Society for Youth and Second-generation A-bomb Victims in 1972. Further evidence of widening interest in problems of the A-bomb victims appeared in the formation, by those who had been active in the movement opposing the Vietnam War, of the Citizens' Group to Convey Testimonies of Hiroshima and Nagasaki; in August 1971 it published an English-language book, *Give Me Water; Testimonies of Hiroshima and Nagasaki*, that treats A-bomb experiences and appeals, Korean A-bomb victims, and current problems. This group also held a series of ten seminars (often with all-night discussions) that helped breathe new life into citizens' movements in Tokyo.

A variety of citizens' movements have since 1964 functioned with considerable zeal and originality. They have carried out a wide range of antinuclear activities, including opposition to nuclear generating stations. It cannot be denied, however, that because they were scattered activities without a unifying force or forum for consolidated effort, they did not exert much influence. Hence, there were occasional voices calling for a unified movement, and especially for reunification of Gensuikyō and Gensuikin. From the mid-1970s these voices suddenly grew stronger, insisting upon dialogue among the three major movements; and the needed ethos for unity and joint action intensified. Behind this change in mood lay three key factors. First, and most important, was the unending military build-up of nuclear capabilities and their continuing spread, and the consequent growing despair over nuclear competition. Second, once the split between fractional movements hardened, their competition for members and public support seemed increasingly pointless to the people attending their respective rallies. The younger generation especially could not understand the rationale of divisiveness. Third, those people most directly involved began to doubt the wisdom of tying their movements to the political parties. The need for taking joint action was felt with particular force when the United Nations Special Session on Disarmament was convened in 1978. That is, the movement in the one country that had suffered A-bomb attacks ought to be able to face the world and, with one voice, speak of its experiences and call for a ban on all nuclear weapons. Thus it was that, after many twists and turns, it was finally possible in Hiroshima in 1977, and again in Tokyo, Hiroshima, and Nagasaki in 1978, to hold world peace conferences that welcomed anyone, whatever their ideological convictions or political preferences, to participate freely so long as they sought a ban on all nuclear weapons.

The antinuclear movement in Japan can be said to be now in search of its next new phase; though mistrust among the existing movements remains, and these movements lack broad public support. The U.N. Special Session on Disarmament, for which the nongovernmental organizations (NGO) took major initiative and leadership, was a pivotal event. The approximately five hundred Japanese delegates who attended came from many social classes and localities. They learned anew that the world community knows little of the realities of an atomic bombing, and that those who find out are invariably shocked by what they learn. The need for and the importance of informing the peoples of the world about the facts and experiences of A-bomb damages were clearly recognized by the mayors of Hiroshima and Nagasaki on their joint visit to the United Nations in 1976 (see page 592), and the same realization emerged from the international interaction that took place in the NGO-sponsored International Symposium on A-bomb Damages and After-effects held in Tokyo, Hiroshima, and Nagasaki in 1977. This awakening was fully confirmed, then, by the 1978 U.N. Special Session on Disarmament.

As noted earlier, relief and compensation for the A-bomb victims even now are inadequate. Furthermore, it is difficult to know how to pass the antinuclear cause, based on experiences of the A-bombings, on to the younger generation. Meeting these problems, both old and new, is the task confronting Japan's antinuclear movement today. It must take up the challenge or risk having no tomorrow.

Figure 14.3. The Honorable H. S. Amerasinghe, President of the 31st U. N. General Assembly, in Nagasaki for the August 1977 peace memorial ceremony, visits with patients at Nagasaki A-bomb Hospital on 8 August.

From "White Paper" Movements to Eradication of Nuclear Weapons*

EARLY EFFORTS TO DOCUMENT A-BOMB DAMAGES

"Japan News No. 257," produced by Nippon Eiga-sha [Japan film] Corporation, is a documentary film of the horrors of A-bombed Hiroshima. A month after the atomic bombings this company embarked upon full-scale, serious filming of Nagasaki (from 15 September) and of Hiroshima (from 25 September). But, as explained earlier (pages 509–10), an assistant photographer was apprehended on 17 October in Nagasaki by American military police; and on 12 December, under an official directive issued by the Occupation's Office

* Hiroshima Prefectural Office 1976; Hiroshima-Nagasaki Testimony Association 1975–76; Japan National Preparatory Committee 1977; Kanai 1970; NGO International Symposium 1977*b*, pp. 89–90; and Yuzaki 1977*b*, pp. 279–313.

of Public Information and Education, all film footage was confiscated. The film was turned over to the U.S. Strategic Bombing Survey Team which, with the addition of some footage shot in Nagasaki, edited it under the title "The Effects of Atomic Bombs on Hiroshima and Nagasaki." Further documentary filming by the Japanese of A-bomb scenes was prohibited. Details regarding filming are recorded by Ryūichi Kanō and Hajime Mizuno in their book *Hiroshima Nijūnen* [Hiroshima Twenty Years after the Atomic Bombing (Kanō and Mizuno 1965)]. Twenty-three years later, in 1968, the United States made a 16-millimeter reprint of the original documentary film and returned it to Japan. Because of restrictions imposed by the Ministry of Education, however, no one in Japan save a few medical personnel has ever viewed the film in its entirety.

Despite the imposed Occupation taboo on publicizing A-bomb damages, efforts by the A-bomb victims to record their own experiences in their own words, including denunciation of the atomic bombings, continued throughout the long Occupation period. Some examples are: the special A-bomb issue of the monthly *Chūgoku Bunka* [Culture of Chūgoku] in 1946 (Chūgoku Cultural League); the 1948 *Hiroshima—Genshi-bakudan Tokushū* [Hiroshima—Special Compilation on the Atomic Bombings], edited by Sankichi Tōge; the 1949 *Nagasaki—Nijūni'nin no Genbaku Taiken Kiroku* [Nagasaki—Record of Twenty-two Persons' A-bomb Experiences], edited by the Nagasaki Cultural League; and the 1950 *Genbaku Taikenki* [Recorded A-bomb Experiences], edited by Hiroshima City (Hiroshima Shiyakusho, Social Welfare Bureau, Social Education Section 1950).

DEVELOPMENT OF WHITE PAPERS ON A-BOMB DAMAGES

Following signing of the San Francisco Peace Treaty (1951), testimonies of A-bomb experiences became strongly antinuclear. A whole series of works, beginning with the 1953 *Genbaku ni Ikite—Genbaku Higaisha no Shuki* [Life after the Atomic Bombing—Notes of Atomic Bomb Victims],* recounted the victims' living conditions and demands but went on to condemn nuclear weapons. With the First World Conference against Atomic and Hydrogen Bombs in 1955, a new type of testimony appeared, such as that edited by the Nagasaki-based A-bomb Youth and Maidens Association (1956), *Mō Iya Da—Genbaku no Ikite iru Shōnintachi* [We've Had Enough—Living A-bomb Witnesses].

Table 14.3 is based on the third volume of *Genbaku Hisai Shiryō Sōmokuroku* [General Catalogue of Documents on A-bomb Damages], produced by the Hiroshima Research Group for Documentation of A-bomb Damages

---

* Atomic Bomb Victims' Written Notes Editorial Committee 1953.

TABLE 14.3

Fluctuations in Numbers of Written Testimonies and
Published Articles or Books on A-Bomb Experiences
in Hiroshima, 1946–71

Year	Published Articles or Books	Written Testimonies	Year	Published Articles or Books	Written Testimonies
1946	4	23	1960	12	21
1947	1	1	1961	15	9
1948	2	3	1962	18	77
1949	9	24	1963	14	45
1950	13	47	1964	18	66
1951	16	145	1965	44	205
1952	16	68	1966	32	137
1953	10	59	1967	31	110
1954	11	133	1968	34	113
1955	25	151	1969	41	141
1956	19	31	1970	44	262
1957	10	55	1971	37	228
1958	12	40			
1959	12	40	Total	500	2,234

Source: Hiroshima Prefectural Office, ed. "Genbaku Sanjūnen: Hiroshimaken no Sengoshi"
[In the Thirty Years after the Atomic Bombing—Postwar History of Hiroshima Prefecture] (Hiroshima: Hiroshimaken, 1976), p. 371.

(1972). From this table it is clear that there have been three peaks in the output of records and testimonies in Hiroshima during the postwar era. The first peak came in 1951 when, with the signing of the peace treaty, there was an outburst of public opinion favoring peace and independence. The second peak occurred during the 1954–55 emergence of the movement against nuclear weapons. The third peak came much later, in 1965–71. The peak periods were generally the same in Nagasaki, except that personal testimonies were relatively more numerous in the initial peak period; while output of published works, poems, and personal testimonies was less than in Hiroshima in the later peak periods. In 1970, however, output increased rapidly as highly motivated movements worked to fill a long-neglected gap.

The Hiroshima-Nagasaki Peace Pilgrimage, organized with the help of Barbara Reynolds, on 16 June 1964 had an interview in New York City with U.N. Secretary-General U Thant and presented him with a petition that, in essence, called for a "U.N. commission to investigate the realities of A-bomb damages in Hiroshima, Nagasaki, and Bikini; and for the results to be disseminated throughout the world to help achieve a ban on nuclear weapons." Acknowledging the import of the petition, the Secretary-General, it is reported, expressed his wish that "the Japanese government bring this problem before the United Nations," and also that the U.N. Science Commission should study the problems of radiation. This Peace Pilgrimage also delivered to the United States government a request for the return of the documentary film "The Effects of Atomic Bombs on Hiroshima and Nagasaki" and all scientific documents which the U.S. military had confiscated and taken back to America. These materials were returned to Japan in several installments beginning in 1967.

The "Hiroshima Appeal" issued by the 1955 World Conference against Atomic and Hydrogen Bombs had proclaimed, "The unfortunate situation of the A-bomb victims must be made known to people around the world. Aid to the victims must be hastened through a worldwide relief effort. Such is the foundation of a true antinuclear movement." In discussions at the Third World Conference in 1957, strong appeals were made for a "relief white paper." Thus, in 1961 a committee of experts appointed by Nihon Gensuikyō published the "White Paper on Damages by Atomic and Hydrogen Bombs—The Hidden Truth." The problems raised by this white paper were discussed in an editorial of the *Chūgoku Shinbun* daily and elsewhere. Then, on 5 August 1964, at the Three-Prefecture Liaison Conference on Nuclear Victims,* Toshihiro Kanai proposed that "a white paper on nuclear victims be prepared for presentation to the United Nations." On 3 October of the same year the Peace Problems Research Group (Danwakai), composed of university scholars from Hiroshima, Yamaguchi, and Okayama prefectures, presented a petition to the national government. The gist of this petition was (1) that the 1965 national census include a supplementary survey for determining the damages suffered by all A-bomb victims, including those who have died; (2) that a comprehensive scientific analysis be added to this survey to produce a white paper on A-bomb damages; and (3) that the national government petition the United Nations to compile a report on nuclear damages. The government's response, however, stopped short of this request. The Ministry of Health and Welfare merely conducted a small-scale survey covering only health-book holders registered under the A-bomb Victims Medical Care Law.

On 15 May 1965, Hideki Yukawa and others of the Committee of Seven to Appeal for World Peace issued a statement advocating "the urgent necessity for compiling, from an international standpoint, a scientific white paper on nuclear damages." On 5 August of that year a petition signed by over forty prominent persons—including Hideki Yukawa, Seiji Kaya, Kenzaburō Ōe, the governors of Hiroshima and Nagasaki prefectures, and the mayors of Hiroshima and Nagasaki cities—was taken by five representatives, led by Kazuo Ōkōchi, to then Prime Minister Eisaku Satō to press vigorously the case for compiling a white paper on nuclear damages.

The Committee for Promotion of an A-bomb Damages White Paper (Seiji

* Prefectures of Hiroshima, Nagasaki, and Shizuoka.

Kaya, chairman) was formed on 7 December 1965; and on 27 June of the following year it handed the government a new "Petition for an A-bomb damages white paper to be compiled by the Japanese government." This petition included an appeal for the United States to return documents on A-bomb damages. In both Hiroshima and Nagasaki, citizens' movements arose to promote a nuclear damages white paper, and the municipal assemblies of the two cities passed resolutions supporting early compilation of such a white paper.

The white paper cause was then picked up by the Science Council of Japan in its campaign to found a "Nuclear Damages Documentation Center," as well as by the Hiroshima movement to preserve A-bomb documents, the movement to reconstruct maps of the bombed areas in Hiroshima and Nagasaki, and the testimonial movement. Meantime, due to efforts by the Committee for Promotion of an A-bomb Damages White Paper, U.N. Secretary-General U Thant developed a deep interest in the problem; experts from various countries (including Takashi Mukaibō from Japan) were entrusted with the task of producing a "White Paper on Nuclear Weapons." This led to the publishing, in 1967, of a report by the U.N. Secretary-General, entitled *Effects of the Possible Use of Nuclear Weapons and the Security and Economic Implications for States of the Acquisition and Further Development of These Weapons.* Because this report was compiled before adequate surveys were carried out in Japan, it was not wholly accurate regarding actual conditions, especially the number of deaths resulting from the atomic bombings. Thus, the report was not sufficiently convincing to move many governments. Given the Japanese government's failure to conduct a complete survey of A-bomb victims or to compile a white paper on A-bomb damages, Toshihiro Kanai, Jitsuo Tabuchi, Shigetoshi Itokawa, and others in Hiroshima organized in 1968 the Hiroshima Research Group for Documentation of A-bomb Damages. By 1972 it had produced the three-volume "General Catalogue of Documents on A-bomb Damages." In 1970, Tōmin Harada, Naomi Shohno, and others formed the A-bomb Film Production Committee, which re-edited documentary films made soon after the bombings and arranged for them to be shown at many places throughout the nation. All these activities naturally had a strong impact on Nagasaki, where the city sponsored compilation of the "Catalogue of A-bomb Records" (Nagasaki Shiyakusho 1970), and slightly cut versions of the documentary film returned from America were shown. But no citizens' group for the study of A-bomb documents was formed.

PROMOTION OF MAP RESTORATION FOR A-BOMBED AREAS

In 1950, Sadanobu Oda, Seiji Imahori, and others active in organizing the Peace Problems Research Center at Hiroshima University, secured the help of Hyōe Ōuchi to conduct an economic survey of A-bomb damages, using as a model Charles Booth's *Life and Labour of the People of London* (1892–97). Later, in the 1966 "white paper" petition presented to the national government, reconstruction of maps of the bombed areas was first proposed. Early in 1966 the epidemiology and social medicine sections of Hiroshima University's Research Institute for Nuclear Medicine and Biology undertook an analytical survey of the health and livelihood of A-bomb victims. In the course of this work the focus shifted to victims' families and households in a specific community and thus yielded a more comprehensive analysis of real conditions and their consequences seen from familial and communal perspectives.

About the same time, the NHK-Hiroshima Central Broadcasting Station undertook to reconstruct the map of the central bombed area where today the memorial cenotaph stands in Hiroshima Peace Memorial Park. On 3 August 1966, NHK-Hiroshima televised a "camera report" with the title *Inside the 500-meter Radius of the Hypocenter.* The staffs of NHK-Hiroshima and the university research institute's social medicine section collaborated to sponsor, on 24 June 1967, a meeting of former residents of their common target area to fill in, by their personal testimony, the missing data in the reconstructed map. Thus, the basic lines of map-reconstruction work were laid out. For its television series *Images of the Present Age,* NHK-Hiroshima in August 1967 produced a film called *A Flash beyond the Roof* to show the importance of map reconstruction. This film evoked great interest among A-bomb victims dispersed throughout the country. The Nuclear Medicine and Biology Research Institute's survey of the central bombed area was made the basis of a comprehensive survey of the former Nakajima district, commenced in March 1968. Public response to this project was immense; survivors and citizens with relations to the former district came forth in steady streams to provide testimony and documents. Some even sent in hand-drawn maps of the district. But their offerings were not limited to the Nakajima district; data on areas outside the central bombed area flowed in, as the initial activity expanded into a combined victims-citizens movement to reconstruct maps of the A-bombed city.

While map reconstruction work progressed, the Hiroshima Peace Culture Center made public its list of dead victims. In late March 1969 the Committee for the Map-restoration of A-bombed Areas was formed of citizens and city authorities, and a project to conduct a "survey for a comprehensive picture of A-bomb damages" was initiated. The scope of this project extended far beyond the central bombed area of the earlier survey; it was designed to discover actual damages within 2 kilometers of the hypocenter—that is, encompassing the entire burned-out area. Hiroshima University Nuclear Medicine and Biology Research Institute's original survey of Nakajima district has since been extended to cover the entire central bombed area within a 500-meter radius; and to date over 95 percent of the central area map has been reconstructed. Roughly 80 percent of the area's 2,400 households have been surveyed, and records on approximately 14,000 persons of related households have been compiled.

Survey activity in Nagasaki was prompted by critical reaction to the conclusion, advanced by the Ministry of Health and Welfare's second report of its 1965 Actual Status Survey of Atomic Bomb Survivors (1967*b*, p. 46) that "in terms of health and livelihood there is no noticeable difference between the A-bomb victims and citizens in general." In the absence of a comprehensive survey conducted by either national or local governments, people were aroused to uncover by themselves the real situation of the A-bomb victims. Thus, from May 1968 volunteers from the Nagasaki A-bomb Victims Association, the Nagasaki Constitution Council, the Nagasaki branch of the Japan Scientists Council, the Nagasaki High School Council against Atomic and Hydrogen Bombs, and other groups carried out a three-month survey and compiled the results under the title "Twenty-three Years since that Day— The Conditions and Demands of Nagasaki A-bomb Victims." This survey was continued in 1970, but in the intervening year the initial survey results and recorded testimonies were compiled and published as *Nagasaki no Shōgen* [Testimonies of Nagasaki] (Publications Committee for Testimonies of Nagasaki 1969). This publication sparked a new surge of activity in the Nagasaki testimonial and peace education movements. Breaking a long period of silence and inactivity, a number of vital testimonial works appeared concurrently, such as *Chinmoku no Kabe o Yabutte* [Breaking the Walls of Silence], compiled by the Nagasaki Prefecture Teachers Union, Nagasaki General Branch, and Nagasaki City Hibakusha Teachers Association (1970); *Nagasaki no Gōkyū* [Nagasaki Lamentations], compiled by the Nagasaki Women's Society (1970); *Genbaku Zengo* [Before and After the Atomic Bombing], by former Mitsubishi employees; *Hōbō* [A Scorched People], poems edited by Kan Yamada (1968); the second volume of *Mō Iya Da* [We've Had Enough—Living A-bomb Witnesses], by the Nagasaki A-bomb Youth and Maidens Association (1970); and *Wasurenagusa* [A Forget-Me-Not], edited by Raisuke Shirabe (1968–74). The year 1970 alone saw over twenty testimonial publications.

Hiroshima's reconstruction movement also ignited new activity in Nagasaki. A-bomb map-restoration groups were formed in 1970 by volunteers in Matsuyama and Yamazato townships to reconstruct maps of their respective districts. In May of that year Nagasaki City authorities began compilation of basic documents and, with the active cooperation of news media, extended the project to cover the entire bombed area of the city within 2 kilometers of the hypocenter. Building on the previous reconstruction efforts of citizen volunteers, the city in January 1971 set up in the city hall a survey office for reconstruction of A-bomb damages, which served as a center to promote all reconstruction activity. In March the city organized the Reconstruction Survey Council composed of representatives from each district's reconstruction group. By March 1975, with this extensive set-up, survey results were in on the forty-eight townships within the 2-kilometer radius. Of the 9,860 households entered on the reconstructed maps, those permitting statistical tabulation numbered 7,545 households with 37,512 members. Households that could not be entered on the maps numbered 606; and there were 2,921 households whose family members and relations were undetermined, even though these households could have been entered on the maps. The rate of map completion in several townships *(machi)*, for example, was 94 percent for Matsuyama, 83.9 percent for Yamazato, 78.3 percent for Komaba, 86.2 percent for Oka, 86.7 percent for Hamaguchi, 86.4 percent for Hashiguchi, 74.3 percent for Ōhashi; and the average rate for all forty-eight townships was 88 percent.

The preceding reconstruction activities are recounted in the following books: for Hiroshima, *Genbaku Bakushinchi* [The Atomic Bomb Central Bombed Area of Hiroshima], edited by Kiyoshi Shimizu et al. and published by Japan Broadcasting Publishing Co., Ltd., in 1969; for Nagasaki, *Nagasaki— Bakushinchi Fukugen no Kiroku* [Nagasaki—Record of Reconstruction of the Central Bombed Area], edited by Raisuke Shirabe, T. Yazaki, and Y. Matsuo and published by Japan Broadcasting Publishing Co., Ltd., in 1972, and *Bakushin no Oka nite* [On the Hill Where the Bomb Hit], compiled by the reconstruction groups of Yamazato and Hamaguchi townships and published in 1972 by the Publications Committee of Testimonies of Nagasaki.

FROM ASCERTAINING DATA ON THE ATOMIC BOMBINGS TO THE ABOLITION OF NUCLEAR WEAPONS

The Peace Problems Research Group was formed at Hiroshima University in September 1951. In February 1953, volunteers from universities throughout Hiroshima City organized the University Group to Protect Peace and Learning; and a group with the same name was formed soon after in Matsuyama City in Ehime Prefecture. In Nagasaki, the University Group to Protect Peace and Democracy came into being around 1960, and in 1965 the Nagasaki Constitution Council appeared. These groups engaged in research and held lecture meetings on many problems related to peace.

At the Hiroshima Conference held in November 1970—a citizens' conference involving both Japanese and foreign experts studying peace problems, and also peace movement participants—the Hiroshima-Nagasaki experience was discussed from a comprehensive standpoint, as were current problems of peace. The conference further assessed possibilities for concerted international action to ban nuclear weapons. These questions were tackled again in the Hiroshima International Forum on the thirtieth anniversary of the bombings in August 1975. Two hundred participants, including several dozen foreigners, analyzed the continuing nuclear arms race and discussed prospects for the complete eradication of nuclear weapons. In December 1975 a "national delegation" was dispatched to United Nations headquarters to demand "an international treaty completely banning nuclear weapons and immediate measures to ban their use." In October 1976 the central executive committee responsible for dispatching the delegation sent to the U.N. Secretary-General "An Introductory Report on the Damage and Aftereffects of the Atomic Bombings of Hiroshima and Nagasaki." This was followed by a supplementary document, "The Actual Conditions of Atomic Bomb Damages in Hiroshima and Nagasaki," presented to the U.N. Secretary-General in November 1976 by Hiroshima Mayor Takeshi Araki and Nagasaki Mayor Yoshitake Morotani, to "promote total abolition of nuclear weapons and realization of general and complete disarmament" (Hiroshimashi–Nagasakishi 1976).

With this background of cumulative research and surveys, as well as repeated overtures to the United Nations, plans were laid for the NGO-sponsored International Symposium on the Damage and Aftereffects of the Atomic Bombing of Hiroshima and Nagasaki. From late July to early August in 1977 the main scheduled events were the symposium involving some five hundred experts, A-bomb victims, and representatives of citizens' groups, and a mass rally attended by several thousand. In addition to the symposium's full report, an appeal was proclaimed (2 August 1977) with the challenging title "Life or Oblivion—A Call from the Hibakusha of Hiroshima and Nagasaki to the Hibakusha of the World."* The appeal not only warned of the threat to all life posed by ever more powerful bombs but also called for a united decision by all peoples of the world to rid this earth of all nuclear armaments.† Some of the immediate results of this symposium were: the sending of a Japanese delegation to the NGO International Conference on Disarmament to be held in Geneva in February 1978 and of another delegation to the U.N. Special Session on Disarmament in May and June of that year; an exhibition of Hiroshima and Nagasaki photographs in the United Nations headquarters; and a campaign to collect thirty-five million signatures supporting a general and complete ban on nuclear arms. These efforts have fostered a wide diffusion of antinuclear consciousness among the Japanese people and, at the same time, served to internationalize the meaning of Hiroshima and Nagasaki.

---

* *Hibakusha* means "A-bomb and H-bomb victims."
† Japan National Preparatory Committee 1977; NGO International Symposium 1977*b*.

Peace Education

> "Rest in peace,
> for the mistake shall not be repeated."

These words are carved in the stone of the memorial cenotaph in Hiroshima Peace Memorial Park. The question of "whose mistake?" has been persistently debated (Kosakai 1978, p. 31), but these words should be understood and accepted as a passionate prayer that abides deep in the hearts of the people of Hiroshima. This memorial cenotaph not only serves as a solemn place of repose for countless souls but also stands as a solemn pledge of Hiroshima's citizens—and a fervent appeal to all mankind—to be peacemakers.

Whether the promise not to repeat the mistake of Hiroshima and Nagasaki can be made a lasting reality will depend crucially on the power of education. This task is made all the more difficult by the relentless escalation of the nuclear arms race and by the fact that the younger generation, with no experience of war, now constitutes over half the population. And "Hiroshima and Nagasaki" become less real and compelling as they fade into the past. To teachers in the two cities it has become unmistakably clear that they need to give the atomic bomb experiences a central place in peace education designed to help young people live in a nuclear age. This realization has given rise to a peace education movement in Hiroshima and Nagasaki that necessarily focuses on "A-bomb education."

ATOMIC BOMB EDUCATION—FROM BUD TO BLOSSOM

The course of peace education in Hiroshima and Nagasaki has had intimate connections with general educational trends in Japan since the Second World War. Postwar education in Japan has been guided by public reflections on the prewar education based on nationalism and militarism which, in turn, had their roots in the ideology of the emperor's divinity. Postwar education, accordingly, began as education for peace and democracy, backed by the new war-renouncing Japanese Constitution (1946) and the Fundamentals of Education Law (1947) framed in the spirit of the new constitution. To build a peace-loving nation that abjures military might and to raise up a generation of people who seek peace were the fundamental goals of the new education. Compared with the militaristic education that preceded it, the postwar educational shift was a virtual Copernican revolution. It was a worthy reparation to make to a people forced to endure a long, costly war and the immense tragedy of atomic bombings.

But during the Occupation (1945–52), the A-bomb experiences could not be made a part of the content of public school education. The textbooks authorized during that period by the Japanese Ministry of Education make almost no mention of atomic bomb damages. Even on the monuments erected then to memorialize the dead of Hiroshima and Nagasaki the two Chinese characters for *genbaku* (shortened form of *genshi bakudan*, "atomic bomb") cannot be found (Ubuki 1976, pp. 57–60). It was a time, indeed, ruled by a "*genbaku* taboo."

The basic principles of peace education in that period were nurtured through the writing of compositions. Even in prewar days the writing of "daily life compositions" had been used to foster democratic education. The postwar teachers in Hiroshima and Nagasaki used the same method by having their pupils write about their own A-bomb experiences. Educational seminars led by Shin'ichi Matsunaga and Atsushi Sanagawa were held to collect the many compositions, and the July 1949 issue of the *Hiroshima Kyōiku* [Hiroshima Education] monthly journal* was a special issue filled with selected compositions expressing the children's opposition to war (that is, to the bomb). About the same time in Nagasaki, Takashi Nagai published a volume of children's compositions under the title *Genshigumo no Shita ni Ikite—Nagasaki no Kodomora no Shuki* [Living beneath the Atomic Cloud—Writings by Nagasaki Children] (Nagai 1949*a*). At the Hiroshima Rally to Protect Peace held on 2 October 1949, at the middle school of Hiroshima Jogakuin [girls school], the composition of a child who lost a younger brother in the atomic bombing was read aloud: it was one factor leading to the rally's resolution demanding abolition of atomic bombs.† Also, in those days monuments were erected to memorialize students and teachers who had died in the bombings, and ceremonies to mourn the dead and pray for peace were conducted. These various activities were not, however, particularly conscious and systematic attempts to develop peace education; they were, rather, educational expressions given to the sentiments and needs that arose directly from still vivid experiences of A-bomb damages and suffering.

The Japan Teachers Union (JTU) was organized in June 1947 with approximately 500,000 registered members. Soon after the outbreak of the Korean War, the Japanese government—in response to a memorandum from General MacArthur—established the national Police Reserve Force (forerunner of the present Self-Defense Forces). The JTU was very sensitive to the implicit danger of this revival of an armed militia by the ruling conservative government, and responded by initiating in 1951 numerous educational seminars throughout the nation under the slogan "Don't send our students to the battlefield again" (Japan Teachers Union 1978, pp. 129–32). Each year the local seminars climaxed in a national rally attended not only by teachers but also by a broad representation of scholars and parents. Peace education

---

* Hiroshima Prefecture Teachers Union, Department of Culture 1949.
† Fukagawa 1970; Imahori 1959–60.

was a central theme of these seminars and rallies. The cumulative discussion left an important legacy of self-determined, systematic thinking about peace education among Japanese teachers.

The international and domestic agitation over this issue had a great effect on peace education in Hiroshima and Nagasaki—the essence of which is crystallized in *Genbaku no Ko* [Children of the Atomic Bomb] (October 1951), edited by Arata Osada. This book is a collection of 105 compositions by boys and girls on their experiences in A-bombed Hiroshima. The editor's preface giving his ideas about peace education established a new beachhead for postwar Japanese peace education. To raise up children who think of peacemaking as the highest human morality, he wrote, is the fundamental goal of education. For this, he stressed the importance of using the children's experiences of war as educational aids to make them hate war and to get rid of all their prejudices so that they can develop generous and noble human sentiments and the abilities needed to establish peace.

The children who contributed essays to this book formed, on 17 February 1952, their own Circle of Friends of "Children of the Atomic Bomb." This group continued collecting children's compositions and also drew pictures and wrote plays in order to spread the truth about A-bomb damages. A group of professors and students of Osaka University's science department formed the Kyoto-Osaka-Kobe Circle to Respond to "Children of the Atomic Bomb," which engaged earnestly in seminars and publishing activity. Also, some essays collected by the Circle of Friends that were translated into Russian, Chinese, and German aroused considerable interest.

In this same period, Takashi Nagai, Sankichi Tōge, Tamiki Hara, and others published a number of literary works on the atomic bomb. Excerpts from these and from "Children of the Atomic Bomb" were included in school textbooks—the first time that fairly detailed descriptions of the A-bomb experience had been made available in teaching materials. Meantime, a series of A-bomb films were produced: *Bell of Nagasaki* (1950), *Children of the Atomic Bomb* (1952), *Hiroshima* (1953), *A Thousand [Paper] Cranes* (1955), *Children of Nagasaki* (1957), and others. Shown widely throughout the nation, these films played a major role in informing the public about the realities of the bomb, Hiroshima, and Nagasaki. Peace education was promoted in each prefectural teachers union. The Yamaguchi Prefecture Teachers Union, for example, collected daily diaries used both at home and at primary and middle schools, and excerpts of these were used as teaching aids in peace education. One such piece, for example, from a primary school pupil's 1953 diary, expressed opposition to rearmament—and provoked fiery criticism about "ideologically prejudiced education" from the conservative camp that was pushing the rearmament of Japan. The Nagasaki Prefecture Teachers Union in August

1955 was the first in the nation to open its own Seminar on Peace Education.

From defeat in 1945 to 1951 was the period during which the first buds of A-bomb education sprouted; from 1951 to 1955 these buds blossomed. In the latter period peace education, using as raw materials children's direct experiences of war, became rooted in people's daily lives. A representative example was the movement among Hiroshima middle school children to erect the Statue of the Atomic Bomb Children.* On 20 October 1955, first-grader Sadako Sasaki of the Noborimachi Middle School in Hiroshima died at age twelve on her bed in Hiroshima Red Cross Hospital. She had experienced the atomic bombing of Hiroshima at age two but had grown up healthily without any sign of abnormality until suddenly, in 1955, symptoms of A-bomb sickness appeared. Having heard that "if you fold a thousand [paper] cranes, your sickness will be cured," she lay in bed folding cranes every day. She folded more than a thousand but did not recover. Her classmates were shocked by word of her death and, wishing somehow to respond to her parting plea for peace, hit upon the idea of erecting a memorial statue as a way of directing a peace appeal to the whole world. Contributions for the Statue of the Atomic Bomb Children poured in from all over Japan and ten foreign countries; the statue was completed in Hiroshima Peace Memorial Park and unveiled on 5 May 1958 (figure 14.4). Atop its 9-meter, three-pronged base stands a young girl holding gold-colored cranes over her head. Sadako's perseverance in folding cranes was not in vain, for this imposing statue reminds thousands of visitors to the park that peace is priceless. It is a monument not only to her but also to the many children who wanted to do something for the sake of peace.

ATOMIC BOMB EDUCATION—RETREAT AND RETROGRESSION

Beginning in 1955, just when it appeared that A-bomb education had come to full bloom, it encountered hard times which lasted for a decade. There were several reasons for this development.

For one thing, the antinuclear movement between 1955 and 1958 involved broad sectors of the public and experienced significant growth. The movement's strength and activity were highly visible, but interest in peace education was perceptibly less. Eager to expand military capabilities within the framework of the Japan–U.S. Security Treaty, the conservative government moved against the currents of public peace sentiment by strengthening its position so as to counter movements for peace and democratization. A major policy change, for instance, was made in 1956 when government appointment replaced popular vote as the means of selecting public education committee members. Performance ratings for teachers were introduced in 1957, and

* Atomic Bomb Monument Research Group 1978; Kosakai 1978.

Figure 14.4. Statue of the A-bomb Children in Hiroshima Peace Memorial Park.

the legal binding power of a revised, prescribed curriculum was strengthened in 1958. Increased control over authorization of school textbooks by the Ministry of Education was another prime instance of the centralization of government power over education. As a result of these moves, explanations of the causes of war and of the A-bomb damages largely disappeared from the textbooks.

Among students the rate of enrollment in high schools and universities*

* Neither is compulsory in Japan. (Trans.)

rose rapidly, as Japan in the 1960s pursued a policy of rapid economic growth. The classroom became a staging area for the frantic competition to pass entrance examinations. The competitive pressure of entrance examinations undercut the spirit of democratic education. Moreover, with the passage of two decades, the school-age population had no direct experience of war; methods of peace education that appealed to personal war experiences no longer worked.

The cumulative effect of these factors was that the war—and the atomic bomb—became history, no longer a living experience. Even among children in Hiroshima and Nagasaki, there now were more and more children who did not know who dropped the bomb or when, who were not worried about political trends that left the peace constitution increasingly void of substance, who even—some of them—thought war is "real cool" *(kakko ii)*. As the teachers became aware of these realities, they were stunned—but not immobilized. They soon set about revising "A-bomb education."

ATOMIC BOMB EDUCATION—REBUILDING AND DEVELOPMENT

The Hiroshima Prefecture Teachers Union, in its November 1968 prefecture-wide educational seminar, scheduled a subgroup on "peace education." This was the springboard for renewed efforts for systematic study and action to revitalize peace education throughout the prefecture.* A survey was made of "A-bomb damage awareness"† among some two thousand primary and middle school students, mainly in Hiroshima City. After analyzing the survey results, the teachers devoted themselves anew to peace education in which A-bomb education had a central place. At its national seminar in 1969 the Japan Teachers Union urged all teachers to engage in A-bomb education. A subgroup on "peace education" was also included in Nagasaki's prefecture-wide educational seminar in 1970.

In both Hiroshima and Nagasaki the main agents of A-bomb education were the teachers who were themselves A-bomb victims. They formed their own associations, first in Hiroshima (Akira Ishida, chairman) in 1969 and then in Nagasaki (Shōhei Tsuiki, chairman) in 1970. A national council for associations of A-bomb victim teachers (Akira Ishida, chairman) was founded in 1971 not only to promote their movement but also to develop new materials and methods for A-bomb education. Drawing upon their own experiences, they compiled documentations of their struggles, such as *Mirai o Kataritsuzukete* [Talking About the Future—A-bomb Experience and the Starting Point

* Fujii 1978; Hiroshima Prefecture Educational Research and Peace Education Expert Committee et al. 1970–78.
† Hiroshima Prefecture Teachers Union and Hiroshima Prefecture Hibakusha Teachers Association 1969, pp. 164–65.

of Education] in 1969,* by the Hiroshima association, and *Chinmoku no Kabe o Yabutte* [Breaking the Wall of Silence] in 1970† by the Nagasaki association. The A-bomb victim teachers in Hiroshima and Nagasaki prefectures have made public their "pledge and appeal to continue teaching 'Hiroshima' and 'Nagasaki' "‡ and to work together to develop peace education. Associations have also been formed for A-bomb victim high school teachers in Hiroshima (1970; Hiroshi Morishita, chairman) and Nagasaki (1972; Yoshiteru Sakai, chairman) to promote peace education at that educational level.

As actual involvement in peace education impressed upon the teachers the urgent need for materials, some teachers have themselves produced such works: in Hiroshima, the supplementary reader *Hiroshima—Genbaku o Kangaeru* [Hiroshima—Thinking about the Atomic Bomb (draft)] and *Hiroshima—Kore wa Watashitachi no Sakebi Desu* [Hiroshima—This Is Our Cry (draft)],§ and the English reader *Let's Cry for Peace!*;‖ and in Nagasaki, *Nagasaki no Genbaku Tokuhon* [Nagasaki A-bomb Reader] (three volumes for primary school use, one for middle school use).# Teachers of the two cities collaborated to publish *Asu ni Ikiru* [Living for Tomorrow]** for high school use. Then, after several years of experience, a new supplementary reader, *Hiroshima—Konnichi no Kakujidai o Ikiru* [Hiroshima—Living in the Present Nuclear Age (draft)]†† was published.

These independently produced materials did much to diffuse and deepen peace education in Hiroshima and Nagasaki. A more important step in advancing the cause of peace education was the founding of the Hiroshima Institute for Peace Education (Tsugimaro Imanaka, director). This is a nongovernmental institute established on 1 June 1972 by the Hiroshima Prefecture Teachers Union (with approximately 10,000 members from primary and middle schools), the first independent institute for peace education in the world. Research is conducted in joint projects between classroom teachers and professors from various universities (mainly Hiroshima University). The institute's purpose is "to pass on the lessons of Hiroshima to the next generation for the benefit of all mankind"; and it seeks to achieve this aim by "conducting

* Hiroshima Prefecture Teachers Union and Hiroshima Prefecture Hibakusha Teachers Association 1969, pp. 164–65.
† Nagasaki Prefecture Teachers Union, Nagasaki General Branch, and Nagasaki City Hibakusha Teachers Association 1970.
‡ Hiroshima Prefecture Educational Research and Peace Education Expert Committee et al. 1971, pp. 17–19.
§ Both edited by the Hiroshima Prefecture Peace Education Teaching Materials Editorial Committee and Hiroshima Prefecture Hibakusha Teachers Association 1969, 1970.
‖ Hiroshima Prefecture Peace Education Teaching Materials English Division Editorial Committee and Hiroshima Prefecture Hibakusha Teachers Association 1971.
Nagasaki Prefecture Hibakusha Teachers Association and Peace Education Materials Editorial Committee 1972.
** Hiroshima-Nagasaki Peace Readers Editorial Committee 1974.
†† Hiroshima Institute for Peace Education 1977.

scientific research on peace education and promoting peace education widely throughout the world." Research results are published in the institute's annual report, *Heiwa Kyōiku Kenkyū* [Peace Education Study]; besides this a number of teaching materials and other books are compiled and published. The institute serves nationwide peace education by sponsoring a national symposium, and performs a crucial role as a clearinghouse for international exchange on peace education.

Education for peace in Hiroshima and Nagasaki is not limited to primary, middle, and high school but for several years has been pursued at the preschool and university levels as well. At a number of nurseries and kindergartens in Hiroshima, A-bomb experiences are discussed, and the youngsters draw pictures, visit the Peace Memorial Park, and sometimes put on plays related to peace (Fujii 1978). A special lecture series on "The meaning of 6 August" has been offered at Hiroshima Jogakuin College since 1967. Hiroshima University's department of education has since 1975 included a course on peace education in its required curriculum; lectures, films, and field work are used to elicit interest in peace education among future teachers. From 1977 the university's faculty of integrated arts and sciences has had, for all students, a general lecture course, called "Comprehensive Perspectives on War and Peace"; in it professors from all science fields participate. In 1975, Hiroshima University started the Institute of Peace Science which, beginning with a survey of nuclear problem awareness (Shohno, Nagai, and Ueno 1978), conducts comprehensive research on peace problems (Institute for Peace Science 1977). Nagasaki Institute of Technology in 1978* founded its Nagasaki Institute of Peace Culture (Nagasaki Institute of Technology 1978).

The A-bomb education initiated in Hiroshima and Nagasaki gradually spread to the rest of the nation. The First National Symposium on Peace Education (Japan Peace Education Research Council 1974–77) was held in Hiroshima in 1973. The symposium was held annually in Hiroshima until 1978 when it was moved to Nagasaki. More than one thousand persons— teachers, researchers, peace movement leaders, students, and other citizens— have participated annually. In 1974 the Japan Peace Education Research Council was founded; with headquarters in the Hiroshima Institute for Peace Education, this council aims at organizing programs throughout the country, mainly through its quarterly journal *Heiwa Kyōiku* [Peace Education] (1976, pp. 170–71). Responding to appeals by Hiroshima and Nagasaki teachers, the Japan Teachers Union has, since its twenty-second annual research conference in 1973, included a subgroup on peace education in the "Human Rights and People" section of its conference program; since the twenty-seventh conference held in 1978 in Okinawa, the section title has been "Peace and People."

* In the same year the institute's name was changed to Nagasaki Institute of Applied Science.

A-bomb education has also spread internationally. Masako Shōji and Toshi-hiko Fujii, researchers at Hiroshima Institute for Peace Education, attended the World Peace Education Conference held at Keele University in England in 1974 and presented a report on peace education in Hiroshima (Haavelsrud 1976, pp. 115–36, 201–7). Tatsuo Sora, Hiroshi Morishita, and four other teachers from Hiroshima and Tayori Sakaguchi and five other teachers from Nagasaki participated the following year in the World Peace Education Conference held at Wilmington College (Ohio) in the United States (Sora 1975, pp. 44–58). Then, the NGO International Symposium on the Damage and Aftereffects of the Atomic Bombing of Hiroshima and Nagasaki held in Tokyo, Hiroshima, and Nagasaki, July-August 1977, served further to internationalize A-bomb education.*

The domestic and international growth of peace education has not proceeded unimpeded; not a few social and political factors oppose its spread. The early A-bomb education pioneered in Hiroshima and Nagasaki, as well as the present larger cause of peace education in Japan, have always, except for one brief period, been sustained almost entirely through private institutions, groups, and leadership; and thus this cause has from its inception until now been in conflict with policies of the government's Ministry of Education.

THE FORM AND SUBSTANCE OF PEACE EDUCATION

A-bomb experiences naturally remain central to the peace education developed in Hiroshima and Nagasaki. But the reasons for this are even clearer if one looks at the various school readers (see page 599). Taking A-bomb experiences as their common starting point, these readers cover the entire gamut of peace concerns—the course of the war up to the dropping of the atomic bombs and the reasons for dropping them, the bombs' destructive power and the victims' sufferings that continue to this very day, the realities of today's nuclear arms and the nature of contemporary war potential, the current situation of Japan and the Japan-U.S. Security Treaty, the peace aspirations of children, the evolution of the peace movement, guidelines on how to live in a nuclear age, the prospects for a peaceful world, and, not least, poems of peace. A-bomb education centered on A-bomb experiences, therefore, does not relegate those experiences to past history; it is the basis for making a comprehensive scientific assessment of what war today would be like and, thus, for considering how mankind can live peacefully in a nuclear age.

---

* Japan National Preparatory Committee 1977; NGO International Symposium 1977a, 1977b, pp. 89–90.

Peace education based on A-bomb education is not for use only in special places and times. It must be promoted in and beyond textbooks and classrooms to homes and society—indeed, throughout all of society and at all times. In its earliest phase in Hiroshima and Nagasaki, A-bomb education focused on methods and materials designed only for use in schools on the 6 and 9 August anniversaries of the bombings. Gradually the content of this education became more diverse and inclusive; it was intended for use in longer "peace education week (sometimes ten days, or even a month)" programs. Examples of content diversification include: the use of A-bomb literature and testimonies in Japanese language courses; analysis, in social studies, of war and the strategic aims of dropping the atomic bombs; painting pictures with A-bomb motifs in art classes; peace songs in music classes; and studies of the atomic bomb in science classes. The high school attached to Nagasaki Institute of Applied Science included a "peace problems seminar" in its compulsory curriculum (NGO International Symposium 1977*b*, pp. 89–90). The supplementary readers for primary and middle school students to read during summer vacations have always included materials describing A-bomb damages and fears. Extracurricular activities related to classroom work have also been conducted. These include peace studies for all students in programs held at schools on A-bomb anniversary dates (during summer vacation); excursions to the peace memorial parks and visits to patients in the A-bomb hospitals; performances of A-bomb-related plays at school assemblies; exhibitions of A-bomb materials and peace-related art during schoolwide cultural festivities; showings of slides and movies on the atomic bombs, war, and peace; written reports and compositions based on A-bomb experiences of parents and other adults, as well as inviting A-bomb victims to the schools to talk and answer questions; exchanges with students of other schools throughout the nation; and schoolwide observances of memorial ceremonies for the dead.* Since the 1960s, extracurricular peace education activities have been conducted at various middle and high schools, and since the 1970s the number of primary, middle, and high schools featuring field trips to Hiroshima and Nagasaki has steadily increased. Finally, because audiovisual aids such as slides and movies are particularly effective in transmitting A-bomb education to the younger generation, the Hiroshima

* Fujii 1978; Hiroshima Institute for Peace Education 1973–77; Hiroshima Prefecture Hibakusha Teachers Association and Hiroshima Prefecture Association of Senior High School Teachers– Hibakusha 1977; Hiroshima Prefecture Hibakusha Teachers Association and Hiroshima Prefecture Teachers Union, 1971; Hiroshima Prefecture Senior High School Teachers Union, A-bomb and Peace Education Promotion and Editorial Committee, and Hiroshima Prefecture Hibakusha Teachers Association 1971; Hiroshima Prefecture Educational Research and Peace Education Expert Committee et al. 1973; Hiroshima Prefecture Educational Research and Peace Education Expert Committee et al. 1970–78; Hiroshima Prefecture Teachers Union and Hiroshima Prefecture Hibakusha Teachers Association 1969, pp. 164–65; Ishida 1976; Japan National Preparatory

Peace Education Film Library was established in 1976 as a joint project of the Hiroshima Institute for Peace Education and the Hiroshima Film Center. This library has since loaned peace education films to many schools.

PEACE EDUCATION IN HOME AND SOCIETY

The cities of Hiroshima and Nagasaki have both promoted peace education of various kinds for home and general social use. The impact of this effort has been far from small in fostering a widespread awareness of the A-bomb experiences and the imperatives of peace.

Social Education Activities. In the 1950–59 period, the Hiroshima Municipal Board of Education annually held a public lecture series on peace on the occasion of the 6 August anniversary. The city in 1967 founded the Hiroshima Peace Culture Center,* which has since engaged in the following activities (Hiroshima Peace Culture Foundation 1976, 1978):

1. *Documentation:* The center has the largest collection of books and magazines on A-bomb damages; it has acquired copies of official U.S. documents related to the A-bomb, compiled a list of the A-bomb dead, as well as early records of the bombings, and now houses the materials returned to Japan by the United States.

2. *Documentary films:* In addition to daily showings of films edited from the documentary footage taken soon after the bombings, films are regularly loaned, sold, and presented as gifts. Some films have English sound tracks.

3. *Publications:* The center's major publications are the English-language *A-bomb: A City Tells Its Story; Heiwa no Ayumi* and its English version, *Steps toward Peace; Hiroshima no Shōgen* [Testimonies of Hiroshima]; and *Hiroshima,* a photographic collection.

4. *Exchange with other peace organizations:* Relations have been cultivated in and outside Japan with related organizations, such as the Hiroshima University's Institute of Peace Science, the Hiroshima Appeal Committee (established in 1973; active in cooperation with Wilmington College in the United States), and the World Friendship Center (founded in 1965 by Barbara Reynolds).

5. *Promotion of world federalism:* Through citizens' meetings and world rallies, the center has endeavored to promote awareness of our "global village."

6. *Cultural activities:* The center has supported the Hiroshima Symphony Orchestra and the Hiroshima Wind Ensemble.

Committee 1977; National Education Research Institute 1977; Moritaki 1976; Nagasaki Peace Education Research Society 1976; Nagasaki Prefecture Teachers Union, Peace Education Materials Editorial Committee 1977*b;* Nagasaki Prefecture Hibakusha Teachers Association et al. 1971; Nagasaki Prefecture Hibakusha Teachers Association and Nagasaki Prefecture Teachers Union, Nagasaki General Branch 1972; Nagasaki Prefecture Teachers Union Peace Education Materials Editorial Committee 1975; Nagasaki Prefecture Teachers Union, Nagasaki General Branch and Nagasaki City Hibakusha Teachers Association 1970; NGO International Symposium 1977*a,* 1977*b;* Nagasaki Prefecture Teachers Union Peace Education Materials Editorial Committee 1977*a;* Takeuchi 1968; Yamada et al. 1976.

* Incorporated as a foundation on 1 April 1976.

Figure 14.5. Hiroshima Peace Memorial Museum.

The Hiroshima Peace Memorial Museum (figure 14.5) was opened in 1949 as an exhibition hall for A-bomb materials, the main body of which were items collected immediately after the bombing by Shōgo Nagaoka and the A-bomb Materials Preservation Society. The present building, completed in 1955, houses 5,911 items. In the 1970s annual visitors to the museum often exceeded one million (table 14.4). One section also features items on Nagasaki. The museum's collection is most valuable for gaining an understanding of conditions immediately following the atomic bombing.

Treating both the daily lives and the spiritual situation of the A-bomb victims, the Hiroshima Peace Memorial Hall demonstrates the victims' sufferings as well as their struggle for peace, not only through exhibited materials but also by sponsoring lectures, seminars, and study programs. This hall, along with the museum and Hiroshima City Auditorium, is located in Hiroshima Peace Memorial Park. The Peace Memorial Cenotaph and the A-bomb Dome are also found in this park, which was designed in its entirety by Kenzō Tange to fulfill an educational role in society.

In Nagasaki the A-bomb Records Preservation Committee was formed in April 1949. This committee labored to collect objects that bore witness to the heartrending postbombing conditions, and in May the A-bomb Museum was founded in the center of the bombed area. Subsequent construction of the Nagasaki International Cultural Hall was completed in 1955 (figure 14.6).

TABLE 14.4

*Visitors to the Hiroshima Peace Memorial Museum and the
Nagasaki International Cultural Hall, 1955–78**

Year**	Hiroshima	Nagasaki	Year**	Hiroshima	Nagasaki
1955	115,369	220,671	1968	988,209	997,944
1956	228,940	264,496	1969	963,083	967,921
1957	272,786	313,792	1970	931,508	979,076
1958	230,916	382,243	1971	1,074,465	1,046,154
1959	349,801	459,739	1972	1,107,248	1,105,909
1960	411,185	520,737	1973	951,550	1,150,529
1961	508,494	709,383	1974	880,486	1,118,176
1962	514,584	726,226	1975	1,253,145	1,248,836
1963	714,502	858,086	1976	1,063,103	1,204,081
1964	799,035	910,771	1977	986,709	1,164,787
1965	871,772	970,484	1978	996,117	1,105,858
1966	840,276	946,351			
1967	904,116	983,972	Total	17,957,399	20,356,222

* Both founded in 1955.
** The Japanese fiscal year, beginning 1 April and continuing through 31 March.
Source: Information provided by the Hiroshima Peace Memorial Museum and the Nagasaki
International Cultural Hall.

In the floor of the lobby are embedded stones from the Gotō islands as a memorial to the city's A-bomb dead. The hall's commanding and beautiful view, from its location atop a hill in the center of the bombed area, symbolizes the people's deep desire to rise from the ashes of atomic destruction and fervently to seek peace. The hall's purpose is "to promote international culture and contribute to the establishment of a lasting peace; to this end, it collects, preserves, and exhibits A-bomb materials and sponsors public meetings and exhibitions." The range and the contacts of its programs are generally the same as those of its Hiroshima counterpart. Boasting an extensive collection, visitors to the hall have since 1971 annually exceeded one million (table 14.4).

Because the Nagasaki bomb's destructive capacity exceeded that of Hiroshima, visible ruins were more extensive—a fact that deeply impressed early visitors to the two cities. With the passage of time, however, many of these ruins, including Urakami Cathedral, disappeared as the city was gradually rebuilt. Nagasaki's Peace Park (184,800 square meters) in the central bombed area is skillfully laid out in a setting of woods, ponds, and a river. Its bronze Peace Statue, designed by Seibō Kitamura and 15 meters high, is of a seated Olympian figure whose right hand points skyward "to symbolize the A-bomb" and whose left hand stretches out horizontally "to symbolize peace." His face expresses "a prayer for the eternal happiness of those who died." The stylized figure represents "a human who transcends all mankind."

In 1975 the city of Nagasaki produced a film called *Record of the Atomic Bombing of Nagasaki,* which is largely reproduced film footage from the National Archives in Washington, D.C. Showings in Nagasaki and throughout the nation have had a powerful impact on viewers. The first volume of *Nagasaki Genbaku Sensaishi* [Record of the Nagasaki A-bomb War Disaster], begun in 1973 and published in 1977 by the Nagasaki International Cultural Hall, is intended to "express the sense of mission of Nagasaki citizens to appeal to the world for an everlasting peace and, thus, to fulfill this mission, consists of accurate documentations of the damages caused by the atomic bombing of Nagasaki as well as investigations of all factors and effects related to the bombing." This work is also dedicated to "building the foundations of peace."

Over one hundred memorial monuments and statues have been erected in the memorial parks and places of Hiroshima and Nagasaki. One such is the "Child Praying for Peace" statue in Nagasaki's Peace Park, erected in 1967 by the Nagasaki Peace Paper-Crane Society; on its base is inscribed, "May the grief of Nagasaki's children, crying while clinging to their mothers underneath the A-bomb's mushroom cloud, never be repeated." The red, white, blue, and black "peace stones" of its foundation were donated by fifteen nations and all prefectures of Japan for the sake of "peace without nuclear weapons."

The educational impact of the A-bomb ruins and exhibits on the visitors— children and adults alike—from all over Japan and around the world is powerful, as is clearly evident, for instance, in the "travel memoirs" penned by children on school excursions. Likewise, the exhibits are very effective in making known just what happened in 1945 in Hiroshima and Nagasaki.

Cultural Activities in Home and Community.   Besides the more structured programs we have outlined, a variety of cultural activities extend peace education to both home and community.

The antinuclear comic book *Hadashi no Gen* [Barefoot Gen; also in English] (Nakazawa 1975) is one well-known example. There are also many other significant activities, such as readers, written compositions, and films that link children and parents in peace education (Fujii 1978; NGO International Symposium 1977b).

In 1974 seventy-eight-year-old A-bomb victim Iwakichi Kobayashi sent some of his own A-bomb drawings to NHK-Hiroshima. This inspired many people to try their hands at depicting A-bomb scenes, and their simple but very real representations aroused strong antinuclear feelings among the general public. These new A-bomb resources have now been preserved in a color slide set and a book.*

---

* Hiroshima Peace Culture Foundation 1977; Japan Broadcasting Corporation 1975.

Figure 14.6. Nagasaki International Cultural Hall.

Preparations for the anniversary peace ceremonies held annually each August in Hiroshima and Nagasaki include peace music festivities, poster slogans
created by various peace groups, the solicitation and exhibition of peace
art and literature, and the publication of peace readers.* These activities,
along with the various world peace rallies, have firmly implanted in the
citizens' daily lives the emerging tradition of their home towns as "peace
cities." For three and one-half decades the two cities' citizens have held
ceremonies to mourn and memorialize the A-bomb dead. During these same
years they have composed countless epitaphs and inscriptions for tombstones.
Their thoughts expressed on these occasions have not been addressed solely
to the departed souls; they have also expressed the vows of the living to
work for peace and for abolition of nuclear weapons.†

* Kosakai 1978; Kotani, Maruyama, and Fujii 1979.
† Chūgoku Shinbunsha 1965; Office of the Committee for the Erection of a Monument to
Primary School Teachers and Pupils Killed by the Atomic Bomb 1971; Atomic Bomb Monument
Research Group 1978; Nihon Heiwa Iinkai—Hiroshimaken Heiwa Iinkai 1976; Kosakai 1978;
Nagasaki Peace Education Research Society 1976; and Ubuki 1976, pp. 57–60.

The cooperation of many persons related to newspapers, radio and television broadcasting, and publishing has contributed greatly to enlightening the public and to promoting peace movements. This is especially true of local media in Hiroshima and Nagasaki such as *Chūgoku Shinbun* [regional daily] and *Nagasaki Shinbun* [Nagasaki daily] and other news, radio, and television agencies.*

As these many projects and activities have found their place in the historical and cultural currents of Hiroshima and Nagasaki, they have fostered a new double-edged spiritual ethos of antinuclear and pro-peace passions. It is this ethos that informs the peace education directed toward the younger generation and toward the whole world.

Activities to Tell the Whole World about "Hiroshima" and "Nagasaki." Since the end of the Second World War, the experiences of Hiroshima and Nagaski have in various ways been communicated to all lands and peoples the world over; yet knowledge and understanding of these experiences are far from adequate. Indeed, with the change of generations and the persistent expansion of the nuclear arms race, these experiences fade into the background and are, in fact, in danger of being forgotten.

The thirtieth anniversary of the bombings (1975) became, then, the occasion for renewed efforts to convey, adequately and accurately, the truth about these unprecedented experiences to the next generation and to the whole world. The 1977 NGO symposium was one such effort, as was the May–June 1978 U.N. Special Session on Disarmament, which citizens' representatives of the two cities attended in order to appeal for general and complete disarmament. At the same time the Hiroshima-Nagasaki Photographic Exhibition was held at U.N. headquarters and viewed by approximately seventy-thousand persons. Prior to that, teachers from Hiroshima and Nagasaki who participated in the World Peace Education Conference at Wilmington College in the United States decided to form groups to communicate the A-bomb experiences widely abroad by engaging actively in the translation of A-bomb and peace materials.† Then, taking a hint from the nationwide schoolchildren's exchange programs, a group was founded for the purpose of sending A-bomb materials to children around the world. With the support of many citizens, a pictorial record of A-bomb experiences was completed in 1978 with the title *Hiroshima-Nagaski: A Pictorial Record of the Atomic Destruction* (Hiroshma-Nagasaki Publishing Committee 1978), and efforts are currently under way to distribute this impressive volume throughout the world.

---

* Japan National Preparatory Committee 1977; NGO International Symposium 1977*b*.
† Nagasaki Prefecture Hibakusha Teachers Association and Peace Education Materials Editorial Committee 1977.

APPENDIX

The City of Hiroshima

PEACE DECLARATION

6 August 1980

Change brings change inexorably, and nothing stands still—thirty-five years have now passed since that day of disaster.

On that day, Hiroshima took the brunt of the age of nuclear war, in an infernal and scorching blast. Since that day, she has been ever calling for an end to nuclear weapons, praying for a lasting peace for man.

The world situation, at the present time, deeply troubles Hiroshima. World military expenditure has finally come to exceed one billion dollars per day. Its ever-rising curve affects developing countries, and hastens their armament.

Each element in the conflicts in the Middle East and Southeast Asia bears with it the possibility of a development into total nuclear war, even though this depends on the major powers' political strategies. The massive flow of refugees in these regions casts its dark shadow on us.

Apprehension about nuclear expansion and proliferation, and attempts to save mankind from annihilating itself, have been evident in the Limited Test Ban Treaty, the Treaty on the Non-Proliferation of Nuclear Weapons, the Strategic Arms Limitation Talks between the United States and the Soviet Union, and other concrete results. In particular, in the first-ever Special Session of the United Nations General Assembly devoted to Disarmament, the member nations reached agreement on the principle that the security of a nation should be maintained not by armament but by disarmament. They resolved at the same time that the reduction of nuclear weapons should be given the highest priority in disarmament issues, with the ultimate aim of abolishing nuclear weapons entirely.

This year, a Peace Memorial Exhibition was held at the United States Senate Office Building, focusing on Hiroshima and Nagasaki. It is clear that international concern about the atomic disaster experience of Hiroshima has been growing. We have little doubt that it will usher in a movement not only to prevent any future victims from being exposed to the horrors of nuclear radiation, but to form an international consensus for the complete eradication of nuclear weapons.

But when we take into account the present realities of the international situation, we see that it will be impossible for us to reach the distant shore of peace, unless we conquer intergovernmental distrust, deep-rooted in the folly of the arms race. Hiroshima therefore now proposes that, before the opening of the second Special Session of the U.N. General Assembly devoted to Disarmament, there should be a

World Summit Conference on Peace, with the participation of the leaders of the United States and the Soviet Union. The Government of Japan should take the initiative in advocating this, since, at the first Special Session of the U.N. General Assembly devoted to Disarmament, our Government declared her determination to strengthen still further her diplomatic efforts dedicated to peace and based on international cooperation.

It is now high time for us to call for the solidarity of all mankind, and to shift our common path away from self-destruction towards survival.

Today, on the occasion of the thirty-fifth anniversary of the atomic bombing, we pray devoutly for the repose of the souls of the A-bomb victims; we express our desire for the earliest enactment of the A-bomb victims' relief law, based on the acceptance of national responsibility for indemnity; and we pledge all our efforts to ensure the survival of mankind.

TAKESHI ARAKI
Mayor of Hiroshima

The City of Nagasaki

PEACE DECLARATION

9 August 1980

On August 9, 1945, the city of Nagasaki turned into an inferno beyond human imagination, and more than 70,000 precious lives were obliterated.

Even now, 35 years from that event, a great number of surviving victims are still suffering under the persistent shadow of death.

While the losses and cruelties of the war experienced by the Japanese people, both physical and spiritual, have gradually disappeared, the painful struggle of the atomic bomb victims becomes deeper and more intense with the passing of the months and years.

Now here this common gathering of surviving victims and relatives, youngsters, citizens of Nagasaki, and people from all over our country and from other countries, has paid respect to the souls of the ones who lost their lives on account of the atomic bomb, and, from the bottom of our hearts, we have prayed for their eternal rest and happiness. Out of the sorrow and hate of our relatives and friends who fell victim to the atomic bomb, we have to engrave deeply on our hearts a prayer for peace. Historians of the generations to come will undoubtedly record the cruel atomic bombing as one of the darkest moments of the twentieth century.

The citizens of Nagasaki, now recovered from the suffering and anger of the bombing, have the obligation, the responsibility, and the mission of continuing to urge a stop in the race of nuclear arms proliferation and to advocate total disarmament.

Let us remind ourselves of the existing tense relations between neighboring countries in the world and of how even the light of the dawn of peace has almost been extinguished, how the race of nuclear arms has so fiercely intensified, how the nuclear tests have this year exceeded by far the number of tests held last year. The city of Nagasaki for the last eleven years has protested against the 188 different nuclear tests, but her protests have been totally ignored. Under the pretension of doing it to avoid war, the nations which possess nuclear weapons have expanded them more and more each year. We are sure that unless this dangerous course is reversed, no true peace nor progress will ever be attained on earth.

The world's arsenal of immensely powerful nuclear weapons is capable of erasing several times the whole of mankind. The danger of a technical or supervisory miss leading to an accidental ignition of a nuclear war is a strong reality. Is mankind entering the road of self-destruction? Time is pressing. People of goodwill from all over the world should now give ears to the voice of Nagasaki, open their eyes to wisdom, and stand up with actions and efficient means to stop the proliferation of nuclear arms and to make a reality the total ban of wars. Not only the descendants of the ones who experienced the atomic bomb—the citizens of Nagasaki and Hiroshima—but all our countrymen, and moreover, all mankind should advance in all strength on the way to complete this task. For the realization of true peace we must go beyond countries' borders, beyond beliefs and faiths, in an all-out cooperation.

We now strongly appeal to the government of Japan for a new resolution to stop totally the production of nuclear weapons and for total disarmament, and for the certainty of a policy to help the atomic bomb victims, following the spirit of state compensation.

Here we pray for the eternal repose of the atomic bomb victims and in the name of the citizens of Nagasaki we appeal for a firm advancement in the realization of everlasting world peace and of a total ban on nuclear arms.

HITOSHI MOTOSHIMA
Mayor of Nagasaki

CHRONOLOGY: 1945–78
Events Related to Atomic
Bomb Damages

(For specific times directly related to the dropping of the atomic bombs, see chapter 1.)

1945

July
16 United States successfully tests world's first nuclear (plutonium) device at Alamogordo testing grounds in New Mexico.

August
6 8:15 A.M., atomic (uranium) bomb dropped on Hiroshima City. President Truman and Secretary of War Stimson issue statement concerning the dropping of the atomic bomb on Hiroshima.

7 Japanese Imperial Headquarters announces atomic bombing of Hiroshima.

8 Soviet Union declares war on Japan. Imperial Headquarters survey team enters Hiroshima (headed by Seizō Arimatsu from the General Staff Office, with Yoshio Nishina of the Institute of Physical and Chemical Research and other scientists as members).

9 11:02 A.M., atomic (plutonium) bomb dropped on Nagasaki City. Western Regional Military Headquarters announces atomic bombing of Nagasaki.

10 Japanese government protests (via Swiss government) U.S. use of the new weapon. Imperial Army and Navy's Joint Research Team on Special Bombs concludes in Hiroshima that the new bombs are atomic bombs.

15 Japanese emperor broadcasts end of war. Japanese newspapers report in detail the A-bomb damages.

21 Hiroshima Prefecture compiles summary of A-bomb damages.

23 *Mainichi Shimbun* newspaper reports theory that bombed areas will remain biologically sterile for seventy years.

24 *Asahi Shimbun* and *Yomiuri Hōchi Shinbun* newspapers run same story, with seventy-five-year period.

30 Masao Tsuzuki and others from Tokyo Imperial University reach Hiroshima; Tōichirō Sawada and others from Kyushu Imperial University arrive in Nagasaki.

September

1 Nagasaki Prefecture compiles summary of A-bomb damages.

2 Heavy rains in Nagasaki area alter configuration of A-bomb ruins.

3 Meeting on A-bomb diseases held in Hiroshima, with lectures by Masao Tsuzuki and Masashi Miyake. Occupation press corps enters Hiroshima. Australian journalist Wilfred Burchett enters Hiroshima independently, cables story on local situation.

6 Journalist George Wyler enters Nagasaki to gather information.

9 Special Manhattan Engineer District Investigating Group conducts survey of Hiroshima.

12 Group head T. Farrel denies newspaper reports of theories on biological sterility (press release, Tokyo).

13–14 Manhattan Investigating Group surveys Nagasaki.

14 Ministry of Education establishes Special Committee for Investigation of A-bomb Damages, within Scientific Research Council of Japan.

15 Cameraman Sueo Itō of Nippon Eiga-sha Corporation enters Nagasaki to photograph A-bomb damages in cooperation with Special Committee (see 14 September).

17 Hiroshima hit by Makurazaki typhoon; Kyoto Imperial University survey team buried under landslide.

19 Occupation GHQ issues press code.

21 Advance team of Nippon Eiga-sha enters Hiroshima to photograph A-bomb damages in cooperation with Special Committee (see 14 September).

22 Joint Japan–U.S. survey team holds initial session at Tokyo Imperial University. (Surveys conducted in Nagasaki from 28 September; in Hiroshima, from 12 October.)

25 U.S. Navy engineers begin survey of Nagasaki.

October

17 Nippon Eiga-sha cameraman arrested in Nagasaki by American MPs.

19 Photographing of A-bomb scenes prohibited. (Formal prohibition issued by GHQ on 12 December.)

November

20 GHQ takes over administration of Japan's three atomic research facilities (operated by the Institute of Physical and Chemical Research, Kyoto Imperial University, and Osaka Imperial University).

23 Catholics in Nagasaki observe mass beside ruins of Urakami Cathedral.

24 Destruction of cyclotrons at Japan's atomic research facilities begins.

30 Special Committee for Investigation of A-bomb Damages (Scientific Research Council) presents first report (Tokyo Imperial University). GHQ issues directive requiring prior permission for A-bomb research.

December
  1   Hiroshima War Orphans Foster Home founded.
  9   Hiroshima City and town council heads organize Hiroshima War Damages Reconstruction Council.
 17   GHQ confiscates A-bomb films taken by Nippon Eiga-sha Corporation.
 27   Hiroshima Prefecture police department announces that, as of 30 November, A-bomb dead and lost among civilian population numbered 92,133. Nagasaki Prefecture external affairs section announces 25,677 dead and lost as of 23 October.

1946

February
 28   Special Committee for Investigation of A-bomb Damages (Scientific Research Council) presents second report (Tokyo Imperial University).

March
 10   Hiroshima magazine *Chūgoku Bunka* devotes initial issue to A-bomb damage.

May
 22   Memorial week for A-bomb dead begins in Hiroshima.
 27   Kōshō Ōtani, chief priest of Nishi Honganji temple (Kyoto), visits Hiroshima for memorial services.

June
 29   Manhattan Project team publishes report *The Atomic Bombings of Hiroshima and Nagasaki.*
 30   U.S. Strategic Bombing Survey team completes report *The Effects of Air Attack on the Cities of Hiroshima and Nagasaki.*

August
  5   Citizens Rally for Peace Reconstruction of Hiroshima opens.
  6   Religious groups hold first anniversary memorial services for Hiroshima A-bomb dead.
  9   Memorial services held for Nagasaki A-bomb dead.
 10   Hiroshima City's survey section undertakes survey of city's residents as of 6 August 1945.
 31   *The New Yorker* magazine devotes an entire issue to John Hersey's "Hiroshima"—later published as a book.

November
  3   Japan's new postwar constitution is promulgated (effective from 3 May 1947).
 26   President Truman orders the establishment of the Atomic Bomb Casualty Commission (ABCC) within the National Academy of Sciences—National Research Council (NAS-NRC).

December
  6   The ABCC preparatory survey team arrives in Hiroshima.
  7   The ABCC team departs for Nagasaki.

1947

April
1   Japanese Association of Medical Sciences holds first postwar meeting in Osaka. Special lectures on A-bomb diseases are delivered by Takehiko Kikuchi (Kyoto University), Seiji Kimoto (University of Tokyo), Masanori Nakaizumi (University of Tokyo), and Ryōjun Kinoshita (Osaka University).
7   Special Committee for Investigation of A-bomb Damages presents its third report (Osaka University).

August
1   Hiroshima Prefecture Central Hospital sponsors health examinations. By 7 August, seven leukemia cases have been detected.
6   Hiroshima Peace Festival ceremonies. Mayor issues Peace Declaration. General MacArthur, Supreme Commander for the Allied Powers, sends message.
9   Memorial services for A-bomb dead sponsored by Nagasaki war victims, youth, Buddhist groups; mayor presiding.

December
7   Japanese emperor visits Hiroshima.

1948

March
31   National Institute of Health establishes Hiroshima branch laboratory.

April
4   Consultation held in Honolulu on relief for A-bomb victims.
18   On proposal from American Baptist Federation, committee organized for World Peace Day.

July
14   Opening ceremony for the ABCC in Hiroshima.

August
1   National Institute of Health establishes Nagasaki branch laboratory.
6   Second Hiroshima Peace Festival ceremony. The mayor of Hiroshima sends a peace message to 160 cities around the world.
9   Cultural Festival in Nagasaki's hypocenter area. The mayor of Nagasaki issues a peace declaration. General MacArthur sends message.
10   Hiroshima office of Labor Ministry's Women and Minors Bureau sponsors rally for support of women casualties in Hiroshima Prefecture; eight women A-bomb victims attend.

1949

January
30   Takashi Nagai publishes *Nagasaki no Kane* [Bell of Nagasaki].
April
11   Nagasaki City A-bomb Records Preservation Committee formed
      (dissolved 1 April 1959).
May
6   Preservation Committee decides to open an A-bomb museum in
      Nagasaki.
11   Laws enacted to establish Hiroshima as Peace Memorial City and
      Nagasaki as International Culture City; promulgated 6 and 9 Au-
      gust, respectively.
25   Japanese emperor visits Nagasaki.
29   Ceremony celebrating 400th anniversary of St. Francis Xavier's
      coming to Japan, at A-bomb ruins of Urakami Cathedral in Naga-
      saki.
June
3   Memorial ceremony in Hiroshima for A-bomb dead.
August
29   The Soviet Union conducts first atomic test (Siberia).
September
6   Hiroshima City sends peace petition with 100,000 signatures to
      President Truman.
17   Norman Cousins, in *Saturday Review of Literature,* proposes move-
      ment for foster parents of A-bomb children.
25   A-bomb reference room opened in Hiroshima's Central Community
      Center.
October
2   Hiroshima Rally to Protect Peace adopts resolution to abolish
      atomic weapons.
6   Fourth assembly of Science Council of Japan approves "Petition
      for the establishment of effective international controls of atomic
      energy."
17   Fourth general meeting of National Public Welfare and Child Care
      Committee adopts resolution urging, "Never repeat the tragedy
      of Hiroshima."
November
20   Association for Exchange between Youth of A-bomb Cities formed
      in Hiroshima (dissolved 10 August 1956).

1950

February
8   Iri Maruki and Toshiko Akamatsu hold exhibition of A-bomb
      paintings in Tokyo; later tour the nation.

March
25   World Rally to Preserve Peace issues "Stockholm Appeal."
April
15   Japan P.E.N. Club holds "Hiroshima Meeting."
June
1   Special fifth anniversary issue (no. 5) of *Nagasaki Bunka* features
     "Peace and Nagasaki."
25   Korean War begins.
August
6   Hiroshima's Peace Festival is canceled by Occupation GHQ. Unau-
     thorized peace rallies are held.
9   Unauthorized peace rallies held in Nagasaki.
October
1   The ABCC conducts nationwide survey of A-bomb survivors as
     supplement to national census.

1951

May
1   Hiroshima City undertakes survey of A-bomb deaths.
August
1   Science Council of Japan publishes summary report on its survey
     of A-bomb damages (two volumes of full report published 5 May
     1953).
9   First Kyushu District Peace Rally held in Nagasaki.
27   A-bomb Victims Self-rehabilitation Society organized by churches
     in Hiroshima.
September
8   San Francisco Peace Treaty and Japan–U.S. Security Treaty signed
     (effective 28 April 1952).
October
2   Arata Osada's compilation *Genbaku no Ko* [Children of the Atomic
     Bomb] is published.
16   Hiroshima Colloquium on Peace Problems is organized.
December
9   Hiroshima Association of Medical Sciences and the ABCC sponsor
     a meeting for research reports on A-bomb effects.

1952

January
17   Hiroshima City initiates survey of A-bomb damages with city-ap-
     pointed researchers visiting individual homes.
February
16–17 Fourth assembly of Hiroshima Association of Medical Sciences;
      thirteen research reports on A-bomb diseases are presented.

April

1   Public welfare officials initiate survey of A-bomb damages in Nagasaki.

3   Fourteenth assembly of Japan Hematology Society sponsors symposium on "Radiation and A-bomb Injuries" (Osaka).

4   Class for A-bomb children established in Nagasaki's Shiroyama Primary School.

30   Relief law for war dead and injured is enacted (effective retroactive to 1 April).

June

10   Nine "A-bomb maidens" from Hiroshima go to Tokyo for remedial surgery (three go from Nagasaki on 2 January 1953).

July

1–15 Hiroshima City Association of Surgeons gives free examinations to A-bomb victims.

August

6   Hiroshima City dedicates Memorial Cenotaph to the A-bomb dead. Weekly magazine *Asahi Gurafu* [Asahi graphic] features photographs of Hiroshima-Nagasaki A-bomb damages.

9   Memorial services for A-bomb dead and peace ceremony in Nagasaki.

10   Inaugural ceremony for Hiroshima A-bomb Victims Association.

September

18   Nagasaki Medical University's surgical department gives free examinations to A-bomb victims.

28   Science Council of Japan's A-bomb damages research team (formed in May) holds first reports session (Hiroshima).

October

3   Britain conducts first atomic test on Monte Bello Islands, off the west coast of Australia.

22   A-bomb victim Yoshitaka Mimura relates horrors of atomic bombing to Science Council of Japan (13th assembly).

November

1   The United States explodes first hydrogen bomb device on Eniwetok Atoll, Marshall Islands, Pacific Ocean.

3–6 World Association of World Federalists holds Asian Conference in Hiroshima.

1953

January

13   Hiroshima A-bomb Casualty Council founded (incorporated as foundation on 28 April 1956).

February

21   University Group to Protect Peace and Learning founded in Hiroshima.

22   Hiroshima Society for the Care of Children formed.

May

14   Nagasaki A-bomb Casualty Council founded (incorporated as foundation on 20 September 1958).

23   Nobuo Kusano lectures on A-bomb diseases at International Medical Association conference in Vienna.

June

20   Nagasaki A-bomb Maidens Association formed.

August

1–10   "Help the A-bomb Victims" campaign co-sponsored by Central Community Chest of Japan and Nihon Hōsō Kyōkai (NHK), or Japan Broadcasting Corporation.

3   Lower House of National Diet adopts petition for medical relief to A-bomb victims, presented by mayors of Hiroshima and Nagasaki.

6   Upper House of National Diet adopts this petition.

10   Première showing of movie *Hiroshima* in Tokyo, Hiroshima, and Nagasaki.

12   Soviet Russia tests its first hydrogen bomb, in Central Asia.

November

12   National Institute of Health establishes A-bomb Aftereffects Research Council; first session held.

December

8   President Eisenhower addresses Eighth United Nations General Assembly on peaceful uses of atomic energy.

1954

February

5   Research teams of the ABCC and Science Council of Japan hold joint consultation on A-bomb damages (Tokyo University; till 6 February).

March

1   The United States conducts H-bomb test at Bikini Atoll, Marshall Islands. Micronesian islanders sustain radiation injuries; Japanese tuna fishing vessel *Fukuryū Maru No. 5* is covered with "ashes of death" and returns (14 March) to home port of Yaizu.

27   Yaizu municipal assembly passes resolution against use of atomic weapons.

April

1   Lower House of National Diet adopts resolution for "international control of atomic energy."

5   Upper House adopts resolution for "international control of atomic energy and banning of atomic bombs."

6   Masao Tsuzuki presents report on Hiroshima-Nagasaki-Bikini damages to meeting of Red Cross International Experts Commission in Geneva (till 13 April).

7   Economic Stabilization Board publishes comprehensive report (dated 11 February 1949) on Pacific War damages sustained by Japan.

23 Science Council of Japan (17th assembly) issues "demands for open, democratic, and independent principles concerning research and use of atomic energy" and for "abolition of atomic weapons and establishment of effective international control of atomic energy."

During April and May, various political and scientific bodies issue a series of resolutions and declarations calling for a ban on atomic weapons and nuclear testing.

May

1   Special Research Committee on Radiation Effects is set up by Science Council of Japan.

9   Suginami Council for signature campaign against hydrogen bomb is formed; "Suginami Appeal" is issued.

15 Hiroshima Citizens' Conference against Atomic and Hydrogen Bombs held.

25 Hiroshima municipal assembly passes resolution for government payment of A-bomb victims' medical costs, and another resolution against atomic and hydrogen bombs.

28 Hiroshima prefectural assembly adopts resolutions against atomic weapons and for international control of atomic energy. (Many local governments pass similar resolutions about this time.)

June

20 Hiroshima A-bomb Casualty Council sponsors symposium; Hiroshima doctors present research reports on clinical care of A-bomb patients.

July

2   Hiroshima Prefecture Citizens Movement against Atomic and Hydrogen Bombs establishes headquarters.

August

8   National council for signature campaign against atomic and hydrogen bombs holds inaugural rally (Tokyo).

27 Representatives from Hiroshima and Nagasaki hold consultation on medical costs for A-bomb victims (Nagasaki).

October

11 Ministry of Health and Welfare establishes Liaison Council for Investigation of A-bomb Damages. Hiroshima-Nagasaki branch holds first meeting on 11 November in Hiroshima (second meeting 5 February 1955 in Nagasaki).

November

15–19 Joint Japan–U.S. conference on use and effects of radioactive materials.

November 25
to 3 December Exhibit of Hiroshima-Nagasaki A-bomb materials held at Japanese Red Cross Society headquarters in Tokyo.

1955

February

11　Nagasaki International Cultural Hall completed.

April

25　Three Hiroshima A-bomb victims file suit in Tokyo District Court against the Japanese government, claiming compensation for A-bomb damages. (The court ruled, on 7 December 1963, that dropping the atomic bombs violated international law.)

May

5　Twenty-five "A-bomb maidens" leave for the United States to receive treatment.

May 30–
11 June　World Medical Association sponsors scientific consultations on radiation effects in Tokyo, Osaka, Kyoto, Hiroshima, and Nagasaki.

July

9　Peace declaration issued by Bertrand Russell and Albert Einstein (London).

August

6–8　First World Conference against Atomic and Hydrogen Bombs held in Hiroshima.

7–8　Nagasaki Prefecture peace education seminar held in Nagasaki.

9　Nagasaki Peace Memorial Statue dedicated.

24　Hiroshima Peace Memorial Museum (A-bomb museum) opened.

September

19　Japan Council against Atomic and Hydrogen Bombs (Nihon Gensuikyō) formed.

October

1　Nagasaki A-bomb Youth Association formed.

9　Youth Section (Ayumi group) formed within Hiroshima Society for the Care of Children.

November

11　Committee of Seven to Appeal for World Peace formed (Tokyo).

26　A-bomb victims relief committee formed within Hiroshima Council against Atomic and Hydrogen Bombs.

December

19　Basic Law on Atomic Energy enacted; Atomic Energy Commission established.

1956

February

28　Seiichi Nakano publishes *Genbaku to Hiroshima* [The Atomic Bomb and Hiroshima] as vol. I of *Shinshū Hiroshima-shi Shi* [History of Hiroshima City, New Edition].

May
3   Nagasaki A-bomb Youth and Maidens Association organized (merger of former A-bomb Youth and A-bomb Maidens associations).
27 Inaugural meeting of Hiroshima Prefecture Council of A-bomb Victims Associations.

June
23 Nagasaki A-bomb Victims Council formed.

August
8   Nagasaki A-bomb Youth and Maidens Association publishes *Mō Iya Da—Genbaku no Ikite Iru Shōnintachi* [We've Had Enough—Living A-bomb Witnesses].
9   Second World Conference against Atomic and Hydrogen Bombs held in Nagasaki.
10 Japan Confederation of A- and H-bomb Sufferers Organizations holds inaugural assembly in Nagasaki.
20 Japan Society for the Promotion of Science publishes *Research in the Effects and Influences of the Nuclear Bomb Test Explosions.*

September
20 Hiroshima A-bomb Hospital opens.

December
22 Lower House of National Diet passes resolution for medical treatment for the A-bomb injured.

1957

February
17 Hiroshima Prefecture Society for Sacrificed Students (in wartime mobilization) formed.

March
31 A-bomb Victims Medical Care Law promulgated (effective 1 April).

April
1   Japan Genetics Society and Japan Anthropogenetics Society issue joint warning against harmful effects of radioactivity on genetics.
26 24th assembly of Science Council of Japan issues "Appeal to scientists of the world to stop testing of atomic and hydrogen bombs."

May
15 Britain sets off its first hydrogen bomb, at Christmas Island.

July
1   Japan's Science and Technology Agency founds National Institute of Radiological Sciences.
7–10 International Scientists Council meets in Pugwash, Canada.

October Nagasaki Peace Conference formed.

November
10 Nagasaki Prefecture Society for Sacrificed Students formed.

1958

March	
31	The Supreme Soviet decides to stop nuclear testing.
April	
1	Hiroshima University establishes Institute for Nuclear Radiation Research in its medical school.
May	
5	Statue of the A-bomb Children unveiled in Hiroshima.
28	Nagasaki A-bomb Hospital opens.
June	
13	U.N. Scientific Commission on Effects of Atomic Radiation (established 3 December 1955) adopts report for presentation to U.N. General Assembly.
August	
21	National Institute of Health and the ABCC sign agreement for survey of deaths among A-bomb victims.
22	The United States and Britain announce a one-year moratorium on nuclear tests beginning 31 October.
October 31 to 19 December	The United States, Britain, and the Soviet Union hold consultations on nuclear test moratorium in Geneva.

1959

March	The ABCC decides to publish its findings in the English and the Japanese languages.
June	
13–14	Research Society for Late-effects of Atomic Bomb meets in Hiroshima.
July	
2	Japan A-bomb Aftereffects Research Society founded.
September	
	Hiroshima-Nagasaki strategy committee for revision of A-bomb Victims Medical Care Law formed.
November	
20	U.N. General Assembly approves 82-nation resolution for general and complete disarmament.

1960

January	
19	Japan–U.S. Security Treaty signed in Washington (effective 23 June).

February

13   France conducts its first A-bomb test in the Sahara Desert.

May

7   The United States announces resumption of underground nuclear testing.

July

5   Nagasaki Research Society for Late-effects of Atomic Bombs initiated (second seminar held 19–20 November in Nagasaki).

August

1   "Special A-bomb Victims" classification introduced in A-bomb Victims Medical Care Law; payments of medical care allowances authorized.

October

1   Hiroshima and Nagasaki prefectures carry out A-bomb victims survey in conjunction with national census.

4   U.S. Government contributes $300,000 each to Hiroshima and Nagasaki universities for research on A-bomb damage.

1961

April

1   Hiroshima University establishes Research Institute for Nuclear Medicine and Biology.

July

31   Expert Committee of Japan Council against Atomic and Hydrogen Bombs publishes *Gensuibaku Hakusho—Kakusareta Shinjitsu* [White Paper on Atomic and Hydrogen Bombs—the Hidden Truth].

August

12   Seventh World Conference against Atomic and Hydrogen Bombs opens in Tokyo.

14   Socialist Party of Japan, General Council of Trade Unions in Japan (Sōhyō), National Federation of Regional Women's Organizations, and Japan Youth Council issue joint declaration of nonconfidence in staff of Japan Council against Atomic and Hydrogen Bombs.

30   Soviet Russia announces resumption of nuclear testing.

November

15   National Council for Peace and against Nuclear Weapons (Kakkin Kaigi) organized.

1962

March

31   A-bomb Victims Medical Care Law revised (eligibility for "Special A-bomb Victims" extended from 2 to 3 kilometers from hypocenter at bombing times).

April

1   Atomic Disease Institute established in Nagasaki University medical school.

May

7–9   Scientists consultation held in Kyoto.

August

4–6   Eighth World Conference against Atomic and Hydrogen Bombs in Tokyo; conference ends as opinions split over protest against Soviet nuclear tests.

October

22   The United States announces blockade of Cuba in response to Soviet missile sites built there.

1963

March

1   Nationwide gathering planned for ninth anniversary of Bikini test fails to open due to conflicting opinions.

July

15   The United States, Britain, and the Soviet Union agree upon treaty banning nuclear tests in the atmosphere, in outer space, and under water. (Limited Nuclear Test-ban Treaty). Formal signing completed 5 August; effective from 10 October.

August

5   Ninth World Conference against Atomic and Hydrogen Bombs in Hiroshima, boycotted by Socialist Party of Japan and General Council of Trade Unions, ends in split.

14   Japan signs limited ban on nuclear testing (ratified 15 June 1964).

October

17   Hiroshima-Auschwitz Committee formed in Hiroshima.

1964

July

12   League of Okinawan A-bomb Victims formed.

August

3   Separate world conferences against atomic and hydrogen bombs held in Kyoto and Hiroshima; later separate organizations, Japan Council against Atomic and Hydrogen Bombs (Gensuikyō) and Japan Congress against Atomic and Hydrogen Bombs (Gensuikin), are formed.

5   At Hiroshima conference against nuclear weapons sponsored by Three-Prefecture Liaison Conference, Toshihiro Kanai proposes that a white paper on nuclear damages be produced for presentation to the United Nations.

——   Radiation Research Center of South Korea's Atomic Energy Agency undertakes survey of Korean A-bomb victims; by following year lists 203 names (164 from Hiroshima, 39 from Nagasaki).

October

3   Peace Problems Research Group (Danwakai) of university persons from Hiroshima, Yamaguchi, and Okayama prefectures proposes a white paper on nuclear damages.

16   The People's Republic of China conducts a test explosion of its first atomic bomb (western province).

November

Hiroshima City issues A-bomb health book to a Korean A-bomb victim who entered Japan on a tourist visa.

1965

February

7   In Vietnam War, the United States begins bombing North Vietnam.

March

16   Japan–U.S. consensus reached on medical care of A-bomb victims in Okinawa (still under U.S. administration).

April

6   Okinawan A-bomb victims given medical examinations by medical teams from Nagasaki (8–20 April) and Hiroshima (17–24 April).

June

27   Kinoko-kai (Mushroom Club) formed by parents of microcephalic children who were fetal victims.

August

5   Five representatives of university consultation group (established 3 October 1964) and Committee of Seven to Appeal for World Peace have interview with Prime Minister Eisaku Satō to petition for a white paper on A-bomb damages.

——   Friends of Hiroshima-Nagasaki A-bomb Victims formed in Los Angeles.

October

16–17 Seventh Assembly of Research Society for Late-effects of Atomic Bombs held in Hiroshima, sums up twenty years of findings.

November

1   Ministry of Health and Welfare undertakes the Japanese government's first nationwide survey of actual conditions of A-bomb victims.

December

7   Committee for promotion of an A-bomb damages white paper formed in Tokyo.

23   Hiroshima citizens' group for a ban on atomic and hydrogen bombs holds first consultation (group's name changed to "Citizens' Group to Promote an A-bomb and H-bomb Damages White Paper" at third consultation on 8 February 1966).

1966

April
9   Nagasaki citizens' group formed to promote an A-bomb damages
     white paper; activities begin 1 August 1968.
July
10   Hiroshima society for the care of fetal victims and second-genera-
     tion A-bomb victims formed.
11   Hiroshima municipal assembly votes in favor of permanent preser-
     vation of A-bomb Dome.
August
4–5 Scientists against atomic and hydrogen bombs hold first meeting
     in Hiroshima.
October Japan Confederation of A-bomb and H-bomb Sufferers Organiza-
     tions issues "Crane pamphlet" appealing for relief law recognizing
     special needs of A-bomb victims.

1967

February
11   Founding group of Korean A-bomb Victims Relief Association
     meets in Seoul.
June
1   Specimen Center set up in Hiroshima University's Research Insti-
     tute for Nuclear Medicine and Biology.
12   Committee of Seven to Appeal for World Peace meets with Prime
     Minister Satō to present petition for A-bomb victims relief law.
     (Similar petition jointly signed by Hiroshima and Nagasaki gover-
     nors and mayors presented on 2 September.)
17   The People's Republic of China conducts its first hydrogen bomb
     test.
18   Friends of A-bomb Health-book Holders formed in Nagasaki.
October
13   Hiroshima Peace Culture Center opened.
23   U.N. Secretary-General U Thant issues experts' report on nuclear
     weapons.
November
1   Japanese Ministry of Health and Welfare publishes report of its
     1965 survey on A-bomb victims.
9   A-bomb documentary films confiscated by the United States are
     returned to Japan.
——   Hiroshima-Nagasaki group formed to promote A-bomb victims
     relief.
December
16   Symposium sponsored by A-bomb damages documentation sub-
     committee of the Science Council of Japan's Special Atomic Energy
     Committee.

1968

February
15   Research Group for Documentation of A-bomb Damages founded in Hiroshima.

March
20   Hiroshima University's Research Institute for Nuclear Medicine and Biology initiates preparatory survey for map reconstruction of Nakajima district in central bombed area of Hiroshima.

May
17   Science Council of Japan at 50th assembly recommends collection and preservation of A-bomb records before most are lost.
20   A-bomb Victims Special Measures Law is passed (effective 1 September).

July
1   The United States, Britain, and the Soviet Union sign nuclear non-proliferation treaty.

August
24   France conducts its first hydrogen bomb test in the South Pacific.

October
26   Japan–South Korea A-bomb Victims Relief Council is established in Hiroshima.

1969

March
25   Hiroshima Prefecture A-bomb Teachers Association formed.
31   Hiroshima City forms committee for the Map Restoration of A-bombed Areas.

April
10   Governor Ryōkichi Minobe of Tokyo calls for preservation of *Fukuryū Maru No. 5* fishing vessel.

1970

February
1   A-bomb testimonial society formed in Nagasaki.
3   Japan signs nuclear nonproliferation treaty (ratified on 8 June 1976).

May
16   Nagasaki City Hibakusha Teachers Association formed.

June
26   Map reconstruction started for Matsuyama district in Nagasaki's central bombed area.

August
9   Nagasaki Prefecture Hibakusha Teachers Association formed.

October
1   A-bomb Victims Medical Care Law revised to include persons who were in "black rain" fallout areas.

November 29–
2 December   Hiroshima conference on theme "Conditions for peace in the nuclear age."

1971

January
1   Nagasaki City establishes office for reconstruction surveys of A-bomb damage. (Council for this purpose formed 26 March.)

April
16   Emperor and empress pay respects at Hiroshima's Peace Memorial Cenotaph.

June
17   Agreement for reversion of Okinawa to Japanese administration is signed (effective 15 May 1972).

July
31   National Federation of A-bomb Youth Associations formed in Hiroshima.

August
6   Memorial ceremonies for 26th anniversary of atomic bombing held in Hiroshima; Prime Minister Satō attends.

September
20   Medical team sponsored by Hiroshima citizens' and antinuclear groups leaves for South Korea to give examinations to Korean A-bomb victims.

October
13   American A-bomb Victims Association formed.
17   National Liaison Council of A-bomb Teachers Associations formed.

November
9   Science Council of Japan at 59th assembly approves resolutions calling for "establishment of an A-bomb damage documentation center" and "basic surveys of A-bomb damage records."

December
13   Survey team (sponsored by Japan Congress against Atomic and Hydrogen Bombs) to study H-bomb test damages in Micronesia is denied entry into island zone.

1972

January
1   Hiroshima City undertakes survey of A-bomb orphaned elderly.

March

6   Society for youth and second-generation A-bomb victims formed in Nagasaki.

June

1   Hiroshima Institute for Peace Education opens.

24   Nagasaki mayor calls for "memorial week" (10 days) in honor of A-bomb dead and world peace.

July

2   Japan Confederation of A-bomb and H-bomb Sufferers Organizations initiates movement to search for witnesses on behalf of health-book applicants who have no one to testify that they are A-bomb victims (see page 398).

August

5   Hiroshi Maki, associate director of the ABCC, arrives in Los Angeles to console and survey A-bomb victims residing in the United States.

October

National Liaison Council for War Dead is formed. (First meeting held August 1974 in Nagoya.)

November

1   Nagasaki Prefecture/City undertake basic survey of A-bomb victims and families.

1973

January

1   Hiroshima Prefecture/City carry out first phase of survey of A-bomb victims and families. (Second phase, 1 December; third, 17 September 1974.)

April

2   Japan Confederation of A-bomb and H-bomb Sufferers Organizations draws up petition for A-bomb victims relief law.

May

9   Ministry of Foreign Affairs holds ceremony for return of Hiroshima-Nagasaki A-bomb records confiscated by the United States.

17   A-bomb teacher Akira Ishida appeals to Hiroshima District Court, seeking certification of cataracts as A-bomb injury. (Court rules in Ishida's favor on 27 July 1976.)

August

8   First "Evening for considering the atomic bomb and science, education, and culture" is held in Nagasaki.

25   Ministry of Health and Welfare sets objectives for survey of second-generation victims at consultation (in Nagasaki) with prefectural and municipal authorities of Hiroshima and Nagasaki.

October

1   Ministry of Health and Welfare abolishes distinction between "special" and "ordinary" A-bomb health-book holders.

13–14   First national symposium on peace education held in Hiroshima.

1974

March

29 Four opposition parties present A-bomb victims relief bill to National Diet (voted down 21 May).

April

11 Hiroshima University's Research Institute for Nuclear Medicine and Biology establishes its Medical Records and Specimens Center.

May

16 India conducts its first A-bomb test in Rajasthan state, in northwest India.

June

2 Japan Peace Education Research Council formed.

September

1 Radiation leak occurs during inaugural run of Japan's nuclear-powered ship *Mutsu*.

1975

April

1 Hiroshima and Nagasaki hold opening ceremonies for their respective Radiation Effects Research Foundation facilities (reorganizations of former ABCC facilities in each city).

May

14 Scientific Data Center of Atomic Bomb Disaster established in Nagasaki University's medical school.

July

12–13 Scientists Forum in Tokyo appeals for ban on nuclear weapons.

August

1–5 World Peace Education Conference held at Wilmington College, Ohio, under theme of "Hiroshima after Thirty Years: A Call to World Community."

5 Hiroshima and Nagasaki enter into "Peace Culture Cities Covenant" (Hiroshima).

28 25th Pugwash Conference held in Kyoto (till 1 September).

September

1 Ministry of Health and Welfare undertakes second nationwide survey of A-bomb victims' actual conditions.

December

8 National representatives group appeals to U.N. Secretary-General Kurt Waldheim to promote international agreement for total ban on nuclear weapons.

1976

June
10   Exhibition hall for *Fukuryū Maru No. 5* fishing vessel completed at Tokyo's Yume no Shima.*

August
6   Prime Minister Takeo Miki attends Hiroshima's peace memorial ceremony.

9   Prime Minister Takeo Miki attends Nagasaki's peace memorial ceremony.

October
13–15 National representatives group to appeal for total nuclear bomb ban visits United Nations and presents "An Introductory Report on the Damage and Aftereffects of the Atomic Bombings of Hiroshima and Nagasaki" to U.N. Secretary-General Kurt Waldheim.

December
1   Mayors of Hiroshima and Nagasaki meet with U.N. Secretary-General Kurt Waldheim to present petition for "Total Abolition of Nuclear Weapons and General and Complete Disarmament."

1977

March   Society formed to present a pictorial record of the atomic destruction to children of the world.

May
19   Ichirō Moritaki, head of Gensuikin, and Nobuo Kusano, head of Gensuikyō, reach consensus on reunification of movements against atomic and hydrogen bombs within a year.

July
21   Nongovernmental organizations (NGO) sponsor international investigation of A-bomb problems (Tokyo, Hiroshima, Nagasaki).

July 21
to 2 August   NGO Symposium on Damage and Aftereffects of the Atomic Bombing of Hiroshima and Nagasaki.

August
3–6   Unified World Conference against Atomic and Hydrogen Bombs held in Hiroshima.

6   H. S. Amerasinghe, President of 31st U.N. General Assembly, participates in Hiroshima peace memorial ceremony.

9   Amerasinghe participates in Nagasaki peace memorial ceremony.

* Yume no Shima, or "Dream Island," is a flat area located in Kōtō Ward, Tokyo. It is 1.2 kilometers from east to west and 0.8 kilometers from north to south. The land was reclaimed from the sea with war debris, rubbish, household refuse, garbage, and the like.

1978

February 27
to 2 March — NGO International Disarmament Conference held in Geneva.

May 23
to 28 June — U.N. Special Session on Disarmament held in New York. Mayors of Hiroshima and Nagasaki attend to appeal for total abolition of nuclear weapons. Exhibit of Hiroshima-Nagasaki A-bomb photographs held in U.N. headquarters (23 May–30 June).

August
1 — World conference for total ban on nuclear weapons and relief for A-bomb victims held in Tokyo (1–2 August), Hiroshima (5–6 August), and Nagasaki (9 August). (This was the first unified conference in Nagasaki in fifteen years.)

October
24–30 — U.N. Disarmament Week.

December
16 — 33rd U.N. General Assembly adopts resolution against introduction of nuclear weapons into territories of nonnuclear nations.

22 — First meeting of comprehensive seminar on A-bomb problems held in Hiroshima.

Postscript

When the mayors of Hiroshima and Nagasaki visited the United Nations in 1976, bearing a petition for "total abolition of nuclear weapons" and "general and complete disarmament," they urged that body to do all in its power to avoid repetition of the Hiroshima-Nagasaki holocausts. The petition was drafted by a committee (Seiji Imahori, chairman; Tatsuichirō Akizuki, Tōmin Harada, vice-chairmen*) that took pains to sum up the broad range of scientifically confirmed data on the atomic bomb damages. The original text was presented to the U.N. Secretary-General, and the contents were distributed in booklet form by the two cities to many concerned people. But nothing was prepared at the time for wider public distribution. From the mayors' United Nations visit was born, therefore, a plan to compile into a single volume all available scientific findings on atomic bomb damages in order to pass on to present and future generations the lessons that so clearly necessitate the eradication of nuclear weapons and the establishment of peace. Through the efforts of Seiji Imahori, this plan began to take concrete form in the summer of 1977.

The two cities entrusted the compilation responsibilities to three editors—Soichi Iijima, Seiji Imahori, and Kanesaburo Gushima—who met repeatedly from September 1977 to determine basic policy, the nature and scope of the contents, and a production schedule. Thirty-four specialists in the fields of physics, medicine, social sciences, and the humanities were selected to write the initial basic sections. The selected authors in the three disciplinary areas, along with the three editors, were (in alphabetical order):

MATTERS RELATED TO THE PHYSICAL SCIENCES:

Tadashi Hashizume   Naomi Shohno
Takatoshi Okabayashi   Kenji Takeshita
Shunzō Okajima

* Other members of the committee were Sadamu Ishida, Michito Ichimaru, Shunzō Okajima, Naomasa Okamoto, Hachirō Shimauchi, Naomi Shohno, Issei Nishimori, Shigenobu Miyagi, and Minoru Yuzaki.

MATTERS RELATED TO MEDICAL SCIENCES:

Akio A. Awa   Masuho Konuma
Kanji Chōshi   Minoru Kurihara
Tsugio Dodo   Issei Nishimori
Atsushi Fujiwara   Naomasa Okamoto
Kaichi Fukazawa   Takeshi Ohkita
Fumio Hirose   Hisao Sawada
Michito Ichimaru   Akira Tabuchi
Soichi Iijima (ed.)   Shōji Tokuoka
Hiroo Kato   Tsutomu Yamamoto
Sadahisa Kawamoto

MATTERS RELATED TO SOCIAL SCIENCES AND HUMANITIES:

Kazunari Abe   Masaaki Ogawa
Masayoshi Chūbachi   Kiyoshi Shimizu
Toshihiko Fujii   Toshio Tochigi
Kanesaburo Gushima (ed.)   Satoru Ubuki
Seiji Imahori (ed.)   Shigeru Yamate
Takeshi Itō   Minoru Yuzaki
Sadao Kamata

Each of these three groups held a number of consultations. From spring to fall in 1978 the editors each went over a share of the completed manuscripts and, in the interests of a coordinated whole, made a variety of changes before agreeing on the final form of all manuscripts. Indeed, rewriting was requested in a number of cases, and in not a few instances the editors themselves rewrote passages. This book, then, is not simply a collection of essays; it is, rather, a single work cooperatively produced; and for this reason we have had to rely on the sympathetic understanding of our collaborators. In addition to the staff of Iwanami Shoten (publishers of the original Japanese edition), the editorial work has benefitted particularly from the devoted support of Takeshi Ohkita, Minoru Yuzaki, Naomi Shohno, Takeshi Itō, Kenji Takeshita, and Issei Nishimori. On matters related to content, valuable assistance was received from Hidetsugu Aihara, Tatsuichirō Akizuki, Nobuo Kusano, Yoshimasa Matsusaka, Gorō Ōuchi, Tetsurō Shimamine, Raisuke Shirabe, and Toshiyuki Toyoda. We wish to record here our deep appreciation to all who helped in so many ways. But, as the preceding outline of the editorial process indicates, final responsibility for the content of this book rests entirely with the three editors.

From the time of the bombings to the present a considerable body of surveys, research, and documents has accumulated. Behind this cumulative literature lies the experiences of the countless persons, from which this book too has greatly benefitted. Directly quoted references are appropriately indicated, but significant reports and essays that have since been superseded by later research have been omitted. The authors and editors have endeavored to check all relevant sources and records but, due to time limits, have not necessarily succeeded in every instance. Moreover, in certain fields the needed references were so woefully inadequate that certain planned sections had to be reluctantly canceled. Treatment of these excluded topics must await future research and analysis.

In the compilation of this work, the writings, records, and photographs of Masao Tsuzuki (The Tsuzuki Collection), kindly offered by Masakazu Tsuzuki, were of particular value in grasping the medical situation immediately after the bombings. A rich array of articles, records, and specimens was shared by over a hundred persons, including Tatsuichirō Akizuki, Nobuo Kusano, Kikuo Nishida, Takuya Sasaki, Tetsu-rō Shimamine, and Raisuke Shirabe. The A-bomb Damages Documentation Center at Hiroshima University's Research Institute for Nuclear Medicine and Biology and Nagasaki University's Scientific Data Center of Atomic Bomb Disaster (medical school), Hiroshima Peace Memorial Hall, and Nagasaki International Cultural Hall were all most helpful in providing access to their records and materials. For use of photographs of actual conditions of the bombed areas, we have, wherever possible, checked sources and credited the original photographers, and received their consent for use of the photographs. In many cases we received kind permission to make prints from the carefully preserved original negatives. We could not, however, determine the photographer in all cases; and, thus, for any omissions, unintended as they are, the editors apologize. Many of the tables were used by permission from the sources cited in such cases. Takuya Sasaki and Masanobu Tsutsumi worked hard and long to produce most of the maps; a few maps were researched and drawn by Michio Shimomura. As much as possible we have relied on records and documents preserved in Japan. In cases where original documents have been lost or were not accessible in Japan, we have relied on the collection returned to Japan by the United States; such instances are noted by the number (#) sign. Even for references among the materials returned by the United States, our policy was to acknowledge original authorship and identity when known. To all the persons, groups, and organizations who cooperated with this effort, we express our warm gratitude.

That the editorial committee members, all of whom hold positions with heavy responsibilities, could accomplish the tasks of compilation in a two-year period was due, above all, to the unfailing support of the cities of Hiroshima and Nagasaki. Mayor Takeshi Araki of Hiroshima, former Mayor Yoshitake Morotani of Nagasaki, and his successor, current Mayor Hitoshi Motoshima, all had a keen appreciation, as heads of their municipal governments, of the importance of a scholarly work of this nature and gave us unstinting encouragement. The staffs of Hiroshima Peace Memorial Hall (Yasutake Hirayama, director) and Nagasaki International Cultural Hall (Kō Hayashida, director) supported the editorial process in all needs, great and small. Likewise, Tōru Midorikawa, Ryōsuke Yasue, Shigeki Kobayashi, Hiromi Katayama, and others at Iwanami Shoten were literally devoted to the successful completion of this venture. The editorial committee is most grateful to all these supporters and co-workers.

The people of Hiroshima and Nagasaki have a profound understanding that the realization of a world without nuclear weapons is absolutely necessary if the human race is to avoid irretrievable destruction. This volume was conceived as one instrument for making that understanding the common possession of people the world over. Working from that premise, the editorial committee has endeavored to analyze objectively the realities of the atomic bomb damages sustained by Hiroshima and Nagasaki and then to convey a clear and comprehensive description of those realities. Such a comprehensive view provides a new point of departure for rethinking the implications of the atomic bomb for all mankind. In that sense, this book, by accurately informing people of the historically unprecedented experiences of suffering and loss wrought by the atomic bombings, should provoke unprecedented vigorous efforts on behalf of peace. Whether we have succeeded in the enormous responsibilities of producing the work we intended, is a question we humbly submit to the opinion of a worldwide audience. In any event, we have done our best to bring clearly and forcefully into focus the efforts of the A-bomb victims, of the citizens of Hiroshima and Nagasaki, and of all concerned people in this nation. Beyond that, we can only hope that the people's own passion for peace will overcome our inadequacies and open up an expanding way toward a peaceful world without nuclear weapons.

The Committee for the
Compilation of Materials on
Damage Caused by the Atomic Bombs
in Hiroshima and Nagasaki

Soichi Iijima
Seiji Imahori
Kanesaburo Gushima

2 June 1979

BIBLIOGRAPHY

Abbreviations

ABCC TR   Atomic Bomb Casualty Commission Technical Report.

CRIABC   Science Council of Japan. 1953. *Genshibakudan Saigai Chōsa Hōko-kushū* [Collection of the Reports on the Investigation of the Atomic Bomb Casualties], 2 vols. Nihon Gakujutsu Shinkōkai, Tokyo. In Japanese.

FMN   Shirabe, R., ed. 1968–74. *Wasurenagusa* [Forget-me-not], vols. I–V. Kyū Nagasaki Ikadaigaku Genbaku Gisei Gakuto Izokukai, Nagasaki. In Japanese.

HAMCH   Hiroshima A-bomb Medical Care History Editorial Committee. 1961. *Hiroshima Genbaku Iryōshi* [Hiroshima A-bomb Medical Care History]. Hiroshima Genbaku Shōgai Taisaku Kyōgikai, Hiroshima. In Japanese.

HH   Japan Hematological Society. 1964, 1962. *Nippon Ketsuekigaku Zensho* [Handbook of Hematology], vol. III, vol. V. Maruzen, Tokyo. In Japanese.

JNIH   Japan National Institute of Health.

ORNL TM   Oak Ridge National Laboratory Technical Manuscript.

PSH   Japan Hematological Society. 1953. *Ketsuekigaku Tōgikai Hōkoku* [Proceedings of the Symposium on Hematology], no. 5. Nagai Shoten, Osaka. In Japanese.

RERF TR   Radiation Effects Research Foundation Technical Report.

RHAWD   Hiroshima Shiyakusho [Hiroshima City Office]. 1971. *Hiroshima Genbaku Sensaishi* [Record of the Hiroshima A-bomb War Disaster], 5 vols. In Japanese.

RNAWD   Nagasaki Shiyakusho [Nagasaki City Office]. 1977. *Nagasaki Genbaku Sensaishi* [Record of the Nagasaki A-bomb War Disaster]. Nagasaki Kokusai Bunka Kaikan [Nagasaki International Cultural Hall], Nagasaki. In Japanese.

SRIABC   Science Council of Japan. 1951. *Genshibakudan Saigai Chōsa Hōko-kusho* [Summary Report of the Investigation of the Atomic Bomb Casualties]. Nihon Gakujutsu Shinkōkai, Tokyo. In Japanese.

USAEC NYO United States Atomic Energy Commission, New York Office.

References

*A-bomb Aftereffects Research Council (chaired by Rokuzō Kobayashi). 1954. "Guide to treatment of late A-bomb disturbances," *The Journal of Japan Medical Association* 32:188.

*A-bomb Aftereffects Research Council (chaired by Rokuzō Kobayashi). 1955. "Guide to treatment of late A-bomb disturbances," *The Journal of Japan Medical Association* 34:676.

*Aihara, H. 1978. Letter to Dr. Masayoshi Chūbachi (dated December 1978). Results of studies based on: Relief Squad dispatched by Hario Marine Corps. 1973; and K. Kenmyō 1975.

*Air Defense Law. 1937. Law no. 47.

*Akazaki, K. 1969. "Comparative studies on the prevalence of latent prostate cancer among Japanese, American, and Colombian males. Director's report, 1968–1969." Nagoya Aichi Cancer Center Research Institute.

*Akizuki, T. 1966. *Nagasaki Genbakuki, Hibaku Ishi no Shōgen* [Document of A-bombed Nagasaki—testimony of A-bombed doctor]. Kōbundō, Tokyo. Translated into English and published privately in Nagasaki by K. Nagata, 1977.

Albright, E. C.; and Allday, E. C. 1967. "Thyroid carcinoma after radiation for adolescent acne vulgaris," *Journal of the American Medical Association* 199:280.

Allen, J. S. 1952. *Atomic Imperialism: The State, Monopoly and the Bomb.* International Publishers, New York.

Amano, S. 1956. "Studies on the pathological changes caused by the atomic bomb explosure in Hiroshima," in *Research in the Effects and Influences of the Nuclear Bomb Test Explosions,* vol. II. Japan Society for the Promotion of Science, Tokyo.

*Amano, S. 1964. "Pathological findings of atomic bomb exposure," in HH, vol. III.

Anderson, R. E. 1971. "Leukemia and related disorders," in "The delayed consequence of exposure to ionizing radiation: Pathology studies at the Atomic Bomb Casualty Commission, Hiroshima and Nagasaki" (symposium), *Human Pathology* 2:505.

Anderson, R. E.; Hoshino, T.; and Yamamoto, T. 1964. "Myelofibrosis with myeloid metaplasia in survivors of the atomic bomb in Hiroshima," *Annals of Internal Medicine* 60:1.

Anderson, R. E.; and Ishida, K. 1964. "Malignant lymphoma in survivors of the atomic bomb in Hiroshima," *Annals of Internal Medicine* 61:853.

*Andō, N. 1958. "Effects of the atomic bomb on physical and mental development of children," *Journal of the Hiroshima Medical Association* (original series) 6:951.

Angevine, D. M.; and Jablon, S. 1964. "Late radiation effects of neoplasia and other diseases in Japan," *Annals of the New York Academy of Science* 114:823.

*Aoki, K.; Yamada, J.; and Murakami, E. 1953. "Investigation report on damages to structure by the atomic bombs," CRIABC, vol. I.

*Arakatsu, B.; Kimura, K.; Shimizu, S.; Hanaya, K.; Ueda, R.; Ishiwari, R.; Takagi, I.; Kondō, S.; Takase, H.; Aoki, K.; Ishizaki, Y.; Hondō, E.; Nishikawa, Y.; Takai, S.; Hori, J.; and Murao, M. 1953. "Report on radiological investigation in Hiroshima City conducted for several days after the A-bomb explosion," in CRIABC, vol. I.

Arakawa, E. T. 1960. "Radiation dosimetry in Hiroshima and Nagasaki atomic-bomb survivors," *New England Journal of Medicine* 263:488.

Arakawa, E. T. 1962. "Residual radiation in Hiroshima and Nagasaki," ABCC TR 2–62.

*Arakawa, E. T.; and Nagaoka, S. 1959. "Determiniation of the burst point of the Hiroshima atomic bomb: Dosimetric significance," *Journal of the Hiroshima Medical Association* 12:1052.

*Arima, M. 1968. "Morphological abnormalities noted among those exposed in utero with A-bomb disturbances—especially in comparison with general feeble-minded patients," *Nagasaki Medical Journal* 43:873.

*Army Medical School, Provisional Tokyo First Army Hospital. 1953. "Medical investigation report on A-bomb casualty of Hiroshima," in CRIABC, vol. I.

Asahi Shimbun [Asahi Newspaper]. 1970a. *Nagasaki Idai Genshi-bakudan Kyūgo Hōkoku* [Nagasaki Medical University A-bomb Relief Activities Report]. Asahi Shimbunsha, Tokyo.

Asahi Shimbun. 1970b. *Genshi-bakudan Kyūgo Hōkoku* [Report of A-bomb Emergency Care]. Asahi Shimbunsha, Tokyo.

* An asterisk denotes that the text of a particular title is *only* in Japanese.

*Asahi Shimbun. 1978. Minryoku [Civilian Power], 1978 edition. Asahi Shimbunsha, Tokyo.
*Asahi Shimbun 1976. "Postwar history of forty-four pupils evacuated from the Hiroshima Fukuromachi Primary School in the A-bomb hypocenter area," 5 August 1976.
*Asayama, R.; and Tsukahara, I. 1955. "About atomic bomb cataract in Kyoto prefecture," Rinshō Ganka [Japanese Journal of Clinical Ophthalmology] 9:1137.
Atomic Bomb Casualty Commission (ABCC). 1961. Bibliography of Publications Concerning Effect of Nuclear Explosions, 1945–1960.
Atomic Bomb Casualty Commission (ABCC). 1947–75. "A general report on the ABCC–JNIH joint research program," ABCC, Hiroshima.
Atomic Bomb Casualty Commission (ABCC). 1958. "ABCC Annual Report for the Period 1 July 1957–30 June 1958," ABCC, Hiroshima.
Atomic Bomb Casualty Commission (ABCC). 1968. "Introduction of ABCC professional staff," Journal of Hiroshima Medical Association 21:1239.
*Atomic Bomb Monument Research Group (Ei Yokoyama, representative). 1978. Genbaku Monyumento Hibunshū [Collection of Inscriptions on the Atomic Bomb Monument]. Hiroshima Daigaku Bungakubu, Hiroshima.
*The Atomic Bomb Victims' Written Notes Editorial Committee. 1953. Genbaku ni Ikite— Genbaku Higaisha no Shuki [Life after the Atomic Bombing—Notes of Atomic Bomb Victims]. San-ichi Shobō, Tokyo.
Auxier, J. A. 1975. "A review of thirty years study of Hiroshima and Nagasaki atomic survivors. I. Dosimetry, A. Physical dose estimates for A-bomb survivors—Studies at Oak Ridge, U.S.A.," Journal of Radiation Research (Tokyo) 16(supplement):1.
Auxier, J. A.; Cheka, J. S.; Haywood, F. F.; Jones, T. D.; and Thorngate, J. H. 1966. "Free-field radiation dose distribution from the Hiroshima and Nagasaki bombings," Health Physics 12:425.
Awa, A. A. 1974. "Cytogenetic and oncogenetic effects of the ionizing radiations of the atomic bomb," in Chromosomes and Cancer, J. German ed., John Wiley & Sons, New York.
Awa, A. A. 1975a. "A review of thirty years study of Hiroshima and Nagasaki atomic bomb survivors. II. Biological effects, B. Genetic study. 2. Cytogenetic study," Journal of Radiation Research (Tokyo) 16(supplement):75.
Awa, A. A. 1975b. "A review of thirty years study of Hiroshima and Nagasaki atomic bomb survivors. II. Biological effects, G. chromosome aberrations in somatic cells," Journal of Radiation Research (Tokyo) 16(supplement):122.
*Awa, A. A. 1975c. "Genetic effects of atomic bomb irradiation, Iden [Heredity] 29:33.
*Awa, A. A. 1976. "Cytogenetic study of the offspring of atomic bomb survivors," Nagasaki Medical Journal 51:273.
Awa, A. A.; Neriishi, S.; Honda, T.; Yoshida, M. C.; Sofuni, T.; and Matsui, T. 1971. "Chromosome-aberration frequency in cultured blood-cells in relation to radiation dose of A-bomb survivors," Lancet 2:903.
Awa, A. A.; Sofuni, T.; Honda, T.; Itoh, M.; Neriishi, S.; and Otake, M. 1978. "Relationship between the radiation dose and chromosome aberrations in atomic bomb survivors of Hiroshima and Nagasaki," Journal of Radiation Research (Tokyo) 19:126.

*Bank of Japan, Statistics Bureau. 1964. Meiji Nijūnen-Shōwa Sanjūshichinen Oroshiuri Bukka Shisū [1887–1962 Wholesale Price Index]. Nihon Ginkō Tōkei Kyoku, Tokyo.
*Bean, M. A.; Yatani, R.; Liu, P. I.; Fukazawa, K.; Ashley, F. W.; and Fujita, S. 1974. "Prostatic carcinoma at autopsy in Hiroshima and Nagasaki," Journal of the Hiroshima Medical Association 27:720.
Beck, J. S. P.; and Meissner, W. A. 1946. "Radiation effects of the atomic bomb among the natives of Nagasaki, Kyushu," American Journal of Clinical Pathology 6:586.
Beck, J. S. P.; and Meissner, W. A. 1947. "Atomic bomb surface burns: Some clinical observations among prisoners of war rescued at Nagasaki, Kyushu," Journal of the Indiana Medical Association 40:515.
Beebe, G. W.; and Hamilton, H. B. 1975. "A review of thirty years study of Hiroshima and Nagasaki atomic bomb survivors. III. Future research and health surveillance, B.," Journal of Radiation Research (Tokyo) 16(supplement):149.
Beebe, G. W.; and Kato, H. 1975. "A review of thirty years study of Hiroshima and Nagasaki atomic bomb survivors: Cancers other than leukemia," Journal of Radiation Research (Tokyo) 16(supplement):97.

Beebe, G.W.; Kato, H.; and Land, C. E. 1970. "JNIH-ABCC life span study Hiroshima-Nagasaki, Report 5, Mortality and radiation dose, October 1950–September 1966," ABCC TR 11–70.

Beebe, G. W.; Kato, H.; and Land, C. E. 1977. "Life span study, Report 8, Mortality experience of atomic bomb survivors, 1950–74," RERF TR 1–77.

Beebe, G. W.; Yamamoto, T.; Matsumoto, Y. S.; and Gould, S. E. 1967. "ABCC-JNIH pathology studies, Hiroshima-Nagasaki, Report 2, October 1950–December 1965," ABCC TR 8–67.

Belsky, J. L.; and Blot, W. J. 1975. "Adult stature in relation to childhood exposure to the atomic bombs of Hiroshima and Nagasaki," *American Journal of Public Health* 65:489.

Belsky, J. L.; Tachikawa, K.; and Jablon, S. 1971. "ABCC-JNIH adult health study. Report 5. Results of the first five examination cycles, 1958–68, Hiroshima and Nagasaki," ABCC TR 9–71.

Belsky, J. L.; Tachikawa, K.; and Yamamoto, T. 1972. "Salivary gland tumors in atomic bomb survivors, Hiroshima-Nagasaki, 1957 to 1970," *Journal of the American Medical Association* 219:864.

Belsky, J. L.; Takeichi, N.; Yamamoto, T.; Cihak, R. W.; Hirose, F.; Ezaki, H.; Inoue, S.; and Blot, W. J. 1975. "Salivary gland neoplasms following atomic radiation. Additional cases and reanalysis of combined data in a fixed population 1957–70," *Cancer* 35:555.

Bizzozero, O. J.; Johnson, K. G.; and Ciocco, A. 1966. "Radiation-related leukemia in Hiroshima and Nagasaki, 1946–1964. Observations on type-specific leukemia, survivorship, and clinical behavior," *Annals of Internal Medicine* 66:522.

Bizzozero, O. J.; Johnson, K. G.; Ciocco, A.; Hoshino, T.; Itoga, T.; Toyoda, S.; and Kawasaki, S. 1966. "Distribution, incidence and appearance time of radiation-related leukemia in Hiroshima and Nagasaki, 1946–1964," *New England Journal of Medicine* 274:1095.

Blackett, P. M. S. 1948. *Military and Political Consequences of Atomic Energy.* Turnstile Press, London.

Block, M. A.; Miller, M. J.; and Horn, R. C. 1969. "Carcinoma of the thyroid after external radiation to the neck in adults," *American Journal of Surgery* 118:764.

Block, M. A.; and Tsuzuki, M. 1948. "Observations of burn scars sustained by atomic bomb survivors," *American Journal of Surgery* 75:417.

Bloom, A. D.; Neriishi, S.; and Archer, P. G. 1968. "Cytogenetics of the in-utero exposed of Hiroshima and Nagasaki," *Lancet* 2:10.

Bloom, A. D.; Neriishi, S.; Awa, A. A.; Honda, T.; and Archer, P. G. 1967. "Chromosome aberrations in leukocytes of older survivors of the atomic bombings of Hiroshima and Nagasaki," *Lancet* 2:802.

Bloom, A. D.; Neriishi, S.; Kamada, N.; Iseki, T.; and Keehn, R. J. 1966. "Cytogenetic investigation of survivors of the atomic bombings of Hiroshima and Nagasaki," *Lancet* 2:672.

Blot, W. J.; and Miller, R. W. 1972. "Mental retardation following in utero exposure to the atomic bombs of Hiroshima and Nagasaki," ABCC TR 36–72.

Blot, W. J.; Moriyama, I. M.; and Miller, R. W. 1972. "Reproductive potential of males exposed in utero or prepubertally to atomic radiation," ABCC TR 39–72.

Blot, W. J.; and Sawada, H. 1971. Fertility among female survivors of the atomic bombs, Hiroshima and Nagasaki," ABCC TR 26–71.

Blot, W. J.; Shimizu, Y.; Kato, H.; and Miller, R. W. 1975. "Frequency of marriage and live birth among survivors prenatally exposed to the atomic bomb," ABCC TR 2–75.

Boice, Jr., J. D.; and Monson, R. R. 1977. "Breast cancer in women after repeated fluoroscopic examinations of the chest," *Journal of the National Cancer Institute* 59:823.

Booth, C. 1892–97. Life and Labour of the People in London, etc. 10 vols. MacMillan & Co., London.

Boué, A.; and Boué, J. 1974. "Chromosome abnormalities and abortion," in *Physiology and Genetics of Reproduction,* part B, E. M. Contino and F. Fuchs, eds. Plenum Press, New York.

Brill, A. B.; Tomonaga, M.; and Heyssel, R. M. 1962. "Leukemia in man following exposure to ionizing radiation: A summary of the findings in Hiroshima and Nagasaki and a comparison with other human experience," *Annals of Internal Medicine* 56:590.

Brode, H. L. 1955. "Numerical solution of spherical blast waves," *Journal of Applied Physics* 26:766.

Brody, H.; and Cullen, M. 1957. "Carcinoma of the breast seventeen years after mammography with thorotrast," *Surgery* 42:600.

Bross, I. D. J.; and Nataraian, N. 1972. "Leukemia from low-level radiation: Identification of susceptible children," *New England Journal of Medicine* 287:107.

*Brues, A. M. 1968. "Kiku to niwaka kōkyū gunzoku—Genbaku chokugo no Hiroshima-Nagasaki e no tabi" [Chrysanthemum and temporary high-level civilian personnel—Trip to Hiroshima and Nagasaki immediately after the atomic bombings], *Journal of the Hiroshima Medical Association* 21:74.

Burke, G.; Levinson, M. J.; and Zitman, I. H. 1967. "Thyroid carcinoma ten years after sodium iodine I^{131} treatment," *Journal of the American Medical Association* 199:247.

Burrow, G. N.; Hamilton, H. B.; and Hrubec, Z. 1964. "Study of adolescents exposed in utero, clinical and laboratory data 1958–59, Nagasaki," *Yale Journal of Biology and Medicine* 36:430.

Burrow, G. N.; Hamilton, H. B.; and Hrubec, Z. 1965. "Study of adolescents exposed in utero to the atomic bomb, Nagasaki, Japan," *Journal of the American Medical Association* 192:357.

*Central Liaison Office, Domestic Affairs Section, Political Affairs Department. 1947. *Keisatsu ni Kansuru Rengōkoku Shireishū* [Directives of Allied Powers Concerning the Police]. Nyūsusha, Tokyo.

Chee, C. A. K.; and Ilbery, P. L. T. 1977. "Cytogenetic findings 30 years after low-level exposure to the Nagasaki atom bomb," *Journal of Radiation Research* (Tokyo) 18:132.

*Chen, H. 1967. "Review of experiences in treatment of one case with atomic bomb radiation injury," *Journal of the Hiroshima Medical Association* 20:851.

*Cheong, G.; Cheong, C.; Kurihara, M.; and Watanabe, S. 1978. "Actual status of atomic bomb survivors in Hapchon County, South Korea," *Nagasaki Medical Journal* 53:298.

Chinnock, F. W. 1970. *Nagasaki—The Forgotten Bomb*. George Allen & Unwin, London.

Chōsen Shinpō [Korean News]. 1965. 15 August.

*Chūbachi, M. 1968. "Structural relationship of life conditions of atomic bomb sufferers: As revealed through the interviews conducted in Hiroshima area," *Mita Gakkai Zasshi* [Mita Journal of Economics], 61 (December):1221. Keio University, Tokyo.

*Chūgoku Cultural League. 1946. *Chūgoku Bunka—Genshi-bakudan Tokushūgō* [Culture of Chūgoku—Special Issue on the Atomic Bombing]. Chūgoku Bunka Renmei, Hiroshima.

Chūgoku Shinbun [Chūgoku Newspaper]. 1945. 5 December.

Chūgoku Shinbun [Chūgoku Newspaper]. 1946a. 22 May.

Chūgoku Shinbun [Chūgoku Newspaper]. 1946b. 21 December.

Chūgoku Shinbun [Chūgoku Newspaper]. 1956. 21 August.

*Chūgoku Shinbunsha. 1965. *Hi wa Mitsumete Iru* [The Monument Is Watching]. Chūgoku Shinbun Bunka Jigyōbu, Hiroshima.

*Chūguku Shinbunsha. 1966. *Hiroshima no Kiroku—Nenpyō-Shiryōhen* [Record of Hiroshima—Volume of Chronological Table and Data]. Miraisha, Tokyo.

*Chūō Kishōdai [Central Meteorological Observatory]. 1945. *Tenkizu* [Weather Chart], no. 221 (6:00 A.M., 9 August 1945). Chūō Kishōdai.

Cihak, R. W.; Ishimaru, T.; Steer, A.; and Yamada, A. 1974. "Lung cancer at autopsy in A-bomb survivors and controls, Hiroshima and Nagasaki, 1961–70. I. Autopsy findings and relation to radiation," *Cancer* 33:1580.

*A Citizens' Group to Convey Testimonies of Hiroshima and Nagasaki. 1972. "Give Me Water; Testimonies of Hiroshima and Nagasaki." Tokyo.

Clark, D. E. 1955. "Association of irradiation with cancer of the thyroid in children and adolescents," *Journal of the American Medical Association* 159:1007.

Cogan, D. G.; Donaldson, D. D.; and Reese, A. B. 1952. "Clinical and pathological characteristics of radiation cataract," *Archives of Ophthalmology* 47:55.

Cogan, D. G.; Martin, S. F.; and Kimura, S. J. 1949. "Atom bomb cataracts," *Science* 110:654.

Cogan, D. G.; Martin, S. F.; Kimura, S. J.; and Ikui, H. 1950. "Ophthalmological survey of atomic bomb survivors in Japan, 1949," *Transcripts of the American Ophthalmological Society* 48:62.

*Committee for the Map Restoration of A-bombed Areas. 1970–76. *Genbaku Hisai Zentaizō Chōsa Jigyō Hōkokusho* [Atomic Bomb Disaster Overall Picture Survey Reports]. Reports for the years 1969–75. Genbaku Hisai Fukugen Iinkai, Hiroshima.

Connor, R. J.; Kawamoto, S.; and Omori, Y. 1971. "Growth and development age 10 to age 17 of children exposed in utero to the atomic bombs, Hiroshima and Nagasaki," ABCC TR 5–71.

Conrad, R. A. 1977. "Summary of thyroid findings in Marshallese, 22 years after exposure to radioactive fallout," in *Radiation-Associated Thyroid Carcinoma*. L. J. De Groot, ed. Grune & Stratton, New York.

Court-Brown, W. M.; and Doll, R. 1957. *Leukemia and Aplastic Anaemia in Patients Irradiated for Ankylosing Spondylitis*. Medical Research Council Special Report Series, no. 295. Her Majesty's Stationery Office, London.

Court-Brown, W. M.; and Doll, R. 1958. "Expectation of life and mortality from cancer among British radiologists," *British Medical Journal* 2:181.

Court-Brown, W. M.; Doll, R.; and Hill, A. B. 1960. "Incidence of leukaemia after exposure to diagnostic radiation in utero," *British Medical Journal* II:1539.

DeCoursey, E. 1948. "Human pathologic anatomy of ionizing radiation effects of atomic bomb explosions," *Military Surgeon* 102:427.

DeCoursey, E. 1949. "Medical aspects of atomic explosion," *Journal of the Tennessee Medical Association* 42:259.

Diamond, E. L.; Schmerler, H.; and Lilienfeld, A. M. 1973. "The relationship of intra-uterine radiation to subsequent mortality and development of leukemia in children: A prospective study," *American Journal of Epidemiology* 97:283.

*Dodo, T. 1962. "State of A-bomb cataracts at the Department of Ophthalmology, Hiroshima University during the recent four years, " *Journal of the Hiroshima Medical Association* 15:878.

*Dodo, T. 1967. "Photographic reproduction of findings on A-bomb cataracts among Hiroshima A-bomb survivors," *Rinshō Ganka* [Japanese Journal of Clinical Ophthalmology], 21:729.

*Dodo, T.; and Toda, S. 1963. "Ophthalmological late effects among A-bomb survivors, especially A-bomb cataracts," in *Genshi Igaku* [Nuclear Medicine], T. Koyama, A. Tabuchi, and S. Watanabe, eds. Kanehara Shuppan, Tokyo.

Doida, Y.; Sugahara, T.; and Horikawa, M. 1965. "Studies on some radiation-induced chromosome aberrations in man," *Radiation Research,* 26:69.

Doll, R.; Muir, C. S.; and Waterhouse, J. A. H., eds. 1970. *Cancer Incidence in Five Continents.* International Union Against Cancer. Springer-Verlag, New York.

Duffy, Jr., B. J.; and Fitzgerald, P. J. 1950. "Thyroid cancer in childhood and adolescence. A report of twenty-eight cases," *Cancer* 3:1018.

Dunlap, C. E. 1942. "Effects of radiation on the blood and the hemopoietic tissues, including the spleen, the thymus and the lymph nodes," *Archives of Pathology* 34:562.

*Economic Planning Agency, Research Bureau. 1978. *Keizai Yōran* [Economics Manual], 1978 ed. Keizai Kikaku Chō, Tokyo.

*Economic Stabilization Board, President's Secretariat, Investigation Section, 1949. *Taiheiyō Sensō ni yoru Wagakuni no Higai Sōgō Hōkokusho* [A Comprehensive Report on the Damages to Our Country Due to the Pacific War]. Keizai Antei Honbu, Tokyo.

*Editorial Committee of Data on the Case of Forced Arrest of Chinese. 1964. *Kusa no Bohyō* [Grave Marker of Grass]. Shin-nihon Shuppansha, Tokyo.

*Editorial Committee for the Fukuryū Maru No. 5. 1976. *Daigo Fukuryū Maru Jiken* [The "Lucky Dragon No. 5" incident]. Yaizu City.

*Education Ministry Scientific Research Grant (Co-operative) "Radiation Effects" Research Team. 1965. *Hōshasen Eikyō Kenkyū no Jūnen* [Ten Years of Radiation Effects Studies].

* Egawa, Y. 1971. "Atomic bomb exposure and relief activities in Saeki County," *Journal of the Hiroshima Medical Association* 24:92.

Evans, H. J. 1977. "Chromosome anomalies among live births," *Journal of Medicine and Genetics* 14:309.

Evans, T. H. 1973. "Testimony of an English atomic bomb survivor," in *Nagasaki no Shōgen* [Testimony of Nagasaki], fifth collection. Nagasaki no Shōgen Kankō Iinkai, Nagasaki.

*Ezaki, H.; and Shigemitsu, T. 1967. "Studies on thyroid cancer induced by A-bomb exposure, and its clinical significance," *Journal of the Hiroshima Medical Association* (special series) 20:336.

*Ezaki, H.; and Shigemitsu, T. 1970. Studies on thyroid cancer induced by A-bomb exposure," *Proceedings of the Hiroshima University Research Institute for Nuclear Medicine and Biology* II:166.

Fillmore, P. G. 1952. "Medical examination of Hiroshima patients with radiation cataracts," *Science* 116:322.

Finch, S. C.; and Anderson, P. S. 1963. "ABCC-JNIH adult health study report 3, 1958–60: cycle of examination, Hiroshima," ABCC TR 19–63.

Folley, J. H.; Borges, W.; and Yamawaki, T. 1952. "Incidence of leukemia in survivors of the atomic bomb in Hiroshima and Nagasaki, Japan," *American Journal of Medicine* 13:311.

Foulds, L. 1939. "The production of transplantable carcinoma and sarcoma in guinea-pigs by injections of thorotrast," *American Journal of Cancer* 35:363.

Francis, T.; Jablon, S.; and Moore, F. E. 1959. "Report of the ad hoc committee for appraisal of ABCC program, 6 November 1955," ABCC TR 33–59.

Freed, F.; and Giovannitti, L. 1965. *The Decision to Drop the Bomb.* Coward-McCann, New York.

Freedman, L. R.; Fukushima, K.; and Seigel, D. G. 1963. "ABCC-JNIH adult health study report 4, 1960–62, cycle of examinations, Hiroshima, Nagasaki," ABCC TR 20–63.

Frieben. 1902. "Cancroid des rechten Handrückens," *Deutsche Medizinische Wochenschrift* 28 (supplement):334.

*Fujii, T., editor-author. 1978. *Yōjiki no Heiwa Kyōiku* [Peace Education in Childhood]. Sa-sa-ra Shobō, Tokyo.

*Fujimoto, Y.; Ishida, S.; Itasaka, K.; Yorita, T.; Matsuura, K.; and Oda, T. 1962. "Lung cancer among A-bomb survivors," *Journal of the Hiroshima Medical Association* 15:935.

*Fujimoto, Y.; Yamamoto, T.; Ishida, S.; and Numata, J. 1959a. "Three autopsy cases of myelogenic leukemia complicated by thyroid cancer seen in A-bomb survivors," *Journal of the Hiroshima Medical Association* 12:1077.

*Fujimoto, Y.; Yamamoto, T.; Numata, J.; and Mori, K. 1959b. "Two autopsy cases of thyroid cancer in young people of atomic bomb survivors," *Journal of the Hiroshima Medical Association* 12:519.

*Fujinaga, Y. 1969. "On the histological study of cataracts of atomic bomb survivors," *Societatis Ophthalmologicae Japonicae* 73:1094.

*Fujinaga, Y. 1970. "Cases of atomic bomb radiation cataract in the last ten years," *Folia Opthalmologica Japonica* 21:233.

*Fujita, T.; Andō, H.; and Tanaka, R. 1977. "Acute effects of atomic bomb on vegetable kingdom plants," in *Seishi no Hi—Hiroshima Daigaku Genbaku Hisai Shi* [Light of Fate—Record of the Hiroshima University A-bomb Disaster], Hiroshima University A-bomb Dead Memorial Functions Committee, ed. Hiroshima Daigaku Genbaku Shibotsusha Irei Gyōji Iinkai, Hiroshima.

*Fukagawa, M. 1970. *Senkyūhyakugojūnen Hachigatsu Muika—Chōsen Sensōka no Hiroshima* [6 August 1950—Hiroshima during the Korean War]. Gensuibaku Kinshi Hiroshimashi Kyōgikai, Hiroshima.

*Fukagawa, M. 1974. *Chinkon no Kaikyō—Kieta Hibaku Chōsenjin Chōyōkō Nihyakuyonjūrokumei* [Channel of Repose of Departed Souls—246 A-bomb Exposed Korean Drafted Workers Who Vanished]. Gendaishi Shuppankai, Tokyo.

*Fukuda, C. 1967. "Twenty years' course of Nagasaki prefectural A-bomb survivors health management activities," *Journal of the Hiroshima Medical Association* (special series) 20:14.

*Fukuoka, T.; and Nita, T. 1953. "Clinical report on ophthalmological disturbance due to atomic bomb in Hiroshima," in CRIABC, vol. I.

*Funahashi, T. 1955a. "Study on the growth and development of children who were born to mothers exposed to the atomic bomb," *Journal of the Hiroshima Medical Association* (original series) 3:139.

*Funahashi, T. 1955b. "Study on the growth and development of children who were born to mothers exposed to the atomic bomb. 2. Growth and development of children conceived after exposure and born as the first child (so-called first-born children)," *Journal of the Hiroshima Medical Association* (original series) 3:991.

Furth, J.; and Furth, O. B. 1936. "Neoplastic diseases produced in mice by general irradiation with X-rays. I. Incidence and type of neoplasm," *American Journal of Cancer* 28:54.

Furth, J.; Upton, A. C.; and Kimball, A. W. 1959. "Late pathologic effects of atomic detonation and their pathogenesis," *Radiation Research* 1(supplement):243.

*Furushō, T. 1976. "Genetic effects of atomic bomb radiation on growth of stature of F_1 generation," *Nagasaki Medical Journal* 51:259.

Gates, O.; and Warren, S. 1961. "Histogenesis of lung carcinoma in mice induced by gamma radiation," *Archives of Pathology* 71:693.

Glasstone, S., ed. 1962. *The Effects of Nuclear Weapons,* rev. ed. United States Atomic Energy Commission, Washington, D.C.

Graham, S.; Levin, M. L.; Lilienfeld, A. B.; Schuman, L. M.; Gibson, R.; Dowd, J. E.; and Hempelmann, L. 1966. "Preconception, intrauterine, and postnatal irradiation as related to leukemia," *National Cancer Institute Monographs* 19:347.

Groves, L. R.; and Groves, R. H. 1962. *Now It Can be Told: The Story of the Manhattan Project.* Harper & Brothers, New York.

Haavelsrud, M., ed. 1976. *Education for Peace—Reflection and Action.* International Publishing Corporation, Science and Technology Press, Guildford, Surrey, England.

Hachiya, M. 1955. *Hiroshima Nikki* [Hiroshima Diary]. Asahi Shimbunsha, Tokyo.

Hall, C. W.; Miller, R. J.; and Nefzger, M. D. 1964. "Ophthalmologic findings in atomic bomb survivors, Hiroshima, 1956–57," ABCC TR 12–64.

Ham, W. T. 1953. "Radiation cataract," *Archives of Ophthalmology* 50:618.

*Hamada, T.; and Ishida, S. 1974. "Lung cancer among atomic bomb survivors: Study of 114 autopsy cases, 1957–72," *Journal of the Hiroshima Medical Association* 27:558.

*Hamai, S.; and Tagawa, T. 1961. "Fund raising for treatment of persons suffering A-bomb disturbances (Request addressed to Nozomu Nakagawa, President of the Central Community Chest of Japan, dated 2 June 1953)," in HAMCH.

*Hamaoka, H. 1959. "On the sterility and infertility of women exposed to the atomic bomb," *Journal of the Hiroshima Medical Association* (special series) 12:96.

Hamilton, H. B.; and Brody, J. A. 1975. "A review of thirty years study of Hiroshima and Nagasaki atomic bomb survivors. III. Future research and health surveillance. A. Health surveillance studies," *Journal of Radiation Research* (Tokyo) 16(supplement):138.

*Hanaoka, M. 1959. "Histological studies on the mice irradiated with neutron-gamma ray, the primary and secondary injuries in the acute radiation," *Symposia of the Society for Cellular Chemistry* 9:201.

*Hanaoka, M. 1964. "Radiation injuries, especially influences to blood and hematopoietic organs by neutron irradiation," in HH vol. III.

Hanford, J. M.; Quimby, E. H.; and Frantz V. K. 1962. "Cancer arising many years after radiation therapy," *Journal of the American Medical Association* 181:404.

*Harada, T. 1967. "Summary report on scar keloids, Hiroshima," *Journal of the Hiroshima Medical Association* (special series) 20:199.

Harada, T.; Ide, M.; Ishida, M.; and Troup, G. M. 1963. "Tumor registry data, Hiroshima-Nagasaki 1957–59, Malignant neoplasms," ABCC TR 23–63.

*Harada, T.; and Ishida, M. 1960. "Neoplasms among A-bomb survivors in Hiroshima: First report of the Tumor Statistical Committee" (Hiroshima City Medical Association, ed.), *Journal of the National Cancer Institute* 25:1253.

*Harano, C.; Tezuka, H.; and Shirabe, R. 1961. "Thyroid tumors among those exposed to radiation from the atomic bomb," *Acta Medica Nagasakiensia* 6:36.

*Harano, C.; Tezuka, H.; and Shirabe, R. 1967. "Thyroid cancer in atomic bomb survivors," *Journal of the Hiroshima Medical Association* (special series) 20:348.

Harley, N. H.; Albert, R. E.; and Shore, R. E. 1976. "Follow-up study of patients treated by X-ray epilation for tinea capitis. Estimation of the dose to the thyroid and pituitary glands and other structures of the head and neck," *Physics in Medicine and Biology* 21:631.

Harris, B. R.; and Stevens, M. A. 1945. "Experiences at Nagasaki, Japan," *Connecticut Medical Journal* 9:1913.

Hashizume, T. 1967. "On instant radiation dose by the atomic bombing," *Journal of the Hiroshima Medical Association* (special series) 20:66.

Hashizume, T.; and Maruyama, T. 1973. "Dose estimation of human fetus exposed in utero to radiations from atomic bombs in Hiroshima and Nagasaki," *Journal of Radiation Research* (Tokyo) 14:346.

Hashizume, T.; and Maruyama, T. 1975a. "A review of thirty years study of Hiroshima and Nagasaki atomic bomb survivors. I. Dosimetry, C. Dose estimation from residual and fallout radioactivity: A simulated neutron activation experiment," *Journal of Radiation Research* (Tokyo) 16(supplement):32.

Hashizume, T.; and Maruyama, T. 1975b. "I. Dosimetry, B. Physical dose estimates for A-bomb survivors—Studies at Chiba, Japan," *Journal of Radiation Research* (Tokyo) 16(supplement):12.

Hashizume, T.; Maruyama, T.; Kumamoto, Y.; Kato, Y.; and Kawamura, S. 1969. "Estimation of gamma-ray dose from neutron-induced radioactivity in Hiroshima and Nagasaki," *Health Physics* 17:761.

*Hashizume, T.; Maruyama, T.; and Nishizawa, K. 1977. "Estimation of exposed radiation dose of atomic bomb survivors," in *Genbaku Shōgaishō Chōsa Kenkyū-han Hōkoku* [Report of the Study Group for Atomic Bomb Disease], Nihon Kōshū Eisei Kyōkai. Tokyo.

Hashizume, T.; Maruyama, T.; Nishizawa, K.; and Fukuhisa, K. 1977. "Mean bone marrow dose of atomic bomb survivors in Hiroshima and Nagasaki," *Journal of Radiation Research* (Tokyo) 18:67.

Hashizume, T.; Maruyama, T.; Nishizawa, K.; and Nishimura, A. 1974. "Estimation of absorbed dose in thyroids and gonads of survivors in Hiroshima and Nagasaki," *Acta Radiologica* 13:411.

Hashizume, T.; Maruyama, T.; Shiragai, A.; Tanaka, E.; Izawa, M.; Kawamura, S.; and Nagaoka, S. 1967. "An estimation of the air dose from the atomic bombs, Hiroshima-Nagasaki," *Health Physics* 13:149.

*Hatanaka, T. 1953. "Relation between the Nagasaki A-bomb exposure and menstruation," in CRIABC, vol. II.

*Hatano, S.; and Watanuki, T. 1953. "A-bomb disaster investigation report—fourth investigation: Chiefly concerned with occurrence of keloids due to thermal burns of atomic bomb," in CRIABC, vol. I.

*Hayashi, I.; Okamoto, N.; Tsuchiyama, H.; and Yamabe, T. 1955. "Atomic bomb and fetal development," *Rinshō Fujinka Sanka* [Clinical Gynaecology and Obstetrics] 9:923.

*Hayashi, T. 1970. "Reminiscences of atomic-bombed Nagasaki," in *Wasurenagusa* [FMN, vol. III]. Kyū Nagasaki Ikadaigaku Genbaku Giseigakuto Izokukai, Nagasaki.

Hazen, R. W.; Pifer, J. W.; and Toyooka, E. T. 1966. "Neoplasms following irradiation of the head," *Cancer Research* 26:305.

Hempelmann, L. H. 1968. "Risk of thyroid neoplasms after irradiation in childhood," *Science* 160:159.

Hempelmann, L. H.; Pifer, J. W.; Burke, G. J.; Terry, R.; and Ames, W. R. 1967. "Neoplasms in persons treated with X-rays in infancy for thymic enlargement. A report of the third follow-up survey," *Journal of the National Cancer Institute* 38:317.

Henshaw, P. S. 1944. "Leukemia in mice following exposure to X-rays," *Radiology* 43:279.

Henshaw, P. S.; Hawkins, J. W.; Meyer, H. L.; Woodruff, J.; and Marshall, J. F. 1944. "Incidence of leukemia in physicians," *Journal of the National Cancer Institute* 4:339.

Hersey, J. 1946. *Hiroshima.* Alfred A. Knopf, New York. First published in August 1946 in *The New Yorker.*

Hesse, O. 1911. "Das Röntgenkarzinom," *Fortschritte auf dem Gebiete der Röntgenstrahlen und der Nuklearmedizin* 15:82.

Heyssel, R. M.; Brill, A. B.; Woodbury, L. A.; Nishimura, E. T.; Ghose, T.; Hoshino, T.; and Yamasaki, M. 1960. "Leukemia in Hiroshima atomic bomb survivors," *Blood* 15:313.

*Hibino, S. 1956. "Clinical survey of A-bomb survivors, especially on hematological findings," *Annual Report of the Cooperative Research Ministry of Education—Medicine* (1955), Nihon Gakujutsu Shinkōkai, Tokyo.

*Hibino, S.; and Yamasaki, K. 1961. "Polycythemia vera in Japan, with special reference to atomic bomb survivors," *Japanese Journal of Clinical Hematology* 2:195.

*Hibino, S.; Yamasaki, K.; and Kurita, S. 1962. "Polycythemia vera," in HH, vol. V.

Higashimura, T.; Ichikawa, Y.; and Sidei, T. 1963. "Dosimetry of atomic bomb radiation in Hiroshima by thermoluminescence of roof tiles," *Science* 139:1284.

*Hirai, G. 1964. "Studies on developmental disturbances in children exposed in utero to the atomic bomb," *Journal of the Hiroshima Obstetrical and Gynecological Society* 3:1.

*Hiraoka, T. 1966. "Visiting A-bomb sufferers in Korea," *Sekai* [World], April 1966 edition. Iwanami Shoten, Tokyo.

*Hiraoka, T. 1969. "Anger and grief of A-bomb exposed Koreans," *Dokyumento Nihonjin 8—Anchihyūman* [Document Japanese 8—Antihuman], Ken'ichi Tanigawa, Shunsuke Tsurumi, and Ichirō Murakami, eds. Gakugei Shorin, Tokyo.

Hirono, T.; and Aihara, K. 1953. "Investigation report on blasts caused by the atomic bombs," in CRIABC, vol. I.

*Hirose, F. 1967. "Prevalence of leukemia among Hiroshima survivors during the past nineteen years (1946-64)," *Journal of the Hiroshima Medical Association* (special series) 20:274.

*Hirose, F. 1968. "Leukemia in atomic bomb survivors, Hiroshima. 1946-67," *Acta Haematologica Japonica* 31:765.

*Hirose, H. 1970. "Letter from an English prisoner of war," in *Genbaku Zengo* [Before and after the Atomic Bomb], vol. III, Hideo Shirai et al., eds. Privately printed by Omoideshū Sewanin.

*Hirose, I.; Fujisawa, H.; Fujino, T.; and Okamoto, A. 1967. "Amplitude of visual accommodation in atomic bomb survivors," ABCC TR 9-67.

*Hirose, I.; and Okamoto, A. 1961. "Interrelationship between lenticular turbidity of the posterior pole and estimated exposure doses of the atomic bomb survivors in Nagasaki" (preliminary report), *Nagasaki Medical Journal* 36:781.

*Hirose, K.; and Fujino, S. 1950. "Cataracts due to atomic bomb exposure," *Acta Societatis Ophthalmologicae Japonicae* 54:449.

Hirose, K.; and Sugito, K. 1953. "Investigation report on atomic bomb disasters to water supply," in CRIABC, vol. I.

Hiroshima A-bomb Medical Care History Editorial Committee (HAMCH). 1961. *Hiroshima Genbaku Iryōshi* [Hiroshima A-bomb Medical Care History]. Hiroshima Genbaku Shōgai Taisaku Kyōgikai, Hiroshima.

*Hiroshima A-bomb Survivors Relief Projects Group. 1978. *Hiroshima Genbaku Yōgo Hōmu Shōwa Gojūsannen Ichigatsubun Jigyō Gaiyō*—Nyūshosha no Kakushitsuwari Jōkyō [Summary of Projects of Hiroshima A-bomb Survivors Home for January 1978—Mode of Assignment of Inmates to Rooms].

*Hiroshima District Meteorological Observatory, Observation Section. 1953. "Weather conditions of Hiroshima at time of the atomic bombing," in CRIABC, vol. I.

*Hiroshima Institute for Peace Education. 1973-77. *Heiwa Kyōiku Kenkyū* [Peace Education Research], annual report, vols. I-V. Hiroshima Heiwa Kyōiku Kenkyūsho Shuppanbu, Hiroshima.

*Hiroshima Institute for Peace Education. 1977. *Hiroshima—Konnichi no Kakujidai o Ikiru (Shian)* [Hiroshima—Living in the Present Nuclear Age (draft)]. Hiroshima Heiwa Kyōiku Kenkyusho Shuppanbu, Hiroshima.

*Hiroshima-Nagasaki Peace Readers Editorial Committee. 1974. *Asu ni Ikiru* [Living for Tomorrow]. Hiroshimaken Nagasakiken Kōtōgakkō Kyōshokuin Kumiai and Hiroshimaken Nagasakiken Kōtōgakkō Hibaku Kyōshi no Kai, Hiroshima-Nagasaki.

*Hiroshima-Nagasaki Publishing Committee. 1978. *Hiroshima-Nagasaki—A Pictorial Record of the Atomic Destruction*. Kodomotachi ni Sekai ni Hibaku no Kiroku o Okuru Kai [Committee of Japanese Citizens to Send Gift Copies of a Photographic & Pictorial Record of the Atomic Bombing to Our Children and Fellow Human Beings of the World], Tokyo.

*Hiroshima-Nagasaki Testimony Association. 1975-76. *Hiroshima-Nagasaki Sanjūnen no Shōgen* [Testimony of Thirty Years, Hiroshima and Nagasaki], 2 vols. Miraisha, Tokyo.

*Hiroshima Peace Culture Foundation. 1977. *Genbaku no E, Hiroshima* [Hiroshima, Picture of the Atomic Bomb]. Dōshinsha, Tokyo.

*Hiroshima Peace Culture Foundation. 1976, 1978. *Heiwa no Suishin* [Promotion of Peace], 1976 and 1978 eds. Hiroshima Heiwa Bunka Sentā, Hiroshima.

*Hiroshima Prefecture Educational Research and Peace Education Expert Committee, Hiroshima Prefecture Hibakusha Teachers Association and Hiroshima Institute for Peace Education. 1973. *Ningen no Ashita e—Heiwa o Kangaeru Hiroshima no Ko* [For the Future of Man— Hiroshima Children Thinking of Peace], first collection. Hiroshima Kyōiku Kaikan Shuppanbu, Hiroshima.

*Hiroshima Prefecture Educational Research and Peace Education Expert Committee, Hiroshima Prefecture Peace Education Teaching Materials Editorial Committee, and Hiroshima Prefecture Hibakusha Teachers Association. 1970-78. *Hiroshima no Heiwa Kyōiku* [Peace Education of Hiroshima], first to fifth collections. Hiroshima Kyōiku Kaikan Shuppanbu, Hiroshima.

*Hiroshima Prefecture Educational Research and Peace Education Expert Committee, Hiroshima Prefecture Peace Education Teaching Materials Editorial Committee, and Hiroshima Prefecture Hibakusha Teachers Association. 1971. "The pledge and appeal to continue teaching

'Hiroshima' and 'Nagasaki,' " in *Hiroshima no Heiwa Kyōiku* [Peace Education of Hiroshima], second collection. Hiroshima Kyōiku Kaikan Shuppanbu, Hiroshima.

*Hiroshima Prefecture Hibakusha Teachers Association and Hiroshima Prefecture Association of Senior High School Teachers–Hibakusha. 1977. *Konokora ni Kataritsugu Mono—Hiroshima Genbaku Hibaku Kyōshokuin no Shuki* [The Experience to Be Handed Down to These Children—Memoirs of Hiroshima Teachers Exposed to the Atomic Bomb], first collection. Yūbunsha, Hiroshima.

*Hiroshima Prefecture Hibakusha Teachers Association and Hiroshima Prefecture Teachers Union. 1971. *Genbaku o Dō Oshieta ka* [How Were the Children Taught about the Atomic Bomb]. Meiji Tosho, Tokyo.

*Hiroshima Prefectural Office. 1972. *Hiroshima Kenshi* [History of Hiroshima Prefecture], A-bomb data volume. Hiroshimaken, Hiroshima.

*Hiroshima Prefectural Office. 1973. *Hiroshima Kenshi* [History of Hiroshima Prefecture], A-bomb data volume. Hiroshimaken, Hiroshima.

*Hiroshima Prefectural Office. 1976. *Genbaku Sanjūnen—Hiroshimaken no Sengoshi* [Thirty Years since the Atomic Bombing—Postwar History of Hiroshima Prefecture]. Hiroshimaken, Hiroshima.

*Hiroshima Prefectural Office, Civil Welfare Department. 1973. *Kōreisha Kihon Jittai Chōsa* [Basic Actual Status Survey of the Aged Persons]. Hiroshimaken Minseibu, Hiroshima.

*Hiroshima Prefectural Office and Hiroshima City Office. 1960. *Shōwa Sanjūsannen Jūgatsu Ichijitsu Hiroshima Shinai Genshibakudan Hibakusha Tōkei Hōkoku* [Report on Statistics of Atomic Bomb Survivors in Hiroshima City as of 1 October 1958]. Hiroshimaken Tōkeika, Hiroshima.

*Hiroshima Prefectural Office and Hiroshima City Office. 1964a. *Hiroshimaken Genbaku Hibakusha Jittai Chōsa Hōkoku* [Hiroshima Prefecture A-bomb Survivors Actual Status Survey Report], 1960. Hiroshimaken-Hiroshimashi, Hiroshima.

*Hiroshima Prefectural Office and Hiroshima City Office. 1964b. *Hiroshimaken Genbaku Hibakusha Jittai Chōsa Kekka Hyō* [Table of Results of Hiroshima Prefecture A-bomb Survivors Actual Status Survey], 1960. Hiroshimaken-Hiroshimashi, Hiroshima.

*Hiroshima Prefectural Office and Hiroshima City Office. 1975. *Genbaku Hibakusha Taisaku Jigyō Gaiyō* [Summary of A-bomb Survivors Measures Projects], Thirtieth A-bomb anniversary ed. Hiroshimaken-Hiroshimashi, Hiroshima.

*Hiroshima Prefecture Peace Education Teaching Materials Editorial Committee and Hiroshima Prefecture Hibakusha Teachers Association. 1969. *Hiroshima—Genbaku o Kangaeru (Shian)* [Hiroshima—Thinking about the Atomic Bomb (draft)]. Hiroshima Kyōiku Kaikan Shuppanbu, Hiroshima.

*Hiroshima Prefecture Peace Education Teaching Materials Editorial Committee and Hiroshima Prefecture Hibakusha Teachers Association. 1970. *Hiroshima—Kore wa Watashitachi no Sakebi Desu (Shian)* [Hiroshima—This Is Our Cry (draft)]. Hiroshima Kyōiku Kaikan Shuppanbu, Hiroshima.

Hiroshima Prefecture Peace Education Teaching Materials English Division Editorial Committee and Hiroshima Prefecture Hibakusha Teachers Association. 1971. *Let's Cry For Peace!* Hiroshima Kyōiku Kaikan Shuppanbu, Hiroshima.

*Hiroshima Prefecture Police History Editorial Committee. 1954. *Shinpen Hiroshimaken Keisatsushi* [History of Hiroshima Prefecture Police, New Edition]. Hiroshimaken Keisatsu Renraku Kyōgikai, Hiroshima.

*Hiroshima Prefecture Senior High School Teachers Union, A-bomb and Peace Education Promotion and Editorial Committee, and Hiroshima Prefecture Hibakusha Teachers Association. 1971. *"Hiroshima" kara Manabu—Kōkōyō Genbaku-Heiwa Kyōiku Kyōzai-shiryō (Shian)* [Learning from "Hiroshima"—A-bomb and Peace Education Teaching Materials for Senior High School Use (draft)]. Hiroshimaken Kōtōgakkō Kyōshokuin Kumiai, Hiroshima.

*Hiroshima Prefecture Teachers Union, Department of Culture. 1949. *Hiroshima Kyōiku* [Hiroshima Education], July edition. Hiroshimaken Kyōshokuin Kumiai Bunkabu, Hiroshima.

*Hiroshima Prefecture Teachers Union and Hiroshima Prefecture Hibakusha Teachers Association. 1969. *Mirai o Kataritsuzukete—Genbaku Taiken to Kyōiku no Genten* [Talking about the Future—A-bomb Experience and the Starting Point of Education]. Rōdō Junpō Sha, Tokyo.

*Hiroshima Promoters Group, World Peace Convention. 1955. *Hachiji Jūgofun—Genbaku Hiro-

shima Jūnen no Kiroku [8:15 A.M.—A Ten-year Record of A-bombed Hiroshima]. Sekai Heiwa Shūkai Hiroshima Sewaninkai, Hiroshima.

*Hiroshima Research Group for Documentation of A-bomb Damages. 1968–72. *Genbaku Hisai Shiryō Sōmokuroku* [General Catalogue of Documents on A-bomb Damages], 3 vols. Hiroshima.

*Hiroshima Shiyakusho.† 1946. *Shōwa Nijūnen Hiroshima-shi Jimu Hōkokusho Narabini Zaisanhyō* [Hiroshima City Administrative Report and Properties Table for 1945]. Mayor's report to Hiroshima City Assembly on 8 March 1946.

*Hiroshima Shiyakusho. 1947. *Hiroshima Shisei Yōran* [Hiroshima City Almanac]. First-anniversary-of-reconstruction issue, 1946 ed.

*Hiroshima Shiyakusho. 1958. *Shinshū Hiroshima-shi Shi* [History of Hiroshima City, new edition], vol. II.

*Hiroshima Shiyakusho. 1970. *Genbaku Hibakusha Taisaku Jigyō Gaiyō* [Summary of A-bomb Survivors Measures Projects].

*Hiroshima Shiyakusho. 1971. *Hiroshima Genbaku Sensaishi* [Record of the Hiroshima A-bomb War Disaster (RHAWD)], 5 vols.

  1971a. Vol I.
  1971b. Vol. II.
  1971c. Vol. V.

*Hiroshima Shiyakusho. 1972. *Genbaku Hibakusha Taisaku Jigyō Gaiyō* [Summary of A-bomb Survivors Measures Projects].

*Hiroshima Shiyakusho. 1973. *Genbaku Hibakusha Taisaku Jigyō Gaiyō* [Summary of A-bomb Survivors Measures Projects].

*Hiroshima Shiyakusho, Public Health Bureau, A-bomb Survivors Measures Section. 1967. *Genbaku Hibakusha Taisaku no Gaiyō* [Summary of A-bomb Survivors Measures]. Hiroshimashi Eiseikyoku Genbaku Higai Taisakuka.

*Hiroshima Shiyakusho, Public Health Bureau, A-bomb Survivors Measures Section. 1968. *Genbaku Hibakusha Taisaku Jigyō Gaiyōsho* [Summary Report of A-bomb Survivors Measures Projects]. Hiroshimashi Eiseikyoku Genbaku Higai Taisakuka.

*Hiroshima Shiyakusho, Public Health Bureau, A-bomb Survivors Measures Section. 1972. *Hiroshimashi Genbaku Korō Jittai Chōsa no Matome* [Summary of Hiroshima City Actual Status Survey of Solitary Old A-bomb Survivors]. Hiroshimashi Eiseikyoku Genbaku Higai Taisakuka.

*Hiroshima Shiyakusho, Public Health Bureau, A-bomb Survivors Measures Department. 1976. *Genbaku Hibakusha Taisaku Jigyō Gaiyō* [Summary of A-bomb Survivors Measures Projects].

*Hiroshima Shiyakusho, Public Health Bureau, A-bomb Survivors Measures Department. 1977. *Genbaku Hibakusha Taisaku Jigyō Gaiyō* [Summary of A-bomb Survivors Measures Projects].

*Hiroshima Shiyakusho, Public Health Bureau, A-bomb Survivors Measures Department. 1978a. *Genbaku Hibakusha Taisaku Jigyō Gaiyō* [Summary of A-bomb Survivors Measures Projects].

*Hiroshima Shiyakusho, Public Health Bureau, A-bomb Survivors Measures Department. 1978b. *Genbaku Higai Zentaizō Chōsa Jigyō Hōkokusho* [A-bomb Disaster Overall Picture Survey Report]. Hiroshimashi Eiseikyoku Genbaku Higai Taisakubu.

*Hiroshima Shiyakusho, Social Welfare Bureau, Social Education Section, ed. 1950. *Genbaku Taikenki* [Recorded A-bomb Experiences]. Hiroshima.

*Hiroshima University, Research Institute for Nuclear Medicine and Biology. 1973. *Report on the Scientific Materials and Data of Atomic Bomb Disasters. On the Returned Materials from the Armed Forces Institute of Pathology*, report no. 1. Hiroshima Daigaku Genbaku Hōshanō-igaku Kenkyūsho, Hiroshima.

*Hiroshima University A-bomb Dead Memorial Functions Committee. 1975. *Seishi no Hi— Hiroshima Daigaku Genbaku Hisai Shi* [Light of Fate—Record of the Hiroshima University A-bomb Disaster]. Hiroshima Daigaku Genbaku Shibotsusha Irei Gyōji Iinkai, Hiroshima.

*Hiroshimashi–Nagasakishi [City of Hiroshima–City of Nagasaki]. 1976. *To the United Nations.* Expert Committee for Compilation of Data to Appeal to the United Nations, ed.

† Hiroshima City Office.

Hirschfelder, J. O.; Parker, D. B.; Kramish, A.; Smith, R. C.; and Glasstone, S., eds. 1950. *The Effects of Atomic Weapons,* rev. ed. U.S. Government Printing Office, Washington, D.C.

Hiyama, Y., ed. 1971. *Hōshasen Eikyō no Kenkyū* [Research in the Effects of Radiation]. University of Tokyo Press.

Hollingsworth, D. R.; Hamilton, H. B.; Tamagaki, H.; and Beebe, G. W. 1963. "ABCC-JNIH adult health study, Hiroshima 1958–59, thyroid disease," *Medicine* 42:47.

Hollingsworth, J. W.; and Anderson, P. S. 1961. "ABCC-JNIH adult health study, Hiroshima 1958–59, preliminary report," ABCC TR 11–61.

*Honda, I.; Hamai, S.; Tagawa, T.; Ikenaga, K.; Mizogami, T.; et al. 1961. "Petition for National Treasury disbursement of treatment expenses for A-bomb disturbance sufferers (September 1954)," in HAMCH.

*Hoshino, T. 1962. "Clinical and statistical observations of polycythemia among Hiroshima A-bomb survivors," *Acta Haematologica Japonica* (abstract) 25:604.

Hoshino, T.; Kato, H.; Finch, S. C.; and Hrubec, Z. 1967. "Leukemia in offspring of atomic bomb survivors," *Blood* 30:719.

*Hoshino, T.; Kawasaki, S.; Okada, H.; Yamamoto, T.; and Kimura, K. 1968. "Polycythemia vera terminating in acute myelogenous leukemia with fibrosis of bone marrow: Case report," *Acta Haematologica Japonica* 30:214.

*Huany, Y. 1972. "Victims of Japanese militarism," in *Asahi Shimbun* [Asahi Newspaper], 22 July (Nagasaki edition).

Hubbell, H. H.; Arakawa, E. T.; Nagaoka, S.; Ueda, S.; and Tanaka, S. 1970. "The epicenters of the atomic bombs. 1. An estimate based on thermal ray shadows, Nagasaki," *Journal of the Hiroshima Medical Association* 23:279; ABCC TR 1966 5–66.

Hubbell, H. H.; Jones, T. D.; and Cheka, J. S. 1969. "The epicenter of the atomic bombs. 2. Re-evaluation of all available physical data with recommended values," ABCC TR 3–69.

*Ichikawa, O. 1953. "Pathological study of atomic bomb diseases in horses," in CRIABC, vol. I.

Ichikawa, Y.; Higashimura, T.; and Sidei, T. 1966. "Thermoluminescence dosimetry of gamma rays from atomic bombs in Hiroshima and Nagasaki," *Health Physiology* 12:395.

*Ichimaru, M. 1968. "Leukemia in survivors of the atomic bombing, Nagasaki," *Acta Haematologica Japonica* 31:772.

*Ichimaru, M. 1976. "Late effect of atomic-bomb radiation at Nishiyama district," *Journal of the Hiroshima Medical Association* 29:294.

*Ichimaru, M. 1979. "A review of thirty years study of atomic bomb survivors. II. Biological effects, D. Prevalence of leukemia among atomic bomb survivors in Nagasaki," in *Shinpan Nippon Ketsuekigaku Zensho* [Handbook of Hematology, new edition], vol. VI. Maruzen, Tokyo.

*Ichimaru, M. 1981. "Radiation and human leukemia," in *Hakketsubyō no Subete* [All of the Leukemias] K. Nakano, ed., Internal Medicine Series No. 6, Second edition. Nankōdō, Tokyo.

Ichimaru, M.; and Ishimaru, T. 1975. "Leukemia and related disorders," *Journal of Radiation Research* (Tokyo) 16(supplement):89.

Ichimaru, M.; Ishimaru, T.; Belsky, J. L.; Tomiyasu, T.; Sadamori, N.; Hoshino, T.; Tomonaga, M.; Shimizu, N.; and Okada, H. 1976. "Incidence of leukemia in atomic bomb survivors, Hiroshima and Nagasaki, 1950–71: By radiation dose, years after exposure, age and type of leukemia," RERF TR 10–76.

*Ichimaru, M.; Ishimaru, T.; Mikami, M.; and Matsunaga, M. 1978a. "Multiple myeloma among atomic bomb survivors," *Nagasaki Medical Journal* 53:404.

*Ichimaru, M.; Tomonaga, Y.; Matsunaga, M.; Sadamori, N.; and Ishimaru, T. 1978b. "Aplastic anemia and related disorders in atomic bomb survivors," *Journal of the Hiroshima Medical Association* 31:484.

Ide, M.; Shimizu, K.; Sheldon, W. F.; and Ishida, M. 1965. "Malignant neoplasms–tumor registry data Hiroshima and Nagasaki 1957–61," ABCC TR 3–65.

*Iijima, S. 1967a. "A-bomb scar keloids: Pathology of keloids," *Journal of the Hiroshima Medical Association* (special series), 20:211.

*Iijima, S. 1967b. "Specimens of A-bomb victims in Hiroshima," *Kagaku* [Science] 37:377.

Iijima, S. 1977. "Address of welcome—The vital meaning of Hiroshima and Nagasaki," in *A Call from Hibakusha of Hiroshima and Nagasaki, Proceedings of International Symposium on the Damage and Aftereffects of the Atomic Bombing of Hiroshima and Nagasaki,* Japan National Preparatory Committee, ed. *Asahi Evening News,* Tokyo.

*Ikeda, H. 1968. "Bombing of Daiichi Office," in *Genbaku Zengo* [Before and after the Atomic Bomb], vol. I, Hideo Shirai, ed. Privately printed by Omoideshū Sewanin, Nagasaki.

*Ikui, H. 1967. "Ocular lesions caused by the atomic bombing of Nagasaki and Hiroshima: Early disorders," *Journal of the Hiroshima Medical Association* (special series) 20:160.

*Imahori, S. 1959–60. *Gensuibaku Jidai—Gendaishi no Shōgen* [A-bomb and H-bomb Age—Testimony of Contemporary History], 2 vols. San-ichi Shobō, Tokyo.

*Imahori, S. 1960. "About the Ayumi Group," *Bunko* 8:2. Published by Iwanami Bunko no Kai.

*Imahori, S. 1971. *Gensuibaku Kinshi Undō* [Movements against Atomic and Hydrogen Bombs]. Ushio Shuppansha, Tokyo.

*Institute for Peace Science, Hiroshima University. 1977. *Hiroshima Heiwa Kagaku* [Hiroshima Peace Science], vol. I. Hiroshima Daigaku, Hiroshima.

International Union Against Cancer. 1970. *Cancer Incidence in Five Continents,* R. Doll, C. S. Muir, and J. A. H. Waterhouse, eds. Springer-Verlag, New York.

"An introductory report on the damage and after-effects of the atomic bombings of Hiroshima and Nagasaki," 1976. Address to the Secretary-General of the United Nations.

*Irie, H.; Ide, I.; Kamoi, A.; Uozumi, K.; Matsuura, K.; Watanuki, T.; and Murakami, K. 1956. "Changes in the peripheral blood of people in the Nishiyama district caused by the atomic bomb explosion at Nagasaki," in *Research in the Effects and Influences of the Nuclear Bomb Test Explosions,* vol. II. Japan Society for the Promotion of Science, Tokyo.

*Irie, H.; and Matsuura, K. 1967. "Clinical observations of A-bomb effects in residents of the Nishiyama district, Nagasaki," *Journal of the Hiroshima Medical Association* (special series) 20:135.

*Iseki, T. 1966. "Cytogenetic studies in atomic bomb survivors," *Journal of the Japanese Society of Internal Medicine* 55:76.

*Ishida, A. 1976. *Hibaku Kyōshi* [A-bomb Exposed Teacher]. Hitotsubashi Shobō, Tokyo.

*Ishida, M. 1959. "Epidemiological study of neoplasms among A-bomb survivors in Hiroshima City," *Journal of the Hiroshima Medical Association* 12:1020.

*Ishida, M. 1960. "Statistical aspects of tumor registry in Hiroshima and Nagasaki," *Kōsei no Shihyō* [Index of Health and Welfare Statistics] 7:28.

Ishida, M.; and Matsubayashi, I. 1961. "An analysis of early mortality rates following the atomic bombs—Hiroshima," ABCC TR 20–61.

*Ishida, T., editor-author. 1973. *Hangenbaku—Nagasaki Hibakusha no Seikatsushi* [Against Atomic Bomb—Life History of Nagasaki Atomic Bomb Survivors] Miraisha, Tokyo.

*Ishida, T., editor-author. 1974. *Zoku Hangenbaku—Nagasaki Hibakusha no Seikatsushi* [More against Atomic Bombs—Life History of Nagasaki Atomic Bomb Survivors]. Miraisha, Tokyo.

*Ishida, Y. 1953. "Formation of clouds due to the atomic bomb detonation as observed from Unzen," in CRIABC, vol. I.

Ishihara, T.; and Kumatori, T. 1965. "Chromosome aberrations in human leukocytes irradiated in vivo and in vitro," *Acta Haematologica Japonica* 28:291. (English abstract)

*Ishikawa, K. 1953. "Seminal findings in A-bomb survivors nine months after explosion (Hiroshima City)," in CRIABC, vol. I.

*Ishikawa, K.; and Asakura, S. 1953. "Seminal changes due to exposure to A-bomb," in CRIABC, vol. I.

Ishimaru, T.; Cihak, R. W.; Land, C. E.; Steer, A.; and Yamada, A. 1975. "Lung cancer at autopsy in A-bomb survivors and controls, Hiroshima and Nagasaki, 1961–1970. II. Smoking, occupation, and A-bomb exposure," *Cancer* 36:1723.

Ishimaru, T.; Hoshino, T.; Ichimaru, M.; Okada, H.; Tomiyasu, T.; Tsuchimoto, T.; and Yamamoto, T. 1971a. "Leukemia in atomic bomb survivors, Hiroshima and Nagasaki, 1 October 1950–30 September 1966," *Radiation Research* 45:216.

Ishimaru, T.; Hoshino, T.; Ichimaru, M.; Okada, H.; Tomiyasu, T.; Tsuchimoto, T.; and Yamamoto, T. 1971b. "Leukemia in atomic bomb survivors in ABCC Master Sample, Hiroshima and Nagasaki 1950–66," *Journal of the Hiroshima Medical Association* 24:1009; in English, ABCC TR 25–69.

Ishimaru, T.; Okada, H.; Tomiyasu, T.; Tsuchimoto, T.; Hoshino, T.; and Ichimaru, M. 1972. "Occupational and other environmental factors in the epidemiology of leukemia, Hiroshima-Nagasaki, 1945–67," *Journal of the Hiroshima Medical Association* 25:623; in English, ABCC TR 26–69 (1969).

Ishimaru, T.; Otake, M.; and Ichimaru, M. 1977. "Incidence of leukemia among atomic bomb survivors in relation to neutron and gamma dose, Hiroshima and Nagasaki, 1950–71," RERF TR 14–77.

*Ishitobi, J. 1973. *Chūgokujin Kyōsei Renkō no Kiroku* [Record of Forced Arrest of Chinese]. Taihei Shuppansha, Tokyo.

*Ishizu, S. 1960. "Statistical studies on stillbirths in Hiroshima," *Journal of the Hiroshima Medical Association* (original series) 8:1077.

*Itō, T. 1960. "The A-bomb Victims' Situation and Their 'Negation' Mentality," *Shisō* [Thought], April (no. 430). Iwanami Shoten, Tokyo.

*Itō, T. 1975. *Hibaku no Shisō to Undō: Hibakusha Engohō no Tame ni* [The Thought and Actions of A-bomb Victims]. Shin Hyōron, Tokyo.

Izumi, N. 1955a. "Investigation of the physical strength and athletic ability of children exposed to the atomic bomb," *Annual Report of the Cooperative Research, Ministry of Education—Medicine and Pharmacy,* 1954. Nihon Gakujutsu Shinkōkai, Tokyo.

Izumi, N. 1955b. "Investigation of the mental and esthetic powers of the children exposed to the atomic bomb," *Annual Report of the Cooperative Research, Ministry of Education—Medicine and Pharmacy,* 1954. Nihon Gakujutsu Shinkōkai, Tokyo.

Izumi, N. 1956. "Effect of the atomic bomb on schoolchildren in Urakami district, Nagasaki," in *Research in the Effects and Influences of the Nuclear Bomb Test Explosions,* vol. II. Japan Society for the Promotion of Science, Tokyo.

Jablon, S.; Angevine, D. M.; Matsumoto, Y. S.; and Ishida, M. 1965. "On the significance of cause of death as recorded on death certificates in Hiroshima and Nagasaki, Japan," *National Cancer Institute Monograph* 19:445.

Jablon, S.; and Kato, H. 1970a. "Childhood cancer in relation to prenatal exposure to atomic bomb radiation," *Lancet* 2:1000.

Jablon, S.; and Kato, H. 1970b. "Sex ratio in offspring of survivors exposed prenatally to the atomic bombs, Hiroshima-Nagasaki," ABCC TR 24–70.

Jablon, S.; and Kato, H. 1972. "Studies of the mortality of A-bomb survivors, fifth report. Relationship between radiation dose and mortality, 1950–70," *Radiation Research* 50:649.

Jablon, S.; Tachikawa, K.; Belsky, J. L.; and Steer, A. 1971. "Cancer in Japanese exposed as children to the atomic bombs, 1950–69, Hiroshima and Nagasaki," *Lancet* 1:927.

Jacower, M. L.; and Miettinen, O. S. 1971. "Neoplasms after childhood irradiation of thymus gland," *Journal of the American Medical Association* 215:753.

Japan Broadcasting Corporation (NHK), ed. 1977. [Unforgettable Fire—Pictures Drawn by Atomic Bomb Survivors]. Nihon Hōsō Shuppan Kyōkai, Japan Broadcasting Publishing Co., Ltd., Tokyo.

*Japan Central Meteorological Observatory. 1945. *Tenkizu* [Daily Weather Maps], no. 225 (6:00 A.M., 9 August 1945). Chūō Kishōdai, Tokyo.

*Japan Confederation of A-bomb and H-bomb Sufferers Organizations, ed. 1966. *Genbaku Higai no Tokushitsu to Hibakusha Engo Hō no Yōkyū: Hibakusha Kyūen Undō no Hatten no Tame ni* [Characteristics of Atomic Bomb Damages and Demand for "Hibakusha Relief Law": For the Development of the Hibakusha Relief Movement]. Nihon Gensuibaku Higaisha Dantai Kyōgikai, Tokyo.

*Japan Council against Atomic and Hydrogen Bombs, ed. 1975. *Gensuibaku Kinshi Sekaitaikai Sengen Ketsugishū 1955–74* [A Collection of Declarations and Resolutions at World Conferences of Atomic and Hydrogen Bombs 1955–74]. Gensuibaku Kinshi Nihon Kyōgikai, Tokyo.

*Japanese Pathological Society. 1965. "Atomic bomb exposure and medical science of Japan (a roundtable talk)," *Saishin Igaku* [Modern Medicine] 20:2569.
*Japan Hematological Society, ed. 1953. *Ketsuekigaku Tōgikai Hōkoku* [Proceedings of the Symposium on Hemalology], no. 5. Nagai Shoten, Osaka.
Japan National Preparatory Committee. 1977. *A Call from the Hibakusha of Hiroshima and Nagasaki, Proceedings of International Symposium on the Damage and Aftereffects of the Atomic Bombing of Hiroshima and Nagasaki.* Asahi Evening News, Tokyo.
*Japan Peace Education Research Council. (1974–77.) *Heiwa Kyōiku Undō* [Peace Education Movement], nos. 1–5. Hiroshima Heiwa Kyōiku Kenkyūsho Shuppanbu, Hiroshima.
*Japan Peace Education Research Council. 1976. *Kikan Heiwa Kyōiku* [Peace Education Quarterly], first issue. Meiji Tosho, Tokyo.
*Japan Political Science Society. *Sengo Nihon no Seiji Katei* [Political Course of Postwar Japan]. Annual Report of Japan Political Science Society, 1953. Iwanami Shoten, Tokyo.
Japan Scientific Council. 1956. *Research in the Effects and Influences of the Nuclear Bomb Test Explosions,* 2 vols. Japan Society for the Promotion of Science, Tokyo.
*Japan Teacher's Union. 1978. "Resolutions and statements of the Japan Teacher's Union concerning peace and peace education," in *Kikan Heiwa Kyōiku* [Peace Education Quarterly], seventh issue. Meiji Tosho, Tokyo.
Junod, M. 1945. *Le Désastre de Hiroshima.* Ancien Délégué du Comité International de la Croix-Rouge.

*Kageura, N.; Tomonaga, M.; Ichimura, T.; Murakami, F.; Nagasawa, H.; Takamori, M.; Matsuda, M.; Nonaka, I.; Hirose, H.; Harada, Y.; Kusunoki, S.; and Azisaka, S. 1955. "Medical survey of atomic bomb survivors in Nagasaki one, two, and three years after the explosion," *Nagasaki Medical Journal* 30:232.
*Kajitani, T.; and Hatano, S. 1953. "Medical survey on acute effects of the atomic bomb in Hiroshima," in CRIABC, vol. I.
Kamada, N. 1969. "The effects of radiation on chromosomes of bone marrow cells. II. Studies on bone marrow chromosomes of atomic bomb survivors in Hiroshima," *Acta Haematologica Japonica* 32:236.
Kamada, N.; Tsuchimoto, T.; and Uchino, H. 1970. "Smaller G chromosomes in the bone-marrow cells of heavily irradiated atomic bomb survivors," *Lancet* 2:880.
Kamada, N.; and Uchino, H. 1976. "Preleukemia states in atomic bomb survivors in Japan," *Blood Cells* 2:57.
Kamada, N.; Kuramoto, A.; Katsuki, T.; and Hinuma, Y. 1979. "Chromosome Aberrations in B Lymphocytes of Atomic Bomb Survivors, *Blood* 53:1140.
*Kamata, S. 1978. "Foreign Hibakusha in Hiroshima and Nagasaki," in *Heiwa Bunka Kenkyū* [Peace Culture Research], first issue. Nagasaki Zōsen Daigaku Nagasaki Heiwa Bunka Kenkyūsho, ed. Nagasaki.
*Kamisugi Primary School Centennial Bulletin Editorial Committee. 1975. *Kyōiku Hyakunen no Ayumi* [Course of Education over One Hundred Years]. Miyoshi Shiritsu Kamisugi Shōgakkō Sōritsu Hyakushūnen Kinen Jikkō Iinkai, Hiroshima.
*Kanai, K. 1953. "Hypocenter of the atomic bomb in Hiroshima," in CRIABC, vol. I.
*Kanai, T. 1970. *Kaku Kenryoku—Hiroshima no Kokuhatsu* [Nuclear Power—Hiroshima's Plea]. Sanseidō, Tokyo.
Kanamaru, H. 1970. "Inochi-biroi Sando [Escape from death thrice]," in *Genbaku Zengo* [Before and after the Atomic Bomb], vol. III, Hideo Shirai et al., eds. Privately printed by Omoideshū Sewanin.
Kanamitsu, M.; Morita, K.; Finch, S. C.; Kato, H.; and Onishi, S. 1966. "Serologic response of atomic bomb survivors following Asian influenza vaccination," *Japanese Journal of Medical Science and Biology* 19:73.
Kandori, F.; and Masuda, Y. 1956. "Statistical observations of atom-bomb cataracts," *American Journal of Ophthalmology* 42:212.
*Kaneko, N.; and Numata, J. 1957. "One autopsy case of leukemia, complicated by thyroid cancer, in a child exposed to the atomic bomb," *Shōni-ka Shinryō* [Journal of Pediatric Practice] 20:478.
*Kanō, R.; and Mizuno, H. 1965. *Hiroshima Nijūnen, Genbaku Kiroku Eiga Seisakusha no Shōgen* [Hiroshima Twenty Years after the Atomic Bombing: Testimony of an A-bomb Documentary Film Producer]. Kōbundō, Tokyo.

Kaplan, E. L. 1948. "Influence of age on susceptibility of mice to development of lymphoid tumors after irradiation," *Journal of the National Cancer Institute* 9:55.

*Katashima, R. 1977. "Zoological investigation on the effects of the atomic bomb," in *Seishi no Hi—Hiroshima Daigaku Genbaku Hisai Shi* [Light of Fate—Record of the Hiroshima University A-bomb Disaster]. Hiroshima University A-bomb Dead Memorial Functions Committee, ed. Hiroshima Daigaku Genbaku Shibotsusha Irei Gyōji Iinkai, Hiroshima.

Kato, H. 1971. "Mortality in children exposed to the A-bombs while in utero, 1945–69," *American Journal of Epidemiology* 93:435.

Kato, H. 1973. "Late effects in children exposed to the atomic bomb while in utero," Igaku no Ayumi [Advances in Medicine], 84:754; in English, ABCC TR 18–73.

*Kato, H. 1975. "A review of thirty years study of Hiroshima and Nagasaki atomic bomb survivors. II. Biological effects, B. Genetic effects. 1. Early genetic surveys and mortality study," *Journal of Radiation Research* (Tokyo) 16(supplement):67.

Kato, H. 1978. "Mortality of children exposed in utero to the atomic bomb and offspring of A-bomb survivors," in *Late Biological Effects of Ionizing Radiation*, vol. I. International Atomic Energy Agency, Vienna.

Kato, H.; Schull, W. J.; and Neel, J. V. 1966. "Survival in children of parents exposed to the atomic bomb, a cohort-type study," *American Journal of Human Genetics* 18:339.

*Katsube, G. 1953. "On the cause of scar and keloid of A-bomb exposed people," in CRIABC, vol. II.

*Kawaguchi, E. 1977. "Hiroshima committing suicide," *Chūō Kōron* [Central Public Opinion], September 1977 issue. Chūō Kōronsha, Tokyo.

*Kawai, T.; Harada, K.; and Tanaka, N. 1969. "Changes in the social life of atomic bomb survivors. (1,2) Social reconstruction process observed in Hiroshima Urban District Case Report Survey," *Hōgaku Kenkyū* [Journal of Law, Politics, and Sociology]. 42:1340, 1472.

Kawamoto, S.; Fujino, T.; and Fujisawa, H. 1964. "Ophthalmologic study of children exposed in utero, Nagasaki," ABCC TR 23–64.

*Kawamoto, S. 1966. "Microcephaly in children exposed to Nagasaki atomic bomb while in utero" (preliminary report), at the Nagasaki meeting of the Japanese Pediatric Society, 11 December 1966.

*Kawata, K. 1961. "Relief of the injured and sick in the atomic bombing of Hiroshima," in HAMCH.

*Kenmyō, K. 1975. "All is death, all is destruction—Records of the Sasebo Naval First Relief Corps," in *Nagasaki no Shōgen* [Testimony of Nagasaki], seventh collection. Nagasaki no Shōgen Kankō Iinkai, Nagasaki.

Kerr, G. D.; and Solomon, D. L. 1976. "The epicenter of the Nagasaki weapon—A reanalysis of available data with recommended values," ORNL-TM–5139.

*Kikuchi, T. 1970. "Formation of Kyoto University A-bomb Casualty Comprehensive Survey Team and its activities," *Journal of the Hiroshima Medical Association* 20(1967), 51; ABCC Shiryō [ABCC Historical Notes], no. 3, ABCC, Hiroshima.

*Kikuchi, T.; Fukase, M.; Sawada, T.; Ishigami, R.; and Yamaso, Y. 1953a. "On blood and bone marrow pictures in A-bomb survivors in Nagasaki, especially Nishiyama district, a year and one-half after explosion," in CRIABC, vol. II. p. 871.

*Kikuchi, T.; and Kimoto, S. 1947. "Clinical observations of atomic bomb exposure," Report at the Twelfth General Assembly of the Japan Medical Association, April 1947, in CRIABC, vol. II.

*Kikuchi, T.; Wakisaka, G.; Setsuta, T.; Anzai, S.; Ōga, T.; Hiraoka, T.; Murata, K.; Itoi, S.; Umeda, T.; Okamoto, J.; Hama, O.; Murakami, T.; Sawada, T.; Ishigami, R.; Teshima, Y.; and Akiyama, S. 1953b. "Result of examination of A-bomb sufferers one year after explosion, especially on their hematological findings," in CRIABC, vol. II.

*Kikuchi, T.; Wakisaka, G.; Setsuta, T.; Yokoyama, T.; Uma, B.; Nishikawa, G.; Tanaka, J.; Yamaso, Y.; and Akiyama, S. 1953c. "Result of examination of A-bomb sufferers in Hiroshima City two years and two months after explosion, especially on their hematological findings," in CRIABC, vol. II.

*Kikuchi, T.; Wakisaka, G.; Yoda, T.; Node, S.; Yamada, H.; and Miki, K. 1953d. "Result of examination of A-bomb sufferers in Nagasaki City one year and four months after explosion, especially on their hematological findings," in CRIABC, vol. II.

*Kimura, M.; and Tajima, E. 1953. "On the burst point of the atomic bomb and the size of the fireball," in CRIABC, vol. I.

Kimura, S. J.; and Ikui, H. 1951. "Atomic bomb radiation cataract: Case report with histopathologic study," *American Journal of Ophthalmology* 34:811.

*Kinoko-kai [Mushroom Club]. 1966. "Course of Kinoko-kai," *Kinoko-kai Kaihō* [Bulletin of Kinoko-kai, Hiroshima] 1:4.

*Kinoshita, R.; and Miyake, M. 1951. "Pathological investigation of atomic bomb injuries," in SRIABC.

*Kitagawa, K. 1963. "Present status and problems of internal urban structure of Hiroshima City," *Shakai to Sono Shūhen* [Society and Its Periphery] 10:139.

*Kiuchi, S. 1953. "Investigation of disasters by the atomic bombs on the relation between topography and development of city," in CRIABC, vol. I.

Knebel, F.; and Bailey II, C. W. 1960. *No High Ground,* Harper & Brothers, New York.

*Komiya, E.; and Yamamoto, S. 1947. "A case of acute leukemia of survivors of the atomic bomb," *Shindan to Chiryō* [Diagnosis and Treatment] 35:88.

*Kondō, T.; Yoshioka, I.; Kida, S.; and Hayakawa, T. 1956. "Psychological study of atomic bomb survivors," *Journal of the Hiroshima Medical Association* 9:95.

*Kondō, Y.; and Saka, S. 1953. "Investigation report on the effects of atomic bomb blast to architecture," CRIABC, vol. I.

*Kōno, H. 1958. "New employees to the bank immediately after war's defeat," in *Haikyo no Naka kara—Jūnenshi* [From the Ruins—A Ten-year History], Hiroshima Bank Employees Union Ten-year History Editorial Committee, ed. Hiroshima Ginkō Jūgyōin Kumiai, Hiroshima.

*Kōno, Y. 1957. "Blood findings of those exposed to the Hiroshima atomic bomb eleven years after the detonation," *Acta Haematologica Japonica* 20(supplement):160.

*Konpira War Comrades Association, ed. 1977. *Senyū* [War Comrades]. Konpira Senyū Kai, Nagasaki.

*Konuma, M. 1954. "Psychiatric and psychosomatic case studies on the aftereffects of A-bomb survivors," *Report of the Cooperative Research, Ministry of Education—Medicine and Pharmacy, 1953.* Nihon Gakujutsu Shinkōkai, Tokyo.

Konuma, M. 1956. "Neuropsychiatric case studies on the atomic bomb casualties at Hiroshima," in *Research in the Effects and Influences of the Nuclear Bomb Test Explosions,* vol. II. Japan Society for the Promotion of Science, Tokyo.

*Konuma, M. 1961. "Interpretation of the complaints and symptoms assuming diencephalon syndrome as a late effect of the atomic bomb," *Nagasaki Medical Journal* 36:158.

*Konuma, M. 1963. "Psychosomatic problems as the late effects of atomic bomb exposure," in *Genshi Igaku* [Nuclear Medicine]. T. Koyama, A. Tabuchi, and S. Watanabe, eds. Kanehara Shuppan, Tokyo.

*Konuma, M. 1967. "Psychiatric atomic bomb casualties," *Journal of the Hiroshima Medical Assocation* (special series) 20:231.

*Konuma, M. 1977. "Neuropsychiatric consideration of the atomic bomb sickness and its sequelae," in *Genbaku to Hiroshima Daigaku—"Seishi no Hi" Gakujutsuhen* [The Atomic Bomb and Hiroshima University—Science Section of "Light of Fate"]. Hiroshima Daigaku Genbaku Shibotsusha Ireigyōji Iinkai, Hiroshima.

*Konuma, M.; Furutani, M.; and Kubo, S. 1953. "Diencephalic syndrome as a delayed A-bomb effect," *Nihon Iji Shinpō* [Japanese Medical Journal] 1547:4853.

*Konuma, M.; Miyake, M.; Furutani, M.; Akamatsu, K.; Hayakawa, T.; and Kubo, S. 1954. "Psychoneurological study concerning A-bomb aftereffects," *Naika no Ryōiki* [Journal of Medicine, Pediatrics, and Dermatology] 2:261.

*Korean History Research Society. 1974. *Chōsen no Rekishi* [History of Korea]. Sanseidō, Tokyo.

Kosakai, Y. 1978. *Hiroshima Tokuhon* [Hiroshima Reader]. Hiroshima Heiwa Bunka Sentā, Hiroshima. English edition was published in 1980.

*Kotani, T.; Maruyama, M.; and Fujii, T. 1979. *Heiwa—Kokka–Kaku–Kyōiku* [Peace—The State–Nuclear Arms–Education]. Hiroshima Heiwa Bunka Sentā, Hiroshima.

*Koyama, A.; and Seki, S. 1959. "Ophthalmological accommodating function of A-bomb survivors," *Journal of the Hiroshima Medical Association* 12:1028.

Kozumi, A. 1956. *Hiroshima wa Uttaeru: Genbaku Hiroshima Jūichinen no Kiroku* [Hiroshima Appeals: Record of Eleven Years Since the Hiroshima Atomic Bombing]. Hiroshima Genbaku Shiryō Shuppan Kai, Hiroshima.

Krebs, C.; Rask-Nielsen, H. C.; and Wagner, A. 1930. "The origin of lymphosarcomatosis and its relation to other forms of leucosis in white mice," *Acta Radiologica* (supplement) 10:1.

Kubo, Y. 1952. Study of human behavior immediately after the atomic bombing of Hiroshima—Socio-psychological study pertaining to the atomic bomb and atomic energy," I, *Shinrigaku Kenkyū* [Japanese Journal of Psychology] 22:103. (English abstract).

*Kumazawa, T.; Matsusaka, Y.; and Teragami, M. 1974. "Investigation of a regular mass examination of atomic bomb survivors," *Journal of the Hiroshima Medical Association* 27:626.

*Kurihara, S. 1970. *Hiroshima Nijūyonen* [Hiroshima Twenty-four Years]. Shakai Shinpō, Tokyo.

*Kurokawa, Y. 1957. "Blood findings of atomic bomb survivors in Tokai district," *Acta Haematologica Japonica* 20(supplement):209.

Kusano, N. 1953a. *Atomic Bomb Injuries.* Tsukiji Shokan, Tokyo.

*Kusano, N. 1953b. "Pathological studies of A-bomb victims in Hiroshima (Autopsy case at Saijō Sanatorium)," in CRIABC, vol. II.

*Kyushu Regional Group to Investigate the Facts Concerning Forced Arrest of Koreans. 1974. *Kyushu Chōsenjin Kyōsei Renkō no Jittai—Shinbun Hōdō Shiryō* [Actual Status of Forced Arrest of Koreans in Kyushu—Newspaper Data]. Kyushu Chihō Chōsenjin Kyōsei Renkō Shinsō Chōsadan.

Lange, R. D.; Moloney, W. C.; and Yamawaki, T. 1954. "Leukemia in atomic bomb survivors. I. General observations," *Blood* 9:574.

Langham, W. H.; Brooks, P. M.; and Graphn, D. 1965. "Radiation biology and space environmental parameters in manned spacecraft design and operations," *Aerospace Medicine* 36 (part 2):1.

Larkin, J. C. 1946. "Distribution of radiation in atomic bombing of Nagasaki," *American Journal of Roentgenology* 55:525.

Laurén, P. 1965. "The two historogical main types of gastric carcinoma: Defuse and so-called intestinal-type of carcinoma—intestinal-type carcinoma," *Acta Pathologica et Microbiologica Scandinavica* 64:31.

Law Concerning Medical Care of Atomic Bomb Survivors. (31 March 1957, Law no. 41).

Law Concerning Special Measures for Atomic Bomb Survivors (20 May 1968, Law no. 53).

LeRoy, G. V. 1947. "Medical sequelae of atomic bomb explosion," *Journal of the American Medical Association* 134:1143.

Liebow, A. A. 1965. "Encounter with disaster: A medical diary of Hiroshima 1945," *Yale Journal of Biology and Medicine* 38:61.

Liebow, A. A.; Warren, S.; and DeCoursey, E. 1949. "Pathology of atomic bomb casualties," *American Journal of Pathology* 25:853.

Lifton, R. J. 1967. *Death in Life—Survivors of Hiroshima.* Random House, New York.

Loke, Y. W. 1967. "Salivary gland tumors in Malaya," *British Journal of Cancer* 21:665.

Looney, W. D. 1949. "Medical aspects of the atomic bomb," *Virginia Medical Monthly* 76:73.

Lorenz, E. 1944. "Radioactivity and lung cancer: A critical review of lung cancer in the miners of Schneeberg and Joachimsthal," *Journal of the National Cancer Institute* 5:1.

Lorenz, E. 1950. "Some biologic effects of long continued irradiation," *American Journal of Roentgenology and Radium Therapy and Nuclear Medicine* 63:176.

Los Alamos Scientific Laboratory. 1944. "Shock hydrodynamics and blast waves," Report AECD-2860.

Lyon, G. M. 1947. "Effects of atomic bomb radiation on human body," *West Virginia Medical Journal* 43:391.

McDougall, I. R.; Kennedy, J. S.; and Thomson, J. A. 1971. "Thyroid carcinoma following I[131] therapy—Report of a case and review of the literature," *Journal of Clinical Endocrinology and Metabolism* 33:287.

McGregor, D. H.; Land, C. E.; Choi, K.; Tokuoka, S.; Liu, P. I.; Wakabayashi, T.; and Beebe, G. W. 1977. "Breast cancer incidence among atomic bomb survivors, Hiroshima and Nagasaki, 1950–69," *Journal of the National Cancer Institute* 59:799.

Mackenzie, I. 1965. "Breast cancer following multiple fluoroscopies," *British Journal of Cancer* 19:1.

MacMahon, B. 1962. "Prenatal X-ray exposure and childhood cancer," *Journal of the National Cancer Institute* 28:1173.

MacMahon, H. E.; Murphy, A. S.; and Bates, M. I. 1947. "Endothelial-cell sarcoma of liver following thorotrast injections," *American Journal of Pathology* 23:585.

*Maeda, E.; Fujisaki, N.; Hada, J.; Fujii, T.; and Namikawa, H. 1955. "Oral clinical examination results of A-bomb survivors." *Journal of the Stomatological Society* 4:196.

*Maekawa, F. 1953. "Stenographic records of the first Report of the Special Committee for Atomic Bomb Casualties: Biology Section," in CRIABC, vol. I.

*Maetani, M. 1955. "Report of ophthalmic examination of the survivors in Ōtake city exposed to the atomic bombing of Hiroshima," *Rinshō Ganka* [Japanese Journal of Clinical Ophthalmology] 9:1235.

*Majima, M.; Tsutsui, T.; and Suga, Y. 1953. "Radiation temperature and blast pressure of atomic bombs in Hiroshima and Nagasaki," in CRIABC, vol. I.

*Maki, H. 1959. *Kōsei no Shihyō* [Index of Health and Welfare Statistics] ABCC Studies. 6 (1):14.

Mansur, G. P.; Keehn, R. J.; Hiramoto, T.; and Will, D. W. 1968. "Lung carcinoma among atomic bomb survivors, Hiroshima–Nagasaki, 1950–64," ABCC TR 19–68.

March, H. C. 1944. "Leukemia in radiologists," *Radiology* 43:275.

Marx, J. L. 1971. *Nagasaki—The Necessary Bomb?* Macmillan, London.

*Mashimo, S.; Kikuchi, T.; Funaoka, S.; Shimizu, S.; et al. 1953. "Study of A-bomb injuries in Hiroshima" (clinical report), in CRIABC, vol. II.

*Masuda, Y. 1955. "The recent clinical study of the radiation cataract in Hiroshima," *Acta Societatis Ophthalmologicae Japonicae* 59:899.

*Masuda, Y. 1962. "Clinical observations concerning the further development of atomic bomb cataract," *Rinshō Ganka* [Japanese Journal of Clinical Ophthalmology] 16:346.

*Masuda, Y. 1966. "Supplemental clinical study on the atomic bomb cataract in Hiroshima," *Acta Societatis Ophthalmologicae Japonicae* 70:1109.

*Masuda, Y.; and Shōji, Y. 1972. "Atomic bomb cataract," in *Crystalline Lens* [Handbook of Clinical Ophthalmology], vol. V, no. 2. Kanehara Shuppan, Tokyo.

*Masuyama, M. 1953. "Statistical study of human casualties of the atomic bomb, especially of the death rate in the acute stage," in CRIABC, vol. I.

*Matsuoka, S. 1959. "Autopsy findings of deceased caused by A-bomb exposure—Bone marrow of the A-bomb exposed (aleukemic group)," *Journal of the Hiroshima Medical Association* 12:919.

*Matsusaka, Y., ed. 1969. *Hibakusha to Tomo ni—Zoku Hiroshima Genbaku Iryōshi* [With Atomic Bomb Survivors—Hiroshima A-bomb Medical Care History (second series)]. Hiroshima Genbaku Shōgai Taisaku Kyōgikai, Hiroshima.

*Matsusaka, Y. 1972. "Epilation as an acute symptom of A-bomb exposure," *Journal of the Hiroshima Medical Association* 25:356.

*Matsusaka, Y. 1978. "Progress of measures for atomic bomb survivors and mission of the Late A-bomb Effects Research Society," *Journal of the Hiroshima Medical Association* 31:339.

*Miki, C. 1960. "Trend of deaths in children exposed to the atomic bomb," *Journal of the Hiroshima Medical Association* (special series) 13:739.

Miller, R. J.; Fujino, T.; and Nefzger, M. D. 1967. "Lens findings in atomic bomb survivors. A review of major ophthalmic surveys at the Atomic Bomb Casualty Commission, 1949–1962," *Archives of Ophthalmology* 78:697.

Miller, R. J.; Fujino, T.; and Nefzger, M. D. 1968. "Eye findings in atomic bomb survivors, 1963–1964, Hiroshima–Nagasaki," ABCC TR 9–68.

Miller, R. W. 1956. "Delayed effects occurring within the first decade after exposure of young individuals to the Hiroshima atomic bomb," *Pediatrics* 18:1.

Miller, R. W.; and Blot, W. J. 1972. "Small head size after in utero exposure to atomic radiation," *Lancet* 2:784.

Milton, R. C.; and Shohoji, T. 1968. "Tentative 1965 radiation dose (T65D) estimation for atomic bomb survivors, Hiroshima and Nagasaki," ABCC TR 1–68.

*Minami, S. 1953. "Dermatological observations of A-bomb injuries," in CRIABC, vol. II.

*Ministry of Health and Welfare, Public Health Bureau. 1967. *Shōwa Yonjūnendo Genshibakudan Hibakusha Jittai Chōsa* [1965 Actual Status Survey of Atomic Bomb Survivors] Kōseishō Kōshūeiseikyoku, Tokyo.
1967a. Summary of Basic Survey.
1967b. Summary of Health Survey and Living Survey.

*Ministry of Health and Welfare, Public Health Bureau, Planning Section. 1977. *Shōwa Gojūnen*

Genshibakudan Hibakusha Jittai Chōsa [1975 Actual Status Survey of Atomic Bomb Survivors] Kōseishō Kōshūeiseikyoku Kikakuka, Tokyo.
  1977*a*. Basic Survey and Living Survey.
  1977*b*. Case Survey.
  1977*c*. Data Section.
*Ministry of Health and Welfare, Public Health Bureau, Planning Section. 1977*d*. *Shōwa Gojū-nendo Genshibakudan Hibakusha Taisaku no Gaiyō* [Summary of Measures for Atomic Bomb Survivors in 1976]. Kōseishō Kōshūeiseikyoku Kikakuka, Tokyo.
*Ministry of Home Affairs, Security Bureau. 1976. "Status of movements of resident Koreans—'Special Secret Service Police Monthly Report' manuscript 1945," in *Zainichi Chōsenjin Kankeishiryō Shūsei* [Collection of Data on Koreans in Japan], vol. V, Pak Gyeung-sik, ed. San-ichi Shobō, Tokyo.
*Misao, T.; Haraguchi, Y.; and Hattori, K. 1953. "A case of monocytic leukemia developed after the acute symptoms by atomic bomb exposure," in CRIABC, vol. II.
*Misao, T.; Hyōdō, S.; Shirakawa, M.; and Yano, T. 1967. "Health condition of atomic bomb survivors with special reference to the cardiovascular system," *Journal of the Hiroshima Medical Association* (special series) 20:260.
*Misao, T.; Kimura, N.; Mimura, M.; Yadomaru, F.; Kimura, M.; Maeda, M.; Hattori, K.; Fukuda, M.; Mitsutake, Y.; Kanemaru, M.; Gotō, M.; Yanase, T.; Miyazaki, K.; and Yamagata, M. 1953. "Clinical observations on A-bomb injuries," in CRIABC, vol. II.
*Mitani, Y. 1953. "Survey of menarche among girl students in Nagasaki, especially effects of the atomic bomb," *Nippon Sanka Fujinka Gakkai Zasshi* [Journal of the Japanese Obstetrics and Gynecology Society] 5:84.
*Mitani, Y. 1954. "Survey of menarche among girl students in Nagasaki, especially effects of the atomic bomb" (second report), *Clinical Gynaecology and Obstetrics* 8:71.
*Mitani, Y. 1955. "A-bomb effects from the obstetrical and gynecological point of view," *Clinical Gynaecology and Obstetrics* 9:933.
Mitani, Y. 1956. "Investigation of menarche of schoolgirls in Nagasaki, especially of the effects of the atomic bomb," in *Research in the effects and influences of the nuclear bomb test explosions*, vol. II. Japan Society for the Promotion of Science, Tokyo.
*Mitani, Y.; Itō, M.; Nozu, S.; Ikuishi, T.; Iwai, M.; Iwadate, M.; and Watanabe. 1953. "Effects of A-bomb exposure on female sexual function in Hiroshima," in CRIABC, vol. I.
  1953*a*. First report.
  1953*b*. Second report.
*Mitani, Y.; and Kidera, A. 1967. "A survey on the mortality rate of Nagasaki A-bomb survivors in relation to malignant diseases," *Journal of the Hiroshima Medical Association* (special series) 20:406.
*Mitani, Y.; and Mori, S. 1961. "Statistical observations on mortality due to malignant tumor of the atomic bomb survivors in Nagasaki," *Nagasaki Medical Journal* 36:724.
*Miyake, M. 1953*a*. "Pathology of atomic bomb injuries," *Rinshō* [Clinical Medicine] 6:38.
*Miyake, M. 1953*b*. "Pathology of atomic bomb injuries: Acute and subacute stage," in PSH.
*Miyake, M. 1967. "Pathology of acute effects from exposure to the atomic bomb," *Journal of the Hiroshima Medical Association* (special series) 20:92.
*Miyake, M.; Sugano, H.; Yokoyama, T.; Yamaguchi, S.; and Hara, M. 1967. "Atomic bomb injuries: Experimental studies on the induced radioactivity by neutrons," *Igaku no Ayumi* [Advances in Medicine] 60:375.
*Miyamoto, T.; Yamamoto, S.; Kajinishi, M.; and Yamashiro, T. ed. 1960. *Nihon Zankoku Monogatari* [Tales of Japanese Atrocities], part 5; Darkness of Modern Times. Heibonsha, Tokyo.
*Miyata, H. 1957. "Hematological studies on atomic bomb survivors living in or near Tokyo," *Acta Haematologica Japonica* 20(supplement):201.
*Miyata, H., editor-author. 1977. *Rokujūgomannin—Zainichi Chōsenjin* [650 Thousand—Koreans in Japan]. Suzusawa Shoten, Tokyo.
*Mizutani, H.; and Watanabe, T. 1978. *Chikyū* [The Earth], Iwanami Earth Science Series, vol. I, S. Uyeda and H. Mizutani, eds. Iwanami Shoten, Tokyo.
Modan, B.; Baidatz, D.; and Mart, H. 1974. "Radiation-induced head and neck tumors," *Cancer*, 1:277.

*Monden, K. 1955. "Menarche of exposed girls." *Journal of the Hiroshima Medical Association* (original series) 3:1035.
*Monzen, T.; and Kamimatsuse, M. 1954. "An autopsy case of carcinoma of the lung found in a male staying near the hypocenter directly after the atomic bomb explosion in Hiroshima," *Acta Pathologica Japonica* 43:305.
Moorhead, P. S.; Nowell, P. C.; Mellman, W. J.; Battips, D. M.; and Hungerford, D. A. 1960. "Chromosome preparations of leukocytes cultured from human peripheral blood," *Experimental Cell Research* 20:613.
*Mori, T. 1966. "Pathological and radiological studies of chronic thorotrast injury. Part I. Study of human materials," *Nippon Acta Radiologica* 26:1028.
*Mori, T. 1977. "Epidemiological and pathological studies of the late effects of thorotrast injection," *Hōshasen Kagaku* [Radiological Science] 20:82.
*Mori, T.; Nozue, Y.; Okamoto, T.; Tanaka, T.; Sugita, K.; and Tsuda, T. 1966. "Follow-up study of the fate of patients who had been administered thorotrast more than twenty-two years previously," *Nippon Acta Radiologica* 25:1144.
*Morita, Y. 1955. "Changes and present status of treatment of Koreans in Japan," *Hōmu Kenkyū Hōkokusho* [Ministry of Justice Research Reports], 43rd collection, no. 3. Hōmu Kēnshūsho, Tokyo.
*Moritaki, I. 1954. "A-bomb orphans," in *Genbaku to Hiroshima* [The Atomic Bomb and Hiroshima]. University Group to Protect Peace and Learning, ed., Collection of Research Papers of University Group, 1. Hiroshima Kyōshokuin Kumiai Jigyōbu, Hiroshima.
*Moritaki, I. 1976. *Hankaku Sanjūnen* [Thirty Years of Antinuclear Weapons Activities]. Nihon Hyōronsha, Tokyo.
Moriyama, I. M.; and Kato, H. 1973. "JNIH-ABCC life span study. seventh report. Mortality rate of A-bomb survivors, 1970–72 and 1950–72," ABCC TR 15–73.
Morris, J. H.; and Creighton, H. A. 1964. "Thyroid carcinoma in adults following external irradiation," *Archives of Internal Medicine* 113:97.
Morton, J. H.; Kingsley, H. D.; and Pearse, H. E. 1952. "Studies on flash burns; threshold burns," *Surgery, Gynecology and Obstetrics* 94:317.
Muller, H. J. 1927. "Artificial transmission of the gene," *Science* 66:84.
*Munaka, M.; Watanabe, T.; Sumita, H.; Yamamoto, H.; Ueoka, H.; Kodama, M.; Watanabe, M.; and Okamoto, N. 1975. "Study on population mobility among A-bomb survivors. 1. Survivors residing in Hiroshima City in fiscal year 1972," in *Proceedings of Fifteenth Annual Meeting of Late Effects of Atomic Bombs*. Nagasaki Genshi Bakudan Kōshōgai Kenkyūkai, Nagasaki.
Murphy, D. P. 1947. "Maternal pelvic irradiation," in *Congenital Malformations,* 2nd ed. Lippincott, Philadelphia, Pa.
*Mutō, K. 1941. "The destruction due to accumulated force (Study of structural failure from blast pressure)," *Transactions of the Architectural Institute of Japan* 21:246.
*Mutō, K. 1952. "The atomic bombs and buildings," *Nihon Kenchiku Gakukai Kenkyū Hōkoku* [Reports of the Architectural Institute of Japan] 20:295.
*Mutō, K.; and Umemura, K. 1953. "Investigation report on damages to buildings by atomic bombs," CRIABC, vol. I.

*Nagai, T., ed. 1949a. *Genshigumo no Shita ni Ikite—Nagasaki no Kodomora no Shuki* [Living beneath the Atomic Cloud—Writings by Nagasaki Children]. Kōdansha, Tokyo.
*Nagai, T. 1949b. *Nagasaki no Kane* [Bell of Nagasaki]. Hibiya Shuppansha, Tokyo.
*Nagaoka, H. 1977. *Genbaku Minshūshi* [People's History of the A-bomb]. Miraisha, Tokyo.
*Nagasaki A-bomb Youth and Maidens Association, ed. 1956. *Mō Iya da—Genbaku no Ikite iru Shōnintachi* [We've Had Enough—Living A-bomb Witnesses], Ayumi Shuppansha, Nagasaki.
*Nagasaki A-bomb Youth and Maidens Association. 1970. *Mō Iya da* [We've Had Enough], vol. II. Nagasaki Seinen Otome no Kai, Nagasaki.
*Nagasaki City International Cultural Hall, A-bomb Data Section. 1975. *Genbaku Hisai Fukugen Chōsa Jigyō Hōkokusho* [Report of the Restoration Survey on the Atomic Bomb Disaster: From fiscal 1970 to fiscal 1974]. Nagasaki Shiyakusho, Nagasaki.

*Nagasaki Cultural League, ed. 1949. *Nagasaki—Nijūni'nin no Genbaku Taiken Kiroku* [Naga-saki—Record of Twenty-two Persons' A-bomb Experiences]. Jiji Tsūshinsha, Tokyo.

*Nagasaki Institute of Technology, Nagasaki Institute of Peace Culture. 1978. *Heiwa Bunka Kenkyū* [Peace Culture Studies], first issue. Nagasaki Zōsen Daigaku, Nagasaki.

Nagasaki Minyū Shinbun [Nagasaki Citizens' Companion Newspaper], 1952. Article in 18 September 1952 edition.

*Nagasaki Peace Education Research Society. 1976. *Nagasaki Heiwa Annai* [Introduction to the Peace of Nagasaki].

*Nagasaki Prefectural Office and Nagasaki City Office. 1964. *Nagasakiken Genbaku Hibakusha Jittai Chōsa Kekkahyō* [Table of Results of Nagasaki Prefecture A-bomb Survivors Actual Status Survey], 1960. Nagasakiken-Nagasakishi, Nagasaki.

*Nagasaki Prefecture Hibakusha Teachers Association and Nagasaki Prefecture Teachers Union Nagasaki General Branch. 1972. *Keishō no Akashi o Tatazu* [The Transmitted Evidence Will Not Be Given Up]. Peace Education of Nagasaki II. Nagasaki Heiwa Kyōiku Kenkyū-kai, Nagasaki.

*Nagasaki Prefecture Hibakusha Teachers Association, Nagasaki Prefecture Teachers Union Peace Education Materials Editorial Committee, and Nagasaki Prefecture Teachers Union Nagasaki General Branch. 1971. *Genbaku o Dō Oshieru Ka* [How Should We Teach About the Atomic Bomb], Peace Education of Nagasaki I. Nagasaki Heiwa Kyōiku Kenkyū-kai, Nagasaki.

*Nagasaki Prefecture Hibakusha Teachers Association and Peace Education Materials Commit-tee. 1972. *Nagasaki no Genbaku Tokuhon* [Nagasaki A-bomb Reader]. Nagasakiken Kyō-shokuin Kumiai, Nagasaki.

Nagasaki Prefecture Hibakusha Teachers Association and Peace Education Materials Editorial Committee. 1977. *In the Sky over Nagasaki—An A-bomb Reader for Children,* translated by Cheryl-Green Lammers Translation Collective. Nagasaki o Sekai ni Tsutaeru Kai, Naga-saki.

*Nagasaki Prefecture Teachers Union, Nagasaki General Branch, and Nagasaki City Hibakusha Teachers Association. 1970. *Chinmoku no Kabe o Yabutte* [Breaking the Wall of Silence]. Rōdō Junpō Sha, Tokyo.

*Nagasaki Prefecture Teachers Union Peace Education Materials Editorial Committee. 1975. *Heiwa Kyōiku no Ayumi* [Course of Peace Education). Nagasakiken Kyōshokuin Kumiai, Nagasaki.

*Nagasaki Prefecture Teachers Union Peace Education Materials Editorial Committee. 1977a. *Genbaku o Oshietsuzukete* [On Continuing to Teach about the Atomic Bomb]. Peace Educa-tion of Nagasaki III. Nagasaki Heiwa Kyōiku Kenkyūkai, Nagasaki.

*Nagasaki Prefecture Teachers Union Peace Education Materials Editorial Committee. 1977b. *Heiwa no Ayumi—Kenkyū no Tebiki* [Steps toward Peace—Guide to Research], 3 vols. Nagasakiken Kyōshokuin Kumiai, Nagasaki.

*Nagasaki Shiyakusho.† 1970. *Genbaku Shiryō Mokuroku—Ano Hi no Tsumeato* [Catalogue of A-bomb Records—Scars Remaining Since That Day]. Nagasaki Kokusai Bunka Kaikan [Nagasaki International Cultural Hall]. Nagasaki.

*Nagasaki Shiyakusho. 1977. *Nagasaki Genbaku Sensaishi* [Record of the Nagasaki A-bomb War Disaster (RNAWD)], vol. I. Nagasaki Kokusai Bunka Kaikan [Nagasaki International Cultural Hall]. Nagasaki.

*Nagasaki Shiyakusho, A-bomb Survivors Measures Department. 1974. *The A-bombed Area Map.* Nagasaki.

*Nagasaki Shiyakusho, A-bomb Survivors Measures Department, 1978. *Genbaku Hibakusha Taisaku Jigyō Gaiyō* [Summary of A-bomb Survivors Measures Projects], 1978 ed. Nagasaki.

*Nagasaki Shiyakusho, Civil Welfare Department, Social Affairs Section. 1964. *Nagasakishi o Shutosuru Genbaku Hibakusha Jittai Chōsa no Kenkyū* [Study of A-bomb Survivors Actual Status Survey Mainly with Reference to Nagasaki City]. Nagasaki.

*Nagasaki Shiyakusho, Investigation Section. 1949. *Nagasaki Shisei Yōran* [Nagasaki City Alma-nac], 1949 ed. Nagasaki.

*Nagasaki Shiyakusho, Investigation Section. 1951. *Nagasaki Shisei Yōran* [Nagasaki City Alma-nac], 1950 ed. Nagasaki.

*Nagasaki Shiyakusho, General Affairs Department, Investigation and Statistics Section. 1959.

† Nagasaki City Office.

Nagasaki Shisei Rokujūnenshi [Sixty-five-year History of the Municipality of Nagasaki], 3 vols. Nagasaki.

*Nagasaki Women's Society. 1970. *Nagasaki no Gōkyū—Nagasakishi Fujinkai Hibaku Taikenki* [Nagasaki Lamentations—A-bomb Experiences of Nagasaki Women's Society Members]. Nagasakishi Fujinkai, Nagasaki.

*Nakaizumi M.; Tabuchi, A.; Shimizu, K.; and Arima, M. 1967. *Tainaihibaku Shōtōshō no Ekigakuteki Kenkyū narabini Shoki no Shōgai ni Kansuru Kenkyū* [Epidemiological Study of Microcephaly Due to Exposure In Utero and Studies Concerning Various Dysfunctions], Kōseishō Tainai Hibaku Shōtōshō Kenkyū-han Hōkoku (Report of Health and Welfare Ministry's In-utero Exposed Microcephaly Research Team).

*Nakajima, Y.; Ishikawa, K.; Ide, I.; Ozeki, K.; Koga, K.; Hayashi, R.; Sakurai, T.; Kinoshita, T.; Gyōtoku, H.; Jinnai, T.; Yoshida, M.; Katsuhara, O.; Yoshihara, T.; Uozumi, K.; Kanemitsu, K.; Hirayama, G.; Miyagi, N.; Kadota, H.; Tokutomi, H.; Terashima, S.; Kanbara, M.; Nonaka, Y.; Etō, S.; and Kojima, R. 1953. "Investigation of A-bomb damage to human bodies in Nagasaki city," in CRIABC, vol. II.

*Nakamura, K. 1953. "The survey of the A-bomb disaster in Nagasaki," in CRIABC, vol. I.

*Nakamura, K. 1977. "Stomach cancer in atomic bomb survivors," RERF TR 8–77.

*Nakano, S. 1954. "Sociological study of atomic bomb effects," in *Genbaku to Hiroshima* [The Atomic Bomb and Hiroshima], Collection of Research Papers of University Men's Group, first collection. University Group to Protect Peace and Learning, ed. Hiroshimaken Kyōshokuin Kumiai Jigyōbu, Hiroshima.

*Nakano, S. 1978. "Solidarity lives" (first, second, and third parts), *Chūgoku Shinbun* [Chūgoku Newspaper], 16–18 January.

*Nakao, K. 1953. "On the changes in the hematopoiesis of patients exposed to the atomic bombs and of the animals exposed to X-ray irradiation," in PSH.

*Nakao, K.; Kobayashi, G.; Katō, S.; Yano, Y.; and Komiya, M. 1953. "Hematological studies of A-bomb radiation injuries," in CRIABC, vol. I.

*Nakatsuka, A. 1978. "The problem of Korean atomic bomb survivors—A historical study," *Rekishi Hyōron* [Historical Review] 336:38. Azekura Shobō, Tokyo.

*Nakayama, H. 1953. "Biological investigation of atomic bomb disaster, part II, Effect on plants, chapter 4. Radiation effects on plants," in CRIABC, vol. I.

*Nakayama, H. "Nakayama Hiromi Nikki" [Unpublished diary of Hiromi Nakayama]. Property of Hidetsugu Aihara.

*Nakayama, S. 1968. *Shi no Kage* [Shadow of Death]. Nanbokusha, Tokyo.

Nakazawa, K. 1975. *Hadashi no Gen* [Barefoot Gen], 4 vols. Chōbunsha, Tokyo. English edition published by San-yūsha Shuppan, Tokyo, 1979.

National Delegation [from Japan] to the U.N.O. Demanding "An international treaty completely banning nuclear weapons and immediate measures to ban their use." 1976. "An Introductory Report on the damage and aftereffects of the atomic bombings of Hiroshima and Nagasaki—Address to the Secretary-General of the United Nations." Tokyo.

*National Education Research Institute. 1977. *Heiwa Kyōiku no Riron to Jissen* [Theory and Practice of Peace Education]. Sōdobunka, Tokyo.

Neel, J. V.; Kato, H.; and Schull, W. J. 1974. "Mortality in children of atomic bomb survivors and controls," *Genetics* 76:311.

Neel, J. V.; McDonald, D. J.; Morton, N. E.; Kodani, M.; Takeshima, K.; Anderson, R. C.; Wood, J.; Brewer, R.; Wright, S.; Yamazaki, J.; Suzuki, M.; and Kitamura, S. 1953a. "The effect of exposure to the atomic bombs on pregnancy termination in Hiroshima and Nagasaki," *Science* 118:537.

Neel, J. V.; Morton, N. E.; Schull, W. J.; McDonald, D. J.; Kodani, M.; Takeshima, K.; Anderson, R. C.; Wood, J.; Brewer, R.; Wright, S.; Yamazaki, J.; Suzuki, M.; and Kitamura, S. 1953b. "The effect of exposure of parents to the atomic bombs on first-generation offspring in Hiroshima and Nagasaki," *Japanese Journal of Genetics* 28:211.

Neel, J. V.; and Schull, W. J. 1956. "The effect of exposure to the atomic bombs on pregnancy termination in Hiroshima and Nagasaki," National Academy of Sciences, National Research Council, United States, no. 491.

Newmark, N. M.; and Hansen R. J. 1961. *Design of Blast-resistant Structures, Shock and Vibration Hand Book.* McGraw-Hill, New York.

*NGO International Symposium on the Damage and Aftereffects of the Atomic Bombing of Hiroshima and Nagasaki, Hiroshima Expert Committee and Hiroshima Institute for Peace

Education. 1977a. *Hiroshima de Oshieru—Kakujidai no Heiwa Kyōiku* [Teaching in Hiroshima—Peace Education in the Nuclear Age]. Rōdō Kyōiku Sentā, Tokyo.

*NGO International Symposium on the Damage and Aftereffects of the Atomic Bombing, Nagasaki Preparatory Committee and Expert Committee for the Preparation of the Nagasaki Report. 1977b. *Genbaku Hibaku no Jissō—Nagasaki Repōto* [Real Facts of the Damage and Aftereffects of the Atomic Bombing—Nagasaki Report]. NGO Hibakumondai Kokusai Shinpojiumu Nagasaki Junbi Iinkai, Nagasaki.

*Nihon Heiwa Iinkai—Hiroshimaken Heiwa Iinkai. 1976. *Hiroshima Heiwa Annai—Hiroshima no Kokoro o Tazunete* [Introduction to the Peace of Hiroshima—An Inquiry into the Mind of Hiroshima]. Tokyo, Hiroshima.

*Nishida, S. 1956. "Life span in the A-bombed. I. Study on deaths of the A-bombed during the late stage," *Journal of the Hiroshima Medical Association* (original series) 4:886.

*Nishida, S. 1957. "Life span of the exposed. III. Survey for latter period, 1951–55, on birth and stillbirths of the exposed," *Journal of the Hiroshima Medical Association* (special series) 10:35.

*Nishijima, A. 1968. *Genbaku wa Naze Tōka Sareta ka—Nihon Kōfuku o Meguru Senryaku to Gaikō* [Why Was the Atomic Bomb Dropped?—Strategy and Diplomacy Concerning Japan's Surrender]. Aoki Shoten, Tokyo.

*Nishikawa, T.; and Tsuiki, S. 1961. "Psychiatric investigations of atomic bomb survivors," *Nagasaki Medical Journal* 36:717.

*Nishimaru, K. 1969. "Hiroshima and the atomic bomb," *Journal of the Hiroshima Medical Association* 22:56.

*Nishina Memorial Foundation, ed. 1973. *Genshi Bakudan—Hiroshima-Nagasaki no Shashin to Kiroku* [The Atomic Bombs—Photos and Records of Hiroshima and Nagasaki]. Kōfūsha Shoten, Tokyo.

Nishiyama, H.; Anderson, R. E.; Ishimaru, T.; Ishida, K.; Ii, Y.; and Okabe, N. 1973. "The incidence of malignant lymphoma and multiple myeloma in atomic bomb survivors, Hiroshima-Nagasaki 1945–65," *Cancer* 32:1301.

*Ōe, K. 1965. *Hiroshima Nōto* [Hiroshima Notes]. Iwanami Shoten, Tokyo.

*Office of the Committee for the Erection of a Monument to Primary School Teachers and Pupils Killed by the Atomic Bomb. 1971. *Ryūtō—Hiroshima no Ko to Haha to Kyōshi no Kiroku—Genbaku Gisei Kokumin Gakkō Kyōshi to Kodomo Tsuitō no Ki* [Setting Lighted Paper Lanterns Adrift on the Water—Record of Child and Mother and Teacher—An Account in Memory of the Primary School Teachers and Pupils Killed by the Atomic Bomb]. Hiroshima Kyōiku Kaikan Shuppanbu, Hiroshima.

*Oguma, N.; Uchino, H.; Okamoto, M.; Ooya, M.; Kamada, N.; Satow, Y.; Nagata, N.; Hattori, T.; Hino, S.; Yamamoto, H.; Yano, M.; Yuzaki, M.; and Watanabe, T. 1975. "A comparative study on atomic bomb survivors who were exposed proximally. 3. Chromosome aberrations in bone marrow cells and peripheral blood," in *Proceedings of Fifteenth Annual Meeting of Late Effects of Atomic Bombs.* Nagasaki Genshi Bakudan Kōshōgai Kenkyū-kai, Nagasaki.

*Ogura, K. 1953. "Biological investigation of atomic bomb disaster. Part II. Effect on plants. Chapter 1. Outline of the investigation," in CRIABC, vol. I.

*Ohkita, T. 1969. "Recent trends in the incidence of leukemia among Hiroshima A-bomb survivors," *Journal of the Hiroshima Medical Association* 22:379.

Ohkita, T. 1975. "A review of thirty years study of Hiroshima and Nagasaki atomic bomb survivors. II. Biological effects. A. Acute effects," *Journal of Radiation Research* (Tokyo) 16(supplement):49.

*Ohkita, T. 1976. "Leukemia in Hiroshima atomic bomb survivors from 1946 to 1975. A summary of the findings and recent trends," *Proceedings of Hiroshima University Research Institute for Nuclear Medicine and Biology* 17:77.

*Ohkita, T.; Ohara, K.; and Nakanishi, S. 1969. "Clinical and epidemiological studies of leukemia among Hiroshima survivors," *Nihon Rinshō* [Japanese Journal of Clinical Medicine] 27:2151.

*Ohkita, T.; and Takahashi, H. 1970. "Statistical studies of anemia of Hiroshima A-bomb survivors during their pregnancy," *Journal of the Hiroshima Medical Association* 23:1044.

*Ohkita, T.; and Takahashi, H. 1972. "Anemia in pregnancy among Hiroshima A-bomb survivors," *Nagasaki Medical Journal* 47:285.

*Ohkita, T.; Takahashi, H.; Kawakami, M.; Shigeta, C.; and Shimizu, H. 1976. "Leukemia among Hiroshima A-bomb survivors from 1971 to 1975," *Nagasaki Medical Journal* 51:171.

*Ohkita, T.; and Watanabe, S. 1979. "Epidemiology of leukemia. Prevalence of leukemia among Hiroshima atomic bomb survivors," in *Shinpan Nihon Ketsueki-gaku Zensho* [Handbook of Hematology, new edition], vol. VI. Maruzen, Tokyo.

*Oho, G. 1956. "Statistical observation on deaths due to malignant neoplasm in A-bomb survivors," *Nihon Iji Shinpō* [Japanese Medical Journal] 1686:8.

*Oho, G. 1959. "Statistical observation on deaths due to malignant neoplasm in A-bomb survivors, second report," *Nihon Iji Shinpō* [Japanese Medical Journal] 1839:27.

*Oho, G. 1960. "Statistical observation on deaths due to malignant neoplasm in A-bomb survivors, third report," *Journal of the Hiroshima Medical Association* 13:287.

*Oho, G. 1961. "Statistical study on the causes of death occurring among atomic bomb survivors," *Journal of the Hiroshima Medical Association* 14:323.

*Oho, G. 1963. "Statistical observation on deaths due to malignant neoplasm in A-bomb survivors, fourth report," *Nagasaki Medical Journal* (special issue) 38:117.

*Oka, Y., ed. 1959. *Gendai Nihon no Seiji Katei* [Political Course of Modern Japan]. Iwanami Shoten, Tokyo.

*Okada, H. 1977. A written report, in RNAWD, vol. I.

*Okada, K. 1953a. "Biological investigation of atomic bomb disasters. Part I. Effect on animals," in CRIABC, vol. I.

*Okada, K. 1953b. "Stenographic records of the Second Report of the Special Committee for Atomic Bomb Casualties: Biology Section," in CRIABC, vol. I.

*Okada, K.; Shimazono, Y.; and Hakamada, S. 1953. "Cerebral findings in A-bomb victims," in CRIABC, vol. I.

Okajima, S. 1975. "A review of thirty years study of Hiroshima and Nagasaki atomic bomb survivors. I. Dosimetry. C. Dose estimation from residual and fallout radioactivity: Fallout in the Nagasaki-Nishiyama district," *Journal of Radiation Research* (Tokyo) 16(supplement):35.

*Okajima, S.; Shiomi, T.; Norimura, T.; Yoshinaga, H.; Takeshita, K.; Antoku, S.; Russell, W. J.; Fujita, S.; Neriishi, S.; and Kawamoto, S. 1972. "Radioactive fallout effect survey of Nishiyama residents Nagasaki: Result of chromosome examination," *Nagasaki Medical Journal* 47:232.

Okajima, S.; Takeshita, K.; Antoku, S.; Shiomi, T.; Russell, W. J.; Fujita, S.; Yoshinaga, H.; Neriishi, S.; Kawamoto, S.; and Norimura, T. 1975. "Effects of the radioactive fallout of the Nagasaki atomic bomb," ABCC TR 12–75.

Okajima, S.; Takeshita, K.; Antoku, S.; Shiomi, T.; Russell, W. J.; Fujita, S.; Yoshinaga, H.; Neriishi, S.; Kawamoto, S.; and Norimura, T. 1978. "Radioactive fallout effects of the Nagasaki atomic bomb," *Health Physics* 34:621.

*Ōkawa, K.; Ishiwatari, S.; Yamada, S.; and Ishi, H. 1966. *Shihon Sutokku* [Capital Stock] (Chōki Keizai Tōkei 3 [Long-term Economic Statistics III]). Tōyō Keizai Shinpōsha, Tokyo.

*Ōkoshi, M.; Asakura, S.; and Kaseki, T. 1953. "Seminal findings in Hiroshima A-bomb survivors," in CRIABC, vol. I.

*Okumura, N.; and Hikida, H. 1949. "Results of psychoneurological studies on atomic bomb survivors," *Kyushu Shinkei Seishin Igaku* [Kyushu Neuropsychiatry] 1:50.

*Ono, K.; Imai, T.; Gotō, S.; Sakane, H.; Mitsui, N.; and Okabe, N. 1953a. "Pathological findings in A-bomb injuries" (first report), in CRIABC, vol. II.

*Ono, K.; Imai, T.; Mitsui, N.; and Okabe, N. 1953b. "Supplementary report on pathological findings in A-bomb injuries," in CRIABC, vol. II.

Osada, A., ed. 1951. *Genbaku no Ko—Hiroshima no Shōnen Shōjo no Uttae* [Children of the Atomic Bomb—Testament of the Boys and Girls of Hiroshima]. Iwanami Shoten, Tokyo. Published in English by Uchida Rōkakuho, Tokyo; P. Owen, London; and Putnam's, New York (1959).

*Osada, A., ed. 1953. *Genbaku no Ko ni Kotaete* [In Response to Children of the Atomic Bomb]. Maki Shoten, Tokyo.

*Ōta, S. 1958. "The effects of radiation on the development of the jaw," *Journal of Osaka University Dental Society* 3:123.

*Ōta, Y. 177. "Masanobu, let us walk slowly," in *Genbaku no Nokoshita Kora—Tainai Hibaku Shōtōshō no Kiroku* [Children Left behind by the Atomic Bomb—Record of Microcephaly due to Exposure in Utero, Kinoko-kai, ed. Keisuisha, Hiroshima.

*Ōtsuru, S. 1968. "An autopsy case of A-bomb microcephaly in children exposed in utero," *Nagasaki Medical Journal* 43:882.

*Ōuchi, G. 1967. "Clinics [surgery] in the early period after the atomic bombing," *Journal of the Hiroshima Medical Association* (special series) 20:141.

Oughterson, A. W.; Barnett, H. L.; LeRoy, G. V.; Rosenbaum, J. D.; Liebow, A. A.; Schneider, B. A.; and Hammond, E. C. 1951. *Medical Effects of Atomic Bombs: The Report of the Joint Commission for the Investigation of the Effects of the Atomic Bomb in Japan*, vol. VI. United States Atomic Energy Commission, Technical Information Service, Oak Ridge, Tennessee.

Oughterson, A. W.; and Warren, S. 1956. *Medical Effects of the Atomic Bomb in Japan*. McGraw-Hill, New York.

*Ozono, N. 1965. "Effects of radiation on the chromosomes of the bone marrow cells," *Acta Haematologica Japonica* 28:308.

Pace, N.; and Smith, R. E. 1959. "Measurement of the residual radiation intensity at the sites of the Hiroshima and Nagasaki atomic bombs," ABCC TR 26–59.

*Pak, C. 1957. *Zainichi Chōsenjin ni Kansuru Sōgōteki Kenkyū* [Comprehensive Study Concerning Koreans in Japan]. Shinkigensha, Tokyo.

*Pak, G. 1965. *Chōsenjin Kyōsei Renkō no Kiroku* [Record of Forced Arrest of Koreans]. Miraisha, Tokyo.

*Pak, G., ed. 1976. *Zainichi Chōsenjin Kankei Shiryō Shūsei* [Collection of Data on Koreans in Japan]; vol. V (5 vols., 1975–76). San-ichi Shobō, Tokyo.

*Pak, M. 1978. "Liquidation of nuclear weapons and independent peaceful unification of the fatherland: From the course followed by Korean atomic bomb survivors resident in Nagasaki," *Nagasaki no Shōgen* [Testimony of Nagasaki], tenth collection. Nagasaki no Shōgen Kankō Iinkai, Nagasaki.

*Pak, S. 1969. "Forced arrest of Koreans—as told from personal experience," in *Dokyumento Nihonjin 8—Anchihyūman* [Document Japanese 8—Antihuman]. Ken'ichi Tanigawa, Shunsuke Tsurumi, and Ichirō Murakami, eds. Gakugei Shorin, Tokyo.

*Pak, S.; Kwak, K.; and Sin, W. 1975. *Hibaku Kankokujin* [A-bomb–Exposed Koreans]. Asahi Shimbunsha, Tokyo.

Parker, L. N.; Belsky, J. L.; Yamamoto, T.; Kawamoto, S.; and Keehn, R. J. 1973. "Thyroid carcinoma diagnosed between thirteen and twenty-six years after exposure to atomic radiation," ABCC TR 5–73.

Pearse, H. E.; and Kingsley, H. D. 1954. "Thermal burns from the atomic bomb," *Surgery Gynecology and Obstetrics* 98:385.

Penny, L.; Samuels, D. E. J.; and Scorgie, G. C. 1970. "The nuclear explosive yields at Hiroshima and Nagasaki," *Philosophical Transactions of the Royal Society of London* A266:357.

Pifer, J. W.; Toyooka, E. T.; Murray, R. W.; Ames, W. R.; and Hempelmann, L. H. 1963. "Neoplasms in children treated with X-rays for thymic enlargement. I. Neoplasms and mortality," *Journal of the National Cancer Institute* 31:1333.

Plummer, G. 1952. "Anomalies occurring in children exposed in utero, Hiroshima," *Pediatrics* 10:687.

Pochin, E. E.; Myant, N. B.; and Corbett, B. D. 1956. "Leukaemia following radioiodine treatment of hyperthyroidism," *British Journal of Radiology* 29:31.

*Prime Minister's Office, Statistics Bureau. 1948. *Shōwa Jūnen ni Okeru Waga Kokufu Oyobi Kokumin Shotokugaku* [Our National Wealth and National Income in 1935]. Sōrichō, Tokyo.

*Prime Minister's Office, Statistics Bureau. 1949. *Showa Jūgonen Kokusei Chōsa, Shōwa Jūkyūnen Jinkō Chōsa, Shōwa Nijūnen Jinkō Chōsa Kekka Hōkoku Tekiyō* [Summary of Reported Results of 1940 National Census, 1944 Census, 1945 Census and 1946 Census], Nihon Tōkei Kyōkai, Tokyo.

*Prime Minister's Office, Statistics Bureau. 1951a. *Sōrifu Tōkeikyoku Hachijūnenshi Kō* [Draft of Eighty-year History of Statistics Bureau, Prime Minister's Office]. Sōrifu Tōkeikyoku, Tokyo.

*Prime Minister's Office, Statistics Bureau. 1951b. *Shōwa Nijūgonen Kokusei Chōsa Hōkoku* [1950 National Census Report], vol. VI: Settled Population and Present Population. Nihon Tōkei Kyōkai, Tokyo.

*Prime Minister's Office, Statistics Bureau. 1954. Shōwa Nijūgonen Kokusei Chōsa Hōkoku

[1950 National Census Report], vol. VII: Region and Prefectures Section—34: Hiroshima Prefecture. Nihon Tōkei Kyōkai, Tokyo.

*Prime Minister's Office, Statistics Bureau. 1953. *Shōwa Nijūgonen Kokusei Chōsa Hōkoku* [1950 National Census Report], vol. VII: Region and Prefectures Section—42: Nagasaki Prefecture. Nihon Tōkei Kyōkai, Tokyo.

*Prime Minister's Office, Statistics Bureau. 1962. *Shōwa Sanjūgonen Kokusei Chōsa Hōkoku* [1960 National Census Report], vol. IV: Region and Prefectures Section—42: Nagasaki Prefecture. Sōrifu Tōkeikyoku, Tokyo.

*Prime Minister's Office, Statistics Bureau. 1963. *Shōwa Sanjūgonen Kokusei Chōsa Hōkoku* [1960 National Census Report], vol. IV: Region and Prefectures Section—34: Hiroshima Prefecture. Sōrifu Tōkeikyoku, Tokyo.

*Prime Minister's Office, Statistics Bureau. 1966. *Shōwa Sanjūgonen Kokusei Chōsa Hōkoku* [1960 National Census Report], vol. I: Total Number of Population. Sōrifu Tōkeikyoku, Tokyo.

*Prime Minister's Office, Statistics Bureau. 1977a. *Shōwa Jūkyūnen Jinkō Chōsa Shūkei Kekka Tekiyō* [Summary of the Tabulated Results of the 1944 Census], Nihon Tōkei Kyōkai, Tokyo.

*Prime Minister's Office, Statistics Bureau. 1977b. *Shōwa Nijūnen Jinkō Chōsa Shūkei Kekka Tekiyō* [Summary of the Tabulated Results of the 1945 Census], Nihon Tōkei Kyōkai, Tokyo.

*Prisoners of War Information Bureau. 1955. *Furyo Toriatsukai no Kiroku* [Record of Treatment of Prisoners of War], December. Document in the Custody of Investigation Section, Repatriation Bureau, Ministry of Health and Welfare, Japan.

*Professor Seiichi Nakano Commemorative Projects Society, ed. 1965. *Nakama to Tomoni—Nakano Seiichi Kyōju Hiroshima Daigaku Gotaikan Kinen Ronshū* [With Colleagues—Collection of Papers in Commemoration of the Retirement of Professor Seiichi Nakano from Hiroshima University]. Nakano Seiichi Kyōju Kinen Jigyō Kai, Hiroshima.

*Publications Committee of Testimonies of Nagasaki. 1969. *Nagasaki no Shōgen* [Testimonies of Nagasaki]. Ayumi Shuppan, Nagasaki.

*Reconstruction Groups of Yamazato and Hamaguchi Townships. 1972. *Bakushin no Oka nite* [On the Hill Where the Bomb Hit]. Nagasaki no Shōgen Kankō Iinkai, Nagasaki.

*Relief Squad dispatched by Hario Marine Corps. 1973. "Nagasaki City atomic bomb damages investigation report" (dated 12 September 1945), in *Genshi Bakudan—Hiroshima-Nagasaki no Shashin to Kiroku* [The Atomic Bombs—Photographs and Records of Hiroshima and Nagasaki]. Nishina Memorial Foundation, ed. Kōfūsha Shoten, Tokyo.

Report of the British Mission to Japan on an Investigation of the Effects of the Atomic Bombs Dropped at Hiroshima and Nagasaki. English reprint, n.d.

Reynolds, E. L. 1959. "Growth and development of Hiroshima children exposed to the atomic bomb: Three-year study (1951–1953)," ABCC TR 20–59.

*Ri, S. 1977. "The forgotten people—A review of the Korean Hibakusha problems," *Tōitsu Hyōron* [Unified Review], October 1977 issue. Tōitsu Hyōronsha, Tokyo.

Ritchie, R. H.; and Hurst, G. S. 1959. "Penetration of weapons radiation—Application to the Hiroshima-Nagasaki studies," *Health Physics* 1:390.

Rossi, H. H.; and Kellerer, A. M. 1972. "Radiation carcinogenesis at low doses," *Science* 175:200.

Russell, W. J. 1975. "A review of thirty years study of Hiroshima and Nagasaki atomic bomb survivors. I. Dosimetry. D. Diagnostic and therapeutic radiation exposure," *Journal of Radiation Research* (Tokyo) 16(supplement):42.

Russell, W. J.; Keehn, R. J.; Ihno, Y.; Hattori, F.; Kogure, T.; and Imamura, K. 1973. "Bone maturation in children exposed to the atomic bomb in utero," *Radiology* 108:367.

Russell, W. L. 1963. "The effect of radiation dose rate and fractionation on mutation in mice," *Repair from Genetic Radiation Damage*. F. H. Sobel, ed. Pergamon Press, New York.

Saccomanno, G.; Archer, V. E.; Auerbach, O.; Kusehner, M.; Saunders, R. P.; and Klein, M. G. 1971. "Histologic types of lung cancer among uranium miners," *Cancer* 27:515.

*Saeki, F. 1977. "Summary of Hiroshima City war disaster management (Data of Repatriation Bureau, Ministry of Health and Welfare)," in RHAWD, vol. I.

Saenger, E. L.; Silverman, F. N.; Sterling, T. D.; and Turner, M. 1960. "Neoplasia following therapeutic irradiation for benign conditions in childhood," *Radiology* 74:889.

Safa, A. M.; and Schumacker, O. P. 1975. "Long-term follow-up results in children and adolescents treated with radioactive iodine for hyperthyroidism," *New England Journal of Medicine* 292:167.

Sagan, L. A.; and Seigel, D. 1963. "ABCC-JNIH adult health study report 2, 1958–60: Cycle of examination, Nagasaki." ABCC TR 12–63.

*Saito, N. 1961. "Estimation of neutron flux from Hiroshima and Nagasaki atomic bombs— Radiochemical evaluation," in *Monbushō Kenkyū Hōkoku Shūroku, 1960, Hōshasen—Sōgō Kenkyū* [Annual Reports of the Cooperative Research by the Ministry of Education, 1960]. Nihon Gakujutsu Shinkōkai, Tokyo.

Sampson, R. J.; Key, C. R.; Buncher, C. R.; and Iijima, S. 1969a. "Prevalence of thyroid carcinoma at autopsy, Hiroshima 1957–65, Nagasaki 1951–67," *Journal of the American Medical Association* 209:65.

Sampson, R. J.; Key, C. R.; Buncher, C. R.; and Iijima, S. 1969b. "The age factor in radiation carcinogenesis of the human thyroid," ABCC TR 7–69.

Sampson, R. J.; Key, C. R.; Buncher, C. R.; and Iijima, S. 1970a. "The smallest forms of papillary carcinoma of the thyroid. A study of 141 microcarcinomas less than 0.1 cm in greatest dimension," ABCC TR 18–70.

Sampson, R. J.; Key, C. R.; Buncher, C. R.; Oka, H.; and Iijima, S. 1970b. "Papillary carcinoma of the thyroid gland sizes of 525 tumors found at autopsy in Hiroshima and Nagasaki," *Cancer* 25:1391.

Sampson, R. J.; Oka, H.; Key, C. R.; Buncher, C. R.; and Iijima, S. 1970c. "An autopsy study of cervical metastasis from occult carcinoma of the thyroid, Hiroshima, Nagasaki 1957–68," *Cancer* 25:803.

Sasaki, M. S. 1971. "Radiation-induced chromosome aberrations in lymphocytes: Possible biological dosimeter in man," in *Biological Aspects of Radiation Protection*, T. Sugahara and O. Hug, eds. Igaku-Shoin, Tokyo.

Sasaki, M. S.; and Miyata, H. 1968. "Biological dosimetry in atomic bomb survivors," *Nature* 220:1189.

*Satō, C. 1976. "Biological genetic approach to the study of late A-bomb effects," *Nagasaki Medical Journal* 51:271.

*Sawada, H. 1958. "Evaluation of gynecological tumors in atomic bomb survivors," *Hiroshima Journal of Medical Science* 7:187.

*Sawada, H. 1960. "Sexual function of women who survived the atomic bomb," *Journal of the Hiroshima Medical Association* (special series) 13:1158.

Sawada, S.; Wakabayashi, T.; Takeshita, K.; Yoshinaga, H.; and Russell, W. J. 1971. "Radiologic practice since the atomic bombs," *American Journal of Public Health* 61:2455.

*Sawada, T.; Masuya, T.; Oda, H.; Arakawa, H.; and Hayashi, N. 1953. "Clinical study of A-bomb injuries, first report: The effect on people residing in the bombed areas," in CRIABC, vol. II.

Schlaegel, Jr., T. F. 1947. "Ocular histopathology of some Nagasaki atomic bomb casualties," *American Journal of Ophthalmology*, 30:127.

Schreiber, W. M.; Kato, H.; and Robertson, J. D. 1970. "Primary carcinoma of the liver, Hiroshima-Nagasaki 1961–1967," *Cancer* 26:69.

Schull, W. J.; and Neel, J. V. 1958. "Radiation and the sex ratio in man," *Science* 128:343.

Schull, W. J.; Neel, J. V.; and Hashizume, A. 1966. "Some further observations on the sex ratio among infants born to survivors of the atomic bombings of Hiroshima and Nagasaki," *American Journal of Human Genetics* 18:328.

*Science Council of Japan, ed. 1951. *Genshibakudan Saigai Chōsa Hōkokusho* [SRIABC]. Nihon Gakujutsu Shinkōkai, Tokyo.

*Science Council of Japan. 1953. *Genshibakudan Saigai Chōsa Hōkokushū* [CRIABC,], 2 vols. Nihon Gakujutsu Shinkōkai, Tokyo.

*Science Council of Japan. 1974. *Nihon Gakujutsu Kaigi Nijūgonenshi* [Twenty-five-year History of Science Council of Japan]. Nihon Gakujutsu Kaigi, Tokyo.

Segi, M. 1977. "Graphic presentation of cancer incidence by site and by area and population." Compiled from the data published in *Cancer Incidence in Five Continents*, vol. III. Segi Institute of Cancer Epidemiology, Nagoya.

Segi, M.; and Kurihara, M. 1972. *Cancer Mortality for Selected Sites in 24 Countries (1966– 67)*, no. 6. Japan Cancer Society, Nagoya.

670 Bibliography

*Sekai [World]. 1960. "Record of forced arrest of Chinese during the war." May edition. Iwanami Shoten, Tokyo.
*Sekai [World]. 1974. "Sit-in on Hibakusha." January edition. Iwanami Shoten, Tokyo.
Seigel, D. G. 1966. "Frequency of live births among survivors of the atomic bombs, Hiroshima and Nagasaki," Radiation Research 28:278.
Seltser, R.; and Sartwell, P. E. 1965. "The influence of occupational exposure to radiation in the mortality of American radiologists and other medical specialties," American Journal of Epidemiology 81:2.
*Seto, N. 1954–55. "On the fertility of the exposed women," Journal of the Hiroshima Medical Association (original series) 2(1954):864, 3(1955):123.
*Setoguchi, M. 1951. "Effects of the atomic bomb on children," Nika Shinryō [Journal of Pediatric Praxis] 14:467.
*Setsuta, T. 1957. "Hematological observations on the atomic bomb survivors now living in the Kinki area eleven years from the time of the exposure," Acta Haematologica Japonica 20(supplement):213.
Shellabarger, C. J.; Brown, R. D.; Rao, A. R.; Shanley, J. P.; Bond, V. P.; Kellerer, A. M.; Rossi, H. H.; Goodman, L. J.; and Mills, R. E. 1974. "Rat mammary carcinogenesis following neutron or X-radiation," Biological Effects of Neutron Irradiation, vol. I. International Atomic Energy Agency, Vienna.
*Shibata, S. 1978. Gendai no Kadai I—Kakuheiki Haizetsu no Tame ni [Present-day problems I—For the Liquidation of Nuclear Weapons]. Aoki Shoten, Tokyo.
*Shigemitsu, T. 1962. "Study on A-bomb survivors with thyroid cancer in the Department of Surgery, Hiroshima University Hospital," Journal of the Hiroshima Medical Association 15:946.
*Shigemitsu, T. 1965. "Studies on thyroid cancer induced by A-bomb exposure and its clinical characteristics," Medical Journal of Hiroshima University 13:665.
*Shigetō, F. 1967. "General outline of patients observed at Hiroshima Atomic Bomb Hospital— In the nine years since the hospital opened," Journal of the Hiroshima Medical Association (special series) 20:51.
*Shimizu, K. 1960a. "Trend of deaths due to malignant neoplasms in Hiroshima City. Part 1. Comparison of those with and without survivor's health handbooks," Journal of the Hiroshima Medical Association 13:885.
*Shimizu, K. 1960b. "Trend of deaths due to malignant neoplasms in Hiroshima City. Part 2. Trend of deaths among patients with recognized A-bomb disease," Journal of the Hiroshima Medical Association 13:956.
*Shimizu, K. 1961. "Trend of deaths due to malignant neoplasms in Hiroshima City. Part 3. Comparison of those with and without survivors' health handbooks in 1960 and 1958–1960," Journal of the Hiroshima Medical Association 14:578.
*Shimizu, K. 1964. "Socio-medical study on aged atomic bomb survivors in Hiroshima," part 1, Journal of the Hiroshima Medical Association 17:1120.
*Shimizu, K. 1967. "Summary of health management results," Journal of the Hiroshima Medical Association (special series) 20:5.
*Shimizu, K. 1978. "Present status and present-day problem of patients exposed in utero with microcephaly," Journal of the Hiroshima Medical Association 31:401.
*Shimizu, K.; Ishida, S.; Hamada, T.; Tsubokura, A.; Kikkawa, S.; Orimen, A.; Yamamoto, T.; Kato, H.; Schreiber, W. W. W.; Robertson, J. D.; and Ito, C. 1970. "Symposium on the liver function of A-bomb survivors," Journal of the Hiroshima Medical Association 23:1088.
*Shimizu, K.; Munaka, M.; Kumazawa, T.; Ishida, S.; and Aisaka, T. 1976. "The current analysis of medical treatment and of welfare for atomic bomb survivors in the thirtieth year after bombing," Journal of the Hiroshima Medical Association 29:317.
*Shimizu, K.; Watanabe, M.; and Itō, S. 1961. "Social and medical investigation of lung cancer among atomic bomb survivors," part 1, Journal of the Hiroshima Medical Association 14:979.
*Shimizu, K.; Yuzaki, M.; Kanazawa, K.; and Nagaya, T. 1969. Genbaku Bakushinchi [A-bomb Hypocenter]. Kiyoshi Shimizu, ed. Nihon Hōsō Shuppan Kyōkai [Japan Broadcasting Publishing Co., Ltd.], Tokyo.
*Shimizu, K.; Yuzaki, M.; Yamamoto, H.; and Watanabe, S. 1967. "On the changes in the family structure of native families and newly settled families in an urban district: From the actual status survey results on households exposed to the atomic bomb," Daiyonjikkai

Nihon Shakaigakkai Taikai Hōkoku Shiryō [Data reported at the fortieth meeting of the Japan Sociological Society].

*Shimotomai, N.; Horikawa, Y.; Fujita, T.; Fujiwara, I.; Hayashi, K.; and Katsuta, K. 1953. "Biological investigation of atomic bomb disaster. Part II. Effect on plants. Chapter 2: On-the-spot investigation in Hiroshima," in CRIABC, vol. I.

*Shinohara, K.; Ishikawa, K.; et al. 1953a. "Radiation due to the atomic bomb and its damage to the human body," in CRIABC, vol. II.

*Shinohara, K.; Morita, S.; Kōra, K.; Kawai, N.; and Yokota, M. 1953b. "Radiation of the ground in Nagasaki city and vicinity. Part II. Radiation near the Nishiyama reservoir," in CRIABC, vol. I.

*Shinohara, K.; Okada, T.; Morita, S.; Kōra, K.; Inoue, K.; and Kawai, N. 1953c. "Radiation of ground in Nagasaki city and vicinity. Part I. Radioactivity near the hypocenter," in CRIABC, vol. I.

*Shiotsuki, M. 1945. "Experience in the treatment and autopsy of atomic bomb victims in Nagasaki City. Treatise, October 1945.

*Shiotsuki M. 1978. *Hatsushigoto wa Anrakusatsu datta* [My First Work, Mercy Killing]. Kōbunsha, Tokyo.

Shirabe, R. 1953. "Medical survey of atomic bomb casualties," *Military Surgeon* 113:251.

*Shirabe, R. 1967. "Summary report on scar keloids in Nagasaki A-bomb survivors," *Journal of the Hiroshima Medical Association* (special series) 20:212.

*Shirabe, R., ed. 1968–74. *Wasurenagusa* [FMN], vols. I–V. Kyū Nagasaki Ikadaigaku Genbaku Gisei Gakuto Izokukai, Nagasaki.

*Shirabe, R., ed. 1971. "Register of names of A-bomb victims of former Nagasaki Medical University and representatives of bereaved families," in *Wasurenagusa* [FMN], vol. IV. Kyū Nagasaki Ikadaigaku Genbaku Gisei Gakuto Izokukai, Nagasaki.

*Shirabe, R., ed. 1974. *FMN*, Vol. V.

*Shirabe, R. 1978. "A dialogue with Soichi Iijima (21 October 1978)."

*Shirabe, R. 1979. "Nagasaki A-bomb disaster—A diary of a doctor," I, II, III, *Sekai* [World], August–October issues. Iwanami Shoten, Tokyo.

*Shirabe, R.; and Tezuka, H. 1959. "Characteristics of thermal burn scars caused by the atomic bomb and their treatment," *Journal of the Hiroshima Medical Association* 12:897.

*Shirabe, R.; Harano, C.; and Tezuka, H. 1962. "Thyroid diseases of the A-bomb survivors, especially thyroid cancer," *Journal of the Hiroshima Medical Association* 15:1023.

*Shirabe, R.; Tezuka, H.; Harano, C.; and Shigematsu, S. 1964. "Thyroid and breast tumors in A-bomb survivors," *Journal of the Hiroshima Medical Association* 17:788.

*Shirabe, R.; Yazaki, T.; and Matsuo, Y. 1972. *Nagasaki—Bakushinchi Fukugen no Kiroku* [Nagasaki—Record of Reconstruction of the Central Bombed Area], R. Shirabe, ed. Nihon Hōsō Shuppan Kyōkai [Japan Broadcasting Publishing Co., Ltd.], Tokyo.

*Shirai, H. 1956. "Deformation of hair of patients with A-bomb radiation injuries in Hiroshima," *Nippon Acta Radiologica* 16:660.

Shiraki, H. 1951. "Die Pathologie der Gehirne von der atomischen Bombenerkrankung," *Seishin Shinkei-gaku Zasshi* [Psychiatrica Neurologica Japonica] 53:147.

*Shiraki, H. 1953. "Later findings on cerebral degeneration in A-bomb injuries. Cerebral lesions observed in atomic bomb victims," in CRIABC, vol. I.

*Shiraki, H.; and Andō, J. 1956. "Cerebral lesions noted in A-bomb survivors with blood diseases," *Seishin Shinkei-gaku Zasshi* [Psychiatrica Neurologica Japonica] 58:407.

Shiraki, H.; Uchimura, Y.; Matsuoka, S.; Takeya, S.; Tamagawa, C.; Koyano, K.; Amano, S.; Araki, M.; Ayres, W. W.; and Haymaker, W. 1958. "Effects of atomic radiation on the human brain: A study of the brains of Hiroshima and Nagasaki casualties," *Journal of Neuropathology* 17:79.

*Shohno, N. 1967. "Physical observations on the atomic bombs at Hiroshima and Nagasaki. III. Residual radiation," *Journal of the Hiroshima Medical Association* (special series) 20:75.

*Shohno, N.; and Iijima, S. 1975. *Kakuhōshasen to Genbakushō* [Nuclear Radiation and Atomic Bomb Disease]. Nihon Hōsō Shuppan Kyōkai [Japan Broadcasting Publishing Co., Ltd.], Tokyo.

*Shohno, N.; Nagai, H.; and Ueno, H., eds. 1978. *Kaku to Heiwa—Nihonjin no Ishiki* [Nuclear Arms and Peace—Consciousness of the Japanese People]. Hōritsubunkasha, Kyoto.

*Shōji, T.; and Kariya, H. 1947. "Effect of the atomic bomb on menstruation of girl students," *Sanka to Fujinka* [Obstetrics and Gynecology] 14:45.

Shore, R. E.; Albert, R. E.; and Pasternack, B. S. 1976. "Follow-up study of patients treated by X-ray epilation for Tinea capitis," *Archives of Environmental Health* 31:21.

Shore, R. E.; Hempelmann, L. H.; Kowaluk, E.; Mansur, P. S.; Pasternack, B. S.; Albert, R. E.; and Haughie, G. E. 1977. "Breast neoplasms in women treated with X-rays for acute postpartum mastitis," *Journal of the National Cancer Institute* 59:813.

Simpson, C. L.; Hempelmann, L. H.; and Fuller, L. M. 1955. "Neoplasia in children treated with X-rays in infancy for thymic enlargement," *Radiology* 64:840.

Sinskey, R. M. 1955. "The status of lenticular opacities caused by atomic radiation, Hiroshima and Nagasaki, Japan, 1951–1953," *American Journal of Ophthalmology* 39:285.

Snell, F. M.; Neel, J. V.; and Ishibashi, K. 1949. "Hematologic studies in Hiroshima and control city two years after the atomic bombing," *Archives of Internal Medicine* 84:569.

*Society to Transmit the Atomic Bomb Experience. 1975. *Genbaku kara Genpatsu made* [From Atomic Bomb to Atomic Power Generation], 2 vols. Agune, Tokyo.

Socolow, E. L.; Hashizume, A.; Neriishi, S.; and Niitani, R. 1963. "Thyroid carcinoma in man after exposure to ionizing radiation. A summary of the findings in Hiroshima and Nagasaki," *New England Journal of Medicine* 268:406.

*Sodei, R. 1978. *Watakushitachi wa Teki Datta no ka—Zaibei Hibakusha no Mokushiroku* [Were We Enemies?—A Record of the Revelations of Hibakusha in the United States]. Ushio Shuppansha, Tokyo.

Sofuni, T.; Shimba, H.; Ohtaki, K.; and Awa, A. A. 1977. "G-banding analysis of chromosome aberrations in Hiroshima atomic bomb survivors," RERF TR 13–77.

*Sora, T. 1975. "Peace education in the United States and Japan—Report of World Peace Education Conference: Thirty years after 'Hiroshima' and 'Nagasaki' (Wilmington College, Ohio, U.S.A.)," in *Heiwa Kyōiku Kenkyū* [Peace Education Research], annual report, vol. III. Hiroshima Heiwa Kyōiku Kenkyūsho, Hiroshima.

Steer, A.; Moriyama, I.; and Shimizu, K. 1973. "ABCC-JNIH pathology studies, Hiroshima and Nagasaki. Report 3," ABCC TR 16–73.

Steer, A.; Wakabayashi, T.; Kirshbaum, J. D.; Ii, Y.; and Ishida, K. 1973. "Multiple primary malignancies and radiation exposure, Hiroshima and Nagasaki," presented at Sixth International Congress of Cancer Society, 28 June 1973. Perugia, Italy.

Stewart, A.; and Kneal, G. W. 1970. "Radiation dose effects in relation to obstetric X-rays and childhood cancers," *Lancet* 1:1185.

Stewart, A.; Webb, J.; and Hewitt, D. 1958. "A survey of childhood malignancies," *British Medical Journal* 1:1495.

Stimson, H. L. 1947. "The decision to use the atomic bomb," *Harper's Magazine,* February.

*Sugihara, Y.; and Takahashi, Y. 1960, 1961. "Research data on atomic bomb survivors collected by Okayama University Medical School Relief Team," *Transactions of the Societatis Pathologicae Japonicae* 49:805; 50:162.

*Sugimoto, A. 1953. "Determination of number of primary fast neutron particles emitted at the time of the Hiroshima A-bomb explosion," in CRIABC, vol. I.

*Sugimoto, S. 1971. "The fate of A-bomb cataract in relation to radiation dosage," *Rinshō Ganka* [Japanese Journal of Clinical Ophthalmology] 25:1157.

*Sugimoto, S. 1973. "Significance of lenticular opacities in survivors directly exposed to the atomic bomb with special reference to aging," *Journal of the Hiroshima Medical Association* 26:652.

*Sugiyama, S.; Amano, S.; Shimamoto, M.; Kimura, M.; and Unno, G. 1953. "Report on A-bomb injuries" (first to fourth reports), in CRIABC, vol. II.

*Suita, N. 1953. "Biological investigation of atomic bomb disaster. Part II. Effects on plants. Chapter 3. On morphologically unusual plants," in CRIABC, vol. I.

*Survey Committee for the Map Restoration of A-bombed Areas. 1968. "Logic of A-bomb disaster map reconstruction and conception for synthesis survey of the A-bomb disaster," *Journal of the Hiroshima Medical Association* 21:1231.

Sutow, W. W. 1957. "Summary of medical studies on Hiroshima children exposed to the atomic bomb 1951–1953," ABCC Report.

Sutow, W. W.; Hamada, M.; and Kawamoto, S. 1953. "Neurological and psychometric examination of children exposed in utero to the atomic bomb in Nagasaki," USAEC NYO–4472.

Sutow, W. W.; and West, E. 1955. "Studies on Nagasaki (Japan) children exposed in utero to the atomic bomb," *American Journal of Roentgenology & Radium Therapy* 74:493.

*Tabuchi, A. 1955. "Obstetrical and gynecological survey of A-bomb survivors," *Journal of the Hiroshima Medical Association* 8:322.

*Tabuchi, A. 1959. "Obstetrical and gynecological investigation of women exposed to the atomic bomb," *Journal of the Hiroshima Medical Association* 12:958.

*Tabuchi, A. 1967. "Microcephaly due to exposure in utero," *Journal of the Hiroshima Medical Association* (special series) 20:214.

*Tabuchi, A.; and Hirai, G. 1965. "Studies on developmental disturbances in children exposed in utero to the atomic bomb," *Journal of the Hiroshima Obstetrical and Gynaecological Society* 4:236.

Tabuchi, A.; Hirai, G.; Nakagawa, S.; Shimada, K.; and Fujitō, J. 1967. "Clinical findings on microcephalic children exposed in utero," ABCC TR 28–67.

*Tabuchi, A.; and Kinutani, K. 1965. "Summary on disorders of women exposed to the atomic bomb seen at the Department of Obstetrics and Gynaecology, Hiroshima University," *Journal of the Hiroshima Obstetrical and Gynaecological Society* 4:205.

Tabuchi, A.; Nakagawa, S.; Hirata, M.; and Sato, H. 1966. "Summary report on disorders noted among A-bomb exposed women," *Hiroshima Journal of Medical Science* 15:1.

*Tajima, J. 1976. "Anger and grief have no frontiers—Testimony of atomic bomb exposure of the Nagasaki Prisoner of War Camp," in *Nagasaki no Shōgen* [Testimony of Nagasaki], eighth collection. Nagasaki no Shōgen Kankō Iinkai, Nagasaki.

*Tajima, Y. 1972. "Genetic effects of radiation—Hiroshima and Nagasaki," *Nagasaki Medical Journal* 47:336.

*Takahashi, H.; Ohkita, T.; and Enzan, H. 1974. "The recent incidence of leukemia in Hiroshima atomic bomb survivors," *Journal of the Hiroshima Medical Association* 27:538.

*Takahashi, S. 1977. "Recent trends of thorotrast study in the world," *Hōshasen Kagaku* 20:82.

*Takahashi, S.; Kitabatake, T.; Wakabayashi, M.; Koga, Y.; Miyakawa, T.; Yamashita, H.; Masuyama, M.; Hibino, S.; Miyakawa, M.; Okajima, S.; Kaneda, H.; Tachiiri, H.; Anno, Y.; and Irie, H. 1964. "A statistical study on human cancer induced by medical irradiation," *Nippon Acta Radiologica* 23:1510.

*Takahashi, S.; Kitabatake, T.; Yamagata, S.; Miyakawa, T.; Masuyama, M.; Mori, T.; Tanaka, T.; Hibino, S.; Miyakawa, M.; Kaneda, H.; Okajima, S.; Komiyama, K.; Koga, Y.; Adachi, T.; Hashizume, T.; and Hashimoto, Y. 1965. "Statistical study on thorotrast-induced cancer of the liver," *Tōhoku Journal of Experimental Medicine* 87:144.

Takamura, T.; and Ueda, S. 1960. "Hematologic findings for children exposed in utero, Hiroshima," ABCC TR 26–60.

*Takeichi, N.; Hirose, F.; Inoue, S.; Niimoto, M.; and Hattori, T. 1976a. "Parotid gland tumors, observed in the clinic of Research Institute for Nuclear Medicine and Biology, Hiroshima University," *Japanese Journal of Cancer Clinics* 22:15.

Takeichi, N.; Hirose, F.; and Yamamoto, T. 1976b. "Salivary gland tumors in atomic bomb survivors, Hiroshima, Japan. 1. Epidemiologic observation," *Cancer* 38:2462.

*Takeichi, N.; Inoue, S.; Niimoto, M.; Nagata, N.; Ezaki, H.; Hirose, F.; and Kurozumi, S. 1973. "Parotid gland tumors, especially in relation to radiation exposure," *Journal of the Japanese Surgical Society* 74:1170.

*Takeichi, N.; Inoue, S.; Niimoto, M.; Nagata, N.; Hirose, F.; Ezaki, H.; Yamamoto, H.; and Hiramoto, T. 1974. "Salivary gland tumors in atomic bomb survivors in Hiroshima," *Journal of the Hiroshima Medical Association* 27:555.

*Takeshita, K. 1960. "Re-evaluation of the dose from the atomic bomb explosion and its fallout delivered to the residents of Nishiyama district, Nagasaki City. Special consideration of the correlation between blood picture changes and radiation dose," *Fukuoka Acta Medica* 51:1296.

Takeshita, K. 1975. "A review of thirty years study of Hiroshima and Nagasaki atomic bomb survivors. I. Dosimetry. C. Dose estimation from residual and fallout radioactivity—Aerial surveys," *Journal of Radiation Research* (Tokyo) 16(supplement):24.

*Taketomi, Y.; Abe, T.; Kamada, N.; Kuramoto, A.; Takahashi, H.; Ohkita, T.; Ito, C.; and Kimura, H. 1978a. "Clinical survey of blood dyscrasias among Hiroshima A-bomb survivors by the periodical health examination (report 3)," *Journal of the Hiroshima Medical Association* 31:493.

*Taketomi, Y.; Abe, T.; Kamada, N.; Kuramoto, A.; Takahashi, H.; Ohkita, T.; Ito, C.; and

Kimura, H. 1978*b*. Clinical survey of blood dyscrasias among Hiroshima A-bomb survivors by periodical health examination (report 4)," *Nagasaki Medical Journal* 53:325.

*Taketomi, Y.; Kamada, N.; Takahashi, H.; Ohkita, T.; Ito, C.; and Kimura, H. 1976*a*. "Clinical survey of blood dyscrasias among Hiroshima A-bomb survivors by the periodical health examination (Report 2)," *Nagasaki Medical Journal* 51:185.

*Taketomi, Y.; Kamada, N.; Uchino, H.; Takahashi, H.; Ohkita, T.; Ito, C.; and Kimura, H. 1976*b*. "Clinical survey of blood dyscrasias among Hiroshima A-bomb survivors by periodical health examination," *Journal of the Hiroshima Medical Association* 29:235.

*Takeuchi, K. 1971. "Administrative notebook" (extract), in RHAWD, vol. V.

*Takeuchi, Y., ed. 1968. *Boku Ikitakatta—Hibaku Nisei Fumikichan no Shi* [I Wanted to Live—Death of Fumiki-chan, a Child Born to an A-bomb Survivor]. Uno Shoten, Tokyo.

*Tamagawa, C. 1950*a*. "A study of keloids due to exposure to the atomic bomb," *Transactions of the Societatis Pathologicae Japonicae* 39:300.

*Tamagawa, C. 1950*b*. "A study of keloids due to exposure to the atomic bomb in Hiroshima," *Journal of the Okayama Medical Society* (supplement) 60:13.

*Tamagawa, C. 1953*a*. "Autopsy records on nineteen cases of A-bomb injuries in Hiroshima City," in CRIABC, vol. II.

*Tamagawa, C. 1953*b*. "The scar keloid remaining in atomic bomb," *Rinshō Geka* [Journal of Clinical Surgery] 8:231.

*Tamagawa, C. 1958. "Dermal changes in irradiation, cellular changes observed in keloidlike tissue," *Acta Pathologica Japonica* 8(supplement):787.

*Tamagawa, C.; and Katsube, G. 1953. "Study on keloids due to the A-bomb exposure," in CRIABC, vol. II.

*Tamagawa, C.; Katsube, G.; Okamoto, S.; Takeuchi, K.; Hattori, T.; and Sasaki, T. 1950. "Development of keloids caused by exposure to the atomic bomb in Hiroshima," *Journal of the Hiroshima Medical Association* 3:50.

Tamagawa, C.; and Oda, T. 1959. "An electron microscope study on the keloid caused by the exposure to the atomic bomb in Hiroshima," *Symposia of the Society for Cellular Chemistry* 9:253. English abstract: Maruzen, Tokyo.

Tamagawa, C.; Sasaki, T.; and Yokoyama, K. 1952*a*. "A study of keloids due to exposure to the atomic bomb in Hiroshima City (Report 2)," *Gann* [Japanese Journal of Cancer Research] 42:163.

*Tamagawa, C.; Sugihara, Y.; Sasaki, M.; Araki, F.; Otsu, K.; Yokoyama, K.; and Sasaki, T. 1952*b*. "Patho-anatomical observations on 'the atomic bomb injury' corpses exposed to atomic bomb irradiation in Hiroshima City," *Transactions of the Societatis Pathologicae Japonicae* 41:65.

*Tamura, S.; Ikui, H.; Nakano, K.; Hiwatari, R.; and Oshio, S. 1953*a*. "Clinical findings on eye disturbances due to A-bomb exposure," in CRIABC, vol. II.

*Tamura, S.; Ikui, H.; Nakano, K.; Hiwatari, R.; and Oshio, S. 1953*b*. "Patho-histological findings on eye disturbances in A-bomb illness," in CRIABC, vol. II.

*Tanabe, H. 1953. "Autopsy records and charts of atomic bomb victims (ten cases)," in CRIABC, vol. II.

*Tanaka, M.; and Kawahara, H. 1954. "Studies on the physical and psychological development of children exposed to the atomic bomb in Hiroshima (1)," *Nippon Eisei Gakkai Zasshi* [Japanese Journal of Hygiene] 9:108.

*Tanaka, Y. 1953. "Investigation report on the atomic bomb damage to buildings: Report in the second meeting of the Special Committee for A-bomb Casualties," in CRIABC, vol. I.

*Taura, M. 1971. "Attack Fighter Shūsui—An account of the construction of its secret base in Ōmura, *Genbaku Zengo* [Before and After the Atomic Bomb], H. Shirai et al., eds. vol. V, (privately published by) Omoideshū Sewanin.

Terasaki, T.; and Shiota, K. 1953. "Effects of radiation on human dentition—preliminary report, 30 June 1953," USAEC NYO-4464.

*Terasaki, T.; and Shiota, K. 1955. "A-bomb radiation effects on human teeth," *Journal of the Japanese Dental Association* 7:325.

*Tezuka, H. 1967. "Summary report on scar keloids of atomic bomb survivors of Nagasaki City," *Journal of the Hiroshima Medical Association* 20(special series):204.

Timmes, J. J. 1946. "Radiation sickness in Nagasaki: Preliminary report," *United States Navy Medical Bulletin* 46:219.

Tjio, J. H.; and Levan, A. 1956. "The chromosome number of man," *Hereditas* 42:1.

*Toda, K. 1945. *Hiroshima Kushu Higai Chōsa Hōkoku* [Investigation Report on Hiroshima Air Raid Damages], dated 13 August 1945. (Property of Hidetsugu Aihara.)

*Toda, S.; Hosokawa, Y.; Chōshi, K.; Nakano, A.; and Takahashi, M. 1964. "Ocular changes in A-bomb survivors exposed during infancy," *Nihon Ganka Kiyō* [Folia Ophthalmologica Japonica] 15:96.

Tōge S., ed. 1948. *Hiroshima—Genshi-bakudan Tokushū* [Hiroshima—Special Compilation on the Atomic Bombing]. Setonaikai Bunko, Hiroshima.

Tokunaga, M.; Norman, Jr., J. E.; Asano, M.; Tokuoka, S.; Ezaki, H.; Nishimori, I.; and Tsuji, Y. 1977. "Malignant breast tumors among atomic bomb survivors, Hiroshima and Nagasaki, 1950–74," RERF TR 17–77.

*Tokunaga, T. 1953. "Atomic bomb cataracts," *Ganka Rinshō Ihō* [Japanese Review of Clinical Ophthalmology] 47:504.

*Tokunaga, T. 1959. "Atomic bomb radiation cataract in Nagasaki," *Acta Societatis Ophthalmologicae Japonicae* 63:1211.

*Tokunaga, T. 1962. "The latent period of A-bomb cataracts," *Journal of the Hiroshima Medical Association* 15:891.

*Tokunaga, T. 1963. "Histopathological findings of radiation cataract," *Rinshō Ganka* [Japanese Journal of Clinical Ophthalmology] 17:587.

*Tokunaga, T. 1968. "Result of follow-up study of atomic bomb radiation cataracts in Nagasaki," *Acta Societatis Ophthalmologicae Japonicae* 72:1774.

*Tokyo Imperial University, School of Medicine, Department of Pathology. 1953. "Autopsy records of A-bomb victims (twenty-eight cases)," in CRIABC, vol. II.

*Tomisaki, T. 1955. "Effects of A-bomb radiation on domain of human oral cavity," *Journal of the Japanese Stomatological Society* 4:230.

*Tomonaga, M. 1957. "Blood picture of Nagasaki A-bomb survivors," *Acta Haematologica Japonica* 20(supplement):176.

*Tomonaga, M. 1964. Leukemia among A-bomb survivors as a late effect, especially clinical observation on Hiroshima and Nagasaki cases, in HH, vol. III.

Tomonaga, M.; Brill, A. B.; Itoga, T.; and Heyssel, R. M. 1959. "Leukemia in Nagasaki atomic bomb survivors," ABCC TR 11–59.

*Tomonaga, M.; Ichimaru, M.; Danno, H.; Inoue, A.; Okabe, N.; Kinoshita, K.; Matsumoto, Y.; Nonaka, M.; Takahashi, Y.; Tomiyasu, T.; Toyomasu, S.; Tamari, K.; and Kawamoto, M. 1967. "Leukemia in atomic bomb survivors from 1946 to 1965 and some aspects of epidemiology of leukemia in Japan," *Journal of the Kyushu Hematology Research Society* 17:375.

*Tomonaga, Y.; Sadamori, N.; Matsunaga, M.; Tagawa, M.; and Ichimaru, M. 1976. "Cytogenetic studies on bone marrow cells of the atomic bomb survivors in Nagasaki," *Journal of the Hiroshima Medical Association* 29:239.

*Torii, S. 1957. "Blood changes in X-ray technicians," *Nagoya Journal of Medical Science* 19:31.

Tough, I. M.; Buckton, K. E.; Baikie, A. G.; and Court-Brown, W. M. 1960. "X-ray induced chromosome damage in man," *Lancet* 2:849.

Trimble, B. K.; and Daughty, J. H. 1974. "The amount of hereditary disease in human populations," *Annals of Human Genetics* 38:199.

Tsuiki, S.; and Ikegami, A. 1956. "Personality test on the atomic bomb exposed children," in *Research on the Effects and Influences of the Nuclear Bomb Test Explosions,* vol. II. Japan Society for the Promotion of Science, Tokyo.

*Tsuiki, S.; Ueno, K.; Segawa, K.; and Kaburagi, S. 1951. "Clinical experiences in the Department of Psychiatry, Nagasaki University for five years after the end of the Second World War," *Psychiatrica Neurologica Japonica* 53:229.

*Tsuiki, S.; Yuzuriha, T.; Anzo, E.; Ikegami, A.; Suzuki, S.; Karashima, S.; Nishiwaki, M.; Kawasaki, N.; Hironaka, M.; Nagaoka, M.; Fujii, K.; and Nakagawa, Y. 1958. "Psychiatric investigations on people exposed to the atomic bomb," *Nagasaki Medical Journal* 33:637.

*Tsuzuki, M. ca.1945. Data of Masao Tsuzuki (property of Masakazu Tsuzuki).

*Tsuzuki, M., ed. 1951. "A-bomb disaster investigation results, chap. 5, par. 2: Relief measures," in SRIABC.

*Tsuzuki, M. 1954a. *Igaku no Tachiba kara Mita Genshi-bakudan no Saigai* [Atomic Bomb Injury from the Medical Point of View]. Igaku Shoin, Tokyo.

*Tsuzuki, M. 1954b. "Chronic A-bomb diseases," *Nihon Iji Shinpō* [Japanese Medical Journal]
    1556:783.
Tsuzuki, M. 1956. "Keloid problem as a late effect of the atomic bomb injury," in *Research
    in the Effects and Influences of the Nuclear Bomb Test Explosions*, II. Japan Society for
    the Promotion of Science, Tokyo.
*Tsuzuki, M. 1973. "Medical care policy for so-called A-bomb injuries," *Genshi-bakudan—
    Hiroshima-Nagasaki no Shashin to Kiroku* [Atomic Bombs—Photographs and Records of
    Hiroshima and Nagasaki]. Nishina Memorial Foundation, ed. Kōfūsha Shoten, Tokyo.
*Twenty-year History Compilation Committee. 1964. *Hirosen no Ayumi Nijūnenshi* [Twenty-
    year History of Hiroshima Shipyard]. Mitsubishi Zōsen Kabushiki Kaisha Hiroshima Zō-
    sensho, Hiroshima.

*Ubuki, A. 1976. "Ideological nature of the Hiroshima monument," in *Heiwa Kyōiku Kenkyū*
    [Peace Education Research], annual report, vol. IV. Hiroshima Heiwa Kyōiku Kenkyūsho,
    Hiroshima.
Uchimura, Y.; and Shiraki, H. 1952a. "Zur Gehirnpathologie der Atombombenschädigungen,"
    Folia Psychiatrica et Neurologica Japonica 6:155.
Uchimura, Y.; and Shiraki, H. 1952b. "Cerebral injuries caused by bombardment," *Journal of
    Nervous and Mental Disorders* 116:654.
*Uchino, H.; and Kamada, N. 1972. "Detection of preleukemic state," *The Journal of Japan
    Medical Association* 67:1415.
*Uda, M.; Sugahara, Y.; and Kita, I. 1953. "Meteorological conditions related to the atomic
    bomb explosion in Hiroshima," in CRIABC, vol. I.
*Uehara, T. 1972. "A review concerning Korean Hibakusha in Hiroshima (1)," in *Geibi Chihōshi
    Kenkyū* [Geibi Local History Research], ninetieth issue. Geibi Chihōshi Kenkyūkai, Hiro-
    shima.
United Nations. 1967. *Effects of the Possible Use of Nuclear Weapons and the Security and
    Economic Implications for States of the Acquisition and Further Development of these Weap-
    ons—Report of the Secretary-General Transmitting the Study of his Consultative Group*,
    no. 10. New York.
United Nations. 1969. *Report of the United Nations Scientific Committee on the Effects of Atomic
    Radiation, Radiation-induced chromosome aberrations in human cells.*
United Nations. 1972. *Report of the United Nations Scientific Committee on the Effects of Atomic
    Radiations, Ionizing Radiation: Levels and effects.*
The United States Strategic Bombing Survey. 1946. *The Effects of Atomic Bombs on Hiroshima
    and Nagasaki*, Pacific War Reports, no. 3. U.S. Government Printing Office, Washington,
    D.C.
    1946a. "Report of the third survey team, Morale Division," (by Lieutenant H. Nisserson,
    dated 5 November 1945).
    1946b. "Population and casualties of Hiroshima and Nagasaki," United States Strategic
    Bombing Survey memorandum dated 11 March 1946 (based on report by Lieutenant Colonel
    Ōya, dated 10 December 1945).
    1946c. "Population and casualties of Hiroshima and Nagasaki," United States Strategic
    Bombing Survey memorandum dated 11 March 1946 (based on report by Lieutenant Colonel
    Ōya and Lieutenant Colonel Ishiwatari).
The United States Strategic Bombing Survey, Physical Damage Division. 1947a. *Effects of the
    Atomic Bomb on Hiroshima, Japan*, vol. I, sec. X. U.S. Government Printing Office, Washing-
    ton, D.C.
The United States Strategic Bombing Survey, Physical Damage Division. 1947b. *Effects of the
    Atomic Bomb on Nagasaki, Japan*, vol. I, part 2. U.S. Government Printing Office, Washing-
    ton, D.C.
The United States Strategic Bombing Survey, Physical Damage Division. 1947c. *Effects of the
    Atomic Bomb on Hiroshima, Japan*, vol. II, part 3. U.S. Government Printing Office, Wash-
    ington, D.C.
The United States Strategic Bombing Survey, Urban Areas Division. 1947a. *The Effects of Air
    Attack on the City of Hiroshima.* U.S. Government Printing Office, Washington, D.C.
The United States Strategic Bombing Survey, Urban Areas Division. 1947b. *The Effects of Air
    Attack on the City of Nagasaki.* U.S. Government Printing Office, Washington, D.C.

Upton, A. C.; Kimball, A. W.; Furth, J.; Christenberry, K. W.; and Benedict, W. H. 1960. "Some delayed effects of atom-bomb radiations in mice," *Cancer Research* 20(part 2):1.

*Urabe, M.; and Keuke, M. 1953a. "Cachectic state among A-bomb injured," in CRIABC, vol. I.

*Urabe, M.; and Keuke, M. 1953b. "Supplementary report on cachectic state among A-bomb injured," in CRIABC, vol. I.

*Usami, S. 1963. "Data on Chinese prisoners of war as wartime labor force" (1,2), *Hōsei Daigaku Ōhara Shakai Mondai Kenkyūsho Shiryōshitsu Hō* [Report of Data Room, Hosei University Ōhara Social Problems Research Institute], nos. 89, 90.

Vogel, H. H.; and Zaldívar, R. 1972. "Neutron-induced mammary neoplasms in the rat," *Cancer Research* 32:933.

*Wakisaka, G. 1953. "Acute and subacute injuries due to the atomic bomb, with special reference to the peripheral blood picture," in PSH.

*Wakisaka, G. 1961. "Clinical aspects of atomic bomb disease," in HH, vol. III.

Wald, N. 1957. "Blood picture of Hiroshima A-bomb survivors," *Acta Haematologica Japonica* 20(supplement):152.

Wanebo, C. K.; Johnson, K. G.; Sato, K.; and Thorslund, T. W. 1969. "Breast cancer after exposure to the atomic bombings of Hiroshima and Nagasaki," *Journal of the Hiroshima Medical Association* 22:752; *New England Journal of Medicine,* 279(1968):667.

Wanebo, C. K.; Johnson, K. G.; Sato, K.; and Thorslund, T. W. 1968. "Lung cancer following atomic radiation," *American Review of Respiratory Diseases* 98:778.

*War Disaster Editorial Committee. 1973. *Tokyo Daikūshū—Sensaishi* [The Great Tokyo Air Raid—Record of the War Disaster], vol. I. Tokyo Kūshū o Kirokusuru Kai, Tokyo.

Warren, S. 1946. "Medical aspects of atomic bombings," *Rhode Island Medical Journal* 29:907.

Warren, S. 1948. "Nagasaki survivors as seen in 1947," *Military Surgeon* 102:98.

Warren, S. 1961. *The Pathology of Ionizing Radiation.* Charles C Thomas, Springfield, Ill.

Warren, S.; and Draeger, R. H. 1946. "Patterns of injuries produced by atomic bombs at Hiroshima and Nagasaki," *United States Navy Medical Bulletin* 46:1349; *Cincinnati Journal of Medicine* 27:871.

Warren, S.; and Gates, O. 1932. "Multiple primary malignant tumor: Survey of literature and statistical study," *American Journal of Cancer* 16:1358.

* *Wartime Casualty Care Law* (1942, Law no. 71).

*Watanabe, M. 1968. "The crude and standardized death rate of atomic bomb survivors in Hiroshima City, 1965," *Nagasaki Medical Journal* 43:852.

*Watanabe, S. 1958. "Blood findings of A-bomb survivors in Kure City eleven years after exposure," *Annual Report of the Comprehensive Research of the Ministry of Education, Medical and Pharmaceutical Division, 1957.* Nihon Gakujutsu Shinkōkai, Tokyo.

*Watanabe, S. 1959a. "Blood findings of A-bomb survivors residing in Hiroshima city twelve years after the detonation," *Annual Report of the Comprehensive Research of the Ministry of Education, 1958.* Nihon Gakujutsu Shinkōkai, Tokyo.

*Watanabe, S. 1959b. "Pathological studies on leukemia induced by exposure to the atomic bomb, particularly on the behavior of leukemic cells in the process of proliferation and development," *Journal of the Hiroshima Medical Association* 12:905.

Watanabe, S. 1961. "On the incidence of leukemias in Hiroshima during the past fifteen years from 1946 to 1960," *Journal of Radiation Research* (Tokyo) 2:131.

*Watanabe, S. 1964. "Present status of somatic effects in atomic bomb survivors living in Hiroshima," *Acta Haematologica Japonica* 27:121.

Watanabe, S. 1965. "Nuclear hematology: Based on experience with atomic explosions," in *Nuclear Hematology.* E. Szirmai, ed. Academic Press, New York.

Watanabe, S. 1974. "Cancer and leukemia developing among atom-bomb survivors," in *Geschwulste Tumors* I (Handbuch der allgemeinen Pathologie, 6 Bd., 5 Teil). Springer-Verlag, Berlin.

Watanabe, S.; Shimosato, Y.; Ohkita, T.; Ezaki, H.; Shigemitsu, T.; and Kamada, N. 1972. "Leukemia and thyroid carcinoma found among A-bomb survivors in Hiroshima," in *Recent Results in Cancer Research,* vol. XXXIX. E. Grundmann and H. Tulinius, eds. Springer-Verlag, Berlin.

*Watanabe, S.; and Yokoro, K. 1963. "Somatic effects of radiation," in *Genshi Igaku* [Nuclear Medicine], T. Kayama; A. Tabuchi; and S. Watanabe, eds. Kanehara Shuppan, Tokyo.

*Watanabe, S.; and Yokoro, K. 1964. "Late somatic effects and leukemia, especially pathological findings on Hiroshima cases," in HH, vol. III.

*Watanabe, T.; Tagawa, T.; Itō, T.; and Wakiyama, H. 1961. "Petition concerning enactment of Atom Bomb Victims Relief Law (5 November 1956)," in HAMCH.

Wells, W.; and Tsukifuji, N. 1952. "Scars remaining in atom bomb survivors," *Surgery Gynecology and Obstetrics* 95:129.

White, D.C. 1975. *An Atlas of Radiation Histopathology.* Technical Information Center, Office of Public Affairs, United States Energy Research Development Administration.

Winship, T.; and Rossvoll, R. V. 1961. "Childhood thyroid carcinoma," *Cancer* 14:734.

Wohlwill, F. 1942. "Üntersuchungen über die Gewebesreaktion auf Thorotrast," *Schweizerische Zeitschrift fur Allgemeine Pathologie* 5:21.

Wood, J. W.; Johnson, K. G.; Omori, Y.; Kawamoto, S.; and Keehn, R. J. 1967a. "In-utero exposure to the Hiroshima atomic bomb. An evaluation of head size and mental retardation—20 years later," *Pediatrics* 39:355.

Wood, J. W.; Keehn, R. J.; Kawamoto, S.; and Johnson, K. G. 1967b. "The growth and development of children exposed in utero to the atomic bombs in Hiroshima and Nagasaki," *American Journal of Public Health* 57:1374.

Wood, J. W.; Tamagaki, H.; Neriishi, S.; Sato, T.; Scheldon, W. F.; Archer, P. C.; Hamilton, H. B.; and Johnson, K. G. 1969. "Thyroid carcinoma in atomic bomb survivors, Hiroshima and Nagasaki," *American Journal of Epidemiology* 89:4.

Woodbury, L. A.; and Mizuki, M. 1961. "The location of hypocenter and epicenter of the atomic bomb in Hiroshima," *Journal of the Hiroshima Medical Association* 14:127; in English, ABCC TR 12–59 (1959).

*Yamada, A. 1967. "Some pathomorphological considerations on lung cancer observed in Hiroshima A-bomb survivors," *Journal of the Hiroshima Medical Association* (special series) 20:369.

*Yamada, H.; Seki, H.; Nagai, H.; Ishida, A.; and Shohno, N., eds. 1976. *Hiroshima karano Hōkoku—Heiwa-Kyōiku-Hibakusha Mondai o Kangaeru* [Report from Hiroshima—Consideration of Peace, Education and Hibakusha Problems]. Rōdō Kyōiku Sentā, Tokyo.

*Yamada, K., ed. 1968. *Shishi—Hōbō* [Poetry—Scorched People]. Hōbō Sha, Nagasaki.

*Yamaguchi, Y., ed. 1964. *Kāsan to Yobeta—Genbaku no Kora to Aruita Jūichinen no Kiroku* [I Could Call Her "Mother"—Record of eleven years with A-bomb children]. Sōdobunka, Tokyo.

*Yamamoto, T. 1957. "The pathoanatomical study of atypical regeneration or hyperplasia of bone marrow disease among A-bomb survivors," *Acta Haematologica Japonica* 20:59.

*Yamamoto, T.; and Kato, H. 1971a. "Malignant tumor of intestinal tract among fixed population sample in Hiroshima," *Proceedings of the Japanese Cancer Association* 30:112.

Yamamoto, T.; and Kato, H. 1971b. "Two major histological types of gastric carcinoma among the fixed population of Hiroshima and Nagasaki," *Gann* [Japanese Journal of Cancer Research] 62:381.

Yamamoto, T.; and Shimizu, Y. 1978. "Relation of radiation to gastric carcinoma observed in autopsy cases in a fixed population, Hiroshima and Nagasaki," *Journal of Radiation Research* (Tokyo) 19:213.

*Yamamoto, T.; Steer, A.; Liu, P.; Ishimaru, T.; Iijima, S.; Nanba, K.; and Berard, C. W. 1975. "Malignant lymphoma in atomic bomb survivors" (abstract), *Journal of the Hiroshima Medical Association* 28:922.

Yamamoto, T.; and Wakabayashi, T. 1969. "Bone tumors among atomic bomb survivors, 1950–65, Hiroshima-Nagasaki," *Acta Pathologica Japonica* 19:201.

*Yamao, S. 1951. "Menarche of girl students in Nagasaki City after the atomic bomb," *Kyushu Igakukai Kaishi* [Journal of the Kyushu Medical Association] 50:118.

*Yamaoka, K.; Kihara, Y.; Hiyama, S.; Asada, K.; and Sugiyama, M. 1955. "A-bomb illness in the domain of obstetrics and gynecology," *Clinical Gynecology and Obstetrics* 9:943.

*Yamaoka, S.; Yamada, M.; Kuwada, I.; Nakata, S.; Asada, T.; and Ozaki, S. 1953. "Report on damages by the atomic bomb in Hiroshima," in CRIABC, vol. I.

*Yamashina, K. 1967. "Pathology of early effects from exposure to the atomic bomb," *Journal of the Hiroshima Medical Association* (special series) 20:115.

*Yamawaki, T. 1953. "On the incidence of leukemia among atomic bomb survivors in Hiroshima and clinical observations on some of these cases," in PSH.

*Yamawaki, T. 1954a. "Statistical and clinical study on leukemia, especially observation of the survivors of the atomic bomb in Hiroshima. Report II. The incidence of leukemia among the survivors of the atomic bomb explosion in Hiroshima," *Acta Haematologica Japonica* 17:345.

*Yamawaki, T. 1954b. "Statistical and clinical study on leukemia, especially observation on the survivors of the atomic bomb in Hiroshima. Report III. Clinical observation of leukemia in children in Hiroshima after the war," *Acta Haematologica Japonica* 17:360.

*Yamazaki, F. 1953. "Residual radiation in west Hiroshima following the atomic bomb explosion," in CRIABC, vol. I.

*Yamazaki, F.; Sugimoto, A.; and Kimura, K. 1953. "Radioactive phosphorus P^{32} induced in sulphur by atomic bombing in Hiroshima," in CRIABC, vol. I.

Yamazaki, J. N.; Wright, S. W.; and Wright, P. M. 1954. "Outcome of pregnancy in women exposed to the atomic bomb in Nagasaki," *American Journal of Diseases of Children* 87:448.

*Yasuhi, S.; and Yokouchi, H. 1967. "Some studies on liver disorders as a late effect of the atomic bomb," *Journal of the Hiroshima Medical Association* (special series) 20:265.

Yasunaka, M.; and Nishikawa, T. 1956. "On the physical development of the A-bombed children," in *Research in the Effects and Influences of the Nuclear Bomb Test Explosions*, vol. II. Japan Society for the Promotion of Science, Tokyo.

*Yokota, S. 1967. "Clinical observation of atomic bomb survivors," part 6, *Journal of the Hiroshima Medical Association* (special series) 20:41.

*Yokota, S.; Tagawa, D.; Ohtsuru, S.; Nakayama, I.; Neriishi, S.; Namiki, H.; and Hirose, I. 1963. "Autopsy of a case exposed in utero with microcephaly," *Nagasaki Medical Journal* (special issue) 38:92.

*Yoneyama, K.; and Kawai, T. 1965. "The atomic bomb and social changes (I)—A socio-demographic review of atomic bomb sufferers and atomic bomb experience of occupational and work groups," *Hōgaku Kenkyū* [Journal of Law, Politics, and Sociology] 38:1163.

*Yoneyama, K.; Kawai, T.; and Harada, K. 1968. "A-bomb exposure and subsequent social life—A comparative study on the basis of a district case report survey," *Hōgaku Kenkyū* [Journal of Law, Politics, and Sociology] 41:303.

*Yonezawa, T.; Chin, S.; and Takejima, A. 1949. "Patho-anatomical study on keloids," *Mitteilungen aus der Medizinischen Akademie zu Kioto* [Journal of Kyoto Prefectural University of Medicine] 45:345.

York, E. N. 1957. "In communication from M. Mogan, Armed Forces Special Weapons Center, to G. S. Hurst, Oak Ridge National Laboratory," ORNL–CF–57 11–144.

*Yoshimoto, T. 1977. "I want to be loved by my husband—My personal history," in *Genbaku no Nokoshita Kora—Tainai Hibaku Shōtōshō no Kiroku* [Children Left behind by the Atomic Bomb—Record of Microcephaly due to Exposure in Utero]." Kinoko-kai, ed. Keisuisha, Hiroshima.

You, M. 1950. "A-bomb I was attacked by," *Jinmin Nippō* [People's Daily News, Peking], 19 November. Reprinted in *Shinka Geppō* [New China Monthly Report], no. 2, vol. 3 (in Chinese).

*Yuzaki, M. 1972. "In making the survey—Nukui in the twenty-seven years after the atomic bombing: A record of the atomic bombing of a village." Part 1 (13), *Asahi Shimbun* [Asahi Newspaper], 9 March (Hiroshima edition).

*Yuzaki, M. 1975a. "On the actual state of disaster in the A-bomb hypocenter area (II): General condition of human casualties and survivors in the hypocenter area of Hiroshima," in *Daisanjūsankai Nishinihon Shakaigakkai Taikai Hōkoku Shiryō* [Data Reported at the thirty-third meeting of West Japan Sociological Society].

*Yuzaki, M. 1975b. "Summary of hypocenter area retrospective follow-up survey and general condition of human casualties," *Hiroshima Daigaku Genbaku Hōshanō Igaku Kenkyūsho Ekigaku-Shakaiigaku Kenkyū Bumon, Igakubu Kōshūeiseigaku, Dō Eiseigaku Kyōshitsu "Gōdō Shōdoku Kai" Hōkoku Shiryō* [Proceedings of "Joint Seminar" of the Department of Epidemiology and Social Medicine, Research Institute for Nuclear Medicine and Biology and the Department of Public Health and the Department of Hygiene, School of Medicine, Hiroshima University].

*Yuzaki, M. 1976a. "American investigation team and ABCC," in *Genbaku Sanjūnen—Hiroshimaken no Sengoshi* [In the Thirty Years after the Atomic Bombing—Postwar History of Hiroshima Prefecture], Hiroshima Prefectural Office, ed. Hiroshimaken, Hiroshima.

*Yuzaki, M. 1976b. "From the restoration survey of the A-bomb disaster—For the reinstatement of man," in *Hiroshima-Nagasaki Sanjūnen no Shōgen* [Testimony of Hiroshima and Nagasaki on the Thirty Years after the Atomic Bombings], vol. II. Miraisha, Tokyo.

*Yuzaki, M. 1977a. "Family disintegration due to the atomic bomb (part 1)—Actual status as seen from the restoration survey of the 'burned area' of Hiroshima," in *Daigojikkai Nihon Shakaigakkai Taikai Hōkoku Shiryō* [Data Reported at the fiftieth meeting of Japan Sociological Society].

*Yuzaki, M. 1977b. "Concerning the problems of the A-bomb disaster record—Hiroshima University and the 'Research Center for the Materials and Data of the Atomic Bomb Disaster,' " in *Genbaku to Hiroshima Daigaku—"Seishi no Hi" Gakujutsuhen* [The Atomic Bomb and Hiroshima University—Science Section of "Light of Fate"]. Hiroshima Daigaku Genbaku Shibotsusha Ireigyōji Iinkai, Hiroshima.

*Yuzaki, M. 1978. "Facts of the Hiroshima A-bomb disaster," *Rekishi Hyōron* [Historical Review] 336:12.

*Yuzaki, M.; and Ueoka, H. 1976a. "Study of the population exposed to the atomic bomb and of the number of deaths from the viewpoint of population changes—Report 1: The methodology and general condition of Hiroshima," *Journal of the Hiroshima Medical Association* 29:193.

*Yuzaki, M.; and Ueoka, H. 1976b. "Study of the population exposed to the atomic bomb and the number of deaths from the viewpoint of population changes—Report 2: The general condition in Nagasaki," *Nagasaki Medical Journal* 51:135.

*Yuzaki, M.; Watanabe, S.; Watanabe, T.; and Yamamoto, H. 1974. "Actual status of A-bomb exposure in the hypocenter area, with reference to the social effects of the A-bomb disaster," in *Daiyonjūshichikai Nihon Shakaigakkai Taikai Hōkoku Shiryō* [Data Reported at the forty-seventh meeting of Japan Sociological Society].

*Yuzaki, M.; and Watanabe, T. 1972. "Study concerning the social effects of the A-bomb disaster—Actual status of A-bomb exposure in a village in the suburbs of Hiroshima, with reference to study of the life history of atomic bomb survivors and their families," in *Daisanjikkai Seibu Shakaigakkai Taikai Hōkoku Shiryō* [Data Reported at the thirtieth meeting of West Japan Sociological Society].

*Yuzaki, M.; and Yamate, S. 1978. "A-bomb casualties and A-bomb survivors problems, in *Hoken-Iryōshakaigaku no Tenkai 1978—Chiiki Shakai to Hoken-Iryō Mondai* [Health-Medicosociological Development in 1978—Community and Health-Medicosociological Problems], Health-Medicosociology Research Society, ed. Kakiuchi Shuppan, Tokyo.

Zeldis, L. J.; Jablon, S.; and Ishida, M. 1964. "Current status of ABCC-JNIH studies of carcinogenesis in Hiroshima and Nagasaki," *Annals of the New York Academy of Science* 114:225.

INDEX

A-bomb Aftereffects Research Council, 513, 514, 540, 542, 545
A-bomb Children's Memorial, 596
A-bomb Film Production Committee, 588
A-bomb health book, 359, 369, 544; under A-bomb Victims Medical Care Law, 403; foreign holders of, 475, 477; and medical reimbursement, 557; surveys of holders of, 15, **570,** * 587
A-bomb maidens, 565, 574, 579; keloid scar treatment for, 538, 545
A-bomb Materials Preservation Society, 604
A-bomb Records, Catalogue of, 588
A-bomb Records Preservation Committee, 604
A-bomb Victims Association, 565, 574–75, 579
A-bomb Victims Medical Care Law, 544–45, **549,** 555, 567; categories covered by, 403; and certificate record books, 15 (*see also* A-bomb health book); criteria for certification, 558; definition of victims, 359; enactment of, 542, 566; and examination, 330; geographical distribution of victims covered by, 405, **409;** and local government, 559–60, 561; and medical assistance, 429; and microcephaly, 451; problems of, 403, 405; registration for, 404, 405–7, 569; "special" classification under, 557; special measures added to, 547; and survivors, 398, 403–9; symposium on, 540
A-bomb Victims Special Measures Law, 460, 547–48, **550,** 551, 557, 568; and aid to elderly victims, 446; and exposure in utero, 452; and funeral expenses, 558; goals of, 598–99; and guidance to victims, 569
A-bomb Victims Welfare Center, 545, 560, 561, 563, 569
abandonment of families, 14
abdominal pain, 248
ablation in testes, 171, 172
abortion, 214, 218; and chromo-some anomaly, 324; spontaneous, 321; *see also* pregnancy
absorption: of neutrons, 68; of thermal radiation, 34, 36
acentric fragmentation of chromosomes, 313, **314**
acute radiation illness, 115; and Adult Health Study, 328; and amenorrhea, 211; and anxiety, 488; and atomic bomb cataract, 207; and dentition in children, 236; and malaise, 488; and microcephaly following, in mother, 225; symptoms of, 136, 219, 364; and thyroid, 277
acute stage, *see* radiation illness, acute stage
adenocarcinoma, 287, 288
adolescence, mortality in, 219
adrenal cortex: atrophy of, 172, 181; treatment for dysfunction of, 542
adrenal gland pathology, 172, 195
adrenalin compress for bleeding, 532
Adult Health Program, 213
Adult Health Study, 295, 298, 329, 330, 512; and chromosome aberrations, 316–18; and diabetes, 329; methods and results of, 328–30; and thyroid cancer data from, 277–79
adults: exposed in childhood, 236; exposed in utero, 222; leukocytosis in, 151; microcephalic, 452–53; and cancer, 241
age: of autopsied cases, 158; of breast cancer onset, 293, 295; at death from double cancer, 309; and direct explosion injuries, 376; and economic recovery, 432–33; and employment, 412, **413,** 414, 418; and leukemia onset, 266, **268,** 269; of marriage, 421–25 passim; of menstruation, 211, 212; population change by, **368,** 401–3; and post-bomb sperm count, 152; of survivors, 395–97, 398, **399,** 400–3, 407–8; of thyroid cancer onset, 282, 283
age of exposure: and atomic bomb cataract, 207; and cancer, 241, **242,** 273–74, 279, **280,** 295–97, 309–10; and chromosome aberrations, 315; and effect on children, 234–35; and leukemia, 266, **267,**

268, 269; and microcephaly, 450; and salivary gland tumors, 299, 302–3; and stillbirth, 214
aged, *see* aging; elderly
aging, 210, 243, 330, 458, 459; acceleration of, 203; and Adult Health Study, 329; and employment problems, 413, **414,** 428–29, 459, 460; in experimental animals, 237; leukocytosis and, 151; *see also* elderly
agriculture and residual radiation, 79
aid to atomic bomb victims: allowances and, 558, 561; and A-bomb health book, **570;** citizens' group for, 5, 454, 460, 482, 556, 562, 564, 565, 568–69, 576–77; 582; and condolence payments, 558; delays in, 337; and elderly, 444, 445, 446; and foreign survivors, 462; in Hiroshima, 560–61; and Hiroshima Appeal, 578, 587, 603; inadequacy of, 4, 459, 554; and microcephalic victims, 451–53, 561; in Nagasaki, 560; national movement for, 16; and People's Peace Rally, 574; resistance to, 443, 445, 447–48; and U.S. H-bomb test, 552, 554–55; *see also* Atomic Bomb Victims Medical Care Law
Aioi bridge, 48, 82
air burst and radiation, 67
air defense: in Hiroshima, 336, 515–16; in Nagasaki, 336, 526–27; temporary headquarters for, 356, 516
Air Defense Law, 515
air raid, 341
air-raid alert, 21, 23
air-raid shelter, bombing of, 479
alcoholic beverages, and medical care, 534
Allied Occupation: and ABCC survey problems, 512; and attitude toward bombing, 496; and data on surviving residents, 395; end of, 16; medical supplies during, 535; and press code, 497; and rearmament of Japan, 572; and reconstruction plan for Hiroshima, 554; and "Red Purge," 573

* A number in boldface denotes a reference to a table or a figure.